STAFFING ORGANIZATIONS
Tenth Edition

Timothy A. Judge
The Ohio State University

John D. Kammeyer-Mueller
University of Minnesota

Pangloss Industries
Columbus, OH

Mc
Graw
Hill

Dedication

Herb and Susan Heneman

STAFFING ORGANIZATIONS, TENTH EDITION

Published by Pangloss Industries, Inc., 4130 Mountview Road, Columbus, OH 43220, in collaboration with McGraw Hill, LLC, 1325 Avenue of the Americas, New York, NY 10121. Copyright © 2022 by Pangloss Industries, Inc. All rights reserved. Printed in the United States of America. Previous editions © 2019, 2015, and 2012. No part of this publication may be reproduced or distributed in any form or by any means, or stored in a database or retrieval system, without the prior written consent of the publisher, including, but not limited to, in any network or other electronic storage or transmission, or broadcast for distance learning.

Some ancillaries, including electronic and print components, may not be available to customers outside the United States.

This book is printed on acid-free paper.

This publication is designed to provide accurate and authoritative information in regard to the subject matter covered. It is sold with the understanding that the publisher is not engaged in rendering legal, accounting, or other professional services. If legal advice or other expert assistance is required, the services of a competent professional should be sought. (FROM A DECLARATION OF PRINCIPLES JOINTLY ADOPTED BY A COMMITTEE OF THE AMERICAN BAR ASSOCIATION AND A COMMITTEE OF PUBLISHERS.)

1 2 3 4 5 6 7 8 9 LCR 26 25 24 23 22 21

ISBN 978-1-260-70305-4 (bound edition)
MHID 1-260-70305-3 (bound edition)
ISBN 978-1-264-07290-3 (loose-leaf edition)
MHID 1-264-07290-2 (loose-leaf edition)

Associate Portfolio Manager: *Laura Spell*
Marketing Manager: *Lisa Granger*
Content Project Managers: *Maria McGreal, Emily Windelborn*
Senior Buyer: *Laura Fuller*
Designer: *Matt Diamond*
Content Licensing Specialist: *Traci Vaske*
Cover image: Texture: *IronHeart/Moment/ Getty Images*; Symbol: *kovalto1/Shutterstock*
Compositor: *Westchester Publishing Services*

Address orders and customer service questions to:
McGraw-Hill Higher Education
120 South Riverside Plaza
Chicago, IL 60606
1-800-338-3987

Address editorial correspondence to:
Timothy A. Judge
Pangloss Industries
4130 Mountview Road
Columbus, OH 43220
judge.56@osu.edu

Note to the Instructor:

Pangloss and McGraw Hill Education have combined their respective skills to bring *Staffing Organizations* to your classroom. This text is marketed and distributed by McGraw Hill Education. For assistance in obtaining information or supplementary material, please contact your McGraw Hill Education sales representative or the customer services division of McGraw Hill Education at 800-338-3987.

Library of Congress Cataloging-in-Publication Data
Names: Heneman, Herbert G., III, 1944- author. | Judge, Tim, author. | Kammeyer-Mueller, John, author.
Title: Staffing organizations / Herbert G. Heneman III, University of Wisconsin-Madison, Timothy A. Judge, Ohio State University, John D. Kammeyer-Mueller, University of Minnesota.
Description: Tenth Edition. | Dubuque : McGraw-Hill Education, 2021. | Revised edition of the authors' Staffing organizations, [2019]
Identifiers: LCCN 2020034209 | ISBN 9781260703054 (hardcover) | ISBN 9781264072903 (spiral bound) | ISBN 9781264072590 (ebook other) | ISBN 9781264072675 (ebook)
Subjects: LCSH: Employees–Recruiting. | Employee selection.
Classification: LCC HF5549.5.R44 H46 2021 | DDC 658.3/11–dc23
LC record available at https://lccn.loc.gov/2020034209

www.mhhe.com

AUTHOR PROFILES

Timothy A. Judge is the Joseph A. Alutto Chair in Leadership Effectiveness and executive director of the Fisher Leadership Initiative in the Department of Management and Human Resources, Fisher College of Business, The Ohio State University. Prior to receiving his PhD at the University of Illinois, Tim was a manager for Kohl's department stores. Tim has served on the faculties of Cornell University, University of Iowa, University of Florida, and University of Notre Dame. Tim's teaching and research interests are in the areas of personality, leadership and influence behaviors, staffing, and job attitudes. Tim is a former program chair for the Society for Industrial and Organizational Psychology and a past chair of the Human Resources Division of the Academy of Management. He has also served on the Academy of Management Board of Governors. Tim is a Fellow of the American Psychological Association, the Society for Industrial and Organizational Psychology, the American Psychological Society, and the Academy of Management. He has held honorary appointments at University of Cambridge and University College London.

John D. Kammeyer-Mueller is the Curtis L. Carlson Professor of Industrial Relations in the Department of Work and Organizations, Carlson School of Management, University of Minnesota. John's primary research interests include the areas of organizational socialization and employee adjustment, personality and the stress process, employee retention, and career development. He has taught courses related to organizational staffing at the undergraduate, masters, and doctoral levels. His research work has appeared in *Academy of Management Journal*; the *Journal of Applied Psychology*; *Personnel Psychology*; the *Journal of Management*; and the *Journal of Organizational Behavior*, among other outlets. He serves on the editorial boards of the *Journal of Applied Psychology*; *Personnel Psychology*; and *Organizational Research Methods*. In addition to his scholarly work, John has performed consulting work in the areas of employee satisfaction, retention, and workplace safety and health for 3M Corporation, Allegiance Healthcare, Allina Healthcare, and the State of Minnesota. He has also worked with the Florida Nurses Association and the Florida Bar on research projects of interest to their professional membership.

PREFACE

The latest revisions to *Staffing Organizations* were designed to strike a balance between the needs of human resources (HR) professionals and the latest research findings. In the tenth edition, we have incorporated many changes that reflect ongoing developments in the field. Our continued conversations with top HR leaders across many organizations and staffing scholars have informed our revisions, enabling us to ensure the strategic relevance across all topics.

The use of big data and analytics in the HR function has increased exponentially since the last edition. We have updated the chapters to reflect these changes with discussions of artificial intelligence, machine learning, and other cutting-edge tools that are shaping the field. Methods to take advantage of contemporary survey tools and human resource information systems have been included. We have also improved the integration of more conventional statistical concepts, like multiple regression, in a way that is rigorous while keeping the material accessible to the general reader.

Another major change in this edition is the new chapter on the social and legal environment. The social context section now incorporates behavioral research on the employment relationship and updates the discussion of legal obligations and regulations. We have also introduced a major new section covering diversity and inclusion, which adds a discussion of how staffing practices can address the needs of a more diverse workforce. Ideas from this chapter are also woven throughout the book, helping students develop an integrated understanding of the contemporary employment relationship.

We also made changes to facilitate student engagement. Several sections of the book have been extensively revised with an eye toward making key concepts clear, tying together themes, and showing how staffing practices will be relevant to work in organizations. New exhibits also were created to give more of a big-picture view of how staffing accomplishes strategic goals in contemporary organizations.

A note on terminology in discussions of demography:

Terminology used for demographic groups is a key issue when addressing the contemporary workplace. Throughout the book, we have endeavored to use terms that are respectful, inclusive, and maximally relevant for organizational practice. We use "underrepresented group" or "minority" in different sections to reflect the specific issue under consideration and to fit with terminology of the Equal Employment Opportunity Commission (EEOC). We use "Black" to refer inclusively to all individuals in the African diaspora, including African Americans, Afro-Caribbeans, and recent African immigrants. We use the term Hispanic rather than Latino or Latinx to be consistent with legal and research terminology and to recognize the distinction between these terms and cultural groups. We also use LGBT to reference lesbian, gay, bisexual, and transgender individuals for similar reasons when discussing matters of the law rather than LGBTQ or LGBTQA, which are not currently used in most legal or research documents. When discussing matters of recruitment, diversity, and inclusion, we use LGBT+ to represent related communities that may not be included in the LGBT term.

Listed below are updates to each chapter.

Chapter One: Staffing Models and Strategy

- New material on valuing employees as a competitive advantage
- Updated Exhibit 1.1 on the importance of staffing to organizational leaders
- New staffing system example—Marriott: Leveraging Technology for Staffing
- Updated material on the Enterprise Rent-a-Car staffing system example
- New material on person/job match and person/organization fit
- New integrated example to illustrate staffing levels and quality: TOMS shoes
- New and updated material on staffing levels and quality
- Updated example of hiring/retention trade-offs: Ultimate Software
- New example of attraction and relocation: Amazon's establishment of a second headquarters
- Updated definition of staffing ethics from the Society for Human Resource Management

Chapter Two: Social and Legal Environment

- New chapter incorporating legal context with social factors
- Discussion of expectations, economic exchange, and social exchange
- Review of the sources of laws
- Emphasis on diversity and inclusion in contemporary organizations
- Discussion of the business case for diversity and inclusion
- Review of best practices for inclusive staffing

Chapter Three: Planning

- Major revision to chapter structure
- Streamlined discussion of internal and external influences
- Integrated material and strategies for forecasting requirements and availabilities
- Greater integration of competency material

- Forecasting of HR availability significantly updated to reflect contemporary practice
- Updated and expanded discussion of replacement and succession planning
- New application exercise on forecasting demand

Chapter Four: Job Analysis: Requirements, Competencies, and Rewards

- Major revision to chapter structure
- Thematic incorporation of sources to be used for job analysis information across the chapter
- New material on the changing nature of jobs
- Discussion of machine learning and other contemporary approaches to job analysis
- Description of strategic competencies applicable across organizations
- Major update to job rewards section, including information on contemporary strategies
- New exhibit reviewing sources of job analysis information
- New exercises focused on job requirements and assessing job rewards

Chapter Five: External Recruitment

- Major revision to discussion of strategic recruitment goals
- Expanded discussion of diversity and inclusion in recruiting
- New exhibit featuring examples of branded, targeted, and realistic message content
- New exhibit comparing communication media in terms of reach, richness, interactivity, and credibility
- Updated discussion of online recruiting methods
- Major update to material on social media in recruiting
- New summary clarifying the implications of individual, social, and organizational strategies for sourcing candidates
- Streamlined and updated discussion of recruiting practices as they relate to sourcing candidates
- New material on videoconferencing and remote interviewing

Chapter Six: Internal Recruitment

- Updated and expanded discussion of strategic issues in internal recruiting
- Improved integration with the external recruitment chapter
- Major conceptual revision to applicant sourcing material, differentiating short- and long-range sourcing strategies
- Updated discussion of research regarding the outcomes of internal promotion systems

- New discussion of high-potential employees
- Updated discussion of alternative mobility paths and their potential for improving flexibility
- Incorporation of human capital resources perspective

Chapter Seven: Measurement

- New material on the importance and use of measures
- Updated material on and integrative example of the definition of measurement
- New material on employer idiosyncratic evaluations of applicants' responses to interview questions
- Revised material on scores and the correlation between scores
- Updated material on the significance of the correlation coefficient
- New material on "practical significance"
- Updated Exhibit 7.5
- Revised material on reliability and validity
- New Exhibit 7.14 to illustrate the job requirements matrix
- Revised content validity section and updated the illustrative study of the Maryland Department of Transportation
- New material on differential prediction of selection measures

Chapter Eight: External Selection I

- New material on and examples of video résumés
- New material on and examples of résumé fabrications, distortions, and evaluation
- New material on and examples of getting a résumé noticed
- New discussion of the usefulness of a college education and quality of school as educational requirements, including examples
- New material on how prehire work experience is less important as a predictor of performance than once thought
- New material on and examples of the evaluation of application blanks
- Revised section on biographical information
- Revised section on the evaluation of recommendations, references, and background checks
- New material on and examples of video and computer interviews
- Updated Exhibit 8.8 and discussion of the choice of initial assessment methods
- Updated material on legal issues

Chapter Nine: External Selection II

- Reorganized and revised the chapter (as discussed in the introduction) to discuss external selection methods in terms of their correspondence with the job content in the following sequence: (1) performance tests, work samples, and

simulations; (2) situational judgment tests; (3) structured interviews; (4) ability tests; (5) emotional intelligence tests; (6) personality tests; (7) integrity tests; (8) interest, values, and preference inventories; (9) selection for team environments; and (10) selection of leaders
- Updated material on the prevalence and use of external selection methods
- Updated exhibits throughout the chapter
- New material on performance tests, work samples, and situational judgment tests
- Revised section on structured interviews, including the use of critical incidents to write structured interview questions
- Added examples and discussion of the gamification of cognitive ability assessment
- Updated sections on physical abilities
- New material on personality and emotional intelligence tests
- Revised section clarifying the validity of integrity tests, their fakability, and candidate reactions
- New section on the selection of leaders
- New discussion of favoritism, cronyism, and nepotism in discretionary assessment
- Updated discussion of marijuana and other drug testing

Chapter Ten: Internal Selection

- Updated material on the prevalence and use of internal selection methods
- Updated discussion of why organizations may not use talent management systems
- Updated exhibits throughout the chapter
- New section on employee reactions to talent management systems
- New discussion of meta-analytic findings on managerial sponsorship and seniority for promotion decisions
- New section and discussion on role-play exercises in assessment centers, in-basket exercises, and leaderless group discussions
- New Exhibit 10.8 and discussion of dysfunctional aspects of assessment centers
- Revised and updated sections on interview exercises, oral presentations, performance interviews, and the limitations of promotion panels
- Revised discussion of the choice of substantive assessment methods
- Revised section on and examples of discretionary assessment methods, including research on "left behind" employees
- Revised and updated section on the glass ceiling and the glass cliff
- New ethical issues question
- Revised application: Promotion from within at Citrus Glen

Chapter Eleven: Decision Making

- Greater attention to issues related to diversity and inclusion
- New material on selecting for multiple dimensions of performance
- Discussion of incremental validity analyses
- Updated discussion of cut score development procedures
- Expanded discussion of methods of final choice
- New exhibits showing implementation of cut scores and final choice policies

Chapter Twelve: Final Match

- New section covering the employment relationship and setting expectations
- Material integrating perspectives from the social and legal environment chapter
- Updated discussion of arbitration agreements for employment disputes
- Updated material on noncompete agreements
- New coverage of salary negotiation policies
- Major revision to discussion of job offer content
- Major revision to discussion of legal obligations that arise in the job offer process
- New exhibit and discussion of negotiable and nonnegotiable components of a job offer

Chapter Thirteen: Staffing System Management

- New section on analysis of staffing as a system integrated with other functions
- Updated and revised discussion of staffing processes
- Updated material on how human resource information systems are used
- Updated discussion of developing metrics for staffing systems
- New exhibit demonstrating analytics-based methods of evaluating staffing systems
- New exhibit showing a staffing flowchart emphasizing areas of accountability
- New discussion questions
- New application exercise focused on developing staffing policies and procedures

Chapter Fourteen: Retention Management

- New discussion of costs and benefits of retention strategies
- Increased emphasis of the effects of work process disruption due to turnover
- Revised and updated discussion of exit interview methods
- Updated review of methods for performance management strategies
- Revised discussion of methods of progressive discipline

Our first note of thanks is to Herbert G. Heneman III. Without Herb, *Staffing Organizations* would not exist. Herb and his brother Rob started this book in the early 1990s and were kind enough to bring me (Tim) in on the second edition. Rob soon left to pursue other interests, and Herb and I continued our happy and productive work on the book for seven more editions. During that time, we quickly became friends, establishing a friendship that continues to this very day. Starting with the seventh edition, John became an author on the book.

Over the course of nine editions, the book continues to reflect Herb's original vision. *Staffing Organizations* presents a broad view of the entire staffing process, from the proverbial cradle (staffing strategy) to the grave (retention and evaluation). Guiding this inclusive approach has been Herb's premise (which of course we share) that as important as recruitment and selection are, they do not exist in a vacuum. That premise is why topics such as staffing strategy, decision making, staffing system management, and retention management are discrete (and somewhat unique) chapters in the book. While we also want our book to reflect the latest research, most fundamentally we want the book to capture the staffing process as *it should and does exist* in organizations.

This unique perspective is, in our view, probably the most important reason why the book continues to thrive. But Herb added much more than his keen insight. As an author and leader of the project, Herb was methodical, honest, and supportive. Herb never ceased being opinionated about content (thank heavens!) and passionate about the quality of the book. Herb himself would be quick to thank his brother Rob and especially his wife, Sue, for their work and support over the more than quarter century Herb worked on the book.

Herb, thank you for starting this project, for your stewardship over the course of nine editions, for all the virtues you brought to bear on ensuring its success, and most of all for being a model co-author and friend every step of the way. We dedicate this edition, and all subsequent editions, to you.

In preparing previous editions, we have benefited greatly from the critiques and suggestions of numerous people whose assistance was invaluable. They helped us identify new topics, as well as clarify, rearrange, and delete material. We express our gratitude to the following individuals: Amy Banta, Fred Dorn, Hank Findley, Diane Hagan, and Mark Lengnick-Hall.

We extend a special note of thanks to the McGraw Hill Education publishing team—in particular, Michael Ablassmeir, Laura Spell, Maria McGreal, Traci Vaske, and Lisa Granger for their continued support of the number-one staffing textbook in the market. Thanks also to the staff at Westchester Publishing Services for their dedicated work on this collaborative undertaking. We especially want to thank Dr. David R. Glerum for his hard work on manuscript revisions, editing, and preparation. Finally, we wish to thank you, the students and faculty who use the book. If there is anything we can do to improve your experience with *Staffing Organizations*, please contact us. We will be happy to hear from you.

CONTENTS

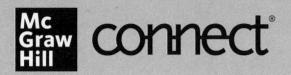

Instructors: Student Success Starts with You

Tools to enhance your unique voice

Want to build your own course? No problem. Prefer to use our turnkey, prebuilt course? Easy. Want to make changes throughout the semester? Sure. And you'll save time with Connect's auto-grading too.

65%
Less Time Grading

Laptop: McGraw-Hill; Woman/dog: George Doyle/Getty Images

Study made personal

Incorporate adaptive study resources like SmartBook® 2.0 into your course and help your students be better prepared in less time. Learn more about the powerful personalized learning experience available in SmartBook 2.0 at **www.mheducation.com/highered/connect/smartbook**

Affordable solutions, added value

Make technology work for you with LMS integration for single sign-on access, mobile access to the digital textbook, and reports to quickly show you how each of your students is doing. And with our Inclusive Access program you can provide all these tools at a discount to your students. Ask your McGraw-Hill representative for more information.

Padlock: Jobalou/Getty Images

Solutions for your challenges

A product isn't a solution. Real solutions are affordable, reliable, and come with training and ongoing support when you need it and how you want it. Visit **www.supportateverystep.com** for videos and resources both you and your students can use throughout the semester.

Checkmark: Jobalou/Getty Images

Students: Get Learning that Fits You

Effective tools for efficient studying

Connect is designed to make you more productive with simple, flexible, intuitive tools that maximize your study time and meet your individual learning needs. Get learning that works for you with Connect.

Study anytime, anywhere

Download the free ReadAnywhere app and access your online eBook or SmartBook 2.0 assignments when it's convenient, even if you're offline. And since the app automatically syncs with your eBook and SmartBook 2.0 assignments in Connect, all of your work is available every time you open it. Find out more at **www.mheducation.com/readanywhere**

> *"I really liked this app—it made it easy to study when you don't have your text-book in front of you."*
>
> - Jordan Cunningham, Eastern Washington University

Calendar: owattaphotos/Getty Images

Everything you need in one place

Your Connect course has everything you need—whether reading on your digital eBook or completing assignments for class, Connect makes it easy to get your work done.

Learning for everyone

McGraw Hill works directly with Accessibility Services Departments and faculty to meet the learning needs of all students. Please contact your Accessibility Services Office and ask them to email accessibility@mheducation.com, or visit **www.mheducation.com/about/accessibility** for more information.

STAFFING
ORGANIZATIONS
Tenth Edition

The Staffing Organizations Model

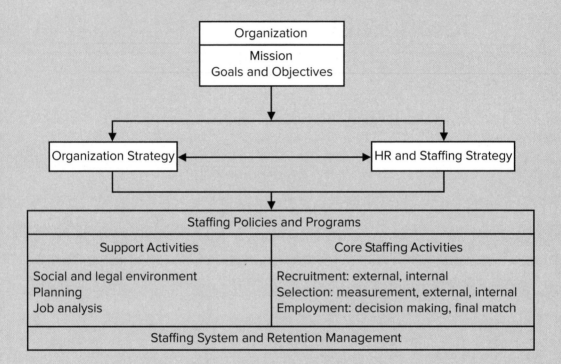

PART ONE

The Nature of Staffing

CHAPTER ONE

Staffing Models and Strategy

LEARNING OBJECTIVES AND INTRODUCTION

Learning Objectives

- Define staffing and consider how, in the big picture, staffing decisions matter
- Review the five staffing models presented, and consider the advantages and disadvantages of each
- Consider the staffing system components and how they fit into the plan for the book
- Understand the staffing organizations model and how its various components fit into the plan for the book
- Appreciate the importance of staffing strategy, and review the 13 decisions that staffing strategy requires
- Realize the importance of ethics in staffing, and learn how ethical staffing practice is established

Introduction

Staffing is a critical organizational function concerned with the acquisition, deployment, and retention of the organization's workforce. As we note in this chapter and throughout the book, staffing is arguably the most critical function underlying organizational effectiveness, because "the people make the place," labor costs are often the highest organizational cost, and poor hiring decisions are not easily undone.

This chapter begins with a look at the nature of staffing. This includes a view of the "big picture" of staffing, followed by a formal definition of staffing, the implications of that definition, and examples of staffing systems.

Five models are then presented to illustrate various facets of staffing. The first model shows how projected workforce head-count requirements and availabilities are compared to determine the appropriate staffing level for the organization. The next two models illustrate staffing quality, which refers to matching a person's qualifications with the requirements of the job or organization. The person/job match model is the foundation of all staffing activities; the person/organization match model, on the other hand, shows how the person/job match could extend to how well the person may fit with the organization. The core staffing components model identifies recruitment, selection, and employment as the three key staffing activities, and it shows that both the organization and the job applicant interact in these activities. The final model, staffing organizations, provides the entire framework for staffing and the structure of this book. It shows that organizations, human resources (HR), and staffing strategy interact to guide the conduct of staffing support activities (legal compliance, planning, and job analysis) and core staffing activities (recruitment, selection, and employment); employee retention and staffing system management are shown to cut across both types of activities.

Staffing strategy is then explored in detail by identifying and describing a set of 13 strategic staffing decisions that may confront any organization. Several of the decisions pertain to staffing levels and the remainder to staffing quality.

The ethics of staffing—the moral principles and guidelines for acceptable practice—is discussed next. Several suggestions that may help guide ethical conduct in staffing are provided, as well as several pressure points that may lead staffing professionals to compromise their ethical standards. Recommendations for how to handle these pressures are also made.

Finally, the plan for the remainder of the book is presented. The overall structure of the book is shown, along with key features of each chapter.

THE NATURE OF STAFFING

The Big Picture

Organizations are combinations of physical, financial, and human capital. Human capital refers to the knowledge, skill, ability, and traits of people and their motivation to use these successfully on the job. The term "workforce quality" refers to an organization's human capital. The organization's workforce is thus a stock of human capital that it acquires, deploys, and retains in pursuit of organizational outcomes such as profitability, market share, customer satisfaction, and environmental sustainability. Staffing is the organizational function used to build this workforce through such systems as staffing strategy, HR planning, recruitment, selection, employment, and retention.

At the national level, the collective workforces of US organizations total over 128 million (down from a peak of nearly 140 million in 2005), with employees spread across nearly eight million work sites. The work sites vary considerably in size, with 23% of employees in work sites with fewer than 20 employees, 55% in work sites with 20–499 employees, and 22% in work sites with 500 or more employees.[1] Each of these work sites likely used some form of a staffing process to acquire its employees. Job creation has continued to expand since recovery from the Great Recession was achieved in April 2014, with 11.7 million jobs created since that date. Since then, the unemployment rate declined to 3.8% in 2019, the lowest in 49 years. During this time, the ratio of unemployed persons to job openings also declined to below 1.0 for the first time. Among the industries contributing to this job growth, service-providing industries such as hospitality, leisure, health care, and professional services have been leading the way (despite major employment decline in the retail sector in 2019). Given the steadily increasing job growth over the last five years, as well as the boon in professional services such as selection and assessment, staffing is a big, $167 billion business for both organizations and job seekers—employing 2% of the US nonfarm workforce.[2]

For most organizations, maintaining a qualified workforce is expensive and a cost of doing business. It is estimated that an average organization's employee cost (wages or salaries and benefits) is over 22% of its total revenue (and generally a higher percentage of total costs).[3] The percentage is much greater for organizations in labor-intensive industries—the service-providing as opposed to goods-producing industries—such as retail trade, information, financial services, professional and business services, education, health care, and leisure and hospitality. Since service-providing industries now dominate our economy, matters of employee cost and whether the organization is acquiring a high-quality workforce are of considerable concern.

A shift is gradually occurring from viewing employees as just a cost of doing business to valuing employees as human capital that creates a competitive advantage for the organization. Experts from around the world collaborated with the International Organization for Standardization to develop guidelines for the reporting of human capital. This new standard is revolutionary in that it provides guidance for organizations, investors, and members of the workforce for indexing human capital, establishing a link with competitive advantages, and benchmarking results across organizations. Since the development of these standards, 22 countries have been actively participating.[4] To illustrate the value of human capital, organizations that deliver superior customer service, much of which is driven by highly knowledgeable employees with fine-tuned customer service skills, have a definite and hopefully long-term advantage over their competitors. In 2015, Ruby Receptionists raised $38.8 million in private equity and doubled its staff through its efforts to forge a culture that values and develops its employees.[5] Research supports the competitive advantage of human capital, with one study of a large fast-food organization demonstrating that improvements in staffing procedures lead to improvements in customer service performance and profits.[6] The competitive advantage derived from human capital has important financial implications.

In addition to direct bottom-line implications, an organization's focus on creating an effective selection system also has indirect implications for a competitive advantage by enhancing employee well-being and retention. One study showed that employees who perceive that their company uses effective selection practices such as formal selection tests and structured job interviews (practices that we will discuss in this book) are more committed to their organizations. In turn, those higher levels of commitment lead to more helping or citizenship behaviors on the part of employees, as well as stronger intentions to remain employed, both of which ultimately contribute to an organization's bottom line.[7]

This renewed focus on establishing a competitive advantage in staffing has also been revolutionized by advancements in technology that have changed the way employees are assessed during the staffing process. These include changes in the delivery of assessments (e.g., computerized adaptive testing [CAT] and mobile assessment); novel ways of assessing applicant knowledge, skill, and ability (e.g., simulation-based training and serious games); and the advanced scoring and reporting of assessments (e.g., electronic scoring and reporting). Although these changes are often financially sound and efficient benefits for organizations, this new paradigm in staffing is not without its limitations, including the potential threat of reduced effectiveness due to decreased face-to-face contact in assessment and a potential for the cognitively demanding nature of electronic assessments to adversely affect members of the applicant pool.[8] Interestingly, this recent "technology effect" suggests that certain technological advancements may be viewed with rose-colored glasses, even without proper evaluation of their effectiveness.[9]

Thus, organizations are increasingly recognizing the value creation that can occur through staffing. Quotes from several organizational leaders attest to this, as shown in Exhibit 1.1. Of course, it should also be noted that effective staffing involves a series of trade-offs in practice, such as between customization and consistency or wide reach and coherence.[10] Furthermore, effective staffing in and of itself is not a silver bullet: a strategic consideration of the context and environment is important for assessing the value of staffing, as staffing practices tend to be more effective in dynamic industries with less collective turnover.[11]

Definition of Staffing

The following definition of staffing is offered and will be used throughout this book:

> Staffing is the process of acquiring, deploying, and retaining a workforce of sufficient quantity and quality to create positive impacts on the organization's effectiveness.

This straightforward definition contains several implications that are identified and explained next.

Implications of Definition

Acquire, Deploy, Retain

An organization's staffing system must guide the acquisition, deployment, and retention of its workforce. Acquisition activities involve external staffing systems that govern the initial intake of applicants into the organization. These involve planning for the numbers and types of people needed, establishing job requirements in the form of the qualifications or knowledge, skills, abilities, and other characteristics (KSAOs) needed to perform the job effectively, establishing the types of rewards the job will provide, conducting external recruitment campaigns, using selection tools to evaluate the KSAOs that applicants possess, deciding which applicants are the most qualified and will receive job offers, and putting together job offers that applicants will hopefully accept.

Deployment refers to the placement of new hires in the actual jobs they will hold, something that may not be entirely clear at the time of hire, such as the specific work unit or geographic location. Deployment also encompasses guiding the movement of current employees throughout the organization through internal staffing

EXHIBIT 1.1   The Importance of Staffing to Organizational Leaders

"The secret of my success is that we have gone to exceptional lengths to hire the best people in the world. And when you're in a field where the dynamic range is 25 to 1, boy, does it pay off."[a]

Steve Jobs, chairman, CEO, and cofounder
Apple

"At most companies, people spend 2% of their time recruiting and 75% managing their recruiting mistakes."[b]

Richard Fairbank, chairman and CEO
Capital One

"I think about this in hiring, because our business all comes down to people. . . . In fact, when I'm interviewing a senior job candidate, my biggest worry is how good they are at hiring. I spend at least half the interview on that."[c]

Jeff Bezos, CEO
Amazon.com—Internet merchandising

"I am convinced that nothing we do is more important than hiring and developing people. At the end of the day, you bet on people, not on strategies."[d]

Lawrence Bossidy (Ret. CEO)
Honeywell

"Obviously, engaging and recruiting people are closer to you achieving your desired goal, but you can't do that until you have found them in the first place. Sourcing and finding people is the most important. You can't recruit, message, or network with someone you haven't found."[e]

Glen Gathey, SVP Digital Strategy and Innovation
Randstad

[a]B. Schlender, "New Wisdom From Steve Jobs on Technology, Hollywood, and How 'Good Management Is Like the Beatles,'" *Fast Company*, April 2012 (*www.fastcompany.com/90449052/what-you-should-know-about-5g-in-2020*).

[b]J. Trammell, "CEOs Must Own Recruiting: 10 Rules for Building a Top-Notch Function," *Forbes*, Apr. 17, 2013 (*www.forbes.com/sites/joeltrammell/2013/04/17/ceos-must-own-recruiting-10-rules-for-building-a-top-notch-function*).

[c]G. Anders, "Taming the Out-of-Control In-Box," *Wall Street Journal*, Feb. 4, 2000, p. 81.

[d]N. M. Tichy and R. Charan, "The CEO as Coach: An Interview With AlliedSignal's Lawrence A. Bossidy," *Harvard Business Review*, March 1995.

[e]LinkedIn Talent Solutions, "35 Inspirational Quotes From Talent Connect San Francisco and London" (slide), Nov. 7, 2014 (*www.slideshare.net/linkedin-talent-solutions/25-quotes-from-talent-connect-san-francisco-that-will-inspire-you*).

systems that handle onboarding, promotions, transfers, and new project assignments. Internal staffing systems mimic external staffing systems in many respects, such as planning for promotion and transfer vacancies, establishing job requirements and job rewards, recruiting employees for promotion or transfer opportunities, evaluating employees' qualifications, and making job offers to employees for new positions.

Retention systems seek to manage the inevitable flow of employees out of the organization. Sometimes these outflows are involuntary on the part of the employee, such as through layoffs or the sale of a business unit to another organization. Other outflows are voluntary in that they are initiated by the employee, such as leaving the organization to take another job (a potentially avoidable turnover by the organization) or leaving to follow one's spouse or partner to a new geographic location (a potentially unavoidable turnover). Of course, no organization can or should seek to eliminate employee outflows, but it should try to minimize the types of turnover in which valued employees leave for greener pastures elsewhere—namely, voluntary-avoidable turnover. Such turnover can be very costly to the organization, as can turnover due to employee discharges and downsizing. Through various retention strategies and tactics, the organization can combat these types of turnover, seeking to retain those employees it thinks it cannot afford to lose.

Staffing as a Process or System

Staffing is not an event, as in, "We hired two people today." Rather, staffing is a process that establishes and governs the flow of people into the organization, within the organization, and out of the organization. Organizations use multiple interconnected systems to manage the flow of people. These include planning, recruitment, selection, decision making, job offer, and retention systems. Events or actions in one system inevitably affect the other systems. If planning activities show a forecasted increase in vacancies relative to historical standards, for example, the recruitment system will need to gear up for generating more applicants than previously needed, the selection system will have to handle the increased volume of applicants needing to be evaluated, decisions about job offers may have to be sped up, and the job offer packages may have to be sweetened to entice the necessary numbers of new hires. Further, steps will have to be taken to retain the new hires and thus avoid having to repeat the above experiences in the next staffing cycle.

Quantity and Quality

Staffing the organization requires attention to both the numbers (quantity) and the types (quality) of people brought into, moved within, and retained by the organization. The quantity element refers to having enough people to conduct business, and the quality element refers to having people with the requisite KSAOs so that jobs are performed effectively. It is important to recognize that it is the combination of quantity and quality of labor that creates a maximally effective staffing system.

Organizational Effectiveness

Staffing systems should be used to contribute to the attainment of organizational goals such as survival, profitability, and growth. A macro view of staffing like this is often lost or ignored because most of the day-to-day operations of staffing systems involve micro activities that are procedural, transactional, and routine in nature. While these micro activities are essential for staffing systems, they must be viewed within the broader macro context of the positive impacts staffing can have on organizational effectiveness. There are many indications of this critical role of staffing.

Leadership talent is at a premium, with very large stakes associated with new leader acquisition. Sometimes leadership talent is bought and brought from the outside to hopefully execute a reversal of fortune for the organization or a business unit within it. For example, in 2012, Yahoo brought in Marissa Mayer, a former executive at Google, to turn around the aging tech giant. Organizations also acquire leaders to start new business units or ventures that will feed organizational growth. The flip side of leadership acquisition is leadership retention. A looming fear for organizations is the unexpected loss of a key leader, particularly to a competitor. The exiting leader carries a wealth of knowledge and skill out of the organization and leaves a hole that may be hard to fill, especially with someone of equal or higher leadership stature. The leader may also take other key employees along, thus increasing the exit impact.

Organizations recognize that a strategic hunt for talent is essential to expand organizational value and provide protection from competitors. Such a strategy is particularly effective if the talent is unique and rare in the marketplace, valuable in the anticipated contributions to be made (such as product creations or design innovations), and difficult for competitors to imitate (such as through training current employees). Talent of this sort can serve as a source of competitive advantage for the organization, hopefully for an extended time period.[12]

Talent acquisition is essential for growth even when it does not have such competitive advantage characteristics. As hiring has steadily picked up since the end of the Great Recession, many companies are scrambling to staff positions in order to keep up with demand. For example, Amazon, Microsoft, and Oracle are each attempting to fill over a whopping 2,000 positions that all pay at least $60,000 a year.[13] Shortages in the quantity or quality of labor can mean lost business opportunities, scaled-back expansion plans, an inability to provide critical consumer goods and services, and even threats to the organization's survival.

Finally, for individual managers, having sufficient numbers and types of employees on board is necessary for the smooth, efficient operation of their work units. Employee shortages often require disruptive adjustments, such as job reassignments or overtime for current employees. Underqualified employees present special challenges to the manager, as they need to be trained and closely supervised. Failure of the underqualified to achieve acceptable performance may require termination, a difficult decision to make and implement.

In short, organizations experience and respond to staffing forces and recognize how critical these forces can be to organizational effectiveness. The forces manifest themselves in numerous ways: acquisition of new leaders to change the organization's direction and effectiveness, prevention of key leader losses, use of talent as a source of growth and competitive advantage, shortages of labor—both quantity and quality—that threaten growth and even survival, and the ability of individual managers to effectively run their work units.

Staffing System Examples

Staffing Jobs Without Titles

W. L. Gore & Associates is a Delaware-based organization that specializes in making products derived from fluoropolymers. Gore produces fibers (including dental floss and sewing threads), tubes (used, for example, in heart stents and oil exploration), tapes (including those used in space exploration), and membranes (used in Gore-Tex waterproof clothing).

Gore employs over 10,000 workers and appears on nearly every "great place to work" list, including *Fortune* magazine's "100 Best Companies to Work For." In addition, it boasts a miniscule 4% full-time voluntary turnover rate. What makes Gore so special? Gore associates say that it is the culture, and the culture starts with the hiring.

Gore has a strong culture that is reflected in its structure: a team-based, flat lattice structure that fosters personal initiative. At Gore, no employee can ever command another employee—all commitments are voluntary, and any employee can say no to any request. Employees are called "associates" and managers are called "sponsors." How do people become leaders at Gore? "You get to be a leader if your team asks you to lead them."[14]

Gore extends this egalitarian, entrepreneurial approach to its staffing process. The focal point of Gore's recruitment process is the careers section of its website, which describes its core values and its unique culture. The website also provides position descriptions and employee perspectives on working at Gore, complete with pictures of the associates and videos. Three Gore associates—Janice, Katrin, and Mike—work on Gore's footwear products, striving to uphold the company's "keep you dry" guarantee. As Mike notes, "The reasons that I chose Gore from the start are the same reasons why I stay at Gore today, and continue to have fun every day: It's the people. Our team is a great team, and I think that is reflected or echoed across the entire enterprise." Hajo, Alicia, and Austin make up a team working on the clinical product Thoracic Endoprosthesis. As Hajo notes, "When you come to work each day, you don't have a boss to give you explicit instructions on what you need to accomplish."

Gore finds that its employee-focused recruitment efforts do not work for everyone, which is exactly what it intends. "Some of these candidates, or prospects in the fields we were recruiting for, told us 'this company probably isn't for me,'" says Steve Shuster, who helped develop the recruitment strategy. Shuster says that this self-selection is another benefit of its recruitment message. Potential recruits who prefer a more traditional culture quickly see that Gore isn't for them. Shuster says, "Rather than have them go through the interview process and invest their time and our time, we wanted to weed that out." Of course, Gore has a culture that fits many. Says Gore associate Hannah, who works on the company's heart device team, "I feel like Gore is not just a job, that it's more of a lifestyle and a huge part of my life."[15]

Leveraging Technology for Staffing

Staffing is immensely important to Marriott—with over 30 brands and more than 7,000 properties in 131 countries, finding talented, motivated people to fill a wide variety of positions is a challenge. Marriott is arguably the model for effectively leveraging social media for recruitment. In order to broaden the talent pool and reach as many people as possible, social media is the way to go: 91% of employers are using social media for talent acquisition and believe that usage will only continue to increase. From a strategic standpoint, social media also enables employers to connect with passive candidates. One survey suggests that 75% of potential hires are not actively searching and that 80% of employers found that using social media has helped them find passive candidates.

So, what does Marriott do to reach more people through social media? First and foremost, Marriott remains actively engaged with potential applicants and customers throughout the world: it boasts over 70 billion reactions and 3.5 million mentions across social media accounts. It maintains engagement by encouraging dialogue on the brand and by connecting person to person. For example, Marriott's MarriottCareers Instagram account enables potential applicants to experience stories and impressions from current employees while advertising for open jobs. Relatedly, its "Where I Belong" campaign focuses on creating a shared sense of space and core values with potential applicants.

One innovative strategy Marriott enacted was through the development of My Marriott Hotel, an online game designed to attract applicants who have little exposure to the hospitality industry. This game enabled Marriott to leverage technology toward several strategic aims: making the recruitment process entertaining, providing a realistic job preview to those unfamiliar with the industry, and gaining a potential advantage over competitors. The decision to design the game was strategic: Marriott was struggling to connect with potential applicants in Indian and Chinese markets, and it knew that in many of these regions potential applicants were moving from rural areas to the city, and primarily used social media to play games and search for new jobs. Such a decision was not without risk, however. As David Kippen of Evviva, the firm that designed the game, noted, "There were risks to consider—what if it didn't work? What if it was lame? What would it mean for the Marriott brand?" Overall, the risk paid off: since its launch, the game has attracted tens of thousands of users from hundreds of countries.[16]

Management Trainees

Enterprise Rent-A-Car is a private company founded in 1957 with locations in the United States, Canada, the UK, Ireland, and Germany. Enterprise boasts 7,600 offices in neighborhoods and airports in over 85 countries. Among its competitors, Enterprise frequently wins awards for customer satisfaction.

To staff its locations, Enterprise relies heavily on recruiting recent college graduates. In fact, Enterprise hires more college graduates—often between 8,000 and 9,000 a year—than any other company. New hires enter Enterprise's management training program, where they learn all aspects of running a branch, including taking reservations, picking up customers, developing relationships with car dealerships and body shops for future rentals, managing the fleet, handling customer issues, and even washing cars. Nearly all promotions at Enterprise occur from within and are strictly performance based, allowing management trainees to see a clear path from their current position to higher positions such as assistant manager, branch manager, and area manager. Typically, the first promotion occurs within 9–12 months of being hired, which speeds the climb up the corporate ladder.

To fill so many positions with college graduates, Enterprise relies on several strategies, including recruiting from an internship program of approximately 1,000 students a year, attending college recruitment fairs, using its website to highlight its performance-driven culture as well as employee testimonials, and devoting a large percentage of its television advertising to the NCAA basketball tournament, which occurs each March and has a high college viewership. Although graduates' grades are important to Enterprise, communication skills are even more essential, says Dylan Schweitzer, northeast manager of talent acquisition.

Although the management trainee program at Enterprise has been described as a grueling process, with many trainees leaving prior to being promoted, its executives often describe it as an "MBA without the IOU" because trainees gain firsthand experience in sales, marketing, finance, and operations.[17]

STAFFING MODELS

Various elements of staffing are depicted in the five staffing models presented in the following sections. Each of these is described in detail to more fully convey the nature and richness of staffing the organization.

Staffing Quantity: Levels

The quantity or head-count portion of the staffing definition means organizations must be concerned about staffing levels and their adequacy. Exhibit 1.2 shows the basic model. The organization, as well as each of its units, forecasts workforce quantity requirements (the needed head count) and then compares these with

---

EXHIBIT 1.2 Staffing Quantity

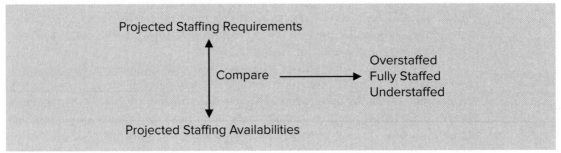

forecasted workforce availabilities (the likely employee head count) to determine its likely staffing level position. If head-count requirements match availabilities, the organization will be fully staffed. If requirements exceed availabilities, the organization will be understaffed, and if availabilities exceed requirements, the organization will be overstaffed.

Making forecasts to determine appropriate staffing levels and then developing specific plans are the essence of planning. Being understaffed means the organization will have to gear up its staffing efforts, starting with accelerated recruitment and carrying on through the rest of the staffing system. It may also require developing retention programs that will slow the outflow of people, thus avoiding costly "turnstile" or "revolving door" staffing. Overstaffing projections signal the need to slow down or even halt recruitment, as well as to take steps to reduce head count, perhaps through early retirement plans or layoffs.

Staffing Quality: Person/Job Match

The person/job match seeks to align characteristics of individuals with jobs in ways that will result in desired outcomes. Casual comments made about applicants often reflect awareness of the importance of the person/job match: "Clark just doesn't have the interpersonal skills that it takes to be a good customer service representative." "Mary has exactly the kind of budgeting experience this job calls for; if we hire her, there won't be any downtime while she learns our systems." "Gary says he was attracted to apply for this job because of its sales commission plan; he says he likes jobs where his pay depends on how well he performs." "Diane was impressed by the amount of challenge and autonomy she will have." "Jack turned down our offer; we gave him our best shot, but he just didn't feel he could handle the long hours and amount of travel the job calls for."

Comments like these raise four important points about the person/job match. First, jobs are characterized by their requirements (e.g., interpersonal skills, previous budgeting experience) and embedded rewards (e.g., commission sales plan, challenge and autonomy). Second, individuals are characterized by their level of qualification (e.g., few interpersonal skills, extensive budgeting experience) and motivation (e.g., need for pay to depend on performance, need for challenge and autonomy). Third, in each of the previous examples, the issue was the likely degree of fit or match between the characteristics of the job and the person. Fourth, there are implied consequences for every match. For example, Clark may not perform very well in his interactions with customers; retention might quickly become an issue with Jack.

These points and concepts are shown more formally through the person/job match model in Exhibit 1.3. In this model, the job has certain requirements and rewards associated with it. The person has certain qualifications, referred to as KSAOs, and motivations. There is a need for a match between the person and the job. To the extent that the match is good, it will likely have a positive impact on outcomes, particularly with attraction of job applicants, job performance, retention, attendance, and satisfaction.

There is a need for a dual match to occur: job requirements to KSAOs, and job rewards to individual motivation. In and through staffing activities, there are attempts to ensure both. Such attempts collectively involve what will be referred to throughout this book as the matching process.

Several points pertaining to staffing need to be made about the person/job match model. First, the concepts shown in the model are not new.[18] They have been used for decades as the dominant way of thinking about how individuals

EXHIBIT 1.3   Person/Job Match

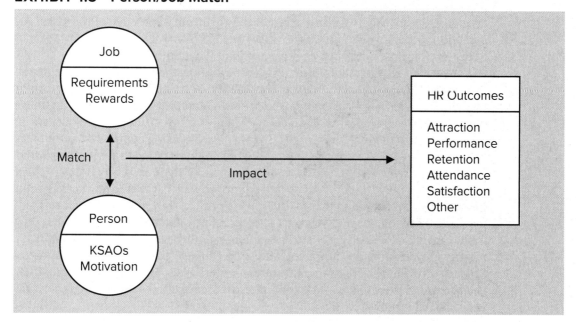

successfully adapt to their work environments. The view is that the positive interaction of individual and job characteristics creates the most successful match. Thus, a person with a given package of KSAOs is not equally suited to all jobs, because jobs vary in the KSAOs required. Likewise, an individual with a given set of needs or motivations will not be satisfied with all jobs, because jobs differ in the rewards they offer. Thus, in staffing, everyone must be assessed relative to the requirements and rewards of the job being filled.

Second, the model emphasizes a dual match of KSAOs to requirements and motivation to rewards. Both matches require attention in staffing. For example, a staffing system may be designed to focus on the KSAOs/requirements match by carefully identifying job requirements and then thoroughly assessing applicants relative to those requirements. While such a staffing system may accurately identify the probable high performers, problems could arise. By ignoring or downplaying the motivation/rewards portion of the match, the organization may have difficulty getting people to accept job offers (an attraction outcome) or having new hires remain with the organization for any length of time (a retention outcome). It does little good to identify the likely high performers if they cannot be induced to accept job offers or to remain with the organization. Paradoxically, a recent research study has demonstrated that although matching the KSAOs to requirements is important for organizations, job advertisements that emphasize the fit between employee needs and employer fulfillment of those needs (e.g., motivation to rewards) actually led to more applications and a higher-quality applicant pool.[19]

Third, job requirements should be expressed in terms of both the tasks involved and the KSAOs needed to perform those tasks. Most of the time, it is difficult to establish meaningful KSAOs for a job without having first identified the job's tasks. KSAOs usually must be derived or inferred from knowledge of the tasks. An exception to this involves very basic or generic KSAOs that are reasonably deemed necessary for most jobs, such as literacy and oral communication skills.

Fourth, job requirements often extend beyond task and KSAO requirements. For example, the job may require punctuality, good attendance, safety toward fellow employees and customers, and travel. Matching an individual to these requirements must also be considered when staffing the organization. Travel requirements of the job, for example, may involve assessing applicants' availability for, and willingness to accept, travel assignments. Integrating this with the second point above, travel issues, which frequently arise in the consulting industry, play a role in both the attraction process (getting people to accept) and the retention process (getting people to stay). "Road warriors," as they are sometimes termed, may first think that frequent travel will be exciting, only to discover later that they find it taxing. Relatedly, job rewards often extend beyond pay and benefits. A recent study has found that organizations should also pay attention to the match between providing developmental career experiences for employees and their need for such experiences—doing so improved commitment to the organization and reduced turnover.[20]

Finally, the matching process can yield only so much by way of impacts on the HR outcomes. The reason for this is that these outcomes are influenced by factors outside the realm of the person/job match. Retention, for example, depends not only on how close the match is between job rewards and individual motivation but also on the availability of suitable job opportunities in other organizations and labor markets. As hiring begins to improve and unemployment continues to drop, organizations are likely to face increased retention pressures as other opportunities present themselves to employees due to more favorable economic conditions. Furthermore, given that fit may change over time, organizations should pay attention to changes in person/job fit: if jobs become more challenging over time or employees lose the KSAOs needed to meet job demands, retention can be affected.[21]

Staffing Quality: Person/Organization Match

Often the organization seeks to determine how well the person matches not only the job but also the organization. Likewise, applicants often assess how well they think they will fit into the organization, in addition to how well they match the specific job's requirements and rewards. For both the organization and the applicant, then, there may be a concern with a person/organization match.[22]

Exhibit 1.4 shows this expanded view of the match. The focal point of staffing is the person/job match, and the job is the bull's eye of the matching target. Four other matching concerns involving the broader organization also arise in staffing: organizational values, new job duties, multiple jobs, and future jobs.

Organizational values are norms of desirable attitudes and behaviors for the organization's employees. Examples include honesty and integrity, achievement and hard work, and concern for fellow employees and customers. Though such values may never appear in writing, such as in a job description, the likely match of the applicant to them is judged during staffing. The effects of a mismatch between an employee and the organization on values can be quite strong, given that the mismatch tends to deplete an individual's regulatory resources, leading to low performance and a decreased ability to adapt.[23]

New job duties are tasks that may be added to the target job over time. Organizations desire new hires who will be able to successfully perform these new duties as they are added. In recognition of this, job descriptions often contain the catchall phrase "and other duties as assigned." These other duties are usually vague at the time of hire, and they may never materialize. Nonetheless, the organization would like to hire people it thinks could perform these new duties. Having such people will provide the organization the flexibility to complete new tasks without having to hire additional employees. As we will discuss later in this book, certain types of individuals are better than others at adapting to changing circumstances, and organizations with evolving job duties are well advised to select them.

Flexibility concerns also enter the staffing picture in terms of hiring people who can perform multiple jobs. Small businesses, for example, often desire new hires

EXHIBIT 1.4 Person/Organization Match

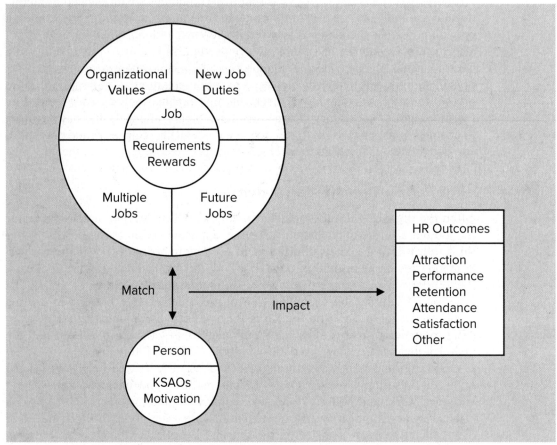

who can function as jacks-of-all-trades. Organizations experiencing rapid growth may require new employees who can handle several job assignments, splitting their time among them on an as-needed basis. Such expectations obviously require assessments of person/organization fit.

Future jobs represent forward thinking by the organization and the person as to which job assignments the person might assume beyond the initial job. Here the applicant and the organization are thinking of long-term matches over the course of transfers and promotions as the employee becomes increasingly seasoned for the long run. As technology and globalization cause jobs to change at a rapid pace, more organizations are engaging in "opportunistic hiring," where an individual is hired into a newly created job or a job that is an amalgamation of previously distributed tasks. In such cases, person/organization match is more important than person/job match.[24]

In each of the four concerns, the matching process is expanded to consider requirements and rewards beyond those of the target job as it currently exists. Though the dividing line between person/job and person/organization matching is fuzzy, both types of matches are frequently of concern in staffing. Ideally, the organization's staffing systems focus first and foremost on the person/job match. This will allow the nature of the employment relationship to be specified and agreed to in concrete terms. Once these terms have been established, person/organization match possibilities can be explored during the staffing process. However, assessing fit reliably is more difficult than it may seem: applicants in tight job markets may strategically "fake fit" in order to land the job.[25] In this book, for simplicity's sake, we will use the term "person/job match" broadly to encompass both types of matches, though most of the time we will be referring to the match with the actual job itself.

Staffing System Components

As noted, staffing encompasses managing the flows of people into and within the organization, as well as retaining them. The core staffing process has several components that represent steps and activities that occur over the course of these flows. Exhibit 1.5 shows these components and the general sequence in which they occur.

As shown in the exhibit, staffing begins with a joint interaction between the applicant and the organization. The applicant seeks the organization and job opportunities within it, and the organization seeks applicants for job vacancies it has or anticipates having. Both the applicant and the organization are thus "players" in the staffing process from the very beginning, and they remain joint participants throughout the process.

At times, the organization may be the dominant player, such as in aggressive and targeted recruiting for certain types of applicants. At other times, the applicant may be the aggressor, such as when he or she desperately seeks employment with a particular organization and will go to almost any length to land a job with it. Most of the time, the staffing process involves a more balanced and natural interplay between the applicant and the organization.

The initial stage in staffing is recruitment, which involves identification and attraction activities by both the organization and the applicant. The organization seeks to identify and attract individuals so that they become job applicants. Activities such as advertising, job fairs, use of recruiters, preparation and distribution of informational brochures, and "putting out the word" about vacancies among its own employees are undertaken by the organization. The applicant identifies organizations with job opportunities by reading advertisements, contacting an employment agency, mass mailing résumés to employers, and so forth. These activities are accompanied by attempts to make one's qualifications (KSAOs and motivation) attractive to organizations, such as by applying in person for a job or preparing a carefully constructed résumé that highlights significant skills and experiences.

EXHIBIT 1.5   Staffing System Components

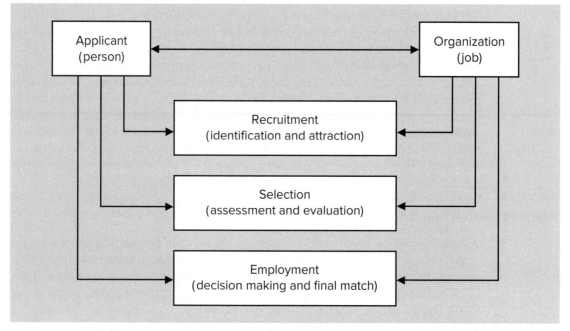

Gradually, recruitment activities phase into the selection stage and its accompanying activities. Now, the emphasis is on assessment and evaluation. For the organization, this means the use of various selection techniques (interviews, application blanks, and so on) to assess applicant KSAOs and motivation. Data from these assessments are then evaluated against job requirements to determine the likely degree of person/job match. At the same time, the applicant is assessing and evaluating the job and organization on the basis of the information gathered from organizational representatives (e.g., recruiters, manager with the vacancy, and other employees), written information (e.g., brochures, employee handbook), informal sources (e.g., friends and relatives who are current employees), and visual inspection (e.g., a video presentation, a work site tour). This information, along with a self-assessment of KSAOs and motivation, is evaluated against the applicant's understanding of job requirements and rewards to determine whether a good person/job match is likely.

The last core component of staffing is employment, which involves decision making and final match activities by the organization and the applicant. The organization must decide which applicants to allow to continue in the process and which to reject. This may involve multiple decisions over successive selection steps or hurdles. Some applicants ultimately become finalists for the job. At that point, the organization must decide to whom it will make the job offer, what the content of the offer will be, and how it will be drawn up and presented to the applicant. Upon the applicant's acceptance of the offer, the final match is complete, and the employment relationship is formally established.

For the applicant, the employment stage involves self-selection, a term that refers to deciding whether to continue in the staffing process or drop out. This decision may occur anywhere along the selection process, up to and including the moment of the job offer. If the applicant continues as part of the process through the final match, the applicant has decided to be a finalist. Their attention now turns to a possible job offer, possible input and negotiation on its content, and making a final decision about the offer. The applicant's final decision is based on their overall judgment about the likely suitability of the person/job match.

Note that the above staffing components apply to both external and internal staffing. Though this may seem obvious in the case of external staffing, a brief elaboration may be necessary for internal staffing, where the applicant is a current employee and the organization is the current employer. As we discussed above, Enterprise Rent-A-Car staffs most of its managerial positions internally. Job opportunities (vacancies) exist within the organization and are filled through the activities of the internal labor market. Those activities involve recruitment, selection, and employment, with the employer and the employee as joint participants. As another example, at the investment banking firm Goldman Sachs, candidates for promotion to partner are identified through a multistep process.[26] They are "recruited" by division heads identifying prospective candidates for promotion (as in many internal staffing decisions, it is assumed that all employees are interested in promotion). Candidates are then vetted based on input from senior managers in the firm and are evaluated from a dossier that contains the candidate's credentials and accomplishments. After this six-month process, candidates are recommended for partner to the CEO, who then makes the final decision and offers partnership to those lucky enough to be selected (partners average $7 million a year, plus perks). When candidates accept the offer of partnership, the final match has occurred, and a new employment relationship has been established.

Staffing Organizations

The overall staffing organizations model, which forms the framework for this book, is shown in Exhibit 1.6. It depicts that the organization's mission, along with its goals and objectives, drives both organization strategy and HR and staffing strategy, which influence each other when they are being formulated. Staffing policies and programs result from these strategies and serve as an overlay to both support activities and core staffing activities. Employee retention and staffing system management concerns cut across these support and core staffing activities. Finally, though not shown in the model, it should be remembered that staffing levels and

EXHIBIT 1.6   Staffing Organizations Model

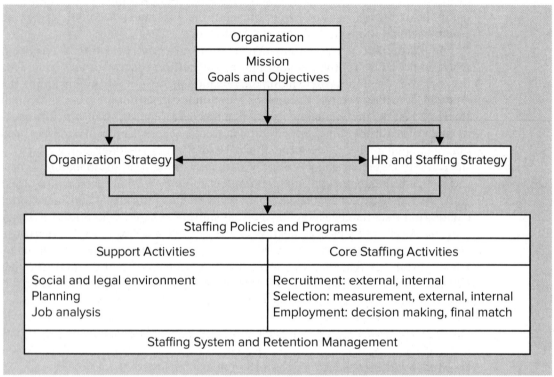

staffing quality are the key focal points of staffing strategy, policy, and programs. A more thorough examination of the model follows next.

Organization, HR, and Staffing Strategy

An organization formulates strategy to express an overall purpose or mission and to establish broad goals and objectives that will help fulfill its mission. For example, TOMS's mission is to "help improve lives through business." With this mission statement, the organization has built a brand presence that emphasizes helping others and harmony with nature. This mission has driven goals and objectives pertaining to product development, sales growth, and competitive differentiation through its efforts to help improve lives, through such aims as alleviating poverty. Although the organization originally began producing shoes and would match every sale with a pair donated to a child in need, it has continued to develop products such as eyewear, coffee, and bags operating under a similar business model, to further its mission. This mission permeates into the staffing function, as the company forges a supportive and collaborative culture to advance TOMS's mission, offers an internship program that develops social entrepreneurship skills so that interns can start their own businesses that change lives, and offers a pathways program that provides employment opportunities to unemployed youth.[27]

Underlying these objectives are certain assumptions about the size and types of workforces that will need to be acquired, trained, managed, rewarded, and retained. HR strategy represents the key decisions about how these workforce assumptions will be handled. Such HR strategy may not only flow from the organization strategy but also may actually contribute directly to the formulation of the organization's strategy. TOMS's mission of improving lives through business assumes that sufficiently qualified and motivated team members are available internally and externally, and assurances from the HR department about availability may have been critical in helping the organization decide on its product development goals. From this general assumption, TOMS's HR strategy may suggest (1) obtaining unemployed applicants with a passion for helping others; (2) building a headquarters facility in a geographic area that is an attractive place to work and facilitates collaboration and socialization (Los Angeles, close to the beach); (3) holding a "Happy Helping Hour," in which members of charitable organizations engage with employees in a community service activity; (4) offering competitive, socially conscious benefits packages that include eight weeks of paid maternity and paternity leave, flexible work schedules, and "no-meeting Mondays"; (5) allowing employees to submit ideas for a socially conscious project that inspires them, vote on them, and award $10,000 and two days off to make it happen; and (6) using seniority-based eligibility for giving trips that enable employees to assist community partners in impoverished countries.[28] In all these ways, HR strategy seeks to align acquisition and management of the workforce with organization strategy.

Staffing strategy deals directly with key decisions regarding the acquisition, deployment, and retention of the organization's workforces. Such decisions guide the development of recruitment, selection, and employment programs. The aforementioned "pathways" program is likely one way in which TOMS's staffing strategy operates: because its target market is socially conscious youth, TOMS continues to engage with this group through talent sourcing and identification.[29] It may also lead to the development of special selection techniques for assessing person/organization match. Indeed, TOMS uses situation-based interview questions that key into its core values, such as long-term vision (e.g., "Tell me about a time in which you made a decision that was unpopular but was important for a long-term goal").[30] In such ways, strategic staffing decisions shape the staffing process.

Support Activities

Support activities serve as the foundation and necessary ingredients for the conduct of core staffing activities. Legal compliance represents knowledge of the myriad laws and regulations, especially equal employment opportunity and affirmative action (EEO/AA), and incorporation of their requirements into all phases of the core staffing activities. Planning serves as a tool for first becoming aware of key external influences on staffing, particularly economic conditions, labor markets, and labor unions. Such awareness shapes the formulation of staffing levels—both requirements and availabilities—the results of which drive planning for the core staffing activities. Job analysis represents the key mechanism by which the organization identifies and establishes the KSAO requirements for jobs, as well as the rewards that the jobs will provide. These are both first steps toward filling projected vacancies through core staffing activities.

Returning to our example, given that TOMS meets the size threshold for coverage (usually 15 or more employees), it must ensure that the staffing system complies with all applicable federal, state, and local laws and regulations. For example, TOMS prepares a supply chain disclosure statement that it includes on its website that outlines the measures TOMS takes to conform with the California Transparency in Supply Chains Act and the UK Modern Slavery Act, to combat human trafficking and forced labor practices.[31]

Planning activities revolve around first determining the major types of jobs that will be necessary, such as computer programmers, Internet specialists, and project managers. For each job, a forecast must be made about the number of employees needed and the likely availability of individuals both externally and internally for the job. Results of such forecasts serve as the key input for developing detailed staffing plans for the core staffing activities. Finally, job analysis will be needed to specify for each job exactly which KSAOs and rewards will be necessary for these sought-after new employees. Once all these support activities are in place, the core staffing activities can begin.

Core Staffing Activities

Core staffing activities focus on recruitment, selection, and employment of the workforce. Since staffing levels have already been established as part of staffing planning, the emphasis shifts to staffing quality to ensure that successful person/job and person/organization matches will be made. Accomplishment of this will require multiple activities, including recruitment methods, communication with potential applicants with a special recruitment message, recruitment media, types of selection tools, deciding which applicants will receive job offers, and job offer packages. Staffing experts and the hiring manager will be involved in these core staffing activities. Moreover, it is likely that the activities will have to be developed and tailor-made for each type of job.

Consider a job of a logistics specialist in TOMS's Logistics + Distribution department. It will be necessary to develop specific plans for issues such as the following: Will we recruit only online, or will we use other methods such as job fairs (recruitment methods)? What exactly will we tell applicants about the job and our organization (recruitment message), and how will we deliver the message, such as on our website or in a brochure (recruitment media)? What specific selection tools—such as interviews, assessments of experience, work samples, and background checks—will we use to assess and evaluate the applicants' KSAOs (selection techniques)? How will we combine and evaluate all the information we gather on applicants with these selection tools and then decide which applicants will receive job offers (decision making)? What exactly will we put in the job offer, and what will we be willing to negotiate (employment)?

Staffing and Retention System Management

The various support and core staffing activities are quite complex, and they must be guided, coordinated, controlled, and evaluated. Such is the role of staffing system management. For example, what will be the role of the HR department, and what types of people will be needed to develop and manage the new staffing system (administration of staffing systems)? How will we evaluate the results of these systems—will we collect and look at cost-per-hire and time-to-hire data (evaluation of staffing systems)? Data such as these are key effective indicators that both general and staffing managers are attuned to.

Finally, voluntary employee departure from the organization is usually costly and disruptive, and it can involve the loss of critical talent that is difficult to replace. Discharges can also be disruptive. Unless the organization is downsizing, replacements must be found in order to maintain desired staffing levels. The burden for such replacement staffing can be substantial, particularly if the turnover is unanticipated and unplanned. Other things being equal, greater employee retention means less staffing, and thus effective retention programs complement staffing programs.

For TOMS, the primary focus would likely be on "staffing up" in order to ensure the company's retail locations are sufficiently staffed with sales supervisors, associates, and baristas. Unless attention is also paid to employee retention, maintaining adequate staffing levels and quality may become problematic. Hence, the organization will need to monitor the amount and quality of employees who are leaving, along with the reasons they are leaving, in order to learn how much of the turnover is voluntary and avoidable. With these data, tailor-made retention strategies and programs to better meet employees' needs can be developed. If these are effective, strains on the staffing system will be lessened.

The remainder of the book is structured around and built on the staffing organizations model shown in Exhibit 1.6.

STAFFING STRATEGY

As noted, staffing strategy requires making key decisions about the acquisition, deployment, and retention of the organization's workforce. Thirteen such decisions are identified and discussed below. Some decisions pertain primarily to staffing levels, and others pertain primarily to staffing quality. A summary of the decisions is shown in Exhibit 1.7. While each decision is shown as an either-or, each is more appropriately thought of as lying on a continuum anchored at the ends by these either-or extremes. When discussing the decisions, continued reference is made to TOMS.

EXHIBIT 1.7 Strategic Staffing Decisions

Staffing Levels
- Acquire or Develop Talent
- Hire Yourself or Outsource
- External or Internal Hiring
- Core or Flexible Workforce
- Hire or Retain
- National or Global
- Attract or Relocate
- Overstaff or Understaff
- Short- or Long-Term Focus

Staffing Quality
- Person/Job or Person/Organization Match
- Specific or General KSAOs
- Exceptional or Acceptable Workforce Quality
- Active or Passive Diversity

Staffing Levels

Acquire or Develop Talent

A pure acquisition staffing strategy would have an organization concentrate on acquiring new employees who can hit the ground running and be at peak performance the moment they arrive. These employees would bring their talents with them to the job, with little or no need for training or development. A pure development strategy would lead to acquisition of just about anyone who is willing and able to learn the KSAOs required by the job. Staffing strategy must position the organization appropriately along this "buy or make your talent" continuum. For the sales associate and barista positions at TOMS, for example, the emphasis would likely be on acquiring talent because of the urgency of sufficiently staffing retail locations. There may not be time to train, and qualified internal candidates may not be available. Thus, in order to align with the business strategy of maximizing sales, a strategy that is focused mostly on acquisition would enable the organization to hire associates who can hit the ground running.

Hire Yourself or Outsource

Increasingly, organizations are outsourcing their hiring activities, meaning they use outside organizations to recruit and select employees. For example, HR professionals at the National Cash Register corporation in Dayton, Ohio, made the decision to outsource their staffing function. Dan Delano, the director of HR operations, outlined the strategy behind this decision: "We've taken a look at the activities, processes, and functions that we have to perform inside the company, and we've decided which ones are core to our business and which ones we really don't need to handle directly, that we could have an outsource vendor do for us."[32] Although there are variations of staffing outsourcing (we will have more to say about it in the planning chapter), in some cases, an organization wholly cedes decision-making authority to the vendor. Why might an organization do this? First, it may believe that the vendor can do a better job of identifying candidates than the organization itself. This is particularly true for small and midsize companies that lack a professional HR function. Second, in labor shortages, an organization may not be able to recruit enough employees on its own, so it may supplement its recruiting or selection efforts with those of a vendor. Finally, outsourcing may also have advantages for legal compliance, as many vendors maintain their own procedures for tracking compliance with equal-opportunity laws. From a strategic standpoint, when does it make the most sense to outsource? You may wish to outsource critical tasks that are not crucial to your strategy, like payroll and benefits, or tasks that would require a substantial investment to complete in-house (e.g., conducting extensive background checks). Considering the time and financial resources of these outsourced hires or staffing processes can help you make an informed, strategic outsourcing decision.[33]

External or Internal Hiring

When job vacancies occur or new jobs are created, should the organization seek to fill them from the external or internal labor market? While some mixture of external and internal hiring will be necessary in most situations, the relative blend could vary substantially. To the extent that the organization wants to cultivate a stable, committed workforce, it will probably need to emphasize internal hiring. This will allow employees to use the internal labor market as a springboard for launching long-term careers within the organization. External hiring might then be restricted to specific entry-level jobs, as well as newly created ones for which there are no acceptable internal applicants. External hiring might also be necessary when there is rapid organizational growth, such that the number of new jobs created outstrips internal supply. In general, Boris Groysberg of Harvard Business School notes, "It's not whether you build or buy, it's figuring out under what conditions you build or buy." In many ways, external and internal hiring is a strategic decision. For example, Daniel Sonsino, VP of talent management at Polycom, uses a combination of internal and external hiring that is based primarily on workforce and succession planning—with HR professionals "thinking inside first" before deciding on an external approach, which may be required if new perspectives or ideas are needed.[34]

Core or Flexible Workforce

The organization's core workforce is made up of individuals who are viewed (and view themselves) as regular full-time or part-time employees of the organization. They are central to the core goods and services delivered by the organization. The flexible workforce is composed of more peripheral workers who are used on an as-needed, just-in-time basis. They are not viewed (nor do they view themselves) as regular employees, and legally, most of them are not even employees of the organization. Rather, they are employees of an alternative organization such as a staffing firm (temporary help agency) or an independent contractor. For example, a demand planner who forecasts the demand for TOMS's products may be considered part of the core workforce, but seasonal sales associates may be part of the flexible workforce, particularly since the need for them will depend on sales seasonality. The organization must decide whether to use both core and flexible workforces, what the mixture of core versus flexible workers will be, and in what jobs and units of the organization these mixtures will be deployed. Ideally, these decisions should be driven by the overall business strategy. For example, the demand planner might find an increased forecasted demand in the Palo Alto area during the coming months, which in turn might lead to the hiring of seasonal sales associates.

Hire or Retain

There are trade-offs between hiring strategies and retention strategies for staffing. At one extreme, the organization can accept whatever level of turnover occurs and simply hire replacements to fill the vacancies. Alternatively, the organization can seek to minimize turnover so that the need for replacement staffing is held to a minimum. For example, Ultimate Software, a company that frequently finds itself on *Fortune* magazine's "100 Best Companies to Work For" list, has an annual turnover rate of 4%, meaning that fewer than 4 out of 100 of its employees leave voluntarily within a 12-month period. The company's ability to retain its employees at such a high level is likely due in part to the generous perks it offers, including free health care, paid maternity and paternity leave, life insurance, disability insurance, and tuition reimbursement.[35] Although offering benefits can help improve retention, an organization could strategically conduct an analysis to determine the costs and benefits of these types of strategies and then strive for an optimal mix to control its inflow needs (replacement staffing) by controlling its outflow (retention staffing).

National or Global

As we noted earlier, one form of outsourcing is when organizations outsource staffing activities. Of course, many organizations outsource more than staffing activities— technical support, database management, customer service, and manufacturing are common examples. A growing number of computer-chip makers, such as IBM, Intel, and Motorola, contract with outside vendors to manufacture their chips; often these companies are overseas. Offshoring is related to, but distinct from, outsourcing. Whereas outsourcing is moving a business process (service or manufacturing) to another vendor (whether that vendor is inside or outside the organization's home country), offshoring is the organization setting up its own operations in another country (the organization is not contracting with an outside vendor; rather, it is establishing its own operations in another country). For example, outsourcing would be if an organization, say, IBM, contracted with an outside vendor to manufacture computer chips. Offshoring would be if IBM set up its own plant in another country to manufacture the chips.

Increasingly, US organizations are engaged in both overseas outsourcing and offshoring, a trend spurred by three forces. First, most nations have lowered trading and immigration barriers, which has facilitated offshoring and overseas outsourcing. Second, particularly in the United States and western Europe, organizations find that by outsourcing or offshoring, they can manufacture goods or provide services more cheaply than they can in their own country. Third, some organizations cannot find sufficient talent in their home countries, so they must look elsewhere. A recent report by ManpowerGroup suggests that the world is currently experiencing the highest talent shortage since 2007, particularly in the IT, skilled trades, and sales industries. Although the cost of talent is often cited as a reason for this shortage (e.g., applicants often look for more pay than what is offered), the most frequently cited reasons why employers cannot fill the positions are a lack of applicants, a lack of technical competencies, and a lack of experience. Notably, nearly one-fifth of those surveyed by ManpowerGroup have resorted to outsourcing or offshoring.[36]

Attract or Relocate

Typical staffing strategy is based on the premise that the organization can attract a sufficient number of qualified people to become employees. Another version of this premise is that it is better (and cheaper) to bring the labor to the organization than to bring the organization to the labor. Some organizations, both established and new ones, challenge this premise and choose locations with ample supplies of labor. The growth of high technology pockets such as Silicon Valley reflects the establishment or movement of organizations to geographic areas where there is ready access to highly skilled labor and where employees would like to live, usually locations with research universities nearby to provide the needed graduates for jobs. One now historical example of relocation was Amazon's bidding process to create a second headquarters (in addition to the location in Seattle). As part of the bidding process, cities had to be of a large enough population and have access to transportation and mass transit—with Arlington, Virginia, as the winning bid. In addition to the creation of jobs that will most likely be sourced from the greater Washington, DC, talent pool, the selection of Arlington was a strategic decision with Amazon gaining over $500 million in grants and tax incentives.[37]

Overstaff or Understaff

While most organizations seek to be fully staffed, some opt for being over- or understaffed. Overstaffing may occur when there are dips in demand for the organization's products or services that the organization chooses to ride out. Organizations may also overstaff in order to stockpile talent, recognizing that the staffing spigot cannot be easily turned on or off. Alternatively, understaffing may occur when the organization is confronted with chronic labor shortages, such as is the case for nurses in health care facilities. Also, prediction of an economic downturn may lead the organization to understaff in order to avoid future layoffs. Finally, the organization may decide to understaff and adjust staffing level demand spikes by increasing employee overtime or using flexible staffing arrangements such as temporary employees. Many have blamed the slow job recovery following the Great Recession on the reluctance of companies to put themselves in an overstaffing situation, instead asking current employees to work longer hours in order to handle increased demand in the company's products or services.

Short- or Long-Term Focus

Although any organization would want to have its staffing needs fully anticipated for both the short term and the long term, optimizing both goals is difficult, so trade-offs are often required. In this case, it often means addressing short-term labor shortages by identifying and developing talent for the long term. When forced to choose, organizations focus on their short-term needs. This is understandable because labor shortages can be debilitating. Even when the overall economy is sluggish, the pool of qualified applicants may be thin. In periods of economic duress, a labor shortage can happen in any industry. The trucking industry, for example, has been plagued by a labor shortage. The American Trucking Association predicts a loss of 175,000 truck drivers by 2025, and some economists have referred to this as "ground zero for labor shortages in the U.S."[38]

Balanced against this short-term "crisis management" focus are long-term concerns. Organizations with a long-term view of their staffing needs have put in place talent management programs. In some cases, this means thinking about the strategic talent, or future skill, needs for the entire organization. The problem with a long-term focus is that long-term needs (demand) and availability (supply) are often unclear. Often, it seems as if calls for an upcoming labor shortage due to baby boomer retirements will never end. In fact, recent projections from the Bureau of Labor Statistics (BLS) predict that by 2024 the labor force will have grown by 7.9 million, an average of 0.5% per year (which is much smaller than the growth rates of previous decades). However, BLS economist Ian Wyatt admits that whereas population and labor force growth can be forecasted accurately, labor demand estimates are far less reliable. The future demand for workers "is a very tough question to answer," Wyatt said. "Perhaps because of this, while most organizations are aware of projected labor shortages, many fewer have any concrete plans to do anything about it." Furthermore, even though the labor force is expected to slowly grow over the next decade, the labor force *participation rate*, or the number of those from the labor force expected to become employed and work, is slated to decrease steadily by 2024.[39]

These long-term forecasting difficulties notwithstanding, growth will occur in some skill areas, while others will decrease in demand. Employers that make no efforts to project future supply and demand risk having their strategies derailed by lack of available labor. As a result of a lack of planning, some companies are facing unanticipated skilled labor shortages. For example, Linda Fillingham cannot find skilled laborers to work in her family's steel plant in Bloomington, Illinois. Fillingham expresses puzzlement as to her labor shortage, given the alleged lack of job growth in manufacturing: "It's there if you want to do it," she said. Perhaps long-term planning would have avoided or ameliorated Fillingham's dilemma.[40]

Staffing Quality

Person/Job or Person/Organization Match

When acquiring and deploying people, should the organization opt for a person/job or person/organization match? As we have discussed, both are important for effective staffing. In part, a person/job match will have to be assessed anytime a person is hired to perform a finite set of tasks. In our example, TOMS might hire a demand planner to run forecasting analyses using a software program like Demantra, and most certainly the organization would want to assess whether applicants meet this specific job requirement. On the other hand, a job may be poorly defined and fluid, making a person/job match infeasible. Such jobs are often found in technology and software development organizations. A person/organization match should also be examined, given its effects on retention, interpersonal dynamics, and job satisfaction. A person/organization match would likely become an important concern in organizations with strong, mission-driven cultures. In general, both forms of fit have their own benefits, and it is possible to maximize both (e.g., finding candidates who fit in both respects). However, certain situations (as mentioned) may require a heavier emphasis on one or the other.

Specific or General KSAOs

Should the organization acquire people with specific KSAOs or more general ones? The former means focusing on job-specific competencies, often of the job knowledge and technical skill variety. The latter requires a focus on KSAOs that will be applicable across a variety of jobs, both current and future. Examples of such KSAOs include flexibility and adaptability, ability to learn, written and oral communication skills, and algebra/statistics skills. An organization expecting rapid changes in job content might position itself closer to the general competencies end of the continuum. However, one should be careful to ensure that the skills, whether broad or specific, are critical for the job at hand and not a wish list—one study suggests that including too many disparate competencies can limit the number of applications you receive.[41]

Exceptional or Acceptable Workforce Quality

Strategically, the organization could seek to acquire a workforce that is preeminent KSAO-wise (exceptional quality) or that is more ballpark variety KSAO-wise (acceptable quality). Pursuit of the exceptional quality strategy would allow the organization to stock up on the "best and the brightest" with the hope that this exceptional talent pool would deliver truly superior performance. The acceptable quality strategy means pursuit of a less high-powered workforce and probably a less expensive one as well. Such a decision is a strategic one: during workforce planning, the minimum level of acceptable performance as well as the utility of exceptional performance should be defined. Depending on the added value of exceptional versus acceptable performance for that job, the organization should strive to hire candidates that strategically meet the standards for the position based on these standards.

Active or Passive Diversity

The labor force is becoming increasingly diverse in terms of demographics, values, and languages. Does the organization want to actively pursue this diversity in the labor market so that its own workforce mirrors it, or does the organization want to more passively let diversity of its workforce happen? Advocates of an active diversity strategy argue that it is legally and morally appropriate and that a diverse workforce allows the organization to be more attuned to the diverse needs of the customers it serves. Those favoring a more passive strategy suggest that diversification of the workforce takes time because it requires substantial planning and assimilation activity. TOMS is up-front on its application materials that it is an equal-opportunity employer—in fact, promoting equal opportunity is one of its philanthropic endeavors. It supports the Magic Bus, a company that ensures that children from diverse and impoverished backgrounds are equipped with the education and skills they need to succeed.[42]

STAFFING ETHICS

Staffing the organization involves a multitude of individuals—hiring managers, staffing professionals, potential coworkers, legal advisors, and job applicants. During the staffing process, all these individuals may be involved in recruitment, selection, and employment activities, as well as decision making. Are there, or should there be, boundaries on these individuals' actions and decisions? The answer is yes, for without boundaries, potentially negative outcomes and harmful effects may occur. For example, staffing is often a hurried process, driven by tight deadlines and calls for expediency (e.g., the hiring manager who says to the staffing professional, "Just get me someone now—I'll worry about how good they are later on"). Such calls may lead to negative consequences, including hiring someone without proper assessment and subsequently having him or her perform poorly, ignoring the many applicants who would have been successful performers, failing to advance the organization's workforce diversity initiatives and possible legal obligations, and making an exceedingly generous job offer that provides the highest salary in the work unit, causing dissatisfaction and possible turnover among other work unit members. Such actions and outcomes raise issues of staffing ethics.

Ethics involves determining moral principles and guidelines for the acceptable practice of staffing. Within the practice of staffing in the workplace, ethics emphasizes adhering to high standards for professional responsibility, undergoing continuous professional development, exercising ethical leadership, promoting fairness and justice, avoiding conflicts of interest, and protecting the rights and information of stakeholders.[43] Generally, organizational ethics seeks to

- Raise ethical expectations
- Legitimize dialogue about ethical issues
- Encourage ethical decision making
- Prevent misconduct and provide a basis for enforcement

While organizations are increasingly developing general codes of conduct, it is unknown whether these codes contain specific staffing provisions. Even the general code will likely have some pertinence to staffing through provisions on such issues as legal compliance, confidentiality and disclosure of information, and use of organizational property and assets. Individuals involved in staffing should know and follow their organization's code of ethics. Several points that pertain to staffing specifically can guide a person's ethical conduct. These points are shown in Exhibit 1.8 and elaborated on below.

The first point is that the staffing professional is serving as an agent of the organization and is duty bound to represent the organization first and foremost. That duty is to bring into being effective person/job and person/organization matches. The second point indicates that the agent must avoid placing their own interests, or that of a third party (such as an applicant or friend), above that of the organization. Point three suggests that even though the staffing professional represents the organization, he or she should remember that the applicant is a participant in the staffing process. How the staffing professional treats applicants may well lead to reactions by them

---

EXHIBIT 1.8 Suggestions for Ethical Staffing Practice

1. Represent the organization's interests.
2. Beware of conflicts of interest.
3. Remember the job applicant.
4. Follow staffing policies and procedures.
5. Know and follow the law.
6. Consult professional codes of conduct.
7. Shape effective practice with research results.
8. Seek ethics advice.
9. Be aware of an organization's ethical climate/culture.

that are favorable to the organization and further its interests, let alone those of applicants. Point four reminds the staffing professional to know the organization's staffing policies and procedures and adhere to them. The fifth point indicates a need to be knowledgeable of the myriad laws and regulations governing staffing, to follow them, and to seek needed assistance in their interpretation and application. Point six guides the staffing professional toward professional codes of conduct pertaining to staffing and HR. For example, the Society for Human Resource Management (SHRM) has a formal code of ethics. The Society for Industrial and Organizational Psychology (SIOP) follows the ethics code of the American Psychological Association (APA) and has issued a set of professional principles to guide appropriate use of employee selection procedures. The seventh point states that there is considerable useful research-based knowledge about the design and effectiveness of staffing systems and techniques that should guide staffing practice. Much of that research is summarized in usable formats in this book. The eighth point suggests that when confronted with ethical issues, it is appropriate to seek ethical advice from others. Handling troubling ethical issues alone is unwise.

The final point is that one must be aware of an organization's climate and culture for ethical behavior. Organizations differ in their ethical climate/culture, and this has two implications for staffing.[44] First, an organization may have expectations for *how* staffing decisions are made. How an organization communicates with recruits (including those who are rejected) and whether selection decisions are made hierarchically or collaboratively are two examples of ethical staffing issues that may well vary from organization to organization. Second, an organization's ethics climate may well affect *which* staffing decisions are made. An organization that has high expectations for ethics may weight selection information differently (placing more weight on, say, background checks) than an organization with more typical expectations.

In both ways, one needs to realize that while some ethics considerations are universal, in other cases, what is considered ethical in one climate may be a breach of ethics in another.

It should be recognized that many pressure points on staffing professionals may cause them to compromise the ethical standards discussed above. Research suggests that the principal causes of this pressure are the felt needs to follow top management's or a supervisor's directive, be a team player, protect the interests of the organization, save others' jobs, meet performance goals, deal with internal competition, and cope with having limited resources.[45]

Being aware of and consciously attempting to follow the suggestions in Exhibit 1.8 constitute a professional and ethical responsibility. But what about situations in which ethical lapses are suspected or observed in others?

One response to the situation is to do nothing—neither report nor attempt to change the misconduct. Research suggests a small proportion (about 20%) chooses to ignore and not report misconduct.[46] Major reasons for this response include the need to report the incident to the person involved, the belief that no action would be taken, a lack of anonymity in the reporting process, and the fear of retaliation from one's boss or senior management. Against such reasons for inaction must be weighed the harm that has, or could, come to the employer, the employee, or the job applicant. Moreover, failure to report the misconduct may well increase the chances that it will be repeated, with continuing harmful consequences. Not reporting misconduct may also conflict with one's personal values and create remorse for not having done the right thing. Finally, a failure to report misconduct may bring penalties to oneself if that failure subsequently becomes known to one's boss or senior management. In short, "looking the other way" should not be viewed as a safe, wise, or ethical choice.

A different way to handle unethical staffing practices by others is to seek advice from one's boss, senior management, coworkers, legal counsel, an ethics officer or ombudsperson, or an outside friend or family member. The guidelines in Exhibit 1.8 can serve as a helpful starting point to frame the discussion and decide what to do.

At times, the appropriate response to others' misconduct is to step in directly to try to prevent or rectify the misconduct. This would be especially appropriate with employees whom one supervises or with coworkers. Before taking such an action, it would be wise to consider whether one has the authority and resources to do so, along with the likely support of those other employees or coworkers.

PLAN FOR THE BOOK

The book is divided into six parts:

1. The Nature of Staffing
2. Support Activities
3. Staffing Activities: Recruitment
4. Staffing Activities: Selection
5. Staffing Activities: Employment
6. Staffing System and Retention Management

Each chapter in these six parts begins with a brief topical outline to help the reader quickly discern its general contents. The "meat" of the chapter comes next. A chapter summary then reviews and highlights points from the chapter. A set of discussion questions, ethical issues to discuss, applications (cases and exercises), and detailed endnotes complete the chapter.

The social and legal contexts for staffing are considered first in the social and legal environment chapter. This chapter reviews principles related to social expectations around the employment relationship, legally recognized forms of employment relationship (i.e., employee, independent contractor, temporary worker), fairness in selection, inclusive staffing policies, and equal employment opportunity law. These social issues are woven through the content of all chapters. Each subsequent chapter also has a separate breakout section labeled "Legal Issues," in which specific legal topics relevant to the chapter's content are discussed.

The endnotes at the end of each chapter are quite extensive. They are drawn from academic, practitioner, and legal sources with the goal of providing a balanced selection from each of these sources. Emphasis is on the inclusion of recent references of high quality and easy accessibility. An overly lengthy list of references to each specific topic is avoided; instead, a sampling of only the best available is included.

The applications at the end of each chapter are of two varieties. First are cases that describe a situation and require analysis and response. The response may be written or oral (such as in class discussion or a group presentation). Second are exercises that entail small projects and require active practice of a particular task. Through these cases and exercises the reader becomes an active participant in the learning process and is able to apply the concepts provided in each chapter.

SUMMARY

At the national level, staffing involves a huge number of hiring transactions each year, is a major cost of doing business (especially for service-providing industries), and can lead to substantial revenue and growth for the organization. Staffing is defined as "the process of acquiring, deploying, and retaining a workforce of sufficient quantity and quality to create positive impacts on the organization's effectiveness." The definition emphasizes that both staffing levels and labor quality contribute to an organization's effectiveness, and that a concerted set of labor acquisition, deployment, and retention actions guides the flow of people into, within, and out of the organization. Descriptions of three staffing systems help highlight the definition of staffing.

Several models illustrate various elements of staffing. The staffing level model shows how projected labor requirements and availabilities are compared to derive staffing levels that represent being overstaffed, fully staffed, or understaffed. The next two models illustrate staffing quality via the person/job match and the person/organization match. The former indicates there is a need to match (1) the person's KSAOs to job requirements and (2) the person's motivation to the job's rewards. In the person/organization match, the person's characteristics are matched to additional factors beyond the target job, namely, organizational values, new job duties for the target job, multiple jobs, and future jobs. Effectively managing the matching process results in positive impacts on HR outcomes such as attraction, performance, and retention. The core staffing components model shows that there are three basic activities in staffing: recruitment (identification and attraction of applicants), selection (assessment and evaluation of applicants), and employment (decision making and final match). The staffing organizations model shows that organization, HR, and staffing strategies are formulated and shape staffing policies and programs. In turn, these meld into a set of staffing support activities (legal compliance, planning, and job analysis), as well as the core activities (recruitment, selection, and employment). Retention and staffing system management activities cut across both support and core activities.

Staffing strategy is both an outgrowth of and a contributor to HR and organization strategy. Thirteen important strategic staffing decisions loom for any organization. Some pertain to staffing level choices, and others deal with staffing quality choices.

Staffing ethics involves determining moral principles and guidelines for practice. Numerous suggestions were made for ethical conduct in staffing, and many pressure points for sidestepping such conduct are in operation. Appropriate ways of handling such pressures will be discussed in the remainder of the book.

The staffing organizations model serves as the structural framework for the book. The first part treats staffing models and strategy. The second part treats the support activities of legal compliance, planning, and job analysis. The next three parts treat the core staffing activities of recruitment, selection, and employment. The last section addresses staffing systems and employee retention management. Each chapter has a section labeled "Legal Issues," as well as discussion questions, ethical issues questions, applications, and endnotes.

DISCUSSION QUESTIONS

1. What are potential problems with having a staffing process in which vacancies are filled (1) on a lottery basis from among job applicants, or (2) on a first come–first hired basis among job applicants?
2. Why is it important for the organization to view all components of staffing (recruitment, selection, and employment) from the perspective of the job applicant?
3. Would it be desirable to hire people only according to the person/organization match, ignoring the person/job match?
4. What are examples of how staffing activities are influenced by training activities? Compensation activities?
5. Are some of the 13 strategic staffing decisions more important than others? If so, which ones? Why?

ETHICAL ISSUES

1. Assume that you are either the staffing professional in the department or the hiring manager of a work unit. Explain why it is so important to represent the organization's interests (see Exhibit 1.8). What are some possible consequences of not doing so?
2. One of the strategic staffing choices is whether to pursue workforce diversity actively or passively. First suggest some ethical reasons for active pursuit of diversity, and then suggest some ethical reasons for a more passive approach. Assume that the type of diversity in question is increasing workforce representation of women and ethnic minorities.

APPLICATIONS

Staffing for Your Own Job

Instructions

Consider a job you previously held or your current job. Use the staffing components model to help you think through and describe the staffing process that led to your getting hired for the job. Trace and describe the process (1) from your own perspective as a job applicant and (2) from the organization's perspective. Listed below are some questions to jog your memory. Write your responses to these questions and be prepared to discuss them.

Applicant Perspective

Recruitment:

1. Why did you identify and seek out the job with this organization?
2. How did you try to make yourself attractive to the organization?

Selection:

1. How did you gather information about the job's requirements and rewards?
2. How did you judge your own KSAOs and needs relative to the requirements and rewards?

Employment:

1. Why did you decide to continue on with the staffing process, rather than drop out of it?
2. Why did you decide to accept the job offer? What were the pluses and minuses of the job?

Organization Perspective

Even if you are unsure of the answers to the following questions, try to answer them or guess at them.

Recruitment:

1. How did the organization identify you as a job applicant?
2. How did the organization make the job attractive to you?

Selection:

1. What techniques (application blank, interview, etc.) did the organization use to gather KSAO information about you?
2. How did the organization evaluate this information? What did it see as your strong and weak points, KSAO-wise?

Employment:

1. Why did the organization continue to pursue you as an applicant, rather than reject you from further consideration?
2. What was the job offer process like? Did you receive a verbal or written offer (or both)? Who made the offer? What was the content of the offer?

Reactions to the Staffing Process

Now that you have described the staffing process, what are your reactions to it?

1. What were the strong points or positive features of the process?
2. What were the weak points or negative features of the process?
3. What changes would you like to see made in the process, and why?

Staffing Strategy for a New Plant

Household Consumer Enterprises, Inc. (HCE) specializes in the design and production of household products such as brooms, brushes, rakes, kitchen utensils, and garden tools. It has its corporate headquarters in downtown Chicago, with manufacturing and warehouse/distribution facilities throughout the north-central region of the United States. The organization recently changed its mission from "providing households with safe and sturdy utensils" to "providing households with visually appealing utensils that are safe and sturdy." The new emphasis on "visually appealing" will necessitate new strategies for designing and producing products that have design flair and imagination built into them. One strategy under consideration is to target various demographic groups with different utensil designs. One group is 25- to 40-year-old professional and managerial people, who are believed to want such utensils for both their visual and conversation-piece appeal.

A tentative strategy is to build and staff a new plant that will have free rein in the design and production of utensils for the 25–40 age group. To start, the plant will focus on producing a set of closely related (design-wise) plastic products: dishwashing pans, outdoor wastebaskets, outdoor plant holders, and watering cans. These items can be produced without too large a capital and facilities investment, can be marketed as a group, and can be on stores' shelves and on HCE's store website in time for holiday sales.

The facility's design and engineering team has decided that each of the four products will be produced on a separate assembly line, though the lines will share common technology and require roughly similar assembly jobs. Following the advice from the HR vice president, Jarimir Zwitski, the key jobs in the plant for staffing purposes will be plant manager, product designer (computer-assisted design), assemblers, and packers/warehouse workers. The initial staffing level for the plant will be 150 employees. Because of the riskiness of the venture and the low initial margins that are planned on the four products due to high start-up costs, the plant will run continuously six days per week (i.e., a 24/6 schedule), with the remaining day reserved for cleaning and maintenance. Pay levels will be at the low end of the market, except for product designers, who will be paid above market. Employees will have limited benefits, namely, health insurance with a 30% employee copay after one year of continuous employment and an earned time-off bank (for holidays, sickness, and vacation) of 160 hours per year. They will not receive a pension plan.

The head of the design team, Maria Dos Santos, and Mr. Zwitski wish to come to you, the corporate manager of staffing, to share their preliminary thinking and ask you some questions, knowing that staffing issues abound for this new venture. They ask you to discuss the following questions with them, which they have sent to you in advance so you can prepare for the meeting:

1. What geographic location might be best for the plant in terms of attracting sufficient quantity and quality of labor, especially for the key jobs?
2. Should the plant manager come from inside the current managerial ranks or be sought from the outside?
3. Should staffing be based on just the person/job match or also on the person/organization match?
4. Would it make sense to initially staff the plant with a flexible workforce by using temporary employees and then shift over to a core workforce if it looks like the plant will be successful?
5. In the early stages, should the plant be fully staffed, understaffed, or overstaffed?
6. Will employee retention likely be a problem, and if so, how will this affect the viability of the new plant?
7. What are some of the ethical issues surrounding and confronting the formation of the staffing strategy? What are the potential pressures? How can these ethical issues be addressed?

Your task is to write out a tentative response to each question that will be the basis for your discussion at the meeting.

ENDNOTES

1. "2017 County Business Patterns," *United States Census Bureau* (*www.census.gov/data/tables/2017/econ/cbp/2017-combined-report.html*), accessed Jan. 21, 2020.
2. American Staffing Association, "Staffing Industry Statistics" (*https://americanstaffing.net/staffing-research-data/fact-sheets-analysis-staffing-industry-trends/staffing-industry-statistics/#tab:tbs_nav_item_1*), accessed Jan. 21, 2020; A. Blank and R. Edwards, "Tight Labor Market Continues in 2018 as the Unemployment Rate Falls to a 49-Year Low," *Monthly Labor Review*, May 2019, pp. 1–33; T. Downing, "Employment Growth Accelerates in 2018, Extending a Lengthy Expan-

sion," *Monthly Labor Review*, May 2019, pp. 1–17; L. S. Essien and M. McCarthy, "Job Openings, Hires, and Quits Reach Historic Highs in 2018," *Monthly Labor Review*, July 2019, pp. 1–20.

3. Paycor, "The Biggest Cost of Doing Business: A Closer Look at Labor Costs," Dec. 2019 (*www.paycor.com/resource-center/a-closer-look-at-labor-costs*), accessed Jan. 21, 2020; Saratoga Institute, *The Saratoga Review* (Santa Clara, CA: author, 2009), p. 10.

4. H. Pothmann and M. Loon, "Lifting the Lid on the Value of a Company's Human Capital," *World Economic Forum: Workplace & Employment*, Dec. 2019 (*www.weforum.org/agenda/2019/12/now -there-s-a-way-to-measure-the-value-of-your-company-s-human-capital/*), accessed Jan. 21, 2020.

5. A. Taylor, "Lessons Learned: Ruby's 15 Years," *Ruby* (blog), June 2, 2018 (*www.ruby.com/ruby -15-birthday/*), accessed Jan. 21, 2020; L. Williams-Staples, "A People-Centric Workplace: Good for Growth and Profits," *Great Place to Work* (blog), Dec. 17, 2015 (*www.greatplacetowork.com /resources/blog/a-people-centric-workplace-good-for-growth-and-profits*), accessed Jan. 21, 2020.

6. C. H. Van Iddekinge, G. R. Ferris, P. L. Perrewé, A. A. Perryman, F. R. Blass, and T. D. Heet-derks, "Effects of Selection and Training on Unit-Level Performance Over Time: A Latent Growth Modeling Approach," *Journal of Applied Psychology*, 2009, 94, pp. 829–843.

7. R. R. Kehoe and P. M. Wright, "The Impact of High-Performance Human Resource Practices on Employees' Attitudes and Behaviors," *Journal of Management*, 2013, 39, pp. 366–391.

8. W. F. Cascio and R. Montealegre, "How Technology Is Changing Work and Organizations," *Annual Review of Organizational Psychology and Organizational Behavior*, 2016, 3, pp. 349–375; D. L. Stone, D. L. Deadrick, K. M. Lukaszewski, and R. Johnson, "The Influence of Technology on the Future of Human Resource Management," *Human Resource Management Review*, 2015, 25(2), pp. 216–231; and N. T. Tippins, "Technology and Assessment in Selection," *Annual Review of Organizational Psychology and Organizational Behavior*, 2015, 2, pp. 551–582.

9. T. Chamorro-Premuzic, D. Winsborough, R. A. Sherman, and R. Hogan, "New Talent Signals: Shiny New Objects or a Brave New World?," *Industrial and Organizational Psychology*, 2016, 9(3), pp. 621–640; and B. B. Clark, C. Robert, and S. A. Hampton, "The Technology Effect: How Perceptions of Technology Drive Excessive Optimism," *Journal of Business Psychology*, 2016, 31(1), pp. 87–102.

10. A. M. Ryan and E. Derous, "Highlighting Tensions in Recruitment and Selection Research and Practice," International Journal of Selection and Assessment, 2016, 24(1), pp. 54–62.

11. Y. Kim and R. E. Ployhart, "Antecedents and Consequences of Firm-Level Selection Practice Usage," *Academy of Management Journal*, 2018, 61(1), pp. 46–66; M. A. Wolfson and J. E. Mathieu, "Sprinting to the Finish: Toward a Theory of Human Capital Resource Complementarity," *Journal of Applied Psychology*, 2018, 103(11), pp. 1165–1180.

12. J. B. Barney and P. M. Wright, "On Becoming a Strategic Partner: The Role of Human Resources in Gaining Competitive Advantage," Human Resource Management, 1998, 37(1), pp. 31–46; J. M. Phillips and S. M. Gully, "Multilevel and Strategic Recruiting: Where Have We Been, Where Can We Go From Here?," *Journal of Management*, 2015, 41(5), pp. 1416–1445.

13. *Forbes*, "The Companies Hiring the Most Right Now" (*www.forbes.com/pictures/efkk45ehhfg/the -companies-hiring-the-most-right-now-2/#669cb20e48db*), accessed Jan. 21, 2020.

14. D. Roberts, "At W. L. Gore, 57 Years of Authentic Culture," *Fortune (Leadership: 100 Best Companies to Work for)*, Mar. 5, 2015 (*fortune.com/2015/03/05/w-l-gore-culture/*), accessed Nov. 7, 2016; G. Hamel, "Five Ways to Evolve Management," *Dividend*, Spring 2011, p. 6.

15. "Mike's Story," *W. L. Gore & Associates* (*www.gore.com/en_gb/careers/associatestories/comfort/comfort_ mike.html*); "Hajo's Story," *W. L. Gore & Associates* (*www.gore.com/en_gb/careers/associatestories/lives1 /lives1_hajo.html*); "Our Culture," W. L. Gore & Associates, 2010 (*www.gore.com/about/culture*).

16. Betterteam, "Social Recruiting Tips," Aug. 26, 2019 (*www.betterteam.com/social-recruiting-tips*); T. David, "The Future of Recruiting," Apr. 4, 2017 (*www.careerarc.com/blog/2017/04/future-of -recruiting-study-infographic/*); A. Guadagno, "A Foray Into Social Recruiting: The Untold Stories

Behind 'My Marriott Hotel,'" *HR Exchange Network*, Aug. 1, 2011 (*www.hrexchangenetwork.com/ hr-tech/columns/my-marriott-hotel-the-untold-stories*); MarriottCareers (Instagram page) (*www.ins-tagram.com/marriottcareers/?hl=en*), accessed Jan. 22, 2020; Netbase, "Social Media Rankings Index" (*www.netbase.com/social-media-rankings/*), accessed Jan. 22, 2020; J. Ordioni, "Why Marriott Is a Social Media Recruiting Superstar," *Brandemix* (blog), Mar. 2, 2015 (*www.brandemix.com /why-marriott-is-a-social-media-recruiting-superstar/*); P. Slezak, "How Marriott Hotels Is Beating Facebook at Their Own Game in Social Recruiting," *Recruiting Blogs*, June 25, 2013 (*https:// recruitingblogs.com/profiles/blogs/how-marriott-hotels-is-beating-facebook-at-their-own-game-in*).

17. CollegeGrad, "Top Entry Level Employers for 2019" (https://collegegrad.com/topemployers), accessed Jan. 22, 2020; A. Fisher, "Graduating This Spring? How to Stand Out From the Crowd," *Fortune*, Mar. 1, 2013 (*http://fortune.com/2013/03/01/graduating-this-spring-how-to-stand-out-from -the-crowd/*), accessed Aug. 28, 2013; S. Pathak, "Frat Boys Get an MBA Without the IOU at Enterprise," *Sales Job Watch*, Mar. 3, 2011 (*https://shareenpathak.contently.com/pub/sales-jobs-fins -com*), accessed Aug. 28, 2013.

18. D. F. Caldwell and C. A. O'Reilly, "Measuring Person-Job Fit With a Profile-Comparison Process," *Journal of Applied Psychology*, 1990, 75, pp. 648–657; R. V. Dawis, L. H. Lofquist, and D. J. Weiss, *A Theory of Work Adjustment (A Revision)* (Minneapolis: Industrial Relations Center, University of Minnesota, 1968); A. E. M. van Vianen, "Person-Environment Fit: A Review of Its Basic Tenets," *Annual Review of Organizational Psychology and Organizational Behavior*, 2018, 5, pp. 75–101.

19. J. A. Schmidt, D. S. Chapman, and D. A. Jones, "Does Emphasizing Different Types of Person-Environment Fit in Online Job Ads Influence Application Behavior and Applicant Quality? Evidence from a Field Experiment," *Journal of Business Psychology*, 2015, 30, pp. 267–282.

20. J. Cao and M. Hamori, "How Can Employers Benefit Most From Developmental Job Experiences? The Needs-Supplies Fit Perspective," *Journal of Applied Psychology*, in press.

21. M. E. Beier, W. J. Torres, G. G. Fisher, and L. E. Wallace, "Age and Job Fit: The Relationship Between Demands-Ability Fit and Retirement and Health," *Journal of Occupational Health Psychology*, in press.

22. M. R. Barrick and L. Parks-Leduc, "Selection for Fit," *Annual Review of Organizational Psychology and Organizational Behavior*, 2019, 6, pp. 171–193; A. L. Kristof, "Person-Organization Fit: An Integrative Review of Its Conceptualizations, Measurement, and Implications," *Personnel Psychology*, 1996, 49, pp. 1–50; C. A. O'Reilly, J. Chatman, and D. F. Caldwell, "People and Organizational Culture: A Profile Comparison Approach to Assessing Person-Organization Fit," *Academy of Management Journal*, 1991, 34, pp. 487–516.

23. H. Deng, C.-H. Wu, K. Leung, and Y. Guan, "Depletion From Self-Regulation: A Resource-Based Account of the Effect of Value Incongruence," *Personnel Psychology*, 2016, 69, pp. 431–465.

24. L. L. Levesque, "Opportunistic Hiring and Employee Fit," *Human Resource Management*, 2005, 44, pp. 301–317.

25. N. Roulin and F. Krings, "Faking to Fit In: Applicants' Response Strategies to Match Organizational Culture," *Journal of Applied Psychology*, in press.

26. S. Craig, "Inside Goldman's Secret Rite: The Race to Become Partner," *Wall Street Journal*, Oct. 13, 2006, pp. A1, A11; J. La Roche, "A Tiny Group of Goldman Sachs Employees Are About to Get the Phone Call of a Lifetime," *Business Insider (Finance)*, Nov. 11, 2014 (*www.businessinsider .com/becoming-a-partner-at-goldman-sachs-2014-11*), accessed Nov. 7, 2016.

27. K. Beasley, "Strategy Matters for Mission Driven Brands," *The Chamber* (blog), Sept. 5, 2019 (*https://chamberphl.com/2019/09/strategy-matters-for-mission-driven-brands/*); S. Mainwaring, "Purpose at Work: Lessons From TOMS on How to Lead With Purpose," *Forbes*, Dec. 13, 2018 (*www.forbes.com/sites/simonmainwaring/2018/12/13/purpose-at-work-lessons-from-toms-on-how -to-lead-with-purpose/#4e986fc83e81*); TOMS, "Jobs at TOMS" (*www.toms.com/jobs*), accessed Jan. 22, 2020.

28. L. Buchanan, "Why This Company's Mission Includes No-Meeting Mondays," *Inc.*, May 2016 (*www.inc.com/magazine/201605/leigh-buchanan/toms-employee-culture-programs.html*).

29. R. Karaim, "TOMS' Formula for Connecting With Young Consumers," *WARC (Event Report)*, Sept. 2017 (*www.warc.com/content/paywall/article/event-reports/toms-formula-for-connecting-with-young-consumers/118021*).

30. Buchanan, "Why This Company's Mission Includes No-Meeting Mondays."

31. TOMS, "Supply Chain Disclosure" (*www.toms.com/supply-chain-transparency*), accessed Jan. 22, 2020.

32. J. Koch, "Are You Ready to Outsource Staffing," *Workforce*, Apr. 1, 2000 (*www.workforce.com/news/are-you-ready-to-outsource-staffing*).

33. C. Cohn, "Strategic Ways to Outsource, and When to Do It," *Forbes*, Mar. 19, 2015 (*www.forbes.com/sites/chuckcohn/2015/03/19/strategic-ways-to-outsource-and-when-to-do-it/#68dd51d42fcb*).

34. E. Krell, "Weighing Internal vs. External Hires," *SHRM*, Jan. 7, 2015 (*www.shrm.org/hr-today/news/hr-magazine/pages/010215-hiring.aspx*).

35. Ultimate Software, "Careers" (*www.ultimatesoftware.com/careers/*), accessed Jan. 22, 2020.

36. ManpowerGroup, 2016/2017 Talent Shortage Survey (*www.manpowergroup.us/campaigns/talent-shortage/assets/pdf/2016-Global-Talent-Shortage-Infographic.pdf*), accessed Nov. 7, 2016.

37. L. Feiner, "Amazon Will Get up to $2.2 Billion in Incentives for Bringing New Offices and Jobs to New York City, Northern Virginia and Nashville," *CNBC*, Nov. 13, 2018 (*www.cnbc.com/2018/11/13/amazon-tax-incentives-in-new-york-city-virginia-and-nashville.html*); A. Selyukh, "Amazon's Grand Search for 2nd Headquarters Ends With Split: NYC and D.C. Suburb," *NPR*, Nov. 13, 2018 (*www.npr.org/2018/11/13/665646050/amazons-grand-search-for-2nd-headquarters-ends-with-split-nyc-and-d-c-suburb*).

38. I. Ivanova, "These Are the Industries With the Biggest Labor Shortages," *CBS News*, Feb. 4, 2019 (*www.cbsnews.com/news/these-are-the-industries-with-the-biggest-labor-shortages/*); J. Kingston, "ATA's Costello Projects Out the Driver Shortage, and It's a Big Number," *FreightWaves*, Apr. 3, 2018 (*www.freightwaves.com/news/driver-shortage-ata-estimates*).

39. K. R. Lewis, "Recession Aside, Are We Headed for a Labor Shortage?," *The Fiscal Times*, Aug. 26, 2010 (*www.thefiscaltimes.com*); K. Gurchiek, "Few Organizations Planning for Talent Shortage as Boomers Retire," *SHRM News*, Nov. 17, 2010 (*www.shrm.org*); M. Toossi, "Labor Force Projections to 2024: The Labor Force Is Growing, but Slowly," *Monthly Labor Review*, December 2015 (*www.bls.gov/opub/mlr/2015/article/labor-force-projections-to-2024.htm*), accessed Nov. 7, 2016.

40. C. Bowers, "Skilled Labor Shortage Frustrates Employers," *CBS Evening News*, Aug. 11, 2010 (*www.cbsnews.com/stories/2010/08/11/eveningnews/main6764731.shtml?tag=mncol;lst;1*).

41. T. S. Mohr, "Why Women Don't Apply for Jobs Unless They're 100% Qualified," *Harvard Business Review*, Aug. 25, 2014 (*https://hbr.org/2014/08/why-women-dont-apply-for-jobs-unless-theyre-100-qualified*); R. Skilbeck, "3 Ways to Identify the Best Person for the Role," *Forbes*, Oct. 29, 2019 (*www.forbes.com/sites/rebeccaskilbeck/2019/10/29/3-ways-to-identify-the-best-person-for-the-role/#174049705a2e*).

42. TOMS, "Careers"; TOMS, "Impact" (*www.toms.com/impact*), accessed Jan. 22, 2020.

43. Society of Human Resource Management, *Code of Ethics*, amended Nov. 21, 2014 (*www.shrm.org/about-shrm/pages/code-of-ethics.aspx*).

44. A. Arnaud and M. Schminke, "The Ethical Climate and Context of Organizations: A Comprehensive Model," *Organization Science*, 2012, 23, pp. 1767–1780.

45. Society for Human Resource Management, *The Ethics Landscape in American Business: Sustaining a Strong Ethical Work Environment*, June 2008 (*www.shrm.org/hr-today/trends-and-forecasting/research-and-surveys/Documents/08%20Ethics_Landscape_in_American_Business%20FINAL.pdf*), accessed Nov. 7, 2016.

46. Ibid.

The Staffing Organizations Model

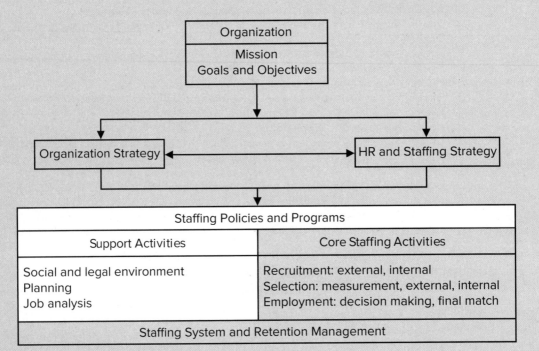

PART TWO

Support Activities

CHAPTER TWO

Social and Legal Environment

Learning Objectives and Introduction
  Learning Objectives
  Introduction

The Employment Relationship
  Social and Legal Foundations
  Economic and Social Exchanges
  Forms of the Employment Relationship

Diversity and Inclusion
  Business Case for Diversity and Inclusion
  Demography of the American Workforce
  Workforce Diversity Measurement and Analysis
  Staffing Practices for Diversity and Inclusion

Legal Framework for Equal Employment Opportunity
  Key Concepts
  Federal Laws Regarding EEO
  Claim Resolution Processes

Social and Legal Issues in Remainder of Book

Summary

Discussion Questions

Ethical Issues

Applications
  To Employ, or Not to Employ?
  Age Discrimination in a Promotion?

Endnotes

LEARNING OBJECTIVES AND INTRODUCTION

Learning Objectives

- Understand the social and legal foundations for the employment relationship
- Appreciate the purpose and sources of staffing regulation
- Evaluate the business case for diversity and inclusion
- Learn how to measure and evaluate workforce diversity
- Understand staffing practices to enhance diversity and inclusion
- Review major federal equal employment opportunity statutes
- Understand the process of employment discrimination cases

Introduction

An employment relationship is established when an organization and an individual develop an agreement about requirements and rewards. Social norms and legal frameworks combine to provide the context in which the relationship plays out. As relationships become more enduring, a set of mutual expectations develops. The relationship shifts from a transactional orientation based on economic exchange to a relational orientation based on social exchange. The employment relationship has been increasingly regulated. The laws and regulations come from many sources and take different forms depending on whether individuals are classified as employees, independent contractors, or temporary workers.

Part of the social context for employment relates to diversity and inclusion. Businesses that successfully draw from the full range of potential talent have a competitive advantage. Inclusivity in staffing also helps organizations ethically promote their goals, benefiting workers and society as a whole. Many methods have been developed to help turn these good intentions into concrete, tangible practices.

The legal system has also endeavored to foster fairness and nondiscrimination in staffing. Laws and accompanying regulations prohibit discrimination on the basis of protected characteristics, such as race, sex, religion, age, and disability. Organizations may not make staffing decisions based on these characteristics. Instead, employers must focus on job-related knowledge, skill, ability, and other characteristics (KSAOs) as the bases for all staffing practices and decisions.

Throughout the chapter, topics and applications of the law are presented. Their intent is to raise awareness about issues covered by the law. Every staffing professional should be aware of the law, while recognizing that compliance requires professional legal counsel.

THE EMPLOYMENT RELATIONSHIP

As the introductory chapter noted, the majority of staffing activities are designed to initiate and maintain relationships with employees. There are many competing theories related to the types of interactions employers and employees will have with one another. We cover some of the most prominent of these below.

Social and Legal Foundations

Work is central to a functioning society. Thus, robust systems of social norms and legal regulations have been developed. Staffing professionals need to understand these forces to be successful in their roles. We start our discussion of social and legal foundations by describing the social and cultural aspects of how work is viewed. Our discussion is rooted in the laws and customs in the United States, but we note cultural factors that produce different legal considerations in other countries.

Social Foundations

The social foundations of paid work are rooted in economics. The unemployment rate and labor productivity are two of the most substantive indicators of the well-being of the economy as a whole. For the great majority of workers, the employment relationship is the main source of income for all their needs. Employment provides health care benefits and retirement income as well. For employers, the employment relationship is a major input into production. This production is, in turn, the source of most goods and services for consumers. Labor costs constitute the single largest expenditure for many organizations.

The social foundations of employment go beyond monetary concerns. We all implicitly recognize the importance of work, since when we first meet someone we often ask, "So what do you do?" The assumption is that the person will mention their job. Most people spend more time engaged in work than in any other activity. This means that a huge part of our identity and role in society is determined by the work we do. The bond between the person who pays for the work and the person who does the work goes beyond exchanging goods and services. People derive motivation and a sense of selfhood not merely from the work they do but from whom they do it for.[1]

Legal Foundations

The centrality of work is reflected in the legal system. Laws and regulations provide specific protections to employees that they are unlikely to get in an unregulated relationship. These protections include the right to organize and collectively bargain, minimum wages, nondiscrimination, overtime pay, and safety and health standards. Individual rights examples include privacy protections and constraints on unilateral termination. Finally, laws and regulations encourage consistency of treatment among employees who have historically faced discrimination.

Employers also benefit from laws and regulations. Laws and regulations not only forbid certain types of discrimination but also outline permissible employment practices. Having a written set of guidelines from administrative agencies makes compliance far easier. Reflecting this desire for certainty, much of the legislative advocacy work performed by the Society for Human Resource Management (SHRM) is directed toward increasing uniformity and clarity in laws. Many of the agencies that regulate employment provide assistance and training to employers. Finally, laws reduce the incentive for employers to save money by underpaying workers, cutting costs in safety procedures, or engaging in discrimination to appeal to the preferences of prejudiced customers. Leveling the playing field through a common set of legal rules helps staffing professionals act in accord with their ethical values.

There are many sources for the laws and regulations that govern the employment relationship. Staffing professionals should recognize that these different sources all come together to influence how a case may be decided, so knowing the major federal laws is only a starting point for knowing how to keep policies and procedures within regulatory guidelines.[2] Exhibit 2.1 outlines how these sources of laws pertain to staffing.

Constitutional Law. Constitutional law is derived from the US Constitution and its amendments. It supersedes any other source of law or regulation. Constitutional law is most commonly referenced when determining whether a statute is consistent with, or in violation of, the constitutional framework. The language of

EXHIBIT 2.1 Sources of Employment Regulations

Source	Examples
Constitutional law	Defines limits for statutes Fifth Amendment Fourteenth Amendment
Statutes	Civil Rights Act Age Discrimination in Employment Act Americans With Disabilities Act Immigration Reform and Control Act State and local laws Civil service laws
Case law	Interpretation of statutes Employment-at-will Definition of torts
Administrative regulations	Equal Employment Opportunity Commission (EEOC) Department of Labor (DOL) Office of Federal Contract Compliance Programs (OFCCP) Department of Homeland Security State fair employment practice (FEP) agencies

constitutional amendments is very broad, so there is comparatively little guidance for staffing policy. Another major application of constitutional law is in the area of public employee rights, particularly their due process rights.

Statutes.   Statutory law is derived from written statutes passed by legislative bodies. These bodies are federal (Congress), state (legislatures and assemblies), and local (municipal boards and councils). Legislative bodies may also create agencies to administer and enforce the law. Staffing professionals need to be especially well informed about statutes since they provide the foundation for nearly all aspects of equal employment opportunity regulation.

The emphasis in this book is on federal laws and regulations. Laws at the state and local levels are equally important. State laws are often patterned after federal law. Basic provisions, however, vary substantially from state to state. State and local laws and regulations often provide protections beyond those contained in the federal laws and regulations. State laws, for example, may apply to employers with fewer than 15 employees, may prohibit kinds of discrimination not prohibited under federal law, and may deviate from federal law with regard to enforcement mechanisms and penalties for noncompliance. Organizations that operate in many locations need to know multiple bodies of law. For multinationals, an even more complicated picture arises since the fundamental assumptions and procedures in American law are not held in many other nations. These variations greatly increase the array of applicable laws to which the organization must attend.

Case Law.   Case law is based on precedents for how cases have been adjudicated across multiple layers of the legal system. Case law in the American system dates back to the colonial era, and therefore overlaps with the foundation found in many countries, such as the United Kingdom, as well as former colonies including Canada, Jamaica, India, Pakistan, and Australia. It consists of the case-by-case decisions of the court, which determine over time permissible and impermissible practices, as well as their remedies. Much of the law regarding the employment relationship and the rights of both employers and employees comes from case law rather than statutes.[3] Case law is often concerned with interpretation of statutes for instances not covered in sufficient detail in the original documents. Nearly all the guidance related to specific employment practices and standards of evidence comes from case law.

Each state develops and administers its own case law. Employment-at-will and workplace tort cases are treated at the state level. Employment-at-will involves the rights of the employer and the employee to terminate the employment relationship at any time for nearly any reason. A tort is a civil wrong that occurs when the employer violates a duty owed to its employees or customers that leads to harm or damages suffered by them. Staffing tort examples include hiring of employees who pose a danger to other employees or customers or who create an unsafe working environment, fraud and misrepresentation regarding employment terms and conditions, defamation of former employees, and invasion of privacy.

Administrative Regulations.   Administrative agencies interpret, administer, and enforce the law. Employees who have concerns about workplace issues often turn to administrative agencies, which act to facilitate investigation and resolution of complaints. Administrative agencies also provide guidance to employers in developing policies and procedures that provide equal employment opportunities, training in best practices in equal employment opportunity, and mediation services to resolve disputes between employers and employees. Agencies document rules, regulations, guidelines, and policy statements and use these to guide their activities.

At the federal level, the two major agencies of concern to staffing are the Equal Employment Opportunity Commission (EEOC) and the Department of Labor (DOL).[4] The EEOC provides guidance and enforcement for federal laws related to race, color, religion, sex, national origin, age over 40, and disability. Several units for administration of employment law are housed within the DOL, most notably the Wage and Hour Division (WHD) and the Occupational Safety and Health Administration (OSHA). The Office of Federal Contract Compliance Programs (OFCCP) oversees compliance with nondiscrimination laws and regulations for organizations that do business with the federal government, including affirmative action. Data related to employment is collected and reported through the DOL's Bureau of Labor Statistics (BLS).

Economic and Social Exchanges

Not all employment relationships are the same. One useful way to differentiate these relationships is to consider economic and social exchanges.[5] Below, we outline some of the social norms related to these exchanges and how they influence behavior. Although these norms are not legally binding, they have bottom-line consequences: employee motivation and behavior come from normative expectations for reciprocity and fair treatment. Legal processes also start from employee perceptions of norms violations—before consulting a lawyer, employees usually check with family, friends, and coworkers about whether they are being treated fairly. In light of this, staffing experts need to be aware that their actions can either foster or undermine high-quality economic and social exchanges. Exhibit 2.2 provides an overview of the employment relationship process and the outcomes of different forms of exchanges.

Economic Exchange

Employment is fundamentally an economic exchange in which employers offer pay and benefits to employees in exchange for labor. Relationships that are marked by economic exchanges are described as having a transactional orientation. A transactional orientation means that employees see the organization largely as a source of well-defined financial outcomes, and the organization sees employees largely as a source of well-defined work outcomes. An employee who is hired for short-term work with no expectation of training or development beyond the bare minimum required to do the job will naturally come to see the organization in this way.

EXHIBIT 2.2   Matching Process and Employment Relationship

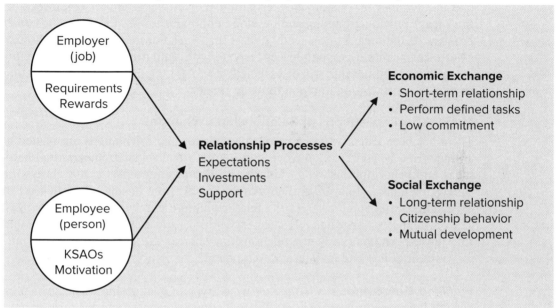

These economic exchanges are largely impersonal. Enforcement mechanisms through formal agreements are common in the absence of a bond of loyalty and trust. Contracts, commissions, and piece-rate pay are all examples of these well-specified economic exchanges. Because of their specific outcome orientation and lack of mutual investment, transactional relationships are generally easy for either party to exit without much economic harm.

Social Exchange

Of course, people do not see others in terms of just pure economic exchanges; there are also elements of social exchange. The term "social exchange" refers to social-emotional interactions in which parties contribute above and beyond written agreements. The social context for these exchanges is based on less concrete but powerful concepts of commitment and loyalty. Such characteristics tend to emerge over time during periods of repeated exchanges. As the employer and the employee invest in one another through repeated interactions, they come to develop a sense of commitment and mutual obligation.[6] Emotionally linked factors like trust and support facilitate more flexibility in meeting expectations over long timelines.[7] In the same way that a relationship marked by economic exchanges tends to foster a transactional orientation, relationships marked by social exchanges tend to foster a relational orientation.

Because they are open-ended and involve positive feelings, social exchanges induce employees to contribute effort exceeding the job description or performance evaluation form. When employers and employees report a relational orientation toward one another, they make more long-term mutual investments. On the employer side, this means providing training and development opportunities that facilitate career progress. If the organization sends signals that a relationship will endure through investment in employees, employees respond with similar investments in developing skills and abilities that will be especially useful for the organization. Motivation to help the organization in broad terms is greater.

Managerial Implications of Relationship Exchange

There has been extensive research on how relationship orientations are related to attitudes and behaviors of employees. While informal social exchanges build attitudes and behaviors that seem desirable to organizations, this is not always the case. Sometimes employers and employees benefit from having an explicit set of expectations that some parts of the relationship are purely economic exchanges. The economic exchange has very clear expectations and is useful for setting ground rules for expectations early in a relationship, whereas the social exchange permits for more flexibility and long-term development.

Fulfilling Expectations.   No matter which type of relationship exchange is present, fulfilling expectations is crucial. When it comes to expectations for performance, established terms can reduce uncertainty for both sides. Explicit terms may result in a more transactional orientation, but they also greatly reduce the likelihood of a violation of expectations. Within a relational orientation, a well-defined path for career development and future investment is welcome. It is easier to develop trust when there are clear signals that the employer sees the relationship as worthy of investment.

Violation of either specific or general terms of employment is related to lower job satisfaction and engagement, increased burnout, and lower job performance.[8] If a transactional orientation prevails and commitment is minimal, violations are likely to represent an immediate point for employee turnover. Given the lack of shared investment, little is lost by leaving the organization. With a relational orientation based on a history of trust and expectation of mutual support, failure to fulfill expectations can be even more damaging.[9] The disruption of the close emotional bond can create an equal and opposite set of strongly negative feelings. When social expectations are violated, the breaking of the relationship will have more emotional impact. Employees in these cases may be more prone to engage in sabotage or complain about the organization both internally and externally. Once damaged, a social exchange is very hard to recover. The organization's investment in the relationship will be squandered.

Perceived Organizational Support.   There are many activities organizations can engage in to build up a relational orientation to the employment relationship.[10] Many of these involve building perceptions of organizational support through mutual exchange investments. Developmental opportunities, job security, and enriching job characteristics are some of the investments employers can make. Organizational support can also be established through honest personal communication. Fit between employee values and the values of the organization contributes to the sense that the organization is supportive, perhaps reflecting the fact that the employer provides treatment consistent with employee expectations and preferences. Workers who have autonomy and the ability to participate in decision making also have higher levels of employee-organization relationship quality. Conversely, poorly defined work roles or conflicts about responsibilities tend to undermine perceptions that the organization is supportive.

The Role of Supervisors.   While the organization may influence social exchanges through general policies and procedures, direct supervisors may have an even stronger role to play. People seldom develop a trusting emotional bond by having social exchanges with an entire organization; instead, supervisors come to embody the organization for employees.[11] Supervisors build up mutual support in the same way that the organization does by treating employees with respect, fulfilling expectations for fair treatment, and giving employees development assistance. Supervisors can also damage the relationship much as the organization can by undermining employees and embarrassing them in front of others.

Outcomes of Economic and Social Exchange.   The outcomes of different relationship orientations have implications for different organizational structures and goals. Organizations that are oriented toward internal employee development and promotion-from-within policies will tend to reap greater rewards from a psychosocial relationship. On the other hand, when relationships are short term, having explicit employment terms may be preferable. Sometimes these expectations are so specific that the relationship is completely governed by a contract that covers starting and ending dates, rates of pay for outcomes (e.g., commissions, piece rates), and grounds under which parties can terminate the relationship before the expected duration.

Social exchanges increase employee feelings of obligation to reciprocate organizational investments.[12] As interactions take on a relational character, employees develop a sense of emotional commitment to the organization. The relationship itself becomes valuable for employees, and employees voluntarily engage in actions to help maintain the relationship. Employees in these social exchange relationships will do extra work beyond the requirements explicitly listed in the job description. Examples of "going the extra mile" include taking time to help newcomers adjust to their jobs, volunteering for difficult assignments, and spreading positive word of mouth about the organization.

Managing Relationships Through Staffing

In light of the preceding material, it is clear that there are desirable elements of both economic and social exchanges. Concerns about the nature of the relationship between employer and employee arise throughout the employee life cycle.

Supportive behavior strategies for recruiting include following through on promises for contact, regular two-way communication, and adequate explanation for all the stages of the process of application and evaluation.[13] Recruiting managers should be thoroughly trained in all of these issues. The issue of establishing accurate expectations during recruiting is further discussed later in the book when we talk about realistic job previews and the development of clear policies for internal promotions.

In the selection context, communicating with candidates about how and why they are being evaluated is extremely important for both forms of relationships. Everyone involved in evaluating candidate KSAOs should be well informed about the policies and procedures so that they can be consistently presented to candidates. There are also signals that might be given to applicants and candidates by different selection tools. For example, the conduct of the interviewer during a selection interview further develops job candidate expectations related to the relationship. Internal selection methods tend to foster a social exchange, especially when the stages for selection are clearly defined for employees and expectations are clear. Even external applicants will see the presence of career possibilities as a signal of their own possible future treatment.

The chapter on final match discusses how to initiate the individual relationship through the job offer and onboarding processes. Research consistently shows that when employees are first hired, they tend to see the relationship in transactional terms. Social exchanges require time for the parties to observe one another and establish trust.[14] This means that new hires should have exceptionally clear and specific expectations for what they are expected to do. If the organization anticipates having a purely economic exchange, employees should be told that performance that is consistent with these expectations will be linked to compensation. When social exchanges are preferred, meeting these expectations can be tied to training and development opportunities.

Finally, the chapter on retention management describes how the nature of the relationship with the organization and others in the organization influences retention decisions.

Forms of the Employment Relationship

Because employment relationships are such a fundamental part of most people's lives and undergird the structure and functions of all organizations, they are featured prominently in the law.[15] Exhibit 2.3 shows some of the features of the two major forms of employment relationships (employer-employee and independent contractor) we discuss below.

Before covering these forms of employment relationships, we will review the principle of employment-at-will because it forms such an important backdrop for employment law in the United States.

EXHIBIT 2.3   Forms of the Employment Relationship

Employer-Employee
- Employer defines hours and location of work
- Employer determines and monitors methods and pace of work
- Relationship can be short or long term
- Employer is liable for employee misconduct on the job
- Employer is responsible for employee safety and health
- Employer must pay employee for time or effort dedicated to work
- Employer must pay employee even if work is unsatisfactory

Independent Contractor
- Contractor defines hours and location of work
- Contractor has full discretion over how work is done
- Relationship must be short term
- Contractor has full legal responsibility for work activities
- Contractor is accountable for own safety and health
- Contractor is paid only for work product
- Contractor is paid only for satisfactory work

Employment-at-Will

Under case law, and in the absence of any contract language to the contrary, employment is at-will, meaning that either the employer or the employee may terminate the employment relationship at any time, for any reason, without prior notification.[16] Although employment is assumed to be at-will unless stated otherwise, it is a good idea to include statements related to the at-will nature of the relationship where relevant in policy and procedure materials. Such information is especially important for companies working with expatriates or recent immigrants to the United States, as the at-will principle is not common in most other countries. Employers in the United States have much more freedom to terminate employment without warning or due process relative to much of the rest of the world.

The employment-at-will principle serves several social functions. For the employer, staffing flexibility makes it possible to quickly terminate employees without the expense of developing an argument defending just cause for termination in a legal proceeding. This does put employees in a somewhat precarious position because they rely on their current employer for most of their economic needs, whereas the organization usually does not have that same level of dependence on a single employee. The greater right of the employee to leave with no warning or cause, without fear of legal consequences partially offsets this imbalance. The right to unilaterally terminate employment is not conditional for employees in any way. No written agreement can abrogate this right.

The concept of employment-at-will is very broad, but it is far from absolute. Several regulations restrict employer rights to terminate the employment relationship.[17] Collective bargaining agreements usually outline grounds and processes for termination, including progressive discipline procedures and a demonstration of just cause. Implicit contracts are also a concern. Even casual oral statements or e-mails from supervisors suggesting that an employee will be retained in the organization can be interpreted as contractual promises by the courts. Employers may not terminate employees on the basis of discrimination on protected class status. Employers also cannot fire an employee in retaliation for making a claim related to employment discrimination. Finally, employers may not discharge employees for reasons counter to public policy. This prohibits terminating an employee who refuses to perform an illegal act or violate safety and health laws.

Employer-Employee Relationship

By far the most prevalent form of the employment relationship is that of employer-employee. This arrangement is the result of the organization's usual staffing activities—a culmination of the person/job matching process. As shown in Exhibit 2.2, the employer and the employee negotiate and agree on the terms and conditions that will define and govern their relationship. The terms and conditions of the resulting employment relationship represent the promises and expectations of the parties. Over time, the initial agreement may be modified due to changes in requirements or rewards of the current job, or employee transfer or promotion. Either party may terminate the employment relationship.

Employment agreements come in a variety of forms. They may be written or oral (both types can be legally enforceable), and their specificity varies from extensive to bare bones. Job descriptions and wage offers form a minimal basis for the employment agreement. Written contracts sometimes describe terms and conditions in great detail—collective bargaining agreements and contracts for professional athletes, entertainers, and upper-level executives are examples. At the other extreme, agreements may be little more than some oral promises about job features agreed to with a handshake.

There are a number of costly features associated with the employment relationship. Employers are legally liable for actions that employees take in the scope of their employment duties; this is embodied in the case law concept of vicarious liability. If an employee behaves in a negligent fashion or harasses subordinates, it is the employer that must pay, even if the employee's behavior is in violation of organizational policy. Employers must withhold payroll taxes such as Social Security and Medicare. There are also taxes associated with unemployment insurance and workers' compensation. Employer-employee relationships also have more regulatory burdens. Policies, procedures, and reporting are required to demonstrate compliance with equal employment opportunity laws in the treatment of employees. This represents a cost in terms of time and money even for organizations that are strongly committed to and invest resources in creating an inclusive workplace. Organizations must adhere to minimum wage and overtime pay requirements. Safety and health regulations are also enforced for employees.

Independent Contractor Relationship

Alternatively, the employer may hire independent contractors.[18] The employer has fewer responsibilities for an independent contractor than for an employee. Classifying a person as an independent contractor frees the employer of the tax withholding, tax payment, and benefits obligations it has for employees. Vicarious liability is reduced. Independent contractor status reduces employer reporting requirements under wage and hour laws. In sum, there is an increasing desire for the staffing and labor cost advantages of using independent contractors such as on-demand workers, project-based freelancers, or gig workers.

There are legal constraints on classifying a worker as an independent contractor, and misclassification can lead to costly penalties. For example, FedEx reached a $228 million settlement for misclassifying 2,300 of its truck drivers as independent contractors. While the drivers owned their trucks, they had to follow standards for delivery times and schedules, paperwork, customer service, safe driving, and personal appearance. The courts therefore concluded that FedEx exercised so much control over the drivers that they were indeed employees. This is not an isolated case. In a four-year period, the DOL assessed $1.1 billion in penalties to employers for misclassifying employees as independent contractors.[19]

So, what is the dividing line between employees and independent contractors? There is no single, bright-line test. Instead, there are two related administrative guidelines, both using multiple criteria to guide the employer's classification judgment.[20] The approach used by the Internal Revenue Service emphasizes the degree of employer control and worker independence. By this standard, a person is more likely to be an independent contractor if the person works without supervision, sets own work hours, pays business and travel expenses, and works on relatively short projects with a definite completion date. The other approach, used by the DOL, is based on the economic realities test. It determines whether a person is economically dependent on the business (i.e., an employee) or is in business for himself or herself (i.e., an independent contractor). Under these criteria, a person is more likely to be an independent contractor when the work is not integral to the employer's business, there is not a permanent relationship, and the person controls meaningful aspects of the work.

Employers can avoid misclassifications by developing agreements that address the criteria described above. For example, an agreement should specify the project to be completed along with an agreed upon flat fee. Also, the contractor uses all of their own materials and equipment. Finally employers should be careful not to provide a contractor with a job description, training and supervision, or employee benefits.[21]

Temporary Employees

Temporary employees are considered employees of the staffing firm that obtained them through its own staffing process. Temporary employees are given job assignments with other employers by the staffing firm. During these assignments, the temporary employee remains on the payroll of the staffing firm, and the client employer reimburses the staffing firm for its wage and other costs. The client employer has a limited right to control temporary employees that it utilizes because they are not its employees but employees of the staffing firm.

Use of temporary employees often raises issues of joint employment, in which the client employer and the staffing firm share the traditional role of employer.[22] Because both function as employers to an extent, their obligations and liabilities under various laws need to be sorted out. The EEOC provides guidance on coverage and responsibility requirements for staffing firms and their client organizations.[23] When both the firm and the client exercise control over the temporary employee, they are considered joint employers.

The demarcation between an employee and a temporary employee becomes increasingly blurred when an employer uses a set of temporary employees from a staffing firm on a long-term basis, resulting in so-called permatemps. Court cases suggest that these individuals are in fact employees of the client employer rather than of the staffing firm, particularly because of the strong degree of control the client employer typically exercises over those people. Hence, to help ensure that permatemps will not be legally considered the client's employees, the client must give up, or never exercise, direct control over these people and treat them as truly separate from regular employees. This may require, for example, not training or supervising them, not listing them in the company's directory, and not giving them an organizational e-mail account. In practice, this is difficult to do.[24]

Unpaid Interns and Trainees

A final form of relationship exists for unpaid interns and trainees. An individual must meet six requirements to be classified as an unpaid intern or trainee.[25] The requirements are that (1) the training must be similar to that given in an educational setting, (2) the training experience is to benefit the intern, (3) the trainee does not displace another person and works under close supervision of the employer's staff, (4) the employer does not gain an immediate advantage from the trainee's activities, and on occasion operations may be hampered, (5) the trainee is not entitled to a job at the end of training, and (6) the employer and the trainee must understand that the trainee is not entitled to any pay for time spent.

DIVERSITY AND INCLUSION

Human resources professionals in general, and staffing professionals in particular, are frequently given primary responsibility for ensuring that the organization provides equal employment opportunity and enhances workforce diversity through inclusive practices. What do all these terms mean for staffing managers? We provide the following definitions for our own discussion:

- Equal employment opportunity means that all interested individuals are treated in a similar manner, with no policies or procedures serving to give advantage to any demographic group.
- Diversity means that employees are representative of the available workforce.
- Inclusion in staffing means that the culture, policies, and practices of the organization create an open and supportive environment for individuals from a variety of backgrounds and perspectives.

These definitions apply broadly, but the methods for achieving these ends require considerable thought and discussion within each organization's unique internal and external context.

Business Case for Diversity and Inclusion

There is a strong impetus for effectively managing diversity and inclusion. Human resources professionals need to familiarize themselves with the key outcomes of inclusive practices so they can communicate the business case for such practices.[26] Because staffing leaders have access to much data and information on how the workforce is composed and have direct influence over practices that shape employee opportunity, they are ultimately accountable for communicating the current status of the organization's efforts and advocating for positive change.

There is an ethical need to treat all employees fairly and with respect. There is also a financial imperative to manage diversity effectively.[27] Many investigations of diversity and firm performance show that increasing the number of people from diverse backgrounds in the organization does little to help firm performance. The potential gains from a diverse workforce are realized only when a culture is supportive of diversity. As we discussed in the introductory chapter, there are two ways organizations can address issues related to diversity. In passive diversity planning, the organization reviews all policies and practices to ensure there is no discrimination on the basis of race, religion, national origin, gender, disability status, age, or other protected classes covered locally. In active diversity planning, the organization goes a step further by encouraging underrepresented groups to apply for positions, actively recruiting from a variety of sources that are likely to be seen by underrepresented groups, and providing additional training and mentoring to encourage the advancement of underrepresented groups.

There are advantages of actively pursuing diversity and inclusion. Exhibit 2.4 illustrates ways in which an effective diversity and inclusion management strategy can enhance organizational effectiveness in several domains. These are not speculative outcomes—all are supported by prior research across many organizations. In some areas, like legal compliance, the goal is to minimize negative consequences. However, it is more productive for an organization to emphasize diversity management

EXHIBIT 2.4   Making the Business Case for Diversity

Area of Concern	Effective Diversity Management
Legal and policy compliance	• Avoids lawsuits • Minimizes operational disturbances • Reduces negative press
Staffing levels	• Broadens base of applicants • Increases diversity of employee KSAOs • Improves potential to respond to changing business environment • Improves retention of employees
Employee attitudes and behavior	• Enhances engagement • Creates perceptions of justice • Fosters cooperation and collaboration
Product/service market	• Increases insight into diverse customer groups' preferences • Heightens sensitivity in interacting with the public • Improves relationships with communities and regulatory agencies

as an opportunity for gain rather than as a way of protecting against a threat. Emphasizing the positive impact that all workers will see when diversity is managed effectively enhances employee engagement in creating an inclusive environment.[28]

There are costs associated with these active diversity efforts that must be considered, as additional recruiting, selection, and training programs do not come for free. Empirical evidence suggests that despite the conceptual advantages of having more diverse points of view in work groups, demographically diverse teams are not more effective than more homogenous teams.[29] Active diversity efforts that are directed to some groups of employees and not others may unintentionally send a message to members of the demographic majority that they are less welcome in the organization. Therefore, an organization needs to carefully consider how to engage in active diversity and inclusion and select the right mix of passive and active strategies to ensure that all employees are engaged in the process. Messaging around the advantages of inclusion for the organization in achieving its mission is crucial.

Demography of the American Workforce

Organizations need to take diversity into account because the workforce has become more diverse. There has been a massive shift in the makeup of the American workforce over the past 30 years.[30] Once excluded from large portions of the workforce, women now make up half of the labor force, along with making up a majority of university graduates. There has also been a dramatic increase in ethnic and racial diversity. Immigration has increased the proportion of Hispanics and Asians in the workforce. Progress of civil rights legislation has removed previous barriers to employment faced by Blacks and increased representation in professional roles. Legislation and technology have combined to make accommodations that facilitate inclusion of individuals with disabilities. The age diversity of the workforce has increased over time, as greater numbers of individuals continue working into their sixties and seventies. There has also been an increased presence of openly lesbian, gay, bisexual, and transgender (LGBT+) employees in the workplace, accompanied by more inclusive attitudes in the workforce and society at large.[31]

These shifts in the makeup of the workforce have permanently altered the requirements for successful HR management. Companies that are not able to attract, hire, and retain a diverse workforce are increasingly limiting the pool of human capital from which they can draw. This is an especially acute problem as the gap between employee skills and organizational needs grows. Surveys conducted by SHRM suggest that managers are especially concerned about the loss of skills due to the retirement of baby boomers, about increases in medical expenses that arise as the workforce ages, and about employee elder-care responsibilities.[32] A host of other issues have been identified as arising from demographic changes, including providing work-life benefits for dual-career couples and developing multilingual training materials for workers who primarily speak a language other than English.

Workforce Diversity Measurement and Analysis

As we have seen, there is ample evidence that the workforce in the United States has become more diverse, but this diversity is not reflected in managerial or professional roles. Surveys, focus groups, and interviews with individual employees can evaluate the climate for inclusion. The representation of employees through the staffing process can also be evaluated through data on applicant flows, utilization statistics, and concentration statistics.

Employee Perceptions of Inclusion Climate

Measurement of the climate for inclusion often takes the form of surveys, focus groups, and interviews. All of these techniques ask employees to indicate their own experiences with diversity in the organization. More open-ended information gathering from focus groups and interviews yields richer insights and can also more readily surface issues that staffing managers may not have thought to ask about in a survey.

Surveys with Likert-type scales (e.g., strongly agree to strongly disagree) are useful because they can capture the opinions of far more people and responses are more amenable to statistical analyses. Surveys can also be made anonymous, thereby reducing employee discomfort or concerns about being retaliated against. Templates for such surveys are readily available and can be implemented through online survey tools, so they need not cost much in terms of staff time.[33]

Broad questions about fairness or voice may get an overall impression of the workplace, but for staffing practice, questions about specific actions by the organization can be more informative. When responses are broken out into topics like external recruiting practices, internal promotion practices, selection methods, and career development, it is much more straightforward to create inclusive practices. As noted above, having diverse perspectives may enhance the breadth of actions. Employees should therefore also be asked how they feel the organization can improve the climate for inclusion as part of the data collection process.

Measures of Representation

There are multiple techniques for evaluating the extent to which all components of the staffing process result in a workforce that best represents the diversity of the potential applicant pool across all layers of the organization. Here, we discuss three of the most common types of statistical evidence for representation. As we show in Exhibit 2.5, representation statistics can address applicant flows, the utilization of workers relative to the available qualified workforce, and the concentration of workers in organizational roles.[34] These tables represent three versions of the widely used "2 by 2" table, providing an easily calculated and interpreted presentation of relevant data.[35] Such tables can also be further broken out into subcategories of multiple racial and ethnic groups (White, Black, Hispanic, Asian) or subdivided into intersectional categories (e.g., White male, White female, Black male, Black female).

The first type of data shown in the exhibit involves applicant flows, which looks at the proportion of applicants hired among different groups. Large differences suggest that the selection system may be discriminatory. In the example, 18 out of 40 women who applied for the job are hired, for a selection rate of 45%, and 22 out 40 men who applied for the job are hired, for a selection rate of 55%. The final part of the analysis is computing the ratio of the hiring rates for women versus men; this is the bottom-line evaluation of the extent of differences across groups. If groups being examined are equally likely to be hired, the ratio will equal 1.00, with larger deviations from 1.00 indicating larger discrepancies in selection. In this case, the ratio is 0.82, meaning that women are 82% as likely to be hired as are men.

The second type of data involves utilization statistics. Here, the percentage of employees in a job category is compared with availability in the relevant population. Relevant is defined in terms of qualified individuals in the occupation in the relevant labor market, which could be obtained from the Bureau of Labor Statistics or other occupational surveys. The analysis process is very similar to the analysis of applicant flows. In this example, the organization employs 24 of the 490 qualified individuals over the age of 40 in the relevant labor market, for a utilization rate of 4.9%. The organization employs 15 of the 210 qualified individuals under the

EXHIBIT 2.5   **Representation Statistics**

FLOW STATISTICS

Applicants		Hired		Selection Rate		
Women	Men	Women	Men	Women	Men	Ratio
40	40	18	22	18/40 = 45%	22/40 = 55%	45/55 = 0.82

UTILIZATION STATISTICS

Available Qualified		Current Workforce		Representation Rate		
Over 40	Under 40	Over 40	Under 40	Over 40	Under 40	Ratio
490	210	24	15	24/490 = 4.9%	15/210 = 7.1%	4.9/7.1 = 0.69

CONCENTRATION STATISTICS

All Employees		Managers		Representation Rate		
Black	White	Black	White	Black	White	Ratio
99	159	20	35	20/99 = 20%	35/159 = 22%	20/22 = 0.91

age of 40, for a utilization rate of 7.1%. The ratio of these utilization rates is 0.69, meaning that older workers are significantly less likely to be in this organization relative to the qualified workforce. Even though the majority of this organization's workforce is over the age of 40, it still does not mirror the broader labor market, since the organization skews younger than the available workforce.

The third type of data involves the use of concentration statistics. Here, the percentages of demographic groups are compared to see if they are concentrated in certain workforce categories. Such analyses are especially useful to determine if management and leadership positions represent the broader workforce. In the example shown, there are 99 Black employees in the workforce, and 20 are managers, so the representation rate is 20%. There are 159 White employees in the workforce, and 35 are managers, so the representation rate is 22%.

The different types of statistics have very different managerial implications. Differential hiring rates shown in applicant flow statistics suggest that there is a potential problem with the organization's external selection practices. An audit of interviewing techniques and other selection tools is suggested. Differences between the available workforce and those in the organization revealed through utilization statistics may indicate a problem with recruiting practices, as certain groups are underrepresented in the applicant pool.[36] Finally, differences in representation of groups across occupations or levels of management revealed through concentration statistics suggest there may be a problem with the organization's internal recruiting and promotion practices.

Several interpretive issues should be borne in mind when examining representation statistics. The definition of all terms involves judgment calls. The organization needs to determine which applicants are qualified for flow statistics. A similar judgment regarding qualified or eligible workers needs to be made in analyzing utilization statistics. Choosing demographic groupings also influences results. Results from aggregate categories of "majority" versus "minority" will yield very different inferences from investigating multiple subgroups. It is also worth considering trends in the data or changes in practices carefully.[37] For example, the concentration statistics in Exhibit 2.5 show that Black workers are underrepresented in management at the time of analysis. However, this could represent progress from lower rates of inclusion in the recent past, or could represent lack of progress over time. There is not just one right answer to evaluating whether the workforce is representative. Rather, the data should be examined using a variety of methods of classification and then interpreted in light of the assumptions each model makes.

Staffing Practices for Diversity and Inclusion

Employers can use many strategies to ensure that the staffing process is inclusive. While diversity training for staffing managers and other decision makers may be a part of the process, evidence clearly shows that structural changes in procedures are far more effective in producing change.[38] Organizational leaders should recognize competence in inclusion as a critical skill for managerial effectiveness. Clear accountability for success in fostering inclusion is also needed. Absent top management buy-in to the strategies described below, diversity and inclusion are difficult to achieve in a systematic and sustainable manner.

Acknowledge and Address Group Differences

Recognizing the reality of group differences is a starting point. This approach is sometimes called a multicultural or diversity-conscious view of the workplace.[39] Recognizing and appreciating differences across groups has been consistently shown to be associated with more positive intergroup relationships. Rather than only countering stereotypes, a multicultural approach encourages individuals to recognize and value differences while also not assuming any group characteristic applies to a single individual. This multicultural approach can undermine prejudice and discrimination. Conversely, research shows that emphasizing assimilation, in which members of underrepresented groups are encouraged to behave like the dominant group, tends to have the opposite effect. Such an approach is exemplified by strategies to train women to lead and negotiate more like men, or encouraging all racial and ethnic groups to behave like those already in power. Put differently, pushing people to think and act alike tends to have the opposite of the intended effect, because it tends to treat differences as a problem. Recognizing the value of differences tends to improve the organization's climate.

Acknowledging differences also means acknowledging biases. The forms of bias that people have can be direct, in the form of overt racism or sexism, for example. However, there are many unspoken or unacknowledged forms of bias. Research on implicit biases has demonstrated that most people have some prejudices that they may not be aware of but that influence their decisions. While few people openly acknowledge that they are prejudiced, rigorous research often shows that discriminatory behavior is common. Building from this premise, human resources scholars suggest that the most effective starting point for inclusion is to recognize that biases may be present.[40] It is not necessary, or even helpful, to recognize one's own biases as part of the process. This tends to produce more blame and defensiveness than progress. A better focus is looking at how some may be excluded by staffing practices, and then modifying those practices accordingly.

Create Diverse Policy Development Teams

Given the differences in perspective across groups, having representation of diversity in the staffing policy development process is vital. Assumptions people have about the challenges and opportunities available to other groups are often not correct. Such problems are more effectively addressed when people who have different experiences are included in the process. Discussion across diverse groups can reveal hidden or unintentional sources of exclusion in the staffing process. For example, wording in advertising may prevent some candidates from seeking a job in the recruiting phase. The demographic makeup of the recruiting team may send signals about the organization's diversity (or lack thereof). Some culturally specific standards for expected social behavior in interviews may tend to limit the degree to which some individuals would be considered qualified. These issues could be surfaced and resolved when groups affected by selection decisions are represented in the policy development process.

Review Job Requirements Rigorously

Unstated assumptions about what makes a "good candidate" can undermine inclusion. The characteristics or traits associated with success in the current workforce may not be relevant for other groups. Underrepresented applicants may not have as much access to formal education institutions, for example, but could have developed the requisite skills from other life experiences. Similarly, individuals with disabilities may have all the requisite KSAOs and would be able to do the job if given sufficient developmental assistance and support. The process of reviewing KSAO requirements should also compare multiple well-researched predictors of performance and then select measurement strategies that maximize the diversity of the qualified applicant pool (this means selecting job-related predictors that minimize disparate impact, as discussed later in the chapter).[41]

To ensure that all qualified individuals are given due consideration in the recruiting and selection process, the nature of the work itself should be evaluated. An audit of current recruiting selection procedures should follow from this process.[42] All selection tools should be focused on these tasks, duties, and responsibilities. Interviewers and interviewees should also be trained to review all questions and scoring procedures to ensure that the focus is on job requirements as well. Procedures for assessing the necessary KSAOs for a job are covered later in the book, as are methods for structuring interviews.

Make Reasonable Accommodations

Although the concept of "reasonable accommodation" is described in the Americans With Disabilities Act (ADA), such accommodations can also extend to other forms of inclusion. For example, religious holidays or times for worship may be accommodated through flexible scheduling. Policies, procedures, and training materials may also be provided in multiple languages as an accommodation to facilitate inclusion across ethnicity and differences in language. Forms of accommodation for disabilities include leaves of absence and other work schedule changes, physical changes in the workplace, adjustment of supervisory methods, medication monitoring, job restructuring, telework, purchase of adaptive devices, provision of qualified readers and interpreters, and adjustments in testing and training material. A suggested four-step problem-solving approach for handling a reasonable accommodation request from an applicant or employee is as follows.[43] First, conduct a job analysis to determine the job's essential functions. Second, identify performance barriers that would hinder the person from doing the job. Third, work with the person to identify potential accommodations. Fourth, assess each accommodation and choose the most reasonable one that would not be an undue hardship.

Enforce Policies and Procedures

Well-defined policies and procedures should be created on the basis of the methods of inquiry outlined above. All parties to the staffing process should receive training from organizational leaders covering inclusive policies and procedures related to recruiting, promotions, test administration, review of applications, interviewing, negotiating job offers, and onboarding.[44] As noted earlier, tracking workforce demographics and holding individuals accountable for progress constitutes the most effective strategy for achieving more equitable representation across all layers of management.[45] This process of evaluation based on diversity outcomes should not be confused with using quotas. Rather, leaders who effectively implement inclusive staffing procedures focused on job-relevant KSAOs should be recognized. Proficiency in establishing effective inclusion strategies can be a recognized competency taken into consideration for advancement and promotion. When data tracking shows problems exist in workforce representation, staffing managers and other human resource professionals should evaluate the current procedures and determine where potential barriers to inclusion exist. Those in positions of accountability need to change their practices. If these individuals are not following existing practices, there should be tangible consequences.

LEGAL FRAMEWORK FOR EQUAL EMPLOYMENT OPPORTUNITY

In this section, the general provisions of major federal equal employment opportunity (EEO) laws are summarized. Mechanisms for enforcement of the laws are also discussed.[46]

Key Concepts

We start by reviewing a few key terms that cut across areas of different statutes, case law areas, and administrative regulations.

Unlawful Employment Practices

Title VII of the Civil Rights Act of 1964 contains a comprehensive statement regarding unlawful employment practices. Specifically, it is unlawful for an employer

1. "to fail or refuse to hire or to discharge any individual, or otherwise discriminate against any individual with respect to his compensation, terms, conditions, or privileges of employment, because of such individual's race, color, religion, sex, or national origin"; or
2. "to limit, segregate, or classify his employees or applicants for employment in any way which would deprive or tend to deprive any individual of employment opportunities or otherwise adversely affect his status as an employee because of such individual's race, color, religion, sex, or national origin."

These two statements are the foundation of civil rights law. They are very broad and inclusive, applying to virtually all staffing practices of an organization. There are also separate statements for employment agencies and labor unions. Subsequent laws and regulations have added other protected characteristics to the list, such as age over 40 and disability status, but the basic form of the prohibitions is the same.

Permitted Employment Practices

Besides specifying prohibited criteria for employment decision making, statutes and administrative guidelines clarify some employer practices that are allowed. The law explicitly permits the use of seniority and merit systems as a basis for applying different terms and conditions to employees. Examples of merit systems in external staffing include choosing to recruit at institutions like universities where employees receive job-relevant training, hiring on the basis of job knowledge or competence, and interview performance. Examples of merit systems in internal staffing include training performance, demonstrated competence, and supervisor performance ratings. Employers have the discretion to determine what constitutes "merit," so long as the definition does not disproportionately disadvantage employees on the basis of protected characteristics. Any seniority or merit system must be "bona fide," meaning that it is demonstrably linked to performance on the job. It may not be the result of an intention to discriminate. This provision is particularly relevant to internal staffing systems. It in essence allows the employer to take into account seniority (experience) and merit (e.g., KSAOs, promotion potential assessments) when making internal staffing decisions.

The law permits the use of tests in staffing. The employer may "give and act upon the results of any professionally developed ability test, provided that such test, its administration, or action upon the basis of results is not designed, intended, or used to discriminate because of race, color, religion, sex, or national origin." Interpretation of this provision comes, in part, through the Uniform Guidelines on Employee Selection Procedures (UGESP), although many selection researchers and practitioners believe this document is in need of major updating and revision.[47]

Essential Job Functions

Essential job functions are the major, nontrivial tasks required of an employee. According to the ADA, "consideration shall be given to the employer's judgment as to what functions of a job are essential, and if an employer has prepared a written description before advertising or interviewing applicants for the job, this description shall be considered evidence of the essential functions of the job." Subsequent regulations amplify what are essential job functions; these are explored in the chapter on job analysis and rewards.

Organizations are prohibited from using screening or selection criteria that are likely to reduce the likelihood of hiring individuals with disabilities, unless the criteria can be shown to be related to performance in the job. These provisions mean that if selection procedures cause disparate impact, the employer must show that the procedures are job related and consistent with business necessity, and that employment tests are accurate indicators of the KSAOs they attempt to measure.

Protected Characteristics

Equal employment laws in the United States focus on protected characteristics rather than demarcated protected groups. This means that coverage is extended to everyone, regardless of which group they belong to. So rather than covering men as a group or women as a group from discrimination, gender as a whole is the protected characteristic, and both men and women are covered (it should be noted that the federal law does not address nonbinary gender identification, but many states have protections for gender identity and expression). Taking another example, race and ethnicity are covered as a whole, so protections extend across Blacks, Asian, Pacific Islander, Hispanic, Native American, and Whites as groups. One way to think of this is that US law is based on the premise that no decisions should be made according to which groups one belongs to. It is possible for men to file and win cases in which they have received discriminatory treatment, however, the great majority of cases arise when underrepresented groups are the recipients of inequitable treatment.

Limitations on EEO-Enhancing Practices

Although there are many ways companies can legally work to improve workforce diversity, there are some practices that are also specifically prohibited. Most court decisions have found that using quotas or setting aside jobs for individuals in underrepresented groups is a form of discrimination. Test scores are not to be altered to make them more fair; test scores should speak for themselves. It is an unlawful employment practice "to adjust the scores of, use different cutoff scores for, or otherwise alter the results of employment-related tests" on the basis of protected characteristics.[48] This provision bans race or gender norming, in which people's scores are compared only with those of members of their own group and separate cutoff or passing scores are set for each group.

To understand these limitations, recall that American law prohibits all discrimination on the basis of protected characteristics. Quotas and set-asides deliberately incorporate characteristics into selection decisions. On the other hand, the methods that we described earlier under diversity and inclusion—auditing current practices, ensuring that recruiting makes knowledge of job openings available to all potential applicants, ensuring job qualifications are sufficiently job related, providing training and development for those who have not had access to such training and development in the past, and rewarding employees for achieving diversity goals—are all policies that allow an organization to take a proactive stance while still treating all potential employees equitably. Many other countries do use quotas to address social inequality, so employers operating in multinational contexts should be aware of how laws differ across borders.

Federal Laws Regarding EEO

Exhibit 2.6 contains a summary of the basic provisions of federal laws pertaining to coverage and prohibited discrimination. These laws are appropriately labeled "major" for several reasons. First, the laws are very broad in their coverage of employers. Second, they prohibit discrimination on the basis of multiple categories of characteristics. Exhibit 2.6 shows that for some laws, the number of employees in the organization determines whether the organization is covered.

EXHIBIT 2.6   Federal Laws and Regulations

Statute	Coverage	Prohibited Discrimination
Civil Rights Act (1964, 1978, 1991)	Private employers with 15 or more employees Federal, state, and local governments Educational institutions Employment agencies Labor unions	Race, color, religion, national origin, sex (includes sexual orientation and gender identity), pregnancy
Age Discrimination in Employment Act	Private employers with 20 or more employees Federal, state, and local governments Employment agencies Labor unions	Age (40 and over)
Americans With Disabilities Act	Private employers with 15 or more employees Federal, state, and local governments Educational institutions Employment agencies Labor unions	Qualified individuals with a disability
Immigration Reform and Control Act	Employers with 4 or more employees	Requires verification of employment status; prohibits discrimination on the basis of national origin in the verification process

Individuals who oppose unlawful practices, participate in proceedings, or request accommodations are protected from retaliation under the laws shown in Exhibit 2.6. The term "retaliation" is broadly interpreted by the courts and the EEOC to include refusal to hire, denial of promotion, termination, other actions affecting employment (e.g., threats, unjustified negative evaluations), and actions that deter reasonable people from pursuing their rights (e.g., assault, unfounded civil or criminal charges). The EEOC has issued guidance on what constitutes evidence of retaliation, as well as special remedies for retaliatory actions by the employer.[49]

Guidance on the meanings of protected characteristics, given by the EEOC, is shown in Exhibit 2.7. Note the generally expansive definitions of the characteris-

EXHIBIT 2.7   EEOC Protected Classes and Their Characteristics

(I) Race/Color
- Of a certain race
- Of personal characteristics associated with a race (e.g., facial features)
- Of skin color complexion
- Of marriage/association with person of particular race/color
- Of connection with an organization associated with people of race/color

(II) National Origin
- Of a particular country or part of the world
- Of ethnicity or accent
- Of a certain background
- Of marriage/association with person of particular national origin
- Of connection with an ethnic organization or group

(III) Sex
- Of the person's sex, which includes gender identity, transgender status, and sexual orientation
- Of connection with an organization or group of a certain sex

(IV) Religion
- Of religious beliefs in a traditional, organized religion
- Of sincerely held religious, ethical, or moral beliefs
- Of marriage/association with a person of a particular religion
- Of connection with a religious organization

(V) Disability
- A qualified person with a disability
- Has a history of a disability
- Believed to have a physical or mental impairment
- Of a relationship with a person with a disability

(VI) Age
- Of the person's age, if age 40 or older

SOURCE: Equal Employment Opportunity Commission, 2016.

tics. Third, separate agencies have been created for administration and enforcement of these laws. Finally, these agencies have issued numerous rules, regulations, and guidelines to assist in interpreting, implementing, and enforcing the law. The specifics of these regulations will be discussed in subsequent chapters.

An overview of the broad, sweeping nature of the employment practices affected by the federal EEO laws is shown in Exhibit 2.8.

EXHIBIT 2.8   Employment Practices Covered Under EEOC Enforcement

- Job advertisements, recruitment, and job referrals
- Application and hiring
- Job assignments and promotion
- Employment references
- Preemployment inquiries
- Discipline and discharge
- Pay and benefits
- Reasonable accommodation and disability, religion
- Training and apprenticeship programs
- Harassment
- Terms and conditions of employment
- Dress code
- Constructive discharge (forced to resign)

Civil Rights Acts (1964, 1978, 1991)

The form of all subsequent employment discrimination law in the United States is derived from the structure and provisions of Title VII of the Civil Rights Act of 1964. The Civil Rights Acts of 1964, 1978, and 1991 are combined for discussion purposes here. Title VII prohibits discrimination on the basis of race or color, national origin, gender, and religion. Many countries have adopted similar legislation, with provisions that are similar to those in American law as modified for local situations (e.g., political opinion, social origin, or caste).

The Civil Rights Act was passed during a period of transformation in American society.[50] Systematic discrimination was being publicly questioned through protest and legislative action. The main thrust of the law at this time was to limit rampant discrimination against African Americans, Hispanics, religious minority groups, and women. Since then, there has been significant fluidity in some of these definitions socially, and in the law. This means interpretation of the law is in flux. Definition of race and ethnicity is subject to shifting social boundaries. Recognition of this reality has resulted in greater nuance in terms of identification, as reflected in documents like the EEOC's official EEO-1 reporting forms.[51] Classifications now recognize that individuals may see themselves as belonging to multiple racial and ethnic categories. Moreover, while there was a prevalent tendency to divide the workforce into categories of "White" as contrasted with "minority," the very different experiences and outcomes across racial and ethnic groups have led courts to consider different forms of grouping employees.

Legal decisions have found that practices that relate to normative behavior across ethnic groups cannot necessarily be used in employment decision making. Language is certainly a feature of different cultural traditions, so making decisions on the basis of language fluency will likely lead to disparate impact. However, in many jobs, proficiency in English is necessary to do core job tasks. In other jobs, the ability to speak multiple languages is necessary, so evaluating candidates on the basis of proficiency in a language other than English becomes both a source of disparate hiring rates and a job-relevant skill. Generally, if proficiency in a language is required to do a job, it is seen as a business-related necessity. However, strict rules forbidding employees to speak another language are less likely to be recognized as valid criteria for decision making, as such rules are not related to a business necessity and create a potentially hostile environment across protected characteristics.

Gender roles and gender identification have also come to be defined less in terms of a dichotomy.[52] The legal system has ruled consistently that employers cannot enforce gender-normative patterns of dress and appearance. For example, employers cannot enforce "grooming codes" requiring individuals to wear clothing or behave in a way that corresponds to traditional conceptualizations of what is appropriate for men or women. This certainly applies to evaluating applicant dress or behavior in the selection interview context. Gender-inclusive standards of business-appropriate behavior and dress, however, can be valid grounds for hiring and promotion decisions. Similar rules regarding business-appropriate but inclusive dress rules may apply to religiously linked dress, such as wearing of the hijab or kippah. It goes without saying that whether the legal system interprets a dress code issue as being permissible or not, organizations should still strive for inclusivity and require certain modes of dress or appearance only when job related.

Age Discrimination in Employment Act

The Age Discrimination in Employment Act (ADEA) prohibits discrimination against those aged 40 and older. The provisions of the law have been interpreted to mean that it is not unlawful to favor an older worker over a younger worker, even if both workers are aged 40 or older. This is a rare case in which US law does not apply consistently across a protected characteristic.

The employer may use reasonable factors other than age (RFOA) in making employment decisions. Interpretation of this provision is given by the EEOC. In the case of disparate impact (but not disparate treatment) claims, the employer can seek to justify its occurrence as being based on an RFOA (as opposed to business necessity). An employment practice is based on an RFOA if it is reasonably designed and administered to achieve a legitimate business purpose in light of circumstances. Reasonableness depends on the extent to which (1) a measured factor (e.g., job skill) is related to the employer's business purpose, (2) the factor has been accurately and fairly identified and applied, (3) managers and supervisors were given guidance or training about how to use the factor and avoid discrimination, (4) limits were placed on supervisors' discretion to assess employees subjectively, (5) disparate impact against older workers was assessed, including the degree of harm to older workers, and (6) steps were taken to reduce the harm.

Americans With Disabilities Act (1990, 2008)

The ADA's basic purpose is to prohibit discrimination against individuals with disabilities who are qualified for the job, and to require the employer to make reasonable accommodation for such individuals unless that would cause undue hardship for the employer. The law broadly says that an employer may not "discriminate against an individual on the basis of disability in regard to job application procedures, the hiring, advancement, or discharge of employees, employee compensation, job training, and other terms, conditions, and privileges of employment." We expand on these core concepts in detail below because of the complexities that arise in the legal determination of whether a person has a disability.

To determine whether a person is covered under the ADA, it must be determined whether the person has a disability and is qualified for the job. The definition is interpreted in favor of broad coverage of individuals. There are three prongs to the definition. The language from the act is retained below, although for organizational practice, describing people in terms of "impairment" is stigmatizing and therefore inappropriate for creating an inclusive environment:

1. A physical or mental impairment that substantially limits one or more major life activities
2. A record of physical or mental impairment that substantially limited a major life activity
3. When an employer takes an action prohibited by the ADA because of an actual or perceived impairment that is not both transitory and minor

To be considered as having a disability under the law, the person must be substantially limited in performing a major life activity compared with individuals who do not have the condition. Temporary, non-chronic impairments of short duration with little or no residual effects usually are not considered disabilities. An impairment that is episodic or in remission is a disability if it substantially limits a major life activity when active (e.g., major depression, seizure disorder). The use of mitigating measures (with the exception of eyeglasses and contact lenses) that eliminate or reduce the symptoms or impact of a disability must be ignored when determining whether there is an impairment that substantially limits a major life activity. The long list of mitigating measures includes medications, assistive devices, and various types of therapy. In terms of addiction as an impairment, current users of illegal drugs are not covered by the law; recovering drug users and both current and recovering alcoholics are covered.

Prior to making a job offer, the employer may not conduct medical exams of job applicants, inquire whether or how severely a person is disabled, or inquire whether the applicant has received treatment for a mental or emotional condition. Inquiries about a person's ability to perform essential job functions, however, are permitted. After a job offer has been made, the employer may require the applicant to take a medical exam, including a psychiatric exam if job relevant. The job offer may be contingent on the applicant successfully passing the exam. All applicants must be required to take and pass the same exam regardless of disability status. Medical exams must be job related and consistent with business necessity. Exam results are confidential.

Immigration Reform and Control Act (1986)

A final major federal EEO-related law is the Immigration Reform and Control Act (IRCA).[53] Unlike the other laws covered here, the purpose of the IRCA and its amendments is to prohibit the employment of unauthorized aliens and to provide civil and criminal penalties for violations of this law. We include this federal law here because of its bearings for workforce composition and provisions related to discrimination, but the spirit and foundations should be recognized as entirely different from those of the Civil Rights Act, the ADEA, and the ADA.

The law states that "it is unlawful for a person or other entity to have, or to recruit or refer for a fee, for employment in the United States an alien knowing the alien is an unauthorized alien with respect to such employment" and that "it is unlawful for a person or other entity, after hiring an alien for employment . . . to continue to employ the alien in the United States knowing the alien is (or has become) an unauthorized alien with respect to such employment." The law also specifies that reporting should not be based on national origin or citizenship status. The purpose of this provision is to discourage employers from attempting to comply with the prohibition by screening against applicants on the basis of stereotypes related to appearance or accents.

Employers must use the I-9 form to gather documents from the new employee that establish proof of both identity and eligibility (authorization) for work. To verify eligibility information, federal contractors and subcontractors must use E-Verify, which conducts electronic verification checks against federal databases. Other employers may voluntarily participate in E-Verify. The employer may apply for temporary visas for up to six years for foreign workers who have highly specialized qualifications (H1-B visas) or for nonagricultural temporary workers (H2-B visas) who can augment an employer's regular workforce during times of peak load, seasonal, or intermittent needs.

Sexual Orientation and Gender Identity

Starting in the 1990s, numerous state and local statutes began to address the employment rights of LGBT+ applicants and employees. By 2020, nearly half of all states and most large metropolitan areas prohibited employment discrimination on the basis of sexual orientation, gender identity, or both. As these were local laws, employers had to comply with myriad definitions and enforcement mechanisms. Bringing clarity to the patchwork of state and local laws, in June 2020 the United States Supreme Court concluded that sexual orientation and gender identity fall under the definition of "sex" as a protected characteristic in Title VII of the Civil Rights Acts.[54] This means that sexual orientation and gender identity are therefore also protected characteristics that cannot be used in employment decision making across the United States. This decision was in line with policies that had become common in many large organizations. Surveys showed that 98% of Fortune 100 companies and 91% of Fortune 500 companies had nondiscrimination policies that include sexual orientation, and 97% of Fortune 100 companies and 83% of Fortune 500 companies had nondiscrimination policies that include gender identity even before the Supreme Court decisions.[55]

Claim Resolution Processes

Evidentiary Bases for Claims

Case law has come to recognize a difference between forms of evidence for discrimination. If discrimination can be shown to reflect on a clear difference in standards or processes for different groups, it is called disparate treatment, whereas if only differences in outcomes can be shown, it is called disparate impact.

Claims of disparate treatment involve allegations of intentional discrimination in which the employer knowingly and deliberately discriminated on the basis of protected characteristics. The evidence might, for example, refer to an e-mail between colleagues stating that "women should not be hired for this job." The situation may not involve such blatant action but may consist of what is referred to as a mixed motive. Here, both a prohibited characteristic (e.g., sex) and a legitimate reason (e.g., job qualifications) are mixed together to contribute to a negative decision about a person, such as a failure to hire or promote. Finally, the discrimination may be such that evidence of a failure to hire or promote because of a protected characteristic must be inferred from situational factors. One common staffing example of such inference would be when a qualified person applies for a job, the employer turns the person down, and the employer continues to search for other applicants who are equally qualified to the person who was rejected until someone who is from a different group within the protected class is identified.

Disparate impact, also known as adverse impact, focuses on the effect of employment practices rather than on the motive or intent underlying them. Accordingly, the emphasis here is on the need for direct evidence that, as a result of a protected characteristic, people are being adversely affected by a practice. Statistical evidence must be presented to support a claim of disparate impact.[56] Representation statistics, like those shown in Exhibit 2.5, are central to such claims. For legal purposes, these differences are usually evaluated on the basis of statistical significant testing, although the exact form and interpretation of these statistics have not been strictly codified and the statutes concerning employment discrimination provide no guidance on using or interpreting data.

Methods of Adjudication

Court cases involving employment disputes make the news, so it may seem like this is the main way that employment law is enforced. In reality, very few legal complaints make it to the courtroom. Instead, formal complaints are more commonly routed through alternative resolution processes such as internal dispute resolution, mediation, administrative judgments, and arbitration before they get to court. The general standards for processing claims and the language of these claims are similar across all of these methods of adjudication, but the actual processes become increasingly formal as we move from internal processes to court cases. The EEOC is responsible for enforcing the Civil Rights Act, the ADEA, and the ADA. Though each law requires separate enforcement mechanisms, some generalizations about their collective enforcement are possible.[57]

Internal Dispute Resolution.   The first stage for many claims of employment discrimination is an internal process. Inclusive organizations encourage employees to report violations of organizational policies or employee rights to either the human resources department or a delegated ombudsperson. To facilitate social exchanges with employees, organizations should build trust by acting fairly and resolving these concerns through due process. An organization should thoroughly document all communication with the employee bringing the claim, as this will serve as evidence of the organization's actions if the employee continues to escalate the complaint to external parties. While an organization may recommend the use of internal dispute resolution, and administrative bodies do encourage internal dispute resolution, employees are legally entitled to pursue their claim externally.

Mediation.   Employees who feel that internal dispute resolution has been ineffective or that they will not be treated fairly in an internal process can request that the organization turn to an outside mediator to resolve the situation. A neutral third party mediates the dispute between the employer and the employee and obtains an agreement between them that resolves the dispute. Participation in mediation is voluntary, and either party may opt out for any reason. Mediation proceedings are confidential. Any agreement reached between the parties is legally enforceable. More than 70% of complaints that go to mediation are resolved, and 96% of employers that use the EEOC mediation program say they would do so again.[58] In short, the EEOC prefers settlement to litigation.

Arbitration.   Binding arbitration procedures have many of the features of a court case. Both sides bring evidence before a third party with the authority to issue a legally binding resolution. This is a point of contrast with mediation. Mediators do not have formal power to decide outcomes, they only facilitate negotiation. Arbitrators are given formal power to decide on outcomes. When a dispute enters arbitration, the employer and the employee will typically be making their arguments through a lawyer. In practice, many contemporary organizations encourage employees to use binding arbitration rather than the court system for disputes, and require employees to sign agreements to use binding arbitration as part of the hiring process. Arbitration processes are preferred because they tend to be lower cost and faster than court cases, and they are less likely to be reported in the media. However, there are concerns about the fairness of arbitration for workers, since employers have more experience and skill in working through the arbitration process.[59]

Administrative Judgments.   If employees take their concerns regarding discrimination to outside administrative agencies, such as the EEOC or DOL, a formal investigative process will begin if the original concern is found to have merit.[60] The EEOC itself may also file a charge. In states where there is an EEOC-approved fair enforcement practice (FEP) law, the charge is initially deferred to the state. The charge is investigated to determine whether there is reasonable cause to believe discrimination has occurred. If reasonable cause is not found, the charge is dropped by the agency. If sufficient evidence is found, the EEOC attempts conciliation of the charge. Conciliation is a voluntary settlement process that seeks agreement by the employer to stop the practice(s) in question and abide by proposed remedies. This is the EEOC's preferred method of settlement. Whenever the EEOC decides not to pursue a claim further, it will issue a "right to sue" letter to the complaining party, allowing a private suit to be started against the employer. At this stage, mediation may also occur.

Court Cases.   The final stage in the process of employment discrimination complaints is the courtroom. This is a highly formal procedure, and the decisions rendered by the court have the full force of law behind them. We cover the formal process of litigation below.

Process of Litigation

Should conciliation fail, suit is filed in federal court. The ensuing litigation process under Title VII is shown in Exhibit 2.9. As can be seen, the charge of the plaintiff (charging party) will follow either a disparate treatment or a disparate impact route.[61] In either event, the plaintiff has the initial burden of proof. Such a burden requires the plaintiff to establish a prima facie case that demonstrates reasonable cause to assume discrimination has occurred. Assuming this case is successfully presented, the defendant must rebut the charge and accompanying evidence.

Disparate Treatment.   In disparate treatment cases, the defendant must provide nondiscriminatory reasons during rebuttal for the practice(s) in question. In disparate impact cases, the employer must demonstrate that the practices in question are job related and consistent with business necessity. In disparate treatment cases, the plaintiff must ultimately prove that the defendant's practices are discriminatory.

Following rebuttal, the plaintiff may respond to the defense provided by the defendant. In disparate treatment cases, that response hinges on a demonstration that the defendant's reasons for a practice are a pretext, or smoke screen, for the

EXHIBIT 2.9   Basic Litigation Process Under Title VII

	Charge	**Defendant Rebuttal**	**Plaintiff Response**
	Disparate treatment → (intentional practice)	Nondiscriminatory reason(s) for → practice	Reason is a pretext for discrimination

Plaintiff (charging party) alleges occurrence of discrimination

Decision → *Remedies*

	Disparate impact (effect of practice)	Practice is job related and consistent with business necessity	Practice is not job related; employer refuses to adopt affirmative employment practice that causes less disparate impact

practice. Intentional discrimination with staffing practices is prohibited, and the employer may not use a claim of business necessity to justify intentional use of a discriminatory practice.

An employer may attempt to justify explicit use of a protected characteristic as being a bona fide occupational qualification (BFOQ). Such a defense would be used if the employer specifies through recruiting and selection practices that only individuals from specific demographic categories will be applied. As an example, an employer may claim that to be a Catholic priest, the applicant must be Catholic, or to be a rabbi, the applicant must be Jewish. Personal privacy concerns for health professions can also be a BFOQ, such as when individuals prefer to have a physician or nurse of one gender. In some cases, preferences for gender may be stated, such as requiring women for modeling women's clothing, but even this is also a very narrowly construed and sometimes contentious area. Customer preferences cannot be used to defend a BFOQ—simply because biased customers prefer to have a male financial analyst or a female flight attendant is not a valid basis for a BFOQ.

The scope for claiming a BFOQ is extremely narrow.[62] The employer must be able to demonstrate that such discrimination is "a bona fide occupational qualification reasonably necessary to the normal operation of that particular business or enterprise."[63] However, the employer must be able to show that using protected class information as employment criteria is a business necessity, and that someone outside of the specified group could not actually do the job.

Disparate Impact.   In disparate impact cases, the plaintiff's response will focus on showing that the defendant has not shown its practices to be job related and/ or that the employer refuses to adopt a practice that causes less disparate impact. This is a different standard of evidence compared with disparate treatment. Disparate impact can exist even if everyone is treated exactly the same. For example, if all employees take the exact same test for employment, and tests are scored the same way, but scores differ across protected characteristics, a prima facie case for disparate impact has been made. Disparate impact is therefore a matter of numbers and statistics.

Staffing practices that may seem unfair, outrageous, or of dubious value to the employer but do not cause disparate impact are not regulated (assuming, of course, that no intention to discriminate underlies them). Thus, they are a matter of legal concern only if their usage causes disparate impact. Staffing practices that the plaintiff initially shows through numerical evidence to have caused disparate impact enter the legal arena unless the employer can successfully rebut the charges. To do this, the employer must show that the practices are "job related for the position in question and consistent with business necessity."[64] Practices that fail to meet this standard are unlawful.

After statistical evidence has been provided, the defendant rebuttal will involve an attempt to prove that the challenged practice is supported by a reasonable factor other than protected class status, and the plaintiff response will attempt to prove that the factor cited is unreasonable and not the true reason for the practice.

Outcomes

The plaintiff and the defendant have an opportunity to end their dispute through a consent decree. This is a voluntary, court-approved agreement between the two parties. The consent decree may contain an agreement to not only halt certain practices but also implement certain remedies, such as various forms of monetary relief and affirmative action plans.

In the absence of a consent decree, the court will fashion its own remedies from those permitted under the law, of which several are available. First, the court may enjoin certain practices (i.e., to require the defendant to halt the practices). Second, the court may order the hiring or reinstatement of individuals. Third, the court may fashion various forms of monetary relief, such as back pay, front pay, attorney's fees, and compensatory and punitive damages. Compensatory and punitive damages may be applied only in cases involving disparate treatment, and may be considerable. Finally, under the Civil Rights Act and the ADA, the court may order "such affirmative action as may be appropriate," as well as "any other equitable relief" that the court deems appropriate. Through these provisions, the court has considerable latitude in the remedies it imposes, including the imposition of affirmative action plans.

SOCIAL AND LEGAL ISSUES IN REMAINDER OF BOOK

There are many complex norms, laws, and regulations applicable to staffing practices. This chapter emphasized the social underpinnings of the employment relationship, the sources of law, management of relationships, management of diversity, and general provisions of the law and the provisions that pertain to staffing activities. Because of the importance of these issues, we cover them in each chapter throughout the rest of the book.

In the remaining chapters of the book, we continue to give guidance and suggestions on how to align staffing practices with the social and legal context. The issues so addressed, and the chapter in which they occur, are shown in Exhibit 2.10. This exhibit reinforces the importance accorded norms, laws, and regulations as external influences on staffing activities.

EXHIBIT 2.10   Social and Legal Issues in Other Chapters

Chapter Title	Topics
Planning	Planning for diversity and affirmative action
	Legal status of diversity and affirmative action
	EEO and temporary workers
Job Analysis: Requirements, Competencies, and Rewards	Identifying job-related KSAOs
	Evaluating job rewards
	Defining essential job functions
External Recruitment	Definition of a job applicant
	Targeting for a diverse applicant pool
	Realistic recruiting
	Fraud and misrepresentation
Internal Recruitment	Internal promotion and development systems
	Relationships after denied promotions
	Affirmative action for internal promotion systems
Measurement	Standardization
	Statistics relevant to job relatedness

EXHIBIT 2.10 Continued

Chapter Title	Topics
External Selection I	Disclaimers Background and reference checks Preemployment inquiries Bona fide occupational qualifications
External Selection II	Medical exams Uniform Guidelines on Employee Selection Procedures Compliance with the Americans With Disabilities Act
Internal Selection	Talent management and succession systems Seniority systems The glass ceiling
Decision Making	Workforce diversity and assessment methods Defining cut scores and minimal qualifications Incorporating diversity into final choice
Final Match	Setting expectations Contractual obligations Socialization to establish employment relationships Negligent hiring Employment-at-will
Staffing System Management	Creating fair policies and procedures Record keeping and privacy EEO reporting and legal audits Dispute resolution
Retention Management	Building and maintaining employee commitment Performance management Separation lawsuits and regulations

SUMMARY

At its core, staffing is concerned with fostering a productive employment relationship. To clarify rights and responsibilities in these relationships, a combination of statutes, case law, and administrative regulations has arisen. There are also many unwritten norms that guide expectations. Exchanges between employers and employees can take on both economic and social characteristics. To keep the relationship on positive footing, employers should make sure that they fulfill employee expectations and provide support. Staffing practices can help facilitate these relationships. Some key activities include communicating frequently with applicants and candidates, providing clear and accurate messages, and fairly administering hiring and promotion methods.

To capitalize on the diversity in today's workforce, organizations need to create an inclusive environment. Inclusive staffing practices make it possible for organizations to access the broadest set of possible applicants, increase the diversity of KSAOs, foster collaboration, understand diverse perspectives of customers, and improve the organization's relationship with communities and regulatory agencies. To evaluate the organization's climate for diversity, both surveys and representation statistics can be examined. Methods to improve inclusion in the staffing process are rooted in recognizing the pervasiveness of biases. Once sources of potential bias are identified, techniques like creating diverse policy development teams and reviewing job requirements can help staffing professionals foster a truly inclusive and fair organization.

In addition to organizational efforts, there have also been many legal precedents that work to equalize opportunity in staffing. The Civil Rights Act, Age Discrimination in Employment Act, and Americans With Disabilities Act prohibit practices that discriminate on the basis of race or color, religion, gender, national origin, age, and disability status. Recent case law has clarified that these protections extend to sexual orientation and gender identity. Best practices in the legal domain mirror best practices in inclusion: focus the staffing system on identifying job-relevant KSAOs while actively working to investigate and redress factors that have impeded equal opportunity.

Legal issues will continue to be addressed throughout the remainder of this book. The emphasis will be on explanation and application of the laws' provisions to staffing practices. The issues will be discussed at the end of each chapter, beginning with the next one.

DISCUSSION QUESTIONS

1. What are your expectations from the employment relationship? What do you think an employer should give you, and what should you give as an employee?
2. How have expectations about employment changed over time in response to social and economic events? How might they change in the future?
3. What types of organizations benefit most from developing a transactional orientation based on economic exchanges? What types of organizations benefit most from developing a relational orientation based on social exchanges?
4. Which factors need to be balanced in creating an effective diversity and inclusion strategy? What are the trade-offs that organizations will need to consider?
5. What are the limitations of disparate impact statistics as indicators of potential staffing discrimination?
6. What activities can organizations undertake to minimize the risk of legal problems?

ETHICAL ISSUES

1. Some organizations strictly adhere to the law in their relationships with employees and job applicants, but beyond that anything goes in terms of tolerated staffing practices. What are the ethical implications of such a stance?

2. Assume that you are the staffing manager in an organization that informally discourages you and other managers from hiring people with disabilities. The organization's rationale is that reasonable accommodations are too expensive and detract from more profitable investments. Do staffing managers have an ethical obligation to try to change the stance, and if so, how might you go about that?

APPLICATIONS

To Employ, or Not to Employ?

Greater Boston Homes (GBH) is a moderately sized company that does home construction in and around Boston. Although the organization was not terribly creative when coming up with a name, it has been quite successful in developing a market niche for itself by providing a user-friendly experience in the process of design and construction for its customers. GBH is known for its distinctive style of futuristic, neocolonial homes. To maintain a brand image and consistently high quality, the company has used full-time employees to perform most of the work, contracting out only those tasks that are more peripheral to the look and feel of the finished homes. This makes it an exception in the industry.

When it comes to creating software for applicant tracking, however, GBH is behind the curve. Its systems for evaluating recruiting and selection processes are cumbersome, out of date, and not well integrated with compensation, budgeting, and accounting. GBH already has a full-time staffing manager (Sophie Wang) as part of its HR function. Ms. Wang is highly skilled in using all the major software platforms available in the market. In addition to maintaining and analyzing all records related to staffing, she also oversees the recruiting and selection process for the entire organization, so there is no spare time in her schedule to also design a new applicant tracking system.

The company is hoping to have an independent contractor perform the work. After the system is set up, the day-to-day management could be handed off to Ms. Wang. GBH prefers to have the work done in its own offices so that it can track progress on the project and change specifications as needed throughout the process. However, it has also considered having an employee do the work. Given the current growth of the organization and its demand for top-quality analytics, it could reassign Ms. Wang to a purely technology management role in designing the system. It is within her capability. If she did take over the role, GBH could hire a less skilled full-time employee to do the more administrative and direct-contact side of recruiting. Other technology management roles in the organization may open up in the future, so there might be a need for Ms. Wang's skills in these other areas if she received sufficient development.

After costing out the process, the company believes that the costs of adding a full-time employee may be somewhat greater in the short run, but all of the other factors described above suggest there may be long-term advantages to keeping development in-house.

1. What would be the advantage of having an independent contractor perform this job?
2. What expectations for the relationship would you set for an independent contractor?
3. What actions would you have to take to ensure that the relationship remains that of independent contractor?
4. What would be the advantage of having Ms. Wang perform this job?
5. How would you clarify expectations for Ms. Wang about her role at present and in the future?
6. What actions would you take to get the most out of the employee-employer relationship?
7. Given the considerations above, which form of relationship seems more appropriate for this job, and why?

Age Discrimination in a Promotion?

Best Protection Insurance Company (BPIC) handles a massive volume of claims each year in the corporate claims function, as well as in its four regional claims centers. The corporate claims function is headed by the senior vice president of corporate claims (SVPCC); reporting to the SVPCC are two managers of corporate claims (MCC-Life and MCC-Residential) and a highly skilled corporate claims specialist (CCS). Each regional office is headed by a regional center manager (RCM); the RCM is responsible for both supervisors and claims specialists within the regional office. The RCMs report to the vice president of regional claims (VPRC). The organization is structured as follows:

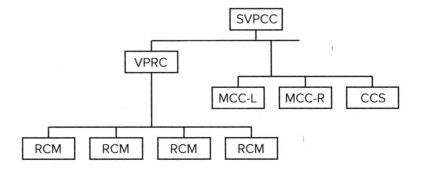

BPIC decided to reorganize its claims function by eliminating the four regional offices (and the RCM position) and establishing numerous small field offices throughout the country. The other part of the reorganization involved creating five new CCS positions. The CCS job itself was to be redesigned and upgraded in terms of knowledge and skill requirements. These new CCS positions would be staffed through internal promotions from within the claims function.

The SVPCC asked Gus Tavus, a 52-year-old RCM, to apply for one of the new CCS positions since his job was being eliminated. The other RCMs, all of whom were over 40 years of age, were also asked to apply. Neither Gus nor the other RCMs were promoted to the CCS positions. Other candidates, some of whom were also over age 40, were also bypassed. The promotions went to five claims specialists and supervisors from within the former regional offices, all of whom were under age 40. Two of these newly promoted employees had worked for, and reported to, Gus as RCM.

Upon learning of his failure to be promoted, Gus sought to find out why. What he learned led him to believe that he had been discriminated against because of his age. He then retained legal counsel, attorney Bruce Davis. Bruce met informally with the SVPCC to try to determine what had happened in the promotion process and why his client had not been promoted. He was told that there were numerous candidates who were better qualified than Gus and that Gus lacked adequate technical and communication skills for the new job of CCS. The SVPCC refused to reconsider Gus for the job and said that all decisions were etched in stone. Gus and Bruce then filed suit in federal district court, claiming a violation of the Age Discrimination in Employment Act. They also subpoenaed numerous BPIC documents, including the personnel files of all applicants for the CCS positions.

After reviewing the documents and discussing things with Gus, Bruce learned more about the promotion process actually used by BPIC. The SVPCC and the two MCCs conducted the entire process; they received no input from the VPRC or the HR department. There was no formal, written job description for the new CCS position, nor was there a formal internal job posting as required by company policy. The SVPCC and the MCCs developed a list of employees they thought might be interested in the job, including Gus, and then met to consider the list of candidates. At that meeting, the personnel files and previous performance appraisals of the candidates were not consulted. After deciding on the five candidates who would be offered the promotion (all five accepted), the SVPCC and MCCs scanned the personnel files and appraisals of these five (only) to check for any disconfirming information. None was found. Bruce's inspection of the files revealed no written comments suggesting age bias in past performance appraisals for any of the candidates, including Gus. Also, there was no indication that Gus lacked technical and communication skills. All of Gus's previous appraisal ratings were above average, and there was no evidence of decline in the favorability of the ratings. Finally, an interview with the VPRC (Gus's boss) revealed that he had not been consulted at all during the promotion process, that he was "shocked beyond belief" that Gus had not been promoted, and that there was "no question" but that Gus was qualified in all respects for the CCS job.

1. Prepare a written report that presents a convincing disparate treatment claim that Gus had been intentionally discriminated against on the basis of his age. Do not address the claim as one of disparate impact.
2. Present a convincing rebuttal, from the viewpoint of BPIC, to this disparate treatment claim.

ENDNOTES

1. O. Farooq, D. E. Rupp, and M. Farooq, "The Multiple Pathways Through Which Internal and External Corporate Social Responsibility Influence Organizational Identification and Multifoci Outcomes: The Moderating Role of Cultural and Social Orientations," *Academy of Management Journal*, 2016, 60, pp. 954–985; G. C. Banks, S. Kepes, M. Joshi, and A. Seers, "Social Identity and Applicant Attraction: Exploring the Role of Multiple Levels of Self," *Journal of Organizational Behavior*, 2016, 37, pp. 326–345.
2. K. R. Murphy, "The Legal Context of the Management of Human Resources," *Annual Review of Organizational Psychology and Organizational Behavior*, 2018, 5, pp. 157–182.
3. Murphy, "The Legal Context of the Management of Human Resources."
4. Department of Labor Statistics (*www.dol.gov*), accessed Apr. 10, 2020; Equal Employment Opportunity Commission (*www.eeoc.gov*), accessed Apr. 10, 2020.
5. L. M. Shore, J. A.-M. Coyle-Shapiro, and C. Chang, "Exchange in the Employee–Organization Relationship," in D. S. Ones, N. Anderson, C. Viswesvaran, and H. K. Sinangil (eds), *The Sage Handbook of Industrial, Work & Organizational Psychology* (London: Sage, 2018), pp. 499–536.
6. B. O'Neill and M. Adya, "Knowledge Sharing and the Psychological Contract: Managing Knowledge Workers Across Different Stages of Employment," *Journal of Managerial Psychology*, 2007, 22, pp. 411–436.
7. Shore, Coyle-Shapiro, and Chang, "Exchange in the Employee–Organization Relationship."
8. L. Jiang, T. M. Probst, and W. L. Benson, "Organizational Context and Employee Reactions to Psychological Contract Breach: A Multilevel Test of Competing Theories," *Economic and Industrial Democracy*, 2017, 38, pp. 513–534.
9. M. Tomprou, D. M. Rousseau, and S. D. Hansen, "The Psychological Contracts of Violation Victims: A Post-Violation Model," *Journal of Organizational Behavior*, 2015, 36, pp. 561–581; O. N. Solinger, J. Hofmans, P. M. Bal, and P. G. W. Jansen, "Bouncing Back From Psychological Contract Breach: How Commitment Recovers Over Time," *Journal of Organizational Behavior*, 2016, 37, pp. 494–514.
10. J. N. Kurtessis, R. Eisenberger, M. T. Ford, L. C. Buffardi, K. A. Stewart, and C. S. Adis, "Perceived Organizational Support: A Meta-Analytic Evaluation of Organizational Support Theory," *Journal of Management*, 2017, 43, pp. 1854–1884.
11. J. D. Mackey, R. E. Frieder, J. R. Brees, and M. J. Martinko, "Abusive Supervision: A Meta-Analysis and Empirical Review," *Journal of Management*, 2017, 43 (6), pp. 1940–1965; C.-M. Alcover, R. Rico, W. H. Turnley, and M. C. Bolino, "Understanding the Changing Nature of Psychological Contracts in 21st Century Organizations: A Multiple-Foci Exchange Relationships Approach and Proposed Framework," *Organizational Psychology Review*, 2017, 7, pp. 4–35.

12. Kurtessis, Eisenberger, Ford, Buffardi, Stewart, and Adis, "Perceived Organizational Support: A Meta-Analytic Evaluation of Organizational Support Theory."

13. M. G. Gonzalez-Morales, M. C. Kernan, T. E. Becker, and R. Eisenberger, "Defeating Abusive Supervision: Training Supervisors to Support Subordinates," *Journal of Occupational Health Psychology*, 2018, 23, pp. 151–162.

14. D. M. Rousseau, S. D. Hansen, and M. Tomprou, "A Dynamic Phase Model of Psychological Contract Processes," *Journal of Organizational Behavior*, 2018, 39(9), pp. 1081–1098.

15. M. W. Bennett, D. J. Polden, and H. J. Rubin, *Employment Relationships: Law and Practice* (New York: Aspen, 2004).

16. D. D. Bennett-Alexander and L. P. Hartman, *Employment Law for Business*, 9th ed. (New York: McGraw-Hill Education, 2019); D. J. Walsh, *Employment Law for Human Resource Practice*, 6th ed. (Boston: Cengage Learning, 2019).

17. Society for Human Resource Management, "Involuntary Termination of Employment in the United States," Dec. 19, 2019 (*www.shrm.org*).

18. Society for Human Resource Management, "Employing Independent Contractors," Dec. 19, 2019 (*www.shrm.org*); Walsh, *Employment Law for Human Resource Practice*.

19. J. Eidelson, "Designated Drivers," *Business Week*, Oct. 20, 2014, pp.19–20; J. Deschenaux, "Calif.: FedEx Agrees to Settle Drivers' Misclassification Claims for $228M," June 18, 2015 (*www.shrm.org*); J. Cohen, "Misclassification Headaches," *HR Magazine*, Dec. 2015/Jan. 2016, pp. 62–63.

20. Bennett-Alexander and Hartman, *Employment Law for Business*, pp. 12–16; US Department of Labor, "Administrator's Interpretation No. 2015-1," July 2015 (*www.dol.gov/whd/workers /Misclassification/AI-2015_1.htm*); US Internal Revenue Service, "Independent Contractor (Self-Employed) or Employee?" Apr. 8, 2020 (*www.irs.gov*) accessed Apr. 20, 2020.

21. Walsh, *Employment Law for Human Resource Practice*; A. A. Idalski, "Contracting Trouble," *HR Magazine*, Apr. 2015, pp. 68–69; Society for Human Resource Management, "Employing Independent Contractors."

22. Walsh, *Employment Law for Human Resource Practice*.

23. Equal Employment Opportunity Commission, *EEOC Policy Guidance on Temporary Workers* (Washington, DC: author, 1997); Equal Employment Opportunity Commission, *Enforcement Guidance: Application of the ADA to Contingent Workers Placed by Temporary Agencies and Other Staffing Firms* (Washington, DC: author, 2000); N. Greenwald, "Use of Temporary Workers Also Invites Exposure to Lawsuits," *Workforce Management Online*, Mar. 2010 (*www.workforce.com*), accessed Mar. 25, 2010.

24. R. J. Bohner, Jr., and E. R. Salasko, "Beware the Legal Risks of Hiring Temps," *Workforce*, Oct. 2003, pp. 50–57; Walsh, *Employment Law for Human Resource Practice*, pp. 40–46; L. E. O'Donnell, "Is Our Unpaid Intern Legit?" *HR Magazine*, Apr. 2013, pp. 77–79.

25. US Department of Labor, "Fact Sheet #71: Internship Programs Under the Fair Labor Standards Act," Apr. 2010 (*www.dol.gov/whd/regs/compliance/whdfs71.htm*).

26. G. Kirton and A. Greene, "Telling and Selling the Value of Diversity and Inclusion—External Consultants' Discursive Strategies and Practices," *Human Resource Management Journal*, 2019, 29, pp. 676–691.

27. S. E. Jackson, A. Joshi, and N. L. Erhardt, "Recent Research on Team and Organizational Diversity: SWOT Analysis and Implications," *Journal of Management*, 2003, 29, pp. 801–830; A. Hajro, C. Gibson, and M. Pudelko, "Knowledge Exchange Processes in Multicultural Teams: Linking Organizational Diversity Climates to Teams' Effectiveness," *Academy of Management Journal*, 2015, online before print: amj.2014.0442; S. R. Fitzsimmons, "Multicultural Employees: A Framework for Understanding How They Contribute to Organizations," *Academy of Management Review*, 2013, 38, pp. 525–549; Y. Chung, H. Liao, S. E. Jackson, M. Subramony, S. Colakoglu,

and Y. Jiang, "Cracking but Not Breaking: Joint Effects of Faultline Strength and Diversity Climate on Loyal Behavior," *Academy of Management Journal*, 2015, 58, pp. 1495–1515.

28. R. R. Hastings, "Diversity Efforts Should Include White Employees," *SHRM HR Topics and Strategy*, July 7, 2012 (*www.shrm.org*); Society for Human Resource Management, *Global Diversity and Inclusion: Perceptions, Practices, and Attitudes* (Alexandria, VA: author, 2009).

29. S. T. Bell, A. J. Villado, M. A. Lukasik, L. Belau, and A. L. Briggs, "Getting Specific About Demographic Diversity Variable and Team Performance Relationships: A Meta-Analysis," *Journal of Management*, 2011, 37, pp. 709–743; S. K. Horwitz and I. B. Horwitz, "The Effects of Team Diversity on Team Outcomes: A Meta-Analytic Review of Team Demography," *Journal of Management*, 2007, 33, pp. 987–1015; H. van Dijk, M. L. van Engen, and D. van Knippenberg, "Defying Conventional Wisdom: A Meta-Analytical Examination of the Differences Between Demographic and Job-Related Diversity Relationships With Performance," *Organizational Behavior and Human Decision Processes*, 2012, 119, pp. 38–53.

30. L. Lieber, "Changing Demographics Will Require Changing the Way We Do Business," *Employment Relations Today*, Fall 2009, pp. 91–96; A. Fox, "At Work in 2020," *HR Magazine Online*, Jan. 1, 2010.

31. M. P. Bell, M. F. Özbilgin, T. A. Beauregard, and O. Sürgevil, "Voice, Silence, and Diversity in 21st Century Organizations: Strategies for Inclusion of Gay, Lesbian, Bisexual, and Transgender Employees," *Human Resource Management*, 2011, 50, pp. 131–146.

32. J. Coombs, J. Schramm, and A. Alonso, *Workplace Visions: Generational Change in the Workplace* (Alexandria, VA: Society for Human Resource Management, 2014).

33. Society for Human Resource Management, "Diversity Survey," *SHRM HR Forms* (*www.shrm.org*), accessed Apr. 13, 2020.

34. D. Kuang and M. Ramos, "Workforce Composition and Utilization Analyses," in S. B. Morris and E. M. Dunleavy (eds.), *Adverse Impact Analysis: Understanding Data, Statistics, and Risk* (New York: Routledge, 2017), pp. 125–145.

35. D. Cohen, E. Tison, and D. S. Fortney, "Structuring a Traditional EEO Adverse Impact Analysis: The 2 x 2 Table," in S. B. Morris and E. M. Dunleavy (eds.), *Adverse Impact Analysis: Understanding Data, Statistics, and Risk* (New York: Routledge, 2017), pp. 48–69.

36. Kuang and Ramos, "Workforce Composition and Utilization Analyses."

37. S. B. Morris, E. M. Dunleavy, and M. Lee, "Many 2 x 2 Tables: Understanding Multiple Events in Adverse Impact Analyses," in S. B. Morris and E. M. Dunleavy (eds.), *Adverse Impact Analysis: Understanding Data, Statistics, and Risk* (New York: Routledge, 2017), pp. 146–168.

38. Q. M. Roberson, "Diversity in the Workplace: A Review, Synthesis, and Future Research Agenda," *Annual Review of Organizational Psychology and Organizational Behavior*, 2019, 6, pp. 69–88; L. H. Nishii, J. Khattab, M. Shemla, and R. M. Paluch, "A Multi-Level Process Model for Understanding Diversity Practice Effectiveness," *Academy of Management Annals*, 2018, 12, pp. 37–82; Kirton and Greene, "Telling and Selling the Value of Diversity and Inclusion—External Consultants' Discursive Strategies and Practices."

39. L. M. Leslie, J. E. Bono, Y. (Sophia) Kim, and G. R. Beaver, "On Melting Pots and Salad Bowls: A Meta-Analysis of the Effects of Identity-Blind and Identity-Conscious Diversity Ideologies," *Journal of Applied Psychology*, 2020, 105, pp. 453–471.

40. D. Wilkie, "Bringing Bias Into the Light," *HR Magazine*, Dec. 2014, pp. 22–27.

41. H. K. Cheung, E. King, A. Lindsey, A. Membere, H. M. Markell, and M. Kilcullen, "Understanding and Reducing Workplace Discrimination," *Research in Personnel and Human Resources Management*, 2016, 34, pp. 101–152.

42. Equal Employment Advisory Council, *Equal Employment Self-Audit Checklist* (Washington, DC: author, 2016); Society for Human Resource Management, *Employment Labor Law Audit* (Alexandria, VA: author, 2016).

43. J. R. Mook, "Accommodation Paradigm Shifts," *HR Magazine*, Jan. 2007, pp. 115–120.

44. A. Smith, "Managerial Training Needed as Hiring Resumes" (*www.shrm.org*), accessed Mar. 16, 2010; D. G. Bower, "Don't Cut Legal Compliance Training," *Workforce Management*, Feb. 2009 (*www.workforce.com*).

45. Nishii, Khattab, Shemla, and Paluch, "A Multi-Level Process Model for Understanding Diversity Practice Effectiveness."

46. Society for Human Resource Management, "Managing Equal Employment Opportunity" (*www.shrm.org*), Apr. 13, 2018; Bennett-Alexander and Hartman, *Employment Law for Business*; C. H. Fleischer, *The SHRM Essential Guide to Employment Law* (Alexandria, VA: Society for Human Resource Management, 2018).

47. Murphy, "The Legal Context of the Management of Human Resources."

48. Equal Employment Opportunity Commission, "Employment Tests and Selection Procedures" (*www.eeoc.gov*), accessed Apr. 20, 2020.

49. Equal Employment Opportunity Commission, *EEOC Guidance on Investigating, Analyzing Retaliation Claims* Aug. 25, 2016 (*www.eeoc.gov*).

50. J. R. Aiken, E. D. Salmon, and P. J. Hanges, "The Origins and Legacy of the Civil Rights Act of 1964," *Journal of Business and Psychology*, 2013, 28, pp. 383–399; Murphy, "The Legal Context of the Management of Human Resources."

51. US Equal Employment Opportunity Commission, "EEO-1 Survey" (*www.eeoc.gov*), accessed Apr. 10, 2020.

52. Bennett-Alexander and Hartman, *Employment Law for Business*.

53. Equal Employment Opportunity Commission, "Immigration Control and Reform Act" (*eeoc.gov/eeoc/history/35th/thelaw/irca.html*), accessed Jan. 18, 2020.

54. J. D. Allen Smith and L. Nagele-Piazza, "Supreme Court to Decide If Civil Rights Act Prohibits LGBT Discrimination," Apr. 22, 2019 (*www.shrm.org*); L. Nagele-Piazza "Supreme Court Says Federal Anti-Bias Law Protects LGBTQ Workers," SHRM Employment Law, June 15, 2020 (*www.shrm.org*).

55. Human Rights Campaign, "Workplace Discrimination Laws and Policies" (*www.hrc.org*), accessed Apr. 13, 2020; J. D. Allen Smith, "Companies Oppose Government's Retraction of Transgender Rights," Nov. 5, 2018 (*www.shrm.org*).

56. R. Tonowski, "Thoughts From an EEO Agency Perspective," in S. B. Morris and E. M. Dunleavy (eds.), *Adverse Impact Analysis: Understanding Data, Statistics, and Risk* (New York: Routledge, 2017), pp. 277–296.

57. M. W. Bennett, D. J. Polden, and H. J. Rubin, *Employment Relationships: Law and Practice* (Frederick, MD: Aspen, 2004).

58. K. Tyler, "Mediating a Better Outcome," *HR Magazine*, Nov. 2007, pp. 63–66.

59. T. J. St. Antoine, "Labor and Employment Arbitration Today: Mid-Life Crisis or New Golden Age?," *Ohio State Journal on Dispute Resolution*, 2017, 32, pp. 1–28.

60. Equal Employment Opportunity Commission, "Resolving a Charge" (*www.eeoc.gov/employers/resolving.cfm*), accessed Mar. 23, 2020; Equal Employment Opportunity Commission, "What You Can Expect After a Charge Is Filed" (*www.eeoc.gov/employers/process.cfm*), accessed Mar. 23, 2020.

61. Walsh, *Employment Law for Human Resource Practice*.

62. Fleischer, *The SHRM Essential Guide to Employment Law*.

63. Equal Employment Opportunity Commission, "Title VII of the Civil Rights Act of 1964" (*www.eeoc.gov*), accessed Apr. 20, 2020.

64. Equal Employment Opportunity Commission, "Title VII of the Civil Rights Act of 1964."

CHAPTER THREE

Planning

Learning Objectives and Introduction
Learning Objectives
Introduction

Internal and External Influences
Organizational Strategy
Organizational Culture
Labor Markets
Technology

Human Resource Planning
Strategic Planning
Forecasting HR Requirements
Forecasting HR Availabilities
Reconciliation and Gaps Example

Staffing Planning
Staffing Planning Process
Core Workforce
Flexible Workforce
Outsourcing

Individual Internal Staffing Plans
Replacement Planning
Succession Planning

Diversity and Affirmative Action Planning
Planning for Diversity
Affirmative Action Plans

Legal Issues
Legality of AAPs and Diversity Programs
AAPs for Veterans and Individuals With Disabilities
EEO and Temporary Workers

Summary

Discussion Questions

Ethical Issues

Applications
Forecasting Demand
Deciding Whether to Use Flexible Staffing

Endnotes

LEARNING OBJECTIVES AND INTRODUCTION

Learning Objectives

- Recognize internal and external influences that will shape the planning process
- Understand how strategic plans integrate with staffing plans
- Become familiar with statistical and judgmental techniques for forecasting HR requirements and availabilities
- Know the similarities and differences between replacement and succession planning
- Understand the advantages and disadvantages of a core workforce, a flexible workforce, and outsourcing strategies for different groups of employees
- Learn how to incorporate diversity into the planning process
- Recognize the fundamental components of an affirmative action plan

Introduction

Human resource (HR) planning is the process of forecasting strategic needs for employee competencies and then developing action plans to fulfill these needs. HR planning forms the basis of all other activities conducted during staffing. An organization that thoroughly considers its staffing needs and how these needs fit with the external environment will find it much easier to recruit the right number and type of candidates, develop methods for selecting the right candidates, and then evaluate whether its programs are successful.

HR planning involves learning about the employment environment, determining how many employees an organization will need in the future, and assessing the availability of employees in both the internal and external markets. The HR planning process involves several specific components that we cover in this chapter, including making initial planning decisions, forecasting HR requirements and availabilities, determining employee shortages and surpluses, and developing action plans.

The chapter begins with an overview of internal and external influences on the HR planning process, like organizational strategy and culture, labor markets, and technology. Next, we provide an overview of the process of HR planning, including a review of methods for forecasting HR requirements and availability. The staffing planning process includes distinguishing between the core and flexible workforces, as well as understanding the environment for outsourcing. Diversity programs have become an increasingly important part of the staffing planning process, so they are also discussed. The major legal issue for HR staffing planning is that of affirmative action plans (AAPs). A different legal issue, that of equal employment opportunity (EEO) coverage for temporary employees and their agencies, is also discussed.

INTERNAL AND EXTERNAL INFLUENCES

Planning does not occur in a vacuum. All aspects of the planning process must consider both internal and external influences. The two most important internal influences on the planning process are the organization's strategy and the organization's culture. The two major sources of external influence on HR and staffing planning are labor markets and technology. Exhibit 3.1 provides specific examples of these influences, which are discussed next.

Organizational Strategy

The first, and most important, influence on the planning process is the organization's overall strategy. To make a convincing business case for HR, staffing managers must be intimately familiar with all aspects of the organization's future plans and goals so they can respond by hiring the right number of people with the right KSAOs (knowledge, skill, ability, and other characteristics) in a timely manner. Although some of the techniques we will review for staffing planning are based on a view of the organization's historical staffing levels, all planning must be conducted with an eye to the future as well.

EXHIBIT 3.1   Examples of Internal and External Influences on Staffing

ORGANIZATIONAL STRATEGY
- Current financial and human resources in the organization
- Demand for products and/or services
- Competitors and partners
- Financial and marketing goals

ORGANIZATIONAL CULTURE
- The expressed vision of executives
- The degree of hierarchy and bureaucracy
- Style of communication

LABOR MARKETS
- Labor demand
- Labor supply
- Shortages and surpluses
- Employment arrangements

TECHNOLOGY
- Elimination of jobs
- Creation of jobs
- Changes in skill requirements

The Society for Human Resource Management (SHRM) proposes that strategic planning involves a thorough knowledge of the organization's current situation as well as a sense of the strategic vision of the organization.[1] Breaking down the organization's strengths, weaknesses, opportunities, and threats (SWOT) is a common method for understanding strategy. The internal assessment phase of the SWOT analysis focuses on physical and financial resources, as well as structure and culture. The external assessment phase looks to learn about economic, demographic, and technological trends that will influence the organization in the future.

Effective staffing planning begins with a dialogue between HR representatives and organizational leaders. HR managers should be aware of core aspects of the organization's operations, including financial and marketing considerations. Additionally, it is important to see how the organization sees itself changing in the future, so that staffing strategies to meet these needs can be developed. Participating in activities like annual planning meetings and reviewing financial statements are essential. Strategic HR experts emphasize that this dialogue must be a two-way communication. In many cases, the current workforce and its capabilities will influence overall organizational plans. HR managers who are aware of internal human capital resources will be much more effective in an advisory capability when discussing future plans with the other executives.[2]

Organizational Culture

Organizational culture is a very complex topic, in part because culture is so difficult to define. In essence, culture is the set of intangibles that influences attitudes and behavior in organizations. Some of the factors that can influence an organization's culture include the expressed vision of executives, the degree of hierarchy and bureaucracy, the history of interactions among departments, and the style of communication throughout the organization. For example, an established company in the insurance industry might value structure and predictability, and so will engage in consistent, conservative practices that ensure that all employees have KSAOs, values, and work styles compatible with existing practices. Companies with a greater need for an innovative culture, like a consumer electronics producer that focuses on keeping up with the latest trends, will put more emphasis on flexible HR plans that can constantly adapt to external situations, and prioritize having a workforce with a variety of KSAOs, values, and work styles. The relationship between the organization and labor unions or other employee organizations (such as professional organizations like the American Medical Association or the state bar association) is also an extremely important part of culture.

Just because culture is intangible does not mean it is not important.[3] Evidence from multiple studies across a wide variety of organizations has demonstrated that HR policy effectiveness requires manager acceptance and understanding of these policies. Buy-in at all levels of the organization is essential to consistent implementation of strategically linked HR plans. Acceptance and understanding by managers is achieved by ensuring that HR is tightly integrated with culture. Michael Davis, former chief human resources officer at General Mills, encourages HR managers to build "an integrated set of programs and policies that reinforce and bring value to life." He further notes that when the company's espoused values are inconsistent with the practices that employees encounter on a day-to-day basis, problems with motivation, communication, and retention will follow.[4]

Matching culture to planning occurs in numerous ways. To understand culture, HR managers should spend time talking with senior executives, administer and evaluate employee survey data, and conduct focus groups. These conversations can help determine the attitudes and values needed to achieve person/organization fit. An organization with a participative culture should ensure that planning involves representatives from many different perspectives. Succession planning should also be influenced by the degree to which the organization's members value opportunities for growth and development relative to stability and predictability. The decision to use temporary or flexible staffing practices is also contingent on how the culture will react to these practices.

External and Internal Staffing Policies

External and internal staffing policies directly shape the nature of the staffing system, sending signals to applicants and employees alike about the organization as an employer. Exhibit 3.2 highlights the advantages and disadvantages of external and internal staffing. Clearly there are trade-offs to consider in deciding the optimal internal-external staffing mix.

The outcomes of external versus internal hiring processes have been studied extensively.[5] External hires are often selected as a way to increase organizational innovation. The "outsider" perspective appears to have significant advantages in this regard, as organizations that engage in more external hiring have higher levels of innovation. External hires may be able to reach job productivity faster if they have experience in a job similar to the one they will be taking, whereas internal hires are promoted into jobs they have not previously held. On the other hand, internal job changers have an advantage in terms of person/organization fit because they are already familiar with the relationships among organizational members as well as the culture, policies, and procedures of the organization. The possibility of future promotion and career development increases motivation and retention. A robust internal labor market can also help knowledge spread through the organization, as employees who are transferred share their knowledge and skills with other departments and divisions.

Diversity and Inclusion

Every organization should recognize the importance attached to being an inclusive employer, and determine which practices support inclusion in its workforce. As described in the previous chapter, an organization's overall philosophy toward diversity and inclusion will be shaped by the cultural value the organization attaches

---

EXHIBIT 3.2 Staffing Philosophy: Internal Versus External Staffing

	Advantages	**Disadvantages**
Internal	• Positive employee reactions to promotion from within • Quick method to identify job applicants • Less expensive • Less time required to reach full productivity	• No new KSAOs into the organization • May perpetuate current underrepresentation of minorities and women • Small labor market to recruit from • Inexperienced employees may require more training time
External	• Brings in employees with new KSAOs • Larger number of minorities and women to draw from • Large labor market to draw from • Experienced employees may require less training time	• Negative reaction by internal applicants • Time-consuming to identify applicants • Expensive to search external labor market • More time required to reach full productivity

to diversity and inclusion, as well as the business-related consequences of diversity-related practices. Many choices throughout the staffing process follow from the organization's attitudes toward diversity and inclusion, such as deciding where to recruit, how to develop inclusive talent pipelines, and what qualifications are most important for new hires.

Labor Markets

In and through labor markets, organizations express specific labor preferences and requirements (labor demand), and persons express their own job preferences and requirements (labor supply). Ultimately, person/job matches occur from the interaction of demand and supply forces. Both labor demand and supply contain quantity and quality components, as described below. Labor shortages, labor surpluses, and a variety of possible employment arrangements are also discussed.

Labor Demand

Knowing the organization's strategy and projections for future KSAO needs will guide the search for labor demand information. In particular, the labor market for the occupations the organization needs to staff will be greatly affected by the product market. For example, in the field of software design, the increased use of tablet computers has increased demand for programmers who have skills in designing applications for related operating systems. In the business-to-business domain, a rapid increase in the availability of large datasets on customer behavior has resulted in a dramatic increase in demand for analytics experts.

National employment statistics provide data about employment patterns and projections for industries, occupations, and organization size. Most organizations will need to examine not just aggregated statistics, like the overall unemployment rate, but also occupational and regional employment data. As an example, the US Bureau of Labor Statistics (BLS) in 2013 estimated that the unemployment rate for structural iron and steel workers was 21.9%, and the rate for telemarketers was 23.1%. At the other extreme, the unemployment rate for physician assistants was 1.2%, and the rate for petroleum engineers was 0.6%.[6]

Employment projections through 2024 indicate that demand is expected to be especially strong for health care practitioners and health care support occupations. Computer and mathematical occupations, and business and financial occupations, will see continued growth. Employment in occupations related to agriculture and production is expected to continue to decline.[7]

KSAO requirements or preferences of employers are not widely measured, except for education requirements. Data collected by the BLS suggest a continued increase in demand for individuals with college degrees or higher. The number of jobs requiring a bachelor's, master's, and doctoral degree are all expected to rise twice as fast as the number of jobs requiring only short-term on-the-job training. The increasing demand for education most likely reflects advances in technology that have made many jobs more complex and technically demanding.[8]

Employers are also interested in a broader set of skills that are not provided through specific educational degree programs. Surveys of HR professionals and employers consistently reveal that communication skills, critical thinking skills, creativity, diversity management, ethics, and a lifelong learning orientation are especially relevant for today's employees.[9]

Labor Supply

The US Department of Labor provides periodic reports of the quantity of labor supplied, along with projections for the near future. An example of data from one of these reports is given in Exhibit 3.3. It shows that there has been significant growth in the working age population and labor force since the 1990s, but that the labor force participation rate has been declining. The data and projections also show a consistent upward trend in the median age of the labor force.

Several labor force trends have particular relevance for staffing organizations. Labor force growth is slowing. The annual growth rate in the early 1990s was around 2%, but had decreased 1% by the year 2018. There are fewer new entrants to the labor force. This trend, coupled with the severe mismatch between organizational demand for KSAOs and workforce qualifications, creates major adaptation problems for organizations.

Demographically, the labor force has become more diverse, and this trend will continue. A trend toward nearly equal labor force participation for men and women and large proportional growth in the representation of Hispanics and Asians has been found beginning in the 1990s and continuing through the present day, and is projected to continue. There will also be a dramatic shift toward fewer younger workers and more workers over the age of 55. These age-related changes are partially a reflection of labor force participation. Today, individuals in their late teens are much less likely to be working, whereas workers over 55 are much more likely to be working.

Surveys conducted by the Society for Human Resource Management consistently find that employers see key shortages in technical skills, written communication, and basic computer skills. The job categories that have been the hardest to fill include engineers, highly skilled medical jobs, computer specialists, scientists, managers, and technicians. Applied skills in problem solving, critical thinking, creativity, and communication are all in high demand not just in the United States but

EXHIBIT 3.3   Labor Force Statistics

	1994	2004	2014	2024 (projected)
Civilian noninstitutional population (in millions)	197	223	248	269
Civilian labor force (in millions)	131	147	156	164
Labor force participation rate (%)	66.6	66	62.9	60.9
Unemployment rate (%)	6.1	5.5	6.2	5.2
Median age of the labor force	37.7	40.3	41.9	42.4

SOURCE: K. J. Byun and B. Nicholson, "The U.S. Economy to 2024," *Monthly Labor Review*, Dec. 2015 (*www.jstor.org/stable/monthlylaborrev.2015.12.005*).

also around the world.[10] There are also shortages of employees with the high skill levels required in contemporary manufacturing environments.[11]

Analysis of labor market data suggests that the problem of skill mismatch is partially the result of poor communication and coordination between employers and workers, and partially a reflection of the failure of specific educational programs to meet the needs of specific occupations.[12] In sum, it appears the problem is that demand for advanced skills is increasing and employer-employee matches are challenging, not that the supply of skilled workers is decreasing. These results also suggest that organizations can address the skills gap through active strategies to advertise their needs and embed themselves more in high schools, technical colleges, and universities.

Shortages and Surpluses

When demand exceeds supply, organizations experience employment shortages. Shortages tend to be job or occupation specific. Low unemployment rates, surges in labor demand in certain occupations, and skill deficiencies fuel labor quantity and labor quality shortages for many organizations. The shortages cause numerous responses:

- Increased pay and benefit packages
- Hiring bonuses and stock options
- Alternative work arrangements to attract and retain older workers
- Use of temporary employees
- Recruitment of immigrants
- Lower hiring standards
- Partnerships with high schools, technical schools, and colleges
- Increased mandatory overtime work
- Increased hours of operation

These responses are lessened or reversed when there are labor surpluses relative to labor demand.

Employment Arrangements

Though labor market forces bring organizations and job seekers together, the specific nature of the employment arrangement can assume many forms.

One arrangement is whether the person will be employed full time or part time. Data show that about 82% of people work full time and 18% work part time.[13]

A second arrangement involves flexible scheduling and shift work. The proportion of the workforce covered by flexible shifts has steadily grown over time. Many of these workers are covered by formal flextime programs. About 25% of full-time employed adults work evening, night, or rotating shifts. Some of the seeming flexibility in work hours has meant that workers on average work three hours from home per day, often during evenings and weekends, with some averaging significantly more than this.[14]

Two other types of arrangements, often considered in combination, are (1) various alternative arrangements to the traditional employer-employee relationship, and (2) the use of contingent employees. Alternative arrangements include the organization filling its staffing needs through the use of independent contractors, on-call workers and day laborers, temporary help agency employees, and employees provided by a contract firm that provides a specific service (e.g., accounting). Those working through online intermediary services like Uber, Lyft, and TaskRabbit, sometimes referred to as the "gig" workforce, also account for a small but growing number of work hours. Contingent employees do not have an explicit or implicit contract for long-term employment; they expect their employment to be temporary rather than long term.

Data collected over the period from 1995 to 2015 show that the prevalence of alternative work arrangements has increased significantly.[15] Construction and business services organizations have historically been the most likely to use alternative work arrangements, but since 2000 there has been a growing trend toward use of alternative work arrangements in education and health services. Roughly half of those in alternative work arrangements are self-employed, while the other half are employees of contract or temporary help firms. There is wide variability in how positively individuals in alternative work arrangements see their situations. On the one hand, over three-quarters of temporary help agency workers would prefer to have a permanent job, and about half of on-call workers would rather have jobs with more regular hours. On the other hand, over three-quarters of individuals who are independent contractors prefer to work for themselves.

Exhibit 3.4 shows several other workforce trends identified in surveys of HR professionals. Many of these issues are directly affected by the increasing influence of

---

EXHIBIT 3.4   Major Workforce Trends

- Creating better relationships between workers and technology
- Continuing high cost of health care in the United States
- Increased use of flexible work schedules
- Increased attention to mental health issues
- Addressing workforce skills gaps
- Preparing the newest generations of workers for the workforce
- Preventing burnout due to constant contact outside of regular work hours
- Greater need for cross-cultural understanding in business settings

SOURCE: J. Nagele-Piazza, *Top 10 Workplace Trends for 2019* (Alexandria, VA: Society for Human Resource Management, 2019).

information technology on the places people work, the types of work arrangements people are provided, and the competencies needed to match employer needs.

Technology

Changes in technology can influence the staffing planning process significantly. In some cases, technology can serve as a substitute for labor by either eliminating or dramatically reducing the need for certain types of workers. The economy as a whole has shown decreased demand for positions like clerical workers and manufacturing operators as technology has replaced labor as an input to production. Ironically, changes in software that have made computers easier for non-specialists to use have eliminated many jobs in computer programming.

At the same time, technology can create new jobs as new business opportunities emerge. In place of the jobs that are eliminated, demand for technical occupations like robotics engineers, systems and database analysts, and software engineers has increased. The expansion of e-commerce and other Internet-based services has increased demand for those who design and manage websites. Increasing productivity as a result of technological change can also spur increased firm performance, which in turn will create more jobs. Often these new jobs will require a completely different set of KSAOs than previous jobs, meaning that increased staffing resources will have to be devoted to either retraining or replacing the current workforce. Research conducted in the United States, Britain, and Germany shows that computerization has led to an increase in the demand for highly educated specialists, leading to an overall increased market demand for skills in science and mathematics, which has led to dramatic increases in wages for individuals with these skills.[16] Employers that adopt new technology for any aspect of their operations will also have to consider how to tap into labor markets that have these skills.

HUMAN RESOURCE PLANNING

After acquiring a solid understanding of the internal and external environments, a more detailed set of plans to strategically address organizational needs can be considered. Human resource planning (HRP) is an ongoing process and set of activities undertaken to forecast an organization's labor demand (requirements) and labor supply (availabilities), to compare these projections to determine employment gaps, and to develop action plans for addressing these gaps. Action plans include planning to arrive at desired staffing levels and staffing quality.

A general model depicting the process of HRP is presented first, followed by an operational example of HRP. The major components of HRP are then discussed in detail. Best practices in contemporary organizations suggest that to be effective, HRP must be an ongoing activity, supplemented with data from human resources

EXHIBIT 3.5   The Basic Elements of Human Resource Planning

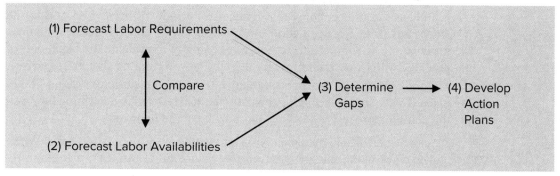

information systems. This presentation reviews only a single cycle of HRP, but it is better to think of HRP as a continuous process that is updated and reviewed at least once a quarter, if not more frequently.[17]

The basic elements of virtually any organization's HRP are shown in Exhibit 3.5. As can be seen, the HRP process involves four sequential steps:

1. Determine future HR requirements to meet strategic business requirements
2. Determine future HR availabilities
3. Reconcile requirements and availabilities—that is, determine gaps (shortages and surpluses) between the two
4. Develop action plans to close the projected gaps

Strategic Planning

We have already discussed the need to integrate organizational strategy into the HRP process. The development of a complementary strategy for HR should be the first element of HRP.[18] Several key decisions should be made before more concrete plans are considered:

- A vision based on the overall organizational strategy should be developed. This often means deciding what values and core competencies all members of the organization should possess, and considering principles that will support these values and competencies.
- Potential strategies for achieving planning process goals should be discussed. It is best at this point to think of whole systems of goals (e.g., integrate all KSAO information for the workforce and future planning needs) rather than specific concrete goals (e.g., conduct recruiting at a local college campus). Too much focus on implementation details early in the strategic planning process can lead to a patchwork of practices that do not fit together well.

- Contingency plans should be developed and considered. For example, what happens if certain key employees leave the organization? What happens if there is a change in the economy that reduces the supply of needed KSAOs in the labor market? Use of simulation software that shows potential future outcomes for a variety of actions and responses is one way to evaluate the likelihood of potential worst-case scenarios and plan for how to respond should they arise.
- Methods for obtaining feedback relative to goals and objectives should be in place. This involves specifying the data that will be used to determine how well the planning process is working and how it can be improved.

HRP can be performed on a plan basis, project basis, or population basis. When HRP takes place as an integral part of an organization's strategic planning process, it is referred to as plan-based HRP. This helps integrate the entire organization's strategic planning process with HR implications. Organizational responses to changes to specific projects or activities are referred to as project-based HRP. In addition, many organizations do HRP for critical groups of employees on a regular basis. This often occurs for jobs in which there are perennial shortages of employees. Planning focused on a specific employee group is referred to as population-based HRP. As we noted earlier, best practices suggest that these activities must be done on an ongoing basis.

Current and Future Competencies Demanded

The strategic process described above for HRP will lead to an understanding of what KSAOs and competencies are needed for the organization. The HRP process at this point takes the broad plan, project, and population business goals and then identifies the quantity of work that needs to be done and the types of KSAOs that will be needed. In subsequent chapters, we discuss the process of evaluating current and future competency needs in much greater detail.

To account for the amount of scheduled time worked by each employee required to accomplish the strategic plan, staffing needs are stated in terms of full-time equivalents (FTEs). Start by estimating how many person-hours might be needed overall to complete the required tasks. These estimated hours of work are then translated into FTEs. Define what constitutes full-time work in terms of hours per week (or other time unit) and count each employee in terms of scheduled hours worked relative to a full workweek. If full time is defined as 40 hours per week, a person who normally works 20 hours per week is counted as a .50 FTE, a person normally working 30 hours per week is a .75 FTE, and so on.

After evaluating which competencies are needed and in what quantity, management usually organizes the HRP around job categories and hierarchical level. Understanding job categories facilitates a systematic promotion-from-within program. Despite these advantages, the organization of roles into jobs and hierarchical levels is only one way of representing organizational need for competencies. In organizations with evolving strategic needs, it may be more helpful to think in terms of competencies and then determine whether these should be apportioned to current jobs, divided among multiple jobs, or outsourced altogether.

Planning Time Frame

Since planning involves looking into the future, the logical question for an organization to ask is, how far into the future should our planning extend? Typically, plans are divided into long term (three years and more), intermediate (one to three years), or short term (one year or less). The higher-level organizational plans tend to focus on the long term, whereas specific project planning is conducted more frequently.

For plan-based HRP, the time frame will be the same as that of the business plan. In most organizations, this is between three and five years for so-called strategic planning and something less than three years for operational planning. Planning horizons for project-based HRP vary depending on the nature of the projects involved. Solving a temporary shortage of, say, salespeople for the introduction of a new product might involve planning for only a few months, whereas planning for the start-up of a new facility could involve a lead time of two or more years. Population-based HRP will have varying time frames, depending on the time necessary for labor supply (internal as well as external) to become available. As an example, for top-level executives in an organization, the planning time frame will be lengthy.

Roles and Responsibilities

Both line managers and HR specialists are involved in HRP, so the roles and responsibilities of each must be determined. As noted previously, in an ideal situation there would be a constant flow of information among those involved in HRP, with line managers indicating how needs are expected to change, and HR staff describing the KSAO resources within and outside the organization that can be used to meet these needs in the future. To ensure that HRP is effective, experts also emphasize the importance of having a higher-level executive to champion this workforce planning process. This can ensure plans are integrated with the company's strategic plans, and it facilitates line manager engagement in the process.

The process begins with line staff evaluating their current capabilities and future needs based on strategic plans for the organization. The HR staff then takes the lead in proposing which types of HRP will be undertaken and when, and in making suggestions with regard to comprehensiveness, planning time frame, and job categories and levels. Final decisions on these matters are usually the prerogative of line management. Once an approach has been decided on, task forces of both line managers and HR staff are assembled to design an appropriate forecasting and action planning process and to do any other preliminary work.

Once these processes are in place, the HR staff typically assumes responsibility for collecting, manipulating, and presenting the necessary data to line management and for laying out alternative action plans (including staffing plans). Action planning usually becomes a joint venture between line managers and HR staff, particularly as they gain experience with, and trust for, one another.

Forecasting HR Requirements

Forecasting HR requirements is a direct derivative of business and organizational planning. As such, it becomes a reflection of projections about a variety of factors, such as sales, production, technological change, productivity improvement, and the regulatory environment. Many specific techniques may be used to forecast HR requirements; these are either statistical or judgmental in nature, and they are usually tailor-made by the organization. In forecasting future needs, it is essential to consider not just the status of the workforce but also the expected changes in needs due to strategic considerations. Forward-thinking HR experts note that data can inform HRP when it comes to prior needs and trends, but effective planning also entails considering how changes in the internal and external environments will alter forecasts.[19]

Statistical Techniques

A wide array of statistical techniques are available for use in HR forecasting. Prominent among these are regression analysis, ratio analysis, trend analysis, time series analysis, and stochastic analysis. Examples of three of these techniques are given in Exhibit 3.6.

The use of integrated workforce planning software, which can be combined with data from other organizational databases, has made it easier to use these statistical techniques. As we noted earlier, HR practitioners are increasingly expected to support their proposals and plans with hard data. The three techniques shown in Exhibit 3.6 have different strengths and weaknesses, as we will see. We present these approaches in order from those requiring the least amount of data collection to those requiring the most.

Trend analysis is the simplest approach, because it uses data only on previous staffing levels over time to predict future needs. Trend analysis is useful when organizations have data mostly on historical staffing levels with less detailed information on specific predictors. The decomposition of data into specific time periods of demand is often used in health care and retail settings, where staffing levels vary greatly over the course of a year and even at different times of the day.

The trend analysis approach implicitly assumes that the pattern of staffing needs in the past will be predictive of the future but does not take any external factors, like the overall state of the economy or product market demand, into account.

Ratio analysis is a more sophisticated approach that uses data from prior sales figures or other operational data to predict expected head count. In the example in Exhibit 3.6, estimates of sales growth are used to predict how many employees will be needed. This technique is useful for incorporating data from other functional areas to predict the future. However, this model cannot directly account for any changes in technology or skill sets that might change these ratios.

EXHIBIT 3.6 Examples of Statistical Techniques to Forecast HR Requirements

(A) Trend Analysis

1. Gather data on staffing levels over time and arrange in a spreadsheet with one column for employment levels and another column for time.
2. Predict trend in employee demand by fitting a line to trends in historical staffing levels over time (this can be done by using regression or graphical methods in most spreadsheet programs).
3. Calculate period demand index by dividing each period's demand by the average annual demand.

> Example: January demand index = Avg. January FTE/Avg. annual FTE

4. Multiply the previous year's FTEs by the trend figure, then multiply this figure by the period's demand index.

> Example: A retail store finds that the average number of employees over the past five years has been 142, 146, 150, 155, and 160. This represents a consistent 3% increase per year; to predict the next year's average demand, multiply 160 by 1.03 to show a 3% expected increase. Over this same time period, the store averaged 150 FTEs per month, with an average of 200 FTEs in December. This means the December demand index is 200/150 = 1.33, so its estimate for next year's December FTE demand will be (160 × 1.03) × 1.3 = 219 FTEs.

(B) Ratio Analysis

1. Examine historical ratios involving workforce size.

> Example: $\dfrac{\$ \text{ sales}}{1.0 \text{ FTE}} = ?$ $\dfrac{\text{No. of new customers}}{1.0 \text{ FTE}} = ?$

2. Assume ratio will be true in future.
3. Use ratio to predict future HR requirements.

> Example: (a) $\dfrac{\$40,000 \text{ sales}}{1.0 \text{ FTE}}$ is past ratio
>
> (b) Sales forecast is $4,000,000
>
> (c) HR requirements = 100 FTEs

(C) Regression Analysis

1. Statistically identify historical predictors of workforce size.

> Example: FTEs = $a + b_1$ sales + b_2 new customers

2. Only use equations with predictors found to be statistically significant.
3. Predict future HR requirements, using equation.

> Example: (a) FTEs = 7 + .0004 sales + .02 new customers
>
> (b) Projected sales = $1,000,000
>
> Projected new customers = 300
>
> (c) HR requirements = 7 + 400 + 6 = 413

The regression analysis technique can be used with historical predictors and can make more statistically precise estimates of future expectations by taking several factors into account simultaneously. In the example, sales data and new customer data from organizational records are used to predict staffing needs in the past. Then the estimates from these predictions are combined with projections for the future to generate future FTE requirements. This procedure is more thorough than the ratio analysis approach, which incorporates only a single predictor of workforce size. However, collecting enough data to make good estimates can be time-consuming and requires judgment calls.

Limitations of Statistical Techniques.   Statistical techniques are extremely useful for getting an accurate aggregate picture for larger organizations engaged in workforce planning. However, there are limitations.

The first and most fundamental limitation is that of sample size, or the number of FTEs being estimated. Employment requirements based on small samples yield unstable estimates of future availabilities. The job category/level combinations created to serve as the unit of analysis can also be problematic. These must be meaningful to the organization for the HRP purposes of both forecasting and action planning. Thus, extremely broad categories (e.g., managers or researchers) and categories without any level designations should be avoided. Note that this recommendation may conflict somewhat with organizations with a non-bureaucratic or team-based structure.

A second limitation is that estimated needs reflect only gross, average figures for large groups and not location-specific needs. Stated differently, all subsets of employees and departments included in a single analysis are treated as facing the same underlying conditions. This is unrealistic because each situation has unique and complex influences. This is where manager discretion should supplement data-based estimates.

Judgmental Techniques

Judgmental techniques represent human decision-making models that are used for forecasting HR requirements. Unlike statistical techniques, judgmental techniques use a decision maker who collects and weighs the information subjectively and then turns it into forecasts of HR requirements. The decision maker's forecasts may or may not agree very closely with those derived from statistical techniques. This is not necessarily a weakness of either approach. Ideally, the precision of statistical techniques should be coupled with on-the-ground knowledge represented by judgmental techniques to provide estimates that have both rigor and relevance.

Implementation of judgmental forecasting can proceed from either a top-down or bottom-up approach. In the former, top managers of the organization, organizational units, or functions rely on their knowledge of business and organizational plans to predict what future head counts should be. At times, these projections may, in fact, be dictates rather than estimates, necessitated by strict adherence to the business plan. Such dictates are common in organizations undergoing significant change, such as restructuring, mergers, and cost-cutting actions.

In the bottom-up approach, lower-level managers make initial estimates for their unit (e.g., department, office, or plant) on the basis of what they have been told or presume are the business and organizational plans. These estimates are then consolidated and aggregated upward through successively higher levels of management. Then, top management establishes the HR requirements in terms of numbers.

Scenario Planning

Scenario planning is a technique that has been explored in a variety of fields to predict future outcomes in an uncertain environment.[20] The previous methods we have described are all designed to give a specific estimate of the number of people who will be needed in the organization in the future. Scenario planning provides a range of estimates based on various possible changes in the external and internal environments. For example, ratio analysis uses forecasts of future product demand to predict how many FTEs will be required; in our example in Exhibit 3.6, 100 FTEs will be required based on sales forecasts. Scenario planning provides a range of possible FTE requirements based on a variety of potential product demand levels; thus, three distinct estimates of FTE requirements will be developed for worst-case, expected, and best-case demand levels.

The advantage of scenario planning is that it allows HRP to incorporate uncertainty and prepare for the unexpected. Because it explicitly acknowledges ways that the future might be different from the past, it also incorporates judgmental techniques. Considering all the complex factors that go into various scenarios is often challenging, so simulation software is often part of the process. These programs allow managers to change various features of a situation to see how an outcome (in this case, projected FTEs) will change. Evidence suggests that the process of doing scenario planning can change the ways decision makers think by promoting more holistic views of a problem that incorporate a wide range of factors.[21]

Forecasting HR Availabilities

When developing forecasts in HR availability, FTE data are given for the current workforce and their availability as forecast in each job category/level. These forecasted figures take into account movement into and out of each job category/level and exit from the organizational unit or the organization. These forecasts can then be combined with estimates of external labor market availabilities. As with forecasting HR requirements, there are both quantitative and judgmental tools available.

External Market Availability Forecasts

Forecasting external market availabilities can involve some of the same methods described earlier, but the focus changes from predicting FTE requirements to predicting the quantity of available workers with a given set of KSAOs.

The most basic method for evaluating the availability of KSAOs in a labor market is by extrapolating from trends across time. In this case, the HR professional will gather data on individuals who have had given levels of qualifications over time. Such information is often available from state and federal labor departments, such as the BLS. If an organization has estimated that it will need 45 engineers in the coming year, data on the number of qualified individuals seeking work in that occupation over the past ten years can be found and then the trend can be extended to the coming years.

Typically, more thorough analyses bring in additional predictors of labor availability. For example, besides using just the general pattern of available workers with a given skill over time, changes in the competition to hire these workers, patterns of retirement in this occupation, the makeup of students in relevant education and training programs, and the demographic shifts in the region will all be relevant. Like the forecasting of HR requirements, all of this information can be combined through regression analysis to create a starting point for estimating external availability.

Internal Availability and Movement: Markov Analysis

Markov Analysis is a quantitative technique that is uniquely related to the forecasting process for internal availabilities and the movement among jobs. This approach models historical patterns of job stability and movement among employees. Consider Figure 3.7. Note that between any two time periods, the following possibilities exist for each employee in the internal labor market:

1. Job stability (remain in A1, A2, B1, or B2)
2. Promotion (move to a higher level: A1 to A2, A1 to B2, B1 to B2, or B1 to A2)
3. Transfer (move at the same level: A1 to B1, B1 to A1, A2 to B2, or B2 to A2)
4. Demotion (move to a lower level: A2 to A1, A2 to B1, B2 to B1, or B2 to A1)
5. Exit (move to another organizational unit or leave the organization)

These possibilities may be thought of in terms of flows and rates of flow or movement rates. Past flows and rates may be measured and then used to forecast the future availability of current employees. For example, if it is known that the historical promotion rate from A1 to A2 is .10 (10% of A1 employees are promoted to A2), we might predict that A1 will experience a 10% loss of employees due to promotion to A2 over the relevant time period.

An example of the elements of Markov Analysis is shown in Exhibit 3.7. Refer first to part A of Exhibit 3.7, where movement rates between two time periods (T and T+1) are calculated for four job category/level combinations. For each job category/level, take the number of employees at time period T and use this number as the denominator for calculating job stability and movement rates. Next, for each of these employees, determine which job category/level they were employed in at

EXHIBIT 3.7 Use of Markov Analysis to Forecast Availabilities

A. Transition Probability Matrix

Job Category and Level		A1	A2	**T + 1** B1	B2	Exit
	A1	.60	.10	.20	.00	.10
T	A2	.05	.60	.00	.00	.35
	B1	.05	.00	.60	.05	.30
	B2	.00	.00	.00	.80	.20

B. Forecast of Availabilities

	Current Workforce				
A1	100	60	10	20	0
A2	20	1	12	0	0
B1	200	10	0	120	10
B2	15	0	0	0	12
		71	22	140	22

T+1. Then, sum up the number of employees in each job category/level at T+1 and use these as the numerators for calculating stability and movement rates. Finally, divide each numerator separately by the denominator. The result is the stability and movement rates expressed as proportions, also known as transition probabilities. The rates for any row (job category/level) must add up to 1.0.

For example, consider job category/level A1. Assume that at time T in the past, A1 had 400 people. Further assume that at T+1, 240 of these employees were still in A1, 40 had been promoted to A2, 80 had been transferred to B1, 0 had been promoted to B2, and 40 had exited the organizational unit or the organization. The resulting transition probabilities, shown in the row for A1, are .60, .10, .20, .00, and .10. Note that these rates sum to 1.0.

By referring to these figures, and the remainder of the transition probabilities in the matrix, an organization can begin to understand the workings of the unit's internal labor market. For example, it becomes clear that 60%–80% of employees experienced job stability and that exit rates varied considerably, ranging from 10% to 35%. Promotions occurred only within job categories (A1 to A2, B1 to B2), not between job categories (A1 to B2, B1 to A2). Transfers were confined to the lower of the two levels (A1 to B1, B1 to A1). Only occasionally did demotions occur, and only within a job category (A2 to A1). Presumably, these stability and movement rates reflect specific staffing policies and procedures that were in place between T and T+1.

With these historical transitional probabilities, it becomes possible to forecast the future availability of the current workforce over the same time interval, T and T+1, assuming that the historical rates will be repeated over the time interval and that staffing policies and procedures will not change. Refer now to part B of Exhibit 3.7. To forecast availabilities, simply take the current workforce column and multiply it by the transition probability matrix shown in part A. The resulting availability figures appear at the bottom of the columns: A1 = 71, A2 = 22, B1 = 140, and B2 = 22. The remainder of the current workforce (80) is forecast to exit and will not be available at T+1.

Judgmental Techniques

Much like in forecasting HR requirements, after estimating HR availability through quantitative techniques, individual manager judgment comes into play. This is especially appropriate in smaller organizations or in ones that lack centralized workforce internal mobility data.

To provide reliable estimates, the manager must be very knowledgeable about both organizational business plans and individual employee plans or preferences for staying in their current job versus moving to another job. Knowledge of business plans will be helpful in judging the likely internal mobility opportunities for employees. Business expansion, for example, will likely mean expanding internal mobility opportunities. Knowledge of employee plans or preferences will help pinpoint which employees are likely to change jobs or leave the work unit or organization.

Reconciliation and Gaps Example

An example of HRP, including results from forecasting requirements and availabilities, is shown in Exhibit 3.8. The exhibit shows a partial HRP conducted by an organization for a specific unit (sales and customer service). It involves only two job categories (sales [A] and customer service [B]) and two hierarchical levels for each category (entry level [1] and managerial level [2]). All of the HRP steps are confined to this particular organizational unit and its job categories/levels, as shown.

The current workforce size (number of employees) is given for each job category/level. Requirements and availabilities are predicted for one year, and the results are shown in the relevant columns. After the reconciliation process, final gap figures are agreed on and entered in the gap column.

These gap data serve as the basic input to action planning. Because the gaps show both shortages and a surplus, and because the gaps vary in severity relative to the current workforce, a specific action plan will probably have to be developed and implemented for each job category/level. The resulting four staffing (and other) plans should bring staffing into an orderly balance of requirements and availabilities over the course of the planning period.

Attention is now directed to the reconciliation and gaps column. It represents the requirements and availability forecasts paired with the results of external and internal environmental scanning. Gap estimates are entered in the column, along with potential explanations for the gaps.

EXHIBIT 3.8 Operational Format and Example of Human Resource Planning

Organizational Unit: Sales and Customer Service

Job Category and Level	Current Workforce	Forecast for Workforce— One Year		Reconciliation and Gaps	Action Planning
		Requirements	Availabilities		
A1 (Sales)	100	110	71	−39 (shortage)	Recruitment Selection
A2 (Sales manager)	20	15	22	+7 (surplus)	Employment Retention
B1 (Customer service representative)	200	250	140	−110 (shortage)	Compensation Training and development
B2 (Customer service manager)	15	25	22	−3 (shortage)	
	335	400	255	−145 (shortage)	

Let's first consider job category/level A1. A relatively large shortage is projected due to a mild expansion in requirements coupled with a substantial drop in availabilities. This drop is not due to an excessive exit rate but to losses through promotions and job transfers.

For A2, decreased requirements coupled with increased availabilities lead to a projected surplus. Clearly, changes in current staffing policies and procedures will have to be made to stem the availability tide, such as a slowdown in the promotion rate into A2 from A1, or to accelerate the exit rate, such as through an early retirement program.

Turning to B1, note that a huge shortage is forecast. This is due to a major surge in requirements and a substantial reduction in availabilities. To meet the shortage, the organization could increase the transfer of employees from A1. While this would worsen the already-projected shortage in A1, it might be cost-effective and would beef up the external staffing for A1 to cover the exacerbated shortage. Alternately, a massive external staffing program could be developed and undertaken for B1 alone. Or, a combination of internal transfers and external staffing for both A1 and B1 could be attempted. To the extent that external staffing becomes a candidate for consideration, this will naturally spill over into other HR activities, such as establishing starting-pay levels for A1 and B1. Finally, a very different strategy would be to develop and implement a major retention program for employees in customer service.

For B2 there is a small projected shortage. This gap is so small, however, that for all practical purposes it can be ignored. The HRP process is too imprecise to warrant concern over such small gap figures.

In short, the reconciliation and gap phase of HRP involves coming to grips with projected gaps and the likely reasons for them. Quite naturally, thoughts about future implications begin to creep into the process. Even in the simple example shown, it can be seen that considerable action will have to be contemplated and undertaken to respond to the forecasting results for the organizational unit. That will involve mixtures of external and internal staffing, with compensation as another likely HR ingredient. Through action planning, these possibilities become real.

STAFFING PLANNING

After the HRP process is complete, it is time to move toward the development of specific plans for staffing. This is a vital phase of the planning process, in which staffing objectives are developed and alternative staffing activities are generated. The objectives are the targets the organization establishes to determine how many employees will be needed and in which job categories. The activities are the specific methods, including recruiting and selection strategies, that will be used to meet these objectives. We devote special attention in this section to one of the most critical decisions made during staffing planning: Should the organization use a core workforce or a flexible workforce, or should parts of the workforce be outsourced?

Staffing Planning Process

Identifying Staffing Objectives

Staffing objectives are derived from identified gaps between requirements and availabilities. Thus, these objectives respond to both shortages and surpluses. They may require the establishment of quantitative and qualitative targets.

Quantitative targets should be expressed in head count or FTE form for each job category/level and will be very close in magnitude to the identified gaps. Indeed, to the extent that the organization believes in the gaps as forecast, the objectives will be identical to the gap figures. A forecast shortage of 39 employees in A1, for example, should be transformed into a staffing objective of 39 accessions (or something close to it) to be achieved by the end of the forecasting time interval. Exhibit 3.9 illustrates these points. For each cell, enter a positive number for head-count additions and a negative number for head-count subtractions.

Qualitative staffing objectives refer to the qualities of people in KSAO-type terms. For external staffing objectives, these may be stated in terms of averages, such as average education level for new hires and average scores on ability tests. Internal staffing objectives of a qualitative nature may also be established. These may reflect desired KSAOs in terms of seniority, performance appraisal record over a period of years, types of on- and off-the-job training, and so forth.

The results of replacement and succession planning, or something similar to that, will be very useful to have as well.

EXHIBIT 3.9   Setting Numerical Staffing Objectives

Job Category and Level	Gap	Objectives					Total
		New Hires	Promotions	Transfers	Demotions	Exits	
A1	−39	52	−6	−3	0	−4	+39
A2	+7	0	+2	−8	0	−1	−7
B1	−110	+140	−5	−3	−2	−20	+110
B2	−3	+2	+4	−1	0	−2	+3

NOTE: The objective is to close each gap exactly.

Generating Alternative Staffing Activities

With quantitative and, possibly, qualitative objectives established, it is necessary to begin identifying possible ways of achieving them. At the beginning stages of generating alternatives, it is not wise to close the door prematurely on any of them. Exhibit 3.10 provides a full range of options for dealing with employee shortages and surpluses. As with previous planning processes, the focus is not on specific programs at this stage but rather on broad classes of potential activities.

As shown in the exhibit, both short- and long-term options for shortages, involving a combination of staffing and workload management, are possible. Short-term options include utilizing current employees better (through more overtime, productivity increases, and buybacks of vacation and holidays), outsourcing work to other organizations (subcontracts, transferring work out), and acquiring additional employees on a short-term basis (temporary hires and assignments). Long-term options include staffing additional employees (recalling former employees, transferring in employees from other work units, adding new permanent hires), enhancing skills (retraining), and pushing work to other organizations (transferring work out). There are also short- and long-term options for surpluses. Short-term options include hiring freezes, retraining current workers for new roles, cutting back the number of days worked per week, providing more voluntary leave, temporarily reassigning surplus employees to do work in areas with shortages, or temporarily suspending operations and laying off employees until need for their work increases. Long-term options are generally permanent versions of the short-term responses.

EXHIBIT 3.10   Staffing Alternatives to Deal With Employee Shortages and Surpluses

Employee Shortage		Employee Surplus	
Short-Term Options	**Long-Term Options**	**Short-Term Options**	**Long-Term Options**
• Subcontracting	• Hiring	• Hiring freeze	• Long-term hiring freeze
• Increase productivity	• Permanent transfer into role	• Retraining	• Permanent transfer out of role
• Increase overtime or part time	• Recall of retired employees	• Reduce workweek	• Retirement incentives
• Buy back vacation or holidays	• Retraining	• Increase leave availability	• Downsizing or long-term layoff
• Temporary assignments	• Outsourcing	• Temporary reassignment	
• Temporary hires		• Temporary shutdown or layoff	

Assessing and Choosing Alternatives

As should be apparent, a veritable smorgasbord of alternative staffing activities are available to address staffing gaps. Each of these alternatives needs to be assessed systematically to help decision makers choose from among them.

The goal of assessment is to identify one or more preferred activities. A preferred activity offers the highest likelihood of attaining the staffing objective within the time limit established, at the least cost or at a tolerable cost, and with the fewest negative side effects. A wide variety of metrics are available to assess potential activities. First, a common set of assessment criteria (e.g., time for completion, cost, and probability of success) should be identified and agreed on. Second, each alternative should be assessed according to each of these criteria. In this way, all alternatives will receive equal treatment, and tendencies to jump at an initial alternative will be minimized.

All of these alternatives must be considered within the broader context of how the organization creates and structures its workforce. This involves the key strategic issue of core versus flexible workforce usage. The choice should be considered in light of the organization's staffing philosophy, in particular, the difference between an internal and external emphasis. Many of the staffing activity alternatives are more applicable to one type of workforce than another.

Core Workforce

A core workforce is defined as regular full-time and part-time employees of the organization. The key advantages of a core workforce are stability, continuity, and predictability. The organization can depend on its core workforce and build strategic plans based on it. Several other advantages accrue to the organization from using a core workforce. The regularity of the employment relationship fosters a sense of commitment and shared purpose toward the organization's mission. In addition, the organization maintains the legal right to control employees working on its behalf, in terms of both work process and expected results, rather than having to divide or share that right with organizations providing a flexible workforce, such as temporary employment agencies. Finally, the organization can directly control how it acquires its workforce and the qualifications of those it employs through the management of its own staffing systems. By doing so, the organization may build not only a highly qualified workforce but also one more likely to be retained, thus lessening pressure to continually restaff.

A core workforce also has several disadvantages. The implied permanence of the employment relationship "locks in" the organization's workforce, with a potential loss of staffing flexibility to rapidly increase, reduce, or redeploy its workforce in response to changing market conditions and project life cycles. Reducing the core workforce can be very costly in terms of severance pay packages, low morale, and damage to the organization's reputation as a good employer. Additionally, the labor costs of the core workforce may be greater than those of the flexible workforce due to (1) higher wages, salaries, and benefits for the core workforce, and (2) the fixed nature of these labor costs, relative to the more variable costs associated with a flexible workforce. By using a core workforce, the organization incurs numerous legal obligations—particularly taxation and employment law compliance—that could be fully or partially avoided through the use of flexible workforce providers, which would be the actual employer. Finally, use of a core workforce may deprive the organization of new technical and administrative knowledge that could be infused into it by use of flexible workers such as programmers and consultants.

Consideration of these numerous advantages and disadvantages needs to occur separately for various jobs and organizational units covered by the HR plan. In this way, usage of a core workforce proceeds along selective, strategic lines. Referring back to the original example in Exhibit 3.8, staffing planners should do a unique core workforce analysis for the sales and customer service unit, and within that unit, for both sales and customer service jobs at the entry and managerial levels. The analysis may result in a decision to use only full-time core workers for the managerial jobs, both full-time and part-time core workers for sales jobs, and full-time core customer service representatives augmented by both full-time and part-time temporary customer service representatives during peak sales periods. Once the job and work unit locations of the core workers have been determined, specific staffing planning for effective acquisition must occur. This involves planning of recruitment, selection, and employment activities; these topics will be covered in subsequent chapters.

Flexible Workforce

The two major components of the flexible workforce are temporary employees provided by a staffing firm and independent contractors. Planning for usage of the flexible workforce must occur in tandem with core workforce planning; hence, it should begin with a review of the advantages and disadvantages of a flexible workforce.[22]

The key advantage is staffing flexibility. The flexible workforce may be used for adjusting staffing levels quickly in response to changing technological or consumer demand conditions and to ebbs and flows of orders for products and services. Other flexibility advantages are the ability to quickly staff new areas or projects and the ability to fill in for core workers absent due to illness, vacations, and holidays. Relative to the core workforce, the flexible workforce may also present labor cost advantages in the form of lower pay and benefits, more variable labor costs, and reduced training costs. Another advantage for the organization is possibly being relieved of many tax and employment law obligations, since flexible workers are often not considered employees of the organization.

The flexible workforce, especially in the professional and technical ranks, may also be an important source of new knowledge about organizational best practices and new skills not present in the core workforce. In a related vein, organizations use temporary or interim top executives to fill in until a permanent hire is found, to spur change, and to launch special projects requiring their expertise. However, most evidence suggests that temporary or interim executives often perform significantly worse than their more established, permanent counterparts, so the decision to use a flexible managerial workforce needs to be undertaken carefully, and only if it is a good match to the organization's strategic needs.[23]

These numerous advantages must be weighed against several potential disadvantages. Research clearly demonstrates that contingent workers are significantly less committed to their employers, and therefore are less likely to engage in extra-role behaviors, like volunteering to help coworkers, providing creative suggestions, or exerting exceptional effort during times of high demand. The legal loss of control over flexible workers is another major concern. Although the organization has great flexibility in initial job assignments for flexible workers, it is very limited in the amount of supervision and performance management it can conduct for them. Exacerbating the situation, frictions between core and flexible workers may also arise. Core workers, for example, may feel that flexible workers lack knowledge and experience, and do not act like committed team players. Also, flexible workers may lack familiarity with equipment, policies, procedures, and important customers; such deficiencies may be compounded by a lack of training in specific job requirements. Finally, the quality of the flexible workforce depends heavily on the quality of the staffing and training systems used by the provider of the flexible workers. The organization may end up with flexible but poorly qualified workers.

Staffing Firms

Recall that staffing firms (also called temporary help agencies) are the legal employers of the workers being supplied, though matters of co-employment may arise. Hence, the staffing firm conducts recruitment, selection, training, compensation, performance appraisal, and retention activities for the flexible workers. The firm is also responsible for on-site supervision and management, as well as all payrolling and the payment of legally required insurance premiums. For such services, the firm charges the organization a general fee for its labor costs (wages and benefits) plus a markup percentage of labor costs (usually 40%–50%) to cover these services' costs plus provide a profit. There may be additional charges for specially provided services, such as extra testing or background checks or skill training. Temp-to-perm workers may be hired away from the firm (with its permission and for a special fee) by the organization to become regular employees in the core workforce. For larger clients the firm may provide an on-site manager to help the organization plan its specific staffing needs, supervise and appraise the performance of the temporary workers, handle discipline and complaints, and facilitate firm-organization relations. With such additional staffing services, the firm functions increasingly like a staffing partner rather than just a staffing supplier.

Use of a staffing firm requires advanced planning, rather than a panicky phone call to a firm at the moment of staffing need. In addition to becoming aware of firms that might be accessed, it is wise to become familiar with their characteristics and services. Shown in Exhibit 3.11 are the various factors and issues to become knowledgeable about for any firm.

EXHIBIT 3.11   Factors to Consider When Choosing a Staffing Firm

Factor	Issues
Agency and Its Reputation	How long in business; location; references from clients available.
Types of Workers Provided	What occupation and KSAO levels; how many available.
Planning and Lead Time	Does agency help client plan staffing levels and needs; how quickly can workers be provided.
Services Provided	
Recruitment	What methods are used; how targeted and truthful is recruitment process.
Selection	What selection techniques are used to assess KSAOs.
Training	What types of training, if any, are provided before workers are placed with client.
Wages and Benefits	How are wages determined; what benefits are provided.
Orientation	How does the agency prepare workers for assignment with client; does agency have an employee handbook for its workers.
Supervision	How does agency supervise its workers on site of client; does agency provide on-site manager.
Temp-to-Perm	Does agency allow client to hire its temporary workers as permanent employees.
Client Satisfaction	How does agency attempt to gauge client satisfaction with services, workers, costs.
Worker Effectiveness	
Punctuality and Attendance	Does the agency monitor these; what is its record with previous clients.
Job Performance	Is it evaluated; how are the results used.
Retention	How long do workers remain on an assignment voluntarily; how are workers discharged by the agency.
Cost	
Markup	What is the percentage over base wage charged to client (often it is 50% to cover benefits, overhead, profit margin).
For Special Services	What services cost extra beyond the markup (e.g., temp-to-perm); what are those costs.

When the organization chooses a firm, both parties should enter into a formal written agreement. The agreement should cover such matters as specific services to be provided, costs, steps to ensure that the flexible workers are employees of the firm (such as having an on-site manager for them), and the process for terminating the firm-organization relationship. It is best to have legal counsel prepare and review the agreement.

The organization may decide to establish its own in-house staffing firm. When this is done, the employees of the firm may even be employees of the organization. Managers thus have readily available flexible workers to whom they can turn, without having to go through all the planning steps mentioned above.

Independent Contractors

An independent contractor (IC) provides specific task and project assistance to the organization, such as maintenance, bookkeeping, advertising, programming, and consulting. The IC can be a single individual (self-employed, freelancer) or an employer with its own employees. Neither the IC nor its employees are intended to be employees of the organization utilizing the IC's services, and care should be taken to ensure that the IC is not treated like an employee.[24]

As with staffing firms, the organization must take the initiative to identify and check out ICs for possible use in advance of when they are actually needed. It is desirable to solicit and examine references from past or current clients of the IC. In addition, as much as possible the organization should seek to determine how the IC staffs, trains, and compensates any employees. This could occur during a preliminary meeting with the IC. If a single individual will be working as an IC, it is advisable to use some of the same tools we describe later in the book for assessing job candidates, including an assessment of KSAOs through a standardized interview process and collection of references related to these characteristics.

Outsourcing

Outsourcing of work functions can be defined as the transfer of a business process to an external organization. This is a more drastic step than simply using ICs or temporary employees. The primary difference is that when processes are outsourced, the organization expects to receive a completely finished product from the external source. This means the organization does not direct or control the way in which work is performed; rather, it only receives the end result of the work.

Within the HR department, it has become the norm for organizations to completely outsource routine or highly specialized tasks, including payroll, benefits, legal compliance, or development of online recruiting strategies. Other core functions like employee training, performance tracking, compensation system administration, and recruiting system management can also be outsourced. Smaller organizations without the resources for multiple HR staff are especially likely to use outsourcing.[25]

Organizations outsource for a variety of reasons. An obvious reason for outsourcing of manufacturing and routine information-processing tasks is the availability of less expensive labor in the global market. Often, specialized vendors can achieve economies of scale for routine tasks that are performed across a variety of organizations. Organizations also outsource functions that have highly cyclical demand so that they do not have to make major capital outlays and go through the cost of hiring and training permanent workers to perform tasks that may not be needed in the future. Sometimes organizations outsource functions that require specific expertise that cannot be economically generated in-house. Smaller organizations that require legal services, for example, often choose to hire an external law firm rather than establish their own pool of legal specialists. As we have noted, many organizations also outsource routine business functions, such as having third-party vendors take care of payroll or benefits administration tasks.

One variant of outsourcing is termed "offshoring," which means that products or services are provided by an external source outside the country where the organization's core operations take place.[26] The outsourcing of manufacturing to lower-wage countries has a long history, and this practice is likely to continue unabated. For example, in the computer industry it is common for large companies to have many subcomponent electronic parts manufactured by third-party vendors overseas, with final assembly of products performed domestically. Many companies have outsourced routine computer programming and telephone help services to third-party providers in India because of the availability of a highly skilled labor force that typically draws only a fraction of the wages paid in North America. Offshoring is no longer limited to blue- and pink-collar jobs. There has been an increase in offshoring white-collar technical and professional work in the twenty-first century, fueled by improvements in global education, an increasingly positive climate for business in China and India, and increased demand for products and services in multinational organizations. Many of these jobs have also been outsourced domestically, as a growing proportion of white-collar work is being done in remote locations.

The decision to outsource is likely to be controversial. Outsourcing is usually done for activities that have low added value for the organization. Normal transactional or procedural work that is easily replicated is likely to be outsourced. Best practices identified by research across many studies suggest that outsourcing of routine functions that is focused on enhancing efficiency and cost savings can have a positive outcome for firm performance, at the price of reduced flexibility and responsiveness created by the bureaucracy needed to manage the relationship with an external partner. Other firms also engage in outsourcing for the purpose of acquiring technical knowledge that they cannot replicate in-house. Such interactions can increase innovation, especially if the company maintains a "hands-off" relationship with the external partner so they can truly generate innovative solutions to problems. On the other hand, a simpler picture emerges when it comes to outsourcing core functions related to strategy development and implementation. Outsourcing these functions almost always leads to worse performance.[27]

Additionally, offshoring has been the focus of media and political scrutiny. Extremely low wages and dangerous working conditions provided by external partners in foreign countries have created a backlash against certain companies that have offshored manufacturing jobs. Negative press about poor working conditions in overseas "sweatshops" has been especially prominent in the clothing industry. When outsourcing, an organization needs to make certain that it is not losing too much control over its major work processes. Just because a business process has been outsourced does not mean that the organization has lost the responsibility (and this sometimes includes legal liability) for the actions of external partners.

INDIVIDUAL INTERNAL STAFFING PLANS

All of the techniques we have described up to this point have highlighted methods for staffing the organization as a whole. Replacement and succession planning focus on identifying individual employees who will be considered for promotion. This form of planning incorporates elements of training and professional development as a method to help current employees fulfill their future job requirements as they move through the organization.

When effective, a process of thoughtful replacement and succession planning can meet many business needs, including identifying exactly where training and development is needed to build KSAOs, retaining institutional knowledge, and demonstrating to employees that there is a potential for growth in the organization. Through replacement and succession planning, the organization constructs internal talent pipelines that ensure steady and known flows of qualified employees to higher levels of responsibility and impact. An increasing body of research suggests that effective succession planning at top executive ranks is associated with superior firm performance, while ineffective succession plans can have catastrophic consequences.[28]

Replacement and succession planning can occur at any and all levels of the organization. They are most widely used at the management level, starting with the chief executive officer and extending downward to the other officers or top managers. They can also be used throughout the entire management team, including the identification and preparation of individuals for promotion into entry-level management and for positions that are critical to organization effectiveness, such as senior scientists in the research and development function of a technology-driven organization.

Replacement Planning

Replacement planning focuses on identifying individual employees who will be considered for promotion and thoroughly assessing their current capabilities and deficiencies. Training and development plans to improve the fit between capabilities and requirements are also developed. The focus is thus on both the quantity and the quality of availability. The results of replacement planning are shown on a replacement chart, an example of which is shown in Exhibit 3.12. The chart is

EXHIBIT 3.12   Replacement Chart Example

Organizational Unit: Merchandising—Soft Goods
Replacement for: Department Sales Manager (A2)
Pipelines for Replacement: Department Sales (A1)—preferred; External Hire—last resort
Minimum Eligibility Requirements: Two years' full-time sales experience; overall performance rating of "exceeds
expectations"; promotability rating of "ready now" or "ready in < 1 yr."

Department: Menswear   Store: Cloverdale

Incumbent Manager	Years in Job	Overall Performance Rating		
Seng Woo	7	X Exceeds expectations	___ Meets expectations	___ Below expectations
Promote to		**Promotability Rating**		
Group Sales Manager		X Ready now	___ Ready in < 1 yr.	___ Ready in 1–2 yrs.	___ Not promotable

Replacement	Years in Job	Overall Performance Rating		
Shantara Williams	8	X Exceeds expectations	___ Meets expectations	___ Below expectations
Promote to		**Promotability Rating**		
Sales Manager		X Ready now	___ Ready in < 1 yr.	___ Ready in 1–2 yrs.	___ Not promotable

Replacement	Years in Job	Overall Performance Rating		
Lars Stemke	2	X Exceeds expectations	___ Meets expectations	___ Below expectations
Promote to		**Promotability Rating**		
Sales Manager		___ Ready now	X Ready in < 1 yr.	___ Ready in 1–2 yrs.	___ Not promotable

based on the previous sales–customer service unit in Exhibit 3.8. The focus is on replacement planning for the sales manager (A2) from the ranks of sales associates (A1) as part of the organization's "grow your own," promotion-from-within HR strategy. The top part of the chart indicates the organizational unit and jobs covered by replacement planning, as well as the minimum criteria for promotion eligibility. The next part shows the information for the incumbent department manager (Woo) and the two eligible sales associates (Williams and Stemke) in the menswear department at the Cloverdale store. The key data are length of service, overall performance rating, and promotability rating. When the incumbent sales manager (Woo) is promoted to group sales manager, both sales associates will be in the promotion pool. Williams will likely get the position because of her "ready now" promotability rating. Given his relatively short length of service and readiness for promotion in less than one year, Stemke is probably considered a "star" or a "fast tracker" whom the organization will want to promote rapidly. Similar replacement charts could be developed for all departments in the store and for all hierarchical levels up to and including store manager. Replacement chart data could then be aggregated across stores to provide a corporate composite of talent availability.

The process of replacement planning has been greatly accelerated by human resources information systems (HRISs).[29] HRISs with integrated succession planning functionality make it possible to easily keep data on KSAOs for each employee based on job history, training, and outside education, and then link that information with the needs for specific roles and functions in the organization. Software also allows organizations to create lists of employees who are ready to move into specific positions, and to assess potential risks that managers or leaders will leave the organization. The ability to keep track of employees across the organization by standardized inventories of skill sets means that staffing managers will be able to compare a variety of individuals for new job assignments quickly and consistently. A large database of candidates also makes it possible to seek out passive internal job candidates who are not actively looking for job changes but might be willing to take new positions if offered. Many organizations that use integrated database systems to track candidates across a variety of locations report that they are able to consider a larger pool of candidates than they would with a paper-based system. Some HRISs automatically alert HR when key positions become open, and thus the process of finding a replacement can get under way quickly.

Succession Planning

Succession plans build on replacement plans and directly tie into leadership development. The intent is to ensure that candidates for promotion will have the specific KSAOs and general competencies required for success across their careers. The key to succession planning is building a process that considers both people and positions. Considering people entails assessing each promotable employee for KSAO or competency gaps and then creating employee training and development plans that will close those gaps. Considering positions entails assessing which functions in the organization require extensive internal development and where long-term commitment to the organization's internal culture and strategic goals is important.[30]

Continuing the example from replacement planning, Exhibit 3.13 shows a succession plan for the two promotable sales associates. The organization has developed a set of general leadership competencies for all managers, and for each management position (such as department sales manager), it indicates which of those competencies are required for promotion, in addition to the minimum eligibility requirements. It is the focus on these competencies, and the development plans to instill them in candidates for promotion who lack them, that differentiates replacement and succession planning.

It can be seen that Williams, who is "ready now," has no leadership competency gaps, with the possible exception of an in-house training course on budget preparation and monitoring, which she is currently completing. Stemke, while having "star"

EXHIBIT 3.13 Succession Plan Example

Organizational Unit: Merchandising—Soft Goods
Department: Menswear
Position to Be Filled: Department Sales Manager (A2)
Leadership Competencies Required
  • Plan work unit activities
  • Budget preparation and monitoring
  • Performance management of sales associates

Eligible Replacement	Promotability Rating	Competency Gaps	Development Plans
S. Williams	Ready now	Budget prep	Now completing in-house training course
L. Stemke	Ready in < 1 year	Plan work	Shadowing sales manager
		Budget prep	Starting in-house training course
		Perf. mgt.	Serving as sales manager 10 hours per week
			Taking course on performance management at university extension

potential, must undertake development work. When he successfully completes that work, he will be promoted to sales manager as soon as possible. Alternatively, he might be placed in the organization's acceleration pool. This pool contains high-potential individuals like Stemke from within the organization who are being groomed for management positions generally, and for rapid acceleration upward, rather than progressing through the normal promotion paths.

Succession planning requires both training and managers' time and expertise. Effective performance appraisal and training and development systems are also necessary. For example, overall performance and promotability ratings, assessment of competency gaps, and development plans need to be integrated as regular components of the organization's practices and culture. Promotability and development assessments require managers to make tough and honest decisions. Surveys suggest that only one in three executives believes that their organization has a sufficient succession plan in place. This problem is made worse because many leaders are reluctant to plan for their own replacements, and boards of directors seldom engage directly in the process of routinely evaluating the performance of executives other than the CEO. Underdeveloped succession plans can also lead to cynicism from other senior managers who believe that they will be sufficiently informed or trained before they need to move up to the next level of responsibility. A study of successful succession management in several Fortune 500 organizations concluded that an effective succession plan depends on a willingness to differentiate individual performance, resources allocated to train and develop future leaders, and honest and direct communication.[31]

DIVERSITY AND AFFIRMATIVE ACTION PLANNING

Diversity planning in staffing requires developing an inclusive strategy to recruit, select, and develop a diverse group of employees. To foster workforce diversity and to help strengthen the diversity–organizational effectiveness link, organizations have designed and implemented a wide variety of diversity initiatives and programs. Many of these initiatives involve staffing, as a diverse workforce must be actively identified, acquired, deployed, and retained. Most organizations supplement the staffing component of their diversity initiatives with many other programs, including diversity training for managers and employees to heighten awareness and acceptance of diversity, mentoring relationships, work/life balance actions such as flexible work schedules, team building, and special career and credential-building job assignments.

Planning for Diversity

Whether an organization adopts an active or passive diversity strategy, there are several ways that workforce diversity should be taken into account in the staffing planning process. First and foremost, top management must state that diversity goals are important and will be measured.[32] Clear communications regarding diversity strategies should be made, and updated frequently, to remind employees of the importance of nondiscrimination for the organization's mission.

Many recruiting activities can help enhance the diversity of the workforce. One such activity is to advertise positions in media sources that target a variety of demographic groups.[33] Organizations that wish to increase the diversity of their workforce may also consider recruiting at colleges, universities, and other institutions that have large numbers of underrepresented minorities. These efforts can have a major impact on employee attitudes. Studies show that women and minorities prefer to work at companies that show a commitment to diversity in their recruiting efforts. Internally, organizational promotion efforts should target qualified members of underrepresented groups, possibly supplemented with mentoring programs to overcome gaps in skills.[34]

There are also techniques that can incorporate diversity into the selection process. Requirements that might lead to lower representation of traditionally underrepresented groups should be considered carefully, and if they are not absolutely necessary for job performance, they should be eliminated. Additionally, efforts to incorporate objective standards for judging candidate qualifications and policies that encourage nondiscrimination have been shown to diminish the extent of discrimination in the hiring process.[35]

Unfortunately, evidence suggests that many organizations do not take demographic shifts in the workplace into account when developing staffing plans. Programs to help dual-career couples manage work and child-care arrangements are implemented in a rather scattered fashion, with some organizations doing little to recognize the needs of such families. Other organizations have failed to adequately address the needs of employees with disabilities, even though disability rights advocates note that most accommodations are relatively inexpensive and do not affect core job tasks. Often, the needs of older workers are also overlooked. A survey of over 700 organizations found that 77% of companies had not analyzed projected retirement rates of their workforce or had done so to only a limited extent.[36] Similarly, data show that about a third of employers report that they do not have enough programs for the recruitment and training of older workers.[37]

Research shows that diversity-oriented staffing practices, including targeted recruitment, inclusion of women and Blacks on the top management team, work/family accommodations, the creation of AAPs, and diversity councils, can increase the racial and gender diversity of the organization's entire managerial workforce.[38] The effects of such practices on the composition of the nonmanagerial workforce are not well known, nor have the effects of these practices on organizational performance been documented. Similar programs with a strong behavioral component designed to improve the representation of individuals with disabilities and older workers should also be considered. An increasing body of research shows that diversity and AAPs are successful only when there is individual accountability in management for improving representation. Measurement of diversity across all layers of the organization is extremely important as well. It is interesting to note that while concrete actions like those mentioned above facilitate workforce diversity, attitude-based diversity training interventions are much less effective.

The Aging Workforce

The aging workforce has proven to be a recent staffing challenge facing organizations (and individuals seeking employment). It is estimated that the number of individuals who are more than 74 years old and still employed has increased by a whopping 172% over the 1977–2007 period. However, this growth significantly tapered off after the Great Recession, with employment rising by a mere 3% between 2007 and 2016.[39] Although many older individuals continued to work after the Great Recession out of financial necessity (many saw their retirement portfolios shrink to substandard levels), their continued push for employment, even as the economy has rebounded, is due to other factors. Not only are people living longer, but many jobs are not as physically demanding as they were in previous generations, allowing individuals to work well past the traditional retirement age.

Older workers are frequently burdened by myths and stereotypes that may influence employers' perceptions of their competence and potential for success. Such myths include perceptions that older workers are poor performers, unmotivated, unhealthy, and resistant to change and skill acquisition. A recent meta-analysis of these stereotypes found that most are exaggerations. Less willingness to train on the part of older workers was the sole exception, although the magnitude of this effect was not great. Thus, the increasing number of older individuals seeking employment presents both opportunities and challenges for selection systems.[40]

Affirmative Action Plans

AAPs are organization-specific plans that have a legal origin and basis. They precede diversity programs, which organizations typically undertake for strategic business reasons rather than legal ones. Often, however, the structure and content of AAPs and diversity programs are very similar. While AAPs are organization specific, they all share a common architecture composed of three major components: availability analysis of women and minorities, placement (hiring and promotion) goals derived from comparing availability with incumbency (percentages of women and minority employees), and action-oriented programs for meeting the placement goals. These components, and accompanying details, are spelled out in the federal regulations put forth and enforced by the Office of Federal Contract Compliance Programs (OFCCP). The Federal Contractor Compliance Manual may also be consulted (*dol.gov/ofccp*).

Affirmative Action Programs Regulations

All but very small federal contractors must develop and implement AAPs according to the OFCCP's affirmative action regulations. Below are a summary of those regulations and a sample of an AAP for small employers from the OFCCP website. The contractor must develop a separate AAP for each of its establishments with more than 50 employees. With advance approval from the OFCCP, the contractor may sidestep separate establishment plans by developing a functional plan that covers employees in discrete functional or business units, even though they are in different locations. All employees must be included in either AAP. The description that follows is for an establishment plan. It uses race, ethnicity, and job category designations on the EEO-1 form (see the staffing system management chapter). OFCCP race, ethnicity, and job category designations are somewhat different. Usage of either EEOC or OFCCP designations is acceptable.

Organization Display. An organization display depicts the staffing pattern within an establishment. It provides a profile of the workforce at the establishment, and it assists in identifying units in which women or minorities are underrepresented. Key elements are a showing of organizational structure of lines of progression (promotion) among jobs or organization units, the total number of job incumbents, the total number of male and female incumbents, and the total number of male and female incumbents in each of the following groups: Hispanic, Whites, Blacks, Native Hawaiian or other Pacific Islander, Asian, American Indian or Alaskan Native, and two or more races.

Job Group Analysis. Jobs with similar content, wage rates, and opportunities (e.g., promotion, training) must be combined into job groups, and each group must include a list of job titles. Small establishments (fewer than 150 employees) may use the categories on the EEO-1 form: executives/senior level officials and managers, first/mid-level officials and managers, professionals, technicians, sales workers, administrative support workers, craft workers, operatives, laborers and helpers, and service workers. The percentage of minorities and the percentage of women (determined in the previous step) employed in each job group must be indicated.

Availability Determination. The availability of women and minorities must be determined separately for each job group. At a minimum, the following two factors should be considered when determining availability:

1. The percentage of minorities or women with requisite skills in the reasonable recruitment area
2. The percentage of minorities or women among those promotable, transferable, and trainable within the organization

Current census data, job service data, or other data should be consulted to determine availability. When there are multiple job titles in a job group, with different availability rates, a composite availability figure for the group must be calculated. This requires summing weighted availability estimates for the job titles.

Exhibit 3.14 shows an example of availability determination for a single job group based on the EEO-1 form. Listed on the left are the two availability factors

EXHIBIT 3.14   Determining Availability of Minorities and Women

Job Group: 1	Raw Statistics		Value Weight	Weighted Statistics		Source of Statistics	Reason for Weighting
	Female	Minority		Female	Minority		
1. Percentage of minorities or women with requisite skills in the reasonable recruitment area	41.8%	9.4%	50.0%	20.9%	4.7%	2000 Census Data The reasonable recruitment area for this job group is the St. Louis, MO–IL metropolitan statistical area (MSA).	50% of placement into this job group is made from external hires.
2. Percentage of minorities or women among those promotable, transferable, and trainable within the contractor's organization	53.3%	26.7%	50.0%	26.7%	13.4%	The group of promotable employees in job group 2	50% of placement into this job group is made from internal promotions.
Totals:			100%	**47.6%**	**18.1%**	<Final Factor	

SOURCE: Sample Affirmative Action Program for Small Employers, 2020 (www.dol.gov/ofccp).

that must be considered. Shown next are the raw statistic availability estimates for females and minorities (summed across the four minority groups) for both of the availability factors (refer to the "Source of Statistics" column to see the sources of data for these estimates). Next, the value weights represent an estimate of the percentages of the total females and minorities available according to each availability factor (50% for each group). The weighted statistics represent the raw statistics multiplied by the value weight (e.g., 41.8% × .50 = 20.9%). A summation of the weighted statistics yields the total availability estimate percentages (47.6% for female, 18.1% for minority).

Comparison of Incumbency With Availability.   For each job group, the percentages of women and minority incumbents must be compared with their availability. When the percentage employed is less than would reasonably be expected by the availability percentage, a placement goal must be established.

Exhibit 3.15 compares incumbency with availability for eight job groups, including job group 1. The comparisons are shown separately for females and minorities. Where incumbency is less than availability, the organization may decide to establish a placement goal. In job group 1, it was concluded that the differences between availability and incumbency percentages for both females and minorities were sufficient to warrant placement goals (47.6% for females and 18.1% for minorities). Note that an incumbency percentage less than an availability percentage does not automatically trigger a placement goal (e.g., females in job group 5).

How does the organization decide whether to set a placement goal for females or minorities in a job group? The OFCCP permits some latitude. One possibility is to set a placement goal whenever incumbency is less than availability, on the theory that any differences between availability and incumbency represent underutilization of females and minorities. A second possibility is based on the theory that some differences in percentages are due to chance, so some amount of tolerance of differences is permissible. The suggested rule is 80% tolerance. This means that if the ratio of incumbency percentage to availability percentage is greater than 80%, no placement goal is needed. If the ratio is less than 80%, a placement goal must be set. The 80% rule was followed in Exhibit 3.15. Though the incumbency percentage for females was less than the availability percentage in both job groups 1 and 5, the difference was less than 80% in only job group 1, triggering a placement goal just for that group.

Placement Goals.   If an annual placement goal is set, it should at least equal the availability percentage for women or minorities in a job group. These placement goals are also used to measure progress toward achieving equal employment opportunity.

Designation of Responsibility.   An official of the organization must be designated as responsible for the implementation of the AAP.

EXHIBIT 3.15 Determining Affirmative Action Goals: Comparing Incumbency With Availability and Annual Placement Goals

Job Group	Female Incumbency	Female Availability	Establish Goal? Yes/No	If Yes, Goal for Females	Minority Incumbency	Minority Availability	Establish Goal? Yes/No	If Yes, Goal for Minorities
1	0.0%	47.6%	Yes	47.6%	11.1%	18.1%	Yes	18.1%
2	45.5%	43.8%	No		18.2%	8.2%	No	
4	20.0%	34.5%	Yes	34.5%	0.0%	12.4%	Yes	12.4%
5	83.3%	87.7%	No		43.3%	27.6%	No	
6	9.3%	5.5%	No		34.9%	23.2%	No	
7	10.0%	6.3%	No		30.0%	37.5%	No	
8	6.3%	19.1%	Yes	19.1%	37.5%	26.3%	No	

NOTE: The 80% rule is followed in declaring underutilization and establishing goals when the actual employment of minorities or females is less than 80% of their availabil ty. If the female/minority incumbency percentage (%) is less than the female/minority availability percentage (%) and the ratio of incumbency to availability is less than 80%, a placement goal should be included in the appropriate "If Yes" column.
SOURCE: Sample Affirmative Action Program for Small Employers, 2020 (*www.dol.gov/ofccp*).

Identification of Problem Areas.   The organization must evaluate the following:

- Problems of minority or female utilization or distribution in each job group
- Personnel activity (applicant flow, hires, terminations, and promotions) and other personnel actions for possible selection disparities
- Compensation systems for possible gender-, race-, or ethnicity-based disparities
- Selection, recruitment, referral, and other procedures to see whether they result in disparities in employment or advancement of minorities or women

Action-Oriented Programs.   The organization must develop and execute action-oriented programs to correct any identified problem areas and attain placement goals. Specific examples of these programs are shown in Exhibit 3.16.

Internal Audit and Reporting.   An auditing system must be developed that periodically measures the effectiveness of the total AAP.

LEGAL ISSUES

The major legal issues in HR and staffing planning are AAPs and diversity programs. AAPs originate from many sources: voluntary employer efforts, court-imposed remedies for discriminatory practices, conciliation or consent agreement, and requirements as a federal contractor. Regardless of the source, all AAPs seek to rectify the effects of past employment discrimination by increasing the representation of certain groups (minorities, women, veterans, and qualified individuals with disabilities) in the organization's workforce. This is achieved through establishing and actively pursuing hiring and promotion goals for these groups. As described above, diversity programs are undertaken for competitive reasons, rather than as a legal response to discrimination. However, diversity programs may share components with AAPs.

Legality of AAPs and Diversity Programs

AAPs have been controversial since their inception, and there have been many challenges to their legality. Questions of legality involve complex issues of constitutionality, statutory interpretations, differences in the structure of the AAPs being challenged in the courts, claims that affirmative action goals represent hiring quotas, and, very importantly, differences in the amount of weight placed on race or gender in the ultimate selection decisions made about job applicants.

Despite these problems, it is possible to provide several conclusions and recommendations regarding affirmative action. AAPs in general are legal in the eyes of the Supreme Court. However, to be acceptable, an AAP should be based on the following guidelines:[41]

- The plan should have as its purpose the remedying of specific and identifiable effects of past discrimination.

EXHIBIT 3.16   Examples of Action-Oriented Programs for an AAP

1. Conducting annual analyses of job descriptions to ensure they accurately reflect job functions;

2. Reviewing job descriptions by department and job title using performance criteria;

3. Making job descriptions available to recruiting sources and to all members of management involved in the recruiting, screening, selection, and promotion processes;

4. Evaluating the total selection process to ensure freedom from bias through:

   a. Reviewing job applications and other preemployment forms to ensure information requested is job related;

   b. Evaluating selection methods that may have a disparate impact to ensure that they are job related and consistent with business necessity; and

   c. Training in EEO for management and supervisory staff.

5. Using techniques to improve recruitment and increase the flow of minority and female applicants:

   a. Include the phrase "Equal Opportunity/Affirmative Action Employer" in all printed employment advertisements;

   b. Place help-wanted advertisements, when appropriate, in local minority news media and women's interest media;

   c. Disseminate information on job opportunities to organizations representing minorities, women, and employment development agencies when job opportunities occur;

   d. Encourage all employees to refer qualified applicants;

   e. Actively recruit at secondary schools, junior colleges, and colleges and universities with predominantly minority or female enrollment; and

   f. Request employment agencies to refer qualified minorities and women.

6. Hiring a statistical consultant to perform a self-audit of compensation practices; and

7. Ensuring that all employees are given equal opportunity for promotion:

   a. Post promotional opportunities;

   b. Offer counseling to assist employees in identifying promotional opportunities, and offer training and educational programs to increase promotions and opportunities for job rotation or transfer; and

   c. Evaluate job requirements for promotion.

SOURCE: Adapted from Sample Affirmative Action Program for Small Employers, 2010 (*www.dol.gov/ofccp*).

• The plan should address the current underutilization of women and/or minorities in the organization.
• The plan should be temporary and should be eliminated once affirmative action goals have been achieved.
• All candidates for positions should be qualified for those positions.
• The plan should include organizational enforcement mechanisms as well as a grievance procedure.

Court rulings on the constitutionality of federal and state government AAPs suggest that even more strict guidelines than these may be necessary. Insofar as these programs are concerned, racial preferences are subject to strict constitutional scrutiny. They may be used only when there is specific evidence of identified discrimination, when the remedy has been narrowly tailored to only the identified discrimination, when only those who have suffered discrimination may benefit from the remedy, and when other individuals will not carry an undue burden, such as job displacement, from the remedy. Lesser scrutiny standards may apply for gender preferences.[42] Some states have even banned the use of AAPs by government employers, contractors, and educational institutions.[43]

In response to questions and controversies regarding AAPs, the EEOC has several specific guidelines for employers implementing these plans.[44] First, the EEOC emphasizes that AAPs are active diversity initiatives, in that the organization is taking a planned and coordinated effort to reach the goal of having a workforce composition that mirrors the relevant labor pool. All employment decisions must be made in a nondiscriminatory manner, which means that organizations may not extend preferences to any individual based on protected class status. The EEOC specifically notes that placement goals may not supersede attention to essential qualifications. Set-aside programs and quotas are expressly prohibited as part of the placement goals. These rules correspond to general preferences expressed in research on AAPs described earlier—the goal of any AAP should be to increase the representation of the available workforce by taking active steps to ensure equality of opportunity.

AAPs for Veterans and Individuals With Disabilities

There are specific AAP regulations for federal contractors under the Vietnam Era Veterans' Readjustment Assistance Act and the Rehabilitation Act. Though each law has its own regulations, the regulations include many common requirements, most importantly for staffing:

1. Establishing an annual hiring goal (8% for veterans and 7% for qualified individuals with disabilities)
2. Conducting a review of personnel processes to ensure they provide for careful, thorough, and systematic consideration of the job qualifications of applicants and employees for job vacancies filled by hiring or promotion and for training opportunities

3. Reviewing all physical or mental job qualifications to ensure that they do not tend to screen out individuals with disabilities or veterans, and that the qualifications are job related and consistent with business necessity

4. Providing reasonable accommodation for physical and mental limitations, unless it would impose an undue hardship on the operation of the business

5. Undertaking appropriate outreach and positive recruitment activities (many suggested activities are listed) and evaluating their effectiveness annually

6. Inviting voluntary self-identification by applicants pre-offer, and employees post-offer, of disabilities and veteran status

EEO and Temporary Workers

The EEOC has provided guidance on coverage and responsibility requirements for temporary employment agencies (and other types of staffing firms) and their client organizations.[45] When both the agency and the client exercise control over the temporary employee and both have the requisite number of employees, they are considered employers and jointly liable under the Civil Rights Act, the Age Discrimination in Employment Act (ADEA), the Americans With Disabilities Act (ADA), and the Equal Pay Act. It should be noted that these laws also apply to individuals placed with organizations through welfare-to-work programs. The agency is obligated to make referrals and job assignments in a nondiscriminatory manner, and the client may not set discriminatory job referral and job assignment criteria. The client must treat the temporary employees in a nondiscriminatory manner; if the agency knows this is not happening, the agency must take any corrective actions within its control. The agency, the client, or both parties could face substantial penalties for noncompliance (e.g., back pay, front pay, and compensatory damages). There is special guidance for ADA-related issues.

SUMMARY

Internal and external forces shape the conduct and outcomes of HRP. The key forces and trends that emerge are organizational strategy, organizational culture, labor markets, and technology.

HRP is a process and set of activities conducted to forecast future HR requirements and availabilities, resulting in the identification of likely employment gaps (shortages and surpluses). Action plans are then developed for addressing the gaps. Before HRP begins, initial decisions must be made about its comprehensiveness, planning time frame, job categories and levels to be included, how to "count heads," and the roles and responsibilities of line and staff (including HR) managers.

A variety of statistical and judgmental techniques may be used in forecasting. Those used in forecasting requirements are typically used in conjunction with business and organization planning. For forecasting external availabilities, data on the relevant labor market over time can be used as a starting point, with additional factors taken into account through regression analysis. For forecasting internal availabilities, techniques must be used that take into account the movements of people into, within, and out of the organization, on a job-by-job basis. Here, manager judgment, Markov Analysis, and replacement and succession planning are suggested as particularly useful techniques.

Staffing planning is a form of action planning. It is shown to generally require setting staffing objectives, generating alternative staffing activities, and assessing and choosing from among those alternatives. A fundamental alternative involves the use of core or flexible workforces, as identified in staffing strategy. Plans must be developed for acquiring both types of workforces, and the advantages and disadvantages of each type should be reviewed to reaffirm strategic choices about the use of each. After this step, planning can begin. For the core workforce, this involves matters of staffing philosophy that will guide the planning of recruitment, selection, and employment activities. For the flexible workforce, the organization should establish early contact with the providers of the flexible workers (i.e., staffing firms and independent contractors). Organizational leaders should also consider the advantages and disadvantages of outsourcing some jobs at this point.

Changes in the demographic makeup of the workforce suggest that organizations need to take employee diversity into account in the planning process. Activities to address a diverse workforce include recruiting, selection, training, development, and retention.

AAPs are an extension and application of general HR and staffing planning. AAPs have several components. The Affirmative Action Programs Regulations, which apply to federal contractors, specify requirements for these components. The legality of AAPs has been clearly established, but the courts have fashioned limits to their content and scope. To clarify how EEO laws apply to temporary employees and agencies, the EEOC has issued specific guidance.

DISCUSSION QUESTIONS

1. What are ways in which the organization can minimize KSAO deficiencies in its workforce?
2. What are the potential limitations and benefits of HR and staffing planning? What costs might be incurred in the process of HR and staffing planning (e.g., staff time gathering and communicating information)?
3. Why are decisions about job categories and levels so critical to the conduct and results of HRP?
4. What are the advantages and disadvantages of doing succession planning for all levels of management instead of just top management?
5. What is meant by reconciliation, and how can it be useful as an input to staffing planning?

6. What criteria would you suggest using for assessing the staffing alternatives shown in Exhibit 3.10?

7. What problems might an organization encounter in creating an AAP that it might not encounter in regular staffing planning?

ETHICAL ISSUES

1. Does an organization have an ethical responsibility to share with all of its employees the results of its forecasting of HR requirements and availabilities? Does it have an ethical responsibility not to do this?

2. Identify examples of ethical dilemmas an organization might confront when developing an AAP.

APPLICATIONS

Forecasting Demand

TechFriend provides advice to customers on how to use a wide variety of consumer electronics. Its tagline is "Helping you find your way through the digital maze." The advice it provides is designed to fill in a gap in typical manufacturing customer assistance. One specific way that TechFriend differentiates itself is by providing in-home consultations with individuals. Its services are also designed to ensure cross-device compatibility and integration. For example, TechFriend employees might show a family how to keep their Internet service, smartphone, and computers all working together. They also can provide impartial advice on purchases (as they receive no commissions for sales).

TechFriend has established itself in the twelve largest metropolitan areas in Georgia and Florida, with several small offices in large cities such as Atlanta, Miami, and Tampa. In total, there are 39 offices, with staffing levels for customer service agents ranging between 50 and 80 FTEs per office. These levels of staffing have evolved over time to match customer demand, so they are close to the capacity for each area. TechFriend intends to expand its reach to 10 new offices in urban areas in South Carolina and Tennessee, and it wants to develop forecasts of how many individuals will be needed in each area.

To estimate the needed staffing levels, central HR representatives worked with their operations team to estimate a regression equation, in which the optimal number of FTE service agents per location was predicted by population data (in thousands) for different regions. Population figures were taken from census information and divided into group A (18 to 24 years old), group B (25 to 44 years old), group C (45 to 65 years old), and group D (65+ years old). The following regression equation was estimated:

$$FTE = 10 + 0.10(\text{group A}) + 0.20(\text{group B}) + 0.20(\text{group C}) + 0.05(\text{group D}).$$

This regression equation can be used to predict the number of FTE service agents needed to meet customer demand. For example, in one expected service area of the Nashville metropolitan area, the approximate population is about 50,000 in group A, 170,000 in group B, 100,000 in group C, and 60,000 in group D. The estimated regression equation is then:

$$FTE = 10 + 0.10 \times 50 + 0.20 \times 170 + 0.20 \times 100 + 0.05 \times 60,$$

which equals:

$$FTE = 10 + 5 + 34 + 20 + 3.$$

So, this region would need about 72 FTEs.

Using this information, answer the following questions:

1. How many FTE customer service agents are needed in another region of the Nashville metropolitan area that has a population of potential customers that equals approximately 40,000 in group A, 120,000 in group B, 80,000 in group C, and 40,000 in group D?

2. How many FTE customer service agents are needed in a region of the greater Charleston metropolitan area that has a population of potential customers that equals approximately 60,000 in group A, 180,000 in group B, 120,000 in group C, and 60,000 in group D?

3. Is there any other information that you might want to incorporate into your estimate of how many FTE customer service agents are needed in these regions? Where might you find out what other factors should be taken into account for staffing these regions?

4. How would you incorporate managerial judgment into your estimate of staffing levels? How would you communicate your conclusions to TechFriend managers?

Deciding Whether to Use Flexible Staffing

The Kaiser Manufacturing Company (KMC) has been in existence for over 50 years. Its main products are specialty implements for use in both the crop and the dairy herd sides of the agricultural business. Products include special attachments for tractors, combines, and discers and add-on devices for milking and feeding equipment that enhance the performance and safety of the equipment.

KMC has a small corporate office and four manufacturing plants (two in the Midwest and two in the South). It has a core workforce of 725 production workers, 30 clerical workers, 32 engineers and professional workers, and 41 managers. All employees are full time, and KMC has never used either part-time or temporary workers. Those in charge of staffing feel very strongly that the strategy of using only a core workforce has paid big dividends over the years in attracting and retaining a committed and highly productive workforce.

Sales have been virtually flat at $175 million annually since 2012. At the same time, KMC has begun to experience more erratic placement of orders for its products, making sales less predictable. This appears to be a reflection of more turbulent weather patterns, large swings in interest rates, new entrants into the specialty markets, and general uncertainty about the future direction and growth of the agricultural industry. Increased unpredictability in sales has been accompanied by steadily rising labor costs. This is due to KMC's increasingly older workforce, as well as shortages of all types of workers (particularly production workers) in the immediate labor markets surrounding the plants.

Assume you are the HR manager responsible for staffing and training at KMC. You have just been contacted by a representative of the Flexible Staffing Services (FSS) Company, Mr. Tom Jacoby. Mr. Jacoby has proposed meeting with you and the president of KMC, Mr. Herman Kaiser, to talk about FSS and how it might be of service to KMC. You and Mr. Kaiser agree to meet with Mr. Jacoby. At that meeting, Mr. Jacoby makes a formal presentation to you in which he describes the services, operation, and fees of FSS and highlights the advantages of using a more flexible workforce. During that meeting, you learn the following from Mr. Jacoby.

FSS is a recent entrant into what is called the staffing industry. Its general purpose is to furnish qualified employees to companies (customers) on an as-needed basis, thus helping the customer implement a flexible staffing strategy. It furnishes employees in four major groups: production, clerical, technical, and professional/managerial. Both full-time and part-time employees are available in each of these groups. Employees may be furnished to the customer on a strictly temporary basis ("temps") or on a "temp-to-perm" basis, in which the employees convert from being temporary employees of FSS to being permanent employees of the customer after a 90-day probationary period.

For both the temp and the temp-to-perm arrangements, FSS offers the following services. In each of the four employee groups it will recruit, select, and hire people to work for FSS, which will in turn lease them to the customer. FSS performs all recruitment, selection, and employment activities. It uses a standard selection system for all applicants, composed of an application blank, reference checks, drug testing, and a medical exam (given after making a job offer). It also offers customized selection plans in which the customer chooses from among a set of special skill tests, a personality test, an honesty test, and background investigations. Based on the standard and/or custom assessments, FSS refers to the customer what it views as the top candidates. FSS tries to furnish two people for every vacancy, and the customer chooses from between the two.

New hires at FSS receive a base wage that is similar to the market wage, as well as close to the wage of the customer's employees with whom they will be directly working. In addition, new hires receive a paid vacation (one week for every six months of employment, up to four weeks), health insurance (with a 25% employee co-pay), and optional participation in a 401(k) plan. FSS performs and pays for all payroll functions and deductions. It also pays the premiums for workers' compensation and unemployment compensation.

FSS charges the customer as follows. There is a standard fee per employee furnished of 1.55 × base wage × hours worked per week. The 1.55 is labeled "markup"; it covers all of FSS's costs (staffing, insurance, benefits, and administration) plus a profit margin. On top of the standard fee is an additional fee for customized selection services. This fee ranges from .50 to .90 × base wage × hours worked per week. Finally, there is a special one-time fee for temp-to-perm employees (a finder's fee of one month's pay), payable after the employee successfully completes the 90-day probationary period and becomes an employee of the customer.

Mr. Jacoby concludes his presentation by stressing three advantages of flexible staffing as provided by FSS. First, use of FSS employees on an as-needed basis will give KMC greater flexibility in its staffing to match fluctuating product demand, as well as movement from completely fixed labor costs to more variable labor costs. Second, FSS provides considerable administrative convenience, relieving KMC of most of the burden of recruitment, selection, and payrolling. Finally, KMC will experience considerable freedom from litigation (workers' comp, EEO, torts) since FSS and not KMC will be the employer.

After Mr. Jacoby's presentation, Mr. Kaiser tells you he is favorably impressed, but that the organization clearly needs to do some more thinking before it embarks on the path of flexible staffing and the use of FSS as its provider. He asks you to prepare a brief preliminary report including the following:

1. A summary of the possible advantages and disadvantages of flexible staffing
2. A summary of the advantages and disadvantages of using FSS as a service provider
3. A summary of the type of additional information you recommend gathering and using as part of the decision-making process

ENDNOTES

1. W. Bliss, "Engaging in Strategic Planning," *SHRM Templates and Toolkits*, Mar. 21, 2013 (*www.shrm.org*).
2. P. M. Wright and M. D. Ulrich, "A Road Well Traveled: The Past, Present, and Future Journey of Strategic Human Resource Management," *Annual Review of Organizational Psychology and Organizational Behavior*, 2017, 4, pp. 45–65; D. Ulrich, J. Younger, W. Brockbank, and M. Ulrich, *HR From the Outside In* (New York: McGraw-Hill, 2012); P. M. Wright, J. W. Boudreau, D. A. Pace, E. Sartain, P. McKinnon, and R. L. Antoine, *The Chief HR Officer: Defining the New Role of Human Resource Leaders* (San Francisco: Jossey-Bass, 2011).
3. N. Fu, P. C. Flood, D. M. Rousseau, and T. Morris, "Line Managers as Paradox Navigators in HRM Implementation: Balancing Consistency and Individual Responsiveness," *Journal of Management*, 2020, 46, pp. 203–233; T. J. M. Mom, Y.-Y. Chang, M. Cholakova, and J. J. P. Jansen,

"A Multilevel Integrated Framework of Firm HR Practices, Individual Ambidexterity, and Organizational Ambidexterity," *Journal of Management*, 2019, 45, pp. 3009-3034; Y. Li, M. Wang, D. D. van Jaarsveld, G. K. Lee, and D. G. Ma, "From Employee-Experienced High-Involvement Work System to Innovation: An Emergence-Based Human Resource Management Framework," *Academy of Management Journal*, 2018, 61, pp. 2000-2019.

4. M. L. Davis, "The CHRO as Cultural Champion," in P. M. Wright, J. W. Boudreau, D. A. Pace, E. Sartain, P. McKinnon, and R. L. Antoine (eds.), *The Chief HR Officer: Defining the New Role of Human Resource Leaders* (San Francisco: Jossey-Bass, 2011), pp. 93-97.

5. T. Wang and C. D. Zatzick, "Human Capital Acquisition and Organizational Innovation: A Temporal Perspective," *Academy of Management Journal*, 2019, 62, pp. 99-116; J. DeVaro, A. Kauhanen, and N. Valmari, "Internal and External Hiring," *ILR Review*, 2019, 72, pp. 981-1008; J. Keller, "Posting and Slotting: How Hiring Processes Shape the Quality of Hire and Compensation in Internal Labor Markets," *Administrative Science Quarterly*, 2018, 63, pp. 848-878; K. Slavova, A. Fosfuri, and J. O. De Castro, "Learning by Hiring: The Effects of Scientists' Inbound Mobility on Research Performance in Academia," *Organization Science*, 2016, 21, pp. 72-89.

6. S. Hargreaves, "Jobs With the Lowest (and Highest) Unemployment," *CNN Money*, Jan. 7, 2013 (*money.cnn.com*).

7. A. Hogan and B. Roberts, "Occupational Employment Projections to 2024," *Monthly Labor Review*, Dec. 2015 (*www.bls.gov/opub/mlr/2015/article/occupational-employment-projections-to-2024.htm*).

8. A. Spitz-Oener, "Technical Change, Job Tasks, and Rising Educational Demands: Looking Outside the Wage Structure," *Journal of Labor Economics*, 2006, 24, pp. 235-270.

9. Society for Human Resource Management, *Critical Skills Needs and Resources for the Changing Workforce* (Alexandria, VA: author, 2008).

10. Society for Human Resource Management, *SHRM Research: Workforce Readiness and Skills Shortages* (Alexandria, VA: author, 2015); Society for Human Resource Management, *The Global Skills Shortage: Bridging the Talent Gap With Education, Training, and Sourcing* (Alexandria, VA: author, 2019).

11. M. Rich, "Factory Jobs Return, but Employers Find Skills Shortage," *New York Times Online*, July 1, 2010 (*www.nytimes.com/2010/07/02/business/economy/02manufacturing.html*).

12. A. Weaver and P. Osterman, "Skill Demands and Mismatch in U.S. Manufacturing," *ILR Review*, 2017, 70, pp. 275-307; T. Bol, C. Ciocca Eller, H. G. van de Werfhorst, and T. A. DiPrete, "School-to-Work Linkages, Educational Mismatches, and Labor Market Outcomes," *American Sociological Review*, 2019, 84, pp. 275-307.

13. Bureau of Labor Statistics, "Employed and Unemployed Full- and Part-Time Workers by Age, Race, Sex and Hispanic or Latino Ethnicity," Feb. 2016 (*www.bls.gov*).

14. Bureau of Labor Statistics, "American Time Use Survey" Aug. 2019 (*www.bls.gov/tus/*), accessed Mar. 21, 2020; S. Sweet, M. Pitt-Catsouphes, E. Besen, and L. Golden, "Explaining Organizational Variation in Flexible Work Arrangements: Why the Pattern and Scale of Availability Matter," *Community, Work, and Family*, 2014, 17, pp. 115-141.

15. L. F. Katz and A. B. Krueger, "The Rise and Nature of Alternative Work Arrangements in the United States, 1995-2015," *ILR Review*, 2019, 72, pp. 382-416.

16. M. Goos and A. Manning, "Lousy and Lovely Jobs: The Rising Polarization of Work in Britain," *Review of Economics and Statistics*, 2007, 89, pp. 118-133; T. Kristal, "The Capitalist Machine: Computerization, Workers' Power, and the Decline in Labor's Share Within US Industries," *American Sociological Review*, 2013, 78, pp. 361-389; Spitz-Oener, "Technical Change, Job Tasks, and Rising Educational Demands: Looking Outside the Wage Structure."

17. HR Council for the Nonprofit Sector, "HR Planning" (*www.hrcouncil.ca/hr-toolkit/planning -strategic.cfm*), accessed Sept. 10, 2016 (site discontinued); J. Clarke, "Making the Case for More

Effective Workforce Planning," *Workforce Online*, Jan. 2010 (*www.workforce.com*); Society for Human Resource Management, "Practicing the Discipline of Workforce Planning," Dec. 2015 (*www.shrm.org*).

18. L. Rubis, "Strategic Planning Not So Hard If Done Right," *HR News*, June 26, 2011 (*www.shrm.org*); Society for Human Resource Planning, "Practicing the Discipline of Workforce Planning."

19. F. Hansen, "Strategic Workforce Planning in an Uncertain World," *Workforce Management Online*, Sept. 7, 2011 (*www.workforce.com*).

20. S. Overman, "Staffing Management: A Better Forecast," *Staffing Management Magazine*, Apr. 1, 2008 (*www.shrm.org*); T. J. Chermack, *Scenario Planning in Organizations: How to Create, Use, and Assess Scenarios* (San Francisco: Berrett-Koehler, 2011).

21. M. B. Glick, T. J. Chermack, H. Luckel, and B. Q. Gauck, "Effects of Scenario Planning on Participant Mental Models," *European Journal of Training and Development*, 2012, 36, pp. 488–507.

22. S. J. Ashford, E. George, and R. Blatt, "Old Assumptions, New Work: The Opportunities and Challenges of Research on Nonstandard Employment," *Academy of Management Annals*, 2007, 1(1), pp. 65-117; C. L. Wilcin, "I Can't Get No Satisfaction: Meta-Analysis Comparing Permanent and Contingent Workers," *Journal of Organizational Behavior*, 2013, 34(1), pp. 47-64; J. G. Weikamp and A. S. Göriz, "Organizational Citizenship Behavior and Job Satisfaction: The Impact of Occupational Future Time Perspective," *Human Relations*, 2016, 69(11), pp. 2091-2115; R. Maurer, "The Temp Trend Is Permanent," *HR Magazine*, Sept. 2015, p. 24; I. Speizer, "Special Report on Contingent Staffing," *Workforce Management*, Nov. 2009 (*www.workforce.com*).

23. Schumpeter, "Talent on Tap," *Economist*, Dec. 10, 2009, p. 74; C. H. Mooney, M. Semadeni, and I. F. Kesner, "Selection of an Interim CEO: Boundary Conditions and the Pursuit of Temporary Leadership," *Journal of Management*, 2014, 43(2), 455-475; J. Greenstone Miller and M. Miller, "The Rise of the Supertemp," *Harvard Business Review*, May 2012, pp. 50-62.

24. D. Weil, *Administrator's Interpretation No. 2015-1* (Washington, DC: US Department of Labor, 2015); Society for Human Resource Management, *Independent Contractor: Audit Checklist for Maintaining Independent Contractor Status* (Alexandria, VA: author, 2014).

25. Society for Human Resource Management, *Outsourcing the HR Function* (Alexandria, VA: author, 2015).

26. A. Ozimek, "Report: Overboard on Offshore Fears," Press Release, Upwork.com, 2019, (*www.upwork.com/press/economics/report-overboard-on-offshore-fears*), accessed Mar. 21, 2020; B. Tai and N. R. Lockwood, *Outsourcing and Offshoring HR Series Part I* (Alexandria, VA: Society for Human Resource Management, 2006); R. J. Moncarz, M. G. Wolf, and B. Wright, "Service-Providing Occupations, Offshoring, and the Labor Market," *Monthly Labor Review*, Dec. 2008, pp. 71-86.

27. A. Fox, "The Ins and Outs of Customer Contact Centers," *HR Magazine Online*, May 2010; O. Bertrand and M. J. Mol, "The Antecedents and Innovation Effects of Domestic and Offshore R&D Outsourcing: The Contingent Impact of Cognitive Dissonance and Absorptive Capacity," *Strategic Management Journal*, 2013, 34, pp. 751-760; A. Rodríguez and M. Nieto, "Does R&D Offshoring Lead to SME Growth? Different Governance Modes and the Mediating Role of Innovation," *Strategic Management Journal*, 2016, 37(8), pp. 1734-1753; W. L. Tate and L. M. Ellram, "Service Supply Management Structure in Offshore Outsourcing," *Journal of Supply Chain Management*, 2012, 48, pp. 8-29; S. Lahiri, "Does Outsourcing Really Improve Firm Performance? Empirical Evidence and Research Agenda," *International Journal of Management Reviews*, 2016, 18, pp. 464-497.

28. E. Harrell, "Succession Planning, What the Research Says," *Harvard Business Review*, Dec. 2016, pp. 70-74; I. A. Weisblat, "Literature Review of Succession Planning Strategies and Tactics," in P. A. Gordon and J. A. Overbey (eds.), *Succession Planning: Promoting Organizational Sustain-*

ability (New York: Springer International Publishing, 2018), pp. 11–22; W. J. Rothwell, *Effective Succession Planning: Ensuring Leadership Continuity and Building Talent From Within* (New York: AMACOM, 2015); Society for Human Resource Management, "Engaging in Succession Planning," *SHRM Resources and Tools*, Aug. 2019 (*www.shrm.org*).

29. E. Frauenheim, "Software Products Aim to Streamline Succession Planning," *Workforce Management*, Jan. 2006 (*www.workforce.com*).
30. Society for Human Resource Management, "Engaging in Succession Planning."
31. B. Leonard, "Some Executives Doubtful Succession Plans Really Work," *SHRM Resources and Tools*, Feb. 2015 (*www.shrm.org*); E. Harrell, "Succession Planning, What the Research Says," *Harvard Business Review*, Dec. 2016, pp. 70–74; B. Leonard, "Create a Succession Plan That Works," *SHRM Resources and Tools*, Mar. 2015 (*www.shrm.org*); D. E. Smith, "What's the Plan on Succession Planning," *Workforce Online*, Dec. 2014 (*www.workforce.com*); P. Duarte, "What's a Succession Plan for an Aging Workforce?" *Workforce Online*, Jan. 2014 (*www.workforce.com*).
32. K. Gurchiek, "12 Truths About Spearheading Diversity and Inclusion," *Society for Human Resource Management*, Oct. 2016 (*www.shrm.org*); L. H. Nishii, "The Benefits of Climate for Inclusion for Gender-Diverse Groups," *Academy of Management Journal*, 2013, 56, pp. 1754–1774.
33. D. R. Avery and P. F. McKay, "Target Practice: An Organizational Impression Management Approach to Attracting Minority and Female Job Applicants," *Personnel Psychology*, 2006, 59, pp. 157–187; D. R. Avery, S. D. Volpone, R. W. Stewart, A. Luksyte, M. Hernandez, P. F. McKay, and M. R. Hebl, "Examining the Draw of Diversity: How Diversity Climate Perceptions Affect Job-Pursuit Intentions," *Human Resource Management*, 2013, 52, pp. 175–193; D. A. Newman and J. S. Lyon, "Recruitment Efforts to Reduce Adverse Impact: Targeted Recruiting for Personality, Cognitive Ability, and Diversity," *Journal of Applied Psychology*, 2009, 94, pp. 298–317.
34. S. B. Welch, "Diversity as Business Strategy: Company Faced Racial Tensions Head On," *Workforce Management Online*, Apr. 2009; L. Lieber, "Changing Demographics Will Require Changing the Way We Do Business," *Employment Relations Today*, Fall 2009, pp. 91–96.
35. J. Levashina, C. J. Hartwell, F. P. Morgeson, and M. A. Campion, "The Structured Employment Interview: Narrative and Quantitative Review of the Research Literature," *Personnel Psychology*, 2014, 67, pp. 241–293; C. Ziegert and P. J. Hanges, "Employment Discrimination: The Role of Implicit Attitudes, Motivation, and a Climate for Racial Bias," *Journal of Applied Psychology*, 2005, 90, pp. 553–562.
36. P. J. Kiger, "Few Employers Addressing Impact of Aging Workforce," *Workforce Management*, Jan. 2010, pp. 6–7.
37. A. Nancherla, "Getting to the Foundation of Talent Management," *T + D*, Feb. 2010, p. 20.
38. E. Hirsh and Y. Cha, "Mandating Change: The Impact of Court-Ordered Policy Changes on Managerial Diversity," *ILR Review*, 2017, 70, pp. 42–72; M. E. Graham, M. A. Belliveau, and J. L. Hotchkiss, "The View at the Top or Signing at the Bottom? Workplace Diversity Responsibility and Women's Representation in Management," *ILR Review*, 2017, 70, pp. 223–258; A. Kalev, F. Dobins, and E. Kelley, "Best Practices or Best Guesses? Assessing the Efficacy of Corporate Affirmative Action and Diversity Policies," *American Sociological Review*, 2006, 71, pp. 589–617.
39. Bureau of Labor Statistics, "Older Workers," July 2008 (*https://stats.bls.gov*); D. DeSilver, "More Older Americans Are Working, and Working More, Than They Used To," *Pew Research Center*, June 20, 2016 (*www.pewresearch.org/fact-tank/*).
40. C. Dugas, "Tips for Gray-Haired Job Searchers; It Can Be Tough, but Programs Are Out There to Help," *USA Today*, Apr. 24, 2013, p. 6B; C. Dugas, "More Older Americans Remaining Part of the Workforce," *USA Today*, Jan. 14, 2013, p. 2B; T. W. H. Ng and D. C. Feldman, "Evaluating Six Common Stereotypes About Older Workers With Meta-Analytical Data," *Personnel Psychology*, 2012, 65, pp. 821–858.

41. D. J. Walsh, *Employment Law for Human Resource Practice*, 5th ed. (Boston: Cengage Learning, 2016), pp. 368–372; D. D. Bennett-Alexander and L. P. Hartman, *Employment Law for Business*, 8th ed. (New York: McGraw-Hill Education, 2015), pp. 231–236.

42. R. U. Robinson, G. M. Franklin, and R. F. Wayland, *Employment Regulation in the Workplace* (Armonk, NY: M. E. Sharpe, 2010), pp. 182–219; Walsh, *Employment Law for Human Resource Practice*, pp. 272–282.

43. M. P. Crockett and J. B. Thelen, "Michigan's Proposal 2: Affirmative Action Law Shifts at the State Level," *Legal Report*, Society for Human Resource Management, July/Aug. 2007, pp. 5–8.

44. Electronic Code of Federal Regulation, Coverage as of January 23, 2020 (*www.dol.gov/general /topic/hiring/affirmativeact*).

45. Equal Employment Opportunity Commission, *Enforcement Guidance: Application of the ADA to Contingent Workers Placed by Temporary Agencies and Other Staffing Firms* (Washington, DC: author, 2000).

CHAPTER FOUR

Job Analysis: Requirements, Competencies, and Rewards

Ethical Issues

Applications
Integrating Competencies and Job Requirements
Designing a Job Rewards Analysis

Endnotes

LEARNING OBJECTIVES AND INTRODUCTION

Learning Objectives

- Understand the rationale behind different forms of job analysis
- Compare sources of information about jobs
- Distinguish job requirements, competency modeling, and job rewards techniques for job analysis
- Learn about methods for conducting the different forms of job analysis
- Learn about methods for linking job analysis to organizational goals
- Recognize how job rewards analysis can address the employee value proposition
- Become familiar with the legal issues surrounding job analysis

Introduction

Once the planning process is complete, the next step in developing an effective, strategic staffing system is to develop a thorough understanding of the jobs to be filled. The process of studying and describing the purpose of, tasks of, and KSAOs (knowledge, skill, ability, and other characteristics) needed for a job is called job analysis. Anyone who has ever looked for a job is familiar with a traditional job description, which lists the major tasks, duties, and responsibilities of a job. Such descriptions are just part of the wealth of information collected during the job analysis process. As we will see later in the book, job analysis information can be used for identifying recruiting pools, designing selection tools, and assessing and improving employee performance.

At first blush, describing a job may seem to be a straightforward task. However, there is more to the process than just writing up a quick paragraph listing what an incumbent typically does. Different techniques have been developed and refined over time to ensure a thorough description of the purpose of the job, how the work is done, and what characteristics are needed to successfully do the work. In many cases, a traditional task-based job requirements analysis is sufficient to cover both the operational and legal requirements of an organization's staffing strategy. In other cases, it will make more sense to focus on a general set of KSAOs or competencies that span a wide variety of jobs, divisions, and levels. Other times it will be most important to know what rewards are associated with the job. And in many cases, describing a job will require a combination of all three of these techniques.

The chapter begins by explaining the rationale behind job analysis, reviewing the challenges that arise when developing a description of jobs in a changing environment, and evaluating what different sources of information provide in the process. Then, methods for performing job analysis are discussed. The first approach, job requirements analysis, is guided by the job requirements matrix, which includes tasks, KSAOs, and job context. Second, the competency modeling approach starts from the organization's mission and goals and then develops a list of the general KSAOs that will help the organization meet these needs. Third, job rewards analysis describes both intrinsic and extrinsic rewards that jobs may provide to employees. Finally, legal issues pertaining to job analysis are addressed.

THE NEED FOR JOB ANALYSIS

Jobs are the building blocks of an organization, in terms of both job content and the hierarchical relationships that emerge among them. They are explicitly designed and aligned in ways that enhance the production of the organization's goods and services. Job analysis thus must be considered within the broader framework of the design of jobs and the organization as a whole. The information from job analysis will be used in every single phase of the staffing process. With thorough and accurate information about job requirements and/or competencies, the organization will be more successful in its attempts to acquire a workforce that matches its needs. Thus, job analysis is the foundation upon which successful staffing systems are constructed.

Types of Job Analysis

Job analysis is the process of gathering, analyzing, synthesizing, and reporting information about job requirements and rewards. Note that job analysis is an overall *process* as opposed to a specific method or technique. An organization can approach the job analysis process in several different ways. A job requirements analysis seeks to identify and describe the specific tasks, KSAOs, and job context for a particular job. This type of job analysis aims to be objective, and has a very well-developed body of techniques to support its implementation. A second type of job analysis, competency modeling, attempts to identify and describe job requirements in the form of general KSAOs required across a range of jobs. Competency-based approaches focus on how jobs relate to organizational strategy. A third approach to job analysis focuses on the rewards employees receive from their work. Unlike the job requirements and competency-based approaches, the rewards-based approach is used to assess what types of positive outcomes employees receive from performing a job. From a staffing perspective, knowing the rewards of a job can be very useful in attracting individuals to apply for, and ultimately accept, jobs in the organization.

To help demonstrate the differences and similarities among job requirements, competency, and rewards methods of job analysis, Exhibit 4.1 describes the method, process, and staffing implications of each of the three types. As can be seen, every phase of the staffing process is rooted in job analysis, from initial planning to retention. Each technique contributes different information. Job requirements analysis is mostly rooted in documenting what employees currently do, competency analysis focuses on how executives see work roles contributing to strategy, and rewards

EXHIBIT 4.1   Comparison of Types of Job Analysis

	Job Analysis Technique		
	Job Requirements	**Competency**	**Job Rewards**
Method	Collect information on activities performed on the job and use this information to assess needed KSAOs for each job	Collect information on company strategy and use this information to determine KSAOs and behavioral capabilities needed across the organization	Collect information from employees on preferences and outcomes of jobs and combine with preferences identified in the labor market as a whole
Process	Review occupational requirements; collect data on tasks, duties, and responsibilities from incumbents and supervisors; develop job requirements matrix	Discuss strategy with executives to determine overall goals, then meet with division or department leaders to review how each job fits with the overall goals	Develop a list of potential rewards for a job and survey job incumbents and leaders
Staffing Implications	Document task requirements for legal purposes and determine specific KSAOs for selection	Link organizational strategy with planning process and determine broad KSAOs for selection	Provide guidance for how to develop recruiting materials and retention strategies

analysis determines what employees get from their jobs. These techniques are not mutually exclusive, and organizations can benefit from using all three methods of analysis simultaneously.

The Changing Nature of Jobs

The traditional way of designing a job is to identify and define its elements and tasks precisely and then incorporate them into a job description. These more traditional jobs have clear lines of demarcation between them in terms of both tasks and KSAOs, and there is little overlap among jobs. Each job also has its own set of extrinsic and intrinsic rewards. Such job design is marked by formal organizational charts, clear and precise job descriptions and specifications, and well-defined relationships between jobs in terms of mobility (promotion and transfer) paths.

One challenge to this traditional perspective is that jobs are constantly evolving.[1] For an example close to home for many working in staffing functions, consider how the role of human resource (HR) managers has shifted over time. As technology has increased the level of data and speed of processing information, less time is needed for traditional record keeping and routine administrative functions. These changes led to new KSAO requirements such as planning and coordination skills, use of interactive HR management systems, and knowledge of workforce analytics. As a result, HR representatives need a broader perspective on the business overall and must be able to coordinate with multiple functional areas. Jobs may also evolve due to changing organizational forms and social factors, as well as employee-initiated changes through a process of job crafting. Task changes may be dictated by changes in production schedules, client demands, or technology. Many small-business owners, general managers of start-up strategic business units, and top management members perform such flexible jobs. Recent developments in job analysis encourage raters to explicitly describe potential changes in future job requirements in an effort to adapt to these forces.[2]

Team-based work enhances the need for flexibility and further complicates the process of job analysis. A work team is an interdependent collection of employees who share responsibility for achieving a specific goal. Examples of such goals include developing a product, delivering a service, winning a game, conducting a process, developing a plan, and making a joint decision. No matter its form or function, every team is composed of two or more employees and has an identifiable collection of tasks to perform. Usually, these tasks are grouped into specific clusters, and each cluster constitutes a position or job. A project management team, for example, may have separate jobs and job titles for budget specialists, technical specialists, coordinators, and field staff. While teams differ in many respects, two differences are very important in terms of their job analysis and staffing implications. Many team members perform multiple jobs (rather than a single job). In such cases, staffing must emphasize recruitment and selection for both job-specific KSAOs and job-spanning KSAOs. Many job-spanning KSAOs involve flexibility, adaptability, and the ability to quickly learn skills that will facilitate performing, and switching between, multiple jobs.[3] Therefore, job analysis for team-based work has to account for this highly varied and constantly evolving set of task demands.

Finally, the more open and flexible nature of work described above has suggested a need to identify factors that make people go beyond what is simply written in a job description. As more and more organizations emphasize employee engagement, the analysis of jobs needs to take motivational factors into account.[4] A large-scale study of 7,939 business units showed that organizations whose employees reported above-average levels of engagement performed significantly better (63% of such organizations had above-average levels of performance) than those whose employees were below average on engagement (37% of such organizations had above-average levels of performance). It is advisable to consider traits and goals linked to engagement in competency modeling, coupled with identifying job characteristics that increase engagement in job rewards analysis. As one reviewer of the engagement literature suggests, "Identify those candidates who are best-suited to the job and your organization's culture."

Sources of Information

Determining the best sources of information for a job analysis has profound implications. Exhibit 4.2 reviews some of the reasons why each source of information might be consulted for each form of job analysis, alongside shortcomings. One rather obvious conclusion from evaluating different sources is that there is not one "best" choice. Ultimately, the choice should be informed by the goal of the job analysis process. Individuals who provide information are collectively called subject matter experts (SMEs). We break out internal SMEs into leaders, supervisors,

EXHIBIT 4.2   Sources of Information

	Job Requirements	Competency	Job Rewards
Organizational Leaders	Remote or abstract knowledge of job-specific activities	Expertise in organizational strategies, goals, and future needs	Knowledge of organizational career paths and future rewards for continued development
Supervisors	Direct knowledge of how the job should be done	Mid-level perspective between overall organizational goals and specific activities in jobs	Control over providing job rewards and knowledge of how rewards relate to performance
Job Incumbents	Direct knowledge of how the job typically is done	May have difficulty assessing how immediate job tasks are linked to strategic goals	Recipient of job rewards for the position; direct knowledge of how rewards are perceived by others in the role
External SMEs	Expert information on occupations or work as a whole; knowledge regarding how to conduct analysis	Outsider perspective on how tasks are typically organized; fresh perspective, but lacking strategic and cultural expertise	May have knowledge of rewards of the job as perceived by individuals in other organizations

and incumbents here but address external SMEs collectively. Whatever the sources of SMEs, a common requirement is that they have recent, firsthand knowledge of the job being analyzed.[5]

Organizational Leaders

To ensure that the job analysis process addresses strategic and operational needs, organizational leaders should be consulted at the outset of the process. Leaders will have the best perspective on work design for the organization as a whole.[6] The competency modeling method focuses squarely on top management, and from this information staffing managers can make certain that KSAO targets in recruiting, selection, and placement are in line with strategic priorities. Leaders can provide a holistic view of work in the organization, which often means their evaluation of the gap between current work functions and needed work functions can result in complete redesign or reorganization of tasks. The leader perspective does have its shortcomings, however. Most top managers have limited knowledge of specific job roles and even less knowledge of the day-to-day tasks. After years of working with competency models, many job analysts have come to the conclusion that a top-down leader perspective does not provide the fine-grained detail that is needed for most staffing functions, so a hybrid approach that also incorporates information from supervisors, incumbents, and external experts may be needed to supplement leaders' perspective.

Supervisors

Supervisors are the main source of information for most job analyses. Evidence suggests there are significant advantages to using supervisors, but also some reasons for concern.[7] Evidence has shown that supervisors make the most accurate judgments in the job analysis process. They not only supervise employees performing the job to be analyzed but may also participate in defining job content for evolving and flexible jobs. Understanding job tasks and the right way to do them is the core of a supervisor's role. Moreover, because supervisors ultimately have to accept the resulting descriptions and specifications for jobs they supervise, including them as a source is a good way to ensure such acceptance. The chief problem with supervisors as a source of information is that they will likely realize that the job analysis process is a key opportunity to increase their status and gain resources, and therefore may overstate the importance of their own role.

Job Incumbents

Job incumbents are a natural source of information to be used in job analysis. Incumbents are intimately familiar with tasks, KSAOs, and job context. In addition, job incumbents may become more accepting of the job analysis process and its results through their participation. Including incumbents in decisions about work tasks signals respect and can build engagement.[8] However, job incumbents do have shortcomings as a source of job analysis information.[9] They may lack the knowledge or insights necessary to understand how the job should be done at a higher level. Some employees may also have difficulty describing the tasks involved in their job or being able to infer and articulate the underlying KSAOs, especially complex bundles of competencies. There are also concerns about job incumbents not responding to job analysis surveys; most studies show that fewer than half of job incumbents voluntarily respond to job analysis surveys. Incumbents' motivation can also be an issue, similar to supervisors. For example, incumbents may intentionally fail to report certain tasks as part of their job so that those tasks are not incorporated into the formal job description. Incumbents may also deliberately inflate the importance ratings of tasks in order to elevate their own importance.

External SMEs

External SMEs can also be useful for gathering information. These experts could include consultants or members of professional organizations (state bar associations for lawyers, the American Medical Association, engineering societies, and so on). External experts offer a fresh, outside perspective since they are neither manager nor incumbent of the jobs analyzed. Consultants who work with job analysis and competency models have specialized training and experience in developing a rigorous and thorough job analysis system. Other external SMEs can help identify best practices in a field or occupation. Despite such advantages, reliance on external SMEs as a job information source is not without limitations. Since they are outsiders, they may not be seen as legitimate by incumbents and supervisors. This perception may raise questions about the SME's relevance, cultural knowledge, and trustworthiness. This may be an accurate perception by insiders. External SMEs may, in fact, lack detailed knowledge of the idiosyncratic nature of jobs in organizations. The best external SMEs are aware of these limitations and combine their perspective with an internal view.

JOB REQUIREMENTS ANALYSIS

Overview

As noted earlier, job requirements analysis identifies the tasks, KSAOs, and context for a job. Concepts underlying job requirements can be arranged in a hierarchy from observable tasks up to job families. Job requirements analysis starts with tasks, which are identifiable work activities that are logical and necessary steps in the performance of the job. Task dimensions are groups of similar types of tasks. A job is a grouping of positions that have similar tasks. Jobs that are similar to one another can be grouped into job categories. Finally, a job family is a grouping of jobs according to function. For example, within the community and social service job family there are categories of jobs like health workers, counselors, and social workers. Under the counselor category are specific jobs like mental health counselor and rehabilitation counselor. Tasks like collecting information, developing treatment plans, and counseling clients make up the job of mental health counselor. A position is a grouping of task dimensions that constitutes the total work assignment of a single employee; there are as many positions as there are employees.

Job requirements analysis begins by identifying the specific tasks and job context for a particular job.[10] After these have been identified, the KSAOs necessary for performing these tasks within the work context are inferred. For example, after identifying the task of "developing and writing monthly sales and marketing plans" for a sales manager's job, the job analysis would proceed by inferring which KSAOs are necessary to perform this task. The task might require knowledge of intended customers, arithmetic skills, creative ability, and willingness and availability to travel frequently to various organizational units. Particular job context factors, such as physical demands, may not be relevant to performance of this task or to its required KSAOs. The task and job context information is recorded in a job description, whereas the KSAO requirements are placed in a job specification. In practice, these are often contained within a single document.

Job Requirements Matrix and Job Descriptions

The job requirements matrix shows the key components of the job requirements analysis, each of which must be explicitly considered for inclusion. Job information, including the specific tasks, task dimensions, task importance, specific KSAOs, and their importance, must be gathered, analyzed, synthesized, and expressed in a usable form.

A completed job requirements matrix, a portion of which is shown in Exhibit 4.3 for the job of administrative assistant, serves as the basic informational source or document for the requirements of any job. The resultant information serves as a basic input and guide to all subsequent staffing activities.

Referring to Exhibit 4.3, five specific tasks identified via job analysis are listed. Note that only a portion of the total tasks of the job is shown. In turn, these have been categorized into two general task dimensions: supervision and document preparation. Their importance to the overall job is indicated with the percentage of time spent on each—30% and 20%, respectively. For each task dimension and its specific tasks, several KSAOs have been inferred to be necessary for performance. The nature of these KSAOs is presented, along with a 1-5 rating of how important each KSAO is for performance of the task dimension. At the bottom of the matrix are indications of job context factors pertaining to work setting (indoors), privacy of work area (cubicle), attire (business clothes), body positioning (mostly sitting and standing), and physical work conditions (no environmental or job hazards).

Task Statements

Job analysis begins with the development of task statements. Task statements are objectively written descriptions of the major tasks an employee performs in a job.

EXHIBIT 4.3   Portion of Job Requirements Matrix for Job of Administrative Assistant

Tasks			KSAOs	
Specific Tasks	Task Dimensions	Importance (% time spent)	Nature	Importance to Tasks (1–5 rating)
1. Arrange schedules with office assistant/volunteers to ensure that office will be staffed during prescribed hours	A. Supervision	30%	1. Knowledge of office operations and policies	4.9
			2. Ability to match people to tasks according to their skills and hours of availability	4.6
2. Assign office tasks to office assistant/volunteers to ensure coordination of activities	A. Supervision		3. Skill in interaction with diverse people	2.9
			4. Skill in determining types and priorities of tasks	4.0
3. Compose and edit letters, memos, and reports based on supervisory direction	B. Document preparation	20%	1. Knowledge of typing formats	3.1
			2. Knowledge of grammar and style rules	5.0
4. Prepare graphs and other visual material to supplement reports	B. Document preparation		3. Knowledge of graphics display software	2.0
			4. Ability to proofread and correct work	5.0
5. Proofread typed copy and correct grammar, punctuation, and typographical errors in order to produce high-quality materials	B. Document preparation		5. Skill in use of MS Word (most current version)	4.3
			6. Skill in creating visually appealing and understandable graphs	3.4

Job Context: Indoors, cubicle, business clothes, mostly sitting and standing, no environmental or job hazards.

They serve as the building blocks for the remainder of the job requirements analysis. The statements are made in simple declarative sentences.

Ideally, each task statement will indicate:

1. What does the employee do?
2. To whom or what?
3. With what expected outcome?

When writing task statements, focus only on major tasks and activities. An exception to this recommendation is when an infrequent task is judged to have great importance to the job. Also, ensure that the list of task statements is reliable.[11] Have two or more people (analysts) independently evaluate the task statement list in terms of both inclusiveness and clarity. If there is disagreement, the nature of the disagreement can be discussed and the task statements can be appropriately modified. Differences in task statements are not necessarily an indication of error. Different incumbents may perform their jobs in different ways.[12] The final job analysis document should reflect these varying perspectives clearly. Failure to acknowledge this variety can lead to legal problems if the job analysis documents used to make decisions do not reflect the various ways jobs are actually performed.

Task Dimensions

It is useful to group sets of task statements into task dimensions and then attach a name to each such dimension. Other terms for task dimensions are "duties," "accountability areas," "responsibilities," and "performance dimensions."

A useful way to facilitate the grouping process is to create a task dimension matrix. Each column in the matrix represents a potential task dimension. Each row in the matrix represents a particular task statement. Cell entries in the matrix represent the assignment of task statements to task dimensions (the grouping of tasks). The goal is to have each task statement assigned to only one task dimension.

There are many different grouping procedures, ranging from straightforward judgmental ones to highly sophisticated statistical ones.[13] For most purposes, a simple judgmental process is sufficient, such as having the people who created the task statements also create the groupings as part of the same exercise. As a rule, there should be four to eight dimensions, depending on the number of task statements, regardless of the specific grouping procedure used.

Task/Dimension Importance

Tasks/dimensions of a job are not of equal importance, so job requirements analysis should take this variability into account.

Before actual weighting can occur, two decisions must be made: (1) the specific attribute of importance to be assessed must be decided (e.g., time spent on the task/

dimension, ratings of criticality), and (2) whether the attribute will be measured in categorical terms (e.g., essential or nonessential) or continuous terms (e.g., percentage of time spent, 1–5 rating of importance). Exhibit 4.4 shows examples of the results of these two decisions in terms of commonly used importance attributes and their measurement. Task importance judgments are likely to vary across raters even more than task statements, so it is necessary to collect judgments from several sources.[14]

KSAOs

KSAOs are inferred or derived from knowledge of the tasks and task dimensions themselves. The inference process requires that the analysts think explicitly in specific cause-and-effect terms. For each task or dimension, the analysts must in essence ask themselves, "Exactly which KSAOs do I think will be necessary for performance of this task or dimension?"

Our discussion of KSAOs is grounded in information provided by the US Department of Labor's Occupational Information Network, or O*NET. The development

---

EXHIBIT 4.4   **Ways to Assess Task/Dimension Importance**

A.   **Relative Time Spent**

For each task/dimension, rate the amount of time you spend on it, relative to all other tasks/dimensions of your job.

1	2	3	4	5
Very small amount		Average amount		Very large amount

B.   **Percentage (%) of Time Spent**

For each task/dimension, indicate the percentage (%) of time you spend on it (percentages must total to 100%).

Dimension _____   % Time spent _____

C.   **Importance to Overall Performance**

For each task/dimension, rate its importance to your overall job performance.

1	2	3	4	5
Minor importance		Average importance		Major importance

and refinement of the O*NET database is ongoing, and many new observations from both job incumbents and trained analysts are being added regularly.[15] O*NET contains extensive research-based taxonomies in several categories: occupational tasks, knowledge, skills, abilities, education and experience/training, work contexts, organizational contexts, occupational interests and values, and work styles.[16] Occupational information remains a crucial issue for understanding the workforce, since many workers obtain highly specialized training for their occupations, look for work based on occupational titles, and identify themselves with occupational roles.

Additionally, O*NET contains ratings of specific factors within each category for many occupations, and ratings for additional occupations are continually being added. Statistical techniques link O*NET KSAO ratings for a job to specific selection tools, like standardized literacy tests.[17] Use of O*NET information is helpful in preparing KSAO statements, but they will probably have to be supplemented with more job-specific statements crafted by the job analyst.

Exhibit 4.5 provides an overview of the distinction among knowledge, skill, ability, and other characteristics. For each KSAO category, brief examples are given, along with an explanation of their relevance. As the exhibit shows, making a distinction across the categories can have important implications for staffing. For example, abilities must be possessed by the candidate at the point of hire, whereas knowledge can be acquired through formal class sessions and skills can be developed while working.

Knowledge.   Knowledge is a body of information (conceptual, factual, procedural) that can be applied directly to the performance of tasks. It tends to be quite focused or specific in terms of the job, organization, or occupation. O*NET provides definitions of 33 types of knowledge that might generally be necessary in varying levels in certain occupations, including areas like business and management, manufacturing and production, engineering and technology, mathematics and science, health services, education and training, arts and humanities, law and public safety, communications, and transportation. Knowledge is often divided into declarative and procedural categories. Declarative knowledge is factual in nature, whereas procedural knowledge concerns processes. A surgeon, for example, has declarative knowledge of the symptoms of heart disease and can state them, and also has procedural knowledge of the steps to perform open-heart surgery. Both declarative and procedural knowledge should be reflected in job analysis documents.[18]

Skill.   Skill refers to an observable competence for working with or applying knowledge to perform a particular task or a closely related set of tasks. A skill is not an enduring characteristic of the person; it depends on experience and practice. Skill requirements are directly inferred from observation or knowledge of tasks

EXHIBIT 4.5   Knowledge, Skill, Ability, and Other Characteristics

KSAO Category	What Is It?	Examples	Workplace Relevance
Knowledge	Information that can be applied to tasks	• Knowing what a solid state drive is and why it's useful for a computer • Knowing the steps in writing a job description	• Easily assessed with factual questions • Forms the basis for communication • Knowledgeable individuals can train others
Skill	Competence for working with or applying knowledge	• Skill in diagnosing and repairing problems with solid state drives • Skill in efficiently collecting job analysis information and writing task statements	• Assessed with job simulations or experience • Directly linked to performance of the job • Can be learned on the job with guidance
Ability	Underlying trait useful for learning about and performing a task	• Ability to perform fine motor activities • Ability to understand complex, multistep instructions	• Assessed through abstract tests • Linked to future potential • Must be present at selection; very hard to develop
Other characteristics	Characteristics that guide or direct actions	• Motivation to perform well • Being responsible and organized • Values consistent with organizational norms	• Challenging to assess because subjective • Very important for turning KSAs into performance

performed. Returning to our example, skill refers to the actual demonstrated capacity of the surgeon to perform an operation in an efficient and competent manner.

O*NET identifies and defines 42 skills applicable across the occupational spectrum. These include basic skills involving acquiring and conveying information, such as reading comprehension, actively listening, mathematics, science, and critical thinking, as well as cross-functional skills more directly related to task performance, such as social skills, complex problem solving, resource management, technical skills, and system skills.

Ability.   An ability is an underlying, enduring trait of the person that is useful for learning about and performing a range of tasks. It differs from a skill in that it is less likely to change over time and that it is applicable across a wide set of tasks encountered in many different jobs. One can think of ability as the underlying personal characteristics that determine how quickly one can acquire and to what degree one can master the knowledge and skills required for a job.[19] Four general categories of abilities are commonly recognized: cognitive (e.g., verbal, quantitative, perceptional, spatial, and memory abilities), psychomotor (e.g., fine manipulative, control movement, and reaction time abilities), physical (e.g., strength, endurance, and coordination abilities), and sensory (e.g., visual and auditory abilities).

Other Characteristics.   "Other characteristics" are a variety of factors that are important for determining how individuals will act on the job. These characteristics can be personality traits that describe a person's preferences or typical behavioral tendencies. While knowledge, skills, and abilities reflect whether someone can do a task, "other characteristics" mostly focus on whether a person wants to do a task or how much effort the person will expend. They can also be a general state of motivation or liking for a specific type of job task, such as a preference for routine or variety, or a preference for working alone or with others. Values are another important set of other characteristics that are crucial for facilitating person/ organization match.

All of these traits can be difficult to measure, because they are often more subjective or loosely defined relative to KSAs, and it is often possible for a job applicant to pretend that he or she has a trait. Despite these difficulties, as we will see later in the book, traits like conscientiousness have been shown to differentiate good from poor performers.

KSAO Importance

As suggested in the job requirements matrix, the KSAOs of a job may differ in their weight or contribution to task performance.

As with task importance, deriving KSAO importance requires two decisions. First, what will be the specific attribute(s) on which importance is judged? Second, will the measurement of each attribute be categorical (e.g., required, preferred) or continuous (e.g., 1–5 rating scale)? Examples of formats for indicating KSAO importance are shown in Exhibit 4.6. O*NET uses a 1–5 rating scale format and also provides actual importance ratings for many jobs.

Ratings of KSAO importance generally can be divided into time and importance.[20] Time-oriented measures include things like time spent, frequency, and duration scales. Importance includes things like criticality, difficulty, and overall importance. In most organizations, time spent and importance are completely distinct, and so both should be measured to get a full picture of the job's requirements. There are systematic differences in ratings of time spent and importance across observers. For example, new employees may spend more time developing relation-

---

EXHIBIT 4.6 Ways to Assess KSAO Importance

A. Importance to (acceptable) (superior) task performance
   1 = minimal importance
   2 = some importance
   3 = average importance
   4 = considerable importance
   5 = extensive importance

B. Should the KSAO be assessed during recruitment/selection?
   ☐ Yes
   ☐ No

C. Is the KSAO required, preferred, or not required for recruitment/selection?
   ☐ Required
   ☐ Preferred
   ☐ Not required (obtain on job and/or in training)

ships, whereas established employees spend time maintaining relationships. Thus, multiple perspectives will need to be integrated.

Job Context

As shown in the job requirements matrix, tasks and KSAOs occur within a broader job context. A job requirements analysis should consider the job context and the factors that are important in defining it. These factors may have an influence on tasks and KSAOs. Information about the context may be used in the recruitment and selection of job applicants. For example, the information may be given to job applicants during recruitment, and consideration of job context factors may be helpful in assessing likely person/organization fit during selection.

O*NET contains a wide array of job and work context factors useful for characterizing occupations. The job context information contained in O*NET involves interpersonal, physical, and structural characteristics, as shown in Exhibit 4.7. These characteristics can be useful for determining additional KSAO requirements and may be especially important for determining whether a job can or cannot be modified to accommodate an individual with a disability.

Job Description and Job Specification

As previously noted, it is common practice to express the results of job requirements analysis in job descriptions and job specifications. The sections of the job requirements matrix pertaining to tasks and job context are similar to a job description, and the section dealing with KSAOs is similar to a job specification.

EXHIBIT 4.7   Job Context Contained in O*NET

Interpersonal Relationships
- Communication
- Role relationships
- Responsibility for others
- Conflictual contact

Physical Work Conditions
- Work setting
- Environmental conditions
- Job hazards
- Body positioning
- Work attire

Structural Job Characteristics
- Criticality of position
- Routine vs. challenging work
- Competition
- Pace and scheduling

There are no standard formats or other requirements for either job descriptions or job specifications. In terms of content, however, a job description should include the following: job family, job title, job summary, task statements and dimensions, importance indicators, job context indicators, and the date that the job analysis was last updated. A job specification should include job family, job title, job summary, KSAOs (separate section for each), importance indicators, and date of last update. An example of a combined job description/specification is shown in Exhibit 4.8.

Collecting Job Requirements Information

Job requirements analysis involves the types of information (tasks, KSAOs, and job context) to be collected and the methods, sources, and processes to be used. There are many alternatives to choose from for developing an overall job analysis system for any particular situation. Potential inaccuracies and other limitations of the alternatives will also be pointed out.[21]

Methods

Job analysis methods represent procedures or techniques for collecting job information. Many specific techniques and systems have been developed and named (e.g., Functional Job Analysis, Position Analysis Questionnaire [PAQ]). Rather than discuss each technique separately, we will concentrate on the major generic methods that underlie all specific techniques and applications.[22]

Prior Information.   Organizations that have performed job analysis in the past will have information on the tasks, duties, and responsibilities of the job as well as

EXHIBIT 4.8   Example of Combined Job Description/Specification

FUNCTIONAL UNIT: CHILDREN'S REHABILITATION
JOB TITLE: REHABILITATION SPECIALIST
DATE: 12/5/15

JOB SUMMARY

Works with children with disabilities and their families to identify developmental strengths and weaknesses, develop rehabilitation plans, deliver and coordinate rehabilitation activities, and evaluate effectiveness of those plans and activities.

PERFORMANCE DIMENSIONS AND TASKS   **Time Spent (%)**

1. Assessment   **10%**

Administer formal and informal motor screening and evaluation instruments to conduct assessments. Perform assessments to identify areas of strengths and need.

2. Planning   **25%**

Collaborate with parents and other providers to directly develop the individualized family service plan. Use direct and consultative models of service in developing plans.

3. Delivery   **50%**

Carry out individual and small-group motor development activities with children and families. Provide service coordination to designated families. Work with family care and child care providers to provide total services. Collaborate with other staff members and professionals from community agencies to obtain resources and specialized assistance.

4. Evaluation   **15%**

Observe, interpret, and report on client to monitor individual progress. Assist in collecting and reporting intervention data in order to prepare formal program evaluation reports. Write evaluation reports to assist in developing new treatment strategies and programs.

JOB SPECIFICATIONS

1. License: License to practice physical therapy in the state

2. Education: B.S. in physical or occupational therapy required; M.S. preferred

3. Experience: Prefer (not required) one year experience working with children with disabilities and their families

4. Skills: Listening to and interacting with others (children, family members, coworkers)
Developing treatment plans
Organizing and writing reports using Microsoft Word

JOB CONTEXT: Indoors, office, business clothes, no environmental or job hazards.

the corresponding KSAOs. While such information can be helpful, the changing nature of work suggests that all older information should be considered carefully and evaluated relative to the current set of requirements. A discrepancy between the job on record and the job as it is actually performed can lead to legal problems.

O*NET is a natural starting point for job requirements information. Obvious advantages of O*NET are its flexibility (it can be applied to many different types of jobs) and its ease of use.[23] Because data were collected by professionals across a wide variety of locations over time, they are highly reliable. The chief disadvantage of O*NET is that it describes occupations and not jobs. Occupational information indicates what individuals performing a certain job title do across a wide variety of organizational contexts, whereas job information reflects the unique characteristics of how work is done in a specific company. In other words, while O*NET has a very well-developed description of what marketing managers do, it cannot say anything about the specific nature of a marketing manager job at Apple.

Observation.   Observing job incumbents performing the job is an excellent way to learn about tasks, KSAOs, and context. It is the most direct form of gathering information, because it does not rely on intermediary information sources like job incumbents and supervisors.

Observation is most appropriate for jobs with physical or interpersonal components (rather than cognitive components) and relatively short job cycles (i.e., amount of time required to complete job tasks before repeating them). Observers need to be trained to know what to look for in each job. Supervisors and incumbents also need to feel comfortable with being observed as they work. As noted earlier in our discussion of sources, incumbents being observed may distort their behavior during observation in self-serving ways, such as making tasks appear more difficult or time-consuming than they really are or performing at a higher level than they typically do.

Interviews.   Interviewing job incumbents and others, such as their managers, has many potential advantages. It respects the interviewee's vast source of information. The interview format allows the interviewer to explain the purpose of the job analysis and how the results will be used, thus enhancing likely acceptance of the process by the interviewees. It can be structured in format to ensure standardization of collected information.

However, it can take a great deal of time and expertise to conduct proper interviews. The quality of the information obtained, as well as interviewee acceptance, depends on the skill of the interviewer. The interviewers should thus be carefully selected and trained. Finally, the success of the interview also depends on the skills and abilities of the interviewee, such as the person's verbal communication skills and the ability to accurately report on what their work entails.

Task Questionnaire.   A typical task questionnaire contains a lengthy list of task statements that cut across many different job titles and is administered to incumbents. For each task statement, the respondent is asked to indicate (1) whether the task applies to the respondent's job and (2) task importance (e.g., a 1–5 scale rating difficulty or time spent).

The advantages of task questionnaires are numerous. They are standardized in content and format, and thus constitute a uniform method of information gathering. They can obtain considerable information from large numbers of people and are economical to administer and score. Additionally, anonymous task questionnaires can enhance respondent participation, honesty, and acceptance.[24]

The development of task questionnaires has also facilitated the development of linkages between task dimensions and required KSAOs. Some of these developments have involved a technique called synthetic validation, which helps determine the most appropriate types of selection tools for a job.[25] As the databases linking task dimensions to KSAOs have increased in size and scope over time, it has become possible to know which selection predictors are most appropriate for a given job without having to resort to a local validation study, as will be discussed in the measurement chapter.

A task questionnaire does have limitations. Because task statements are very general to cover a wide variety of situations, task questionnaires are not useful for describing idiosyncratic tasks. As with other reporting methods, respondents need to have the underlying intelligence, experience, and education to answer accurately. Respondents also need to be motivated to complete the questionnaire accurately.

Machine Learning.   Machine learning is a term capturing a variety of "big data" analytics methods. Machine learning is increasingly used for describing work and associated KSAOs.[26] Text mining is the specific form of machine learning that has been most often employed in this area. In machine learning, computer-trained algorithms comb through enormous amounts of data and extract themes. These themes can then create "profiles" of qualifications, in the same way online retailers use machine learning to combine information from search histories and online purchases to create "profiles" of consumers.

A machine learning approach can save many hours, especially when processing a combination of data from organizational records, written job descriptions, interviews, Internet searches, and questionnaires. This process can not only find ways to describe jobs quickly but also help create a system for rigorously understanding how different jobs are similar or dissimilar based on tasks and KSAOs. For example, one study used machine learning to evaluate the entire database from O*NET and create a numerical score to assess the extent to which prior work experiences are relevant to another job. This application of job analysis would take months if human coders were needed for these choices. The chief drawback of machine learning is the difficulty in understanding or explaining how the algorithmic systems actually combine information. The underlying process that ultimately determines how to cluster information into themes is sometimes not easy for even the individuals designing the system to understand because the algorithms are using combination methods that are driven by incredibly complex systems of equations that build on themselves. Automated processes are often referred to as "black box" because it is so hard to see what is going on inside them. Fortunately, techniques for topic modeling that start from easily explained and theoretically grounded categories of tasks and KSAOs are available and can help overcome these problems and produce results that are easier to interpret.

Committee or Task Force.   Job analysis is often guided by an ad hoc committee or task force. Members of this group typically include job experts—both managers and employees—as well as an HR representative. They may conduct a number of activities, including (1) reviewing existing information and gathering sample job descriptions; (2) interviewing job incumbents and managers; (3) overseeing the administration of job analysis surveys and analyzing the results; (4) writing task statements, grouping them into task dimensions, and rating the importance of the task dimensions; and (5) identifying KSAOs and rating their importance. A committee or task force brings considerable job analysis expertise to the process, facilitates reliability of judgment through conversation and consensus building, and enhances acceptance of the final results.

Criteria for Choice of Methods.   Some explicit choices regarding methods of job requirements analysis need to be made. One set of choices involves deciding whether to use a particular method of information collection. An organization must decide whether to use an off-the-shelf method or its own particular method that is suited to its own needs and circumstances. A second set of choices involves how to blend together a set of methods that will be used in varying ways and degrees in the actual job analysis. Some criteria for guidance in such decisions are shown in Exhibit 4.9. In practice, job analysis is usually conducted through a combination of these methods so that the weaknesses of any one method are offset by the strengths of another.

Job Requirements Analysis Process

Collecting job information through job analysis requires development and use of an overall process. Unfortunately, there is no uniformly best process to be followed; the process has to be tailor-made to suit the specifics of the situation in which it occurs. Decisions need to be made about purpose; scope; organization and coordination; analysis, synthesis, and documentation; and maintenance of the system.

Purpose.   The purpose(s) of job analysis should be clearly identified and agreed on. Since job analysis is a process designed to yield job information, the organization should ask exactly what job information is desired and why. Here, it is useful to refer back to the job requirements matrix to review the types of information that can be sought and obtained in a job requirements analysis. Management must decide exactly what types of information are desired (task statements, task dimensions, and so forth) and in what format. Once the desired output and the results of

EXHIBIT 4.9   **Criteria for Guiding Choice of Job Analysis Methods**

Method	Sources	Advantages and Disadvantages
Prior information	Current job descriptions Training manuals Performance appraisals O*NET	Readily available Inexpensive External sources may not match jobs in your organization Focus is on how jobs have been done previously, not how they will be done in the future
Observation	Trained job analysts or HR professionals watch incumbents perform the job	Thorough, rich information Does not rely on intermediary information sources Not appropriate for jobs that are largely mental in character Incumbents may behave differently if they know they're being observed
Interviews	HR professionals discuss job requirements with job incumbents and managers	Takes the incumbent's knowledge of the position into account Time-consuming and costly Quality depends on the knowledge and ability of the interviewee and skill of the interviewer
Task questionnaire	Job incumbents, managers, and HR professionals complete a standardized form with questions regarding the job	Standardized method across a variety of jobs Can combine information from large numbers of incumbents quickly Developing questionnaires can be expensive and time-consuming Requires that incumbents be capable of completing the forms accurately
Machine learning	Multiple sources, including prior information, observation, interviews, task questionnaires, and online databases	Efficiently combines large amounts of data from different sources Can demonstrate how groups of tasks and qualifications relate to one another across jobs Can be difficult to understand the process Requires expert judgment in the early stages of the process to ensure results are meaningful
Committee or task force	Managers, representatives from HR, and incumbents meet to discuss job descriptions	Brings expertise of a variety of individuals into the process Increases reliability of the process Enhances acceptance of the final product Significant investment of staff time

job analysis have been determined, the organization can then plan a process that will yield the desired results.

Scope.   The issue of scope involves which job(s) to include in the job analysis. Decisions about actual scope should be based on (1) the importance of the job to the functioning of the organization, (2) the number of job applicants and incumbents, (3) whether the job is entry level and thus subject to constant staffing activity, (4) the frequency with which job requirements (both tasks and KSAOs) change, and (5) the amount of time that has lapsed since the previous job analysis.

Organization and Coordination.   Job requirements analysis for any organization can be complicated, and without organization and coordination the process can become inefficient or may remain incomplete. First, an organizational member should be appointed as project manager for the total process. If consultants are used, they should report to this project manager. The project manager should be assigned overall accountability for the project and should have the authority, time, and resources to make the process successful. Second, the roles and relationships for everyone who will be participating in the process, including HR staff, project staff, line managers, and job incumbents, must be clearly established. Third, the workflow and time frame showing critical completion dates for project phases need to be in place.

Analysis, Synthesis, and Documentation.   Once collected, job information must be analyzed and synthesized through the use of various procedural and statistical means. These should be planned in advance and incorporated into the work-flow and time-frame requirements. Likewise, provisions need to be made for preparation of information, especially job descriptions and job specifications, and their incorporation across all elements of the organization's decision-making systems.

Maintenance of the System.   Mechanisms must be developed and put into place to maintain the job analysis and information system over time. As we noted earlier, jobs are constantly changing, so there should be an easy way to update information as the needs of the organization change. Factors that might require a reanalysis include (1) changes in the organization's strategic direction; (2) organizational redesign, restructuring, and realignment; and (3) changes in the technology or processes involved in doing the work. In short, job requirements analysis must be an ongoing organizational process.

Example of Job Analysis Process.   Because of the many factors involved, there is no best or required job analysis process. Rather, the process must be designed to fit each particular situation. Exhibit 4.10 shows an example of the job analysis process with a narrow scope, namely, for a single job—that of administrative assistant. This was a specially conducted job analysis that used multiple methods (prior

EXHIBIT 4.10   Example of Job Requirements Analysis

1. Meet with manager of the job, discuss project → 2. Gather existing job information from O*NET, current job description, observation of incumbents → 3. Prepare tentative set of task statements →

4. Review task statements with incumbents and managers; add, delete, rewrite statements → 5. Finalize task statements, get approval from incumbents and managers → 6. Formulate task dimensions, assign tasks to dimensions, determine % of time spent (importance) for each dimension →

7. Infer necessary KSAOs, develop tentative list → 8. Review KSAOs with incumbents and managers; add, delete, and rewrite KSAOs → 9. Finalize KSAOs, get approval from incumbents and manager →

10. Develop job requirements matrix and/or job description in usable format → 11. Provide matrix or job description to parties (e.g., incumbents, managers, HR department) → 12. Use matrix or job description in staffing activities, such as communicating with recruits and recruiters, developing the selection plan →

information, observation, and interviews) and multiple sources (job analyst, job incumbents, and supervisors). A previous job holder (SME) conducted the job analysis and prepared a written job description as the output of the process, which took about 20 hours over a 30-day period.

COMPETENCY MODELING

Job requirements analysis was originally developed in the first half of the twentieth century to catalog the requirements for well-defined job roles with very specific and observable characteristics that would be the same across many organizations. As the pace of change increased, new technology rendered many of these jobs obsolete, and organizations adopted more flexible roles; thus, the relevance of job requirements analysis came into question.[27] As a result, the competency-based type of job analysis came into being. Competency models reflect a desire to (1) underscore the importance of behavior to organizational strategy, (2) evaluate KSAOs that extend across multiple jobs, (3) increase flexibility in job design and job assignments, and (4) make it easier to adapt jobs to a changing organizational context.

Overview

The chief difference between job requirements analysis and competency modeling is the direction of information flow. The job requirements analysis begins by looking at very specific tasks and then aggregates these from the bottom up to form jobs and job categories that are found throughout an organization. Due to its linkage with overall organizational capacities, competency modeling has become closely aligned with the strategic perspective on HR management. Because of this explicit link to organizational strategy, and the use of terminology that is consistent with strategic plans, most job analysts find that executives are much more supportive of competency-based analysis relative to job requirements analysis.[28]

Many techniques have been developed over time that facilitate competency modeling, such that it has progressively become a much more rigorous approach than it once was.[29] Ironically, the net result is that competency modeling has come to incorporate many of the practices used in job requirements analysis. Competency analysis begins by considering the organization's internal and external environments and then determines how each job corresponds to the associated strategic goals. Competency models should explicitly consider the organizational context. This is a key point, because the top-down approach of competency modeling makes it much easier to address how jobs fit together and complement one another to produce goods and services compared with the task focus of job requirements analysis. Finally, because competency models are tied to the organization's strategy, requirements can change over time. Competencies should be sufficiently general to address both present and future organizational needs.

Nature of Competencies

A competency is an underlying characteristic of an individual that contributes to role performance and to organizational success.[30] Competencies specific to a particular job are the familiar KSAO requirements established through job requirements analysis. Competency requirements may extend beyond job-specific ones to those of multiple jobs, general job categories, or the entire organization. These competencies are much more general or generic KSAOs, such as technical expertise or adaptability. A competency model is a combination of the several competencies deemed necessary for a particular job or role.

Despite the strong similarities between competencies and KSAOs, there are two notable differences. First, competencies may be job spanning, meaning that they contribute to success in multiple jobs. Members of a work team, for example, may each hold specific jobs within the team but may be subject to job-spanning competency requirements, such as adaptability and teamwork orientation. Such requirements ensure that team members will interact successfully with one another and will even perform portions of others' jobs if necessary. As another example, competency requirements may span jobs within the same category, such as sales jobs or managerial jobs. All sales jobs may have product knowledge as a competency requirement, and all managerial jobs may require planning and results orientation. Such requirements allow for greater flexibility in job placements and job assignments within the category.

Second, competencies serve to align requirements of all jobs with the mission and goals of the organization. A job requirements analysis can easily miss out on these broader features. A restaurant, for example, may have "customer focus" as a defining characteristic that contributes to competitive advantage. Customer service orientation should therefore be a competency requirement for all jobs as a way of indicating that servicing customer needs is a key component of all jobs. Research has shown that diversity-related organizational outcomes can be enhanced by incorporating diversity management as a job-spanning competency.[31]

Competency Example

An illustration of the competency approach to job requirements is shown in Exhibit 4.11. The Green Care Corporation produces several lawn maintenance products. The organization is in a highly competitive industry. To survive and grow, its core mission consists of product innovation and product reliability; its goals are to achieve 10% annual growth in revenues and 2% growth in market share. To help fulfill its mission and goals, the organization has established four general (strategic) workforce competencies—creativity/innovation, technical expertise, customer focus, and results orientation. These requirements are part of every job in the organization. At the business unit (gas lawn mowers) level, the organization has also established job-specific and job-spanning requirements. Some jobs, such as design engineer, are traditional or slowly evolving jobs and, as such, have only job-specific KSAO or

EXHIBIT 4.11 Examples of Competencies

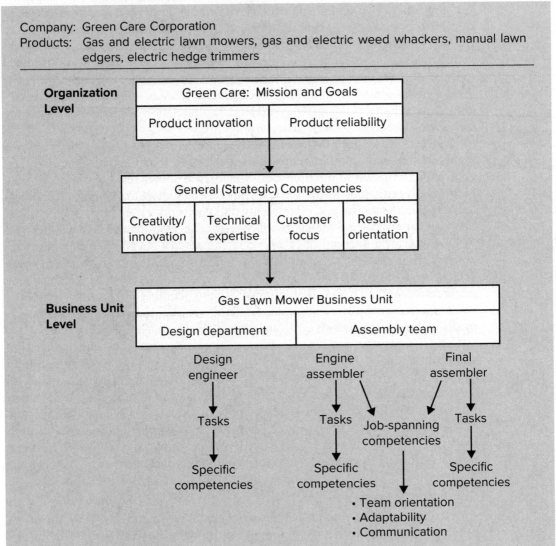

Company: Green Care Corporation
Products: Gas and electric lawn mowers, gas and electric weed whackers, manual lawn edgers, electric hedge trimmers

Organization Level

Green Care: Mission and Goals

Product innovation | Product reliability

General (Strategic) Competencies

Creativity/innovation | Technical expertise | Customer focus | Results orientation

Business Unit Level

Gas Lawn Mower Business Unit

Design department | Assembly team

Design engineer → Tasks → Specific competencies

Engine assembler → Tasks → Specific competencies

Job-spanning competencies

Final assembler → Tasks → Specific competencies

- Team orientation
- Adaptability
- Communication

competency requirements. Because the products are assembled via team processes, jobs within the assembly team (such as engine assembler or final assembler) have both job-specific and job-spanning competency requirements. The job-spanning competencies—team orientation, adaptability, and communication—are general and behavioral. They are necessary because of task interdependence between engine assembly and final assembly jobs and because employees may be shifted between the two jobs in order to cover sudden employee shortages due to unscheduled absences and to maintain smooth production flows. Each job in the business unit thus has four general competency requirements, multiple job-specific competency requirements, and where appropriate, job-spanning competency requirements.

Organization Usage

Organizations have increasingly developed competency models and have used them as the underpinnings of several HR applications.[32] Research indicates that the experimentation is occurring in organizations of all sizes, but especially in large ones. The three key strategic HR reasons for doing competency modeling are to (1) create awareness and understanding of the need for change in business, (2) enhance skill levels in the workforce, and (3) improve teamwork and coordination.

Most of the emphasis has been on establishing general competencies, as illustrated by the "Great Eight" competencies used in one framework, or strategic competencies identified in another framework that combined information from leaders in multiple organizations.[33]

The "Great Eight" competencies are as follows:

- Leading (initiates action, gives direction)
- Supporting (shows respect, puts people first)
- Presenting (communicates and networks effectively)
- Analyzing (thinks clearly, applies expertise)
- Creating (thinks broadly, handles situations creatively)
- Organizing (plans ahead, follows rules)
- Adapting (responds to change, copes with setbacks)
- Performing (focuses on results, shows understanding of organization)

The strategic competencies are as follows:

- Visioning (establishes and communicates a long-term view)
- Alignment (considers multiple stakeholder perspectives in determining strategic direction)
- Environmental awareness (understands external business influences)
- Assessment and evaluation (uses economic, financial, industry, and customer data to identify opportunities)
- Strategy creation (meets evolving goals and objectives)
- Plan development (links objectives with plans for implementation)
- Implementation (executes plans)

Competency models are being used for many HR applications, especially staffing, career development, performance management, and compensation. Pertaining to staffing, one important application is in HR and staffing planning. Here, workforce requirements are specified in competency terms and compared with current workforce competency levels to identify competency gaps. Such comparisons may be particularly appropriate in replacement and succession planning. Another important staffing application is in external and internal selection, where applicants are assessed not only for job-specific competencies but also for general competencies. For external hiring, competency-based interviews with applicants are conducted to gauge general competencies as a key factor in selection decisions and in job placement decisions for new incumbents. For promotion decisions, competency-based interviews are used in conjunction with supervisory assessments of promotability.[34]

Collecting Competency Information

General competencies at the organizational (strategic) level are established by top management, with guidance from strategic HR managers.[35] At a minimum, effective establishment of general competency requirements would seem to demand the following. First, it is crucial that the organization articulate its mission and goals prior to determining competency requirements. Clarity at this level ensures that general competencies are derived from knowledge of mission and goals, much as job-specific competencies are derived from previously identified job tasks. Second, the general competencies should be truly important at all job levels so that their usage as job requirements will focus and align all jobs with the organization's mission and goals. This principle also holds in the case where general competency requirements are at the strategic business unit or subunit level instead of at the organizational level. Third, all general competencies should have specific behavioral definitions, not just labels. These definitions provide substance, meaning, and guidance to all concerned.

For job-spanning competencies, these definitions will necessarily be more task specific. It is crucial to know the major tasks for which the competencies are to be established, meaning that some form of job requirements analysis should occur first. Internal and external SMEs familiar with all the jobs or roles to which the competencies will apply should be part of the process. Definitions of the competencies will also be necessary. Training programs can improve the quality of competency information.[36] Establishing a common frame of reference across raters has been shown to improve accuracy of job analyses in extensive reviews of the results across studies (i.e., meta-analysis). In one instance, managers who attended a program that included an explanation of the competency modeling approach, specific guidance in translating the required behaviors of a role into competencies, and feedback on the quality of practice exercises produced competency data that were more accurate, more detailed, and more consistent across raters relative to competency data produced by managers who had not received training.

When competency modeling first appeared, staffing experts expressed concern about the lack of agreement across multiple raters when evaluating the same job's competencies. One rater might claim that a job entails a high level of interpersonal skill, while another might emphasize the analytical demands of the job. Increasingly, it has been recognized that this inconsistency might be an accurate reflection of the many ways people can do the same job.[37] In particular, in complex jobs with high levels of personal autonomy and discretion, different job incumbents engage in completely different behaviors requiring completely different skills. Competency data may be more likely to show differences across raters than job requirements analysis because competency analysis is more likely to focus on complex jobs with high autonomy. Indeed, evidence suggests that decisions based on well-designed and implemented competency-based job analyses can be as rigorous and accurate as those based on job requirements approaches.[38]

Example of Competency Modeling Process

Similar to our previous example of a job requirements analysis in Exhibit 4.10, an example of competency modeling is presented in Exhibit 4.12. A number of

EXHIBIT 4.12   Example of Competency Modeling

1. Evaluate organizational strategy and goals with executive team
2. Consult lists from existing competency models to establish a baseline for comparison
3. Develop initial set of organization-spanning competencies with executive team
4. Interview business-unit-level directors to develop initial set of job-spanning competencies
5. Interview managers and supervisors to develop initial set of job-specific competencies
6. Evaluate fit across levels of competencies and identify areas of potential inconsistency
7. Develop systems and hierarchies of relationships among competencies
8. Revise competency statements in conjunction with executives and directors
9. Create competency system in easily interpreted format across organizational, unit, and job levels
10. Provide competency system information to all parties, including executives, directors, and managers
11. Incorporate competency system into plans for internal career development and promotion
12. Use competency-based system in staffing activities including recruiting, selection, and placement

key differences are immediately apparent. Unlike the job requirements approach, which can focus on a single job category, the competency-based approach is usually conducted at the organizational level and incorporates a large variety of jobs. The vital importance of coordinating competencies across levels of the organization is reflected in the meetings involving executives, business unit directors, and supervisors. In the end, a competency-based approach will focus on an entire system of relationships across levels, so ensuring consistency and coherence is a key concern. As one might expect, conducting this sort of whole-organization analysis is more time-consuming than analyzing a single predefined role, especially in terms of executive time involvement. This additional effort is justified if the final product helps integrate the organization's strategic goals and objectives with the whole HR management system.

JOB REWARDS ANALYSIS

In the person/job match model, jobs are composed of requirements and rewards. The focus so far in this chapter has been on job requirements and competencies vis-a-vis the discussion of job analysis. Attention now turns to job rewards. Providing and using rewards is a key staffing strategy for meeting the person demands side of the person/job and person/organization match. Successfully matching the rewards with what employees desire will be critical in attaining HR outcomes.

Types of Rewards

Rewards are commonly classified as either extrinsic or intrinsic in nature. Extrinsic rewards are tangible factors provided to job incumbents (e.g., pay, benefits, work schedule, advancement, job security) as a way to make the job more attractive. Intrinsic rewards are the intangibles that are more internal to the job itself and experienced by the employee as an outgrowth of actually doing the job and being a member of the organization (e.g., variety in work duties, autonomy, feedback, coworker and supervisor relations).[39]

The extrinsic rewards of jobs are usually more objectively verifiable and can serve as a strong selling point to those outside the organization. Extrinsic rewards are also valuable because they can offset less pleasant parts of jobs. The evidence on the effects of extrinsic rewards is clear: pay, benefits, and other outcomes of work are strongly associated with applicant attraction, motivation, and retention. There is, at the same time, equally clear evidence that intrinsic rewards have positive effects as well. Intrinsically rewarding job tasks are the best predictors of engagement at work. Intrinsic and extrinsic rewards are not an either-or proposition when it comes to making jobs attractive: the most effective HR systems combine both.[40]

Employee Value Proposition

The totality of rewards, both extrinsic and intrinsic, associated with the job constitutes the employee value proposition (EVP).[41] The EVP is akin to the "package" or "bundle" of rewards provided to employees and to which employees respond by joining, performing for, and remaining with the organization. It is the "deal" or "bargain" struck between the organization and the employee, first as a promise to the prospective employee and later as a reality to the actual new employee. The EVP thus functions as the glue that binds the employee and the organization.

The challenge to the organization is to create EVPs for various employee groups that, on average, are both attractive and affordable (how to create an individual EVP in the form of a formal job offer to a prospective employee is considered in the final match chapter). No reward, extrinsic or intrinsic, is costless; the organization must figure out what it can afford as it creates its EVPs. The dual affordability-attractiveness requirements for EVPs highlight the need to determine the right magnitude, right mix, and right distinctiveness of the rewards of a job.[42] Right magnitude refers to a package of rewards that is large enough to attract and retain workers but not so great that it causes strain on the organization's financial or operational system. A package of rewards that is seen as inadequate or noncompetitive can have negative effects at any stage of the staffing process. Such perceptions may arise very early in the applicant's job search, before the organization is even aware of the applicant, due to word of mouth, online feedback, or electronic recruitment information. Alternatively, an inadequate rewards package may become an issue later in the job search process, as the offer and negotiation process unfolds. Either way, the perception that the EVP is not met can be a deal killer that leads the person to self-select out of consideration for the job, turn down the job, or quit. Conversely, an appropriate rewards package requires an eye to financial and operational issues. An overly generous rewards package creates affordability problems for the organization. High wages and exorbitant benefits are a direct drain on financial health. Overly loose scheduling and autonomy can create coordination problems, undermining productivity. These problems may be particularly acute in service organizations, where compensation and benefits costs are a substantial percentage of total operating costs and the human factor is a major determinant of employee motivation.

Above and beyond the magnitude of rewards, the mix of rewards is also worth consideration. A good mix refers to a situation in which the composition of the rewards package is in sync with the preferences of prospective or current employees. A package that provides excellent retirement benefits, long-term performance incentives, and job security is likely to be more attractive to more experienced employees who are seeking stable employment. A package that provides opportunities for constant travel, a competitive environment, and extensive skill development is a more appealing mix for new labor market entrants.

Finally, rewards packages should be distinctive, helping to build an employer brand.[43] Organizations often compete for employees by providing rewards that are not otherwise available. For example, companies in the fashion industry give their employees deep discounts on clothing and accessories that would not be easy to acquire from other companies. Some companies provide opportunities for high-performing employees to develop relationships with high-powered mentors within and outside the organization. Still others give employees a chance to contribute their time and energy to devote paid hours to nonprofit organizations that fit with the mission and values of employees. From these examples, it should be obvious that there are many very different ways for organizations to be distinctive; no two ways of being unique are quite the same!

Collecting Job Rewards Information

Learning about job rewards involves looking both within and outside the organization. Armed with knowledge about employee preferences and perceived rewards, the organization can begin to build EVPs that are of the right magnitude, mix, and distinctiveness. A meaningful job rewards analysis must be specific to each job category for assessing person/job fit. A broader approach to assessing job rewards distributed across the organization as a whole can address issues of person/organization fit.

Within the Organization

The two most prominent sources of information for learning about job rewards are interviews and surveys.

Interviews.   The interview approach requires decisions about who will guide the process, interview content, sampling confidentiality, data recording and analysis, and reporting of the results. The following are a few suggestions to guide each of those decisions. First, a person with special expertise in the employee interview process should guide the total process. This could be a person within the HR department, a person outside HR with the expertise (such as in marketing research), or an outside consultant.

Second, the interviews should be structured and guided. The major content areas and specific questions should be decided in advance, tested on a small sample of employees as to their clarity and wording, and then placed in a formal interview protocol to be used by the interviewer. Potential questions are shown in Exhibit 4.13. Note that the major content areas covered in the interview are rewards offered, reward magnitude, reward mix, and reward distinctiveness.

Third, employees from throughout the organization should be part of the sample. In small organizations, it might be possible to include all employees; in larger organizations, random samples of employees will be necessary. When sampling, include employees from all job categories, organizational units, and organizational levels.

EXHIBIT 4.13 Examples of Job Rewards Interview Questions

Rewards Offered
- What are the most rewarding elements of your job? Consider both the work itself and the pay and benefits associated with your job.
- Looking ahead, are there any changes you can think of that would make your job more rewarding?

Reward Magnitude
- Overall, do you think the level of complexity and challenge in your job is too much, too little, or about right, compared with that of other jobs in the organization?
- Describe the amount of potential for growth and development in your job.
- Do you feel like the pay and benefits provided for your job are adequate for the work you do? If not, what would you change?

Reward Mix
- If you could change the mix of rewards provided in your job, what would you add?
- Of the rewards associated with your job, which two are the most important to you?
- What types of rewards associated with your job are irrelevant to you?

Reward Distinctiveness
- Which rewards that you receive in your job are you most likely to tell others about?
- Which of our rewards really stand out to you? To job applicants?
- What rewards could we start offering that would be unique?

Fourth, the interviews should be confidential, so the responses of individuals should be seen only by those recording and analyzing the data. At the same time, it would be useful to gather (with their permission) interviewees' demographic information and organizational information (e.g., job title, organizational unit) since this will permit breakouts of responses during data analysis. Such breakouts will be very useful in decisions about whether to create separate EVPs for separate employee groups or organizational units.

Surveys. A survey of employees should proceed along the same lines as the employee interview process, following many of the same recommendations. The biggest difference is the mechanism for gathering the data—namely, a written set of questions with response scales rather than a verbally administered set of questions with open-ended responses. To construct the survey, a listing of rewards must be developed. These could be chosen from a listing of the job's current extrinsic and intrinsic rewards or derived from focus groups and interviews. An example of a partial employee reward preferences survey is shown in Exhibit 4.14. Questions

EXHIBIT 4.14 Example of Job Rewards Survey

To what extent are the following job rewards important to you?

	Not at All Important	Unimportant	Somewhat Important	Important	Very Important
Extrinsic Rewards					
Base pay	1	2	3	4	5
Incentive pay	1	2	3	4	5
Health insurance	1	2	3	4	5
Intrinsic Rewards					
Using my skills	1	2	3	4	5
Doing significant tasks	1	2	3	4	5
Relationships with coworkers	1	2	3	4	5

To what extent does your job provide the following rewards to you?

	Very Low Extent	Low Extent	Moderate Extent	High Extent	Very High Extent
Extrinsic Rewards					
Base pay	1	2	3	4	5
Incentive pay	1	2	3	4	5
Health insurance	1	2	3	4	5
Intrinsic Rewards					
Using my skills	1	2	3	4	5
Doing significant tasks	1	2	3	4	5
Relationships with coworkers	1	2	3	4	5

involve both extrinsic and intrinsic rewards and ask about the importance of various rewards as well as the extent to which each job provides these rewards.

As with interviews, a person with special expertise should guide the project, sampling should include employees throughout the organization, employees should be assured of confidentiality, results should be thoroughly analyzed, and reports of the findings should be prepared for organizational representatives.

Which to Use?   Should the organization opt to use interviews, surveys, or both? Interviews are certainly more personal; employees are allowed to respond in their own words. Questions can probe individual perceptions regarding reward magnitude, mix, and distinctiveness. The resulting data provide insights beyond mere rating-scale responses. On the downside, interviews are costly to schedule and conduct, data analysis is messy and time-consuming, and statistical summaries and analysis of the data are difficult. Surveys are easier to administer (especially online), and they permit statistical summaries and analyses that are very helpful in interpreting responses. Unfortunately, surveys cannot reveal information that the survey designer did not know about.

Assuming adequate resources and expertise, a combined interview and survey approach would be best. This would allow the organization to capitalize on the unique strengths of each approach, as well as offset some of the weaknesses of each. In such cases, interviews usually are done first and then the information gathered from the open-ended responses is used as a springboard to develop specific survey questions.

A final cautionary note is that both interviews and surveys of current employees miss out on two other groups from whom reward preference information would be useful. The first group is departing or departed employees, who may have left due to dissatisfaction with the EVP. The retention management chapter discusses the exit interview as a procedure for learning about this group. The second group is potential job applicants. Presumably the organization could conduct interviews and surveys with this group, but that could be administratively challenging (especially with Internet applicants). Additionally, applicants might feel they are "tipping their hand" to the organization in terms of what they desire or would accept in a job offer. The more common way to learn about applicant reward preferences is from surveys of employees outside the organization, who might represent the types of applicants the organization will encounter.

Outside the Organization

Other Employees.   Data on the reward preferences of employees outside the organization are available from surveys of employees in other organizations. To the extent these employees are similar to the organization's own applicants and employees, the data will likely provide a useful barometer of preferences. An example is the Job Satisfaction survey routinely conducted by the Society for Human Resource

Management (SHRM). Employees rated the importance of several extrinsic and intrinsic rewards. The most frequently endorsed rewards are shown in Exhibit 4.15.

As in most surveys of this type, a mix of both intrinsic and extrinsic factors is apparent. Many of the top intrinsic factors have to do with the social environment; like communication, trust, and respect. On the extrinsic side, wages, benefits, and security all rank high in importance. It is also clear that there is a substantial difference between the percentage of employees rating a factor as "very important" and the percentage rating themselves as "very satisfied" with that factor.

EXHIBIT 4.15   **"Very Important" Versus "Very Satisfied" Aspects of Employee Job Satisfaction**

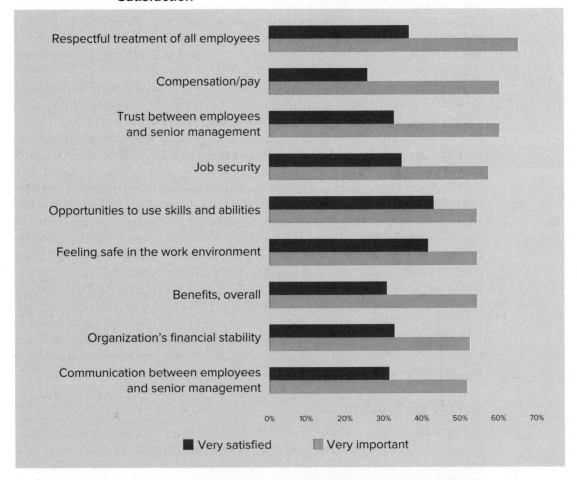

SOURCE: Society for Human Resource Management, *2017 Employee Job Satisfaction and Engagement* (Alexandria, VA: author).

One other important finding stands out from large-scale surveys of employers and employees. When HR professionals are asked to predict the importance that employees attach to rewards, the HR professionals' predictions often do not correspond all that closely to the actual employee ratings.

Another way to gather information about external employee preferences is to check online message boards and discussions. Discussions of the best and worst features of an organization are easy to find. Websites such as GlassDoor or LinkedIn provide a rich database of information about how an organization is perceived and what people are looking for. This online word of mouth may be difficult to manage and frustrating to read (your most disgruntled employees are probably more likely to vent online), but it can also be one of the best ways to learn how people really talk about your jobs and give organizational leaders ideas for how to improve these external perceptions.

Organizational Practices.   A less direct way to assess the importance of rewards to employees is to examine the actual rewards that other organizations provide their employees. The assumption here is that these organizations are attuned to their employees' preferences and try to provide rewards that are consistent with them. Since pay and benefits loom large in most employees' reward preferences, it is particularly important to become knowledgeable of other organizations' pay and benefit practices to assist in the development of the EVP.

The single best source of pay and benefit information comes from the National Compensation Survey, conducted by the Bureau of Labor Statistics (BLS) within the Department of Labor (*www.bls.gov/ncs/*). The pay part of the survey reports average pay for employees, broken out by occupation, private-public sector, organization size, and geographic area. The benefits part of the survey presents detailed data about the percentage of employees who have access to a benefit or are provided an average level of benefits. Data on the following benefits are provided: retirement, health care coverage (medical, dental, and vision) and required employee contributions, short- and long-term disability, paid holidays, paid vacation, child care, flexible workplace, wellness programs, and several others. The data are broken out by occupation, industry, and geographic area.

Another important source of information about benefits is the Society for Human Resource Management Annual Benefits Survey (*www.shrm.com*). It provides very detailed information about specific benefits provided in each of the following areas: family friendliness, housing and relocation, health care and wellness, personal services, finances, business travel, leave, and other benefits. The data are broken out by organization size.

Expert Opinion.   There is a large body of research that has been assembled and cited throughout this book coming from researchers in both the private and public sectors, including consultants and professors. The information from these studies, nearly all of which is derived from real organizational settings, has the advantage of being gathered systematically and with an eye to rigorously evaluating the causal relationship between job rewards and employee attitudes and behavior. Similar information regarding the rewards researchers have found associated with jobs is in O*NET. Every job in O*NET has accompanying salary information. There is also a set of work values associated with each job, evaluating the extent to which a job provides intrinsic rewards like achievement, independence, recognition, relationships, support, and working conditions. Expert opinion may be rigorous but has the disadvantage of being assembled from sources that may not be similar to your own organization. Results from statistical studies across a variety of settings will need to be supplemented with information from your own organization's employees.

LEGAL ISSUES

Job analysis plays a crucial role in establishing the foundations for staffing activities, and that role continues from a legal perspective. Job analysis becomes intimately involved in court cases involving the job relatedness of staffing activities. It also occupies a prominent position in the Uniform Guidelines on Employee Selection Procedures (UGESP). Additionally, the Americans With Disabilities Act (ADA) requires that the organization determine the essential functions of each job, and job analysis can play a pivotal role in that process. The job requirements matrix and its development are very relevant to these issues.

Job Relatedness and Court Cases

In equal employment opportunity and affirmative action (EEO/AA) court cases, the organization is confronted with the need to justify its challenged staffing practices as being job related. Common sense suggests that this requires the organization to conduct some type of job analysis to identify job requirements. If the case involves an organization's defense of its selection procedures, the UGESP requires conducting a job analysis. In addition, specific features or characteristics of the job analysis make a difference in the organization's defense. Specifically, an examination of court cases indicates that for purposes of legal defensibility the organization should conform to the following recommendations:

1. "Job analysis must be performed and must be for the job for which the selection instrument is to be utilized.
2. Analysis of the job should be in writing.
3. Job analysts should describe in detail the procedure used.
4. Job data should be collected from a variety of current sources by knowledgeable job analysts.
5. Sample size should be large and representative of the jobs for which the selection instrument is used.

6. Tasks, duties, and activities should be included in the analysis.
7. The most important tasks should be represented in the selection device.
8. Competency levels of job performance for entry-level jobs should be specified.
9. Knowledge, skills, and abilities should be specified, particularly if a content validation model is followed."[44]

These recommendations are consistent with our view of job analysis as the basic foundation for staffing activities. Moreover, even though these recommendations were made many years ago, there is little reason to doubt or modify any of them on the basis of more recent court cases.

Essential Job Functions

Recall that under the ADA, the organization must not discriminate against a qualified individual with a disability who can perform the "essential functions" of the job, with or without reasonable accommodation. This requirement raises three questions: What are essential functions? What is the evidence of essential functions? What is the role of job analysis?

Essential Functions

The ADA employment regulations provide the following statements about essential functions:

1. "The term essential functions refers to the fundamental job duties of the employment position the individual with a disability holds or desires. The term essential function does not include the marginal functions of the position; and
2. A job function may be considered essential for any of several reasons, including but not limited to the following:
   • The function may be essential because the reason the position exists is to perform the function;
   • The function may be essential because of the limited number of employees available among whom the performance of that job function can be distributed; and/or
   • The function may be highly specialized so that the incumbent in the position is hired for their expertise or ability to perform the particular function."

Evidence of Essential Functions

The employment regulations go on to indicate what constitutes evidence that any particular function is in fact an essential one. Exhibit 4.16 shows the major types of evidence, along with examples and explanations. Other evidence might also be used.

EXHIBIT 4.16   Types of Essential Job Function Evidence

- The employer's judgment. Is this a "must do" task or expected result? An employer requires a customer service representative to handle customer complaints and resolve them within one week.

- A written job description prepared before advertising or interviewing job applicants. Identify the most important—essential—functions of the job.

- Amount of time spent performing the job. The higher the percentage of work time spent on a task or function, the more likely it is essential.

- The consequences of not requiring a person to perform a task. There may be pre-surgery protocols for ensuring patient safety, and not requiring nurses to follow the protocols could threaten patient safety and surgical outcomes.

- The terms of a collective bargaining agreement. The CBA may contain job descriptions or duties.

- The work experience of previous or current employees on the job. Learning which tasks are done can help identify which tasks are essential.

Role of Job Analysis

Behind each of the evidence types lies some type of implicit, informal job analysis. In this sense the regulations touch on job analysis. The separate technical assistance manual from the Equal Employment Opportunity Commission mentions, and provides examples of, more formal job analysis that might be done to help identify essential job functions. It makes four major points about such job analysis.[45] First, while job analysis is not required by law as a means of establishing the essential functions of a job, it is strongly recommended. Second, the job analysis should focus on tasks associated with the job. Where KSAOs are studied or specified, they should be derived from an explicit consideration of their probable links to the essential tasks. Third, with regard to tasks, the focus should be on the tasks themselves and their outcome or results, rather than the methods by which they are performed. Finally, the job analysis should be useful in identifying potential reasonable accommodations.[46]

SUMMARY

Organizations design jobs to fit their strategic and operational needs. As the internal and external environments change, jobs change, and ways to continually assess how to match work needs to jobs are required. This is where different forms of job analysis come in. Job analysis is described as the process used to gather, analyze, synthesize, and report information about job content. The job requirements approach to job analysis focuses on job-specific tasks, KSAOs, and job context. Competency modeling seeks to identify more general KSAOs that apply across jobs and roles. The job rewards approach focuses on understanding the outcomes of work for employees.

The job requirements approach is guided by the job requirements matrix. The matrix calls for information about tasks and task dimensions, as well as their importance. In a parallel fashion, it requires information about KSAOs necessary for the tasks, plus indications about the importance of those KSAOs. The final component of the matrix deals with numerous elements of the job context.

Competency modeling seeks to identify general competencies (KSAOs) necessary for all jobs because the competencies support the organization's mission and goals. Within work units, other general competencies (job-spanning KSAOs) may also be established that cut across multiple jobs. Techniques and processes for collecting competency information were suggested.

Jobs offer a variety of rewards, both extrinsic and intrinsic. The totality of these rewards constitutes the EVP. To help form EVPs, it is necessary to collect information about employee reward preferences and rewards given to employees at other organizations. Numerous techniques for doing this are available.

From a legal perspective, job analysis is very important in creating staffing systems and practices that comply with EEO/AA laws and regulations. The employer must ensure (or be able to show) that its practices are job related. This requires not only conducting a job requirements analysis but also using a process that itself has defensible characteristics. Under the ADA, the organization must identify the essential functions of the job. Though this does not require a job analysis, the organization should strongly consider it as one of the tools to be used.

DISCUSSION QUESTIONS

1. What is the purpose of each type of job analysis, and how can the three types described in this chapter be combined to produce an overall understanding of work in an organization?

2. How should task statements be written, and what sorts of problems might you encounter in asking a job incumbent to write these statements?

3. Would it be better to first identify task dimensions and then create specific task statements for each dimension, or should task statements be identified first and then used to create task dimensions?

4. What would you consider when deciding what criteria (e.g., percentage of time spent) to use for gathering indications about task importance?

5. What are the advantages and disadvantages of using multiple methods of job analysis for a particular job? Multiple sources?

6. What are the advantages and disadvantages of identifying and using general competencies to guide staffing activities?

7. Referring back to Exhibit 4.15, why do you think employees tend to be only moderately satisfied with many of the job rewards that are most important to them? What are the implications for creating the EVP?

ETHICAL ISSUES

1. It has been suggested that ethical conduct be formally incorporated as a general competency requirement for any job within the organization. Discuss the pros and cons of this suggestion.

2. Assume you are assisting in the conduct of job analysis as an HR department representative. You have encountered several managers who want to delete certain tasks and KSAOs from the formal job description that have to do with employee safety, even though they clearly are job requirements. How should you handle this situation?

APPLICATIONS

Integrating Competencies and Job Requirements

The analysis of work for staffing requires attention to both person/organization and person/job matches. Staffing specialists and HR executives can put these pieces together by becoming knowledgeable about both top-down (competency) and bottom-up (job requirements) methods of analyzing work.

To understand this process, select an organization you are familiar with. It can be your school, your workplace, or an organization where you would like to work. Within that workplace, identify at least three different jobs at various levels as a starting point. For example, you might study administrative staff, professors, and deans at a university; customer service representatives, managers, and executives in a retail environment; waitstaff, cooks, and managers at a restaurant; nurses, doctors, and administrators at a hospital, and so on.

To conduct the competency portion of the analysis, review the material in the chapter and create a plan for learning about job-spanning competencies. Determine who is most likely to have the relevant information and, if possible, contact at least three people in the organization who can provide relevant information on competencies. Pay particular attention to the organization's strategic goals, mission, and cultural profile when collecting this information. This information can be supplemented by looking at the organization's website or annual reports.

To conduct the job requirements portion of the analysis, again review the relevant material in the chapter and create a plan for learning about job requirements and their associated KSAOs. If possible, contact at least three people in the organization who can describe their own jobs. Pay particular attention to the tasks individuals complete regularly, evaluate the relative proportion or time of each task, and then match tasks to KSAOs. This information can be supplemented by looking at O*NET.

Once you have the information on competencies and job requirements, evaluate the following questions:

1. What differences did you find in the process of collecting information? Did you identify different KSAOs from your competency model relative to your job requirements analysis?
2. How does job requirements information give additional insight above and beyond what you learned from competency modeling? How does competency modeling give additional insight above and beyond what you learned from job requirements information?
3. How would you use the information you have gathered for developing recruiting, selection, and retention strategies?

Designing a Job Rewards Analysis

CleanBody Organics is a national distributor of natural soap, moisturizers, and shampoo and conditioner. It has a brick-and-mortar store in Asheville, North Carolina, which serves as a conduit for learning more about its customers, but the majority of its sales are from online distribution. As the organization expands, it has decided to supplement its previous strategic profile of directly selling to consumers with plans to also distribute its products in co-ops and organic grocery stores.

The greatest concern in the planned expansion is ensuring that new employees have a strong sense of engagement and cultural values similar to those of current employees. The company's CEO, Eve Libertine, wants to find out what motivates her current workforce, in hopes that she can use this message to hire and retain individuals with similar values and motivations in the future. As an astute student of staffing best practices, you have recommended that a careful job rewards analysis is a good way to achieve this goal.

Ms. Libertine has three key job categories that she wants to focus her analysis on. The first job is customer consultant, which other organizations refer to as a customer service representative. Individuals in this job respond to calls, e-mails, and online chats from customers with questions or complaints about products. This is a key job for the organization because of the large number of individuals occupying this role, as well as the strategic importance of maintaining customer satisfaction. The second job is a product development manager. These individuals are currently responsible for learning about the market for CleanBody products and will have an expanded role in determining how to market products to other retailers. The third job is in production work. Individuals in this job make, cut, pack, and ship the soap, along with performing associated production-area tasks like keeping records and cleaning production areas. This is another job that is expected to greatly expand in numbers as the push into retail sales increases.

1. Find three job titles on O*NET that are relatively similar to the jobs at CleanBody and identify the interests, work styles, and values that are compatible with these jobs.
2. Based on the overall culture of the organization, describe three or four key goals or values that may intrinsically motivate individuals to work at CleanBody.
3. Develop three to five questions for an open-ended survey sent out to current CleanBody employees that will help refine your understanding of job rewards.

ENDNOTES

1. J. I. Sanchez and E. L. Levine, "The Rise and Fall of Job Analysis and the Future of Work Analysis," *Annual Review of Psychology*, 2012, 63, pp. 397–425.
2. F. P. Morgeson, M. T. Brannick, and E. L. Levine, *Job and Work Analysis*, 3rd ed. (Thousand Oaks, CA: Sage, 2020).
3. Morgeson, Brannick, and Levine, *Job and Work Analysis*; S. Krumm, J. Kanthak, K. Hartmann, and G. Hertel, "What Does It Take to Be a Virtual Team Player? The Knowledge, Skills, Abilities, and Other Characteristics Required in Virtual Teams," *Human Performance*, 2016, 29, pp. 123–142.
4. R. J. Vance, *Employee Engagement and Commitment* (Alexandria, VA: Society for Human Resource Management, 2006); J. K. Harter, F. L. Schmidt, and T. L. Hayes, "Business-Unit-Level Relationship Between Employee Satisfaction, Employee Engagement, and Business Outcomes: A Meta-Analysis," *Journal of Applied Psychology*, 2002, 87, pp. 268–279.
5. R. G. Jones, J. I. Sanchez, G. Parameswaran, J. Phelps, C. Shop-taught, M. Williams, and S. White, "Selection or Training? A Two-Fold Test of the Validity of Job-Analytic Ratings of Trainability," *Journal of Business and Psychology*, 2001, 15, pp. 363–389; D. M. Truxillo, M. E. Paronto, M. Collins, and J. L. Sulzer, "Effects of Subject Matter Expert Viewpoint on Job Analysis Results," *Public Personnel Management*, 2004, 33(1), pp. 33–46.
6. M. A. Hitt, S. E. Jackson, S. Carmona, L. Bierman, C. E. Shalley, and D. M. Wright, "The Imperative for Strategy Implementation," in M. A. Hitt, S. E. Jackson, S. Carmona, L. Bierman, C. E. Shalley, and D. M. Wright (eds.), *The Oxford Handbook of Strategy Implementation* (New York: Oxford University Press, 2017) pp. 1–21; D. J. Ketchen, Jr., T. R. Crook, S. Y. Todd, J. G. Combs, and D. J. Woehr, "Managing Human Capital: A Meta-Analysis of Links Among Human Resource Practices and Systems, Human Capital, and Performance," in Hitt, Jackson, Carmona, Bierman, Shalley, and Wright (eds.), *The Oxford Handbook of Strategy Implementation*, pp. 283–310.
7. J. A. Weekley, J. R. Labrador, M. A. Campion, and K. Frye, "Job Analysis Ratings and Criterion-Related Validity: Are They Related and Can Validity Be Used as a Measure of Accuracy?" *Journal of Occupational and Organizational Psychology*, 2019, 92, pp. 764–786; C. P. McAllister, B. P. Ellen, and G. R. Ferris, "Social Influence Opportunity Recognition, Evaluation, and Capitalization: Increased Theoretical Specification Through Political Skill's Dimensional Dynamics," *Journal of Management*, 2018, 44, pp. 1926–1952.

8. M. Kim and T. A. Beehr, "Organization-Based Self-Esteem and Meaningful Work Mediate Effects of Empowering Leadership on Employee Behaviors and Well-Being," *Journal of Leadership & Organizational Studies*, 2018, 25, pp. 385–398; N. A. Bowling, K. J. Eschleman, Q. Wang, C. Kirkendall, and G. Alarcon, "A Meta-Analysis of the Predictors and Consequences of Organization-Based Self-Esteem," *Journal of Occupational and Organizational Psychology*, 2010, 83, pp. 601–626.

9. F. P. Morgeson, M. Spitzmuller, A. S. Garza, and M. A. Campion, "Pay Attention! The Liabilities of Respondent Experience and Carelessness When Making Job Analysis Judgments," *Journal of Management*, 2016, 42, pp. 1904–1933; T. A. Stetz, J. M. Beaubien, M. J. Keeney, and B. D. Lyons, "Nonrandom Response and Variance in Job Analysis Surveys: A Cause for Concern?" *Public Personnel Management*, 2008, 37, pp. 223–241.

10. For excellent overviews and reviews, see Morgeson, Brannick, and Levine, *Job and Work Analysis*; R. D. Gatewood, H. S. Feild, and M. Barrick, *Human Resource Selection*, 9th ed. (Orlando, FL: Harcourt, 2018).

11. E. T. Cornelius III, "Practical Findings From Job Analysis Research," in S. Gael (ed.), *The Job Analysis Handbook for Business, Industry and Government*, Vol. 1 (New York: Wiley, 1988), pp. 48–70.

12. Sanchez and Levine, "The Rise and Fall of Job Analysis and the Future of Work Analysis."

13. C. J. Cranny and M. E. Doherty, "Importance Ratings in Job Analysis: Note on the Misinterpretation of Factor Analysis," *Journal of Applied Psychology*, 1988, 73, pp. 320–322.

14. Sanchez and Levine, "The Rise and Fall of Job Analysis and the Future of Work Analysis."

15. F. P. Morgeson and E. C. Dierdorff, "Work Analysis: From Technique to Theory," in S. Zedeck (ed.), *APA Handbook of Industrial and Organizational Psychology*, Vol. 2 (Washington, DC: American Psychological Association, 2011), pp. 3–41; Sanchez and Levine, "The Rise and Fall of Job Analysis and the Future of Work Analysis."

16. E. C. Dierdorff, "Toward Reviving an Occupation With Occupations," *Annual Review of Organizational Psychology and Organizational Behavior*, 2019, 6, pp. 397–419; N. G. Peterson, M. D. Mumford, W. C. Borman, P. R. Jeanneret, E. A. Fleishman, K. Y. Levin, M. A. Campion, M. S. Mayfield, F. S. Morgeson, K. Pearlman, M. K. Gowing, A. R. Lancaster, M. B. Silver, and D. M. Dye, "Understanding Work Using the Occupational Information Network: Implications for Research and Practice," *Personnel Psychology*, 2001, 54, pp. 451–492.

17. C. C. LaPolice, G. W. Carter, and J. W. Johnson, "Linking O*NET Descriptors to Occupational Literacy Requirements Using Job Component Validation," *Personnel Psychology*, 2008, 61, pp. 405–441.

18. Morgeson, Brannick, and Levine, *Job and Work Analysis*.

19. Morgeson, Brannick, and Levine, *Job and Work Analysis*.

20. Sanchez and Levine, "The Rise and Fall of Job Analysis and the Future of Work Analysis."

21. F. P. Morgeson, K. Delaney-Klinger, M. S. Mayfield, P. Ferrara, and M. A. Campion, "Self-Presentation Processes in Job Analysis: A Field Experiment Investigating Inflation in Abilities, Tasks, and Competencies," *Journal of Applied Psychology*, 2004, 89, pp. 674–686.

22. For detailed treatments, see Morgeson, Brannick, and Levine, *Job and Work Analysis*; M. Mader-Clark, *The Job Description Handbook* (Berkeley, CA: Nolo, 2006).

23. R. Reiter-Palmon, M. Brown, D. L. Sandall, C. B. Buboltz, and T. Nimps, "Development of an O*NET Web-Based Job Analysis and Its Implementation in the U.S. Navy," *Human Resource Management Review*, 2006, 16, pp. 294–309.

24. Morgeson, Brannick, and Levine, *Job and Work Analysis*.

25. P. D. G. Steel and J. D. Kammeyer-Mueller, "Using a Meta-Analytic Perspective to Enhance Job Component Validation," *Personnel Psychology*, 2009, 62, pp. 533–552; P. D. G. Steel, A. I. Huffcutt, and J. D. Kammeyer-Mueller, "From the Work One Knows the Worker: A Systematic Review

of the Challenges, Solutions, and Steps to Creating Synthetic Validity," *International Journal of Selection and Assessment*, 2006, 14, pp. 16-36.

26. V. B. Kobayashi, S. T. Mol, H. A. Berkers, G. Kismihók, and D. N. Den Hartog, "Text Mining in Organizational Research," *Organizational Research Methods*, 2018, 21, pp. 733-765; S. Sajjadiani, A. J. Sojourner, J. D. Kammeyer-Mueller, and E. Mykerezi, "Using Machine Learning to Translate Applicant Work History Into Predictors of Performance and Turnover," *Journal of Applied Psychology*, 2019, 104, pp. 1207-1225.

27. M. C. Campion, D. J. Schepker, M. A. Campion, and J. I. Sanchez, "Competency Modeling: A Theoretical and Empirical Examination of the Strategy Dissemination Process," *Human Resource Management*, 2019, pp. 1-16; G. W. Stevens, "A Critical Review of the Science and Practice of Competency Modeling," *Human Resource Development Review*, 2013, 12, pp. 86-107.

28. M. A. Campion, A. A. Fink, B. J. Ruggeberg, L. Carr, G. M. Phillips, and R. B. Odman, "Doing Competencies Well: Best Practices in Competency Modeling," *Personnel Psychology*, 2011, 64, pp. 225-262.

29. Campion, Fink, Ruggeberg, Carr, Phillips, and Odman, "Doing Competencies Well: Best Practices in Competency Modeling."

30. J. S. Schippman, "Competencies, Job Analysis, and the Next Generation of Modeling," in J. C. Scott and D. H. Reynolds (eds.), *Handbook of Workplace Assessment* (San Francisco: Jossey-Bass, 2010), pp. 197-231; J. S. Schippman, R. A. Ash, M. Battista, L. Carr, L. D. Eyde, B. Hesketh, J. Kehoe, K. Pearlman, E. P. Prien, and J. I. Sanchez, "The Practice of Competency Modeling," *Personnel Psychology*, 2000, 53, pp. 703-740.

31. J. G. Carstens and F. S. De Kock, "Firm-Level Diversity Management Competencies: Development and Initial Validation of a Measure," *International Journal of Human Resource Management*, 2017, 28, pp. 2109-2135.

32. Schippman, "Competencies, Job Analysis, and the Next Generation of Modeling."

33. E. Goldman and A. R. Scott, "Competency Models for Assessing Strategic Thinking," *Journal of Strategy and Management*, 2016, 9, pp. 258-280; D. Bartram, "The Great Eight Competencies: A Criterion-Centric Approach to Validation," *Journal of Applied Psychology*, 2007, 90, pp. 1185-1203.

34. Campion et al., "Doing Competencies Well: Best Practices in Competency Modeling"; Schippman et al., "The Practice of Competency Modeling."

35. Campion et al., "Doing Competencies Well: Best Practices in Competency Modeling"; Schippman et al., "The Practice of Competency Modeling."

36. S. G. Roch, D. J. Woehr, V. Mishra, and U. Kieszczynska, "Rater Training Revisited: An Updated Meta-Analytic Review of Frame-of-Reference Training," *Journal of Occupational and Organizational Psychology*, 2012, 85, pp. 370-395; F. Lievens and J. I. Sanchez, "Can Training Improve the Quality of Inferences Made by Raters in Competency Modeling? A Quasi-Experiment," *Journal of Applied Psychology*, 2007, 92, pp. 812-819.

37. F. Lievens, J. I. Sanchez, D. Bartram, and A. Brown, "Lack of Consensus Among Competency Ratings of the Same Occupation: Noise or Substance?" *Journal of Applied Psychology*, 2010, 95, pp. 562-571; Sanchez and Levine, "The Rise and Fall of Job Analysis and the Future of Work Analysis."

38. V. M. Catano, W. Darr, and C. A. Campbell, "Performance Appraisal of Behavior-Based Competencies: A Reliable and Valid Procedure," *Personnel Psychology*, 2007, 60, pp. 201-230.

39. R. V. Dawis, "Person-Environment Fit and Job Satisfaction," in C. J. Cranny, P. C. Smith, and E. F. Stone (eds.), *Job Satisfaction* (New York: Lexington, 1992), pp. 69-88; G. Ledford, P. Mulvey, and P. LeBlanc, *The Rewards of Work* (Scottsdale, AZ: WorldatWork/Sibson, 2000).

40. B. Gerhart and M. Fang, "Pay, Intrinsic Motivation, Extrinsic Motivation, Performance, and Creativity in the Workplace: Revisiting Long-Held Beliefs," *Annual Review of Organizational Psychology and Organizational Behavior*, 2015, 2, pp. 489-521.

41. E. E. Ledford and M. I. Lucy, *The Rewards of Work* (Los Angeles: Sibson Consulting, 2003).

42. Ledford and Lucy, *The Rewards of Work*, p. 12.

43. S. Milligan, "Use Your Company's Brand to Find the Best Hires," *HR Magazine*, Fall 2019 (*www .shrm.org*).

44. D. E. Thompson and T. A. Thompson, "Court Standards for Job Analysis in Test Validation," *Personnel Psychology*, 1982, 35, pp. 865–874.

45. Equal Employment Opportunity Commission, *Technical Assistance Manual on the Employment Provisions (Title 1) of the Americans With Disabilities Act* (Washington, DC: author, 1992), pp. II-19 to II-21.

46. K. E. Mitchell, G. M. Alliger, and R. Morgfopoulos, "Toward an ADA-Appropriate Job Analysis," *Human Resource Management Review*, 1997, 7, pp. 5–26; F. Lievens, J. I. Sanchez, and W. De Corte, "Easing the Inferential Leap in Competency Modelling: The Effects of Task-Related Information and Subject Matter Expertise," *Personnel Psychology*, 2001, 57, pp. 847–879; Lievens and Sanchez, "Can Training Improve the Quality of Inferences Made by Raters in Competency Modeling: A Quasi-Experiment."

The Staffing Organizations Model

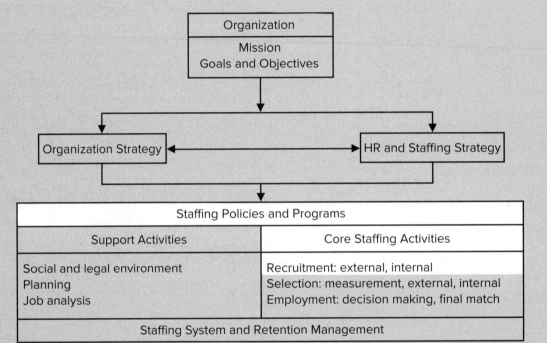

PART THREE

Staffing Activities: Recruitment

CHAPTER FIVE

External Recruitment

Learning Objectives and Introduction
Learning Objectives
Introduction

Strategic Recruitment Planning
Defining Strategic External Recruitment Goals
Open Versus Targeted Recruitment
Organization and Administration

Applicant Reactions
Reactions to Job and Organizational Characteristics
Reactions to Recruiters
Reactions to the Recruitment Process
Diversity and Inclusion

Communication
Communication Message
Communication Media

Applicant Sourcing
Individual Recruitment Sources
Social Recruitment Sources
Organizational Recruitment Sources
Recruitment Metrics

Transition to Selection

Legal Issues
Definition of a Job Applicant
Affirmative Action Programs
Electronic Recruitment
Job Advertisements
Fraud and Misrepresentation

Summary

Discussion Questions

Ethical Issues

Applications
Improving a College Recruitment Program
Internet Recruitment

Endnotes

LEARNING OBJECTIVES AND INTRODUCTION

Learning Objectives

- Engage in strategic recruitment planning activities
- Understand the difference between open and targeted recruitment
- Create a persuasive communication message
- Learn about a variety of recruitment media
- Recognize how applicant reactions influence the effectiveness of a recruitment plan
- Utilize a variety of recruitment sources
- Evaluate recruitment based on established metrics

Introduction

An effective recruitment process is the cornerstone of an effective staffing system. If the recruitment system works, high-quality applicants will be attracted to the organization, the best candidates will be available for selection and eventual hiring, and the organization will have a much easier time reaching its strategic staffing goals. Conversely, if recruitment fails to attract enough qualified applicants, none of the other components of the staffing system can function properly—after all, you cannot hire people who do not apply.

In external recruitment, the organization is trying to sell itself to potential applicants, so many marketing principles are applied to improve recruitment yields. You will learn how recruiters choose from three types of messages—employment brand, targeted, or realistic—to attract the right types of candidates. Over the course of this chapter, you will also learn about advantages and disadvantages of sources of applicants, such as social media, corporate websites, employee referrals, college job fairs, and many others.

The recruitment process begins with a strategic planning phase, during which strategic recruitment goals are defined, a decision is made about whether an open or targeted technique will be employed, and organizational and administrative plans are developed. Following strategy formation, the message to be communicated to job applicants is established, along with the media that will be used to convey the message. Finally, the organization will implement a sourcing strategy, which entails choices about how and where applications will be obtained. Legal concerns include consideration of the definition of job applicant, disclaimers, targeted recruitment, electronic recruitment, job advertisements, and fraud and misrepresentation.

STRATEGIC RECRUITMENT PLANNING

Recruitment is a process that attracts potential future employees who have KSAOs (knowledge, skill, ability, and other characteristics) that will help the organization achieve its strategic goals. If strategic goals are to be fulfilled, each step must flow from the foundation established during the recruitment planning process. Exhibit 5.1 provides an overview of how this process should operate.

Consistent with this model, three issues must be resolved before the organization can begin attracting applicants. First, the organization needs to define its strategic goals for the recruitment process. The needs that were identified in the planning process will guide the process of identifying exactly what types of employees need to be recruited, how quickly these needs will be fulfilled, and the time frame for

EXHIBIT 5.1   Planning, Communicating, and Implementing Strategic Recruitment

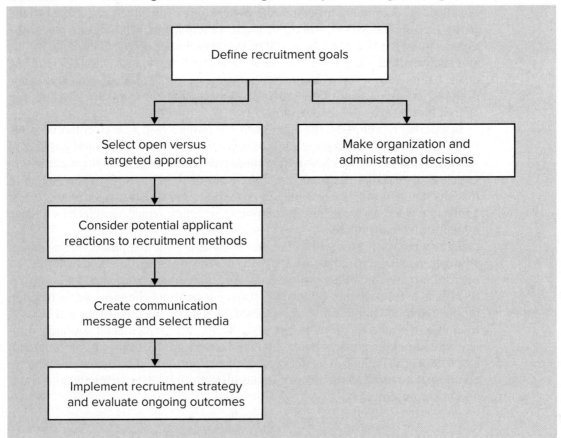

the recruitment process. Next, the organization needs to decide how broadly it will recruit. Finally, organizational and administrative issues need to be considered, including who will do the recruitment and budgeting.

Defining Strategic External Recruitment Goals

Defining strategic goals for the process can ensure that the organization can concentrate its efforts on applicants who will contribute most to overall organizational success.[1] These goals include attracting the right types of applicants, getting the right number of applicants, and having applicants ready at the right time.

Goal 1: The Right Types of Applicants

Knowing how to recruit effectively and strategically begins by knowing the organization's current and future needs for KSAOs. In the planning chapter we mentioned how to incorporate ideas about the external and internal environment into developing strategies. The job analysis chapter furthered these ideas with techniques for assessing organizational competencies and job-specific KSAOs. All of this analysis should flow directly into the process of defining what types of candidates are needed. For example, a global computer hardware manufacturer considering international expansion will need to consider what national cultures and languages its employees will need to understand. A pharmaceutical company in a dynamic market will need to think of the expertise of current employees as well as recruits' ability to learn and develop as the business environment evolves.

The next step is to determine from the job requirements analysis what types of applicants are most likely to have the required KSAOs. After KSAO statements are developed, goals can be formed about identifying the type of people who have the desired characteristics. Do you need a highly educated workforce or one with lots of practical experience? Is this a job that requires more technical expertise or are interpersonal skills important? After defining the types of people you think will match your job demands, think about which of the recruitment sources we discuss later in the chapter are most likely to attract them.

Following from competency modeling, the techniques for recruitment should closely match the organization's culture, values, and job-spanning competencies. Companies that pride themselves on environmental sustainability and a team-oriented environment will want to send a message to new recruits that is much different from the message of companies that have a revenue-driven culture that promotes aggressive growth. Companies that have a high operational need for coordination across functions will want to find recruits who have the right background knowledge and communication skills to match these needs. Everything from the areas of the country where recruitment will take place to the types of media that will be employed will send a message to potential applicants about what the organization's culture is like, so choices about recruitment should always take these considerations into account.

Goal 2: The Right Number of Applicants

A second goal is getting the right number of applicants. As we reviewed in the planning chapter, there are several techniques for evaluating how many employees are needed for ongoing operations. A strategic approach to recruiting requires thoughtful evaluation of what current needs are, alongside estimates of what needs will look like in the future. An expanding area of a business may have plans for recruiting more individuals than are currently needed, since operational needs can quickly turn a strategy of filling all vacancies into a shortage. The result is loss of revenue and market position—hardly a desirable state for a company in an especially opportune moment for growth. Conversely, it can also be advisable to limit recruiting for positions if there is a possibility that a job will go away. Payroll is expensive, and a struggling area of a business cannot afford to be overstaffed.

Determining the right number of applicants also relates to the selectivity of the employment system and the number of applicants who take jobs when offered. We will cover questions of selectivity of a staffing system in later chapters, but for now it suffices to say that if a company rejects a large number of applicants in the selection process, it will be necessary to have a much larger recruiting pool. Even the best selection system is not effective if the number of applicants is so low that the company has to take all of them. Applicants are more likely to turn down jobs if their particular labor market is especially active, so as unemployment decreases and competition increases, recruiting efforts must have a proportional increase as well.

Goal 3: Applicants at the Right Time

While goals for attraction answer the question of what types of job seekers the organization needs to attract, goals for speed answer the question of how fast the organization needs to attract applicants. When an organization needs to fill a position quickly with an employee who will contribute right away, recruitment will have to focus on methods that contact highly qualified and experienced individuals who are probably doing similar work already. Attracting these candidates does not involve the same strategy that would be employed if an organization wants to attract applicants with raw talent and ability who can be molded to fit the needs of the organization with training and experience.

As staffing managers have been increasingly called on to show concrete results for their work, the importance of documenting the time to fill requisitions has grown. These deadlines are very important for procedural justice and even legal defensibility, as both current employees and potential applicants expect the organization to abide by the specified date requirements. Once a goal for the time frame is established, the organization should not pursue a certain applicant before the deadline or consider applicants who apply after the deadline.

Goals for speed can also influence the ways an organization recruits in more immediate ways as well. On the one hand, when an organization needs to fill a position quickly, techniques that identify a large pool of interested individuals who want to start right away should be implemented. On the other hand, the organization's long-term hiring strategy should include establishing personal relationships with a broad pool of talented individuals, regardless of their immediate availability, through ongoing networking. Some technology companies start the recruitment process by providing scholarships and mentoring opportunities for college students, with the hope of identifying and attracting individuals who will be interested in a job when they graduate.

Open Versus Targeted Recruitment

One of the most difficult aspects of recruitment is knowing where to look for applicants. In theory, the pool of potential job applicants is the eligible labor force (i.e., employed, unemployed, discouraged workers, new labor force entrants, and labor force reentrants). In practice, the organization must narrow down this vast pool into segments or strata of workers believed to be the most desirable applicants. To do so, organizations can use open or targeted recruitment methods.

Open Recruitment

With an open recruitment approach, organizations cast a wide net to identify potential applicants for specific job openings. Very little effort is made in segmenting the market into applicants with the most desirable KSAOs. This approach is very passive in that anyone can apply for an opening, and all who apply for a position are considered, regardless of their qualifications. An advantage of the open recruitment method is that applicants often see it as being fair in that everyone has the opportunity to apply. Open recruitment helps ensure that a diverse set of applicants are given a fair shot at being considered. Another advantage of open recruitment is that it is useful—perhaps even essential—when large numbers of applicants must be hired. The disadvantage of this approach is that a large number of applications must be considered, leading to extensive screening costs. Unfortunately, with the growth of web-based recruitment, many employers have found that open recruitment yields too many applicants, making it very time-consuming to review all the résumés and other application materials.[2]

Targeted Recruitment

A targeted recruitment approach is one whereby the organization identifies segments in the labor market where qualified candidates are likely to be. Often, this is done to find applicants with specific characteristics pertinent to person/job or person/organization fit. Some experts propose that a targeted strategy may be more effective because it allows the organization to prepare a specific message that appeals to the audience, rather than relying on a general message that is mildly appealing to some candidates but strongly appealing to none.[3]

Following is a list of some of the potential target recruitment groups (of course, these categories are not mutually exclusive):

- *Key KSAO holders*—the objective here is to identify applicants with specific new areas of knowledge or "hot" skills
- *Diverse job seekers*—organizations sometimes need to make special efforts to reach underrepresented groups
- *Passive job seekers or non-candidates*—individuals who are already employed are often the best qualified
- *Employment-discouraged*—long-term unemployed, welfare recipients, teenagers, and people with disabilities
- *Reluctant applicants*—individuals who have interest in an organization but are conflicted; research shows that flexible work arrangements may help attract such individuals[4]

Making the Choice

The choice between open and targeted recruitment dictates recruitment methods and sources. This is not to suggest that open and targeted recruitment necessarily achieve different goals. For example, whereas open recruitment achieves inclusiveness by encouraging everyone to apply, targeted recruitment may achieve inclusiveness by reaching out to groups who might otherwise not see the recruiting message.

Recruitment experts say it is not advisable to use just one strategy.[5] An organization might choose a very open strategy for jobs that are not core to its performance, such as clerical and administrative functions, but then use a much more targeted approach for employees who need highly specific KSAOs. Accenture Consulting, for example, suggests that retailers identify the most critical segments of the workforce, analyze the performance of the most successful employees, and then target the recruitment to attract employees sharing relevant characteristics with star performers in these high-leverage positions. For less critical positions, a less resource-intensive process might be advisable. Exhibit 5.2 reviews the advantages of open and targeted recruitment and suggests when each approach is appropriate.

Organization and Administration

Once the organization has a good idea of which types of candidates to recruit, decisions must be made regarding how the process will proceed. Recruitment can be coordinated mostly in-house, or in conjunction with an external recruitment partner. Given the flexibility of this process, authority to recruit will have varying degrees of centralization as well.

Centralizing Versus Decentralizing Recruitment

An organization can centralize or decentralize different components of the recruiting process. For centralized functions, one group coordinates the recruitment activities,

---
EXHIBIT 5.2 Choosing Between Open and Targeted Recruitment

	Technique	Advantages	Best When
Open	Advertising positions with a message appealing to a wide variety of job seekers in a variety of media outlets that will reach the largest possible audience	Ensures that a diverse set of applicants are contacted and considered	Large numbers of applicants are required
Targeted	Focusing advertising and recruiting efforts by tailoring message content to attract segments of the labor market with specific KSAOs or demographic characteristics	Narrows the pool of potential applicants, allowing the organization to concentrate efforts on the most qualified Facilitates a more personal approach to each applicant	The organization needs specific skill sets that are in short supply Hiring for high-leverage positions

usually HR professionals in the corporate offices. For decentralized functions, individual business units or managers coordinate the recruitment activities. Although the ultimate hiring decisions reside in the business unit, most organizations centralize the administrative activities associated with recruitment and screening applicants.

One advantage of centralizing recruitment is that efforts are not duplicated. For example, when recruiting at a school, only one advertisement is placed, rather than separate ads for multiple organizational business units. Another advantage is that a centralized approach ensures that policy is being interpreted consistently across business units. Also, centralizing a function helps ensure compliance with relevant laws and regulations. Another factor that facilitates centralized recruitment is the growth in staffing software, as discussed in later chapters.

Some conditions call for decentralizing functions. Case studies suggest that research and development departments, for example, often develop specialized recruitment messages to attract talent. These strategies are focused on university recruitment and emphasize projects that are likely to interest highly educated and intrinsically motivated researchers.[6] One advantage of decentralizing recruitment functions is that when there are fewer people to recruit, placement can happen more quickly than when a centralized approach is used. Also, the recruitment search may be more responsive to the business unit's specific needs because the local managers involved with recruitment may be closer to the day-to-day operations of the business unit than are their corporate counterparts.

Incorporating In-House and External Recruitment Partners

With the growth of software services to facilitate recruitment, the need to process large amounts of applicant data, and the complexity of media for disseminating recruitment messages, it has become difficult for an organization to manage its recruitment function completely by itself.[7] Thus, organizations need to determine which recruitment functions should be fulfilled in-house and which should be conducted by external partners. Even large organizations with dedicated human resources staff can benefit from external partnerships. Responsibility for developing an integrated recruitment strategy needs to remain in-house.

External partners have a vital role to play in facilitating recruitment. There are many software platforms that can be used to collect, track, and analyze data from recruits. Companies often enter into long-term partnerships with these software providers to customize functions. Specialized recruitment firms are constantly in touch with a wide variety of applicants and therefore have detailed knowledge of many potential candidates. Recruitment firms also often have databases of available applicants that they have collected over time, which can mean very rapid access to many interested individuals.

However, in-house recruiters know much about their organization's culture and can convey that information to recruits more credibly because they actually work for the company. Additionally, employees may perceive that a company that does its own recruitment is more interested in the applicants and has a more people-oriented culture than an organization that leaves this process to an outside firm. Taken as a whole, it is best to use external partners for activities that involve developing specialized application portals, coordinating activities across social media and other online sources, and tracking applicants, whereas crafting messages and making contact with applicants are best handled in-house. Despite the scope for automated communication, direct contact with candidates still needs to be personalized by managers.

Timing

Defining a time frame means determining how long the position will be advertised prior to consideration of applications, and at what point a final offer for selection tests and interviews will be sent to applicants. General principles for determining how long a job will remain open are considered in light of strategic goals for the jobs to be filled. Determining the time frame during which recruitment will take place can be particularly important in a legal sense because the applicant pool definition depends on the length of time applicants will have to apply.

When an organization is seeking applicants for a very specific, in-demand position, the time frame should be similarly specific, with applications accepted only until a firm deadline is reached, after which no other applications will be accepted or considered. If an organization has the goal of filling a large number of positions that traditionally have relatively high turnover, such as sales or customer service jobs, then recruitment may not have a termination point. Instead, recruitment will be considered ongoing, as with a policy of "always taking applications."

Although managers would like to fill each position immediately when a vacancy arises, this is not possible because of the process of finding, screening, and selecting applicants. It is possible, however, to minimize the delay. Effective planning requires that top management prioritize job openings so that they can be filled in the order that best meets the needs of the business. Recruiters must also have recruiting messages and methods for receiving applications worked out in advance. Furthermore, hiring today has largely become continuous given the growth of Internet recruitment. For example, many large organizations keep a list of job openings on their websites that are continually updated through their HR information systems.

In a successful recruitment program, the stages involved in the process are clearly defined and sequenced in a logical order. A staffing flowchart should be used to organize all components of the recruitment process and when they occur. The sequence of recruitment activities will affect the amount of time needed to fill job vacancies. Time-lapse statistics can be used to provide data on the average length of time between various phases in the recruitment process.

Recruitment Budget and Return on Investment

The recruitment process is a very expensive component of organizational staffing. Costs include staff time developing a recruitment message, a website, advertising, personal contacts and follow-up with potential candidates, and logistics for on-site candidate visits. Because recruitment is such an expensive proposition, it is vital for HR to track both the costs and the returns of its recruitment practices.[8] The use of applicant tracking systems makes it easier for leaders to estimate metrics from a variety of recruitment practices.

The high costs of recruitment also point to the importance of establishing a well-developed recruitment budget. An example of a recruitment budget is shown in Exhibit 5.3. It accounts for staff time, the salaries of recruiters, and other expenses incurred in a recruitment drive, including memberships with online recruitment sources and social media, hiring external vendors to assist with the development and dissemination of recruitment materials, and travel costs that may be incurred when candidates are geographically dispersed.

Once a budget is in place and the recruitment techniques are implemented, assess the effectiveness of the chosen techniques. An applicant tracking system makes it possible to assess how many individuals are attracted and hired through each source, and identify which recruitment sources lead applicants to the organization. For example, one can determine how many candidates learned about the job opening from media advertisements, the organization's website, campus visits and job fairs, employee referrals, or other sources. It is also possible to track how

---

EXHIBIT 5.3   Example of a Recruitment Budget for 500 New Hires

Administrative Expenses

Staff	32,000
Supplies	45,000
Equipment	10,000
	$87,000

Recruiter Expenses

Salaries	240,000
Benefits	96,000
Expenses	150,000
	$486,000

Candidate Expenses

Travel	320,000
Lodging	295,000
Fees	50,000
Relocation	150,000
	$815,000

Total Recruitment Expenses

87,000 + 486,000 + 815,000 = $1,388,000

Total Cost per Hire

$1,388,000 / 500 new hires = $2,776

---

many candidates are hired from each source. From this information on the number of applicants and hires coupled with budget figures, the cost per applicant (total media cost divided by number of applicants) and the cost per hire (total media cost divided by number of hires) can be calculated. Cost-effective methods for attracting candidates can then become the focal part of the organization's recruitment strategy, and those that have lower returns on investment can be eliminated.

Development of a Recruitment Guide

A recruitment guide is a formal document that details the process to be followed to attract applicants to a job. It should be based on the organization's staffing flowcharts, if available. Included in the guide are details such as the time, money, and staff required to fill the job as well as the steps taken to do so. An example of a recruitment guide is shown in Exhibit 5.4.

Although a recruitment guide takes time to produce—time that may be difficult to find in the face of an urgent requisition to be filled—it is an essential document. It clarifies expectations for both the recruiter and the requesting department as to what will be accomplished, what the costs will be, and who will be held accountable

---

EXHIBIT 5.4   Recruitment Guide for Director of Claims

Position: Director, Claims Processing

Reports to: Senior Director, Claims Processing

Qualifications: 4-year degree in business
8 years' experience in health care, including 5 in claims, 3 of which should be in management

Relevant labor market: Regional Midwest

Timeline: week of 1/17: Conduct interviews with qualified applicants
2/1: Targeted hire date

Activities to undertake to source well-qualified candidates:

Regional newspaper advertising

Post job opening on company website

Request employee referrals

Contact regional health and life insurance associations

Call HR departments of regional health and life insurance companies to see if any are outplacing any middle managers

Contact, if necessary, executive recruiter to further source candidates

Staff members involved:

HR Recruiting Manager
Senior Director, Claims Processing
VP, Human Resources
Potential peers and direct reports

Budget:

$3,000–$5,000

---

for the results. A guide also ensures the recruitment plan is followed in a consistent fashion and in accordance with organization policy as well as relevant laws and regulations. In short, a recruitment guide safeguards the interests of the employer, the applicant, and the recruiter.

Process Flow and Record Keeping

Before deciding where and how to look for applicants, the organization must prepare for the high volume of data that accompanies the filling of vacancies. To manage the process flow and record-keeping requirements, an information system must be created for recruitment efforts. An effective system allows the candidate, the hiring manager, and HR representatives to know the candidate's status at any time. The information system tracks the applicant's file as it flows through the organization's recruitment process. The information system can also periodically issue reports on how timely and accurately the applicant's information is being processed.

The process of managing data and records has been transformed by online applications.[9] On the one hand, data entry and record maintenance are facilitated in that applications are immediately transferred into a searchable standardized database. Online applications often permit candidate screening by checking qualifications and administering online skills tests. This can greatly reduce the time spent weeding out résumés sent in by unqualified candidates. On the other hand, online applications generate much more data, including applications from individuals who are poorly motivated to join the organization or are obviously unqualified for the position. To facilitate combing through all this information, many web-based recruitment systems have integrated screening tools to eliminate unqualified applicants early in the process.

As the applicant progresses through the hiring process, additional record keeping is required, such as who has reviewed the file, how long each individual has had the file to be reviewed, what decision has been reached (e.g., reject, invite for a visit, conduct a second interview), and what step needs to be taken next (e.g., arrange for a flight and accommodations, schedule an interview). Throughout the process, communications with the applicant must also be tracked so the applicant knows whether their credentials will receive further review and whether they need to take any additional steps to secure employment.

Even when an applicant is rejected for a position, there are record-keeping responsibilities. The applicant's file should be stored in the event that another search arises that requires someone with the applicant's qualifications. The applicant's file should be stored for a maximum of one year (see "Legal Issues" at the end of the chapter).

APPLICANT REACTIONS

After the organization has a clear idea of its strategic plan and implementation, the reactions of potential applicants should be considered. Applicant views of an organization change significantly over time, and the direction of these changes is related to later job choice decisions.[10] The first impression an applicant has of an organization has a very strong impact on their later feelings of fit, so it is a good idea to devote significant time and energy to improving these reactions. However, it is just as important to maintain a good impression later on. Applicants can lose interest if the organization fails to maintain their interest.

Collect as much information as possible about potential applicant reactions at all phases of the process, including initial intentions to apply, interest in taking a job if offered, and final choice. Different factors can be important at different stages. For example, the influence of the recruiter on the applicant is likely to be greater in the initial stage than in the latter stages of the recruitment process. In the latter stages, actual job characteristics carry more weight in the applicant's decision. Understanding how applicants react to various features of the recruitment process will help determine which type of communication message content and media should be employed, as well as help facilitate implementation of effective strategies.

Reactions to Job and Organizational Characteristics

In a marketing sense, the job and the organization are the products the organization is trying to "sell" to potential applicants, so any recruitment strategy will have to take these characteristics into account.

Job Characteristics

At the job level, research suggests that applicants are most interested in working for organizations that offer sufficient wages, opportunities for growth and development, and interesting work characteristics.[11] In particular, opportunities for challenges and development are most strongly associated with applicant attraction. Of course, not all jobs have these desired features, so managers will need to decide exactly how much information about the job should be shared.

In some industries, the payment strategy may help attract candidates who match the job demands. For example, to attract entrepreneurial financial advisors, some financial services firms entice potential applicants with a well-publicized opportunity to run their shops independently and keep 100% of their advisory fees. Attracting such individuals supports an organizational strategy that focuses on innovation, personal initiative, and achievement.

Organization Characteristics

At the organization level, applicants are most drawn to prestigious organizations that have a reputation for treating their employees well.[12] The social environment of the organization also matters, with many applicants being attracted to companies where they believe they will work with good coworkers in a positive social environment. Although some research suggests that most potential applicants prefer a supportive organizational culture to a competitive culture, a large proportion of workers clearly prefer an organization that emphasizes individual work and ambition.[13] Most experts advise that organizations should accurately portray their culture in recruitment so they attract employees who will fit well within the organization.

Reactions to Recruiters

Considerable research has been conducted and reviewed on the reactions of job applicants to the behavior and characteristics of recruiters.[14] This literature shows that the main function of an effective recruiter is to communicate the features of the job and organization in an accurate, thorough, and engaging manner. Effective recruiters display warmth and competence. Warmth can be expressed by being enthusiastic, personable, empathetic, and helpful in dealings with the candidate. Another important behavior of recruiters is to communicate knowledge about the job. This can be conveyed by being well versed in the job requirements matrix and the job rewards matrix.

Organizations can use this information to their advantage by selecting and training recruiters well. Recruiters should be knowledgeable about applicant tracking systems, organization and job characteristics, social media strategies, recruitment targets, policies and procedures, and the legal environment around recruitment.[15] Recruiters can be trained on how to do market research, how to find job candidates in the market, and how to identify what candidates want. Recruiters may be able to collaborate with marketing to achieve a brand image that not only sells products to customers but sells the organization to prospective hires as well. Interpersonal skills training should include practice scripts, strategies to put recruits at ease, and role-playing exercises.

Research shows that the importance of recruiters should not be overstated. Although recruiters influence job applicant reactions, they do not have as much influence as actual job or organization characteristics. The recruiter cannot be viewed as a substitute for a well-defined and well-communicated recruitment message showing the actual characteristics of the job and organization. The influence of the recruiter is more likely to be felt in the initial attitudes of the job applicant than in their behavior. That is, an applicant who has been exposed to a talented recruiter may walk away with a favorable impression of the recruiter, but will not necessarily be more likely to take the job offer.

Reactions to the Recruitment Process

Some administrative components of the recruitment process have been shown to have an impact on applicant reactions.[16] Research suggests that above all else, applicants want a system that is fair. First, job applicants are more likely to have favorable reactions to the recruitment process when the screening devices used to narrow the applicant pool are seen as job related. That is, the process used should be closely related to the content of the job as spelled out in the job requirements matrix. Applicants also see recruitment processes as more fair if they have an opportunity to perform or demonstrate their ability to do the job.

Second, delays in the recruitment process have a negative effect on applicants' reactions. In particular, a long delay between the applicant's expression of interest and the organization's response may lead the applicant to form a negative reaction about the organization but not about themselves. This is especially true of the better-qualified candidate, who is likely to act on these feelings by accepting another job offer.

Online recruitment can create additional concerns. Specifically, some applicants may find contacts through social media invasive if not handled appropriately.

Attempts to learn more about an applicant by viewing online profiles and tracking social media connections can lead to negative reactions and even legal repercussions. It is therefore crucial to ensure that recruits are able to control when and how they interact with the organization's social media efforts.

As with general recruitment, perhaps the most important factor is the degree and speed of follow-up; delays greatly harm the image of the recruiting organization, so organizations need to make sure that online applications are followed up. Also, research shows that job seekers are more satisfied with organizational websites when specific job information is provided and security precautions are taken to preserve the confidentiality of the information submitted.[17]

Diversity and Inclusion

In addition to tailoring messages to reach employees with specific KSAO profiles, some organizations also target specific underrepresented groups. Most research suggests that the race or gender of a recruiter has relatively little influence on applicant attraction, and there is not strong support for the idea that individuals react more positively when recruited by someone of their own demographic group. However, the content of the recruitment message and choice of recruitment sources can have an influence.

Research suggests that applicants react more positively to ads that reflect their own demographic group, which should be taken into account when developing a media campaign.[18] Such efforts are among the most effective, and the least controversial, elements of affirmative action programs (AAPs). One of the most common methods for increasing the diversity of applicant pools is to advertise in media sources that will reach underrepresented job seekers. Surveys show that women and minorities are especially interested in working for employers that endorse diversity through policy statements and in recruitment materials. Advertisements depicting groups of diverse employees are seen as more appealing to even majority group job seekers, which is probably why most organizations depict workforce diversity prominently in their recruitment materials. Inclusive marketing should take job functions into account as well; diversity advertisements that fail to show members of underrepresented groups in positions of organizational leadership undermine an inclusive message.[19]

Some organizations are also aiming to increase the age diversity of the workforce. Many traditional recruitment methods, like campus recruitment and job fairs, draw in a primarily younger workforce. However, as noted in the planning chapter, there has been an increase in the proportion of the workforce over 50 years of age. These older workers are often highly qualified and experienced, and thus attractive candidates for recruitment, but a different targeted approach is required to bring them in. Mature workers are attracted by flexible schedules, health and pension benefits, and part-time opportunities, so the presence of such programs should be noted in recruitment advertisements.

COMMUNICATION

Once the strategic planning phase is completed, it is time to consider how the position will be marketed to potential applicants. Reaching out to the job market requires developing a message and then selecting a medium to communicate that message. Both phases are considered in turn.

Communication Message

Types of Messages

Recruitment experts have studied the ways in which the content of the recruitment message can influence potential applicants' thinking about the position. The communication message can vary in the extent to which it focuses on the employment brand, information targeted to a specific group of applicants, or realistic information about the organization or job.

The example messages in Exhibit 5.5 show that messages differ in terms of their focus. The branded message starts from the question, What about this organization would attract someone to work here? The focus is clearly on the organization as a whole, which could come from a job rewards analysis focused on culture and

EXHIBIT 5.5 **Example Communication Messages**

Type of Message	Example Message
Branded	**Example focus:** Tech savvy financial services company
	Example message: Our organization lives on the cutting edge. We have been developing new methods for meeting client needs, including the most fully featured app-based portfolio management tools on the market. Employees will be part of a culture known for rewarding creativity, initiative, and innovation.
Targeted	**Example focus:** Recruiting new college graduates
	Example message: We provide the perfect place to start your career. Our training and development programs offer a world of opportunities to try out a variety of roles and functions, building out your skill set with each new assignment.
Realistic	**Example job requirement:** Frequent travel
	Example message: While working in this organization provides opportunities to do a variety of tasks, it does require extensive travel. New hires can expect to be on the road for at least one week per month, and sometimes more.

image. The targeted message starts from the question, What about this job and organization would appeal to someone from this audience? Now the focus is on the group of people who will be receiving the message, which could come from a job rewards analysis focused on the features most desired and appreciated by a specific group of potential applicants. The realistic message starts from the question, What characteristics of this job or organization might not be appealing to someone? Here the focus is on a specific feature of the job, which might come from a job requirements analysis.

Employment Brand Message. An employment brand is an appealing message that places the image of the organization as being a great place to work or employer of choice in the minds of potential applicants.[20] Organizational impression management efforts to create a brand come in many forms, but a few central themes emerge from analyzing a wide variety of branding strategies.[21] To signal that a company values achievement, organizations play up the quality of their products, describe successes, and show how competently they are run. A company can show that it is stimulating by emphasizing a fun and friendly culture in the media. To show that it values benevolence and social responsibility, an organization can highlight integrity and reputation in its mission statement and media. All of these strategies are effective in creating the desired image, but not all are equally effective. Evidence suggests that integrity-based messages are especially effective in increasing applicant interest in a job.

An organization's employment brand is closely tied to its product market image. As with general product awareness, the more "customers" (in this case, potential applicants) are aware of an organization's employment brand, the more interested they are in pursuing a job. Organizations that are well known by potential applicants may not need to engage in much advertising for their jobs. Big-name organizations that market well-known products, such as Microsoft, Apple, Sony, and Disney, often have many more applicants than they need for most openings. Organizations with lower profiles may have to actively advertise their employment brand to bring in more applicants. Experts in corporate branding encourage employers to compare their own employee value proposition with those of the competition to see how they are unique, and then highlight these unique advantages in recruitment messages. For example, the US Marine Corps emphasizes how the Marines are an elite group of warriors under its branding strategy, rather than focusing on the financial advantages of enlistment. Beyond reputation, another employment brand may be value or culture based. For example, Netflix has promoted its high performance expectations to attract achievement-oriented applicants seeking commensurate rewards.

An organization's website is often used to convey information regarding its culture and to emphasize its employment brand. Most organizational websites provide information on the organization's history, culture, diversity, benefits, and specific job information under a "careers" heading. It is informative to look at a series of these organizational websites to see how organizations cater to applicants. For example,

Merck's corporate website shows an organization that conveys a message of professional development and social responsibility, whereas Goldman Sachs's emphasizes performance and success, and Coca-Cola's emphasizes global opportunities and fun.

Branding has several benefits.[22] Of course, establishing an attractive employment brand may help attract desired applicants to the organization. Moreover, an established product brand may help retain employees who were attracted to the brand to begin with. Research suggests that identifiable employment brands can foster interest from job seekers and commitment on the part of newly hired employees. Applicants are attracted to companies with a reputation for corporate social responsibility because this is seen as a signal that the company will treat employees well. Employment brands associated with empowerment and high compensation have also been shown to be especially attractive to applicants.

Research shows that having a unique employment brand can attract applicants to an organization, even beyond job and organizational attributes. Evidence also suggests that employers are most able to get their brand image out when they engage in early recruitment activities such as advertising or generating publicity about the organization.[23]

Targeted Message.   One way to improve upon matching people with jobs is to target the recruitment message to a particular audience. The targeted message is a natural complement to a targeted search. Different audiences may be looking for different rewards from an employer. Unlike the branded recruitment message, where the focus is on the organization and what it offers to everyone, the targeted message focuses on the unique preferences of specific segments of the potential applicant pool.

To develop a targeted message, an organization can use principles from marketing research.[24] First, employers can look to media used by different groups or visit social media sites. Organizational representatives can also conduct focus groups and interviews with different groups of potential applicants, and then design messages that highlight features of a job that will fit with these different groups. Having members of targeted groups participate in message crafting is key, to avoid messages that come across as inauthentic or even insulting.

Human resources practitioners have developed recruitment messages designed to reach groups that differ in terms of both demographic and deeper level diversity.[25] Examples of demographic groups that might be targeted include underrepresented minorities, teenagers, older workers, welfare recipients, people with disabilities, veterans, and displaced homemakers, all of whom may have special interests or preferences. Older workers, for example, may be looking for employers that can meet their financial needs and provide job security. College students appear to be attracted to organizations that provide rewards and promotions on the basis of individual rather than group performance. Members of underrepresented groups look for evidence of a positive climate for diversity and signals that their group is represented in leadership roles.

Messages can also be targeted toward those with specific interests and values. Evidence suggests that messages targeting those with specific values may have a stronger effect on applicant interests than messages targeting specific demographic groups.[26] It is easy to find examples of such policies. Companies like REI emphasize their commitment to the environment and opportunities to use outdoor gear in hopes of attracting employees who share these values. Companies in the health care industry emphasize patient care. Emphasizing inclusive policies in recruitment not only serves to increase interest among members of underrepresented minority groups but also can appeal to majority group members who value diversity as well.

Realistic Recruitment Message. A realistic recruitment message portrays the organization and the job as they really are, rather than describing what the organization thinks job applicants want to hear. Message content that focuses on accuracy, to the point of incorporating negative information, is called a realistic job preview (RJP).[27] According to this practice, job applicants are given a "vaccination" by being told what the actual job is like. The hope is that some potential applicants will realize the job is a poor fit and not apply. When an applicant self-selects out, the organization does not face the costs associated with recruiting, selecting, training, and compensating someone who will quickly leave the organization.

A great deal of research has been conducted on the effectiveness of RJPs, and their use appears to lead to somewhat higher job satisfaction and lower turnover.[28] This appears to be true because providing applicants with realistic expectations about future job characteristics helps them cope with job demands once they are hired. RJPs also appear to foster the belief in employees that their employer is honest and concerned with employee well-being, which leads to higher levels of organizational commitment.

RJPs may lead applicants to withdraw from the recruitment process, although reviews of studies suggest that RJPs have little effect on such attrition. This may be good news for employers interested in using RJPs: Providing applicants with realistic information provides employers with more satisfied and committed employees while still maintaining applicant interest in the position. Unfortunately, research does suggest that while the negative effects of RJPs on applicant attraction are weak, the most qualified applicants are the most likely to self-select out.[29]

Although RJPs appear to have both weakly positive consequences (slightly higher job satisfaction and lower turnover among new hires) and negative consequences (slightly reduced ability to hire high-quality applicants), the way an RJP is delivered makes a difference. A meta-analytic review of the research on RJPs suggests that they are most effective when presented later in the hiring process, and when delivered in person.[30] These findings suggest that RJPs should be given personally (rather than in writing or by showing a video) and that it is probably best to reserve their use for later in the recruitment process (RJPs should not be part of the initial exposure of the organization to applicants).

Choice of Messages

The different types of messages—branded, realistic, and targeted—are not likely to be equally effective under the same conditions. Which message to convey depends on the labor market, vacancy characteristics, and applicant characteristics. The three types of messages are summarized in Exhibit 5.6.

The information in the exhibit can help address specific organizational goals. For example, if the employment objective is simply to fill job slots in the short run and worry about turnover later, a realistic message will have counterproduc-

---

EXHIBIT 5.6   Comparing Types of Messages

	Information Conveyed	Applicant Reactions	Potential Drawback	Best For
Branded	An appealing description is developed based on marketing principles, emphasizing unique features of the organization	Positive view of the organization, increased intention to apply for jobs, and better prehire information about benefits of the job	Overly positive message may result in employee dissatisfaction after hire	Tight labor markets or higher-value jobs
Targeted	Advertising themes are designed to attract a specific set of employees	Better fit between application message and specific applicant groups	May dissuade applicants who are not interested in the work attributes featured in the message from applying	Specific KSAOs, or seeking a specific type of applicant
Realistic	Both positive and negative aspects of a job and organization are described	Some applicants self-select out; those who remain will have a better understanding of the job and will be less likely to leave	The best potential applicants may be more likely to leave	Loose labor markets or when turnover is costly

tive effects. Conversely, when applicants are abundant and turnover is an immediate problem, a realistic message is appropriate. When applicants are plentiful, the branded and targeted approaches may be costlier than necessary to attract an adequate supply of labor. Also, they may set up false expectations concerning what life will be like on the job and thus lead to turnover.

The job itself will play a role in which approach is appropriate. Job applicants will know more about the characteristics of highly visible jobs than those of less visible jobs. It may be redundant to give a realistic message when recruiting for highly visible jobs in the service sector, such as that of cashier. Other jobs, such as an outside sales position, are far less visible to people. These jobs may seem glamorous (e.g., sales commissions) to prospective applicants who fail to see the less glamorous aspects of the job (e.g., a lot of travel and paperwork).

Some applicants are less likely than others to be influenced in their attitudes and behaviors by the recruitment message. One study showed that a realistic message is less effective for those with considerable job experience.[31] Highly experienced candidates are more likely than less experienced candidates to be persuaded by high-quality, detailed advertisements.[32] Different segments of the labor market have different contrast points: individuals who are new to the labor market compare jobs against their history in school and might contrast the job against further education, employed job seekers compare jobs against their current job and may see an offer as negotiating leverage in their current job, and those who have recently lost a job compare their job against unemployment.[33]

Communication Media

Not only is the message itself an important part of the recruitment process, so, too, is the selection of media to communicate the message. The most common communication media include advertisements, organizational websites, videoconferencing, and direct contact. Although these are all potential ways to get the message out, the most common method of learning about a job is through word of mouth, which is a difficult communication medium for an organization to manage.

Effective communication media are high in reach, richness, interactivity, and credibility. Reach refers to how many individuals can learn about a job through the method of delivery. A source that can be seen by nearly anyone across many platforms is high in reach, whereas a source that needs to be sought out and can be accessed by only a few individuals is low in reach. Rich media channels allow for a variety of methods for conveying messages (e.g., visual images, text, figures and charts). Interactive media sources can be customized to each respondent's specific needs and provide timely personal feedback to questions. Credible media channels transmit information that is honest, accurate, and thorough. If the information is seen as coming directly from the employees, rather than from the organization's recruitment offices, the message will likely be seen as more honest and unbiased.

Research has shown that respondents have more positive images of organizations that transmit information that is rich, interactive, and credible.[34] Greater employer involvement with prospective applicants is likely to improve the image of the organization, which increases the number of applicants pursuing employment.[35] The media with the least richness and credibility usually have an advantage in that they can reach a large number of people at low cost, so they should not be overlooked. Given the various advantages and disadvantages of the methods we review below, organizations usually select a variety of media that support one another. For example, some organizations use the broad reach of advertising to get the word out to many potential candidates, and then direct these candidates to the organization's website for a richer presentation.

Exhibit 5.7 gives an overview of different forms of communication media, along with an overall summary of their reach, richness, interactivity, and credibility. The descriptions of characteristics are not absolute but represent the characteristics of each method on average. There is a range for any media type. For example, organizational websites can be low in credibility but could be enhanced by providing video testimonials of current employees. Throughout our discussion we will emphasize strategies to maximize the strengths of each method while minimizing the weaknesses.

Advertisements

Given limitations in space, time, and attention spans, ads are often short and to the point. Unfortunately, these ads typically cannot provide rich information because of their short durations. Given that advertisements are obvious attempts at persuasion, they tend to have relatively low credibility. They can have a very broad reach, though, so they should be seriously considered if the organization wishes to reach a broad market.

Ads appear in a variety of places other than business publications and can be found in local, regional, and national news media; on social media; on television

---

EXHIBIT 5.7   Comparing Communication Media

Media Type	Reach	Richness	Interactivity	Credibility
Advertisements	High	Medium	Low	Low
Recruitment Brochures	Medium	High	Low	Low
Organizational Websites	Medium	High	Medium	Low
Videoconferencing	Low	High	High	Medium
Direct Contact	Low	High	High	Medium
Word of Mouth and Social Media	Medium	High	High	High

and radio; and in bargain shopper inserts, door hangers, direct mail, and welcome wagon packets. Advertisements can thus be used to reach a broad market segment. Messages can also be distributed to target specific audiences. For example, a classical music radio station will likely draw in different applicants than a contemporary pop music radio station; an all-sports network will draw in different applicants than a cooking program. Media outlets often have detailed demographic information available to potential advertisers. Online sources can use more sophisticated real-time matching of advertising to a target audience by using browsing history and other big data analytics techniques. Anyone who has ever received targeted advertising while browsing online or watching videos is familiar with this phenomenon.

Here are some of the most prominent forms of advertising:

- *Classified advertisements*. Classified ads appear in the "help wanted" section of newspapers or job posting sites. These ads are used most often for quick résumé solicitation for low-level jobs at a low cost. Although there has been a major shift toward the use of electronic recruitment, surveys suggest that print is still a useful complement to an online classified advertisement for some job types.[36]

- *Display ads*. Display ads are more polished and involved than classified ads, and they are usually developed in conjunction with a professional advertising agency. These ads allow for freedom of design and can incorporate a variety of visual display elements. These ads are often found in professional publications or on websites as part of a targeted marketing strategy.

- *Banner ads*. Banner ads are posted to online sites that an organization believes will be visited by potential applicants, including social media sites, occupation-specific websites, and news media sites. They are limited in size, but viewers can easily click over to the organization's official site for a more extensive description of the job. Banner ads can be either relatively cheap or quite expensive, depending on which website the organization chooses to place the ad.

- *Radio, television, and streaming video ads*. These types of ads provide opportunities to deliver a salient message by combining voice, music, and visual elements. The advantage of these broadcast media is their reach. Individuals who are already searching for jobs generally read help-wanted ads, whereas those who are not currently looking for jobs are more likely to hear radio and television ads.

Other media outlets that have been explored less frequently might offer a recruiter a competitive advantage. For example, a large technology firm in Belgium experimented with a decidedly old-fashioned method of recruitment by sending handwritten postcards to potential applicants rather than using e-mail. This strategy paid off, with applicants recruited through the postcard method being more likely to reply, more qualified on average, and, among those who did apply, more likely to be invited for a job interview. In another unusual example of innovative media recruitment, the US Army has used a very popular online video game called *America's Army* to draw in thousands of recruits.[37]

Recruitment Brochures

A recruitment brochure is often sent or given directly to job applicants, or a "virtual brochure" may be included as part of the organization's website. A brochure not only covers information about the job but also communicates information about the organization and its location. It may include pictures in addition to written narrative in order to illustrate various aspects of the job, such as the city in which the organization is located and the actual employees. These various means of demonstrating the features of the organization enhance the richness of this recruitment technique. The advantage of a brochure is that the organization targets who receives a copy. Also, it can be lengthier than an advertisement. A disadvantage is that it can be quite costly to develop, and because it is obviously a sales pitch made by the organization, it might be seen as less credible.

A successful brochure possesses (1) a unique theme or point of view relative to other organizations in the same industry and (2) a visual distinctiveness in terms of design and photographs. A good format for the brochure is to begin with a general description of the organization, including its history and culture (values, goals, "brand"). A description of the hiring process should come next, along with a sense of future career prospects.

Organizational Websites

Organizational websites have become the single most important medium through which organizations communicate with potential applicants. Nearly every organization has a "career opportunities" page on its website. Websites are a powerful means of not only communicating information about jobs but also reaching applicants who otherwise would not bother to apply. Thus, care must be taken to ensure that the organizational website is appealing to potential job candidates. Most websites do double duty by communicating information about the job or organization to potential applicants, and providing methods to submit an application.

Research has shown that organizations can successfully convey cultural messages on their websites by describing organizational policies, showing pictures, and including testimonials. Effective websites also permit users to customize the information they receive by asking questions about their preferences and providing relevant information.[38]

How can web designers put these findings into practice? The three core attributes driving the appeal of an organization's website are engagement, functionality, and content. First, the website must be vivid and attractive to applicants. Second, the website must be functional, meaning that it should be quick to load, easily navigable, and interactive. A website that is overly complex may be vivid, but it will only generate frustration if it is hard to decipher or slow to load. Websites must also have cross-platform compatibility and function on smaller screens, since a large proportion of applicants will access the site through a mobile device or smartphone. Third, an organizational website must convey the information prospective applicants want to see, including current position openings, job requirements, and steps for applying. Many organizations offer video testimonials from current employees to give a more personal view of what work is like.[39]

Of course, there is more to designing an organizational website than the three attributes discussed above. Exhibit 5.8 provides a list of additional features to keep in mind.

EXHIBIT 5.8   Factors for Designing Organizational Websites

1. *Keep it simple*—surveys reveal that potential job candidates are overwhelmed by complex, difficult-to-navigate websites; never sacrifice clarity for a flashy display—remember, a good applicant is there for the content, not for the bells and whistles.
2. *Make access easy; the web page and links should be easy to download*—studies reveal that individuals will not wait more than about eight seconds for a page to download (some recent research even suggests that this number is as low as two seconds), so the four-color page that looks great will backfire if it takes the user too much time to download it (also make sure that the link to the recruiting site on the home page is prominently displayed).
3. *Provide an online application form*—increasingly, potential candidates expect to be able to submit an application online; online forms are not only desired by candidates, organizations can load responses directly into searchable databases.
4. *Provide information about company culture*—allow applicants to self-select out if their values clearly do not match those of the organization.
5. *Include selected links to relevant websites*—the words "selected" and "relevant" are key here; links to include might be a cost-of-living calculator and a career advice area.
6. *Make sure necessary information is conveyed to avoid confusion*—clearly specify job title, location, etc., so applicants know which job they are applying for and, if there are several jobs, do not apply for the wrong job.
7. *Keep the information current*—make sure position information is updated regularly (e.g., weekly).
8. *Evaluate and track the results*—periodically evaluate the performance of the website on the basis of various criteria (number of hits, number of applications, application/hits ratio, quality of hires, cost of maintenance, user satisfaction, time to hire, etc.) or set up a software program to track the response data.

SOURCES: P. W. Braddy, A. W. Meade, and C. M. Kroustalis, "Online Recruiting: The Effects of Organizational Familiarity, Website Usability, and Website Attractiveness on Viewers' Impressions of Organizations," *Computers in Human Behavior*, 2008, 24, pp. 2992–3001; S. Selden and J. Orenstein, "Government E-Recruiting Web Sites: The Influence of E-Recruitment Content and Usability on Recruiting and Hiring Outcomes in US State Governments," *International Journal of Selection and Assessment*, 2011, 19, pp. 31–40.

Videoconferencing

Videoconferencing via Skype, WebEx, Zoom, Google Hangouts, or other providers is another common way to communicate with applicants.[40] Nearly all devices (laptop, tablet, and smartphone) have the technology needed for videoconferencing, so most applicants can participate easily. Most importantly, this technology makes it possible to screen applicants at multiple or remote locations without either the applicant or recruiters having to invest in expensive and disruptive travel. Videoconferencing has most of the advantages of face-to-face communication because it is personal and the applicant and the recruiter can quickly communicate. Videoconferencing also makes it easy to record interviews so that they can be referenced later by hiring managers.

Videoconferencing has high richness because the recruiter can answer questions, and it is highly credible because most people trust personal communication with an identifiable person more than they trust a prepackaged message from an organization. Those familiar with videoconferencing are also aware of the pitfalls of this approach, including poor quality connections, confusion from too many individuals on the call, or distracted interviewers. Before relying on videoconferencing, adequate investment in information technology to bypass these problems must be in place or else applicants can infer that the organization is unprofessional or lacking in competence.

Direct Contact

The most expensive, but potentially the most powerful, method for communicating with potential applicants is through direct contact. Telephone messages, text messages, e-mail, and contact through professionally oriented social media (e.g., LinkedIn) are common methods. These techniques are much more personal than the other methods of recruitment because the applicants are specifically approached by the organization. Personal contacts are likely to be seen as more credible by respondents. In addition, messages delivered through direct contact often allow respondents to ask personally relevant questions, which obviously should enhance the richness of the information.

However, in the age of spamming, it is important to remember that most individuals will regard mass e-mails or automated telephone messages with even less enthusiasm than they would for junk mail. Most e-mail programs filter spam, and the more mass messages that are sent, the more likely it is that mail servers will identify the organization's address as a problem. Direct contact should be communicated in a way that makes it clear that the receiver is one of a small number of people who will receive the message. The messages should be highly personal, reflecting an understanding of the candidate's unique qualifications. Providing a response e-mail address or telephone number that allows respondents to ask questions about the job opening will also help increase the yield for the direct contact method. However, personalization and customized responding to questions obviously will increase the cost per individual contacted, so the trade-offs in terms of reach must be considered.

Word of Mouth and Social Media

One of the most powerful methods for communicating about a potential job opportunity is one that organizations cannot directly control: word of mouth.[41] This refers to the informal information regarding an organization's reputation, employment practices, and policies that can exert a powerful impact on job seekers' impressions of an employer. Because word of mouth usually comes from individuals who do not have a vested interest in "selling" the job, the messages are likely to be seen as more credible. The fact that job seekers can ask and have questions answered also makes word of mouth a very rich source of information.

Some word of mouth is no longer conveyed face-to-face, as blogs and social media can also be used to communicate information about employers.[42] The largest social media sites with employment connections, including Facebook, LinkedIn, and Glassdoor, have reached such a level of prevalence that an employer might regard an applicant who *didn't* extensively research the company's online reputation with suspicion. These sites convey information that an organization might prefer not to have made public to applicants, such as interpersonal conflicts in various divisions, information about inequitable pay practices, or critiques of career paths. For applicants, this increased transparency may make it easier for them to find a good fit. For recruiters, however, it is necessary to regularly scan online content regarding the organization and ensure that the company has answers to common criticisms.

How can organizations influence word of mouth? One technique is to carefully cultivate relationships with current employees, recognizing that the way they are treated will come to influence the ways that other potential applicants believe they will be treated. This means making certain that jobs are as intrinsically and extrinsically satisfying for the current workforce as possible. Organizations should also make conscious efforts to shape the perception of their employment brand by using online testimonials from current employees. These testimonials act as a sort of virtual equivalent of word of mouth. Although job seekers will likely be somewhat skeptical of any information on a corporate website, a testimonial from someone who works at the organization is still likely to be more persuasive than a conventional sales pitch. There are demonstrated advantages to taking a proactive approach in managing online word of mouth. A growing body of evidence shows that companies that actively use social media to craft a compelling message to candidates are seen as more credible. In fact, these social media messages are seen as more credible than organizational websites.[43]

APPLICANT SOURCING

Once the recruitment planning phase is complete and the organization has spread the word about the job opening through various communication media, the next phase is applicant sourcing. This process involves gathering applications from a variety of sources and evaluating the quantity of applicants, the quality of applicants, the cost of using each source, and the impact on HR outcomes.

Individual Recruitment Sources

The first category of recruitment sources we consider are those that focus on the individuals the organization is attempting to contact. These sources target active job seekers who are submitting applications to a number of potential employers. This means that it is incumbent on the job seeker to actively participate in the process early on. Applicants generally apply only to organizations they believe are hiring, so effective use of communication media is necessary to elicit enough applications.

Applicant Initiated

Applicant-initiated recruitment is among the most traditional and well-accepted techniques for finding a job. Most employers accept applications from job applicants who physically walk into the organization to apply for a job, who call the organization, or who contact the organization through the corporate website. The typical point of contact for walk-ins or phone inquiries is the receptionist in smaller organizations and the employment office in larger organizations. In most organizations, however, the process either starts as or transforms into an online process as applicant materials are put into the company's HR information systems by the applicant (usually) or a representative of the organization.[44]

As we noted previously, a company's website can blend the process of spreading information about a job opening with the process of submitting an application. Many of these websites do not live up to their potential, as they are little more than post office boxes where applicants can send their résumés. All of the principles we described earlier in website design should be kept in mind when it comes to the application pages. In particular, the application portal should be simple, easy to use, informative, interactive, and up to date.[45]

Several principles exist for improving the applicant experience. When applications are accepted, a contact person responsible for processing such applicants needs to be assigned. Procedures must be in place to ensure that data from all applicants are routed into the applicant flow process. Recruits are often frustrated by complex application systems, especially those that require them to enter the same data multiple times. To keep potential applicants from feeling disconnected from the online recruitment process, keep in touch with them at every stage of the process. Integrated applicant tracking systems allow applicants to track the status of their applications and provide feedback. Some organizations inform applicants immediately if there is a mismatch between the information they provided and the job requirements; thus they can know immediately that they are not under consideration. Quickly eliminating unacceptable candidates also allows recruiters to respond more quickly to applicants who do have sufficient KSAOs. A review of online job solicitations found that the best website advertising offered special features to potential applicants, including opportunities to check where they are in the hiring process, examples of a typical "day in the life" at an organization, and useful feedback to applicants regarding their potential fit with the organization and job early in the process.

Employment Websites

Employment websites have evolved from their original function as job boards and database repositories of jobs and résumés to become fully featured recruitment and screening centers.[46] For employers that pay a fee, many employment websites provide services like targeted advertising, video advertising, preemployment screening, and applicant tracking. For job seekers, there are resources to facilitate exploring different career paths, information about the communities where jobs are offered, and access to message boards where current and former employees can sound off on the culture and practices of different organizations.

Millions of job seekers submit their résumés to employment websites every year, and there are thousands of job sites to which they can apply. Although it is difficult to obtain precise data on the use of employment websites, some estimates suggest that they are second only to referrals as a source of new hires. On the other hand, research suggests that solicitations for employment from electronic bulletin boards are seen as especially less informative and low in credibility relative to organizations' websites or face-to-face meetings at campus placement offices. Therefore, these methods should not be used without having some supporting practices that involve more interpersonal contact.[47]

General Employment Websites. Most readers of this book are likely familiar with the biggest employment websites, so it is easy to forget that they have had a major impact on the job search process for only the past 20 years. Since that time, a few early movers and larger entrants have grabbed the lion's share of the market. Three of the biggest employment websites are Monster, CareerBuilder, and Indeed. Glassdoor is another very popular employment website that has done an especially good job of integrating various social media into its approach.

General employment websites are not limited to simple advertising, as noted earlier. Services are rapidly evolving for these sites, and many now offer the ability to create and approve job requisitions online, manage recruitment tasks, track the progress of open positions and candidates, and report on recruitment metrics like time to hire, cost per hire, and equal employment opportunity (EEO). Several of the larger employment websites have developed extensive cross-listing relationships with local newspapers, effectively merging the advantages of local media in terms of credibility and name recognition with the powerful technological advances and large user base of employment websites.[48]

Niche Employment Websites. Although there are advantages to open recruitment, as described earlier, it is also possible to conduct a more targeted web-based recruitment effort through niche employment websites.[49] These sites focus on specific occupations (there are employment websites for jobs ranging from nurses to geologists to metal workers), specific industries (e.g., sports, chemicals, transportation, human services), and specific locations (e.g., cities, states, and regions often have their own sites). Recruiters looking for examples of niche job sites for a specific occupation can simply do an Internet search of "employment websites" coupled with the occupation of interest. Although any one niche job board is unlikely to have a huge number of posters, these specialized websites have been estimated to collectively account for two-thirds of Internet hiring. Experienced recruiters claim that the audience for niche employment websites is often more highly qualified and interested in specific jobs than are applicants from more general job sites.

Niche job sites that cater to specific demographic groups have also been developed. Organizations that want to improve the diversity of their work sites or that are under an AAP should consider posting in a variety of such specialized employment websites as part of their search strategy. Survey data suggest that applicants believe that companies that advertise on these targeted websites are more inclusive, further serving to enhance the usefulness of diversity-oriented advertising.[50]

Social Recruitment Sources

A second major type of recruitment source is social networks. These recruitment sources rely on the relationships that potential employees have with either those who currently work for the organization or others who might endorse the organization. Although it is generally the case that these interpersonal recruitment sources will yield fewer applicants than broader media-based recruitment sources used in the individual approaches, there are some distinct advantages to social networks that we review below.

Employee Referrals

Employees are a valuable source for finding job applicants.[51] Most estimates suggest that referrals are one of the most commonly used recruitment methods. The vast majority of organizations accept referrals, though only about half have formal programs. In some organizations, a cash bonus is given to employees who refer job candidates who prove to be successful on the job for a given period of time. To ensure adequate returns on bonuses for employee referrals, it is essential to have a good performance appraisal system in place to measure the performance of the referred new hire. There also needs to be a good applicant tracking system to ensure that new hire performance is maintained over time before a bonus is offered.

Referral programs have many potential advantages, including low cost per hire, high-quality hires, decreased hiring time, and an opportunity to strengthen bonds with current employees.[52] Research also shows that individuals hired through referrals are less likely to leave. There is even evidence that the job performance and retention of the employee who makes the referral may improve.

Former employees can be an ideal source of future applicants, either by recruiting them to come back to the organization or by asking them to provide referrals. As return employees, they will know the organization, its jobs, and its culture and will also be well known to those inside the organization. This not only cuts down on orientation costs but also means they can get into the flow of work more quickly. As referral sources, they can convey their personal observations to other job seekers, and thus those who decide to apply will be better informed. Using former employees as a recruitment source naturally means that the organization must remain on good terms with departing employees and keep channels of communication open after employees leave. Many organizations that undergo cyclical layoffs or downsizing in lean times might also seek to rehire those who were laid off previously when the organization returns to an expansionary strategy.[53]

Social Media

Another way of finding applicants is through social media, where friends or acquaintances are used to connect those looking for applicants to those looking for jobs. Many recruiters have turned to social networking websites such as Twitter, LinkedIn, and Facebook as sources for finding qualified job candidates.[54] The use of social networking has become so prevalent that recruitment software integrates these sites into the applicant tracking process. Some social media sites have developed apps that facilitate job seekers in completing application forms through mobile devices. Job seekers are also aware of the trend toward social media: 50% or more of job candidates include their social media profiles on their résumés. Recruiters can automatically post openings to social media sites and receive reports on which channels are resulting in the most leads and the best candidates.[55]

The use of social media has a number of advantages. The great majority of organizations that use social media in recruiting use it as a method to recruit passive job candidates and to increase employer brand recognition. In fields where the unemployment rate is very low, such as engineering, health care, and information technology (IT), passive candidates may be the primary source of potential applicants. Because many of the connections between users are based on professional background or shared work experiences, networking sites often provide access to groups of potential employees with specific skill sets. Some social networking websites geared toward professionals encourage users to indicate the industry and area in which they work. Recruiters can set up their own profile pages with these websites, encouraging potential applicants to apply by making personal contacts. Surveys suggest that social media job postings are especially effective in decreasing time to fill openings (but are less effective in attracting qualified applicants). Some research supports the idea that staffing professionals can indeed make valid inferences about potential applicant qualifications and personality through a structured review of LinkedIn profiles.[56]

Despite these advantages, organizations can face troubling legal and ethical quandaries when using social media, because candidates' personal information, such as marital status, health status, and demographics, is often publicly available on personal pages. To avoid these problems, recruiters are strongly advised not to ask potential applicants to provide access to personal information when conducting networking-based recruitment. Only publicly available information should be viewed. Although social media for recruiting has increased, there has been a switch from general sites like Facebook to employment-focused sites like LinkedIn. This approach is one way to reduce legal concerns because LinkedIn profiles are specifically designed to advertise qualifications—in other words, the job seeker knows that the information will be used for employment purposes and will therefore be less likely to feel the information is a violation of privacy. Companies should establish strong guidelines for the use of social media, because managers may be using personal information without the company's knowledge or consent.[57]

Recruiters have identified some best practices to facilitate social media campaigns that are not prone to these privacy concerns.[58] Effective campaigns begin by making potential applicants aware of the organization and by creating easy ways for them to follow up on their initial interest. The choice to engage with the organization initially is left up to the applicant. If an individual indicates interest in the position, the organization works to respond quickly to the candidate, providing customized answers to questions and following up regularly. Unlike one-way media campaigns, once a candidate has indicated interest through social media, it is possible to track their level of engagement and likely interests. This information can then be used to identify key developments and other events that might be likely to interest those in the system.

Professional Associations and Meetings

Organizations can take advantage of the relationships their employees have with professional associations. Through networking with others who do similar work, employees can develop contacts with potential new recruits. This contact can be established informally by reaching individuals via e-mail or through message boards. Professional associations sometimes have a formal placement function that is available throughout the year. For example, the websites of professional associations often advertise both positions available and interested applicants. Others may have a computerized job and application database.

Many technical and professional organizations meet around the country at least once a year. Many of these groups run a placement service for their members, and some may charge a fee to recruit at these meetings. This source represents a way to attract applicants with specialized skills or professional credentials. Also, some meetings are an opportunity to attract underrepresented groups.

Organizational Recruitment Sources

External organizations form a third major category of potential recruitment sources. These connections tend to be more formal than social networks, and so they tend not to provide some of the relational advantages of individual contact. However, external organizations provide access to a large number of potential applicants. Organizational recruitment sources can also help narrow down the applicant pool by providing formal screening services.

Colleges and Placement Offices

Colleges are a valuable source of individuals with specialized skills for professional positions. Most colleges have a placement office or officer who is in charge of ensuring that a match is made between the employer's interests and the graduating student's interests. Research has shown that campus recruitment efforts are seen as more informative and credible than organization websites or electronic bulletin boards.[59] In fact, recruitment experts found that members of the tech-savvy millennial generation are reluctant to use social networking and other Internet job search tools, and that they prefer campus career placement offices to find jobs.[60]

In most cases, the placement office is the point of contact with colleges. Additional points of contact for students at colleges include professors, department heads, professional fraternities, honor societies, recognition societies, and national professional societies.

It can be difficult to decide which colleges and universities to target for recruitment efforts. Some organizations focus their efforts on schools with the best return on investment and invest in those programs more heavily. Other organizations, especially large ones with relatively high turnover, find they need to cast a much broader net. In the end, the decision of breadth versus depth comes down to the number of individuals who need to be hired, the recruitment budget, and a strategic decision about whether to invest deeply in a few programs or more broadly in more programs.

Some organizations develop a talent pipeline that includes individuals in educational institutions who may not take a job immediately, but may be attracted to the organization in the future. Some organizations develop early relationships with incoming college freshmen in hopes that they will consider the organization as a potential employer when they graduate. Organizations that engage in large-scale collaborative research and development efforts with universities cultivate relationships with faculty, with the hope of eventually luring them into private sector work. Many organizations establish folders or databases of high-potential individuals who are still receiving an education or who work for other companies and then regularly send materials to those individuals about potential career prospects within the organization. Intel has hosted a competition called the Cornell Cup, in which student teams from a number of universities compete to design the best engineering projects. Those who perform well are not only given cash prizes but also invited to take on summer jobs or internships.[61]

Staffing Agencies

Staffing agencies, like Manpower, Randstad, and Adecco, are one traditional source of nonexempt employees and lower-level exempt employees.[62] These agencies contact, screen, and present applicants to employers for a fee. The fee is contingent on successful placement of a candidate with an employer and is usually a percentage of the candidate's starting pay. In a temp-to-hire arrangement, the employee has a trial period in which their contract is contingent on performance, and then after a period of time the employee will be taken on as a permanent employee of the organization. This gives both the applicant and the employer a chance to observe each other and assess the quality of the fit. Best practices in the area emphasize the need to ensure that when using staffing agencies, it is crucial to routinely evaluate the quality and reliability of the agency. One survey found that more than one in three organizations that use staffing agencies had problems with "ghost bookings," meaning that the agency promised to staff a job without having valid employees ready.

Although staffing agencies have traditionally focused on individuals with comparatively low skill levels, many agencies have expanded to include individuals with specialized or technical skills. There are even staffing agencies that specialize in areas like health care and engineering, which require very high levels of expertise. Some of these agencies provide recruitment and screening services for potential employers, and then employees receive an offer of a permanent position like recruits from any other source. However, even for these technical fields, temp-to-hire arrangements are not unheard of.

Executive Search Firms

For higher-level professional and executive positions, executive search firms, or "headhunters," may be used.[63] Like staffing agencies, these firms contact and screen potential applicants and present résumés to employers. The difference between staffing agencies and search firms lies in two primary areas: (1) search firms typically deal with higher-level positions than those of staffing agencies, and (2) search firms are more likely to operate on the basis of a retainer than on a contingency. Executive search firms are, by design, high-contact, low-reach sources for applicants. The emphasis is on quality of fit rather than quantity.

To make the most out of a relationship with a search firm, make sure you exercise due diligence in evaluating its process. No search firm can possibly look across all markets, so experts advise finding firms that know your organization and industry well. Although search firms are used to tap into a pool of exceptionally qualified individuals, research evidence shows that many firms do not adequately evaluate candidates and attend more to job titles than to qualifications. Policies for ensuring adequate information flow between the organization and the search firm are vital. The search firm should proactively ask questions about the organization and its needs. Building a sense of trust is similarly a crucial factor. Search firms that do not make thorough inquiries or do not establish themselves as attentive and honest should be dropped from consideration as soon as possible.[64] A final factor to consider is the nature of the contract. Search firms that operate on a retainer are paid regardless of whether a successful placement is made. The advantage of operating this way, from the hiring organization's standpoint, is that it aligns the interests of the search firm with those of the organization. Thus, search firms operating on retainer do not feel compelled to put forward candidates just so their contingency fee can be paid. Conversely, working with a contingency-based contract means that the company is paid only if the search is successful.

Social Service Agencies

All states have an employment or job service. These services are provided by the state to help secure employment for those seeking it, particularly those currently unemployed. For jobs to be filled properly, the hiring organization must maintain a close relationship with the employment service. The US Department of Labor has allocated funding for states to develop one-stop career centers that will provide workers with various programs, benefits, and opportunities related to finding jobs. The centers' emphasis is on customer-friendly services that reach large segments of the population and are fully integrated with state employment services. These centers now offer a variety of skills certification programs, such as the National Work Readiness Credential and the National Career Readiness Certificate, which are highly sought after by employers.[65] For example, the state of Washington has introduced a workforce development program called WorkSourceWA that links nonprofit agencies with companies, providing targeted recruiting, screening, and training for thousands of employers.[66] Texas has a similar program within the Texas Workforce Commission that provides job postings and grants for customized job training and apprenticeship programs for businesses, with special attention to training individuals who might otherwise have difficulty finding work.[67] These are just two examples; most states have similar programs.

The federal Job Corps program is another option. Job Corps is designed to help individuals between 16 and 24 years of age obtain employment. The program targets individuals with lower levels of education and prepares them for entry-level jobs through a combination of work ethic training and general job skills. For employers, Job Corps can provide specialized training, prescreening of applicants, and tax benefits. Some agencies in local communities may also provide outplacement assistance for the unemployed who cannot afford it. Applicants who use these services may also be listed with a state employment service. Community agencies may also offer counseling and training.

Job Fairs

Industry associations, schools, groups of employers, the military, and other interested organizations often hold career or job fairs to attract applicants. Typically, the sponsors of a job fair will meet in a central location with a large facility in order to provide information, collect résumés, and screen applicants. Often, there is a fee for employers to participate. Job fairs may provide both short and long-term gains. In the short run, the organization may identify qualified applicants. In the long run, it may be able to enhance its visibility in the community, which, in turn, may improve its image and ability to attract applicants for jobs.

One strength of job fairs is also a weakness—although a job fair enables the organization to reach many people, the typical job fair has a large number of employers vying for the attention of applicants. Given a typical ratio of 25 applicants for every employer, contact with an applicant is probably shallow. In response, some employers instead (or also) devote their resources to information sessions geared toward a smaller group of specially qualified candidates. During these sessions, the organization presents information about itself, including its culture, work environment, and career opportunities. Studies show that job fairs that allow for interpersonal interactions between job seekers and organization representatives are seen as especially informative by job seekers. Thus, both applicants and employers find information sessions a valuable alternative, or complement, to job fairs.[68]

Co-ops and Internships

A large number of educational institutions, including many high schools and nearly all technical colleges and universities, require some or all of their students to get work experience as part of their degree programs. Co-ops and internships are two ways that employers can recruit applicants.[69] Under a co-op arrangement, the student works with an employer on an alternating quarter basis. In one quarter the student works full time and in the next quarter the student attends school full time. Under an internship arrangement, the student has a continuous period of employment with an employer for a specified amount of time. These approaches allow an organization to not only obtain services from a part-time employee for a short period of time but also assess the person for a full-time position after graduation. In turn, interns have better employment opportunities as a result of their experiences.

Increasingly, colleges and universities are giving students college credit for—in some cases, even instituting a requirement for—working as part of their professional degree.[70] A student in social work, for example, might be required to work in a welfare office for a summer. Occasionally, some internships and co-op assignments do not provide these meaningful experiences that build on the qualifications of the student. To lessen the chances of this happening, a preestablished learning contract that serves as a job description can guide the student's activities. Learning contracts clarify expectations for both sides.[71]

Recruitment Metrics

Each recruitment source has strengths and weaknesses. Determining the best method for an organization entails assessing the costs and benefits of each method and then selecting the optimal combination of sources to meet the organization's strategic needs. Exhibit 5.9 provides an overview of the metrics that might be expected for the categories of recruitment activities, along with issues considered relevant to each source. Conclusions for the number and types of applicants

EXHIBIT 5.9   **Potential Recruitment Metrics for Different Sources**

Recruiting Source	Quantity	Quality	Costs	Impact on HR
Applicant initiated	Contingent on how widely the company's brand is known	Highly variable KSAO levels if no skill requirements are posted	Application processing and clerical staff time	Higher training costs, lower performance, higher turnover
Employment websites	Often opens to very large pool, although niche sites have a more narrow pool	Can provide specific keywords to limit applications to those with specific KSAOs	Subscription fees or user fees from database services	Good tracking data, potentially lower satisfaction, and higher turnover
Employee referrals	Generates a small number of applicants	Better fit because current employees will inform applicants about the culture	Signing bonuses are sometimes provided to increase quantity	Higher performance, higher satisfaction, lower turnover, lower diversity
Social networking sites	Potentially a large number of individuals, depending on employee use of networks	Depends on whether networks are made up of others with similar skills and knowledge	Time spent searching through networks and soliciting applications	Potentially similar results to referrals, although results are unknown
Professional associations and meetings	Comparatively few candidates will be identified for each job opening	Those attending professional meetings will be highly engaged and qualified	Cost of attending meetings and direct interviewing with staff can be very high	Superior performance, although those seeking jobs at meetings may be job-hoppers
Colleges and placement offices	About 50 individuals can be contacted at each university per day	High levels of job-relevant human capital, usually screened on the basis of cognitive ability, little work experience	Time costs of establishing relationships, traveling to college locations	Initial training and development for inexperienced workers; can increase average KSAO levels

(continued)

EXHIBIT 5.9 **Continued**

Recruiting Source	Quantity	Quality	Costs	Impact on HR
Staffing agencies	Many applicants for lower-level jobs, fewer applicants available for managerial or executive positions	Applicants will be prescreened; organizations are often able to try out candidates as temps prior to hiring	Fees charged by staffing agencies	Reduced costs of screening candidates, improved person/job match
Executive search firms	Only a small number of individuals will be contacted	Search firms will carefully screen applicants, usually experienced candidates	Fees for executive searches can be more than half of the applicant's annual salary	Reduced staff time required because the search firm finds applicants; very high costs for firms
Social service agencies	Usually only a limited number of individuals are available, although this varies by skill level	Applicants may have had difficulty finding jobs through other routes because of lack of skills	Often there are direct financial incentives for hiring from these agencies	Potentially greater training costs, higher levels of diversity
Job fairs	About 40 applicants can be contacted per recruiter per day	Often draws in individuals with some knowledge of the company or industry	Advertising and hosting costs are considerable, although this is an efficient way to screen many candidates	Higher levels of diversity if targeted to diverse audiences; effects on performance, satisfaction unknown
Co-ops and internships	Only a small number of interns can be used in most organizations	High levels of formal educational preparation, but few interns will have work experience	Cost of paid interns can be very high; unpaid interns are a huge cost savings although they often require staff time	Those who are hired will be prescreened, and should have higher performance and lower turnover

SOURCES: D. S. Chapman, K. L. Uggerslev, S. A. Carroll, K. A. Piasentin, and D. A. Jones, "Applicant Attraction to Organizations and Job Choice: A Meta-Analytic Review of the Correlates of Recruiting Outcomes," *Journal of Applied Psychology*, 2005, 90, pp. 928–944; M. A. Zottoli and J. P. Wanous, "Recruitment Source Research: Current Status and Future Directions," *Human Resource Management Review*, 2000, 10, pp. 353–382.

drawn by each method are informed by a number of studies comparing recruitment sources. Although broad generalizations can be made regarding quantity, quality, cost, and impact on HR outcomes for different recruitment methods, each organization's unique labor market situation will need to be considered since the research evidence shows considerable variety in the effects of recruitment variables on applicant attraction.

Sufficient Quantity

The more broadly transmitted the organization's search methods, the more likely it is that a large number of individuals will be attracted to apply. Other methods of recruitment naturally tend to be more focused and will draw a comparatively small number of applicants. While broad recruitment methods such as advertising and Internet postings are able to reach thousands of individuals, it might be to an organization's advantage not to attract too many applicants, because of the costs associated with processing all the applications.

Sufficient Quality

Recruitment methods that link employers to a database of employees with exceptional skills enable an employer to save money on screening and selection processes. But if the search is too narrow, the organization will likely be engaged in a long-term process of looking.

Cost

The costs of any method of recruitment are the direct expenses involved in contacting job seekers and processing their applications. Some sources, such as radio advertisements, search firms, and sophisticated website portals that customize information and provide employees with feedback, are quite expensive to develop. These methods may be worth the cost if the organization needs to attract a large number of individuals, if KSAOs for a job are in short supply, or if the job is crucial to the organization's success. On the other hand, organizations that need fewer employees or that require easily found KSAOs discover that lower-cost methods like applicant-initiated recruitment or referrals are sufficient to meet their needs. Some fee-based services, like staffing agencies, are able to process applications inexpensively because the pool of applicants is prescreened for relevant KSAOs.

Impact on HR Outcomes

A considerable amount of research has been conducted on the effectiveness of various recruitment sources and can be used as a starting point for which sources are likely to be effective. Research has defined effectiveness as the impact of recruitment sources on increased employee satisfaction, job performance, diversity, and retention. Evidence suggests that, overall, referrals and job trials are likely to attract applicants who have a good understanding of the organization and its culture, and therefore they tend to result in employees who are more satisfied, more productive, and less likely to leave. Conversely, sources like staffing agencies can produce employees who are less satisfied and productive. Any general conclusions regarding the effectiveness of recruitment sources should be tempered by the fact that the location of an organization, the compensation and benefits packages provided, the type of workers, and the typical applicant experience and education levels will moderate the efficacy of these practices.

TRANSITION TO SELECTION

Once a job seeker has been identified and attracted to the organization, the organization needs to prepare the person for the selection process. In preparation, applicants need to be made aware of the next steps in the hiring process and what will be required of them. If the recruitment organization overlooks this transition step, it may lose qualified applicants who mistakenly think that delays between steps in the hiring process indicate that the organization is no longer interested in them or who are fearful that they "didn't have what it takes" to successfully compete in the next steps.

The process one sees in many college career placement offices demonstrates how recruitment and selection are often tied together. Visiting corporations will often host information sessions and social events to advertise themselves to student job seekers. This is usually part of a strong branded-message campaign. In these sessions, job seekers are given information regarding what types of jobs are available, along with previews of the process of selection and hiring. While providing job seekers an opportunity to assess their fit with potential careers with the organization, many of these social events are structured so that recruiters can get a preliminary sense of what the job applicants are like. Preliminary selection decisions can be made during informal recruitment dinners.

Campus recruiters also conduct preliminary interviews with candidates in the college career center. These interviews involve multiple information-exchange opportunities. At this point, recruiters often introduce some realistic job information into the discussion, describing what jobs are like and who candidates are likely to meet if they do an interview at the organization's offices. This is another opportunity for the organization to explain to the recruits what the selection process consists of. Candidates who have a strong grasp of what processes are used in selection and how they fit together are likely to have a strong sense of trust in the organization.

To successfully prepare applicants for the transition to selection, organizations should consider reviewing the selection method instructions with the applicants, describing the rationale behind components of the selection method, and giving applicants opportunities to discuss the selection method. These steps should be followed for all selection methods in the hiring process that are likely to be unfamiliar to applicants or uncomfortable for them.

LEGAL ISSUES

External recruitment practices are subject to considerable legal scrutiny and influence. During recruitment there is ample room for the organization to exclude certain applicant groups (e.g., minorities, women, and people with disabilities) as well as to deceive in its dealings with applicants. Various laws and regulations seek to limit these exclusionary and deceptive practices.

Legal issues regarding several of the practices are discussed in this section. These include the definition of a job applicant, AAPs, electronic recruitment, job advertisements, and fraud and misrepresentation.

Definition of a Job Applicant

Both the Equal Employment Opportunity Commission (EEOC) and the Office of Federal Contract Compliance Programs (OFCCP) require the organization to keep applicant records. Exactly what is a job applicant and what records should be kept? It is necessary to provide guidance on the answer to this question in terms of both traditional hard-copy applicants and electronic applicants.

Hard-Copy Applicants

The original (1979) definition of an applicant by the EEOC is in the Uniform Guidelines on Employee Selection Procedures (UGESP). It reads as follows: "The precise definition of the term 'applicant' depends on the user's recruitment and selection procedures. The concept of an applicant is that of a person who has indicated an interest in being considered for hiring, promotion, or other employment opportunities. This interest may be expressed by completing an application form, or might be expressed orally, depending on the employer's practice."

This definition was created prior to the existence of the electronic job application. It remains in force for hard-copy applications. Because it is so open-ended, it is important to develop and communicate (including to applicants) policies about what the organization considers a written applicant. Examples of such policies include requiring all applicants to file a written application, stating specific qualifications required, stating that a separate application must be submitted for each opening, not accepting open-ended applications, returning unsolicited applications, having a specific closing date for applications, and applying these policies to search firms and third-party vendors.[72]

Internet Applicants

The OFCCP regulations (the Internet Applicant rule) provide a definition of an Internet applicant for federal contractors, as well as establish record-keeping requirements.

According to the OFCCP, an individual must meet all four of the following criteria to be considered an Internet applicant:[73]

- The individual submits an expression of interest in employment through the Internet or related electronic data technologies.
- The employer considers the individual for employment in a particular position.
- The individual's expression of interest indicates that the individual possesses the basic qualifications for the position.
- At no point in the employer's selection process does the individual remove themself from further consideration or indicate that they are no longer interested in the position.

"Internet or related electronic data technologies" includes e-mail, résumé databases, job banks, electronic scanning technology, applicant tracking system/applicant service providers, applicant screeners, and résumé submission by fax. Mobile devices are also likely included. "Basic qualifications for the position" are those established in advance and advertised to potential applicants. They must be non-comparative across applicants, objective (e.g., BS in biology), and relevant to performance in the specific position.

The employer must keep records of the following:

- All expressions of interest submitted through the Internet and contacts made with the job applicant
- Internal résumé databases—including date of entry, the position for which each search was made, the date of the search, and the search criteria used
- External résumé databases—including the position for which each search was made, the date of the search, search criteria used, and the records for each person who met the basic qualifications for the position

The OFCCP regulations also require the employer to make every reasonable effort to gather race/gender/ethnicity data from both traditional and Internet applicants. The preferred method for doing so is voluntary self-disclosure, such as through tear-off sheets on an application form, postcards, or short forms to request the information or as part of an initial telephone screen. Observation may also be used. A series of questions and answers related to the regulations provides additional information and clarification.

Affirmative Action Programs

Both the EEOC and the OFCCP require that the organization undertake strong, positive recruitment and outreach activities as part of its AAP. Passive and informal recruitment is not sufficient. Beyond this general requirement, both agencies provide suggested activities for meeting the recruitment obligation.

The EEOC presents a generic list of suggested best-practice recruitment ideas, shown in Exhibit 5.10. It applies to recruitment of persons in any protected class category.

EXHIBIT 5.10   Best-Practice Recruitment Ideas From the EEOC

- Establish a policy for recruitment and hiring, including criteria, procedures, responsible individuals, and applicability of diversity and affirmative action.

- Engage in short-term and long-term strategic planning:
  —Identify the applicable barriers to equal employment opportunity;
  —Delineate aims;
  —Make a road map for implementing the plan.

- Ensure that there is a communication network notifying interested persons of opportunities, including advertising within the organization and, where applicable, not only with the general media but with minority, persons with disabilities, older persons, and women-focused media.

- Communicate the competencies, skills, and abilities required for available positions.

- Communicate about family-friendly and work-friendly programs.

- Where transportation is an issue, consider arrangements with the local transit authority.

- Participate in career and job fairs and open houses.

- Work with professional associations, civic associations, and educational institutions with attractive numbers of minorities, women, persons with disabilities, and/or older persons to recruit.

- Use recruiter, referral, and search firms with instructions to present diverse candidate pools to expand search networks.

- Partner with organizations that have missions to serve targeted groups.

- Use internships, work/study, co-op, and scholarship programs to attract interested persons and to develop interested and qualified candidates.

- Develop and support educational programs and become more involved with educational institutions that can refer a more diverse talent pool.

- Ensure that personnel involved in the recruitment and hiring process are well trained in equal employment opportunity responsibilities.

- Explore community involvement options that will raise the company's profile and thus may attract more interested persons.

- Eliminate practices that exclude or present barriers to minorities, women, persons with disabilities, older persons, or any individual.

- Include progress in equal employment opportunity recruitment and hiring as a factor in management evaluation.

SOURCE: EEOC, "Best Practices of Private Sector Employees," 2013 (*www.eeoc.gov/eeoc/task_reports /best_practices.cfm*).

Veterans and persons with disabilities are targeted separately in regulations for the OFCCP.[74] Lists of recruitment actions that are consistent with the EEOC suggestions are provided. The lists include examples of many organizations that should be targeted because of their special interest or expertise in recruiting veterans and persons with disabilities. One suggestion from the OFCCP, not found among the EEOC ideas, is to hold a formal briefing session on the organization's premises with representatives from recruiting sources. The session should include "contractor facility tours, clear and concise explanations of the current and future job openings, position descriptions, worker specifications (i.e., VSAOs), explanations of the company's selection process, and recruiting literature." Moreover, "formal arrangements should be made for the referral of applicants, follow up with sources, and feedback on the disposition of applicants."

Finally, though not AAP focused, a special resource guide for employment of people with disabilities is available. Developed by several federal agencies, it contains a wealth of information and references on how to legally and proactively recruit, select, promote, and retain people with disabilities.[75]

Electronic Recruitment

Technology, particularly via websites and social media, has flooded the recruitment process for both the organization and job applicants. Numerous legal issues may arise.

Access and Usage

The use of electronic recruitment technology may potentially create artificial barriers to employment opportunities.[76] In the case of websites, it is assumed that potential applicants have access to computers and the skills necessary to apply online. These may be poor assumptions, especially for some racial minorities and the economically disadvantaged. To guard against legal challenge and to ensure accessibility, the organization might do several things. One action is to supplement online recruitment with other widely used sources of recruitment, such as newspaper advertisements or other sources that organizational experience indicates are frequently used by women and minorities. Alternately, online recruitment and application could be restricted to certain jobs that have strong computer-related KSAO requirements. These applicants in all likelihood will have easy access to computers and online recruitment, as well as the skills necessary to successfully navigate and complete the application.

Another issue is the use of recruitment software that conducts résumé searches within an applicant database using keyword search criteria. Staffing specialists or hiring managers often specify the search criteria to use, and they could select non-job-related criteria that cause disparate impact against women, minorities, or people with disabilities. Examples of such criteria include preferences for graduation from an elite college or university, age, and physical requirements. To guard against such a possibility, the organization should set only job-related KSAO requirements, restrict the search criteria to those KSAOs, and train recruiters in the appropriate specification and use of search criteria.

Social Media

Social networking sites (e.g., LinkedIn, Facebook, Twitter), while widely used by applicants and organizations, present challenges. The lack-of-access and usage problems noted above are troublesome since research indicates that Blacks and Hispanics have lower social media usage rates than other groups. Reliance on some social media sites thus may lead to disproportionately screening out certain protected groups from application to, or consideration by, the organization. Casting wider recruitment nets and using multiple recruitment sources and media are necessary to counteract such possible disparate impact.

The organization should also ensure that its recruitment messages do not discourage applications based on EEO protected characteristics and, conversely, that the messages portray welcoming openness toward applicant diversity. In addition, the organization should make sure that its recruitment information is accurate and does not make any false promises about job offer content or future business and employment opportunities (see "Fraud and Misrepresentation" below).[77]

People With Disabilities

The OFCCP provides specific regulations for people with disabilities.[78] If the employer routinely offers applicants various methods (including online) of applying for a job and all are treated equally, that may be sufficient for compliance purposes. All application systems must be made accessible to everyone. Examples include making the organization's website compatible with screen readers and using assistive technology and adaptive software. The regulations also indicate that the employer is obligated to provide reasonable accommodation to the applicant. Examples include the following:

- Making job vacancy application information accessible for individuals using assistive technology and adaptive software systems
- Providing readers, interpreters, or similar assistance during the application process
- Extending the time limit for completing an online examination
- Making testing locations fully accessible to those with mobility impairments

Job Advertisements

Job advertising that indicates preferences or limitations for applicants based on legally protected characteristics is generally prohibited (see the social and legal environment chapter). Questions continually arise as to exceptions or less blatant forms of advertising, as the following examples indicate.[79]

Title VII permits indicating preferences based on sex, religion, or national origin (but not race or color) only if they are bona fide occupational qualifications (BFOQs). The organization should be sure about the legality and validity of any BFOQ claims before conducting such advertising. Use of gender-specific job titles such as "waitress" or "repairman," however, should be avoided.

Using the phrase "women and minorities are encouraged to apply" in a job advertisement is OK because it is an inclusive effort to generate the largest pool of qualified applicants. An indication that the organization is "seeking" a particular type of applicant (e.g., stay-at-home moms), however, is not permitted, because it connotes a preference for a particular group rather than an encouragement to apply.

Regarding age preferences, advertisements cannot limit or deter potential older applicants from seeking a position. One example is the term "recent graduate," which could signal a younger age preference and hence should not be used. Another example is "digital native," which could imply a desire for someone under 40 and therefore also should not be used. It is permissible, however, to show a preference for older workers, using phrases such as "over age 60," "retirees," or "supplement your pension."

These examples show that the line between permissible and prohibited ad content is quite murky. The organization thus should monitor the construction and content of all its job advertisements.

Fraud and Misrepresentation

Exaggerated promises, half-truths, and even outright lies are all encountered in recruitment under the guise of selling the applicant on the job and the organization. Too much of this type of selling can be legally dangerous. When it occurs, under workplace tort law, applicants may file suit claiming fraud or misrepresentation.[80] Claims may cite false statements of existing facts (e.g., the nature and profitability of the employer's business) or false promises of future events (e.g., promises about terms and conditions of employment, pay, promotion opportunities, and geographic location). It does not matter if the false statements were made intentionally (fraud) or negligently (misrepresentation). Both types of statements are a reasonable basis for a claim by an applicant or newly hired employee.

To be successful in such a suit, the plaintiff must demonstrate that

1. A misrepresentation of a material fact occurred
2. The employer knew, or should have known, about the misrepresentation
3. The plaintiff relied on the information to make a decision or take action
4. The plaintiff was injured because of reliance placed on the statements made by the employer

Though these four requirements may appear to be a stiff set of hurdles for the plaintiff, they are by no means insurmountable, as many successful plaintiffs can attest.

Avoidance of fraud and misrepresentation claims in recruitment requires straightforward action by the organization and its recruiters. First, provide applicants with the job description and specific, truthful information about the job rewards. Second, be truthful about the nature of the business and its profitability. Third, avoid specific promises about future events regarding terms and conditions of employment or business plans and profitability. Finally, make sure that all recruiters follow these suggestions when they recruit job applicants.

SUMMARY

The objective of the external recruitment process is to identify and attract qualified applicants to the organization. To meet this objective, the organization must conduct strategic recruitment planning. The single most important issue at this stage is developing a strong link between organizational strategy and the goals of the recruitment process. The organization will also choose whether to implement an open strategy or a targeted strategy. At this stage, attention must also be given to both organizational issues (e.g., centralized versus decentralized recruitment function) and administrative issues (e.g., size of the budget).

The next stage is to develop a message for the job applicants and to select a medium to convey that message. The message may be branded, targeted, or realistic. There is no one best message; it depends on the characteristics of the labor market, the job, and the applicants. The message can be communicated through several different media, each of which has strengths and weaknesses.

Applicants are influenced by characteristics of recruiters and the recruitment process. Through proper attention to these characteristics, the organization can help provide applicants with a favorable recruitment experience.

Choices the organization makes about which sources to use follow from the previous stages. The applicant sourcing process involves comparing individual, social, and organizational sources and evaluating their effectiveness through a variety of recruitment metrics. After a sufficient number of individuals have applied, the organization begins the process of transition to selection.

Recruitment practices and decisions come under intense legal scrutiny because of their potential for discrimination at the beginning of the staffing process. The legal definition of a job applicant creates record-keeping requirements for the organization that, in turn, have major implications for the design of the entire recruitment process. Affirmative Action Programs Regulations likewise affect the entire recruitment process, prodding the organization to set targeted placement goals for women and minorities and to be aggressive in recruitment outreach actions. Job advertisements may not contain applicant preferences regarding protected characteristics such as age and gender. Finally, recruitment communication with applicants must be careful to avoid false statements or promises, lest problems of fraud and misrepresentation arise.

DISCUSSION QUESTIONS

1. List and briefly describe each of the administrative issues that needs to be addressed in the planning stage of external recruitment.
2. List 10 sources of applicants that organizations turn to when recruiting. For each source, identify needs specific to the source, as well as pros and cons of using the source for recruitment.
3. In designing the communication message to be used in external recruitment, what kinds of information should be included?
4. What are the advantages of conveying a realistic recruitment message as opposed to portraying the job in a way that the organization thinks that job applicants want to hear?
5. What strategies are organizations using to ensure that they attract women and underrepresented racioethnic groups?

ETHICAL ISSUES

1. Many organizations have adopted a targeted recruitment strategy. For example, some organizations target workers 50 years of age and older in their recruitment efforts, which includes advertising specifically in media outlets frequented by older individuals. Other organizations target recruitment messages toward women, minorities, or those with the desired skills. Do you think targeted recruitment systems are fair? Why or why not?
2. Most organizations have job boards on their web page where applicants can apply for jobs online. What ethical obligations, if any, do organizations have to individuals who apply for jobs online?

APPLICATIONS

Improving a College Recruitment Program

The White Feather Corporation (WFC) is a rapidly growing consumer products organization that specializes in the production and sales of specialty household items such as lawn furniture cleaners, spa (hot tub) accessories, mosquito and tick repellents, and stain-resistant garage floor paints. The organization has 400 exempt employees and 3,000 nonexempt employees, almost all of whom are full time. In addition to its corporate office in Clucksville, Arkansas, the organization has five plants and two distribution centers at various rural locations throughout the state.

Two years ago WFC created a corporate HR department to provide centralized direction and control for its key HR functions—planning, compensation, training, and staffing. In turn, the staffing function is headed by the senior manager of staffing, who receives direct reports from three managers: the manager of nonexempt employment, the manager of exempt employment, and the manager of EEO/AA. Marianne Collins, the manager of exempt employment, has been with WFC for 10 years and has grown with the organization through a series of sales and sales management positions. She was chosen for her current position as a result of WFC's commitment to promotion from within, as well as her broad familiarity with the organization's products and customers. When Marianne was appointed, her key area of accountability was defined as college recruitment, with 50% of her time to be devoted to it.

In her first year, Marianne developed and implemented WFC's first-ever formal college recruitment program. Working with the HR planning person, WFC set a goal of 40 college graduate new hires by the end of the year. They were to be placed in the production, distribution, and marketing functions; specific job titles and descriptions were to be developed during the year. Armed with this forecast, Marianne began the process of recruitment planning and strategy development.

The result of Marianne's work was the following recruitment process. Recruitment was to be conducted at 12 public and private schools throughout the state. Marianne contacted the placement office at each school and set up a one-day recruitment visit. All visits were scheduled during the first week in May. The placement office at each school set up 30-minute interviews (16 at each school) and made sure that applicants completed and had on file a standard application form. To visit the schools and conduct the interviews, Marianne selected three young, up-and-coming managers (one each from production, distribution, and marketing) to be the recruiters. Each manager was assigned to four of the schools. Since none of the managers had any recruitment experience, Marianne conducted a recruitment briefing for them. During that briefing she reviewed the overall recruitment (hiring) goal, provided a brief rundown on each of the schools, and explained the specific tasks the recruiters were to perform. Those tasks were to pick up the application materials of the interviewees at the placement office prior to the interviews, review the materials, conduct the interviews in a timely manner (the managers were told they could ask any questions they wanted to that pertained to qualifications for the job), and at the end of the day complete an evaluation form on each applicant. The form asked for a 1–7 rating of overall qualifications for the job, written comments about strengths and weaknesses, and a recommendation of whether to invite the person for a second interview in Clucksville. These forms were to be returned to Marianne, who would review them and decide which applicants to invite for a second interview.

After the campus interviews were conducted, problems began to surface. Placement officials at some of the schools contacted Marianne and lodged several complaints. Among those complaints were that (1) one of the managers failed to pick up the application materials of the interviewees, (2) none of the managers were able to provide much information about the jobs they were recruiting for, especially jobs outside their own functional area, (3) the interviewers got off schedule early on, so some applicants were kept waiting and others had shortened interviews as the managers tried to make up time, (4) none of the managers had any written information describing the organization and its locations, (5) one of the managers asked female applicants very personal questions about marriage plans, use of drugs and alcohol, and willingness to travel with male coworkers, (6) one of the managers talked incessantly during the interviews, leaving the interviewees little opportunity to present themselves and their qualifications, and (7) none of the managers were able to tell interviewees when they might be contacted regarding a second interview. In addition to these complaints, Marianne had difficulty getting the managers to complete and turn in their evaluation forms (they claimed they were too busy, especially after being away from the job for a week). From the reports she did receive, Marianne extended invitations to 55 of the applicants for a second interview. Of these, 30 accepted the invitation. Ultimately, 25 people were given job offers, and 15 accepted.

To put it mildly, the first-ever college recruitment program was a disaster for WFC and Marianne. In addition to her embarrassment, Marianne was asked to meet with her boss and the president of WFC to explain what went wrong and to receive "guidance" from them as to their expectations for next year's recruitment program. Marianne subsequently learned that she would receive no merit pay increase for the year and that the three managers all received above-average merit increases.

To turn things around for the second year of college recruitment, Marianne realized that she needed to engage in a thorough process of recruitment planning and strategy development. As she began this undertaking, her analysis of past events led her to conclude that one of her key mistakes was to naïvely assume that the three managers would actually be good recruiters and were motivated to do the job effectively. This time around, Marianne decided to use 12 managers as recruiters, assigning one to each of the 12 campuses. She also decided that more than a recruitment briefing was needed. She determined that an intensive, one-day training program must be developed and given to the managers prior to the beginning of the recruitment season.

You work in HR at another organization in Clucksville and are a professional acquaintance of Marianne's. Knowing that you have experience in both college recruitment and training, Marianne calls you for some advice. She asks you if you would be willing to meet and discuss the following questions:

1. What topics should be covered in the training program?
2. What materials and training aids will be needed for the program?
3. What skills should the trainees practice during the training?
4. Who should conduct the training?
5. What other changes might have to be made to ensure that the training has a strong impact on the managers and that during the recruitment process they are motivated to use what they learned in training?

Internet Recruitment

Selma Williams is a recruiter for Mervin/McCall-Hall (MMH), a large publisher of educational textbooks (K-12 and college). Fresh out of college, Selma has received her first big assignment at MMH, and it is a tough one—develop an Internet recruitment strategy for the entire organization. Previously, MMH had relied on the traditional recruitment methods—college recruitment, word of mouth, newspaper advertisements, and search firms. As more and more of MMH's textbook business is connected to the web, however, it became clear to Selma's boss, Jon Beerfly, that MMH needs to consider upgrading its recruitment process. Accordingly, after Selma had acclimated herself to MMH and had worked on a few smaller recruitment projects (including doing a fair amount of recruitment at college campuses in the past three months), Jon described her new assignment, concluding, "Selma, I really don't know much about this. I'm going to leave it to you to come up with a set of recommendations about what we ought to be doing. We just had a new intern come into the office for a stint in HR, and I'm going to assign this person to you to help on this project." Assume that you are the intern.

At your first meeting, you and Selma discuss many different issues and agree that regardless of whatever else is done, MMH must have a recruitment area on the corporate website. After further discussion, Selma gives you several assignments toward this objective:

1. Look at three to five corporate websites that have a recruitment area and note their major features, strengths, and weaknesses.
2. Interview three to five students who have used the recruitment area on a corporate website and ask them what they most liked and disliked about it.
3. Prepare a brief report that (1) summarizes your findings from assignments #1 and #2 and (2) recommends the design features that you and Selma will develop for inclusion in the MMH website.

ENDNOTES

1. G. Dessler, *A Framework for Human Resource Management*, 7th ed. (Upper Saddle River, NJ: Pearson, 2013); E. Page, "Linking Business Strategy to Recruiting Strategy," *Journal of Corporate Recruiting Leadership*, 2010, 5(4), pp. 3-6; J. Sullivan, "The 20 Principles of Strategic Recruiting," *ERE*, July 7, 2008 (*www.ere.net/2008/07/07/the-20-principles-of-strategic-recruiting*).
2. D. H. Freedman, "The Monster Dilemma," *Inc.*, May 2007, pp. 77-78; J. Barthold, "Waiting in the Wings," *HR Magazine*, Apr. 2004, pp. 89-95; A. M. Chaker, "Luring Moms Back to Work," *New York Times*, Dec. 30, 2003, pp. D1-D2.
3. L. Ryan, "10 Ways to Fix Broken Corporate Recruiting Systems," *BusinessWeek*, June 13, 2011, p. 3.
4. B. L. Rau and M. M. Hyland, "Role Conflict and Flexible Work Arrangements: The Effects on Applicant Attraction," *Personnel Psychology*, 2002, 55, pp. 111-136.
5. F. Hansen, "Recruiting the Closer: Dealing With a Deal Maker," *Workforce Management Online*, Oct. 2007 (*www.workforce.com*).

6. P. O. Ángel and L. S. Sánchez, "R&D Managers' Adaptation of Firms' HRM Practices," *R&D Management*, 2009, 39, pp. 271–290.

7. P. Cappelli, "Your Approach to Hiring Is All Wrong," *Harvard Business Review*, June 2019, pp. 48–58; R. J. Grossman, "Alternatives to Recruitment Process Outsourcing," *HR Magazine*, July 1, 2012 (*www.shrm.org*).

8. J. Whitman, "The Four A's of Recruiting Help Enhance Search for Right Talent," *Workforce Management Online*, Nov. 2009 (*www.workforce.com*).

9. R. J. Faberman and M. Kudlyak, "What Does Online Job Search Tell Us About the Labor Market?" *Economic Perspectives*, 2016, 40, pp. 1–15; M. Ferguson, "Recruiting by Numbers," *Workforce*, Aug. 2015 (*www.workforce.com*); A. Adams, "Technology and the Labour Market: The Assessment," *Oxford Review of Economic Policy*, 2018, 34, pp. 349–361.

10. B. W. Swider, R. D. Zimmerman, and M. R. Barrick, "Searching for the Right Fit: Development of Applicant Person-Organization Fit Perceptions During the Recruitment Process," *Journal of Applied Psychology*, 2015, 100, pp. 880–893; G. Beenen and S. Pichler, "Do I Really Want to Work Here? Testing a Model of Job Pursuit for MBA Interns," *Human Resource Management*, 2014, 53, pp. 661–682.

11. D. S. Chapman, K. L. Uggerslev, S. A. Carroll, K. A. Piasentin, and D. A. Jones, "Applicant Attraction to Organizations and Job Choice: A Meta-Analytic Review of the Correlates of Recruiting Outcomes," *Journal of Applied Psychology*, 2005, 90, pp. 928–944; K. L. Uggerslev, N. E. Fassina, and D. Kraichy, "Recruiting Through the Stages: A Meta-Analytic Test of Predictors of Applicant Attraction at Different Stages of the Recruiting Process," *Personnel Psychology*, 2012, 65, pp. 597–660; Anonymous, "Recruiting Today: In a Tight Marketplace, the Lures Come Out," *Financial Planning*, Aug. 2013, pp. 14–16.

12. Uggerslev, Fassina, and Kraichy, "Recruiting Through the Stages: A Meta-Analytic Test of Predictors of Applicant Attraction at Different Stages of the Recruiting Process."

13. D. Catanzaro, H. Moore, and T. R. Marshall, "The Impact of Organizational Culture on Attraction and Recruitment of Job Applicants," *Journal of Business and Psychology*, 2010, 25, pp. 649–662; J. E. Slaughter and G. J. Greguras, "Initial Attraction to Organizations: The Influence of Trait Inferences," *International Journal of Selection and Assessment*, 2009, 17, pp. 1–18.

14. M. L. Connerley, "Recruiter Effects and Recruitment Outcomes," in D. M. Cable and K. Y. T. Yu (eds.), *The Oxford Handbook of Recruitment* (New York: Oxford University Press, 2013), pp. 21–34; A. M. Saks and K. L. Uggerslev, "Sequential and Combined Effects of Recruitment Information on Applicant Reactions," *Journal of Business and Psychology*, 2010, 25, pp. 351–365.

15. S. A. Carless and A. Imber, "The Influence of Perceived Interviewer and Job and Organizational Characteristics on Applicant Attraction and Job Choice Intentions: The Role of Applicant Anxiety," *International Journal of Selection and Assessment*, 2007, 15, pp. 359–371; K. Dunn, "Blame the User, Not the Technology," *Workforce*, Aug. 2016 (*www.workforce.com*).

16. A. C. Klotz, S. P. Motta Veiga, M. R. Buckley, and M. B. Gavin, "The Role of Trustworthiness in Recruitment and Selection: A Review and Guide for Future Research," *Journal of Organizational Behavior*, 2013, 34(S1), S104–S119; Chapman, Uggerslev, Carroll, Piasentin, and Jones, "Applicant Attraction to Organizations and Job Choice: A Meta-Analytic Review of the Correlates of Recruiting Outcomes"; W. R. Boswell, M. V. Roehling, M. A. LePine, and L. M. Moynihan, "Individual Job-Choice Decisions and the Impact of Job Attributes and Recruitment Practices: A Longitudinal Field Study," *Human Resource Management*, 2003, 42, pp. 23–37; A. M. Ryan, J. M. Sacco, L. A. McFarland, and S. D. Kriska, "Applicant Self-Selection: Correlates of Withdrawal From a Multiple Hurdle Process," *Journal of Applied Psychology*, 2000, 85, pp. 163–179.

17. B. R. Dineen, S. R. Ash, and R. A. Noe, "A Web of Applicant Attraction: Person-Organization Fit in the Context of Web-Based Recruitment," *Journal of Applied Psychology*, 2002, 87, pp. 723–734; D. C. Feldman and B. S. Klaas, "Internet Job Hunting: A Field Study of Applicant Experiences

With On-Line Recruiting," *Human Resource Management*, 2002, 41, pp. 175–192; K. Maher, "The Jungle," *Wall Street Journal*, July 18, 2002, p. B10; D. L. Van Rooy, A. Alonso, and Z. Fairchild, "In With the New, Out With the Old: Has the Technological Revolution Eliminated the Traditional Job Search Process?" *International Journal of Selection and Assessment*, 2003, 11, pp. 170–174.

18. D. R. Avery, "Reactions to Diversity in Recruitment Advertising: Are the Differences Black and White?" *Journal of Applied Psychology*, 2003, 88, pp. 672–679; D. R. Avery and P. F. McKay, "Target Practice: An Organizational Impression Management Approach to Attracting Minority and Female Job Applicants," *Personnel Psychology*, 2006, 59, pp. 157–187.

19. P. F. McKay and D. R. Avery, "What Has Race Got to Do With It? Unraveling the Role of Racioethnicity in Job Seekers' Reactions to Site Visits," *Personnel Psychology*, 2006, 59, pp. 395–429; Avery, "Reactions to Diversity in Recruitment Advertising: Are the Differences Black and White?"; Avery and McKay, "Target Practice: An Organizational Impression Management Approach to Attracting Minority and Female Job Applicants."

20. F. Lievens and J. E. Slaughter, "Employer Image and Employer Branding: What We Know and What We Need to Know," *Annual Review of Organizational Psychology and Organizational Behavior*, 2016, 3, pp. 407–440; C. J. Collins, "The Interactive Effects of Recruitment Practices and Product Awareness on Job Seekers' Employer Knowledge and Application Behaviors," *Journal of Applied Psychology*, 2007, 92, pp. 180–190; P. J. Kiger, "Talent Acquisition Special Report: Burnishing the Brand," *Workforce Management*, Oct. 22, 2007, pp. 39–45.

21. K. Y. T. Yu, "Influencing How One Is Seen by Potential Talent: Organizational Impression Management Among Recruiting Firms," *Journal of Applied Psychology*, 2019, 104, pp. 888–906.

22. S. Highhouse, M. E. Brooks, and G. Greguras, "An Organizational Impression Management Perspective on the Formation of Corporate Reputations," *Journal of Management*, 2009, 35, pp. 1481–1493; D. Jones, C. Willness, and S. Madey, "Why Are Job Seekers Attracted by Corporate Social Performance? Experimental and Field Tests of Three Signal Based Mechanisms," *Academy of Management Journal*, 2014, 57, pp. 383–404; T. Vanacker and D. P. Forbes, "Disentangling the Multiple Effects of Affiliate Reputation on Resource Attraction in New Firms," *Organization Science*, 2016, 27, pp. 1525–1547.

23. C. J. Collins and C. K. Stevens, "The Relationship Between Early Recruitment-Related Activities and the Application Decisions of New Labor-Market Entrants: A Brand Equity Approach to Recruitment," *Journal of Applied Psychology*, 2002, 87, pp. 1121–1133; F. Lievens and S. Highhouse, "The Relation of Instrumental and Symbolic Attributes to a Company's Attractiveness as an Employer," *Personnel Psychology*, 2003, 56, pp. 75–102.

24. S. D. Volpone, K. M. Thomas, P. Sinisterra, and L. Johnson, "Targeted Recruiting: Identifying Future Employees," in Cable and Yu (eds.), *The Oxford Handbook of Recruitment*, pp. 110–125; R. Sheth, "Recruit Talent Using a Marketing Mindset," *T+D*, 2014, 68(5), pp. 76–77; E. Dhawan, "Recruiting Strategies for a Tight Talent Market," *Harvard Business Review*, Apr. 2016 (*www.hbr.org*).

25. S. M. Gully, J. M. Phillips, W. G. Castellano, K. Han, and A. Kim, "A Mediated Moderation Model of Recruiting Socially and Environmentally Responsible Job Applicants," *Personnel Psychology*, 2013, 66, pp. 935–973.

26. W. J. Casper, J. H. Wayne, and J. G. Manegold, "Who Will We Recruit? Targeting Deep- and Surface-Level Diversity With Human Resource Policy Advertising," *Human Resource Management*, 2013, 52, pp. 331–332.

27. J. E. Baur, M. R. Buckley, Z. Bagdasarov, and A. S. Dharmasiri, "A Historical Approach to Realistic Job Previews: An Exploration Into Their Origins, Evolution, and Recommendations for the Future," *Journal of Management History*, 2014, 20, pp. 200–223; R. S. Landis, D. R. Earnest, and D. G. Allen, "Realistic Job Previews: Past, Present, and Future," in Cable and Yu (eds.), *The*

Oxford Handbook of Recruitment, pp. 423–436; G. Kranz, "New Employees: 'We Were Jobbed About This Job,'" *Workforce Management*, Feb. 2013 (*www.workforce.com*).

28. D. R. Earnest, D. G. Allen, and R. S. Landis, "Mechanisms Linking Realistic Job Previews With Turnover: A Meta-Analytic Path Analysis," *Personnel Psychology*, 2011, 64, pp. 865–897.

29. R. D. Bretz, Jr., and T. A. Judge, "Realistic Job Previews: A Test of the Adverse Self-Selection Hypothesis," *Journal of Applied Psychology*, 1998, 83, pp. 330–337.

30. J. M. Phillips, "Effects of Realistic Job Previews on Multiple Organizational Outcomes: A Meta-Analysis," *Academy of Management Journal*, 1998, 41, pp. 673–690.

31. R. J. Vandenberg and V. Scarpello, "The Matching Model: An Examination of the Processes Underlying Realistic Job Previews," *Journal of Applied Psychology*, 1990, 75(1), pp. 60–67.

32. H. J. Walker, H. S. Feild, W. F. Giles, and J. B. Bernerth, "The Interactive Effects of Job Advertisement Characteristics and Applicant Experience on Reactions to Recruitment Messages," *Journal of Occupational and Organizational Psychology*, 2008, 81, pp. 619–638.

33. W. R. Boswell, R. D. Zimmerman, and B. W. Swider, "Employee Job Search: Toward an Understanding of Search Context and Search Objectives," *Journal of Management*, 2012, 38, pp. 129–163.

34. D. M. Cable and K. Y. T. Yu, "Managing Job Seekers' Organizational Image Beliefs: The Role of Media Richness and Media Capability," *Journal of Applied Psychology*, 2006, 91, pp. 828–840

35. R. D. Gatewood, M. A. Gowen, and G. Lautenschlager, "Corporate Image, Recruitment Image, and Initial Job Choice Decisions," *Academy of Management Journal*, 1993, 36(2), pp. 414–427.

36. M. Baum and R. Kabst, "The Effectiveness of Recruitment Advertisements and Recruitment Websites: Indirect and Interactive Effects on Applicant Attraction," *Human Resource Management*, 2014, 53, pp. 353–378.

37. A. Tarki and K. Kanara, "How Recruiters Can Stay Relevant in the Age of LinkedIn," *Harvard Business Review Digital Articles*, pp. 2–5, Feb. 2019; S. Cromheeke, G. Van Hoye, and F. Lievens, "Changing Things Up in Recruitment: Effects of a 'Strange' Recruitment Medium on Applicant Pool Quantity and Quality," *Journal of Occupational and Organizational Psychology*, 2013, 86, pp. 410–416.

38. T. Harrison and D. L. Stone, "Effects of Organizational Values and Employee Contact on E-Recruiting," *Journal of Managerial Psychology*, 2018, 33, pp. 311–324; D. G. Allen, R. V. Mahto, and R. F. Otondo, "Web-Based Recruitment: Effects of Information, Organizational Brand, and Attitudes Toward a Web Site on Applicant Attraction," *Journal of Applied Psychology*, 2007, 92, pp. 1696–1708; P. W. Braddy, A. W. Meade, J. J. Michael, and J. W. Fleenor, "Internet Recruiting: Effects of Website Content on Viewers' Perception of Organizational Culture," *International Journal of Selection and Assessment*, 2009, 17, pp. 19–34; B. R. Dineen and R. A. Noe, "Effects of Customization on Application Decisions and Applicant Pool Characteristics in a Web-Based Recruitment Context," *Journal of Applied Psychology*, 2009, 94, pp. 224–234.

39. D. S. Onley, "Mobile Recruiting on the Rise," Mar. 2014 (*www.shrm.com*); M. Wisniewski, "In Battle for IT Talent, Banks Deploy High-Tech Recruiting Tactics," *American Banker*, Aug. 1, 2013, p. 8.

40. D. E. Holmes, "Expanding the Pool," *Harvard Business Review*, June 2019, pp. 58–61; T. Cottereau, "The Future of Live Video Interviews for Recruitment," *HR Magazine*, Nov. 1, 2014 (*www.shrm.com*).

41. K. J. Frasca and M. R. Edwards, "Web-Based Corporate, Social and Video Recruitment Media: Effects of Media Richness and Source Credibility on Organizational Attraction," *International Journal of Selection and Assessment*, 2017, 25, pp. 125–137; B. R. Dineen, G. V. Hoye, F. Lievens, and L. M. Rosokha, "Third Party Employment Branding: What Are Its Signaling Dimensions, Mechanisms, and Sources?" *Research in Personnel and Human Resources Management*, 2019, 37, pp. 173–226; H. J. Walker, H. S. Feild, W. F. Giles, A. A. Armenakis, and J. B. Bernerth, "Displaying Employee Testimonials on Recruitment Websites: Effects of Communication Media,

Employee Race, and Job Seeker Race on Organizational Attraction and Information Credibility," *Journal of Applied Psychology*, 2009, 94, pp. 1354–1364.

42. M. Etter, D. Ravasi, and E. Colleoni, "Social Media and the Formation of Organizational Reputation," *Academy of Management Review*, 2017, 44, pp. 28–52; L. A. McFarland and R. E. Ployhart, "Social Media: A Contextual Framework to Guide Research and Practice," *Journal of Applied Psychology*, 2015, 100, pp. 1653–1677; A. M. Sivertzen, E. R. Nilsen, and A. H. Olafsen, "Employer Branding: Employer Attractiveness and the Use of Social Media," *Journal of Product Brand Management*, 2013, 22, pp. 473–483.

43. Frasca and Edwards, "Web-Based Corporate, Social and Video Recruitment Media: Effects of Media Richness and Source Credibility on Organizational Attraction," *International Journal of Selection and Assessment*, 2017, 25, pp. 125–137; M. Carpentier, G. Van Hoye, and B. Weijters, "Attracting Applicants Through the Organization's Social Media Page: Signaling Employer Brand Personality," *Journal of Vocational Behavior*, 2019, 115, 103326.

44. Faberman and Kudlyak, "What Does Online Job Search Tell Us About the Labor Market?" *Economic Perspectives*, 2016, 40, pp. 1–15.

45. G. Ruiz, "Studies Examine the Online Job Hunting Experience," *Workforce Management Online*, July 2005 (*www.workforce.com*).

46. Freedman, "The Monster Dilemma"; R. Zeidner, "Companies Tell Their Stories in Recruitment Videos," *HR Magazine*, Dec. 2007, p. 28; E. Frauenheim, "Logging Off Job Boards," *Workforce Management*, June 2009, pp. 25–29.

47. D. M. Cable and K. Y. T. Yu, "Managing Job Seekers' Organizational Image Beliefs: The Role of Media Richness and Media Credibility," *Journal of Applied Psychology*, 2006, 91, pp. 828–840.

48. G. Ruiz, "Newspapers, Job Boards Step Up Partnerships," *Workforce Management*, Dec. 11, 2006, pp. 17–18.

49. R. Maurer, "Niche Job Boards Muscle Into Recruiting Marketplace," *HR Magazine*, Feb. 2017 (*www.shrm.org*).

50. Avery and McKay, "Target Practice: An Organizational Impression Management Approach to Attracting Minority and Female Job Applicants."

51. I. Weller, B. C. Holtom, W. Matiaske, and T. Mellewigt, "Level and Time Effects of Recruitment Sources on Voluntary Employee Turnover," *Journal of Applied Psychology*, 2009, 94, pp. 1146–1162; J. R. Pieper, J. M. Greenwald, and S. D. Schlachter, "Motivating Employee Referrals: The Interactive Effects of the Referral Bonus, Perceived Risk in Referring, and Affective Commitment," *Human Resource Management*, 2018, 57, pp. 1159–1174.

52. J. R. Pieper, "Uncovering the Nuances of Referral Hiring: How Referrer Characteristics Affect Referral Hires' Performance and Likelihood of Voluntary Turnover," *Personnel Psychology*, 2015, 68, pp. 811–858; J. R. Pieper, C. O. Trevor, I. Weller, and D. Duchon, "Referral Hire Presence Implications for Referrer Turnover and Job Performance," *Journal of Management*, 2019, 45, pp. 1858–1888; A. Pallais and E. G. Sands, "Why the Referential Treatment? Evidence From Field Experiments on Referrals," *Journal of Political Economy*, 2016, 124, pp. 1793–1828.

53. P. Weaver, "Tap Ex-Employees' Recruitment Potential," *HR Magazine*, July 2006, pp. 89–91.

54. Society for Human Resource Management, "Using Social Media for Talent Acquisition," Sept. 17, 2017 (*www.shrm.org*).

55. Society for Human Resource Management, "Using Social Media for Talent Acquisition"; S. F. Gale, "In E-Recruiting, There's a New Recruit in Town," *Workforce Management*, Aug. 2013, p. 8.

56. N. Roulin and J. Levashina, "LinkedIn as a New Selection Method: Psychometric Properties and Assessment Approach," *Personnel Psychology*, 2019, 72, pp. 187–211.

57. B. Busch, "Professional Employer Organizations, Social Media, and the Workplace," *Business People*, Aug. 2013, p. 72.

58. S. Greengard, "Recruit Like a Marketer," *Workforce*, July 2016 (*www.workforce.com*).

59. Cable and Yu, "Managing Job Seekers' Organizational Image Beliefs: The Role of Media Richness and Media Credibility."

60. S. Overman, "Do Your Hiring Homework," *Staffing Management Magazine*, Jan. 1, 2009 (*www.workforce.com/topics/staffing-management/*).

61. B. Perkins, "Jousting for Jobs," *Computerworld*, Aug. 12, 2013, p. 40.

62. T. Lytle, "How to Minimize Staffing Agency Snags," *Society for Human Resource Management*, Oct. 24, 2017 (*www.shrm.org*); R. J. Grossman, "The Art of Choosing a Staffing Agency," *HR Magazine*, Mar. 1, 2012 (*www.shrm.org*).

63. M. Feffer, "How to Work Effectively With an Executive Search Firm," *Society for Human Resource Management*, July 18, 2016 (*www.shrm.org*); M. Hamori, "Who Gets Headhunted—and Who Gets Ahead?" *Academy of Management Perspectives*, 2010, 24(4), pp. 46–59.

64. Feffer, "How to Work Effectively With an Executive Search Firm."

65. US Department of Labor, "Career One Stop," (*www.careeronestop.org*) accessed Feb. 14, 2020.

66. WorkSource (*worksourcewa.com*), accessed Feb. 14, 2020.

67. Texas Workforce Commission (*twc.texas.gov*), accessed Feb. 14, 2020.

68. Cable and Yu, "Managing Job Seekers' Organizational Image Beliefs: The Role of Media Richness and Media Credibility"; Society for Human Resource Management, "How Can I Make the Most Out of Career Fairs?" (*www.shrm.org*), accessed Nov. 19, 2019.

69. J. Stremersch and G. Van Hoye, "Searching Hard Versus Searching Smart: The Role of Search Process Quality in an Internship Context," *International Journal of Selection and Assessment*, 2020, 28, pp. 31–44.

70. Stremersch and Van Hoye, "Searching Hard Versus Searching Smart: The Role of Search Process Quality in an Internship Context"; A. Jaime, J. J. Olarte, F. J. García-Izquierdo, and C. Domínguez, "The Effect of Internships on Computer Science Engineering Capstone Projects," *IEEE Transactions on Education*, 2020, 63, pp. 24–31.

71. G. Beenen and D. M. Rousseau, "Getting the Most From Internships: Promoting Intern Learning and Job Acceptance," *Human Resource Management*, 2010, 49, pp. 3–22.

72. Equal Employment Opportunity Commission, "Records Management" (*www.eeoc.gov*), accessed Dec. 23, 2019.

73. Office of Federal Contract Compliance Programs, "Internet Applicant Recordkeeping Rule" (*www.dol.gov/ofccp*), accessed Feb. 14, 2020.

74. Office of Federal Contract Compliance Programs, "The New Regulations: Vietnam Era Veterans' Readjustment Assistance Act" (*dol.gov/ofccp/regs/compliance/vevraa.htm*); Office of Federal Contract Compliance Programs, "New Regulations: Section 503 of the Rehabilitation Act" (*dol.gov/ofccp/regs/compliance/section503.htm*).

75. A. Iyer and S. Masling, *Recruiting, Hiring, Retaining and Promoting People With Disabilities* (Washington, DC: Whitehouse, 2015).

76. J. Arnold, "Online Job Sites: Convenient but Not Accessible to All," *Society for Human Resource Management*, July 31, 2007 (*www.shrm.org*); S. Bates, "Use Social Media Smartly When Hiring," *Society for Human Resource Management*, Mar. 19, 2013 (*www.shrm.org*).

77. L. S. Rosen, *The Safe Hiring Manual*, 2nd ed. (Tempe, AZ: BRP Publications, 2013), pp. 413–436; J. A. Segal, "Dancing on the Edge of a Volcano," *HR Magazine*, Apr. 2011, pp. 83–86; J. A. Segal, "Widening Web of Social Media," *HR Magazine*, June 2012, pp. 117–120.

78. Office of Federal Contract Compliance Programs, "Disability Issues Related to Online Application Systems," periodically updated (*www.dol.gov*), accessed Feb. 2, 2020.

79. Equal Employment Opportunity Commission, "Prohibited Employment Policies/Practices" (*www.eeoc.gov/laws/practices*), accessed Jan. 28, 2020.

80. D. J. Walsh, *Employment Law for Human Resource Practice*, 5th ed. (Mason, OH: Cengage Learning, 2016), pp. 136–137.

CHAPTER SIX

Internal Recruitment

LEARNING OBJECTIVES AND INTRODUCTION

Learning Objectives

- Be able to engage in effective internal recruitment planning activities
- Apply concepts of closed, open, and hybrid recruitment to the internal recruitment process
- Recognize which recruitment sources are available for internal candidates
- Evaluate internal recruitment based on established metrics
- Recognize how applicant reactions influence the effectiveness of a recruitment plan
- Understand why and how affirmative action plans are implemented for internal recruitment

Introduction

Internal recruitment is the process of identifying and attracting current employees for open jobs. Internal recruits have numerous advantages: they already know the organization's culture, they have already developed relationships with coworkers, and they may require less training than external hires. The nearly ubiquitous presence of internal labor markets underscores the importance of effective internal recruitment. Surveys of human resource (HR) professionals show that as a result of recruitment, selection, training, and development costs, organizations are increasingly looking internally to staff positions.[1] Some estimates suggest that around half of all open jobs are filled through internal hires. Over three-quarters of those surveyed reported that managing their internal talent pool was either a high or a very high strategic priority in their organization. The development of internal talent was seen as a more important talent management task than the acquisition of talent.

Unfortunately, despite the imperative placed on talent management, surveys show that only a quarter of organizations have a formal talent management strategy, and about an eighth of small businesses have a formal talent management system. This relatively limited implementation of effective formal talent management systems means there is much room for improvement. At the same time, a poorly managed internal talent management system can lead to accusations of favoritism, bias, or discrimination. Great care must be taken to ensure that any internal recruitment system is seen as fair.

The first step in the internal recruitment process is recruitment planning. The second step is developing a strategy for where, how, and when to look for recruits. Knowing where to look requires an understanding of open, closed, and hybrid internal recruitment systems. Knowing how to look requires an understanding of job postings, intranets, intra-placement, talent management systems, nominations, in-house temporary pools, replacement and succession plans, and career development centers. Knowing when to look requires an understanding of lead time and time sequencing concerns. The third step consists of the communication message and medium for notification of the job vacancy. The fourth step in the process is developing a job posting system and providing applicants with an understanding of the selection process and how to best prepare for it. The fifth step in the process is the consideration of legal issues. Specific issues to be addressed include Affirmative Action Program regulations, bona fide seniority systems, and the glass ceiling.

STRATEGIC RECRUITMENT PLANNING

Like the external recruitment process, the internal recruitment process involves matching employee KSAOs (knowledge, skill, ability, and other characteristics) to organizational needs. Unlike external recruitment, the management of an internal recruitment process is directed toward channeling and enhancing existing capabilities rather than bringing in new capabilities from the external market. Internal recruitment must be integrated with employee training and development programs. Before identifying and attracting internal applicants to vacant jobs, attention must be directed to organizational and administrative issues that facilitate the effective matching of those applicants with available positions.

Defining Strategic Internal Recruitment Goals

The goals of an internal recruitment system will flow from the organization's overall strategic goals. Much like external recruitment, an internal perspective on recruitment entails defining goals for the right type of applicants, the right number of applicants, and applicants at the right time. As noted below, internal recruiting does add some additional considerations.

Goal 1: The Right Type of Applicants

Defining current and future KSAO needs through the staffing planning and job analysis process is just as important for internal recruiting as it is for external recruiting. Companies can track KSAO levels among their employees and can therefore quickly target their recruiting efforts to individuals who have the appropriate capabilities when the need arises. An internal recruiting strategy is especially valuable when the needed KSAOs are not available on the open market. Expertise with proprietary technology, familiarity with the organization's policies and procedures, knowledge of relationships among different internal stakeholder groups, and skill in leveraging organizational culture to achieve goals are all examples of these types of human capital resources that can be uniquely developed through an internal staffing strategy.[2]

Goal 2: The Right Number of Applicants

Determining the internal-external mix for recruiting depends on whether there are enough internal applicants to fill needs. The planning chapter described some tools that are used for estimating the number of internal applicants that are available for a job. Tools like Markov Analysis and replacement charts highlight one important factor in using internal recruitment: every person who moves into a new role creates a vacancy in their previous role. As we discuss later, casting too wide a net in internal recruiting creates problems since there could be many employees who apply for but are not offered an internal option.

Goal 3: Applicants at the Right Time

Strategic talent management means that the organization identifies crucial skills that will be needed for future positions and begins cultivating these skills in the workforce well in advance.[3] By proactively developing needed skills, the organization will be able to significantly reduce the lead time to fill positions with very specific KSAO requirements. The ability to build KSAOs in the current workforce in anticipation of future staffing needs is the key advantage of an internal recruiting system. Internal hires are also often able to leverage their knowledge of internal processes and culture, and therefore reach full productivity more quickly than external hires.[4] Many of the applicant sourcing strategies we discuss in this chapter, like talent management systems and succession plans, explicitly incorporate a long-term perspective.

Mobility Paths and Policies

The internal recruitment system will be crucially dependent on the mobility paths and policies that have been established in the organization. Just as the external labor market can be divided into segments or strata of workers believed to be desirable job applicants, so, too, can the internal labor market of an organization be divided into segments. This division is often done informally inside organizations. For example, managers might talk about the talented pool of managerial trainees this year and refer to some of them as "high-potential employees." As another example, people in the organization talk about their "techies," an internal collection of employees with the technical skills needed to run the business.

Mobility Paths

A mobility path consists of possible employee movements within the internal labor market structure. Mobility paths are determined by many factors, including KSAO requirements, workforce characteristics, organizational culture, and labor market characteristics. Mobility paths are of two types: hierarchical and alternative. Both types determine who is eligible for a new job in the organization.

Hierarchical Mobility Paths. Examples of hierarchical mobility paths are shown in Exhibit 6.1. As can be seen, the emphasis is primarily on upward mobil-

EXHIBIT 6.1 **Hierarchical Mobility Paths**

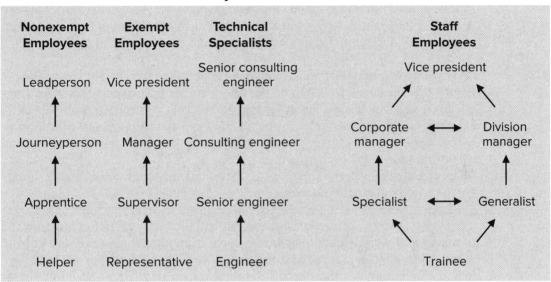

ity in the organization. Due to their upward nature, hierarchical mobility paths are often labeled "promotion ladders." This label implies that each job is a step toward the top of the organization. Employees often see upward promotions as prizes because of the promotions' desirable characteristics. For example, a promotion might lead to a higher rate of pay, and a transfer may result in a move to a better work location. A great deal of research has been conducted on these types of "tournaments" for higher pay and promotions, with evidence clearly suggesting that individuals increase their effort when faced with the prospect of a large payoff.[5] However, this same research suggests that competition can lead to counterproductive behavior, like sabotaging other employees or turnover among those who do not receive promotions.

An exception to the primarily upward mobility in the promotion ladders in Exhibit 6.1 shows the lateral moves that sometimes occur for the staff member who has both generalist and specialist experience as well as corporate and division experience. This staff member is considered more well-rounded and better able to work within the total organization. Experience as a specialist gives the person familiarity with technical issues. Experience as a generalist gives the employee a breadth of knowledge. Corporate experience provides a policy and planning perspective, whereas division experience provides greater insight into day-to-day operational matters.

Hierarchical mobility paths make it easy, from an administrative vantage point, to identify where to look for applicants in the organization. For promotion, one looks at the next level down in the organizational hierarchy, and for transfer, one looks over. Although such a system is straightforward to administer, it is not very flexible and may inhibit matching the best person to the job. For example, the best person for the job may be two levels down and in another division from the vacant job. It is very difficult to locate such a person under a hierarchical mobility path.

Alternative Mobility Paths.   Examples of alternative mobility paths are shown in Exhibit 6.2. The emphasis here is on movement in the organization in any direction—up, down, and side to side. Employee movement is emphasized to ensure that each employee is continuously learning and that they can make the greatest contribution to the organization. This is in direct contrast to the hierarchical promotion ladder, where the goal is for each person to achieve a position with ever-higher status. Many organizations have shifted to alternative mobility paths to be flexible, avoiding the rigidity of strict hierarchies.

Parallel tracks allow for employees to specialize in technical work or management work. Historically, technical specialists had to shift away from technical work to managerial work if they wanted to receive higher-status job titles and pay. In other words, a technical specialist was a dead-end job. Under a parallel track system, however, job titles and salaries of technical specialists are elevated to be commensurate with their managerial counterparts. Such parallel track systems avoid the problem of employees being promoted out of a job they were effective in, and into a role requiring KSAOs they do not possess.[6] For example, hierarchical paths sometimes mean that an excellent engineer is promoted into an administrative role that matches neither her skills nor her interests. In a parallel track system, this

EXHIBIT 6.2   Alternative Mobility Paths

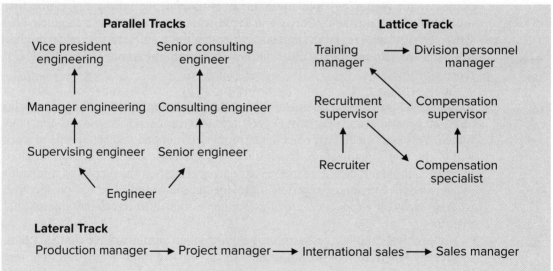

engineer can grow their career by taking on increased responsibility for the part of the job they are best at.

With a lateral track system, there may be no upward mobility at all. The individual's greatest contribution to the organization may be to stay at a certain level for an extended period of time while serving in a variety of capacities. Lateral tracks are quite common, especially in industries and countries with strong labor protections that make hiring and terminations administratively complex and expensive. A lateral track system allows for the flexible assignment of employees within the organization in response to changing strategic and operational needs.[7]

A lattice mobility path has upward, lateral, and even downward movement. For example, a recruiter may be promoted to a recruitment supervisor position, but to continue to contribute to the organization, the person may need to take a downward step to become knowledgeable about all the technical details in compensation. After mastering these details, the person may then become a supervisor again, this time in the compensation area rather than in recruitment. The person may have experience in training from a previous organization and be ready to move to training manager without training experience internal to the organization. Finally, the person may make a lateral move to manage all the HR functions in a division (recruitment, compensation, and training) as a division personnel manager.

Some organizations have adopted a team-based structure, hoping to maximize the information flow, increase flexibility, and minimize boundaries among employees.[8] These organizations may do away with formal job titles and ranks altogether, with workers being reassigned to different roles in various project teams as needed. Such a structure is found mainly in research and development environments. The role of internal recruitment in such organizations changes completely, as talent management is focused on pairing employee KSAOs with unique project demands that are constantly in flux. This means there is a dramatic increase in the need for assessment of employee KSAOs and collaboration with team leaders to reconfigure groups quickly and efficiently. Such team-focused arrangements can be highly motivational for highly skilled individuals who are self-directed and engaged in their profession.

When upward mobility is limited in an organization, as in those using alternative mobility paths, special steps need to be taken to ensure that work remains meaningful to employees. Examples of steps to make work more meaningful include the following:

1. *Alternative reward systems.* Pay increases can be based on an individual's knowledge, skill acquisition, and contribution as a team member. These programs are successful at encouraging employees to develop job-relevant skills.[9]
2. *Team building.* Greater challenge and autonomy in the workplace can be created by having employees work in teams where they are responsible for all aspects of work involved in providing a service or product, including self-management.

3. *Counseling.* Workshops, self-directed workbooks, and individual advising can be used to ensure that employees have a well-reasoned plan for movement in the organization.

4. *Alternative employment.* Arrangements can be made for employee leaves of absence, sabbaticals, and consulting assignments to ensure that workers remain challenged and acquire new knowledge and skills.

Mobility Policies

Mobility paths show the relationships among jobs, but they do not show the rules by which people move between jobs. These rules should specify eligibility criteria.

Policy Development.   It is important to ensure that mobility policies meet organizational goals, are seen as fair by employees, and can be administered easily.[10] Fortunately, many of the same principles that enhance policy fit with strategy enhance perceived justice and also make the system easy to apply. These principles include clarity, objectivity, consistency, and transparency. These are a few key characteristics of an effective mobility policy development process:

- Ensure that organizational leaders who will be affected by the policy have an opportunity to participate in policy creation.
- Provide clear rationales for overall policy frameworks, linking them to organizational strategy and goals. Link specific mobility path policies to performance-relevant qualifications based on job analysis.
- Clearly state rules for how employees will be notified of openings, deadlines, and data to be supplied; how requirements and qualifications are relevant; how the selection process will work; and how job offers will be made.
- Outline employee and supervisor responsibilities and opportunities for development. Develop clear criteria for who is eligible to be considered for a vacancy in a mobility path.
- Communicate procedures and policies to all affected parties.

Policy Implementation.   After the organization has developed its mobility policies, a strong set of supporting practices should ensure they are implemented as planned. To facilitate effective implementation of the policies and practices, the organization should match implementation plans to the components of policy creation:

1. Continually collect data from leaders regarding the fit of mobility policies with organizational goals. If implementing the policies as written is difficult or interferes with organizational effectiveness, they should be revised.

2. Track compliance with preestablished criteria and reinforce why these criteria are important for managers.

3. Use tracking systems that ensure communication and selection procedures are followed and that favoritism and bias are minimized.

4. Document employee development progress. Methods for tracking should be automated (such as through automatic e-mails or posting to a central career management system) and accessible for users.

5. Supervisors and employees should receive regular updates regarding the status of any internal mobility decisions. This can be automated in a manner similar to the development progress system.

Closed, Open, and Hybrid Recruitment

The decision of how to communicate a job announcement to employees is a key component of an internal recruitment system. The choice among closed, open, and hybrid systems can affect employee motivation and perceptions of fairness, so each possibility should be carefully considered.

Closed Internal Recruitment System

Under a closed internal recruitment system, employees are not made aware of job vacancies. The only people made aware of promotion or transfer opportunities are those who oversee placement in the HR department, line managers with vacancies, and contacted employees. Exhibit 6.3 shows how a vacancy is typically filled under a closed system.

EXHIBIT 6.3   Closed Internal Recruitment System

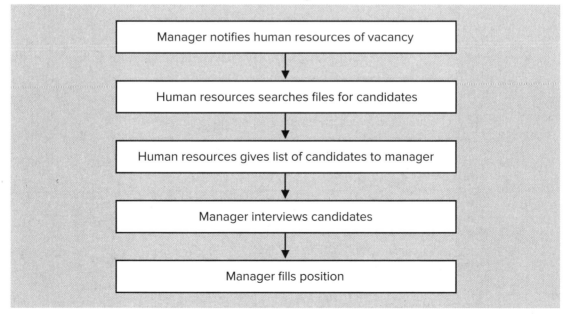

A closed system is very efficient. There are only a few steps to follow, and the time and cost involved are minimal. However, a closed system is only as good as the files showing candidates' KSAOs. If the files are inaccurate or out of date, qualified candidates may be overlooked. Thus, maintaining accurate human resource information systems (HRISs) that track KSAOs regularly is vital.

Open Internal Recruitment System

Under an open internal recruitment system, employees are made aware of job vacancies. Usually this is accomplished by a job posting and bidding system. Exhibit 6.4 shows the typical steps followed in filling a vacancy under an open internal recruitment system.

EXHIBIT 6.4   Open Internal Recruitment System

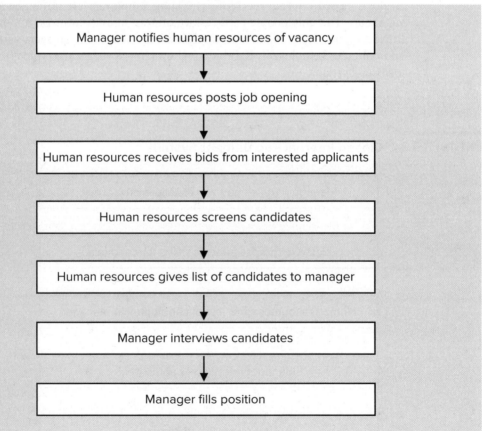

An open system gives employees a chance to measure their qualifications against those required for advancement. It helps minimize the possibility that supervisors will select favorite employees for promotion or transfer, and it often uncovers hidden talent. Some evidence suggests that individuals hired through an open posting system perform better in the job and are less likely to turn over compared with those who are hired through a closed system.[11] Receiving multiple applicants leads managers to treat the process more like a typical external hiring process. Therefore, they pay more attention to evaluating applicant qualifications than they would if evaluating those who are preselected through a closed system.

An open system may, however, create unwanted competition for limited advancement opportunities. It is a very lengthy and time-consuming process to screen all candidates and provide them with feedback. Employee morale may decrease among those who do not advance.

Hybrid System of Internal Recruitment

Under a hybrid system, both open and closed steps are followed at the same time. Job vacancies are posted and the HR department conducts a search outside the job posting system. Both systems are used in order to cast as wide a net as possible. The large applicant pool is then narrowed down by KSAOs, seniority eligibility, demographics, and availability of applicants.

Merico Hotels uses a hybrid system that includes both the training and development of promising employees for specific higher-level positions along with job posting methods.[12] The organization's performance management system encourages employees to specify their potential internal career tracks and indicate which developmental opportunities will help them progress. Those who are identified as high-potential employees receive special training within a formal succession planning system. When jobs open, they are posted via an internal job vacancy software program developed specifically by Merico. Employees who are especially qualified for these openings are alerted by the organization and encouraged to apply.

A hybrid system has four advantages: qualified candidates are identified in advance, a thorough search is conducted, people have equal opportunity to apply for postings, and hidden talent is uncovered. The major disadvantage of a hybrid system is that it entails a time-consuming and costly process.

Criteria for Choice of System

In an ideal world with unlimited resources, one would choose a hybrid system of internal recruitment. However, due to resource constraints, most organizations must choose between open and closed systems. Several criteria need to be thoroughly considered before selecting an internal recruitment system. Exhibit 6.5 reviews these criteria.

EXHIBIT 6.5　**Choosing Among Open, Closed, and Hybrid Internal Recruiting**

Technique	Advantages	Best When
Open	Identifies more candidates, including those who might be overlooked in a closed system	Issues exist about perceived fairness
		Hidden talent might be overlooked
	Makes rules and regulations explicit and open to all employees	
	Sometimes required by labor agreements	
Closed	Less expensive in terms of search costs	Managers need the new candidate to start immediately
	Offers a quicker response	Jobs require a very narrow and specialized set of KSAOs
	Less cumbersome when only a select few meet the minimum requirements	
Hybrid	Finds a large number of candidates	Adequate resources are available to run such a hybrid system
	Everyone has an opportunity to apply	
		Jobs are especially key to organizational success

Although the choice of system is important, the use of staffing software (see the staffing system management chapter) allows bridges to be built between these systems to take advantage of the best features of each.

Organization and Administration

Administrative plans must be established as part of the planning process, including coordination, the budget, and the recruitment guide.

Coordination

Internal and external recruitment efforts need to be coordinated and synchronized via the organization's staffing philosophy. If independent searches are conducted internally and externally, two people may be hired for one vacancy. If only an external recruitment search is conducted, the morale of current employees may suffer if they feel they have been passed over for a promotion. If only an internal recruitment search is conducted, the person hired may not be as qualified as someone from the external market. Because of these possibilities, internal *and* external professionals must work together with the line manager to coordinate efforts before the search for candidates begins.

To coordinate activities, policies need to be created that specify the number and types of candidates sought both internally and externally. External recruiters should stay in frequent contact with internal placement professionals.

Budget

An organization's budgeting process for internal recruitment should closely mirror that of external recruitment. The cost per hire may, however, differ between internal and external recruitment. Targeting current employees does not mean that the cost per hire is necessarily less than the cost per hire for external recruitment. There are time costs because internal candidates who are considered for the job but are not hired may need to be counseled on what to do in order to better compete for the position the next time it is vacant. When an external candidate is rejected, a simple and less costly rejection letter usually suffices.

Recruitment Guide

As with external recruitment, internal recruitment activities involve the development of a recruitment guide, a formal document that details the process to be followed to attract applicants to a vacant job. Included in the plan are details such as the time, money, and staff activities required to fill the job, as well as the steps to be taken to fill the vacancy created by the internal candidate leaving to take on the new job. An example of an internal recruitment guide is shown in Exhibit 6.6.

EXHIBIT 6.6   Internal Recruitment Guide

Position Reassignments Into New Claims Processing Center

Goal: Transfer qualified medical claims processors and examiners from company subsidiary to the new claims processing center. Facilitate outplacement for those whose qualifications no longer fit changed job requirements.

Hiring responsibility: Manager of Claims Processing.

Other resources: Entire human resource department staff.

Time frames:
Positions posted internally on April 2, 2021
Employees may apply until April 16, 2021
Interviews will occur during the week of April 26, 2021

(continued)

EXHIBIT 6.6   Continued

Selections made and communicated by last week in May

Positions available and corresponding qualification summaries:

Total number of available positions: 46

6 claims supervisors—4-year degree with 3 years of claims experience, including 1 year of supervisory experience.

8 hospital claims examiners—12 months of claims data entry/processing experience. Knowledge of medical terminology necessary.

8 physician claims examiners—12 months of claims data entry/processing experience. Knowledge of medical terminology necessary.

8 dental claims examiners—12 months of claims data entry/processing experience and 6 months of dental claims examining experience. Knowledge of dental terminology necessary.

8 mental health claims examiners—12 months of claims data entry/processing experience and 6 months of mental health claims experience. Knowledge of medical and mental health terminology necessary.

8 substance abuse claims examiners—12 months of claims data entry/processing experience and 6 months of substance abuse experience. Knowledge of medical terminology necessary.

Transfer request guidelines: Internal candidates must submit internal transfer request listing all positions for which they are applying, in order of preference, through the company's internal HRIS.

Transfer requests must be endorsed by the employee's supervisor.

Candidate qualification review process: Transfer requests from internal candidates will be reviewed on a daily basis. Those not qualified for positions for which they have applied will be notified immediately through the company's HRIS. Once all candidate qualifications have been received and reviewed, each candidate's transfer packet will be shared with the managers for review and interview selection. Managers will interview only those candidates who meet predefined minimum qualifications.

Selection guidelines: Selection processes will proceed based on the identified competencies developed for each position. Employees should be slotted into a position with a salary grade comparable to their current salary grade. Employees' salaries shall not be reduced due to the involuntary nature of the job reassignment.

Selection notifications: Candidates will be informed whether they have been selected for a position in person by the human resource staff and will be given a confirmation letter specifying starting date, position, reporting relationship, and salary.

A major difference between internal and external recruitment is that internal recruitment not only fills vacancies but also creates them. Each time a vacancy is filled with an internal candidate, a new vacancy is created in the spot vacated by the internal candidate.

Timing

Timing considerations for internal recruiting tend to be more specific to ensure that employees are aware of their prospects. Specific rules about when applications are required and when decisions will be made should be clearly communicated to minimize disruptions to regular work. A flowchart describing the process should also be shared with the individuals who are supervising employees who have applied for a position.

APPLICANT REACTIONS

Internal applicants will have different considerations than external applicants regarding recruitment methods. Their familiarity with the organization's structure, reward practices, and decision-making procedures will allow them to better consider the long-term consequences of pursuing an internal position. Because they are already embedded within the organization, they will probably have a longer time horizon and can consider not just the immediate features of the job but also the future benefits of taking on a new position. From the organization's perspective, it is much easier to evaluate the preferences of internal employees than those of external candidates. Supervisors and other organizational leaders will be able to discuss these preferences at length, and then customize messages to fit individual needs and preferences.

Perceived fairness of an internal recruitment process is extremely important. A potential applicant who feels that a company's external recruitment policy is unfair is unlikely to pursue a job opportunity, and that generally will mark the end of the interaction. An employee who feels that their company's internal recruitment policy is unfair will remain an employee, and the negative perceptions may spill over to reduce motivation, engagement, and performance and might even lead to turnover. As noted earlier in the "Policy Development" and "Policy Implementation" sections, issues of fairness should be resolved through transparency, objectivity, consistency, and clarity. Reviews of the evidence suggest that procedures may be nearly as great a source of dissatisfaction to employees as decisions.[13] In some organizations, dissatisfaction arises because there is no formal policy regarding promotion and transfer opportunities. Ensure that employees are aware of opportunities for which they are qualified, and clearly state the underlying logic for encouraging candidates to take different internal mobility paths.

Individuals who are denied promotion appear to be more likely to turn over, reduce effort, or engage in counterproductive work behaviors.[14] A system for managing the reactions of applicants who do not receive a desired position can head off these negative effects, especially when there are multiple high-potential applicants. Effective policies can focus on providing these individuals with guidance on how they can improve their future prospects. Alternative options should also be evaluated so applicants can identify other attractive opportunities for internal career growth.

COMMUNICATION

Once the planning and strategy development phases have been conducted, it is time to conduct the search. As with external recruitment, informing potential applicants about the opening and the characteristics of the position will have a strong influence on the types of individuals who apply. However, the content of the message and the media through which it will be transmitted are quite different.

Communication Message

Like the external recruitment message, the internal recruitment message can be realistic, targeted, or branded. A realistic message portrays the job as it really is, including positive and negative aspects. A targeted message points out how the job matches the needs of the applicant. A branded message emphasizes the value, culture, and identity of the unit to attract applicants who fit the brand label. Information should clarify how the culture of the new work unit or division differs from other areas of the organization. The internal applicant will have more information about the organization than external applicants, but this information may be in the form of inaccurate word of mouth or uninformed guesses. Therefore, any recruitment message should take the internal image of the job into account.

Branded messages can emphasize how a specific area of the organization offers unique opportunities to internal applicants. This information can be communicated in a way that takes advantage of what employees already know about the job and organization. For example, a company expanding into a new regional market can describe how taking on a position in this new region will be a unique opportunity for personal and professional growth, with detailed information regarding specific products and initiatives that are active in that area, and even mention of key individuals whose reputations might be known in the organization who are also active in that area.

Targeted messages along with inducements are likely to attract experienced internal employees. Because internal applicants will be personally known by coworkers and supervisors, messages can be specifically targeted around each person's identified needs and desires. Targeted messages about the desirability of a position and the actual rewards should come directly from the job rewards matrix. The hiring manager needs to clearly communicate factual information in the job rewards matrix, rather than offers of potential rewards that the manager may not be able to provide.

Realistic messages can be communicated using a realistic job preview (RJP). This technique needs to be carefully applied for internal recruitment because applicants may already have a picture of the job since they are already a member of the organization. It should not be automatically assumed that all internal candidates have accurate information about the job and organization. RJPs are particularly appropriate for internal applicants when they move to an unknown job, a newly created job, or a new geographic area, including an international assignment. Alternatively, it is often possible to give internal recruits informational interviews with future coworkers, site visits, or even hands-on experience in the new work environment, which is less feasible with external recruits.

Communication Media

The actual methods or media used to communicate job openings internally include formal job postings, direct contact with potential supervisors and peers, and word of mouth. In most cases, all three media should be considered as potential parts of the process, although only the first two are encouraged.

A job posting should clearly define the duties and requirements of the job as well as the eligibility requirements. To ensure consistency and fair treatment, job postings are usually coordinated by the HR department. Other documents used to communicate a vacancy may include a description of the work unit and its location as well as a description of the job. A brochure or video can also be created to show and describe what the job and its location are like. Such a message would be important to applicants asked to relocate to a new geographic area or to accept an international assignment.

Potential supervisors and peers can describe to the internal applicant how the position they are considering fits into the larger organizational picture. Supervisors are knowledgeable about how the position fits with the strategic direction of the organization. Hence, they can communicate information regarding the expansion or contraction of the business unit within which the job resides. Moreover, supervisors can convey the mobility paths and requirements for future movement by applicants within the business unit, should they be hired. Peers can supplement these supervisory observations by giving candidates a realistic look at what actually happens by way of career development.

Word of mouth is difficult for the organization to control when it comes to external applicant searches, but it can be much more problematic for internal searches. This can be a highly selective, inaccurate, and haphazard method of communicating information. It is selective because, by accident or design, not all employees hear about vacant jobs. Talented personnel, including underrepresented groups, may thus be overlooked. It is inaccurate because it relies on second- or third-hand information; important details, such as actual job requirements and rewards, are omitted or distorted as they are passed from person to person. Informal methods are also haphazard in that there is no regular communication channel specifying set times for communicating job information. As a result of these problems, the organization should be aware of word-of-mouth influences and attempt to minimize their effect on the applicant identification and attraction process.

APPLICANT SOURCING

After the focus of the strategic recruitment search has been established and communication messages and media have been evaluated, the organization must develop a strategy to access viable internal job applicants. When thinking about sourcing for internal hires, we can think of processes as being mostly focused on a specific position opening and those that address the entire system of job qualifications.

Position-Based Sourcing

First, we consider recruitment sources that are developed around a single job opening. These systems involve managing single job openings and are much more comparable to an external hiring method.

Postings

A job posting system is similar to the use of organizational websites in external recruitment. A posting spells out the duties and requirements of available jobs and provides a portal through which internal applicants can submit their materials. Organizations do not have to build these internal systems from the ground up; many HRIS developers integrate internal job posting systems into their programs. This means that when a job that has been designated as part of the internal market comes open, full posting information based on job analysis records can easily be put on the company intranet in one integrated process. Smaller organizations with less robust internal labor markets may post jobs through e-mails rather than through establishing a dedicated internal recruitment site. E-mail contact with selected individuals can also be part of a closed recruitment system as well.

An example of the type of information found in an internal job posting is shown in Exhibit 6.7. Such information includes the job title, category, compensation, and work schedule. A brief overview of desired qualifications and a job description can be pulled directly into the system from job analysis files. Work unit descriptions can also be developed and standardized to make the process of uploading a new position more efficient. Finally, application instructions link the user to three different portals. The submission portal leads to a series of pages where applicants

EXHIBIT 6.7   Example of Job Posting Information

Job code and title	(75593) Administrative Specialist II
Position title	Assistant to Director of Marketing
Position category	Administrative and clerical
Compensation category	Nonexempt C [$15.00 to $20.00 per hour to start, depending on qualifications]
Work hours	8:30 am–5:00 pm
Work days	MTWThF
Required/preferred qualifications	Prior experience as Administrative Specialist I or II
	Excellent professional communication skills
	Proficiency with word processing, spreadsheet, asset management, database, electronic mail, and Internet browser software
	Knowledge of management principles and functions
Job description	Assist the Director of Marketing with clerical and administrative tasks, including preparing correspondence, organizing a calendar of appointments, communicating with individuals within and external to the organization
Work unit description	The Director of Marketing works in the corporate offices in downtown Chicago. Employees work closely with one another in the marketing department and support one another through their efforts. There is a formal dress code for all employees in this division and professionalism is emphasized.
Application instructions	Click to enter submission portal. ENTER
	Click to submit appraisal information from records: ENTER
	Click to request recommendations: ENTER

can submit their qualifications and statement of interest. The appraisal information portal allows applicants to link their individual application to previous performance appraisal information in the HRIS. Finally, the recommendation portal allows the applicant to request recommendations from other individuals within the organization; these requests generate e-mail messages to the relevant parties with information on how to submit a recommendation to the system. This example shows a very basic, utilitarian format for the posting, but many organizations supplement their postings with images of or personal messages from individuals working in similar roles.

Despite their advantages, internal job posting systems have some drawbacks. Examples of such difficulties include situations where employees believe that someone was selected before the job was posted (a "bagged" job), cumbersome systems where managers and HR personnel are overwhelmed with résumés of unqualified candidates, and criticisms that the HR department is not doing an effective job of screening candidates for positions.

Another important issue with posting systems is in providing feedback. Not only do employees need to know whether they have received the job, but those who did not receive the job need to be made aware of *why* they did not. Providing this feedback serves two purposes. First, it makes job posting part of the career development system of the organization. Second, it invites candidates to bid on future postings. If employees are not given feedback, they may be less likely to bid for another job because they feel that their attempts are futile.

Nominations

Nominations for internal candidates to apply for open positions can be solicited from potential supervisors and peers. These individuals are an excellent source of names of internal candidates, as they are familiar with what is required to be successful in the position. They can help establish the criteria for eligibility and then, through their contacts in the organization, search for eligible candidates. Self-nominations are also useful in that they ensure that qualified candidates are not inadvertently overlooked using other applicant searching methods. Self-nomination is an especially important consideration in the internal recruitment of minorities and women.

In-House Temporary Pools

In-house temporary pools are important to the temporary staffing of organizations, and they are also an excellent source of permanent internal employment. Unlike employees hired through external staffing agencies, those employed through in-house temporary pools are legally treated as employees. Therefore, the full legal liability for these employees falls exclusively on the employer. Using in-house temporary employees has a number of advantages.[15] Internal temporary employees require less orientation to the organization than external hires. Staffing agencies typically charge an employer an hourly fee for each temporary employee. But with an internal system, because the employer does not have to pay an hourly fee to an external agency, the cost savings can be applied to higher levels of compensation and benefits. It is also easier for an organization to ensure the quality and person/organization fit for employees from an in-house pool relative to a pool of external hires. Temporary employment can also serve as an "audition" for full-time employment, allowing the temporary employee to try out a number of positions until the employee and the organization agree on a good person/job match. In health care, it is common to have "float" staff who are assigned to different units regularly, depending on the organization's needs. These pools are especially valuable in this highly specialized field because quality control and knowledge of organizational policies and procedures are crucial for performance. Surveys of health care organizations show that these pools are seen as an important and effective tool for enhancing performance and minimizing costs.[16] Substitute teachers are staffed in a similar manner. Such employees must be adaptable to different situations, and the organization must ensure that the employees have sufficient work. In addition, extra training may be needed for these employees since they are expected to have a broad range of skills in their repertoire.

System-Based Sourcing

Next, we consider internal recruitment sources that are developed around the entire system of jobs in the organization. The key difference is that these internal recruiting systems incorporate training and development across many roles over time. The use of system-based sourcing is consistent with the human capital resources perspective. By thinking of systems of capabilities across numerous employees, organizations can develop capabilities that would be missed by focusing on individual KSAOs. Strategic HR researchers and executives describe these higher-order "synergies" or "emergent properties" derived from a systems-based view of employee capabilities as unique sources of competitive advantage.[17]

Talent Management Systems

A talent management system is a comprehensive method for monitoring and tracking the utilization of employee skills and abilities throughout the organization.[18] The process of talent management is closely aligned with replacement and succession planning: talent management systems track the KSAOs of the workforce, and then replacement and succession planning translates this information into concrete action plans for specific job roles. Although talent management involves performance management and training processes in addition to managing the internal recruitment process, tracking employees' KSAOs and their use in the organization is the key component of talent management systems.

Although a number of different models for implementing talent management systems exist, there are a few key processes common to most. The first stage of the process is identifying the KSAOs required for all jobs in the organization. This information can be obtained from job descriptions and job specifications. The complete set of KSAOs required across the organization will then be compiled into a master list. The current workforce will need to be assessed for its competence in this set of KSAOs, usually as an adjunct to routine performance evaluations. When positions come open, managers make a query to the talent management system to determine which employees are eligible. A process should be in place to make regular comprehensive examinations of the changing nature of KSAO requirements throughout the organization. Information from these analyses can then be used as a springboard for developing comprehensive plans for training and development experiences.

There has been such a strong integration of database software for talent management systems that when staffing managers refer to them, they are often talking about the specific HRIS that is used to facilitate tracking KSAOs in the workforce. While these database applications offer great promise for coordinating information, many managers find operating talent management systems challenging. Most of the problems in implementing the systems in practice do not come from a lack of technology but from an excess of technology that cannot be understood by line managers. A few principles should be borne in mind when developing or evaluating a user-friendly talent management system:

- Keep the format for entering data as simple as possible.
- Have an easy method for updating basic information with each performance evaluation cycle.
- Make it easy to perform database queries.
- Provide varied formats for obtaining reports.
- Ensure that information is confidential.
- Make it possible to perform statistical analyses using relational databases.
- Integrate data with other HR files.

Replacement and Succession Plans

A critical source of internal recruitment that follows from a talent management system is provided by the results of replacement and succession planning. Most succession plans include replacement charts (see the planning chapter), which indicate positions and who is scheduled to fill those slots when they become vacant. Replacement charts usually also indicate when the individual will be ready for the assignment. Succession plans are organized by position and list the skills needed for the prospective position (i.e., "for the employee to be promoted into this position from her current position, she needs to develop the following skills").

It is critical that succession planning be future oriented, lest the organization plan be based on historical competencies that fail to meet new challenges. Software exists to assist organizations with succession planning. The succession planning packages used by many Fortune 500 companies interface with an organization's HRIS. These packages provide replacement charts and competency libraries that allow an organization to identify developmental activities and assignments for individuals in the replacement charts.

Most replacement and succession plans focus their attention on high-potential employees.[19] Such individuals are identified based on performance in their current role as well as signals of competencies required for a higher-level job; talent management systems are usually an important part of the process. Employees who are aware that they have been identified as high potential and whose future internal career paths are being actively cultivated tend to be more motivated and confident. Communication around high-potential status should be carefully managed, however, as it is also clear that overconfidence and resentment from coworkers can occur.

CEO succession has always been an important issue for organizations, but never more so than today. A major retrospective study of CEO transition failures conducted by the Conference Board found that about half of organizations have neither an emergency succession plan nor a long-term succession plan.[20] Key shortfalls identified in CEO succession plans include misalignment of hiring criteria with strategic organization needs, a fear of antagonizing the current CEO by trying to identify potential replacements, and a lack of investment in developing the entire workforce from the bottom up. There is great concern among career development specialists that the mass retirement of baby boomers will lead to a loss of organizational memory and knowledge built up with experience. Having strong succession planning techniques that will enable the more recently hired workforce to acquire knowledge from its experienced coworkers before moving into managerial positions is one way to minimize the impact of mass retirements.

Interviews with executive recruiters and CEOs have found that industry- and organization-specific competencies are highly desirable. This underscores the need to develop these attributes in-house, since they will be hard to find on the open labor market. A succession plan should begin with a thorough job analysis and a listing of the characteristics and behaviors of a successful CEO.[21] The organization should not leave it to the CEO to identify a successor. CEOs are typically not trained or experienced in staffing. Therefore, the board must be deeply involved in the selection process. Boards also need to realize that the succession process should begin well before the CEO departs; in fact, it should be a continuous process. Appropriate succession plans should also examine the pipeline for individuals to replace the top management team members (e.g., chief financial officer, chief operating officer, senior vice presidents) who might replace the CEO. As we saw in the planning chapter, each time an internal promotion occurs, it creates a need to staff the position of the individual who was promoted.

Career Development Centers

To facilitate internal transfers, many organizations have an internal office of career development that helps employees explore career options available within the organization.[22] Career development centers provide employees with opportunities to take interest inventories, assess their personal career goals, and interview with representatives across the organization. The goal of career development centers is twofold. First, employees learn about themselves and have a chance to think about what they really want to achieve in their careers. Second, employers have a chance to explain the career options within the organization and develop methods to structure internal career paths that match the interests of their employees. Surveys conducted in numerous organizations consistently demonstrate that employees are more satisfied when their employers provide them with ample communication and opportunities for internal advancement—an interactive career development center can do both.[23]

The interest inventories provided in career development centers often take the form of multiple-choice questionnaires that ask employees to indicate their preferred work activities. For example, respondents might be asked whether they prefer tasks that involve analytical processes like analyzing financial data or more social tasks like motivating a group of workers. After completing these surveys, employees compare their work preferences with the profiles of activities in a variety of jobs. Career development counselors can help talk employees through their thoughts and concerns about job options. Ideally, these career development inventories, coupled with careful analysis of KSAOs, will be paired with job analysis information to improve the person/job match. If employees lack the required KSAOs, career development counselors can suggest developmental work experiences or training opportunities.

Any assessment of career development centers needs to take the organization's bottom line into account.[24] Having full-time career development staff is a significant cost for any organization, and it is unlikely that small or medium-sized organizations will find it cost-effective to develop a comprehensive career development center. For smaller organizations, it is more advisable to develop smaller-scale informal initiatives based on personal interactions. Smaller organizations can make use of some career development tools by bringing in external career coaches or consultants to work with individuals who are especially interested in career development within the organization. To reduce costs, employees could take their career development profiles and receive initial feedback through web-based surveys. These electronic survey options save money by reducing staff needs, and employees will not need to go to the career development offices to receive initial counseling.

Although career development centers are complicated to develop and expensive to maintain, they offer organizations an opportunity to help employees learn about a large spectrum of careers. By providing employees with a clear sense of how they can direct their own careers, it is hoped that job satisfaction will increase and thus lead to increased retention. Because of the cost of career development services, it is especially important to keep track of the return on investment for these services.

Recruitment Metrics

Like external recruitment sources, each internal recruitment source has strengths and weaknesses. Exhibit 6.8 provides an overview of the metrics that might be expected for the categories of recruitment activities, along with issues considered relevant to each source. There is far less research on the costs and benefits of internal

EXHIBIT 6.8 Potential Recruiting Metrics for Different Sources

Recruiting Method	Quantity	Quality	Costs	Impact on HR
Postings	Often will be the company's entire workforce	Because all employees will be able to apply, quality is variable	Staff time to develop the recruiting message	May reduce turnover, reduced time to full performance
Nominations	Limited to those who receive positive appraisals by supervisors or coworkers	If supervisors make accurate assessments, will be very good person/job match	Many companies keep routine records of employee performance	Can actively identify those who will be good performers and target identified training needs
In-house temporary pools	Based on organization's need for temporary staff coverage	Higher quality if in-house temps receive better benefits than what external staffing firms provide	Start-up costs can be significant; reduces payments to external agencies	More accountability relative to external agencies; increased internal flexibility
Talent management system	Identifies knowledge, skills, and abilities across all employees	High; preselection of applicants based on identified skill sets	Maintenance of databases can be very time and resource intensive	Higher performance, reduced downtime, reduced training costs
Replacement and succession plans	A small number of select workers seen as having high potential	Able to assess skill sets very carefully and consider configurations	HRIS start-up costs, data entry, and checking	Reduces gaps in leadership, protects against shocks due to turnover, reduces turnover
Career development centers	The set of employees who are interested in career development	Assesses employee KSAOs and preferences	Start-up costs, cost of staff, system maintenance	Significant reduction in turnover, increased match between KSAOs and work requirements

recruitment techniques, so our comments here are necessarily somewhat speculative; it is likely that each organization will need to consider its unique needs even more thoroughly than it would when selecting external recruitment methods.

Sufficient Quantity

Because the organization's pool of employees will necessarily be smaller than the general labor market, most internal recruitment methods will have far lower quantity yields. Techniques that permit job postings and use of the organization's intranet will likely produce far more candidates for promotion and advancement than will succession plans.

Sufficient Quality

The degree to which the organization utilizes its own internal information on candidate qualifications and job performance to narrow the pool will determine how qualified the applicants will be. In assessing applicant characteristics, organizations that have internal recruitment systems have a huge advantage over those that use external recruitment systems, so the ability of each source to draw in qualified internal candidates should capitalize on the additional capacity to carefully observe them. Regular performance appraisals of all employees, coupled with talent management systems to track KSAOs, are a vital part of an effective internal recruitment system.

Cost

Internal recruitment methods have a completely different set of costs than external recruitment methods. In some ways, internal recruitment can be far less expensive than external recruitment because the organization's own internal communication systems can usually be utilized. It costs very little to send an e-mail to all qualified staff informing them of job opportunities or to post job advertisements on a physical or an electronic bulletin board. However, more sophisticated systems, such as a corporate intranet or comprehensive talent management system, take more personnel resources to set up and maintain. Career development centers are very costly propositions, and only organizations with considerable internal placement needs will find them cost-effective.

Impact on HR Outcomes

Very little research has been done on the effectiveness of various internal recruitment sources. Thus, it is imperative that organizational leaders consider how their internal recruitment systems affect turnover rates, job performance, and diversity. Despite the lack of research, it should be easier to monitor these outcomes directly, because it is easier to directly measure the applicant pool contacted through internal methods. From anecdotal observations, some preliminary conclusions can be drawn regarding the advantages of internal placement. There is some evidence that internal career opportunities can reduce turnover intentions.[25] Internal recruitment methods may reduce the time it takes for employees to reach full performance once placed, because they will already be familiar with the organization and may know more about the job in question than an external hire would. Any costs of internal recruitment should be compared against the costs of external recruitment, and the replacement of the employee who takes an internal position should also be taken into account.

TRANSITION TO SELECTION

As with external recruitment, once a job seeker has been identified and attracted to a new job, the organization needs to prepare the person for the selection process. It should not be assumed that just because job seekers come from inside the organization they automatically know and understand the selection procedures. With the rapid advances being made in selection methods, the applicant might encounter methods that are different from those they previously experienced. Even if the same selection methods are used, the applicant may need to be refreshed on the process since much time may have elapsed between the current and previous selection decisions.

In many organizations, the most significant internal mobility decisions involve moving an individual from a role as an individual contributor to the management ranks. In this case, the process of "recruitment" incorporates sharing information about what the organization is looking for in a leader and then helping the employee develop these appropriate skills.[26] In other words, recruitment, selection, and development come together in a succession management effort. When an employee has been identified as having some potential for leadership, there should be a gradual process of preparing the individual for the new role with self-development exercises. The employee's interest in the position should be assessed to ensure that they are interested in mobility. The employee's capacity to develop these skills should also be evaluated on an ongoing basis without committing to the mobility decision prematurely. Frequent communication regarding needed skills, job expectations, and responsibilities will help facilitate a smooth transition once the organization decides to offer the employee a higher-level position.

LEGAL ISSUES

The mobility of people within the organization, particularly upward, has long been a matter of equal employment opportunity/affirmative action (EEO/AA) concern. The workings of the internal labor market rely heavily on internal recruitment activities. Like external recruitment activities, internal recruitment activities can operate in exclusionary ways, resulting in unequal promotion opportunities, rates, and results for certain groups of employees—particularly women, minorities, people with disabilities, and veterans. Both the Equal Employment Opportunity Commission (EEOC) and the Office of Federal Contract Compliance Programs (OFCCP) have strong positions on improving advancement for these targeted groups. Seniority systems are likewise subject to legal scrutiny, particularly regarding what constitutes a bona fide system under the law. More recently, promotion systems have been studied as they relate to the glass ceiling effect and the kinds of barriers that have been found to stifle the upward rise of minorities and women in organizations.

Affirmative Action Programs

As is the case with external recruitment, the EEOC and OFCCP require strong actions by the organization to improve promotion opportunities and results for protected groups. The EEOC provides a set of employer best-practice ideas for such actions. The list is shown in Exhibit 6.9.

Bona Fide Seniority Systems

Title VII (see the social and legal environment chapter) explicitly permits the use of bona fide seniority systems as long as they are not the result of an intention to discriminate. This position presents the organization with a serious dilemma. Past discrimination in external staffing may have resulted in a predominantly White male workforce. A change to a nondiscriminatory external staffing system may increase the presence of women and minorities within an organization, but they will still have less seniority than the White males. If eligibility for promotion is based on seniority and/or if seniority is an actual factor considered in promotion decisions, those with less seniority are less likely to be promoted. Thus, the seniority system will have a disparate impact on women and minorities, even though there is no current intention to discriminate. Is such a seniority system bona fide?

Two points are relevant here. First, the law does not define "seniority system." Generally, however, any established system that uses length of employment as a basis for making decisions (such as promotion decisions) is interpreted as a seniority system. Promotions based on ad hoc judgments about which candidates are "more experienced," however, would not likely be considered a bona fide seniority system.[27] Seniority systems can and do occur outside the context of a collective bargaining agreement.

Second, current interpretation is that, in the absence of discriminatory intent, virtually any seniority system is likely to be bona fide, even if it causes disparate impact.[28] This interpretation incentivizes the organization not to change its current seniority-based practices or systems. Other pressures, such as the Affirmative Action Program Regulations or a voluntary affirmative action plan (AAP), create

EXHIBIT 6.9 Best-Practice Promotion Ideas From the EEOC

- Establish a policy for promotion and career advancement, including criteria, procedures, responsible individuals, and the applicability of diversity and affirmative action.
- Engage in short-term and long-term strategic planning:
  —Define aims;
  —Identify the applicable barriers to equal employment opportunity;
  —Make a road map for implementing the plan.
- Establish a communication network notifying interested persons of opportunities, including advertising within the organization and, where applicable, not only with the general media, but with minority, persons with disabilities, older persons, and women-focused media.
- Communicate the competencies, skills, and abilities required.
- Provide for succession planning.
- Build talent pools.
- Develop career plans and programs for high-potential employees.
- Provide sufficient training and opportunities for additional education.
- Ensure that tools for continuous learning and optimum job performance are available.
- Provide tools to enable employees to self-manage careers.
- Provide job transfer/rotation programs for career enhancing developmental experiences.
- Provide employee resource centers, so individuals may have more opportunities to develop career plans.
- Establish mentoring and networking programs and systems to help develop high-potential individuals.
- Eliminate practices which exclude or present barriers to minorities, women, persons with disabilities, older persons, or any individuals.
- Ensure that personnel involved in the promotion and advancement process are well trained in their equal employment opportunity responsibilities.
- Include progress in equal employment opportunity in advancement and promotion as factors in management evaluation.

SOURCE: EEOC, "Best Practices of Private Sector Employees," 2013 (*www.eeoc.gov/eeoc/task_reports /best_practices.cfm*).

an incentive to change in order to eliminate the occurrence of disparate impact in promotion. The organization thus must carefully consider exactly what its posture will be toward seniority practices and systems within the context of its overall AAP.

Under the Americans With Disabilities Act (ADA), there is potential conflict between needing to provide reasonable accommodation to an employee (such as job reassignment) and provisions of the organization's seniority system (such as bidding for jobs based on seniority). According to the Supreme Court, it will ordinarily be unreasonable (undue hardship) for a reassignment request to prevail over the seniority system unless the employee can show some special circumstances that warrant an exception.

The Glass Ceiling

The "glass ceiling" is a term used to characterize strong but invisible barriers to promotion in the organization, particularly to the highest levels, for women and minorities. Evidence demonstrating the existence of a glass ceiling is substantial. At the very top in large corporations, senior-level managers are overwhelmingly White males. As one goes down the hierarchy and across industries, a more mixed pattern of data emerges. EEOC data show that nationwide the percentage of women who are officials and managers has increased over time. In some industries, particularly health care, retail, legal services, and banking, the percentage of women managers is substantially higher. Women account for over half of employees in management, professional, and related occupations. In other industries, such as manufacturing, trucking, and architectural/engineering services, the percentage of women managers is much lower.[29] An important 2015 study of women's representation in the corporate pipeline across 118 diverse companies found that their representation decreased as follows: entry-level professional (43%), manager (37%), senior manager/director (32%), vice president (27%), senior vice president (23%), C-suite (17%). Moreover, women's expected representation at each level was 15% lower than that of men, suggesting broad promotion barriers.[30] Evidence suggests similar underrepresentation of racioethnic minorities and individuals with disabilities in managerial roles as well. Thus, the closer to the top of the hierarchy, the thicker the glass in the ceiling.

Where glass ceilings exist, two important questions should be asked: What are the reasons for a lack of upward mobility and representation for minorities and women at higher levels of the organization? What changes need to be made, especially staffing-related ones, to help shatter the glass ceiling?

Barriers to Mobility

An obvious conclusion from such data is that there are barriers to mobility, many of which originate from within the organization. The Federal Glass Ceiling Commission conducted a four-year study of glass ceilings and barriers to mobility. It identified many barriers: lack of outreach recruitment practices, lack of mentoring training in revenue-generating areas, lack of access to critical developmental assignments, initial selection for jobs in staff areas outside the upward pipeline to top jobs, biased performance ratings, little access to informal networks, and harassment by colleagues. Subsequent research has consistently supported the importance of these same factors across industries, across occupations, and over time.[31] Imbalances in nonwork responsibilities, including childcare and family management, further exacerbate the problem.

The 2015 study mentioned above of women in corporate pipelines looked at representation in line roles (positions focused on core operations and with profit and loss responsibility) and staff roles (support positions for line management, such as legal, accounting, human resources, and IT). Going up the hierarchy, women increasingly held staff roles, while men did not. Since promotion to senior-level line positions usually requires line experience, women's chances of advancement to senior line roles lessened. This finding is consistent with the findings of the Federal Glass Ceiling Commission, and it highlights the critical importance of line role experience for advancement to top leadership positions.[32]

Other causal factors for advancement disparities also were found. These included somewhat less desire by women for a top job (especially due to stress/pressure of the role, and lack of interest in the role); women's perceptions that they have fewer opportunities than men and that their gender has inhibited their advancement success so far; a belief that gender diversity is not a priority for their CEO or direct manager; low participation in work flexibility (e.g., part-time schedule, family leave), professional development (e.g., coaching sessions, executive training), and family-oriented flexibility programs (e.g., maternity leave) due partly to fear of being penalized for using the program; uneven distribution of household/child care chores; and fewer men in women's professional networks.

Overcoming Barriers

It is generally recognized that multiple actions, many of them beyond just staffing-system changes, will be needed to overcome barriers to mobility. Exhibit 6.10 shows a suggested listing of such actions. They include both recruitment and other actions.

An example of a far-reaching diversity initiative to expand the internal diversity pipeline is the Championing Change for Women: An Integrated Strategy program at Safeway, a retail grocery giant. A focal point is the Retail Leadership Development (RLD) program, a formal full-time career development program for entry-level grocery store employees to prepare them for moving up into the management ranks (90% of store managers and above come through the program). The program has a particular focus on women and people of color. Employees apply for the program by taking a retail knowledge and skill exam. Those who complete the program are immediately assigned to a store as an assistant manager—the stepping stone to further advancement. To support the advancement program, all managers attend a managing diversity workshop, receive additional on-the-job education,

---

EXHIBIT 6.10 Overcoming Barriers to Mobility

- Emphasize broad-based scanning for, and communication with, potential candidates in external and internal recruiting processes.
- Create or clarify mobility paths, particularly alternative paths that will facilitate a free-flow of people to jobs and upward movement.
- Communicate paths to top management positions.
- Develop and communicate mobility policies that will foster and encourage upward mobility, accompanied by important KSAOs for that mobility.
- Pay particular attention to job performance, specific job/project experiences, and training or development experiences in decision making.
- Link mobility policies and criteria with replacement and succession planning.
- Identify candidates for promotion well in advance, creating demographically balanced pools for candidate promotion.
- Identify training and experience deficiencies that facilitate advancement for underrepresented groups.

and have access to a toolkit to help them incorporate diversity discussions into their staff meetings. Managers are evaluated in part on their success in meeting diversity goals, and bonus money is riding on that success. Every manager is also expected to serve as a mentor, helping their mentee acquire the KSAOs necessary for continued advancement. Other elements of the program include strong support and participation from the CFO and from women's leadership network groups (for Black, Asian, Hispanic, and LGBT+ employees), modification of a requirement to relocate in order to gain experience, and work/life balance initiatives for employees with and without children. Since the program was initiated, the number of women who qualified for and completed the RLD program has risen 37%, and the number of women store managers has increased by 42% (31% for White women and 92% for women of color).[33]

In summary, solutions to the glass ceiling problem require myriad points of attack. First, women and minorities must have visibility and support at top levels—from the board of directors, the CEO, and senior management. That support must include actions to eliminate prejudice and stereotypes. Second, women and minorities must be provided with job opportunities and assignments that will allow them to develop the depth and breadth of KSAOs needed for ascension to, and success in, top management positions. These developmental experiences include assignments in multiple functions, management of diverse businesses, line management experience with direct profit-loss and bottom-line accountability, diverse geographic assignments, and international experience. Naturally, the relative importance of these experiences will vary according to the type and size of the organization. Third, the organization must provide continual support for women and minorities to help ensure positive person/job matches. Included here are mentoring, training, and flexible work-hour systems. Fourth, the organization must gear up its internal recruitment to aggressively and openly track and recruit women and minority candidates for advancement. Finally, the organization must develop and use valid methods of assessing the qualifications of women and minority candidates (see the external selection chapters).[34]

SUMMARY

The steps involved in the internal recruitment process—planning, strategy development, and communication—closely parallel those in the external recruitment process. With internal recruitment, the search is conducted inside rather than outside the organization. In situations where both internal and external searches are conducted, they need to be coordinated with each other.

The planning stage requires that the applicant population be identified. The process begins by understanding strategic recruitment goals. Next, an understanding of mobility paths in the organization and mobility path policies is a vital part of deciding how to implement internal recruitment. To access the internal applicant population, attention must be devoted in advance of the search to the number and types of contacts, the budget, development of a recruitment guide, and timing. Understanding applicant reactions to internal recruitment policies is also crucial for developing effective systems.

When searching for candidates, the message to be communicated can be realistic, targeted, or branded. Which approach is best depends on the applicants, job, and organization. The message is usually communicated with a job posting. It should, however, be supplemented with other media, including input from potential peers and supervisors. Informal communication methods with information that cannot be verified or that is incomplete are to be discouraged.

There are a variety of internal methods for taking applications in the strategy implementation phase. These include posting information about jobs on the company intranet and career development centers with interest inventories and counseling staff. Just as with external recruitment, multiple criteria must be considered in choosing internal sources.

The organization needs to provide the applicant with assistance for the transition to selection. This assistance requires that the applicant be made fully aware of the selection process and how to best prepare for it. Taking this step, along with providing well-developed job postings and clearly articulated mobility paths and policies in the organization, should help applicants see the internal recruitment system as fair.

Internal recruitment activities have long been the object of close legal scrutiny. Past and current regulations make several suggestions regarding desirable promotion system features. The relevant laws permit bona fide seniority systems, as long as they are not intentionally used to discriminate. Seniority systems may have the effect of impeding promotions for women and minorities because these groups have not had the opportunity to accumulate an equivalent amount of seniority as compared with that of White males. The glass ceiling refers to invisible barriers to upward advancement, especially to the top levels, for minorities and women. Studies of promotion systems indicate that poorly designed internal recruitment practices contribute to this barrier. As part of an overall strategy to shatter the glass ceiling, changes are now being experimented with for opening up internal recruitment. These include actions to eliminate stereotypes and prejudices, training and developmental experiences, mentoring, aggressive recruitment, and use of valid selection techniques.

DISCUSSION QUESTIONS

1. Traditional career paths emphasize strict upward mobility within an organization. How does mobility differ in organizations with innovative career paths? List three innovative career paths discussed in this chapter and describe how mobility occurs in each.
2. A sound promotion policy is important. List the characteristics necessary for an effective promotion policy.
3. Compare and contrast a closed internal recruitment system with an open internal recruitment system.
4. What information should be included in the targeted internal communication message?
5. Exhibit 6.10 contains many suggestions for improving the advancement of women and minorities. Choose the three suggestions you think are most important and explain why.

ETHICAL ISSUES

1. MDN, Inc., is considering two employees for the job of senior manager. An internal candidate, Julie, has been with MDN for 12 years and has received very good performance evaluations. The other candidate, Raoul, works for a competitor and has valuable experience in the product market into which MDN wishes to expand. Do you think MDN has an obligation to promote Julie? Why or why not?
2. Do organizations have an ethical obligation to have a succession plan in place? If no, why not? If so, what is the ethical obligation, and to whom is it owed?

APPLICATIONS

Recruitment in a Changing Internal Labor Market

Mitchell Shipping Lines is a distributor of goods on the Great Lakes. It also manufactures shipping containers used to store the goods while in transit. The subsidiary that manufactures these containers is Mitchell-Cole Manufacturing, and the president and CEO is Zoe Brausch.

Brausch is in the middle of converting the manufacturing system from an assembly line to autonomous work teams. Each team will be responsible for producing a separate type of container and will have different tools, machinery, and manufacturing routines for its particular type of container. Members of each team will have the job title "assembler," and each team will be headed by a leader. Brausch would like all leaders to come from the ranks of current employees, in terms of both the initial set of leaders and the leaders in the future as vacancies arise. In addition, she wants to discourage employee movement across teams in order to build team identity and cohesion. The current internal labor market, however, presents a formidable potential obstacle to her internal staffing goals.

In the long history of the container manufacturing facility, employees have always been treated like union employees even though the facility is nonunion. Such treatment was desired many years ago as a strategy to remain nonunion. It was management's belief that if employees were treated like union employees, they would have no need to vote for a union. A cornerstone of the strategy is use of what everyone in the facility calls the "blue book." The blue book looks like a typical labor contract, and it spells out all terms and conditions of employment. Many of those terms apply to internal staffing and are typical of traditional mobility systems found in unionized work settings. Specifically, internal transfers and promotions are governed by a facility-wide job posting system. A vacancy is posted throughout the facility and remains open for 30 days; identified entry-level jobs that are filled only externally is an exception here. Any employee with two or more years of seniority is eligible to bid for any posted vacancy; employees with less seniority may also bid, but they are considered only when no two-year-plus employees apply or are chosen. Internal applicants are assessed by the hiring manager and a representative from the HR department. They review applicants' seniority, relevant experience, past performance appraisals, and other special KSAOs. The blue book requires that the most senior employee who meets the desired qualifications receive the transfer or promotion. Thus, seniority is weighted heavily in the decision.

Brausch is worried about the current internal labor market, especially for recruitment and choosing team leaders. These leaders will likely be required to have many KSAOs that are more important than seniority, and KSAOs likely to not even be positively related to seniority. For example, team leaders will need to have advanced computer, communication, and interpersonal skills. Brausch thinks that these skills will be critical for team leaders and that they will more likely be found among junior rather than senior employees. Brausch is in a quandary. She asks for your responses to the following questions:

1. Should seniority be eliminated as an eligibility standard for bidding on jobs—meaning the two-year-plus employees would no longer have priority?
2. Should the job posting system simply be eliminated? If so, what should replace it?
3. Should a strict promotion-from-within policy be maintained? Why or why not?
4. How can career mobility paths be developed that would allow across-team movement without threatening team identity and cohesion?
5. If a new internal labor market system is to be put in place, how should it be communicated to employees?

Succession Planning for a CEO

Lone Star Bank, based in Amarillo, is the fourth-largest bank in Texas. Its leader, Harry "Tex" Ritter, has been with the company for 30 years, the last 12 in his current position as president and CEO. The last three years have been difficult for Lone Star, as earnings have been below average for the industry, and shareholders have grown increasingly impatient. Last month's quarterly earnings report was the proverbial last straw for the board. Particularly troublesome was Ritter's failure to invest enough of Lone Star's assets in higher-yielding investments. Though banks are carefully regulated in terms of their investment strategies, Ritter's investment strategy was conservative even for a bank.

In a meeting last week, the board decided to allow Ritter to serve out the last year of his contract and then replace him. An attractive severance package was hastily put together; when it was presented to Ritter, he agreed to its terms and conditions. Although the board feels it has made a positive step, it is unsure how to identify a successor. When the board members met with Ritter, he indicated that he thought the bank's senior vice president of operations, Bob Bowers, would be an able successor. Some members of the board think they should follow Ritter's suggestion because he knows the inner workings of the bank better than anyone on the board. Others are not sure what to do.

1. How should Lone Star go about finding a successor to Ritter? Should Bowers be recruited to be the next CEO?
2. How should other internal candidates be identified and recruited?
3. Does Lone Star need a succession plan for the CEO position? If so, how would you advise the board in setting up such a plan?
4. Should Lone Star have a succession plan in place for other individuals at the bank? If so, why and for whom?

ENDNOTES

1. BMP Forum and Success Factors, *Performance and Talent Management Trend Survey 2007* (San Mateo, CA: author, 2007); G. Crispin and M. Mehler, "Sources of Hire 2013: Perception Is Reality," *CareerXRoads*, 2013 (*www.careerxroads.com*).

2. M. Bidwell and J. R. Keller, "Within or Without? How Firms Combine Internal and External Labor Markets to Fill Jobs," *Academy of Management Journal*, 2014, 57, pp. 1035–1055.

3. D. G. Collings and K. Mellahi, "Strategic Talent Management: A Review and Research Agenda," *Human Resource Management Review*, 2009, 19, pp. 304–313.

4. P. S. DeOrtentiis, C. H. Van Iddekinge, R. E. Ployhart, and T. D. Heetderks, "Build or Buy? The Individual and Unit-Level Performance of Internally Versus Externally Selected Managers Over Time," *Journal of Applied Psychology*, 2018, 103, pp. 916–928; J. DeVaro, A. Kauhanen, and N. Valmari, "Internal and External Hiring," *Industrial and Labor Relations Review*, 2019, 72, pp. 981–1008.

5. B. L. Connelly, L. Tihanyi, T. R. Crook, and K. A. Gangloff, "Tournament Theory: Thirty Years of Contests and Competitions," *Journal of Management*, 2014, 40, pp. 16–47.

6. A. Benson, D. Li, and K. Shue, "Promotions and the Peter Principle," *Quarterly Journal of Economics*, 2019, 134, pp. 2085–2134.

7. S. Belenzon and U. Tsolmon, "Market Frictions and the Competitive Advantage of Internal Labor Markets," *Strategic Management Journal*, 2016, 37, pp. 1280–1303; DeVaro, Kauhanen, and Valmari, "Internal and External Hiring."

8. S. E. Seibert, G. Wang, and S. H. Courtright, "Antecedents and Consequences of Psychological and Team Empowerment in Organizations: A Meta-Analytic Review," *Journal of Applied Psychology*, 2011, 96, pp. 981–1103; C. Chuang, S. E. Jackson, and Y. Jiang, "Can Knowledge-Intensive Teamwork Be Managed? Examining the Roles of HRM Systems, Leadership, and Tacit Knowledge," *Journal of Management*, 2016, 42, pp. 524–554.

9. E. C. Dierdorff and E. A. Surface, "If You Pay for Skills, Will They Learn? Skill Change and Maintenance Under a Skill-Based Pay System," *Journal of Management*, 2008, 34, pp. 721–743.

10. J. Gelens, N. Dries, J. Hofmans, and R. Pepermans, "The Role of Perceived Organizational Justice in Shaping the Outcomes of Talent Management: A Research Agenda," *Human Resource Management Review*, 2013, 23, pp. 341–353; J. A. Colquitt, B. A. Scott, J. B. Rodell, D. M. Long, C. P. Zapata, D. E. Conlon, and M. J. Wesson, "Justice at the Millennium, a Decade Later: A Meta-Analytic Test of Social Exchange and Affect-Based Perspectives," *Journal of Applied Psychology*, 2013, 98, pp. 199–236; A. L. Garcia-Izquierdo, S. Moscoso, and P. J. Ramos-Villagrasa, "Reactions to the Fairness of Promotion Methods: Procedural Justice and Job Satisfaction," *International Journal of Selection and Assessment*, 2012, 20, pp. 394–403.

11. J. Keller, "Posting and Slotting: How Hiring Processes Shape the Quality of Hire and Compensation in Internal Labor Markets," *Administrative Science Quarterly*, 2018, 63, pp. 848–878.

12. R. Fisher and R. McPhail, "Internal Labour Markets as a Strategic Tool," *The Service Industries Journal*, Oct. 2010, pp. 1–16.

13. D. K. Ford, D. M. Truxillo, and T. N. Bauer, "Rejected but Still There: Shifting the Focus in Applicant Reactions to the Promotional Context," *International Journal of Selection and Assessment*, Dec. 2009, pp. 402–416; J. R. Webster and T. A. Beehr, "Antecedents and Outcomes of Employee Perceptions of Intra-organizational Mobility Channels," *Journal of Organizational Behavior*, 2013, 34, pp. 919–941.

14. H. C. Vough and B. B. Caza, "Where Do I Go From Here? Sensemaking and the Construction of Growth-Based Stories in the Wake of Denied Promotions," *Academy of Management Review*, 2016, 42, pp. 103–128; S. Fine, J. Goldenberg, and Y. Noam, "Beware of Those Left Behind: Counterproductive Work Behaviors Among Nonpromoted Employees and the Moderating Effect

of Integrity," *Journal of Applied Psychology*, 2016, 101, pp. 1721–1729; K. Dlugos and J. Keller, "Turned Down and Taking Off? Rejection and Turnover in Internal Talent Markets," *Academy of Management Journal*, 2020 (online first publication).

15. N. Glube, J. Huxtable, and A. Stanard, "Creating New Temporary Hire Options Through In-House Agencies," *Staffing Management Magazine*, June 2002 (*www.shrm.org*).

16. L. J. Weiner, "The Temp Staffing Solution That's Right Under Your Nose," *HealthLeaders Media*, May 18, 2015 (*www.healthleadersmedia.com*); R. Mauer, "Flexible Work Options in Health Care Can Result in a Win-Win," *HR Today*, June 19, 2016 (*www.shrm.org*).

17. R. E. Ployhart, A. J. Nyberg, G. Reilly, and M. A. Maltarich, "Human Capital Is Dead; Long Live Human Capital Resources!" *Journal of Management*, 2014, 40, pp. 371–398.

18. US Office of Personnel Management, *Human Capital Assessment and Accountability Framework* (Washington, DC: author, 2005); A. Gakovic and K. Yardley, "Global Talent Management at HSBC," *Organization Development Journal*, 2007, 25, pp. 201–206; E. Frauenheim, "Talent Management Keeping Score With HR Analytics Software," *Workforce Management*, May 21, 2007, pp. 25–33; K. Oakes, "The Emergence of Talent Management," *T + D*, Apr. 2006, pp. 21–24.

19. M. Ehrnrooth, I. Björkman, K. Mäkelä, A. Smale, J. Sumelius, and S. Taimitarha, "Talent Responses to Talent Status Awareness—Not a Question of Simple Reciprocation," *Human Resource Management Journal*, 2018, 28, pp. 443–461; J. L. Petriglieri and G. Petriglieri, "The Talent Curse," *Harvard Business Review*, 2017, 95, pp. 88–94; J. Gelens, J. Hofmans, N. Dries, and R. Pepermans, "Talent Management and Organisational Justice: Employee Reactions to High Potential Identification," *Human Resource Management Journal*, 2014, 24, pp. 159–175; K. M. Carter, E. Gonzalez-Mulé, M. K. Mount, I.-S. Oh, and L. S. Zachar, "Managers Moving On Up (or Out): Linking Self-Other Agreement on Leadership Behaviors to Succession Planning and Voluntary Turnover," *Journal of Vocational Behavior*, 2019, 115, p. 103328.

20. R. Hooijberg and N. Lane, "How Boards Botch CEO Succession," *MIT Sloan Management Review*, Apr. 21, 2016 (*sloanreview.mit.edu*); G. McKee and K. Froelich, "Executive Succession Planning: Barriers and Substitutes in Nonprofit Organizations," *Annals of Public and Cooperative Economics*, 2016, 87, pp. 587–610.

21. National Association of Corporate Directors, *The Role of the Board in Corporate Succession* (Washington, DC: author, 2006); S. Bates, "Putting a Spotlight on CEO Succession," *HR Magazine*, Dec. 2015, pp. 53–56.

22. M. Wang and C. R. Wanberg, "100 Years of Applied Psychology Research on Individual Careers: From Career Management to Retirement," *Journal of Applied Psychology*, 2017, 102, pp. 546–563; L. H. Bikos, E. C. Dykhouse, S. K. Boutin, M. J. Gowen, and H. E. Rodney, "Practice and Research in Career Counseling and Development—2012," *Career Development Quarterly*, 2013, 61, pp. 290–329.

23. T. Minton-Eversole, "Continuous Learning—in Many Forms—Remains Top Recruitment, Retention Tool," *SHRM Online Recruitment & Staffing Focus Area*, Feb. 2006 (*www.shrm.org*); Society for Human Resource Management, *2007 Job Satisfaction* (Alexandria, VA: author, 2007).

24. I. Speizer, "The State of Training and Development: More Spending, More Scrutiny," *Workforce Management*, May 22, 2006, pp. 25–26.

25. R. Maurer, "Internal Recruitment Critical to Hiring, Retention: But Few Companies Have Formal Programs," *SHRM*, Dec. 2, 2015 (*www.shrm.org/resourcesandtools/hr-topics/talent-acquisition /pages/internal-recruitment-critical-hiring-retention.aspx*).

26. H. Monarth, "Evaluate Your Leadership Development Program," *Harvard Business Review*, Jan. 22, 2015, pp. 2–4; R. Ashkenas and R. Hausmann, "Leadership Development Should Focus on Experiments," *Harvard Business Review*, Apr. 12, 2016, pp. 2–4.

27. D. J. Walsh, *Employment Law for Human Resource Practice*, 2nd ed. (Mason, OH: Thomson Higher Education, 2007), p. 207.

28. Bureau of National Affairs, *Fair Employment Practices* (Arlington, VA: author, 2007), sec. 421: 161–166.
29. Lean In and McKinsey, "Women in the Workplace," *McKinsey&Company*, Sept. 2015 (*womenintheworkplace.com*), accessed Jan. 22, 2016.
30. Federal Glass Ceiling Commission, "Good for Business: Making Full Use of the Nation's Human Capital—Fact-Finding Report of the Federal Glass Ceiling Commission," *Daily Labor Report*, Bureau of National Affairs, Mar. 17, 1995, Special Supplement, p. S6.
31. K. L. McGinn and K. L. Milkman, "Looking Up and Looking Out: Career Mobility Effects of Demographic Similarity Among Professionals," *Organization Science*, 2013, 24, pp. 1041–1060; Q. M. Roberson, "Diversity in the Workplace: A Review, Synthesis, and Future Research Agenda," *Annual Review of Organizational Psychology and Organizational Behavior*, 2019, 6, pp. 69–88; L. H. Nishii, J. Khattab, M. Shemla, and R. M. Paluch, "A Multi-level Process Model for Understanding Diversity Practice Effectiveness," *Academy of Management Annals*, 2018, 12, pp. 37–82.
32. J. Green, "This Is Not a Trend," *Bloomberg Business Week*, Sept. 1, 2014, pp. 19–20.
33. A. Pomeroy, "Cultivating Female Leaders," *HR Magazine*, Feb. 2007, pp. 44–50.
34. K. L. Lyness and D. E. Thompson, "Climbing the Corporate Ladder: Do Male and Female Executives Follow the Same Route?" *Journal of Applied Psychology*, 2000, 85, pp. 86–101; S. J. Wells, "A Female Executive Is Hard to Find," *HR Magazine*, June 2001, pp. 40–49; S. J. Wells, "Smoothing the Way," *HR Magazine*, June 2001, pp. 52–58; S. Shellenbarger, "The XX Factor: What's Holding Women Back?" *Wall Street Journal*, May 7, 2012, pp. B7–B12; D. J. Walsh, *Employment Law for Human Resource Practice*, 5th ed. (Boston: Cengage Learning, 2016), pp. 250–255.

The Staffing Organizations Model

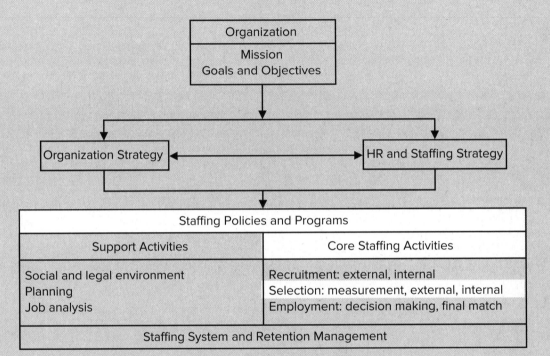

PART FOUR

Staffing Activities: Selection

CHAPTER SEVEN

Measurement

Applications
Evaluation of Two New Assessments for Selecting Telephone Customer
Service Representatives
Conducting Empirical Validation and Disparate Impact Analysis

Endnotes

LEARNING OBJECTIVES AND INTRODUCTION

Learning Objectives

- Define validity and consider the relationship between reliability and validity
- Compare and contrast the two types of validation studies that are typically conducted
- Consider how validity generalization affects and informs validation of measures in staffing
- Review the primary ways assessment data can be collected

Introduction

"I have a good feeling about that candidate—I'm going with this one." Even though you might have a gut feeling about a candidate, this is not the best judgment of whether an individual will perform well in the position.[1] Subjectivity in the selection process can lead to poor decisions.[2] Instead, the best approach to staffing is to use evidence-based measures and procedures that provide you with valid and reliable data for staffing decisions. In staffing, measurement is a process used to gather and express information about people and jobs in numerical form. Measurement is critical to staffing because, as far as selection decisions are concerned, a selection decision can only be as effective as the measures on which it is based.

The first part of this chapter presents the process of measurement in staffing decisions. After showing the vital importance and uses of measurement in staffing activities, the chapter then discusses three key concepts. The first involves measurement itself, along with the issues raised by it—standardization of measurement, levels of measurement, and the difference between objective and subjective measures. The second involves scoring and how to express scores in ways that help facilitate their interpretation. The final concept is that of correlations between scores, particularly as expressed by the correlation coefficient and its significance. Calculating correlations between scores is a very useful way to learn even more about the meaning of scores.

Are the measures used in staffing effective? How well do they represent the attributes being measured? Answers to these questions lie in the reliability and validity of the measures. There are multiple ways of analyzing reliability and validity; these methods are discussed and illustrated by numerous examples drawn from staffing situations. As these examples demonstrate, the quality of staffing decisions (e.g., who to hire or reject) depends heavily on the quality of measures used as inputs to these decisions. Some organizations rely only on common staffing metrics and benchmarks—what leading organizations are doing—to measure effectiveness. Though benchmarks have their value, reliability and validity are the real keys in assessing the quality of selection measures.

An important practical concern in measurement involves the collection of assessment data. Decisions about testing procedures (who is qualified to test applicants, what information should be disclosed to applicants, and how to assess applicants with standardized procedures) need to be made. The collection of assessment data may also include acquiring tests and their manuals or developing the tests themselves. This process will vary depending on whether paper-and-pencil or computerized selection measures are used. Finally, organizations need to attend to professional standards that govern proper use of the assessment data.

Measurement concepts and procedures are directly involved in legal issues, particularly equal employment opportunity and affirmative action (EEO/AA) issues. The law requires collection and analysis of applicant flow and utilization statistics. Also reviewed are methods for determining disparate impact, standardization of measures, and best practices as suggested by the Equal Employment Opportunity Commission (EEOC).

IMPORTANCE AND USE OF MEASURES

Measurement is one of the key ingredients for, and tools of, staffing organizations. Unfortunately, over the past 50 years, it appears as if the focus on quality measurement has shifted. As Peter Cappelli notes, "Employers are missing the forest for the trees: Obsessed with new technologies and driving down costs, they largely ignore the ultimate goal: making the best possible hires."[3] The current assessment landscape is much like the Wild West: the staffing process is largely outsourced, social media networking sites and résumés are scoured for keywords that are important to management, and characteristics as broad as body language and social media posts are assessed (e.g., via machine learning) by an army of vendors, sometimes with little consideration toward whether they are actually predicting future performance.[4] As David Solot, VP of client services at Caliper, notes, "For tests to be truly predictive of individual performance and business outcomes, assessment providers need to have done their research."[5]

Indeed, it is virtually impossible to have any type of systematic staffing process that does not use measures and an accompanying measurement process. Regardless, 29% of companies surveyed in Talent Board's *2019 North American Candidate Experience Research* project reported that they are not using any selection assessments or tests, and about 35% of companies that do use an assessment do not go through the efforts of conducting a validation study.[6] Furthermore, with the rise of the big-data paradigm, along with "fast data" looming on the horizon, the importance of having large-scale, instantaneous, diverse, and readily available data upon which to make dynamic staffing decisions is becoming more and more salient for organizations.[7] Big-data sources such as data obtained through "web scraping" (i.e., mining large amounts of information from websites) and the less widely accessible organization or government agency data repositories are being used more frequently and are poised to change the nature of staffing by catalyzing advancements in disparate impact analyses, leveraging social media for diversity in recruitment initiatives and other staffing processes, and mining internal databases to identify star employees as candidates for promotion.[8] Despite the explosion of interest surrounding this topic, many critics note that most human resources (HR) professionals do not understand big data and that proponents of big data have for the most part failed to connect these approaches to increasing the bottom line. Dan Ariely likened big data to young romance, noting that "everyone talks about it, nobody really knows how to do it, everyone thinks everyone else is doing it, so everyone claims they are doing it."[9] Regardless, big data and HR analytics are important signs of the times that hold clear implications for measurement processes and quality.

Measures are methods or techniques for assessing attributes that are of concern to us. Examples include tests of applicants' knowledge, skills, abilities, and other characteristics (KSAOs) such as personality; evaluations of employees' job performance; and applicants' ratings of their preferences for various types of job rewards. These assessments of attributes are gathered through the measurement process, which consists of (1) choosing an attribute of concern, (2) developing an operational definition of the attribute, (3) constructing a measure of the attribute (if no suitable measure is available), and (4) using the measure to actually assess the attribute.

The goal of the measurement process is to obtain a score for a person on a given attribute, which can then be used to differentiate individuals and make decisions about them. For example, applicants' scores on an ability test, employees' performance evaluation rating scores, and applicants' ratings of rewards in terms of their importance can be used to make decisions about who to hire, who to promote, and how to reward an employee for good performance. Thus, throughout the measurement process, the initial attribute and its operational definition are transformed into a numerical expression of the attribute.

KEY CONCEPTS

This section covers a series of key concepts in three major areas: measurement, scores, and correlation between scores.

Measurement

In the preceding discussion, the essence of measurement and its importance and use in staffing were described. It is important to define the term "measurement" more formally and explore implications of that definition.

Definition

Measurement may be defined as the process of assigning numbers to represent quantities of an attribute. In staffing, the attributes could be critical for an employee to possess, despite the fact that these attributes cannot be physically seen most of the time. However, you can infer these attributes from how well people perform on tasks, tests, or assessments intended to measure the attribute.[10]

For example, let's say you are hiring someone for the position of information technology (IT) analyst. You cannot merely look at an applicant and infer that they know C++, Python, and Java. However, it is critical that the analyst know these programming languages in order to do the job. Exhibit 7.1 depicts the general process of the use of measures in staffing, along with an example for the job of IT analyst. The first step in measurement is to choose and define an attribute (also called a construct) to be measured. In the example, this is knowledge of programming languages. Then, a measure must be developed or obtained for the attribute so that it can be physically measured. In the example, a paper-and-pencil test is developed or purchased from a vendor to measure programming knowledge, and this test is administered to applicants. Once the attribute is physically measured,

EXHIBIT 7.1   Use of Measures in Staffing

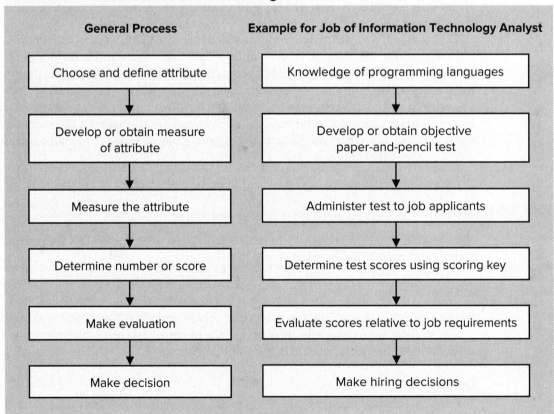

numbers or scores are determined (in the example, the programming knowledge test is scored). At that point, the applicants' scores are evaluated (which scores meet the job requirements) and a selection decision can be made (e.g., hire an IT analyst) using this measure development process.

Of course, in practice, this textbook process is often not followed explicitly, and thus selection errors are more likely. If the methods used to determine scores on an attribute are not explicitly determined and evaluated, the scores themselves may be incorrect. For example, let us say the hiring manager goes through each of the applications and gives each applicant a point or score for "programming knowledge" each time it is mentioned. Although these individuals have a point for this attribute if they pass this stage, there is no way of knowing *how much* they know about programming or even if they know the right programming languages (C++, Java, and Python). Similarly, if the evaluation of the scores is not systematic, each selection decision maker may put their own spin on the scores, thereby defeating the purpose of careful measurement. If Avery interviews a set of candidates on Thursday, and Riley interviews the rest of the candidates on Friday, but they each have their own method for asking about programming knowledge, the information on each candidate will not be consistent. The best way to avoid this problem is for all involved in selection decisions to go through each step of the measurement process depicted in Exhibit 7.1, systematically apply it to the job(s) in question, and reach agreement at each step of the way.

Standardization

The hallmark of sound measurement practice is standardization.[11] Standardization is a means of controlling the influence of extraneous factors on the scores so that the scores obtained closely reflect the attribute measured.

A standardized measure has three basic properties:

1. The content is identical for all objects measured (e.g., all job applicants take the same test)
2. The administration of the measure is identical for all objects (e.g., all job applicants have the same time limit on a test).
3. The rules for assigning scores are clearly specified and agreed on in advance (e.g., a scoring key for the test is developed before it is administered).

These seemingly simple and straightforward characteristics of standardization of measures have substantial implications for the conduct of many staffing activities. These implications will become apparent throughout the remainder of this text. Assessments such as the employment interview often fail to meet the requirements for standardization, and organizations must undertake steps to make them more standardized. For example, if Avery and Riley use different interview protocols and questions, the candidate experience for that position will not be the same.

Levels of Measurement

There are a number of ways to represent differences among object attributes that vary in their precision. Accordingly, there are different levels or scales of measurement.[12] It is common to classify any measure as falling into one of four levels of measurement: nominal, ordinal, interval, or ratio.

Nominal. With nominal scales, a given attribute is categorized, and numbers are assigned to the categories. With or without numbers, however, there is no order or level implied among the categories. The categories are merely different, and none is higher or lower than the others. For example, each job title could represent a different category, with a different number assigned to it: customer service = 1, clerical = 2, sales = 3, and so forth.

Ordinal. With ordinal scales, objects are rank ordered according to how much of the attribute they possess. Thus, objects may be ranked from best to worst or from highest to lowest. For example, five job candidates, each of whom has been evaluated in terms of overall qualification for the job, might be rank ordered from 1 to 5, or highest to lowest, according to their job qualifications.

Though useful for making clear distinctions between objects, rank orderings represent only relative differences among objects; they do not indicate the absolute levels of the attribute. Thus, the rank ordering of the five job candidates does not indicate exactly how qualified each of them is for the job, nor are the differences in their ranks necessarily equal to the differences in their qualifications. In other words, the differences in qualifications between applicants ranked 1 and 2 may not be the same as the differences between those ranked 4 and 5. In practice, care should be taken to avoid making rankings public in staffing applications. Even though it is tempting to think that this can be a motivational tool (e.g., knowing that you are at a lower rank relative to your peers can motivate you to work harder to "rise in the ranks"), research shows this is often not the case: knowing where you rank can actually demoralize employees, make them distrust the process, and undermine teamwork.[13]

Interval. The differences between adjacent points on an interval scale are equal in terms of the attribute, unlike a ranking scale. Standardized tests are great examples of tests that are scored on an interval scale. For example, you may have taken the Graduate Management Admission Test (GMAT) during your academic studies to assess your cognitive abilities as an entrance requirement for graduate school. Because the GMAT is scored on an interval scale, the difference between a 300 and a 350 score is equal to the difference between a 650 and a 700 score. The GMAT does not have an absolute "0" score that represents the "absence of intelligence"; instead, the test ranges from 200 to 800. However, given that there is no absolute "0," you cannot make statements about the ratio of scores (see the next section). For example, someone with a score of 400 is not twice as intelligent as someone with a score of 200.[14] Though this is not a major problem, it does signal the need for HR professionals to exercise caution in interpreting the meaning of differences in scores among people on assessments with interval scales.

Ratio. Like interval scales, ratio scales have equal differences between scale points for the attribute being measured. In addition, ratio scales have a logical or absolute true zero point. Because of this, how much of the attribute each object possesses can be stated in absolute terms.

Normally, ratio scales are involved in counting or weighing things. Examples of ratio scales abound in staffing measurement, including the assessment of how much weight in pounds (lb.) a candidate can carry over some distance for physically demanding jobs such as firefighting or general construction. Perhaps the most common example is counting the years of job experience that job candidates have, where zero is a meaningful number (indicating no job experience).

Objective and Subjective Measures

Frequently, staffing measures are described as either objective or subjective. The term "subjective" is often used in disparaging ways ("I can't believe how subjective that interview was; there's no way they can rate me fairly on the basis of it"). Exactly what is the difference between so-called objective and subjective measures?

The difference, in large part, pertains to the rules used to measure the attribute being assessed. With objective measures, the rules are predetermined and usually communicated and applied through some sort of scoring key or system. For example, in employment contexts, most paper-and-pencil tests with right-or-wrong answers are considered objective. The scoring systems in subjective measures are more elusive and often involve a rater or judge who assigns the numbers. For example, many employment interviews fall into this category, especially those where the interviewer has an idiosyncratic way of evaluating people's responses, one that is not known or shared by other interviewers. Unfortunately, many hiring managers use "oddball," brainteaser interview questions that play into these idiosyncrasies, such as "If you were a pizza delivery man, how would you benefit from scissors?" or "If you were on an island and could only bring three things, what would you bring?"[15] As Laszlo Bock, SVP of people operations at Google, notes: "They don't predict anything. They serve primarily to make the interviewer feel smart."[16]

In principle, any attribute can be measured objectively or subjectively, and sometimes both are used. Research shows that when an attribute is measured by both objective and subjective means, there is often relatively low agreement between scores from the two types of measures. A case in point pertains to job performance. Performance may be measured objectively through quantity of output, and it may be measured subjectively through performance appraisal ratings, yet these two types of measures correlate only weakly with each other.[17] Undoubtedly, the raters' lack of sound scoring systems for rating job performance is a major contributor to the lack of obtained agreement. The use of subjective measures for performance has been subject to much dialogue and scrutiny, given that the raters may be biased or may like certain people more than others.[18] Various forms of rater training, including ensuring that all raters adopt the same "frame of reference" prior to undertaking ratings, have shown promise in improving these issues.[19]

Whatever type of measure is used to assess attributes in staffing, serious attention should be paid to the scoring key. In a sense, this requires having a firm knowledge of exactly what the organization is trying to measure and how to assign numbers to accurately and precisely assess the attribute. It is simply another way of emphasizing the importance of standardization in measurement.

Scores

Measures yield scores or numbers to represent the amount of the attribute being assessed.[20] Once scores have been derived, they can be manipulated in various ways to give them even greater meaning and to better describe characteristics of the objects being scored.

Central Tendency and Variability

Assume that a group of job applicants were administered a programming language knowledge test. The test is scored using a scoring key, and each applicant receives a score, known as a raw score. These are shown in Exhibit 7.2. Some features of this set of scores may be summarized through the calculation of summary statistics. These pertain to central tendency and variability in the scores and are also shown in Exhibit 7.2.

Central tendency is a way to describe data in terms of their middle, or central point. The indicators of central tendency are the mean, the median, and the mode. Since it was assumed that the data are interval-level data, it is permissible to compute all three indicators of central tendency. Had the data been ordinal, the mean (or average) should not be computed. For nominal data, only the mode would be appropriate. This is because it does not make sense to compute the average of the number of customer service employees (assigned the number "1") and clerical employees (assigned the number "2")—only the most frequently occurring category would be useful information.

Variability is a way to describe data in terms of how dispersed or different the data points are from one another. The variability indicators consist of the range and the standard deviation. The range shows the lowest to highest actual scores for the job applicants. The standard deviation shows the amount of deviation of individual scores from the average score. It illustrates the degree to which the scores are spread out, or conversely, tightly clustered. The larger the standard deviation, the greater the variability in the data.

EXHIBIT 7.2 Central Tendency and Variability: Summary Statistics

Data		Summary Statistics
Applicant	**Test Score (X)**	
A	10	A. Central tendency
B	12	Mean ($\overline{X}$) = 338/20 = 16.9
C	14	Median = middle score = 17
D	14	Mode = most frequent score = 15
E	15	
F	15	B. Variability
G	15	Range = 10 to 24
H	15	Standard deviation (SD) =
I	15	
J	17	$\sqrt{\dfrac{\Sigma(X-\overline{X})^2}{n-1}} = 3.52$
K	17	
L	17	
M	18	
N	18	
O	19	
P	19	
Q	19	
R	22	
S	23	
T	24	
Total (Σ) = 338		
n = 20		

Percentiles

A percentile score for an individual is the percentage of people scoring below the individual in a distribution of scores. Refer to the "Data" columns in Exhibit 7.2 (where the applicants are ranked by test score from smallest to largest) and consider applicant B. That applicant's score (12) is at the 5th percentile, given that he or she had the second-lowest score of all applicants (only one person, or 5% of applicants, scored lower); 90% of the applicants scored better than applicant B. Applicant R's score is at the 85th percentile, meaning that 85% of applicants (17 people) scored lower than applicant R. Only two applicants, S and T, scored higher.

Standard Scores

When interpreting scores, you may wish to compare individuals' raw scores with the mean, such as whether scores are above, at, or below the mean. However, a true understanding of how well an individual did relative to the mean considers the amount of variability in scores around the mean (i.e., the standard deviation). The standard score does just that: it depicts an individual's score relative to the mean in standard deviation terms. The standard score thus answers the question, How many standard deviations above or below the mean did a given person score?

The formula for calculating the standard score, or Z score, is as follows:

$$Z = \frac{X - \overline{X}}{SD}$$

Applicant S in Exhibit 7.2 had a raw score of 23 on the test; the mean is 16.9 and the standard deviation is 3.52. Plugging the data into the above formula, applicant S has a Z score of 1.7. Thus, applicant S scored about 1.7 standard deviations above the mean.

Standard scores are also useful for determining how a person performed, in a relative sense, on two or more tests. For example, assume the following data for a particular applicant:

	Test 1	Test 2
Raw score	50	48
Mean	48	46
SD	2.5	.80

On which test did the applicant do better? To answer this question, simply calculate the applicant's standard scores on the two tests. The Z score on test 1 is .80, and the Z score on test 2 is 2.5. Thus, while the applicant got a higher raw score on test 1 than on test 2, the applicant got a higher Z score on test 2 than on test 1. Viewed in this way, it is apparent that the applicant did better on test 2, relatively speaking.

Correlation Between Scores

Frequently in staffing there are scores on two or more measures for a group of individuals (e.g., applicants). For example, an HR professional may have scores on two or more KSAO measures. One set could be scores on a programming language knowledge test, and the other set could be overall ratings of the applicant's probable job success based on the employment interview. As an HR professional, you may want to know whether the test scores and interview ratings are related. Does an increase in knowledge test scores tend to be accompanied by an increase in interview ratings? You may also have a set of scores on a measure of job performance (e.g., performance appraisal ratings) for the same group of individuals. Is there a correlation between the test scores or interview ratings with the job performance scores? In other words, does knowing an individual's score on the knowledge test or interview rating tell you something about their likely job performance? If so, this would provide some evidence about the validity of these measures as predictors of job performance. This evidence would help the organization decide whether to incorporate the use of the test and interview into the selection process for job applicants.

The relationship between two sets of scores can be examined by plotting scatter diagrams and by calculating correlation coefficients.

Scatter Diagrams

Assume two sets of scores for a group of people—scores on a test and scores on a measure of job performance. A scatter diagram is simply the plot of the job performance scores (criterion, or outcome) by the test scores (predictor). Inspection of the plot provides a visual representation of the type of relationship that exists between the two sets of scores. Exhibit 7.3 provides three different scatter diagrams for the two sets of scores. Each X represents a test score and job performance score combination for an individual.

Example A in Exhibit 7.3 suggests very little relationship between the two sets of scores. Example B shows a modest relationship between the scores, and example C shows a somewhat strong relationship between the two sets of scores.

Correlation Coefficient

The relationship between two sets of scores may also be represented numerically by calculating a correlation coefficient. The symbol for the correlation coefficient is r. Numerically, r values can range from $r = -1.0$ to $r = 1.0$. An r value of 0 indicates there is no relationship between the two sets of scores. The larger the absolute value of r, the stronger the relationship. So, $r = -.55$ is stronger in magnitude than $r = .30$. When an r value is shown without a sign (plus or minus), the value is assumed to be positive.

The sign of the correlation coefficient is arbitrary. One could say that job satisfaction is positively related to job performance (a positive r), just as one could say that job *dis*satisfaction is negatively related to job performance (a negative r). Thus, whether r is positive or negative simply depends on how the relationship is worded or considered (and how the measures are scored).

Naturally, the value of r bears a close resemblance to the relationship shown in the scatter diagram. To demonstrate this, Exhibit 7.3 also shows the approximate r value for each of the three scatter diagrams. The r in example A is low ($r = .10$), the r in example B is moderate ($r = .25$), and the r in example C is high ($r = .60$).

Correlations can be easily calculated by a variety of computer programs, including Microsoft Excel. With Excel, scores on each variable are placed in adjacent columns, and Excel's correlate function "(=Correl)" calculates r. However, the calculation of the correlation coefficient is straightforward, even by hand. An example of this calculation and the formula for r are shown in Exhibit 7.4. In the exhibit

EXHIBIT 7.3 **Scatter Diagrams and Corresponding Correlations**

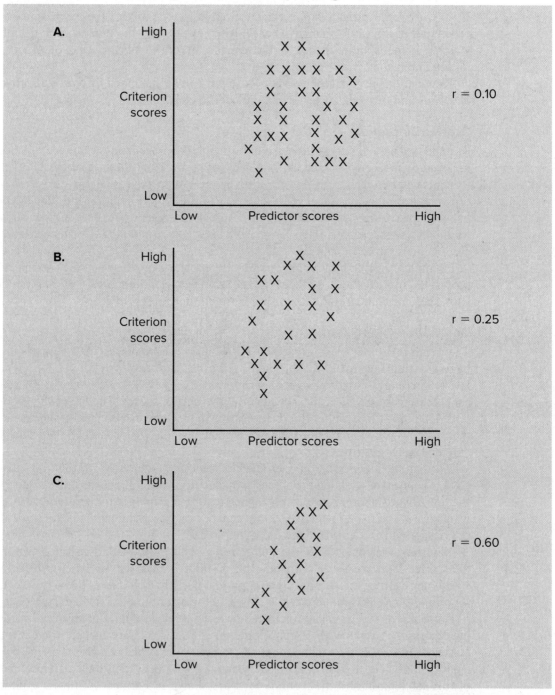

EXHIBIT 7.4 **Calculation of Product-Moment Correlation Coefficient**

Person	Test Score (X)	Performance Rating (Y)	(X^2)	(Y^2)	(XY)
A	10	2	100	4	20
B	12	1	144	1	12
C	14	2	196	4	28
D	14	1	196	1	14
E	15	3	225	9	45
F	15	4	225	16	60
G	15	3	225	9	45
H	15	4	225	16	60
I	15	4	225	16	60
J	17	3	289	9	51
K	17	4	289	16	68
L	17	3	289	9	51
M	18	2	324	4	36
N	18	4	324	16	72
O	19	3	361	9	57
P	19	3	361	9	57
Q	19	5	361	25	95
R	22	3	484	9	66
S	23	4	529	16	92
T	24	5	576	25	120
	$\Sigma X = 338$	$\Sigma Y = 63$	$\Sigma X^2 = 5948$	$\Sigma Y^2 = 223$	$\Sigma XY = 1109$

$$r = \frac{n\,\Sigma XY - (\Sigma X)(\Sigma Y)}{\sqrt{[n\,\Sigma X^2 - (\Sigma X)^2]\,[n\,\Sigma Y^2 - (\Sigma Y)^2]}} = \frac{20\,(1109) - (338)\,(63)}{\sqrt{[20(5948) - (338)^2]\,[20(223) - (63)^2]}} = .58$$

there are two sets of scores for 20 people. The first set is the test scores for the 20 individuals in Exhibit 7.2. The second set of scores is their overall job performance ratings (on a 1–5 rating scale). As can be seen in the exhibit, there is a correlation of r = .58 between the two sets of scores. The correlation succinctly summarizes both the strength and the direction of the relationship between the test scores and performance ratings.

Another useful statistic for staffing professionals is the r-squared (r × r, or r^2). This statistic represents the percentage of common variation between the X and Y scores. Thus, one could interpret r = .50 as indicating that the two variables share 25% ($.5^2 \times 100$) common variation in their scores. As an example, if X was a test of intelligence and Y was a measure of job performance, then one could say that intelligence explains 25% of those differences (hence leaving 75% unexplained and due to other factors).

Despite the simplicity of its calculation, there are several notes of caution regarding the correlation. First, the value of r is affected by the amount of variation in each set of scores. Other things equal, the less variation there is in one or both sets of scores, the smaller the size of the correlation will be. The lack of variation in scores is called the problem of restriction of range. This happens quite often in staffing contexts. For example, if you were to administer the programming knowledge test to all of your current IT analysts (who would, we would hope, all score strongly on this test) and then correlate their scores with their performance evaluations, you may be surprised to find a small correlation. This would be because the "range" of knowledge test scores is "restricted." However, if you were to correlate applicant knowledge test scores with their performance (unrealistically assuming you hire all of the candidates), you may find that the correlation is much higher because the correlation is based on both low and high scores on the knowledge test.

Second, the formula used to calculate the correlation in Exhibit 7.4 assumes that there is a linear relationship between the two sets of scores. This may not always be a good assumption; something other than a straight line may best capture the true nature of the relationship between scores. For example, Nathan Carter has found that a conscientious personality does not always lead to excellent job performance—instead, extremely detail-oriented and conscientious people may experience *drops in performance* after a certain point (a nonlinear relationship).[21] To the extent that two sets of scores are not related in a linear fashion, use of the formula for calculating the correlation will yield a value of r that understates the actual strength of the relationship.

Finally, the correlation between two variables does not imply causation between them. A correlation simply states how two variables relate with one another; it says nothing about one variable necessarily causing the other one.

Significance of the Correlation Coefficient

The statistical significance refers to the likelihood that a correlation is not purely due to chance. Concluding that a correlation is statistically significant in your sample means that there is most likely a correlation in the population.[22] For example, considering the IT analyst position from earlier, 200 applicants to the position (for which we have programming knowledge and interview scores) would be considered a small *sample* of the hundreds of thousands of potential applicants that make up the *population*. If the organization were to use a selection measure based on a statistically significant correlation, the correlation is more likely to be significant again when used to select another sample (e.g., future job applicants).

In order to determine statistical significance for a correlation, one would need to compute the t value of the correlation using the following formula:

$$t = \frac{r}{\sqrt{(1 - r^2)/n - 2}}$$

where r is the value of the correlation, and n is the size of the sample.

A t distribution table, which can be found in any elementary statistics book as well as online, shows the significance level of r.[23] The significance level is expressed as a p value, which represents the probability of concluding that there is a correlation in the population when in fact there is not a relationship. Thus, a correlation with $p < .05$ means there are fewer than 5 in 100 chances of concluding that there is a relationship in the population when in fact there is not one (e.g., a zero correlation). This is a relatively small probability and traditionally leads to the conclusion that a correlation is statistically significant.

An example might help clarify this idea. Taking our previous example of 200 IT analysts, let us say that we found a correlation of $r = .20$ between a measure of programming language knowledge and job performance. How likely is it that we would obtain a correlation of .20 if the "true" correlation between those variables in the population was actually $r = 0$? The t value of our correlation would be 2.87, with our $p = .005$. This means that if we took 100 additional samples of 200 IT analysts (a total of 20,000 analysts) and computed a correlation in each sample, and the true correlation in the population was actually $r = 0$, we would expect to find a correlation of .20 in only half a percent (.005) of those samples. In other words, a correlation of .20 would be extremely rare when the true correlation was 0, and so we conclude that the true correlation is not $r = 0$. The correlation of $r = .20$ is thus deemed "statistically significant."

It is important to avoid concluding that there is a relationship in the population when in fact there is not one (consider the ramifications of concluding that a new drug with harmful side effects drastically reduces the risk of cancer, yet in fact the drug does nothing to reduce that risk). Therefore, one usually chooses a conservative or stringent level of significance that the correlation must attain before concluding that it is significant. Typically, a standard of $p < .05$ or less (another common standard is $p < .01$) is chosen. The actual significance level (based on the t value for the correlation) is then compared with the desired significance level, and a decision is reached as to whether the correlation is statistically significant. Here are some examples:

Desired Level	Actual Level	Conclusion About Correlation
$p < .05$	$p < .23$	Not significant
$p < .05$	$p < .02$	Significant
$p < .01$	$p < .07$	Not significant
$p < .01$	$p < .009$	Significant

Although statistical significance is important in judging the usefulness of a selection measure, caution should be exercised in placing too much weight on this significance. With very large sample sizes, even very small correlations will be significant, and with very small sample sizes, even strong correlations will fail to be significant. Although a finding may be statistically significant, it may not be "practically significant."[24] For example, as mentioned above, one might find a very small correlation (e.g., r = 0.01) that is statistically significant in a sample of 10,000 IT analyst applicants. For the organization, a relationship of .01 might be "too small to be practically important." Therefore, significance is only part of the story; the absolute size of the correlation matters as well.

QUALITY OF MEASURES

For practical reasons, the scores of individuals are treated as if they were the attribute itself rather than merely indicators of the attribute in staffing applications. For example, scores on a mental ability test (e.g., IQ scores) are interpreted as being roughly synonymous with how intelligent individuals are. Alternatively, individuals' ratings from their performance appraisals are viewed as closely representative of their job performance.

Because scores are treated in this way, they become a major input to decision making about individuals. For example, scores on the mental ability test may be used and weighted heavily to decide which job applicants will receive a job offer. Alternatively, performance ratings may serve as a key factor in deciding which individuals will be eligible for an internal staffing move, such as a promotion. In these and numerous other ways, management uses these scores to guide the conduct of staffing activities in the organization. Thus, a lot is at stake in staffing decisions.

The quality of the decisions made and the actions taken depends on the quality of the measures on which they are based. Such concerns are best viewed in terms of reliability and validity of measures.[25]

Reliability of Measures

The reliability of a measure refers to how consistently the measure assesses the attribute.[26] A measure is reliable to the extent that it provides a consistent set of scores to represent an attribute. Perfect reliability is rarely achieved, because of measurement error (see the "Measurement Error" section for a discussion). Therefore, reliability is a matter of degree.

Reliability concerns measurement at a single time period and measurements across multiple time periods. Moreover, reliability is a concern for both objective and subjective measures. These two concerns help create a general framework for understanding reliability.

The key concepts for the framework are shown in Exhibit 7.5. In the exhibit, a single attribute, "A" (e.g., knowledge of programming languages), is being measured. Scores (ranging from 1 to 5) are available for 15 individuals. Attribute A is being measured in time period 1 (T_1) and time period 2 (T_2). In each time period,

EXHIBIT 7.5 **Framework for Reliability of Measures**

	Scores on Attribute A							
	Objective (Test Items)				Subjective (Raters)			
	Time 1		Time 2		Time 1		Time 2	
Person	W_1	X_1	W_2	X_2	Y_1	Z_1	Y_2	Z_2
A	5	5	4	5	5	5	4	5
B	5	4	4	3	5	4	4	3
C	5	5	5	4	5	5	5	4
D	5	4	5	5	5	4	5	5
E	4	5	3	4	4	5	3	4
F	4	4	4	3	4	4	4	3
G	4	4	3	4	4	4	3	4
H	4	3	4	3	4	3	4	3
I	3	4	3	4	3	4	3	4
J	3	3	5	3	3	3	5	3
K	3	3	2	3	3	3	2	3
L	3	2	4	2	3	2	4	2
M	2	3	4	3	2	3	4	3
N	2	2	1	2	2	2	1	2
O	1	2	3	2	1	2	3	2

NOTE: W and X are test items and Y and Z are raters. The subscript "1" refers to T_1, and the subscript "2" refers to T_2.

attribute A may be measured objectively, with two test items (W and X), or subjectively, with two raters (Y and Z). The same two items or raters are used in each time period (in reality, more than two would probably be used, but for simplicity only two are used here). Each item or rater within each time period is a sub-measure of attribute A. There are thus eight sub-measures of A—designated W_1, W_2, X_1, X_2, Y_1, Y_2, Z_1, and Z_2—as well as a score for each. In terms of reliability of measurement, the concern is with the consistency or similarity in the sets of scores. This requires various comparisons of the scores.

As mentioned earlier, the subjective rater-based form of measurement comes with its own assumptions concerning the raters themselves. It is worth mentioning that miscellaneous contextual elements might impact the degree of agreement and reliability between raters. Research within the last two decades suggests that agreement is enhanced when raters share the same goals, have common perceptions of the purposes of the appraisal system, have the same frame of reference in evaluating candidates, and have similar relationships with the ratees. On the other hand, discrepancies are likely to arise when there are systematic differences in what was observed (e.g., when raters observe alternative aspects of a ratee's behavior, do not have the same access to information about the person being rated, vary in their expertise in what is being observed, or use different evaluation processes).[27] Special care should be taken to account for these issues while designing measurement systems and evaluating interrater agreement or reliability.

Comparisons Within T_1 or T_2

Consider the four sets of scores as coming from the objective measure, which used test items. Comparing sets of scores from these items in either T_1 or T_2 is called internal consistency reliability. The relevant comparisons are W_1 and X_1, and W_2 and X_2. It is hoped that the comparisons will show high similarity, because both items are intended to measure attribute A within the same time period.

Now consider the four sets of scores coming from the subjective, rater-based measure. Comparisons of these scores involve what is called interrater reliability. The relevant comparisons are the same as with the objective measure scores, namely, Y_1 and Z_1, and Y_2 and Z_2. Again, it is hoped that there will be high agreement between the raters, because they are focusing on a single attribute at a single moment in time.

Comparisons Between T_1 and T_2

Measurement stability is assessed by comparing scores across time periods. When scores from an objective measure are used, this is referred to as test–retest reliability. The relevant comparisons are W_1 and W_2, and X_1 and X_2. To the extent that attribute A is not expected to change between T_1 and T_2, there should be high test–retest reliability.

When subjective scores are compared between T_1 and T_2, the concern is with intrarater reliability. Here, the same rater evaluates individuals in terms of attribute A at two different time periods. The relevant comparisons are Y_1 and Y_2, and Z_1 and Z_2. To the extent that attribute A is not expected to change, there should be high intrarater reliability.

In summary, reliability is concerned with measurement consistency. There are multiple ways of examining reliability evidence that depend on whether scores are being compared for consistency within or between time periods and whether the scores are from objective or subjective measures. These types of reliability are summarized in Exhibit 7.6. Ways of calculating agreement between scores will be covered shortly, after the concept of measurement error is explored.

Measurement Error

Rarely will comparisons among scores yield perfect reliability. Indeed, none of the comparisons in Exhibit 7.5 appear to suggest complete agreement among the scores. This lack of agreement among the scores may be due to measurement error.

EXHIBIT 7.6 Summary of Types of Reliability

	Compare scores within T_1 or T_2	Compare scores between T_1 and T_2
Objective measure (test items)	Internal consistency	Test–retest
Subjective measure (raters)	Interrater	Intrarater

This type of error represents "noise" in the measure and measurement process. Its occurrence means that the measure did not yield perfectly consistent scores, or so-called true scores, for the attribute.

The scores obtained from the measure thus have two components to them, a true score and measurement error. That is,

$$\text{actual score} = \text{true score} + \text{error}$$

The error component of any actual score, or set of scores, represents the unreliability of measurement. Unfortunately, unreliability is a fact of life for the types of measures used in staffing. To help understand why this is the case, the various types or sources of error that can occur in a staffing context must be explored. These errors may be grouped under the categories of deficiency error and contamination error.[28]

Deficiency Error.   Deficiency error occurs when there is failure to measure some portion or aspect of the attribute assessed. For example, if knowledge of programming languages should involve Java and our test does not have any items (or an insufficient number of items) covering this aspect, the test is deficient. As another example, if a critical aspect of job performance is "planning and setting work priorities" and the raters fail to rate people on that dimension during their performance appraisal, the performance measure is deficient.

Deficiency error can occur in several related ways. First, the attribute may have been inadequately defined in the first place. Thus, the test of knowledge of programming languages may fail to address Java because it was never included in the initial definition of programming knowledge. Alternatively, the performance measure may fail to require raters to rate their employees on "planning and setting work priorities" because this attribute was never considered an important dimension of their work.

A second way that deficiency error occurs is in the construction of measures used to assess the attribute. Here, the attribute may be well defined and understood, but there is a failure to construct a measure that adequately gets at the totality of the attribute. This is akin to poor measurement by oversight, which happens when measures are constructed in a hurried, ad hoc fashion.

Finally, deficiency error occurs when the organization opts to use whatever measures are available because of ease, cost considerations, sales pitches and promotional claims from vendors, and so forth. These measures may turn out to be deficient because the organization selected measures that did not cover all aspects of the attribute in the organization. For example, a vendor might provide a sales performance assessment to an organization, but it might not cover all aspects of sales performance that are unique to that industry.

Contamination Error.   Contamination error represents unwanted or undesirable influences on the measure. These influences muddy the scores and make them difficult to interpret.

Sources of contamination abound, as do examples of them. Several of these sources and examples are shown in Exhibit 7.7, along with some suggestions for how they might be controlled. These examples show that contamination error is multifaceted, making it difficult to minimize and control.

EXHIBIT 7.7   Sources of Contamination Error and Suggestions for Control

Source of Contamination	Example	Suggestion for Control
Content domain	Irrelevant material on test	Define domain of test material to be covered
Standardization	Different time limits for same test	Have same time limits for everyone
Chance response tendencies	Guessing by test taker	Impossible to control in advance
Rater	Rater gives inflated ratings to people	Train rater in rating accuracy
Rating situation	Interviewees are asked different questions	Ask all interviewees the same questions

Calculation of Reliability Estimates

There are a number of procedures for calculating reliability estimates of measures.[29] The first two of these—coefficient alpha and interrater agreement—assess reliability within a single time period. The other two procedures—test-retest reliability and intrarater agreement—assess reliability between time periods. Reliability scores range from 0 (indicating that there is probably nothing but error in the actual scores) to 1.0 (indicating that the actual scores are most likely the "true" scores). As with the squared correlation (r^2), you can think of reliability estimates as the percentage of variation in each measure that is "true" as opposed to "error."

Coefficient Alpha. Coefficient alpha may be calculated in instances in which there are two or more items (or raters) for a particular attribute. Its formula is

$$\alpha = \frac{n\,(\bar{r})}{1 + \bar{r}\,(n-1)}$$

where $\bar{r}$ is the average intercorrelation among the items (raters) and n is the number of items (raters). For example, if there are five items (n = 5) and the average correlation among those five items is $\bar{r}$ = .80, coefficient alpha is .95.

It can be seen from the formula and the example that coefficient alpha depends on two things—the number of items and the amount of correlation between them. This suggests two basic strategies for increasing the internal consistency reliability of a measure—increasing the number of items and increasing the amount of agreement between the items (raters). It is generally recommended that coefficient alpha be at least .70 for a measure to have an acceptable degree of reliability.[30] That means that 70% of the variation in scores is "true" variation and 30% is "error."

Interrater Agreement. When raters serve as the measure, it is often convenient to talk about the degree to which they agree with one another, or interrater agreement. For example, if members of a group or panel interview independently rate a set of job applicants on a 1-5 scale, it is logical to ask how much they agreed with one another.

A simple way to determine this is to calculate the percentage of agreement among the raters. An example of this is shown in Exhibit 7.8.

There is no commonly accepted minimum level of interrater agreement that must be met. Normally, a fairly high level should be set—75% or higher. The more important the end use of the ratings, the greater the minimally acceptable level of agreement should be. Critical usages, such as hiring decisions, demand very high levels of reliability, well in excess of 75% agreement.

Interrater Agreement Versus Coefficient Alpha. It is important to note that reliability (as assessed by coefficient alpha) and interrater agreement can be

---

EXHIBIT 7.8   Calculation of Percentage Agreement Among Raters

Person (ratee)	Rater 1	Rater 2	Rater 3
A	5	5	2
B	3	3	5
C	5	4	4
D	1	1	5
E	2	2	4

$$\frac{\#\ \text{agreements}}{\#\ \text{agreements} + \#\ \text{disagreements}} \times$$

% Agreement
  Rater 1 and Rater 2 = 4/5 = 80%
  Rater 1 and Rater 3 = 0/5 = 0%
  Rater 2 and Rater 3 = 1/5 = 20%

quite different. Specifically, one can have a high coefficient alpha but low agreement, and vice versa. To understand this disparity, consider the data shown in Exhibit 7.9, which, like Exhibit 7.8, involves three raters. However, instead of rating five different applicants, the three raters are rating one applicant on five different skills. Here, there are five items (skills), and the average correlation among those five items (e.g., the correlation between ratings on skill A and skill B; the correlation between ratings on skill A and skill C) is 1.0. This is the case because the ratings are proportionally consistent (although rater 1's ratings are always lower than rater 2's, they differ by the same magnitude each time). Consequently, coefficient alpha is 1.0. However, the raters do not agree at all on how much skill the applicant possesses. Rater 1's average across the five skills is 1.6, rater 2's average is 3.6, and rater 3's average is 4.6.

Now consider Exhibit 7.10. The raters exhibit perfect agreement in their assessment of the candidate. However, coefficient alpha is 0 (technically, it is undefined). Why? Remember that the strength of the correlation coefficient depends on how much variation there is in the items (in this case, skills). Since there is no variation in the items (e.g., skill A is rated 2 by all three raters, as is skill B), the average correlation among the items is 0 and coefficient alpha is 0.

When assessing the reliability of scores where multiple raters are assessing candidates on multiple skills or attributes, keep in mind that coefficient alpha and interrater agreement are assessing different aspects of reliability. Therefore, it is important to consider both.

EXHIBIT 7.9 High Coefficient Alpha but Low Agreement

Skill	Rater 1	Rater 2	Rater 3
Skill A	1	3	4
Skill B	2	4	5
Skill C	2	4	5
Skill D	1	3	4
Skill E	2	4	5

EXHIBIT 7.10 Low Coefficient Alpha but High Agreement

Skill	Rater 1	Rater 2	Rater 3
Skill A	2	2	2
Skill B	2	2	2
Skill C	3	3	3
Skill D	2	2	2
Skill E	2	2	2

Test–Retest Reliability.   To assess test-retest reliability, the test scores from two different time periods are correlated. The correlation may be calculated based on total test scores, or separate correlations may be calculated for each item. The resulting correlation is an indicator of the measurement stability—the higher the correlation (r), the more stable the measure.

Interpretation of the r value is made difficult by the fact that the scores are gathered at two different points in time. Between those two time points, the attribute being measured has an opportunity to change. Interpretation of test-retest reliability thus requires some sense of how much the attribute may be expected to change, and what the appropriate time interval between tests is. Usually, for very short time intervals (hours or days), most attributes are quite stable, and a large test-retest r (r = .90 or higher) should be expected. Over longer time intervals, it is common to expect much lower r's, depending on the attribute being measured. For example, over six months or a year, individuals' knowledge of programming languages might change. If so, there will be lower test-retest reliabilities (e.g., r = .50).

Intrarater Agreement. To calculate intrarater agreement, scores that the rater assigns to the same people in two different time periods are compared. The calculation could involve either computing the correlation between the two sets of scores or using the same formula as for interrater agreement (see Exhibit 7.8).

Interpretation of intrarater agreement is made difficult by the time factor. For short time intervals between measures, a high relationship is expected (e.g., r = .80, or percentage agreement = 90%). For longer time intervals, the level of reliability may reasonably be expected to be lower.

Implications of Reliability

The reliability of a measure has two implications. The first of these pertains to interpreting individuals' scores on the measure and the standard error of measurement. The second implication pertains to the effect that reliability has on the measure's validity.

Standard Error of Measurement. Measures yield scores, which in turn are used as critical inputs for decision making in staffing activities. For example, in Exhibit 7.1 a test of knowledge of programming languages was developed and administered to job applicants. The applicants' scores were used as a basis for making hiring decisions.

The discussion of reliability suggests that measures and scores will usually have some amount of error in them. Hence, scores on the programming language knowledge test most likely reflect both true knowledge and error. Since only a single score is obtained from each applicant, the critical issue is how accurately that particular score assesses the applicant's true level of knowledge.

The standard error of measurement (SEM) addresses this issue. It provides a way to state, within limits, a person's likely score on a measure. The formula for the SEM is

$$SEM = SD_x \sqrt{1 - r_{xx}}$$

where SD_x is the standard deviation of scores on the measure and r_{xx} is an estimate of the measure's reliability. For example, if $SD_x = 10$ and $r_{xx} = .75$ (based on coefficient alpha), SEM = 5.

With the SEM known, the range within which any individual's true score is likely to fall can be estimated. This range is known as a confidence interval or limit. There is a 95% chance that a person's true score lies within ±2 SEM of their actual score. Thus, if an applicant received a score of 22 on the test of knowledge of programming languages, the applicant's true score is most likely to be within the range of 22 ± 2(5), or 12–32.

The use of the SEM allows for care in interpreting scores, as well as the differences between individuals in terms of their scores. For example, using the preceding data, if the test score for applicant 1 is 22 and the score for applicant 2 is 19, what should be made of the difference between the two applicants? Is applicant 1 truly more knowledgeable of programming languages than applicant 2? The answer is probably not. This is because of the SEM and the large amount of overlap between the two applicants' intervals (12–32 for applicant 1, and 9–29 for applicant 2).

In short, there is not a one-to-one correspondence between actual scores and true scores. Most measures used in staffing are unreliable to some degree, meaning that small differences in scores are probably due to error of measurement and should be ignored.

Relationship to Validity. The validity of a measure is defined as the degree to which it measures the attribute it is supposed to be measuring. For example, the validity of the test of knowledge of programming languages is the degree to which it measures that knowledge. There are specific ways to investigate validity, and these are discussed in the next section. Here, we focus more on how reliability is related to validity.

The relationship between the reliability and the validity of a measure is

$$r_{xy} \leq \sqrt{r_{xx}}$$

where r_{xy} is the validity of the measure and r_{xx} is the reliability of the measure.

Thus, the reliability of a measure places an upper limit on the possible validity of a measure. For example, it had been assumed previously that the reliability of the test of knowledge of programming languages was $r = .75$. The validity of that test thus cannot exceed $\sqrt{.75} = 86$. It should be emphasized that this is only an upper limit. A highly reliable measure is not necessarily valid. Reliability does not guarantee validity; it only makes validity possible.

Validity of Measures

The validity of a measure is defined as the degree to which it measures the attribute it is intended to measure.[31] Refer to Exhibit 7.1, which involves the development of a test of knowledge of programming languages that was to be used in selecting job applicants. The validity of this test is the degree to which it truly measures the attribute or construct "knowledge of programming languages."

One can obtain evidence for the validity of a measure by gathering data about the measure, including its development and its relationship with other measures. Depending on the validity evidence of the measure, one can determine whether accurate inferences can be made from scores on the measure. This process can be illustrated in terms of the accuracy of measurement and the accuracy of prediction. These concepts may then be used to demonstrate how the validation of measures occurs in staffing.

Accuracy of Measurement

How accurate is the programming languages knowledge test? This question may be answered by providing evidence about the degree to which the test assesses individuals' true levels of that knowledge. This can be represented as the overlap between the true attribute and the measure of the attribute.

Exhibit 7.11 illustrates accuracy of measurement in Venn diagram form. The circle on the left represents the "knowledge of programming languages" construct, and the circle on the right represents the measure or test of knowledge of programming languages. The overlap between the two circles represents the degree of accuracy of measurement for the test. The greater the overlap, the greater the accuracy of measurement.

Notice that perfect overlap is not shown in Exhibit 7.11. This signifies the occurrence of measurement error with the use of the test. These errors, as indicated in the exhibit, can be found in the errors of deficiency and contamination previously discussed.

So how does accuracy of measurement differ from reliability of measurement since both are concerned with deficiency and contamination? There is disagreement on the answer to this question. Reliability refers to consistency among the

EXHIBIT 7.11   Accuracy of Measurement

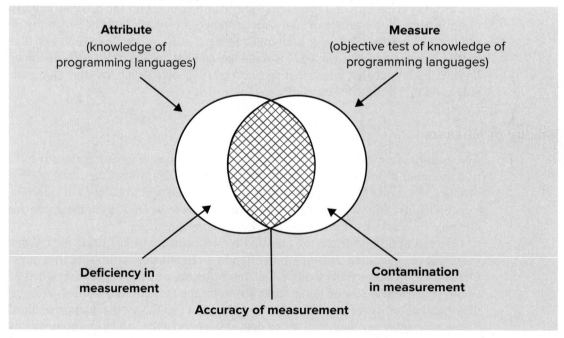

scores on the test, as determined by comparing scores as previously described. Accuracy of measurement goes beyond this to assess the extent to which the scores truly reflect the attribute being measured—the overlap shown in Exhibit 7.11. Accuracy requires reliability, but it also requires more evidence. Accuracy moves beyond determining whether there is consistency among scores on a test toward knowing something. Accuracy also requires evidence concerning how test scores are influenced by other factors: Does the measure contain a sufficient number of questions on each of the programming languages that are important to the organization? Is it missing any? How do scores change as a result of employees attending a training program devoted to providing instruction on programming languages? Accuracy thus demands greater evidence than reliability.

Accuracy of Prediction

Measures are often developed because they provide information about people that can be used to make predictions about them. In Exhibit 7.1, the knowledge test was to be used to help make hiring decisions, which are predictions about which people will be successful at a job. Knowing something about the accuracy with which a test predicts future job success requires examining the relationship between scores on the test and scores on another measure of job success for a group of people. In other words, does the measure accurately predict IT analyst performance as it should?

Accuracy of prediction is illustrated in the top half of Exhibit 7.12. Where there is a job success outcome (criterion) to predict, the test (predictor) will be used to predict the criterion. Each person is classified as high or low on the predictor and high or low on the criterion, based on predictor and criterion scores. Individuals falling into cells A and C represent correct predictions, and individuals falling into cells B and D represent errors in prediction. Accuracy of prediction is the percentage of total correct predictions and can range from 0% to 100%.

The bottom half of Exhibit 7.12 shows an example of the determination of accuracy of prediction using a selection example. The predictor is the test of knowledge of programming languages, and the criterion is an overall measure of job performance. Scores on the predictor and criterion measures are gathered for 100 job applicants and are dichotomized into high or low scores on each. Everyone is placed into one of the four cells. The accuracy of prediction for the test is 70%.

Validation of Measures in Staffing

In staffing, both accuracy of measurement and accuracy of prediction are important aspects of the validity of predictors. It is important to use predictors that accurately represent the KSAOs to be measured, and those predictors need to accurately predict job success. The validity of predictors is explored by conducting validation studies.

EXHIBIT 7.12 Accuracy of Prediction

A. General Illustration

		D	A
High		Errors in predictions	Correct predictions
Low		Correct predictions (C)	Errors in predictions (B)

Actual criterion (vertical axis)

Predicted criterion — Low / High

$$\text{Accuracy} = \frac{A+C}{A+B+C+D} \times 100$$

B. Selection Example (n=100 job applicants)

Actual performance (vertical axis)

	High	20	45
	Low	25	10

Predicted performance (based on test scores) — Low / High

$$\text{Accuracy} = \frac{45+25}{45+10+25+20} \times 100 = 70\%$$

Three types of validation studies are typically conducted: (1) construct validation, (2) criterion-related validation, and (3) content validation. Together, construct, criterion-related, and content validation evidence should be amassed to provide various forms of evidence to support the selection and use of predictors and their measures.[32]

We will discuss construct validation briefly (given that it primarily draws on correlation and reliability evidence, as discussed earlier), followed by discussions of criterion-related validation and content validation.

Construct Validation

Construct validation involves collecting information that shows a test or assessment measures what it was intended to measure. First, reliability evidence assesses the stability and consistency of a measure of a construct (thus, a measure cannot be valid without first being reliable). Second, patterns of correlations between what the measure should be related to and what it should not be related to help provide evidence that the assessment is measuring what it should be measuring. For example, the personality trait of extraversion should be related to sociable behavior but should not be related to problem-solving behavior. Third, patterns of correlations between different kinds of assessments targeted toward different constructs should provide evidence for construct validity. For example, a survey, structured interview question, and situational judgment test that are all intended to assess the personality trait of conscientiousness should be correlated with one another. In other words, three *different types of measures* of conscientiousness should all be related to one another if they are measuring the same thing.

Criterion-Related Validation

Criterion-related validity evidence, which also involves correlational evidence, provides support for the validity of a predictor. Exhibit 7.13 shows the components of criterion-related validation and their usual sequencing.[33] The process begins with job analysis. The results of job analysis lead to the development of criterion and predictor measures. Scores on the predictor and criterion are obtained for a sample of individuals; the relationship between the scores is then examined to make a judgment about the predictor's validity.

Job Analysis.   Job analysis is a procedure used to identify and define the important tasks, duties, and responsibilities of the job. Once these tasks are comprehensively outlined, what it takes to successfully complete them is identified. This is represented by the KSAOs thought to be necessary for performance of these tasks. The results of this process are expressed in the form of the job requirements matrix (Tasks × KSAOs), such as the one shown in Exhibit 7.14; this matrix shows the tasks required and the relevant KSAOs for each task.

For example, let us say that after conducting a job analysis, your team uncovered two critical tasks (among others): task A (troubleshooting and debugging programs) and task B (conferring with clients regarding the nature of system errors). For task A, our "knowledge of programming languages" construct would be an important KSAO to have in order to successfully complete this task. However, would this KSAO also be important for task B? It is likely that a different qualification, such as active listening or another communication skill, will be more important here. Overall, the job requirements matrix is important, as it enables the staffing professional to directly outline the job tasks and the qualifications that are needed to successfully complete them.

EXHIBIT 7.13 Criterion-Related Validation

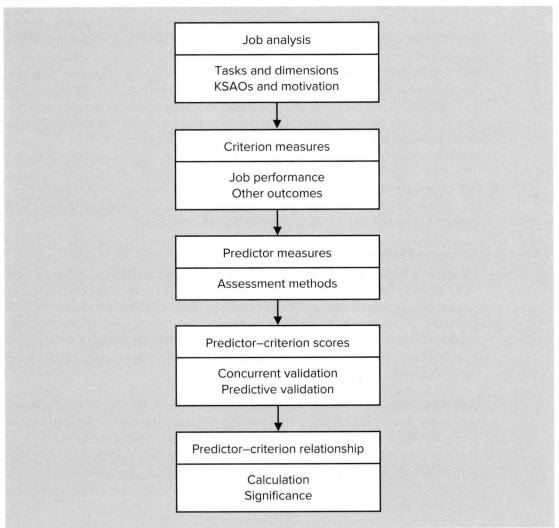

Criterion Measures. Measures of performance on tasks are needed for successful criterion validation. These may already be available as part of an ongoing performance appraisal system, or they may have to be developed. Criterion measures need not be restricted to performance measures. Others may be used, such as measures of attendance, retention, safety, and customer service. In whatever manner these measures are gathered, it is critical that they be as free from measurement error as possible.

EXHIBIT 7.14 Job Requirements Matrix for IT Analyst

	KSAO 1 Communication Skills	KSAO 2 Programming Languages Knowledge	KSAO 3 Problem-Solving Ability	KSAO 4 Planning & Organization Skills
Task A Manage & Plan Projects			X	X
Task B Communicate with Clients	X			
Task C Programming		X		
Task D Troubleshooting Code		X	X	
Task E Train Others to Use Software	X	X		

Predictor Measure. The predictor measure is the measure (e.g., test or assessment) that is being considered for use in the staffing decision. The criterion-related validity of the predictor measure is the focus of criterion-related validation. Ideally, the predictor measure assesses one of the KSAOs identified in job analysis. Also, the type of measure should be the most suitable to assess the KSAO. Knowledge of programming languages, for example, is probably best assessed with some form of written, objective test.

Predictor–Criterion Scores. Predictor and criterion scores must be gathered from a sample of current employees or job applicants. At an absolute minimum, a sample size of 30 (n = 30) is necessary for criterion-related validation. If current employees are used, a concurrent validation design is used. Alternatively, if job applicants are used, a predictive validation design is used. The nature of these two designs is shown in Exhibit 7.15.

Concurrent validation definitely has some appeal. Administratively, it is convenient and can often be done quickly. Moreover, results of the validation study will be available soon after the predictor and criterion scores have been gathered.

EXHIBIT 7.15 **Concurrent and Predictive Validation Designs**

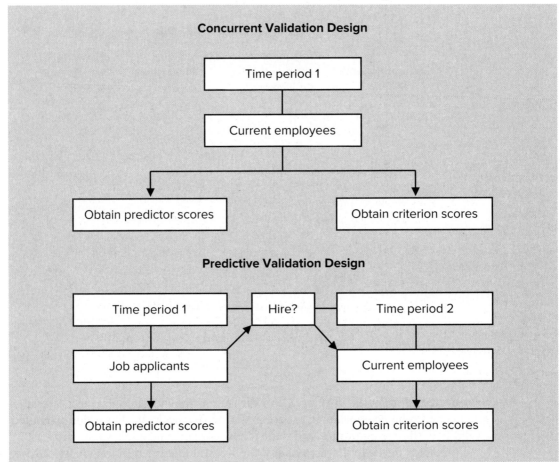

Unfortunately, some serious problems can arise with use of a concurrent validation design. One problem is that if the predictor is a test, current employees may
not be motivated in the same way that job applicants would be in terms of the
desire to perform well. Yet, it is future applicants for whom the test is intended to
be used.

In a related vein, current employees may not be similar to, or representative
of, future job applicants. Current employees may differ in terms of demographics
such as age, race, sex, disability status, education level, and previous job experience. Hence, it is by no means certain that the results of the study will generalize
to future job applicants. In addition, some unsatisfactory employees will have been
terminated, and some high performers may have been promoted. This leads to
restriction of range on the criterion scores (i.e., most employees are high perfor-

mers), which in turn will lower the correlation between the predictor and criterion scores (an issue mentioned earlier in this chapter).

Finally, current employees' predictor scores may be influenced by the amount of experience and/or success they have had in their current job. For example, scores on the programming languages knowledge test may reflect not only that knowledge but also how long people have been on the job and how well they have performed it. This is undesirable because one wants predictor scores to be predictive of the criterion rather than a result of it.

Predictive validation overcomes the potential limitations of concurrent validation since the predictor scores are obtained from job applicants. Applicants will be motivated to do well on the predictor, and they are more likely to be representative of future job applicants. Applicants' scores on the predictor cannot be influenced by success and/or experience on the job, because the scores are gathered prior to their being on the job. Predictive validation also is subject to its own limitations. It is neither administratively easy nor quick. Therefore, results will not be available immediately, as some time must lapse before criterion scores can be obtained. Despite these limitations, predictive validation is considered the sounder of the two designs.

The use of concurrent or predictive designs should also be based on the goals of the validation efforts. For example, research suggests each type of design suffers from its own validity threats, and taking into account the validation goals, the selection of a predictive or concurrent validation study may be more or less appropriate given the situation. Thus, there are certain times when concurrent designs will be preferable. For instance, concurrent designs are best used when the goal is to assess a current skill or when time-related changes in the job or the requirements for the job may be a severe threat. Predictive designs, on the other hand, should be used to test the validity of more unchangeable characteristics (aptitudes, abilities, etc.) and validity stability.[34]

Predictor–Criterion Relationship.   Once predictor and criterion scores have been obtained, the correlation (r), or some variation of it, must be calculated. The value of r is then referred to as the validity of the predictor scores. For example, if r = .35 was found, the validity of the predictor would be .35. Then, the practical and statistical significance of the r should be determined. Only if the r meets desired levels of practical and statistical significance should the predictor be considered valid and thus potentially usable in the selection system.

Illustrative Study.   A state university civil service system covering 20 institutions sought to identify predictors of job performance for clerical employees. The clerical job existed within different colleges (e.g., engineering, humanities) and nonacademic departments (e.g., payroll, data processing). The goal of the study was to have a valid clerical test in two parallel forms that could be administered to job applicants in one hour.

The starting point was to conduct a job analysis, the results of which would be used as the basis for constructing the clerical tests (predictors) and the job performance ratings (criteria). Subject matter experts (SMEs) used job observation and previous job descriptions to construct a task-based questionnaire that was administered to clerical incumbents and their supervisors throughout the system. Task statements were rated in terms of importance, frequency, and essentialness (i.e., if it was essential for a newly hired employee to know how to do this task). From a statistical analysis of the ratings' means and standard deviations, 25 of the 188 task statements were retained as critical task statements. These critical task statements were the input to the identification of key KSAOs and determined the most important aspects of job performance.

Analysis of the 25 critical task statements indicated there were five KSAO components of the job: knowledge of computer hardware and software, ability to follow instructions and prioritize tasks, knowledge and skill in responding to telephone and reception scenarios, knowledge of English language, and ability to file items in alphabetical order. A test was constructed to measure these KSAOs as follows:

- Computer hardware and software—17 questions
- Prioritize tasks—18 questions
- Route and transfer calls—14 questions
- Record messages—20 questions
- Give information on the phone—20 questions
- Correct sentences with errors—22 questions
- Identify errors in sentences—71 questions
- File documents—44 questions
- Type documents—number of questions not reported

To develop the job performance (criterion) measure, a behavioral performance rating scale (1–7 rating) was constructed for each of the nine areas, ensuring a high content correspondence between the tests and the performance criteria they sought to predict. Scores on these nine scales were summed to yield an overall performance score.

The nine tests were administered to 108 current clerical employees to obtain predictor scores. A separate score on each of the nine tests was computed, along with a total score for all tests. In addition, total scores on two short (50-question) forms of the total test were created (Form A and Form B).

Performance ratings of these 108 employees were obtained from their supervisors, who were unaware of their employees' test scores. The performance ratings were summed to form an overall performance rating. Scores on each of the nine tests, on the total test, and on Forms A and B of the test were correlated with the overall performance ratings.

Results of the concurrent validation study are shown in Exhibit 7.16. Seven of the nine specific tests had statistically significant correlations with overall perfor-

EXHIBIT 7.16 **Clerical Test Concurrent Validation Results**

Test	Correlation With Overall Performance
Computer software and hardware	.37**
Prioritize tasks	.29*
Route and transfer calls	.19*
Record messages	.31**
Give information on phone	.35**
Correct sentences with errors	.32**
Identify errors in sentences	.44**
File documents	.22
Type documents	.10
Total test	.45**
Form A	.55**
Form B	.49**

NOTE: *p < .05, **p < .01

SOURCE: Adapted from J. E. Pynes, E. J. Harrick, and D. Schaefer, "A Concurrent Validation Study Applied to a Secretarial Position in a State University Civil Service System," *Journal of Business and Psychology*, 1997, 12, pp. 3–18.

mance (filing and typing did not). Total test scores were significantly correlated with overall performance, as were scores on the two short forms of the total test. The sizes of the correlations suggest favorable practical significance of the correlations as well.

Content Validation

Content validity primarily focuses on the extent to which the content of the measures represents the attribute of interest and the content of the job.[35] Exhibit 7.17 shows the two basic steps in content validation: conducting a job analysis and developing a predictor. These steps are commented on next. Comparing the steps in content validation with those in criterion-related validation (see Exhibit 7.13) shows that they are similar. Because of this, the two types of validation should be thought of as complementary, with content validation being a precursor to criterion-related validation. Content validation can be examined along with criterion-related validation to provide separate pieces of the puzzle of validity in staffing.

Job Analysis. Like criterion-related validation, content validation begins with job analysis, which, in both cases, is undertaken to identify and define tasks and task dimensions and to infer the necessary KSAOs and motivation for those tasks. Results are expressed in the job requirements matrix. Again, special care

EXHIBIT 7.17   Content Validation

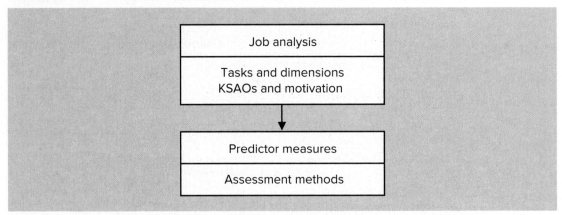

is taken to ensure that tasks and KSAOs are explicitly defined and accurately represent the job.

Predictor Measures.   Sometimes the predictor will be one that has already been developed and is in use. An example here is a commercially available test, interviewing process, or biographical information questionnaire. Other times, such a measure will not be available. This occurs frequently in the case of job knowledge, which is usually very specific to the particular job in question. Lacking a readily available or modifiable predictor means that the organization will have to construct its own predictors.

Now, content validation and the predictor development processes occur simultaneously. Through content-oriented measure development, staffing specialists seek to create a measure prototype that closely matches the construct and maximizes relevance to the job in question.[36] Once a prototype form of the measure is developed, a group of subject matter experts (SMEs) is recruited. These SMEs know the job in question very well and know the KSAOs required to perform the job. The SMEs go through each question in the measure and provide ratings on (a) how well each question matches the construct the question is intended to measure and (b) how important or relevant the question is to representing the construct or the job. SMEs may also be asked to comment on anything they thought was missing from the measure.

With content validation, it is important to continually pay attention to the overlap between the attribute and measurement of that attribute as in Exhibit 7.11. Using the information from the content validation assessment methods, clearly "contaminating" items can be removed from the measure and "deficiencies" can be readily identified (and more questions developed to address these deficiencies). If the measure does not adequately tap into the content domain (deficiency), or if it taps into extraneous, irrelevant content, the measurement will be limited in degree of content validity.

Furthermore, content validity plays into issues of judgments of *face validity* on the part of organizational stakeholders. Both applicants and staffing professionals alike judge the content of the measure and make a connection to eventual job performance. If the content does not contain what it is supposed to or contains attributes that are irrelevant, it will not seem valid, prima facie.

As can be seen from the description, content validation is an important aspect of the validation process that can help improve measurement accuracy. Though content validation has its benefits, including ease of administration, favorable applicant reactions to measures, and legal defensibility, it is not without drawbacks. Critics of content validation argue that, despite the transparent match between job content and measurement content, there is little empirical evidence that predictor measures need to be content-valid to demonstrate criterion-related validity.[37] However, we argue that the three forms of validity are not mutually inclusive and are, rather, pieces of a larger validity puzzle that tap into different aspects of measurement validity (construct-relatedness and prediction).[38]

Illustrative Study.   The Maryland Department of Transportation sought to develop a series of assessment methods for identifying supervisory potential among candidates for promotion to a first-level supervising position anywhere within the department. The content validation process and outputs are shown in Exhibit 7.18. As shown in the exhibit, job analysis was first conducted to identify and define a set of performance dimensions and then infer the KSAOs necessary for successful performance in those dimensions. Several SMEs met to develop a tentative set of task dimensions and underlying KSAOs. The underlying KSAOs were general competencies required of all first-level supervisors, regardless of work unit within the department. Their results were sent to a panel of experienced HR managers within the department for revision and finalization. Three assessment method specialists then set about developing a set of assessments that would (1) be efficiently administered at locations throughout the state, (2) be reliably scored by people at those locations, (3) emphasize the interpersonal skills important for this job, and most importantly, (4) maximize the correspondence between the selected assessments, the KSAOs needed to perform the job successfully, and the content of the job itself. As shown in Exhibit 7.18, five assessment methods were developed: multiple-choice in-basket exercise, structured panel interview, presentation exercise, writing sample, and training and experience evaluation exercise. These assessment methods were designed to match the content of the performance dimensions, tasks, and KSAOs.

After all the various assessments were developed, a separate group of 20 SMEs was formed to review the assessments for content validation purposes. The questions in the in-basket exercise and structured interview, the activities in the presentation exercise, the training exercise, and the writing sample were all reviewed

EXHIBIT 7.18 Content Validation Study

Job Analysis: First-Level Supervisor—Maryland Department of Transportation

Seven performance dimensions and task statements:
Organizing work; assigning work; monitoring work; managing consequences; counseling, efficiency reviews, and discipline; setting an example; employee development

Fourteen KSAOs and definitions:
Organizing; analysis and decision making; planning; communication (oral and written); delegation; work habits; carefulness; interpersonal skill; job knowledge; organizational knowledge; toughness; integrity; development of others; listening

Predictor Measures: Five Assessment Methods

Multiple-choice in-basket exercise
(assume role of new supervisor and work through in-basket on desk)
Structured panel interview
(predetermined questions about past experiences relevant to the KSAOs)
Presentation exercise
(make presentation to a simulated work group about change in their work hours)
Writing sample
(prepare a written reprimand for a fictitious employee)
Training and experience evaluation exercise
(give examples of training and work achievements relevant to certain KSAOs)

SOURCE: Adapted from M. A. Cooper, G. Kaufman, and W. Hughes, "Measuring Supervisory Potential," *IPMA News*, December 1996, pp. 8–18.

and rated by the SMEs for job relevance and representation of the constructs. The assessment specialist reviewed the data generated by the SMEs to refine and hone the assessments to ensure they are job relevant and match the constructs they were intended to assess. Based on these results, several questions were deleted or added, and refinements to the exercises were made. This procedure resulted in a content-valid measure: one that is sufficiently relevant for the job and reflects the construct it was intended to measure.

Validity Generalization

In the preceding discussions of validity, an implicit premise is that validity is situation specific, and therefore validation of predictors must occur in each specific situation. All the examples involve specific types of measures, jobs, individuals, and so forth. Nothing is said about generalizing validity across jobs and individuals. For example, if a predictor is valid for a particular job in organization A, would it be valid for the same type of job in organization B? Or is validity specific to the particular job and organization?

The situation-specific premise is based on the following scenario, which has its origins in findings from decades of previous research. Assume that 10 criterion-related validation studies have been conducted. Each study involves various predictor measures of a common KSAO attribute (e.g., general mental ability) and various criterion measures of a common outcome attribute (e.g., job performance). The predictor will be designated x, and the criterion will be designated y. The studies are conducted in different situations (types of jobs, types of organizations), and they involve different samples (with different sample sizes, n). In each study, the reliability of the predictor (r_{xx}) and the criterion (r_{yy}), as well as the validity coefficient (r_{xy}), is calculated. These results are provided in Exhibit 7.19. At first blush, the results, because of the wide range of r_{xy} values, would seem to support situational specificity. These results suggest that while, on average, there seems to be some validity to x, the validity varies substantially from situation to situation.

The concept of validity generalization questions this premise.[39] It says that much of the variation in the r_{xy} values is due to the occurrence of several "artifacts"—differences across the studies (e.g., differences in reliability of x and y). If these

EXHIBIT 7.19   Hypothetical Validity Generalization Example

Study	Sample Size n	Validity r_{xy}	Reliability Predictor (x) r_{xx}	Reliability Criterion (y) r_{yy}	Corrected Validity r_c
Birch, 2013	454	.41	.94	.94	.44
Cherry, 1990	120	.19	.66	.76	.27
Elm, 1978	212	.34	.91	.88	.38
Hickory, 2009	37	−.21	.96	.90	−.23
Locust, 2000	92	.12	.52	.70	.20
Maple, 1961	163	.32	.90	.84	.37
Oak, 1948	34	.09	.63	.18	.27
Palm, 2007	202	.49	.86	.92	.55
Pine, 1984	278	.27	.80	.82	.33
Walnut, 1971	199	.18	.72	.71	.25

differences were controlled statistically, the variation in values would shrink and converge toward an estimate of the true validity of x. If that true r is significant (practically and statistically), one can indeed generalize validity of x across situations. Validity thus is not viewed as situation specific.

A particular form of validity generalization that has proved useful is meta-analysis. Meta-analysis enables one to produce a statistical average of the correlations across multiple studies weighted by the sample size; this represents a summary of the relationship between two variables (e.g., predictors and criteria) across studies. Indeed, the results in the exhibit reveal that the meta-analytic average (weighted by sample size) validity is $\bar{r}_{xy} = .30$, and the average validity corrected for unreliability in the predictor and criterion is $\bar{r}_{xy} = .36$. In this example, two-thirds (66.62%) of the variance in the correlations was due to study artifacts (differences in sample size and differences in reliability of the predictor or the criterion). Put another way, the variability in the correlations is lower once they are corrected, and the validities do generalize. Meta-analysis is very useful in comparing the relative validity of selection measures, which is precisely what we do in the external selection chapters.

An enormous amount of evidence supporting the validity generalization premise has accumulated. Some experts argue that validity generalization reduces or even eliminates the need for an organization to conduct its own validation study. If validity generalization shows that a selection measure has a statistically significant and practically meaningful correlation with job performance, the reasoning goes, why go through the considerable time and expense to reinvent the wheel (to conduct a validation study when evidence clearly supports use of the measure in the first place)?

There are two caveats to keep in mind in accepting this logic. First, organizations or specific jobs (for which the selection measure in question is intended) can sometimes be unusual. To the extent that the organization or job was not reflected in the validity generalization effort, the results may be inapplicable to the specific organization or job. Second, validity generalization efforts, while undoubtedly offer more evidence than a single study, are not perfect. For example, validity generalization results can be susceptible to "publication bias," where test vendors and academic researchers may report only statistically significant correlations. Although procedures exist for correcting this bias, they assume evidence and expertise usually not readily available to an organization.[40] Thus, as promising as validity generalization is, we think organizations, especially if they think the job in question differs from that in comparable organizations, may still wish to conduct validation studies of their own.

However, future validity generalization work using meta-analysis should pay critical attention to the studies that comprise the meta-analytic databases. Notably, a review of 14 meta-analyses on the validities of cognitive ability and personality traits found that a sizable portion of the meta-analyses did not account for between-study differences in predictive versus concurrent validation, the period of time between measuring the predictor and the criterion, the age of the studies included (most of the studies were conducted in the 1960s or earlier), sample demographics, the culture of the samples, information about the organizations or industries providing the samples, relationships at different levels of analysis (e.g., team-level, department-level relationships), or even reliability information from the primary studies and resultant construction of measurement artifact distributions.[41] Clearly, this information would greatly improve validity generalization efforts and help practitioners determine whether they might expect the validities to be replicated in their own contexts.

Staffing Metrics and Benchmarks

For some time now, HR has sought to prove its value through the use of metrics, or quantifiable measures that demonstrate the effectiveness (or ineffectiveness) of a particular practice or procedure. Staffing is no exception. Fortunately, many of the measurement processes described in this chapter represent excellent metrics. Unfortunately, most HR managers, including many in staffing, may have limited (or no) knowledge of job analysis, validation, and measurement. This lack of knowledge can have the unfortunate side effect of leading to uninformed staffing decisions and a reliance on measures that may not be as effective as alternatives.[42] The reader of this book can "show their stuff" by educating other organizational members about these metrics in an accessible and nonthreatening way. The result may be a more rigorous staffing process that produces higher levels of validity, higher-performing employees, and kudos for you.

Many who work in staffing are likely more familiar with another type of metric, namely, benchmarking. Benchmarking is a process where organizations evaluate their practices (in this case, staffing practices) against those used by industry leaders. Some commonly used benchmarks include cost per hire, forecasted hiring, and vacancies filled. Traditionally, most benchmarking efforts have focused on quantity of employees hired and cost. That situation is beginning to change. For example, Reuters and Dell are tracking "quality of hire," or the performance levels of those hired. Eventually, if enough organizations track such information, they can form a consortium so they can benchmark off one another's metrics for both quantity and quality. More generally, the Society for Human Resource Management (SHRM) regularly offers conferences and mini-conferences on staffing as well as customizable reports that provide benchmarks of current organizational practices.[43]

Such benchmarks can be a useful means of measuring important aspects of staffing methods or the entire staffing process. However, they are no substitute for the other measurement principles described in this chapter, including reliability and validity. Reliability, validity, and other measurement principles are more enduring, and more fundamental metrics of staffing effectiveness.

COLLECTION OF ASSESSMENT DATA

In staffing decisions, the process of measurement is put into practice by collecting assessment data on applicants. To this point, we have discussed the important process of evaluating selection measures. Selection decision makers must be knowledgeable about how to use assessment data; otherwise, the potential value of the data will lie dormant. On the other hand, to put these somewhat theoretical concepts to use, selection decision makers must know how to collect assessment data. Otherwise, the decision makers may find themselves in the unenviable "big hat, no cattle" situation—knowing how to analyze and evaluate assessment data but not knowing where to find the data in the first place.

In collecting assessment data, if a predictor measure is purchased, support services are needed. Consulting firms and test publishers may provide support for scoring the measures. Legal support is also necessary to ensure compliance with laws and regulations. Validation studies are important to ensure the effectiveness of the measures. Training on how to administer the measures is also needed.

Furthermore, practical considerations in staffing should also be examined. For instance, recent research from Glassdoor suggests that employers are taking longer to hire new workers.[44] Andrew Chamberlain, chief economist at Glassdoor, recognizes that although this careful evaluation can lead to better hires, employers could miss out on top talent because their process takes longer than other companies. Therefore, it is important to recognize both mechanical and practical issues when developing a staffing measurement and evaluation system.

Beyond these general principles, which apply no matter what assessment data are collected, there is other information that the selection decision maker must know, such as testing procedures, tests and test manuals, and professional standards.

Testing Procedures

Regardless of whether paper-and-pencil or computerized tests are given, certain guidelines need to be kept in mind.

Qualification

Predictors cannot always be purchased by any firm that wants to use them; many test publishers require the purchaser to have certain expertise, to ensure that the test is used properly. For example, test publishers may want the user to hold a PhD in a field of study related to the test and its use. For smaller organizations, this means hiring the consulting services of a specialist in order to properly use a test.

Security

Care must be taken to ensure that correct answers for predictors are not shared with job applicants (a security leakage).[45] Any person who has access to the predictor answers should be fully trained and should sign a predictor security agreement.

In addition, applicants should be instructed not to share information about the test with fellow applicants. Alternative forms of the test should be considered if the security of the test is in question.

Not only should the predictor itself be kept secure, but also the results of the predictor in order to ensure the privacy of the individual. The results of the predictor should be used only for the intended purposes and by persons qualified to interpret them. Though feedback can be given to the candidate concerning the results, the individual should not be given a copy of the predictor or the scoring key.

Standardization

Finally, it is imperative that all applicants be assessed with standardized procedures. This means that not only should the same or a psychometrically equivalent predictor be used, but individuals should take the test under the same circumstances. The purpose of the predictor should be explained to applicants, and they should be put at ease, be held to the same requirements to complete the measure, and take the measure in the same location.

Internet-Based Test Administration

Increasingly, selection measures are being administered on the Internet. For example, job applicants for hourly positions at Kmart, Publix, and Best Buy take an electronic assessment at in-store kiosks. McDonald's is now even accepting applications through virtual assistants such as Alexa and Google Home.[46]

In general, research suggests that web-based tests work as well as paper-and-pencil tests,[47] as long as special care is taken to ensure that the actual applicant is the test taker and that the tests are validated in the same manner as other selection measures. Test security becomes even more of a concern when using Internet testing, but can be ameliorated with the previously mentioned best practices, along with developing a security plan, preventing and detecting cheating, and engaging in punitive actions.[48] More modern approaches to assessment have utilized mobile assessment modalities. Research here also suggests equivalence between mobile and nonmobile devices for assessment in staffing, although effects may differ depending on applicant anxiety with mobile devices.[49] Some new advancements in technology are also vastly automating scoring procedures that would take much longer and many more resources to accomplish effectively using paper-and-pencil testing formats.[50]

Some organizations, in their rush to use such tests, fail to validate them. The results can be disastrous. The Transportation Security Administration (TSA) was criticized for an "inane" online test. The answers to many questions on the test were obvious to a grade-school student. For example, one question read as follows:

> Why is it important to screen bags for improvised explosive devices (IEDs)?
> a. The IED batteries could *leak and damage* other passenger bags.
> b. The wires in the IED could *cause a short* to the aircraft wires.

c. IEDs can cause *loss of lives*, property and aircraft.

d. The *ticking timer* could worry other passengers.

Obviously, the correct answer is "c." The TSA farmed out the test to a vendor without asking for validation evidence. The TSA's justification was, "We administered the test the way we were told to [by the vendor]." Thus, Internet-based testing can work well and has many advantages, but organizations need to ensure that the tests are rigorously developed and validated.[51]

Acquisition of Tests and Test Manuals

The process of acquiring tests and test manuals, whether digital versions or print versions, requires some start-up costs in terms of the time and effort needed to contact test publishers. Once the selection decision maker is on an e-mail or mailing list, however, they can stay up to date on the latest developments.

Most publishers provide sample copies of the tests and a user's manual that selection decision makers may consult before purchasing the test. Test costs vary widely depending on the test and the number of times the test is given. Discounts can be available for testing a larger numbers of applicants.

Any test worth using will be accompanied by a professional user's manual (whether in print or online). This manual should explicitly describe the development and validation of the test, including validity evidence in selection contexts.[52] A test manual should also include administration instructions, scoring information, interpretation information, and normative data. All this information is crucial to make sure that the test is appropriate and that it is used in an appropriate (valid, legal) manner. Avoid using a test that has no professional manual, as it is unlikely to have been validated. Using a test without a proven track record is akin to hiring an applicant sight unseen. The *Wonderlic Personnel Test User's Manual* is an excellent example of a professional user's manual. It contains information about various forms of the *Wonderlic Personnel Test*, how to administer the test and interpret and use the scores, validity and fairness of the test, and various norms by age, race, gender, and so on.

Publishers of selection tests include Wonderlic, Consulting Psychologists Press (CPP), Institute for Personality and Ability Testing (IPAT), Psychological Assessment Resources (PAR), Hogan Assessments, Shaker, and FurstPerson, Inc. All these organizations have information on their websites that describes the products available for purchase. Furthermore, SHRM has launched the SHRM Talent Assessment Center, whereby SHRM members can review and receive discounts on more than 200 web-based tests, as well as create custom reports based on the results of these tests.[53]

Professional Standards

Revised in 2018 by the Society for Industrial and Organizational Psychology (SIOP) and approved by the American Psychological Association (APA), *Principles for the*

Validation and Use of Personnel Selection Procedures is a guidebook that provides testing standards for use in selection decisions. It covers test choice, development, evaluation, and use of personnel selection procedures in employment settings. Specific topics covered include the various ways selection measures should be validated, how to conduct validation studies, which sources can be used to determine validity, generalizing validation evidence from one source to another, test fairness and bias, how to understand worker requirements, data collection for validity studies, ways in which validity information can be analyzed, and the appropriate uses of selection measures.

Principles was developed by many of the world's leading experts on selection, and therefore any selection decision maker would be well advised to consult this important document, which is written in practical, nontechnical language. This guidebook is free and can be obtained from the APA and SIOP websites.

Principles is consistent with updates made by the joint publication of *The Standards for Educational and Psychological Testing* in 2014. This publication was developed by the American Educational Research Association (AERA), the APA, and the National Council on Measurement in Education (NCME). It constitutes the gold standard for testing in the United States and many other countries. "*The Rights and Responsibilities of Test Takers*" *is one section of the Standards and* enumerates 10 rights and 10 responsibilities of test takers.[54] For example, one of the rights is for the applicant to be treated with courtesy, respect, and impartiality. Another right is to receive prior explanation for the purpose(s) of the testing. One responsibility is to follow the test instructions as given. In addition to enumerating test-taker rights and responsibilities, the document also provides guidelines for organizations administering the tests. For example, the standards stipulate that organizations should inform test takers about the purpose of the test. Organizations testing applicants should consult these guidelines to ensure that these rights are provided wherever possible.

LEGAL ISSUES

Staffing laws and regulations, particularly EEO/AA laws and regulations, place great reliance on the use of measurement concepts and processes.[55] Three key topics are determining disparate impact, standardization of measurement, and best practices suggested by the EEOC.

Determining Disparate Impact

In the social and legal environment chapter, disparate impact was introduced as a way of determining whether staffing practices have potentially illegal impacts on individuals because of protected characteristics. Such a determination requires the compilation and analysis of statistical evidence.

Applicant Flow Statistics

Applicant flow compares selection rates across protected characteristics, and comparisons to see if they are significantly different from one another.

Focusing on flow statistics in Exhibit 2.5, we see the following:

FLOW STATISTICS

Applicants		Hired		Selection Rate		
Men	**Women**	**Men**	**Women**	**Men**	**Women**	**Ratio**
40	40	18	22	18/40 = 45%	22/40 = 55%	45/55 = 0.82

This example shows a difference in selection rates between men and women (45% as opposed to 55%). As we noted in the social and legal environment chapter, the ratio of 0.82 means that qualified women applicants are 82% as likely to be hired as qualified men.

Does this difference indicate disparate impact? The Uniform Guidelines on Employee Selection Procedures (UGESP) speak directly to this question. According to the UGESP, comparisons of selection rates among groups in a job category for purposes of compliance determination should be based on the 80% rule. The UGESP focuses on whether the selection rate for subgroups across protected characteristics "is less than four-fifths (or 80%) of the rate for the group with the highest rate." If this rule is applied to the example, the ratio is 0.82. The UGESP would suggest this is a borderline case. Even if it passes the UGESP 80% test, some observers would say that proof of job relatedness should be provided for a selection procedure that puts women at such a significant disadvantage.

Many experts in the field of selection consider this component of the UGESP test out of date.[56] The 80% rule is not informative as to whether differences between groups could occur if selection is independent of protected characteristics. Statistical tests of contingency tables, based on the chi-squared or Fisher's exact test can describe the likelihood of an observed result. Online calculators can be used to obtain these results. Using the typical language of selection rate tests, 22 men passed the screen, and 18 failed; for women, 18 passed and 22 failed. The value of the test statistics from Fisher's exact test is 0.50, which is not statistically significant. This means a hiring rate difference of this magnitude with this sample size could emerge due to random chance.

This significance testing approach complements, rather than replaces, the use of the 4/5ths rule. In practice, courts will take the ratio of selection rates as an indicator of the practical significance of the difference across characteristics, whereas statistical significance is used to evaluate whether such a difference could be a function of chance.[57]

Applicant Utilization Statistics

Applicant utilization statistics require the calculation of the percentages across protected class status in two areas: (1) employed and (2) available for employment in the population. These percentages are compared in order to identify disparities. The procedure is essentially the same as for flows.

To illustrate, the example from Exhibit 2.5 is shown here:

UTILIZATION STATISTICS

Available Qualified		Current Workforce		Representation Rate		Ratio
Over 40	Under 40	Over 40	Under 40	Over 40	Under 40	
490	210	24	15	24/490 = 4.9%	15/210 = 7.1%	4.9/7.1 = 0.69

This example shows a difference in utilization rates between those over and under 40 (4.9% as opposed to 7.1%), and the ratio of the two is 0.69. Qualified individuals over 40 are only 69% as likely to be represented in this workforce relative to qualified individuals under 40. As with flow statistics, tests of statistical significance should also be performed. For the available workforce over 40, 24 are employed in this organization and 466 are not, as contrasted with 15 employed and 195 not for those under 40. The value of Fisher's exact test is 0.28, which again is not statistically significant even though this hiring procedure does fail the 4/5 rule.

Utilization analysis is an integral part of not only compliance assessment but also affirmative action plans (AAPs). Indeed, utilization analysis is the starting point for the development of AAPs. Affirmative Action Programs Regulations require a formal utilization analysis of the workforce that is (1) conducted by job group and (2) done separately across protected class groups. Though calculation of the numbers and percentages of persons employed is relatively straightforward, determination of their availability is not. The regulations require that the availabilities consider at least the following factors: (1) the percentage of individuals with requisite skills in the recruitment area broken out by protected characteristics, and (2) the percentage of those who are promotable, transferable, and trainable within the organization across protected characteristics.

Accurate measurement of availabilities that consider these factors is difficult. Despite these measurement problems, the regulations require comparison of the percentages employed across protected classes with their availability. When the percentage of workers with a protected characteristic in a job group is less than would reasonably be expected given their availability, underutilization exists and placement (hiring and promotion) goals must be set. Thus, the organization must exercise considerable discretion in the determination of disparate impact using applicant utilization statistics. It would be wise to seek technical and/or legal assistance for conducting utilization analysis (see also "Affirmative Action Plans" in the planning chapter).

Differential Prediction of Selection Measures

The use of selection measures themselves may also lead employers to discriminate in selection decisions. There are several ways to examine bias in selection measures beyond what we have discussed so far.[58] One simple way is to look at subgroup differences between means on predictor scores. For example, White applicants might score .86 standard deviations higher than other applicants on a cognitive ability test;[59] this difference in test scores suggests that White applicants score higher on the test and may be one source for disparate impact. Specific types of selection tests and assessments have been shown to exhibit "differential prediction," in which the measure is predictive for one group when compared with another, resulting in selection decisions exhibiting disparate impact. Special statistics can help in making this determination.[60] These statistics essentially tell us whether the predictor–criterion correlations (discussed earlier) are different for each group. For example, research summarizing hundreds of studies has found that although cognitive ability test scores are higher for Whites, cognitive ability test scores overpredict the performance of Blacks.[61] In other words, cognitive ability tests do not display differential prediction for Blacks. The final (and least often used) form refers to examining whether bias exists not at the predictor level but at the question level. Obviously, this form will not be relevant for all types of predictors but is particularly relevant for surveys and tests. The idea here is that certain questions may have a different meaning (i.e., may be offensive) for members of protected classes.[62] Special statistics (e.g., differential item functioning [DIF]) are used to examine the presence of this form of bias, but large numbers of people are required in order to calculate these statistics. Therefore, they are beyond the scope of this textbook.

Interest in the disparate impact of predictors has resulted in the "diversity-validity" dilemma, in which the best predictors of individual performance and effectiveness (e.g., cognitive ability) are often the ones that are associated with the most disparate impact.[63] Indeed, a review of the meta-analytic literature suggests that many predictors exhibit moderate to large amounts of disparate impact (with the least amount of disparate impact observed for personality tests).[64] One solution has been to design "Pareto-optimal selection systems," in which the selection measures, rules, staging, measurement sequencing, predictor weighting, and flow statistics are all optimized to reduce disparate impact.[65] Furthermore, some research suggests that a combination of low disparate impact predictors (e.g., personality test, structured interview, and biodata) can meet or exceed the validity of a cognitive ability test.[66]

Standardization

A lack of consistency in treatment of applicants is one of the major factors contributing to the occurrence of discrimination in staffing.[67] This is partly due to a lack of standardization in measurement, in terms of both what is measured and how it is evaluated or scored.

An example of inconsistency in what is measured is that the type of background information asked of minority applicants may differ from that asked of nonminority applicants. Minority applicants may be asked about credit ratings and criminal conviction records, while nonminority applicants are not. Alternatively, the type of interview questions asked of male applicants may be different from those asked of female applicants.

Even if information is consistently gathered from all applicants, it may not be evaluated in the same way for all applicants. A male applicant who has a history of holding several different jobs may be viewed as a career builder, while a female with the same history may be evaluated as an unstable job-hopper. In essence, different scoring "policies" may be applied to men and women applicants.

Reducing, and hopefully eliminating, such inconsistencies requires a straightforward application of the three properties of standardized measures discussed previously. Through standardization of measurement comes consistent treatment of applicants and, with it, the possibility of lessened disparate impact.

Best Practices

Based on its long and in-depth involvement in measurement and selection procedures, the EEOC provides guidance to employers in the form of several best practices for testing and selection.[68] These practices apply to a wide range of tests and selection procedures, including cognitive and physical ability tests, sample job tasks, medical inquiries and physical exams, personality and integrity tests, criminal and credit background checks, performance appraisals, and English proficiency tests. The best practices are the following:

- Employers should administer tests and other selection procedures without regard to race, color, national origin, sex, religion, age (40 or older), or disability.
- Employers should ensure that employment tests and other selection procedures are properly validated for the positions and purposes for which they are used. The test or selection procedure must be job related and its results appropriate for the employer's purpose. While a test vendor's documentation supporting the validity of a test may be helpful, the employer is still responsible for ensuring that its tests are valid under the UGESP (discussed in the external selection chapters).
- If a selection procedure screens out a protected group, the employer should determine whether there is an equally effective alternative selection procedure that has less disparate impact and, if so, adopt the alternative procedure. For

example, if the selection procedure is a test, the employer should determine whether another test would predict job performance but not disproportionately exclude the protected group.

- To ensure that a test or selection procedure remains predictive of success in a job, employers should keep abreast of changes in job requirements and should update the test specifications or selection procedures accordingly.
- Employers should ensure that tests and selection procedures are not adopted casually by managers who know little about these processes. A test or selection procedure can be an effective management tool, but no test or selection procedure should be implemented without an understanding of its effectiveness and limitations for the organization, its appropriateness for a specific job, and whether it can be appropriately administered and scored.

Note that these best practices apply to virtually all selection procedures or tools, not just tests. They emphasize the need for fair administration of these tools, the importance of the procedures being job related, usage of alternative valid selection procedures that have less disparate impact, and the updating of job requirements (KSAOs) and selection tools. In addition, casual usage of selection tools by uninformed managers is to be avoided.

SUMMARY

Measurement, defined as a process used to gather and express information about people and jobs in numerical form, is an integral part of the foundation of staffing activities. A standardized, systematic approach to measurement that considers the levels of measurement (i.e., nominal, ordinal, interval, and ratio) as well as the objectivity (or subjectivity) of measurement is important.

Measures yield scores that represent the amount of the attribute being assessed. Statistics can be computed that aid the interpretation of the measure. These include central tendency and variability, percentiles, and standard scores. Scores can also be correlated to learn about the strength and direction of the relationship between two attributes or constructs. The statistical (and practical) significance of the resultant correlation coefficient can then be assessed.

Measurement quality strongly concerns the issues of reliability and validity. Reliability refers to the consistency of measurement, both at a moment in time and between time periods. Various procedures are used to estimate reliability, including coefficient alpha, interrater and intrarater agreement, and test–retest reliability. Reliability places an upper limit on the validity of a measure.

Validity concerns the accuracy of measurement and accuracy of prediction, as reflected by the scores obtained from a measure. Criterion-related and content validation studies are conducted to help learn about the validity of a measure. In criterion-related validation, scores on a predictor (KSAO) measure are correlated with scores on a criterion (HR outcome) measure. In content validation, judgments are made about the content of a predictor relative to the attribute that is intended to be measured as well as the content of the job itself. Traditionally, results of validation studies were treated as situation specific, meaning that the organization ideally should conduct a new and separate validation study for any predictor in any situation in which the predictor is to be used. Recently, studies have suggested that the validity of predictors may generalize across situations, meaning that the requirement of conducting costly and time-consuming validation studies in each specific situation might be relaxed. Staffing metrics such as cost per hire and benchmarks, representing how leading organizations staff positions, can be useful measures, but they are not substitutes for reliability and validity.

Various practical aspects of the collection of assessment data were described. Decisions about testing procedures and the acquisition of tests and test manuals require the attention of organizational decision makers. The collection of assessment data and the acquisition of tests and test manuals vary depending on whether paper-and-pencil or computerized selection measures are used. Finally, organizations need to attend to professional standards that govern the proper use of the collection of assessment data.

Measurement is also said to be an integral part of an organization's EEO/AA compliance activities. When disparate impact is found, changes in measurement practices may be legally necessary. These changes will involve movement toward standardization of measurement and the methods for determining disparate impact. Regardless, organizations should follow best practices in legal compliance, routinely collect legally required data, and ensure that they are not engaging in disparate impact or discriminatory practices.

DISCUSSION QUESTIONS

1. Imagine and describe a staffing system for a job in which no measures are used.
2. Describe how you might go about determining scores for applicants' responses to (a) interview questions, (b) letters of recommendation, and (c) questions about previous work experience.
3. Give examples of when you would want the following for a written job knowledge test: (a) a low coefficient alpha (e.g., $\alpha = .35$) and (b) a low test–retest reliability.
4. Assume you gave a general ability test, measuring both verbal and computational skills, to a group of applicants for a specific job. Also assume that because of severe hiring pressures, you hired all the applicants, regardless of their test scores. How would you investigate the criterion-related validity of the test?

5. Using the same example as in question four, how would you go about investigating the content validity of the test?

6. What information does a selection decision maker need to collect in making staffing decisions? What are the ways in which this information can be collected?

ETHICAL ISSUES

1. Do individuals making staffing decisions have an ethical responsibility to know measurement issues? Why or why not?

2. Is it unethical for an employer to use a selection measure that has high empirical validity but lacks content validity? Explain.

APPLICATIONS

Evaluation of Two New Assessments for Selecting Telephone Customer Service Representatives

The Phonemin Company is a distributor of men's and women's casual clothing. It sells exclusively through its merchandise catalog, which is published four times per year to coincide with seasonal changes in customers' apparel tastes. Customers may order merchandise from the catalog via mail or over the phone. Currently, 70% of orders are phone orders, and the organization expects this to increase to 85% within the next few years.

The success of the organization is obviously very dependent on the success of the telephone ordering system and the customer service representatives (CSRs) who staff the system. There are currently 185 CSRs; that number should increase to about 225 CSRs to handle the anticipated growth in phone order sales. Though the CSRs are trained to use standardized methods and procedures for handling phone orders, there are still seemingly large differences among them in their job performance. CSR performance is routinely measured in terms of error rate, speed of order taking, and customer complaints. The top 25% and lowest 25% of performers on each of these measures differ by a factor of at least three (i.e., the error rate of the bottom group is three times as high as that of the top group). Strategically, the organization knows that it could substantially enhance CSR performance (and ultimately sales) if it could improve its staffing "batting average" by more accurately identifying and hiring new CSRs who are likely to be top performers.

The current staffing system for CSRs is straightforward. Applicants are recruited through a combination of employee referrals and newspaper ads. Because turnover among CSRs is so high (50% annually), recruitment is a continuous process at the organization. Applicants complete a standard application blank, which asks for information about education and previous work experience. The information is reviewed by the staffing specialist in the HR department. Only obvious misfits are rejected at this point; the others (95%) are asked to have an interview with the specialist. The interview lasts 20–30 minutes, and at the conclusion the applicant is either rejected or offered a job. Due to the tightness of the labor market and the constant presence of vacancies to be filled, 90% of the interviewees receive job offers. Most of those offers (95%) are accepted, and the new hires attend a one-week training program before being placed on the job.

The organization has decided to investigate the possibilities of increasing CSR effectiveness through sounder staffing practices. It is not pleased with its current methods of assessing job applicants; it feels that neither the application blank nor the interview provides an accurate and in-depth assessment of the applicant KSAOs that are truly needed to be an effective CSR. Consequently, it engaged the services of a consulting firm that offers various methods of KSAO assessment, along with validation and installation services. In cooperation with the HR staffing specialist, the consulting firm conducted the following study for the organization.

A special job analysis led to the identification of several specific KSAOs likely to be necessary for successful performance as a CSR. Three of these (clerical speed, clerical accuracy, and interpersonal skills) were singled out for further consideration because of their seemingly high impact on job performance. Two new methods of assessment provided by the consulting firm were chosen for experimentation. The first is a paper-and-pencil clerical test assessing clerical speed and accuracy. It contains 50 items and has a 30-minute time limit. The second is a brief work sample that could be administered as part of the interview process. In the work sample, the applicant must respond to four different phone calls: a customer who is irate about an out-of-stock item, a customer who wants more product information about an item than was provided in the catalog, a customer who wants to change an order placed yesterday, and a customer who has a routine order to place. Using a 1–5 rating scale, the interviewer rates the applicant on tactfulness (T) and concern for customers (C). The interviewer is provided with a rating manual containing examples of exceptional (5), average (3), and unacceptable (1) responses by the applicant.

A random sample of 50 current CSRs were chosen to participate in the study. At Time 1 they were administered the clerical test and the work sample; performance data were also gathered from company records for error rate (number of errors per 100 orders), speed (number of orders filled per hour), and customer complaints (number of complaints per week). At Time 2, one week later, the clerical test and the work sample were re-administered to the CSRs. A member of the consulting firm sat in on all the interviews and served as a second rater of performance on the work sample at Time 1 and Time 2. It is expected that the clerical test and work sample will have positive correlations with speed and negative correlations with error rate and customer complaints.

Results for Clerical Test

	Time 1	Time 2
Mean score	31.61	31.22
Standard deviation	4.70	5.11
Coefficient alpha	.85	.86
Test–retest r		.92*
r with error rate	−.31*	−.37*
r with speed	.41*	.39*
r with complaints	−.11	−.08
r with work sample (T)	.21	.17
r with work sample (C)	.07	.15

Results for Work Sample (T)

	Time 1	Time 2
Mean score	3.15	3.11
Standard deviation	.93	1.01
% agreement (raters)	88%	79%
r with work sample (C)	.81*	.77*
r with error rate	−.13	−.12
r with speed	.11	.15
r with complaints	−.37*	−.35*

Results for Work Sample (C)

	Time 1	Time 2
Mean score	2.91	3.07
Standard deviation	.99	1.10
% agreement (raters)	80%	82%
r with work sample (T)	.81*	.77*
r with error rate	−.04	−.11
r with speed	.15	.14
r with complaints	−.40*	−.31*

(Note: * means that r was significant at p < .05)

After reading the description of the study and observing the results above,

1. How do you interpret the reliability results for the clerical test and work sample? Are they favorable enough for Phonemin to consider using them "for keeps" in selecting new job applicants?

2. How do you interpret the validity results for the clerical test and work sample? Are they favorable enough for Phonemin to consider using them "for keeps" in selecting new job applicants?

3. What limitations in the above study should be kept in mind when interpreting the results and deciding whether to use the clerical test and work sample?

Conducting Empirical Validation and Disparate Impact Analysis

Yellow Blaze Candle Shops provides a full line of various types of candles and accessories such as candleholders. Yellow Blaze has 150 shops in shopping malls and strip malls throughout the country. Over 600 salespeople staff these stores, each of which has a full-time manager. Staffing the manager's position, by policy, must occur by promotion from within the sales ranks. The organization is interested in improving its identification of salespeople most likely to be successful store managers. It has developed a special technique for assessing and rating the suitability of salespeople for the manager's job.

To experiment with this technique, the regional HR department representatives reviewed and rated the promotion suitability of each store's salespeople. They reviewed sales results, customer service orientation, and knowledge of store operations for each salesperson and then assigned a 1–3 promotion suitability rating (1 = not suitable, 2 = may be suitable, 3 = definitely suitable) on each of these three factors. Customer service orientation was rated based on supervisor and coworker observations of work behavior. These ratings incorporated evaluations of how often salespeople asked customers how they could help, how effectively salespeople were able to suggest products that matched customer requests, and how well salespeople ensured that customers were happy with their intended purchases at the end of the encounter. In most cases, ratings of customer service orientation were similar across managers and assistant managers, but there were some discrepancies. Knowledge of store operations was evaluated based on a standardized exam consisting of a variety of questions on managerial practices and procedures, refund and exchange policies, and record-keeping requirements. A total promotion suitability (PS) score, ranging from 3 to 9, was then computed for each salesperson.

The PS scores were gathered for all salespeople but were not formally used in promotion decisions. Over the past year, 30 salespeople were promoted to store manager. Now it is time for the organization to preliminarily investigate the validity of the PS scores and see whether their use results in disparate impact against women or minorities. Each store manager's annual overall performance appraisal rating, ranging from 1 (low performance) to 5 (high performance), was used as the criterion measure in the validation study. The following data were available for analysis:

Employee ID	PS Score	Performance Rating	Sex M/F	Minority Status (M = Minority, NM = Nonminority)
11	9	5	M	NM
12	9	5	F	NM
13	9	1	F	NM
14	9	5	M	M
15	8	4	F	M
16	8	5	F	M
17	8	4	M	NM
18	8	5	M	NM
19	8	3	F	NM
20	8	4	M	NM
21	7	5	F	M
22	7	3	M	M
23	7	4	M	NM
24	7	3	F	NM
25	7	3	F	NM
26	7	4	M	NM
27	7	5	M	M
28	6	4	F	NM
29	6	4	M	NM
30	6	2	F	M
31	6	3	F	NM
32	6	3	M	NM
33	6	5	M	NM
34	6	5	F	NM
35	5	3	M	NM
36	5	3	F	M
37	5	2	M	M
38	4	2	F	NM
39	4	1	M	NM
40	3	4	F	NM

Using the data above, calculate the following:

1. Average PS scores for the whole sample, males, females, nonminorities, and minorities.

2. The correlation between PS scores and performance ratings, and its statistical significance (r = .37 or higher is needed for significance at p < .05).

3. Disparate impact (selection rate) statistics for males and females, and non-minorities and minorities. Use a PS score of 7 or higher as a hypothetical passing score (the score that might be used to determine who will or will not be promoted).

4. Average performance rating scores for the whole sample, males, females, nonminorities, and minorities. For each group, evaluate whether the performance rating scores are different for subgroups of employees. Also evaluate whether the magnitude of these differences is sizable enough to warrant concern for Yellow Blaze.

Using the data, results, and description of the study, answer the following questions:

1. Is the PS score a valid predictor of performance as a store manager? Do you see any potential reasons why either the customer service orientation measure or knowledge of store operations measure might be problematic? In answering, consider issues related to reliability and validity.

2. With a cutoff score of 7 on the PS, would its use lead to disparate impact against women? Against minorities? If there is disparate impact, does the validity evidence justify use of the PS anyway?

3. What limitations do you see in the current study design? Do you think that the conclusions you would reach based on this sample of individuals who were promoted to store manager would generalize to the population of all salespeople who are being evaluated for promotion potential? Do you think that the method of rating performance is sufficient as a criterion, and if so, why? If not, what additional steps would you take to ensure that performance is measured adequately?

4. Would you recommend that Yellow Blaze use the PS score in making future promotion decisions? Why or why not? If you said yes, can you think of anything the company could do to make these measures even better than they are already? If you said no, can you think of any ways that this system might be improved?

5. One employee has raised questions regarding whether the performance ratings themselves are biased. This employee has not made a formal legal complaint against Yellow Blaze yet, but the organization wants to evaluate whether there is reason for concern. Based on the calculations you made regarding the differences for performance evaluation ratings for women relative to men, and for minorities relative to nonminorities, do you believe that there is reason for the organization to be concerned regarding this issue? In other words, do the data suggest that there is, in fact, a substantial difference in performance evaluation ratings for different groups of employees? How should the organization respond to this individual employee's concerns?

ENDNOTES

1. Forbes Coaches Council, "14 Bad Hiring Practices and What You Can Do to Improve," *Forbes*, Sept. 20, 2017 (*www.forbes.com/sites/forbescoachescouncil/2017/09/20/14-bad-hiring-practices-and -what-you-can-do-to-improve/#559e52ef749e*).

2. N. R. Kuncel, D. M. Klieger, B. S. Connelly, and D. S. Ones, "Mechanical Versus Clinical Data Combination in Selection and Admissions Decisions: A Meta-Analysis," *Journal of Applied Psychology*, 2013, 98(6), pp. 1060–1072.

3. P. Cappelli, "Your Approach to Hiring Is All Wrong," *Harvard Business Review*, May–June 2019 (*https://hbr.org/2019/05/recruiting?ab=hero-main-text*).

4. Cappelli, "Your Approach to Hiring Is All Wrong"; C. T. Rotolo et al., "Putting an End to Bad Talent Management: A Call to Action for the Field of Industrial and Organizational Psychology," *Industrial and Organizational Psychology*, 2018, 11(2), pp. 176–219.

5. D. Zielinski, "Predictive Assessments Give Companies Insight Into Candidates' Potential," *Society for Human Resource Management* (blog), Jan. 22, 2018 (*www.shrm.org/resourcesandtools/hr -topics/talent-acquisition/pages/predictive-assessments-insight-candidates-potential.aspx*).

6. Talent Board, *2019 North American Candidate Experience Research Report* (Los Angeles: author, 2019).

7. E. E. Chen and S. P. Wojcik, "A Practical Guide to Big Data Research in Psychology," *Psychological Methods*, 2016, 21(4), pp. 458–474; J. Hugg, "Fast Data: The Next Step After Big Data," *InfoWorld*, June 11, 2014 (*www.infoworld.com*); A. Lorentz, "Big Data, Fast Data, Smart Data," *Wired*, Apr. 17, 2013 (*www.wired.com/*); J. Spencer, "Which Do We Need More: Big Data or Fast Data?" *Entrepreneur*, Mar. 12, 2015 (*www.entrepreneur.com*); S. Tonidandel, E. B. King, and J. M. Cortina, "Big Data Methods: Leveraging Modern Data Analytic Techniques to Build Organizational Science," *Organizational Research Methods*, 2018, 21(3), pp. 525–547.

8. Chen and Wojcik, "A Practical Guide to Big Data Research in Psychology"; R. N. Landers, R. C. Brusso, K. J. Cavanaugh, and A. B. Collmus, "A Primer on Theory-Driven Web Scraping: Automatic Extraction of Big Data From the Internet for Use in Psychological Research," *Psychological Methods*, 2016, 21(4), pp. 475–492; Tonidandel, King, and Cortina, "Big Data Methods: Leveraging Modern Data Analytic Techniques to Build Organizational Science."

9. D. Angrave, A. Charlwood, I. Kirkpatrick, M. Lawrence, and M. Stuart, "HR and Analytics: Why HR Is Set to Fail the Big Data Challenge," *Human Resource Management Journal* (Provocation Series Paper), 2016, 26(1), pp. 1–11; J. D. Morrison, Jr., and J. D. Abraham, "Reasons for Enthusiasm and Caution Regarding Big Data in Applied Selection Research," *Industrial-Organizational Psychologist*, 2015, 52(3), pp. 134–139; T. Rasmussen and D. Ulrich, "Learning From Practice: How HR Analytics Avoids Being a Management Fad," *Organizational Dynamics*, 2015, 44, pp. 236–242; D. Ariely, "The New Big Data," Center for Advanced Hindsight (blog), Apr. 1, 2017 (*https://advanced-hindsight.com/blog/new-big-data/*).

10. E. F. Stone, *Research Methods in Organizational Behavior* (Santa Monica, CA: Goodyear, 1978), pp. 35–36; US Department of Labor, Employment & Training Administration, *Testing and Assessment: An Employer's Guide to Good Practices* (Washington, DC: author, 1999).

11. Society for Industrial and Organizational Psychology, *Principles for the Validation and Use of Personnel Selection Procedures*, 5th ed. (Bowling Green, OH: author, 2018).

12. Stone, *Research Methods in Organizational Behavior*, pp. 36–40.

13. P. Korkki, "Why Employee Ranking Can Backfire," *New York Times*, July 11, 2015 (*www.nytimes .com/2015/07/12/business/why-employee-ranking-can-backfire.html*).

14. D. Rukmana, "Interval Scale," in N. J. Salkind (ed.), *Encyclopedia of Research Design*, Vols. 1–10 (Thousand Oaks, CA: Sage, 2010), doi: 10.4135/9781412961288.

15. A. Vaccaro, "25 Crazy Interview Questions (and Why They're a Waste of Time)," *Inc.*, Jan. 17, 2014 (*www.inc.com/adam-vaccaro/25-crazy-interview-questions.html*).

16. A. Bryant, "In Head-Hunting, Big Data May Not Be Such a Big Deal," *New York Times*, June 19, 2013 (*www.nytimes.com/2013/06/20/business/in-head-hunting-big-data-may-not-be-such-a-big-deal.html?pagewanted=all*).

17. W. H. Bommer, J. L. Johnson, G. A. Rich, P. M. Podsakoff, and S. B. McKenzie, "On the Interchangeability of Objective and Subjective Measures of Employee Performance: A Meta-Analysis," *Personnel Psychology*, 1995, 48, pp. 587–606; R. L. Heneman, "The Relationship Between Supervisory Ratings and Results-Oriented Measures of Performance: A Meta-Analysis," *Personnel Psychology*, 1986, 39, pp. 811–826.

18. S. Adler, M. Campion, A. Colquitt, A. Grubb, K. Murphy, R. Ollander-Krane, and E. D. Pulakos, "Getting Rid of Performance Ratings: Genius or Folly? A Debate," *Industrial and Organizational Psychology: Perspectives on Science and Practice*, 2016, 9, pp. 219–252; J. P. Campbell and B. M. Wiernik, "The Modeling and Assessment of Work Performance," *Annual Review of Organizational Psychology and Organizational Behavior*, 2015, 2, pp. 47–74; T. A. O'Neill, M. J. W. McLarnon, and J. J. Carswell, "Variance Components of Job Performance Ratings," *Human Performance*, 2015, 28, pp. 66–91; A. W. Sutton, S. P. Baldwin, L. Wood, and B. J. Hoffman, "A Meta-Analysis of the Relationship Between Rater Liking and Performance Ratings," *Human Performance*, 2013, 26, pp. 409–429.

19. E. C. Dierdorff, E. A. Surface, and K. G. Brown, "Frame-of-Reference Training Effectiveness: Effects of Goal Orientation and Self-Efficacy on Affective, Cognitive, Skill-Based, and Transfer Outcomes," *Journal of Applied Psychology*, 2010, 95, pp. 1181–1191; S. G. Roch, D. J. Woehr, V. Mishra, and U. Kieszczynska, "Rater Training Revisited: An Updated Meta-Analytic Review of Frame-of-Reference Training," *Journal of Occupational and Organizational Psychology*, 2012, 85, pp. 370–395; D. J. Woehr and A. I. Huffcutt, "Rater Training for Performance Appraisal: A Quantitative Review," *Journal of Occupational and Organizational Psychology*, 1994, 67, pp. 189–205.

20. This section draws on F. G. Brown, *Principles of Educational and Psychological Testing* (Hinsdale, IL: Dryden, 1970), pp. 38–45; L. J. Cronbach, *Essentials of Psychological Testing*, 4th ed. (New York: Harper and Row, 1984), pp. 81–120; N. W. Schmitt and R. J. Klimoski, *Research Methods in Human Resources Management* (Cincinnati, OH: South-Western, 1991), pp. 41–87; and US Department of Labor, Employment & Training Administration, *Testing and Assessment: An Employer's Guide to Good Practices*.

21. N. T. Carter, D. K. Dalal, A. S. Boyce, M. S. O'Connell, M. Kung, and K. M. Delgado, "Uncovering Curvilinear Relationships Between Conscientiousness and Job Performance: How Theoretically Appropriate Measurement Makes an Empirical Difference," *Journal of Applied Psychology*, 99(4), 2014, pp. 564–586; N. T. Carter, J. D. Miller, and T. A. Widiger, "Extreme Personalities in Work and in Life," *Current Directions in Psychological Science*, 2018, 27(6), pp. 429–436.

22. For more information, see A. Gallo, "A Refresher on Statistical Significance," *Harvard Business Review*, Feb. 16, 2016 (*https://hbr.org/2016/02/a-refresher-on-statistical-significance*).

23. J. T. McClave and P. G. Benson, *Statistics for Business and Economics*, 3rd ed. (San Francisco: Dellan, 1985); see "t Table" (*www.sjsu.edu/faculty/gerstman/StatPrimer/t-table.pdf*).

24. I. J. Davidson, "The Ouroboros of Psychological Methodology: The Case of Effect Sizes (Mechanical Objectivity vs. Expertise)," *Review of General Psychology*, 2018, 22(4), pp. 469–476; R. E. Kirk, "Practical Significance: A Concept Whose Time Has Come," *Educational and Psychological Measurement*, 1996, 56, pp. 746–759.

25. For excellent reviews, see R. M. Guion, *Assessment, Measurement, and Prediction for Personnel Decisions*, 2nd ed. (New York: Routledge, 2011); Schmitt and Klimoski, *Research Methods in Human Resources Management*, pp. 88–114.

26. This section draws on Carmines and Zeller, *Reliability and Validity Assessment*.

27. K. R. Murphy and R. De Shon, "Interrater Correlations Do Not Estimate the Reliability of Job Performance Ratings," *Personnel Psychology*, 2000, 53, pp. 873–900; F. L. Schmidt, C. Viswesvaran,

and D. S. Ones, "Reliability Is Not Validity and Validity Is Not Reliability," *Personnel Psychology*, 2000, 53, pp. 901–912.

28. D. P. Schwab, *Research Methods for Organizational Studies* (New York: Routledge, 2011).

29. Carmines and Zeller, *Reliability and Validity Assessment*; J. M. Cortina, "What Is Coefficient Alpha? An Examination of Theory and Application," *Journal of Applied Psychology*, 1993, 78, pp. 98–104; Schmitt and Klimoski, *Research Methods in Human Resources Management*, pp. 89–100.

30. R. F. DeVellis, *Scale Development: Theory and Applications*, 3rd ed. (Thousand Oaks, CA: Sage, 2012).

31. This section draws on R. D. Arvey, "Constructs and Construct Validation," *Human Performance*, 1992, 5, pp. 59–69; W. F. Cascio, *Applied Psychology in Personnel Management*, 4th ed. (Englewood Cliffs, NJ: Prentice-Hall, 1991), pp. 149–170; H. G. Heneman III, D. P. Schwab, J. A. Fossum, and L. Dyer, *Personnel/Human Resource Management*, 4th ed. (Homewood, IL: Irwin, 1989), pp. 300–329; N. Schmitt and F. J. Landy, "The Concept of Validity," in N. Schmitt, W. C. Borman, and Associates (eds.), *Personnel Selection in Organizations* (San Francisco: Jossey-Bass, 1993), pp. 275–309; D. P. Schwab, "Construct Validity in Organizational Behavior," in B. M. Staw and L. L. Cummings (eds.), *Research in Organizational Behavior*, Vol. 2 (Greenwich, CT: JAI, 1980), pp. 3–43; S. Messick, "Validity of Psychological Assessment," *American Psychologist*, Sept. 1995, 50, pp. 741–749.

32. J. F. Binning and G. V. Barrett, "Validity of Personnel Decisions: A Conceptual Analysis of the Inferential and Evidential Bases," *Journal of Applied Psychology*, 1989, 74, pp. 478–494; R. P. Bagozzi, Y. Yi, and L. W. Phillips, "Assessing Construct Validity in Organizational Research," *Administrative Science Quarterly*, 1991, 36, pp. 421–458; J. R. Edwards, "Construct Validation in Organizational Behavior Research," in J. Greenberg (ed.), *Organizational Behavior: The State of the Science*, 2nd ed. (Mahwah, NJ: Lawrence Erlbaum, 2003), pp. 311–354.

33. Heneman, Schwab, Fossum, and Dyer, *Personnel/Human Resource Management*, pp. 300–310.

34. M. Sussmann and D. U. Robertson, "The Validity of Validity: An Analysis of Validation Study Designs," *Journal of Applied Psychology*, 1986, 71, pp. 461–468.

35. This section draws on J. C. Anderson and D. W. Gerbing, "Predicting the Performance of Measures in a Confirmatory Factor Analysis With a Pretest Assessment of Their Substantive Validities," *Journal of Applied Psychology*, 1991, 76, pp. 732–740; J. A. Colquitt, T. B. Sabey, J. B. Rodell, and E. T. Hill, "Content Validation Guidelines: Evaluation Criteria for Definitional Correspondence and Definitional Distinctiveness," *Journal of Applied Psychology*, 2019, 104(10), pp. 1243–1265; DeVellis, *Scale Development: Theory and Applications*; T. R. Hinkin and J. B. Tracey, "An Analysis of Variance Approach to Content Validation," *Organizational Research Methods*, 1999, 2, pp. 175–186.

36. Binning and Barrett, "Validity of Personnel Decisions: A Conceptual Analysis of the Inferential and Evidential Bases"; M. L. Tenopyr, "Content-Construct Confusion," *Personnel Psychology*, 1977, 30, pp. 47–54.

37. K. R. Murphy, "Content Validation Is Useful for Many Things, but Validity Isn't One of Them," *Industrial and Organizational Psychology*, 2009, 2, pp. 453–464.

38. Binning and Barrett, "Validity of Personnel Decisions: A Conceptual Analysis of the Inferential and Evidential Bases"; Guion, *Assessment, Measurement, and Prediction for Personnel Decisions*.

39. F. Schmidt and J. Hunter, "History, Development, Evolution, and Impact of Validity Generalization and Meta-Analysis Methods, 1975–2001," in K. R. Murphy (ed.), *Validity Generalization: A Critical Review* (Mahwah, NJ: Erlbaum, 2003), pp. 31–65; K. R. Murphy, "Synthetic Validity: A Great Idea Whose Time Never Came," *Industrial and Organizational Psychology*, 2010, 3(3), pp. 356–359; K. R. Murphy, "Validity, Validation and Values," *Academy of Management Annals*, 2009, 3, pp. 421–461.

40. S. Kepes, G. C. Banks, M. McDaniel, and D. L. Whetzel, "Publication Bias in the Organizational Sciences," *Organizational Research Methods*, 2012, 15, pp. 624–662.

41. N. Schmitt and R. Sinha, "Validation Support for Selection Procedures," in S. Zedeck (ed.), *APA Handbook of Industrial and Organizational Psychology: Selecting and Developing Members for the Organization*, Vol. 2 (Washington, DC: APA, 2011), pp. 399–420.

42. D. J. R. Jackson, C. Dewberry, J. Gallagher, and L. Close, "A Comparative Study of Practitioner Perceptions of Selection Methods in the United Kingdom," *Journal of Occupational and Organizational Psychology*, 2018, 91, pp. 33–56; S. D. Risavy, P. A. Fisher, C. Robie, and C. J. König, "Selection Tool Use: A Focus on Personality Testing in Canada, the United States, and Germany," *Personnel Assessment and Decisions*, 2019, 5(1), pp. 62–72.

43. C. Winkler, "Quality Check: Better Metrics Improve HR's Ability to Measure—and Manage—the Quality of Hires," *HR Magazine*, May 2007, pp. 93–98; Society for Human Resource Management, *SHRM Human Capital Benchmarking Study* (Alexandria, VA: author, 2005).

44. A. Whyte, "Dawdling on Decisions: Hiring Goes From Stat to Analyzing Stats," *Workforce Magazine*, July 13, 2015 (*www.workforce.com/news/dawdling-on-decisions-hiring-goes-from-stat-to-analyzing-stats*).

45. American Psychologist (Editorial), "Test Security: Protecting the Integrity of Tests," *American Psychologist*, 1999, 54(12), p. 1078; T. M. Kantrowitz and A. M. Dainis, "How Secure Are Unproctored Pre-employment Tests? Analysis of Inconsistent Test Scores," *Journal of Business and Psychology*, 2014, 29, pp. 605–616.

46. N. Statt, "McDonald's Is Now Accepting Job Applications Through Alexa and Google Assistant: Presumably Before AI Automates the Job You're Applying For," *The Verge*, Sept. 25, 2019 (*www.theverge.com/2019/9/25/20883007/mcdonalds-apply-thru-amazon-alexa-google-assistant-job-applications-ai-automation*).

47. J. C. Beaty, C. Nye, M. Borneman, T. M. Kantrowitz, F. Drasgow, and E. Grauer, "Proctored Versus Unproctored Internet Tests: Are Unproctored Tests as Predictive of Job Performance?" *International Journal of Selection and Assessment*, 2011, 19, pp. 1–10; N. T. Tippins, "Technology and Assessment in Selection," *Annual Review of Organizational Psychology & Organizational Behavior*, 2015, 2, pp. 551–582.

48. N. Blacksmith and T. Poeppelman, "The Realities of Internet Testing: Security Considerations and Best Practices," *Industrial and Organizational Psychologist (The Modern App: Application of Modern Technology and Social Media in the Workplace)*, 2015, 53, pp. 54–59; Tippins, "Technology and Assessment in Selection."

49. A. J. Illingworth, N. A. Morelli, J. C. Scott, and S. L. Boyd, "Internet-Based, Unproctored Assessments on Mobile and Non-mobile Devices: Usage, Measurement Equivalence, and Outcomes," *Journal of Business and Psychology*, 2015, 30, pp. 325–343; D. D. King, A. M. Ryan, T. Kantrowitz, D. Grelle, and A. Dainis, "Mobile Internet Testing: An Analysis of Equivalence, Individual Differences, and Reactions," *International Journal of Selection and Assessment*, 2015, 23(4), pp. 382–394; N. A. Morelli, R. P. Mahan, and A. J. Illingworth, "Establishing the Measurement Equivalence of Online Selection Assessments Delivered on Mobile Versus Nonmobile Devices," *International Journal of Selection and Assessment*, 2014, 22(2), pp. 124–138.

50. M. Barney and W. P. Fisher, Jr., "Adaptive Measurement and Assessment," *Annual Review of Organizational Psychology and Organizational Behavior*, 2016, 3, pp. 469–490; M. C. Campion, M. A. Campion, E. D. Campion, and M. H. Reider, "Initial Investigation Into Computer Scoring of Candidate Essays for Personnel Selection," *Journal of Applied Psychology*, 2016, 101, pp. 958–975; L. Yao, M. Pommerich, and D. O. Segall, "Using Multidimensional CAT to Administer a Short, Yet Precise, Screening Test," *Applied Psychological Measurement*, 2014, 38, pp. 614–631.

51. J. A. Naglieri, F. Drasgow, M. Schmit, L. Handler, A. Prifitera, A. Margolis, and R. Velasquez, "Psychological Testing on the Internet," *American Psychologist*, 2004, 59, pp. 150–162; R. E. Ployhart, J. A. Weekley, B. C. Holtz, and C. Kemp, "Web-Based and Paper-and-Pencil Testing of Applicants in a Proctored Setting: Are Personality, Biodata, and Situational Judgment Tests Comparable?" *Personnel Psychology*, 2003, 56, pp. 733–752; S. Power, "Federal Official Faults TSA Screener Testing as 'Inane,'" *Wall Street Journal*, Oct. 9, 2003, pp. B1–B2.

52. SIOP, "Seven Questions to Ask a Vendor Before Purchasing a Test" (*www.siop.org/Business -Resources/Employment-Testing/Vendor-Questions*), accessed Jan. 28, 2020.

53. See the Society for Human Resource Management (SHRM), "Talent Assessment Center (TAC)" (*tac.shrm.org*), accessed Jan. 28, 2020.

54. AERA, APA, and NCME, *The Standards for Educational and Psychological Testing* (Washington, DC: AERA Publications, 2014); APA, *The Rights and Responsibilities of Test Takers: Guidelines and Expectations* (*www.apa.org/science/programs/testing/rights*), accessed Jan. 28, 2020; SIOP, *Principles for the Validation and Use of Personnel Selection Procedures*.

55. K. R. Murphy, "The Legal Context of the Management of Human Resources," *Annual Review of Organizational Psychology & Organizational Behavior*, 2018, 5, pp. 157–182.

56. Murphy, "The Legal Context of the Management of Human Resources."

57. R. Tonowski, "Thoughts From an EEO Agency Perspective," in S. B. Morris and E. M. Dunleavy (eds.), *Adverse Impact Analysis: Understanding Data, Statistics, and Risk* (New York: Routledge, 2017), pp. 277–296.

58. SIOP, *Principles for the Validation and Use of Personnel Selection Procedures*.

59. SIOP, *Principles for the Validation and Use of Personnel Selection Procedures*.

60. H. Aguinis, S. A. Culpepper, and C. A. Pierce, "Revival of Test Bias Research in Preemployment Testing," *Journal of Applied Psychology*, 2010, 95(4), pp. 648–680; C. M. Berry, "Differential Validity and Differential Prediction of Cognitive Ability Tests: Understanding Test Bias in the Employment Context," *Annual Review of Organizational Psychology and Organizational Behavior*, 2015, 2, pp. 35–63; Bobko and Roth, "Reviewing, Categorizing, and Analyzing the Literature on Black-White Mean Differences for Predictors of Job Performance: Verifying Some Perceptions and Updating/Correcting Others."

61. Berry, "Differential Validity and Differential Prediction of Cognitive Ability Tests: Understanding Test Bias in the Employment Context"; C. M. Berry and P. Zhao, "Addressing Criticisms of Existing Predictive Bias Research: Cognitive Ability Test Scores Still Overpredict African Americans' Job Performance," *Journal of Applied Psychology*, 2015, 100(1), pp. 162–179.

62. SIOP, *Principles for the Validation and Use of Personnel Selection Procedures*.

63. R. E. Ployhart and B. C. Holtz, "The Diversity-Validity Dilemma: Strategies for Reducing Racio-ethnic and Sex Subgroup Differences and Adverse Impact in Selection," *Personnel Psychology*, 2008, 61, pp. 153–172.

64. Bobko and Roth, "Reviewing, Categorizing, and Analyzing the Literature on Black-White Mean Differences for Predictors of Job Performance: Verifying Some Perceptions and Updating/Correcting Others."

65. W. De Corte, F. Lievens, and P. R. Sackett, "Combining Predictors to Achieve Optimal Trade-Offs Between Selection Quality and Adverse Impact," *Journal of Applied Psychology*, 2007, 92(5), pp. 1380–1393; W. De Corte, P. R. Sackett, and F. Lievens, "Designing Pareto-Optimal Selection Systems: Formalizing the Decisions Required for Selection System Development," *Journal of Applied Psychology*, 2011, 96(5), pp. 907–926; Q. C. Song, S. Wee, and D. A. Newman, "Diversity Shrinkage: Cross-Validating Pareto-Optimal Weights to Enhance Diversity via Hiring Practices," *Journal of Applied Psychology*, 2017, 102(12), pp. 1636–1657.

66. P. Bobko, P. L. Roth, and D. Potosky, "Derivation and Implications of a Meta-Analytic Matrix Incorporating Cognitive Ability, Alternative Predictors, and Job Performance," *Personnel Psychology*, 1999, 52, pp. 561–589; N. Schmitt, W. Rogers, D. Chan, L. Sheppard, and D. Jennings, "Adverse Impact and Predictive Efficiency of Various Predictor Combinations," *Journal of Applied Psychology*, 1997, 82(5), pp. 719–730.

67. SIOP, *Principles for the Validation and Use of Personnel Selection Procedures*.

68. Equal Employment Opportunity Commission, "Employment Tests and Selection Procedures," 2010 (*www.eeoc.gov/policy/docs/factemployment_procedures.html*), accessed July 26, 2013.

CHAPTER EIGHT

External Selection I

LEARNING OBJECTIVES AND INTRODUCTION

Learning Objectives

- Understand how the logic of prediction guides the selection process
- Review the nature of predictors—how selection measures differ
- Understand the process involved in developing a selection plan, along with the selection sequence
- Learn about initial assessment methods and understand how these methods are optimally used in organizations
- Evaluate the relative effectiveness of initial assessment methods to determine which work best, and why
- Review the legal issues involved in the use of initial assessment methods, and understand how legal problems can be avoided

Introduction

External selection—one of the more practically important and heavily researched areas of staffing—refers to the assessment and evaluation of external job applicants. Preliminary issues that guide the use of various assessment methods will be discussed. These issues include the logic of prediction, the nature of predictors, development of the selection plan, and the selection sequence.

Initial assessment methods are used to select candidates from among the initial job applicants. The methods that will be reviewed are résumés and cover letters, application blanks, biographical information, letters of recommendation, reference and background checks, and initial interviews. The factors that should guide the choice of initial assessment methods will be reviewed. These include frequency of use, cost, reliability, validity, utility, applicant reactions, and disparate impact.

The use of assessment methods requires a firm understanding of legal issues—including the use of disclaimers and the legal complexities surrounding reference and background checks. The most important of these details will be reviewed. Finally, bona fide occupational qualifications (BFOQs) are particularly relevant to initial assessment because such qualifications are usually assessed during the initial stages of selection. The legal issues involved in establishing such qualifications will be reviewed.

PRELIMINARY ISSUES

Selection is often equated with one event: the interview. For the best possible person/job match to be made, however, organizations should not rely solely on the interview. Instead, a series of well-thought-out activities need to take place.

Selection is a process, not an event. It is guided by a logic that determines the steps that need to be taken. This logic applies to all predictors that might be used (see the measurement chapter for a discussion of predictor measurement), regardless of their differences. The effective application of the logic of prediction requires a selection plan that guides the selection of predictors and a selection sequence, which is an orderly flow of people through the stages of being an applicant, candidate, finalist, and offer receiver.

The Logic of Prediction

In the staffing models and strategy chapter, the selection component of staffing was defined as the process of assessing and evaluating people for purposes of determining the likely fit between the person and the job. This process is based on the logic of prediction, which holds that indicators of a person's success in past situations should predict how successful they will likely be in new situations. Application of this logic to selection is illustrated in Exhibit 8.1.

A person's knowledge, skills, abilities, and other characteristics (KSAOs) and motivation are the product of their past job, current job, and nonjob experiences and situations. During selection, the organization identifies, assesses, and evaluates samples of KSAOs (presumably) most relevant to the new situation or job, as well as motivation. The results constitute the person's overall qualifications for the new situation or job. These qualifications are then used to predict human resource (HR) outcomes, indicating how successful the person is likely to be in that new job. The logic of prediction works in practice if the organization accurately identifies and measures qualifications relevant to job requirements, and if those qualifications remain stable over time so that the person carries them over to the new job.

The logic of prediction shown in Exhibit 8.1 demonstrates how critical it is to carefully scrutinize the applicant's past situation when making selection decisions.

EXHIBIT 8.1 The Logic of Prediction

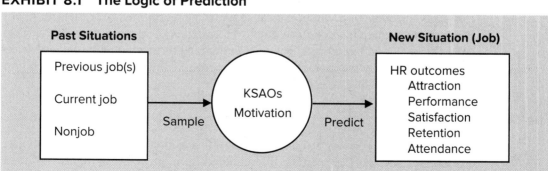

For example, in selecting someone for a division manager position, the success of the applicant in a previous store manager position might be considered a relevant predictor of the likelihood that the applicant will succeed. Alternatively, the fact that the person was previously successful as a front-line cook might be viewed as totally irrelevant.[1] However, considering this role to be irrelevant in this instance might well be an incorrect assessment. Alyssa Gelbard, founder of Resume Strategists, notes that this experience may be directly relevant to the job in ways that may not seem clear on the surface, containing hidden skills or abilities.[2] Specifically, a thorough job analysis can reveal that both jobs rely heavily on troubleshooting, planning, and coordination. Hence, in the absence of a sound job analysis, many qualified applicants may inadvertently be overlooked even though they have some of the characteristics needed to perform the job. Even nonjob experience in the home, in the community, and in other institutions (e.g., volunteering for nonprofit organizations) may be as valuable as employment experiences.

Job titles alone are often not nearly specific enough for making selection decisions (what does a forward brand architect or a senior paradigm associate actually do?). Similarly, the fact that someone has a certain number of years of experience usually does not provide enough detail to make selection decisions. What counts, and what is revealed through job analysis, are the specific types of experiences required (i.e., success on prior job-relevant tasks) and the level of success achieved from each. Similarly, whether someone was a volunteer or a paid employee is not relevant. What counts is the quality of the experience as it relates to success in the new job.[3] In short, the logic of prediction indicates that a point-to-point comparison needs to be made between requirements of the job to be filled and the qualifications applicants have acquired from past situations.

The logic of prediction is also important for recruitment. A number of studies have shown that positive applicant reactions to selection procedures (e.g., assessments) were determined in part by the job relatedness of the procedure. If applicants see the selection process as job related, which should occur if the logic of prediction is used, they are more likely to view the selection process as fair.[4] Applicants who view the selection procedure as fair are more likely to accept a job offer and/or encourage others to apply for a job in the organization.

Finally, the logic of prediction means separating recruitment from selection. For instance many organizations use employee referrals to identify prospective hires (recruitment), as a reference check to select among those who have applied (selection), or both. How they are evaluated as a recruitment device will differ from how they are evaluated as a selection measure.

The Nature of Predictors

Many types of predictors are used in external selection, ranging from interviews to reference checks. They can be differentiated from one another in terms of their content and form.

Content

The substance or content of what is being assessed by a predictor varies considerably and may range from a "sign" to a "sample" to a "criterion."[5] A sign is an aspect of the person that is thought to relate to performance on the job. Personality as a predictor is a good example here. If personality is used as a predictor, the prediction is that someone with a certain personality trait (e.g., abrasiveness) will demonstrate certain behaviors (e.g., rudeness to customers) leading to certain results on the job (e.g., failure to make a sale). As can be seen, a sign is very distant from actual on-the-job results. A sample is closer than a sign to actual on-the-job behavior. Observing a set of interactions between a sales applicant and a customer to see how they interact is an example of a sample. The criterion is very close to actual job performance, such as sales figures in a previous position or during a probationary period for a new employee.

Form

The form or design of the predictor may vary in many ways.

Speed Versus Power. A person's score on some predictors is based on the number of responses completed within a certain time frame. For example, data entry jobs may require an individual to be able to type a certain number of words within an explicit time frame. This is known as a speed test. A power test, on the other hand, presents individuals with items of increasing difficulty. For example, a power test of numerical ability may begin with addition and subtraction, move on to multiplication and division, and conclude with complex problem-solving questions. A speed test is used when speed of work is an important part of the job, and a power test is used when the correctness of the response is essential to the job. Of course, some tests can be both speed and power tests, in which case few individuals would finish.

Paper and Pencil Versus Performance. Many predictors are of the paper-and-pencil variety; applicants are required to fill out a form, write an answer, or complete multiple-choice items (the term "paper-and-pencil" is used loosely here given that many predictors are assessed electronically). Other predictors are performance tests, where the applicant is asked to manipulate an object or operate a machine. Paper-and-pencil tests are frequently used when psychological abilities are required to perform the job; performance tests are used when physical and social skills are required to perform the job. Although many organizations may use one or the other, some use both, as when NFL recruits are timed in the 40-yard dash (a performance test) and given an intelligence test (a paper-and-pencil test). Interestingly, some research suggests that the form of the predictor may influence both applicant reactions and validity. Performance-based responses were found to be better predictors of performance one year later as well as rated more positively by applicants on some dimensions, when compared with paper-and-pencil responses.[6]

Objective Versus Essay. An objective paper-and-pencil predictor uses either multiple-choice questions or true/false questions. These predictors are objective because there are right and wrong answers to these questions. These tests should be used to measure knowledge in specific areas. Another form of a predictor is an essay, where the respondent provides a written answer. Essays are best used to assess written communication, problem-solving, and analytical skills. With the advent of machine learning, advancements have been made that enable staffing professionals to score essays using artificial intelligence.[7]

Oral Versus Written Versus Electronic. Responses to predictor questions can be spoken, written, or electronically recorded. When conducting interviews, some organizations listen to oral responses (either in person or through videoconferencing), read written responses, or read printouts of typed-in responses to assess applicants. As with all predictors, the appropriate form depends on the nature of the job. If the job requires a high level of verbal skill, oral responses should be solicited. If the job requires a large amount of writing, written responses should be required. If the job requires constant interaction with the computer, applicants should use a computer to enter their responses.[8]

Development of the Selection Plan

To translate the results of a job analysis into the actual predictors to be used for selection, a selection plan must be developed. A selection plan describes which predictor(s) will be used to assess the KSAOs required to perform the job. The recommended format for a selection plan, and an example of such a plan for the job of administrative assistant, is shown in Exhibit 8.2. A selection plan can be established in three steps. First, the KSAOs are written in the left-hand column. This list comes directly from the job requirements matrix. Second, for each KSAO, a "yes" or "no" is written to show whether it needs to be assessed in the selection process. Sometimes the answer is no because the applicant will acquire the KSAO once on the job (e.g., knowledge of company policies and procedures). Third, possible methods of assessment are listed for the required KSAOs, and the specific method to be used for each is indicated.

Selection Sequence

Usually, a series of decisions are made about job applicants before they are selected. These decisions are depicted in Exhibit 8.3. The first decision is whether initial applicants who have applied for the job become candidates or are rejected. A candidate is someone who possesses the minimum qualifications to be considered for further assessment but has not yet received an offer.

EXHIBIT 8.2 Selection Plan Format and Example for Administrative Assistant Position

Major KSAO Category	Necessary for Selection? (Y/N)	Method of Assessment								
		WP	CT	DB	LTR	TEF	ML	EM	TM	IRV
1. Ability to follow oral directions/ listening skills	Y			X					X	
2. Ability to read and understand manuals and guidelines	Y	X	X	X	X	X	X	X		
3. Ability to perform basic arithmetic operations	Y			X		X				
4. Ability to organize	Y			X		X	X			
5. Judgments/priority-setting/decision-making ability	Y			X						
6. Oral communication skills	Y								X	X
7. Written communication skills	Y		X		X			X	X	
8. Interpersonal skills	Y		X		X					X
9. Typing skills	N	X			X					
10. Knowledge of company policies and procedures	N									
11. Knowledge of basic personal computer operations	Y	X	X	X	X	X		X		
12. Knowledge of how to use basic office machines	N									
13. Flexibility in dealing with changing job demands	Y						X	X	X	
14. Knowledge of computer software	Y	X	X	X	X	X	X	X		
15. Ability to attend to detail and accuracy	Y	X	X	X	X	X	X	X	X	

WP = Word processing test, CT = Correction test, DB = Database exam, LTR = Letter, TEF = Travel expense form, ML = Mail log, EM = Electronic mail messages, TM = Telephone messages, and IRV = Interview.

SOURCE: Adapted from N. Schmitt, S. Gilliland, R. S. Landis, and D. Devine, "Computer-Based Testing Applied to Selection of Secretarial Positions," *Personnel Psychology*, 1993, 46, pp. 149–165.

EXHIBIT 8.3   Assessment Methods by Applicant Flow Stage

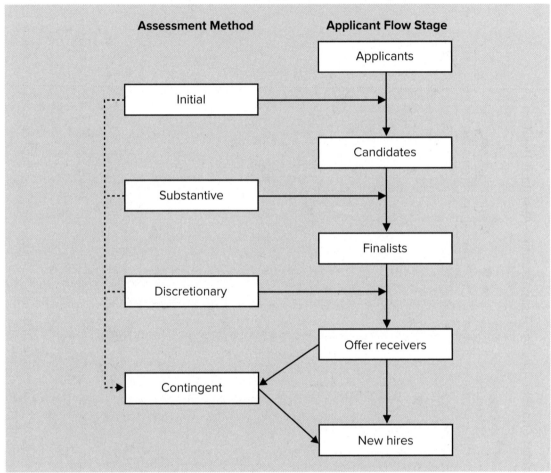

Initial assessment methods are used to choose candidates (these will be discussed later in this chapter). The second decision is to determine which candidates become finalists. A finalist is someone who meets all the minimum qualifications and whom the organization considers fully qualified for the job. Substantive assessment methods, discussed in the next chapter, are used to select finalists. The third decision is to determine which of the finalists receives a job offer. An offer receiver is a finalist to whom the organization extends an offer of employment. Discretionary methods, also discussed in the next chapter, are used to select these individuals. Contingent methods are sometimes used, meaning the job offer is subject to certain qualifications, such as the offer receiver passing a medical exam or drug test. Use of contingent methods, such as drug testing and medical exams, will be reviewed in Chapter 9. Finally, offer receivers may become new hires when they accept their offer and decide to join the organization.

INITIAL ASSESSMENT METHODS

Initial assessment methods, also referred to as preemployment inquiries, are used to minimize the costs associated with substantive assessment methods by reducing the number of people assessed. Predictors typically used to screen applicants include résumés and cover letters, application blanks, biographical information, reference and background checks, and initial interviews. Each of these initial assessment methods will be described in turn. Using meta-analytic results, the average validity (i.e., $\bar{r}$) of each method is also provided if possible. Then, a general evaluation is presented to help guide decisions about which initial assessment methods to use.

Résumés and Cover Letters

The first introduction of the applicant to the organization is often a cover letter and résumé. The applicant controls the introduction concerning the amount, type, and accuracy of information provided. As a result, attempts should be made to verify résumés and cover letters (e.g., through background checks) to ensure that there are accurate and complete data across all job applicants.

One major issue with résumés is with the volume that organizations must process. Some organizations make few provisions for how to file and organize résumés as they filter in, and for how to store them once a hiring decision is made. Most organizations are well advised to produce and maintain an electronic copy of résumés received, both to ease sharing of information among selection decision makers and to track applicants should any questions (legal or otherwise) arise once the applicant is hired.

Most large employers, and even many medium-size employers, encourage submission of résumés via e-mail or through online forms on the organization's website. For example, on the Wal-Mart website, applicants can search an online database for openings and then apply either by completing an online form or, for managerial positions, by attaching their résumé to an e-mail message.

Employers can outsource résumé collection to résumé-tracking services. Many services not only scan résumés but also score them by placing a percentage next to the applicant's name reflecting the number of criteria their résumé meets (methods that have been streamlined by machine learning).[9] Though such methods have powerful time- and cost-saving advantages, there are disadvantages, such as the rejection of résumés that the software could not read (e.g., those on colored paper or that use special formatting like bullets) and applicants who try to beat the system by "fluffing" their résumés with every conceivable skill that appears in the advertisement.[10] Despite these drawbacks, the efficiencies of such services make them particularly attractive for organizations facing large volumes of résumés.

Video Résumés

Video résumés are getting considerable attention in the business press.[11] Companies like Spark Hire help applicants put together video résumés where applicants talk about their qualifications directly to the camera or in a simulated interview. Jared McKinney, a graduate of Brigham Young University, used the program *Screenr* to create a video résumé; he eventually landed a job at a social media firm in Utah, which mentioned the quality of his résumé during his face-to-face interview.[12]

While the topic of video résumés is fashionable, few employers have any experience with them. Despite the popular press touting them as an innovative take on the traditional résumé, a Robert Half survey of executives found that only 3% preferred video résumés, compared with 78% who preferred traditional résumés.[13] One survey indicated that while many hiring managers would view a video résumé, a majority (58%) of those admitted they would do so out of "sheer curiosity." As one career advisor noted, "Most employers don't have much direct familiarity with them yet. Folks are still trying to figure out where the video résumé falls in the calculus in applicant selection."[14]

Furthermore, studies on the effectiveness of video résumés have produced mixed results. Although there may be no differences between paper and video résumés on outcomes such as the likelihood of requesting more information from the candidate, inviting the candidate for an interview, or ratings of the applicant's success, applicants who submitted video résumés tend to be rated as less extroverted and less socially adept, regardless of the richness of information included in the video-based résumé.[15] Self-promotion may also be more easily observed in video-based résumés, leading to diminished hiring outcomes.[16]

Some employers refuse to view video résumés for fear of introducing subjective biasing factors (appearance, race, or a disability) into their decisions.[17] Despite this fear, some initial research suggested that ethnic minority applicants actually react positively to being given the opportunity to submit a video résumé, considering it to be a fairer and more personalized experience.[18] Some job applicants have submitted video résumés only to be the subject of ridicule by their potential employers. Aleksey Vayner, a finance major at Yale, sent a video résumé to bank giant UBS, only to have it posted on blogs and be mocked by others.[19] Some best practices suggest, however, that video-based résumés can be effective if they are brief and professional, tell a story, and are tailored to the employer or relevant for the job (e.g., a performance occupation).[20]

While video résumés could be considered to fall on the more elaborate end of the résumé spectrum, on the more simplistic end of that spectrum is the use of Twitter and LinkedIn. Some firms are avoiding the traditional résumé and instead asking applicants to tweet their qualifications, or they may scour LinkedIn profiles to identify potential applicants.[21] This selection method may be useful when an organization is concerned with how the applicant communicates electronically rather than on paper or face-to-face.[22] Indeed, one study has found that applicants who have a comprehensive LinkedIn profile have a 71% better chance of landing a job interview; on the other hand, applicants with a "bare-bones" profile had a 9% worse chance of landing an interview.[23] Regardless, organizations should exercise caution in using these methods of selection because they may open the door for discriminatory hiring practices (owing to the availability of irrelevant information including race, gender, age, etc.) and because certain qualified applicants may not have complete LinkedIn profiles.[24]

In general, while these alternative résumé formats are receiving a lot of attention in the press, it remains to be seen whether they will be a fad or the wave of the future.

Résumé Issues

Résumés have the advantage of allowing the applicant to control information presented to employers. In evaluating résumés, employers should be aware of fabrications and distortions.[25] Applicants, meanwhile, will want to know how to get their résumés noticed. We consider each of these issues and how to address them below.

Résumé Fabrications and Distortions. Because résumés are prepared by applicants who want to present themselves in a favorable light, distortions are a significant problem. Recent benchmarking surveys have uncovered that a whopping 75%–85% of hiring managers have discovered fabrications on résumés during their careers.[26] Dawn Boyer, an HR consultant, was once hired as an HR manager with a government contractor and assisted with an audit of the résumés for current employees. They found that 50 people lied about their degrees—a finding that resulted in the termination of all these employees (including the vice president) as well as a loss of millions of dollars of revenue.[27] Résumé fabrications continue to be an issue that has resulted in the removal of countless employees, including many well-known CEOs; there is even a hashtag that trends on Twitter (#liesonmyresume) where people brag about lying on résumés.[28]

Like the truth, résumés come in various degrees of accuracy, ranging from small, unintentional mistakes to outright fabrications. Minor embellishments may matter more for applicants who are less desirable, as opposed to applicants who are favored.[29] Furthermore, the degree to which we might call an inaccuracy "distortion" varies. For example, Ellie Strauss's two more recent full-time jobs lasted less than six months. Ellie represented these as freelance jobs, under the heading "Senior Project Manager," to make them look like contract positions.[30] Some might call this deception. Others might call it creative marketing or tailoring. Whatever you call it, it happens a lot. According to a recent survey by Monster, the three biggest areas of distortion (along with examples) are the following:[31]

1. Skill stretching: listing a skill of which you are not really an "expert"
2. Date deception: covering up employment gaps by stretching start and end dates
3. Education embellishments: stretching a completed course as if it were a degree

The best way to combat résumé fraud or fudging is to conduct careful background checks. For example, in light of the false information submitted by applicants, organizations are scrutinizing résumés much more closely. One survey found that although only 49% of hiring professionals verified candidates' credentials, 77% who did use screening methods such as background checks *uncovered an issue that would not have been caught otherwise.*[32] In short, the best protection against résumé fraud is for the hiring organization to do its homework.

***Getting a Résumé* Noticed.** The conscientious job seeker may wonder how to best prepare a résumé. Although there are as many theories on the ingredients of a perfect résumé as there are résumé readers, a few general guidelines may be helpful. First, realize that typos and other minor mistakes could kill your chances. Although some hiring managers may forgive one or two mistakes, an application riddled with errors is likely to send the message that the applicant is not detail oriented, or even appropriate for the job in question.[33] For example, what would you do if an application for a technical writer position you are hiring for ended in, "I asure you that I have the rite skills, kwalifications and ecksperience to add valew to the bisiness"? Second, customize your résumé to the position: try to address how your background, skills, and accomplishments fit the specific job requirements. Third, although résumés are getting somewhat longer, recognize that brevity is highly valued among hiring managers; many will not read résumés that are longer than two pages. However, the traditional advice that the ideal résumé is one page long has also been called into question: a study of nearly 500 hiring managers and 20,000 résumés suggests that the managers were two to three times more likely to prefer two-page résumés over one-page résumés.[34] Fourth, as we noted above, be factual and truthful. As one expert put it, "People are lying when they don't have to." Even if being truthful hurts you in the short run, it is better to pay the price now rather than later, when your entire career might be at stake. Finally, although one should take care to be truthful, a résumé is no time to underplay your accomplishments. Do not just list your job duties; identify your accomplishments as well. Consider your impact on your division or group: What are you proudest of? Can you identify your own strengths from your performance review? Indeed, recent research suggests that low-intensity self-promotion (and even ingratiation, to some extent) can help improve hiring managers' perception of your fit with the job and organization.[35]

Given the widespread use of electronic résumés, there are also several special considerations for submitting your résumé electronically. First, make sure it is scan-ready. This means avoiding unusual fonts and formatting. With today's résumés, form should follow function. In addition, stick to relevant information and traditional résumé formats. When law school graduate Brian Zulberti e-mailed his résumé to potential firms, he attached a picture of himself wearing a T-shirt and showing off his defined biceps. He also posted a shirtless picture of himself on Facebook with the joke to hire him as a lawyer rather than as an escort. Needless to say, the story went viral, with Zulberti drawing laughs from some but scorn from others.[36] Finally, use nouns to describe noteworthy aspects of your background ("nonprofit," "3.75 GPA," "environmental science experience," etc.), as opposed to the traditional emphasis on action verbs ("managed," "guided," etc.), because nouns are more likely to be identified as keywords in scanning software. If the résumé is likely to be scanned, it should be built around such keywords that will be the focus of the scan.[37]

Evaluation of Résumés and Cover Letters. Although some reliability and validity evidence has been provided for résumés, very little research exists on the reliability and validity of cover letters. The research that has been conducted on cover letters suggests that how they are written might matter. Unfortunately, cover letters that are written in an ingratiating tone and that use impression management tactics might result in higher ratings of applicants in some cases and lower ratings in others due to low likability and perceived truthfulness.[38] Moreover, cover letters that contain spelling and grammatical errors may be particularly damaging. One study suggests that applicants are perceived as less hardworking and capable when they submit a cover letter with several errors.[39]

Furthermore, the reliability evidence that exists for résumés suggests that they are, in general, very poor: although some elements of the résumé can be assessed consistently, multiple raters of the same résumé are not usually in agreement.[40] Additional research suggests that ratings and assessments of work experience, extracurricular activities, educational background, and personality inference (e.g., extroversion and conscientiousness) as rated on résumés positively predict employability ratings and hiring recommendations, but none of this research suggests that they actually predict on-the-job performance.[41]

There has been a great amount of interest in the disparate impact of résumés in the past decade. One study conducted in the Netherlands found that résumés with the common Arabic name "Mohammed" were four times as likely to be rejected as résumés with the common Dutch name "Henk." Of additional concern, applicants that belong to more than one minority class (e.g., Arabic women) may be more likely to be rejected when a high-status job is at stake than if they were a woman or a person of Arabic descent alone, a phenomenon known as the "double-jeopardy effect." Other recent research has suggested that disclosure of certain types of information on a résumé, such as a history of cancer, may be negatively interpreted by selection decision makers. These situations are unfortunate given the pervasive use of résumés and cover letters. Thus, organizations using résumés and cover letters in selection should carefully evaluate their effectiveness and make sure to independently verify information they are using in hiring decisions.[42]

Application Blanks

Application blanks are spaces on an application form that request the applicant to provide or write about their educational experiences, training, and job experiences. This information is often on the applicant's résumé as well and may seem unnecessarily duplicated. However, this may not be the case: an application can be used to both verify the data presented on the résumé and obtain data omitted from the résumé, such as employment dates. The major advantage of application blanks over résumés is that the organization, rather than the applicant, can direct the type of information that is presented. As a result, job-critical information is less likely to be omitted by the applicant or overlooked by the reviewer of the résumé. The major issue with application blanks is that the information requested should be critical to job success, following the logic of prediction discussed earlier.

A sample application blank is provided in Exhibit 8.4. As with most application blanks, the major sections are personal information, employment desired, educational background, special interests and abilities, work experience, and suggested references. The only information sought from the application blank should be qualifications or KSAOs that can be demonstrated as relevant to the job. This not only avoids wasting the organization's and the applicant's time but also protects the employer from charges of unfair discrimination (see "Legal Issues" at the end of this chapter) and avoids alienating potentially qualified applicants, discouraging them from continuing with the application.[43] Note the disclaimer statement at the bottom of the application blank. It provides certain legal protections to the organization, which are discussed in "Legal Issues." Asking applicants to sign a disclaimer may also decrease the incentive to distort or falsify information.

Educational Requirements

When soliciting information about educational experiences and performance, special care needs to be taken in wording items on an application blank.[44] The following are several particularly important areas pertaining to educational requirement information on application blanks.

Level of Education.   Often, level of education is measured by the attainment of a degree at various levels (e.g., bachelor's, master's, doctorate). Despite its pervasive use, it is not clear that level of education is a truly useful selection measure. Some economists and sociologists question its importance, and a meta-analysis suggested that the correlation between education and task performance was relatively small (across all measures of task performance, ranges from $\bar{r}_{xy} = .04$ to $\bar{r}_{xy} = .14$).[45]

According to the College Board, the average cost of attending a four-year university has tripled over the last 30 years for public institutions and has doubled over the last 30 years for private institutions, a rapid ascent that has left many questioning the value of a college degree.[46] "Is college worth it?" asks author and former US secretary of education William Bennett. Critics argue that the traditional path of going to a "brick and mortar" college or university and earning a degree is no longer as useful. They also point to famous billionaires such as Mark Zuckerberg and Bill Gates, both of whom dropped out of college. As Mike Hagen, who dropped out of Princeton in 2006 and started a mobile app, noted, in Silicon Valley,

EXHIBIT 8.4   Application for Employment

PERSONAL INFORMATION

DATE _____

NAME _____

SOCIAL SECURITY
NUMBER _____

LAST   FIRST   MIDDLE

PRESENT ADDRESS _____

STREET   CITY   STATE   ZIP

PERMANENT ADDRESS _____

STREET   CITY   STATE   ZIP

PHONE NO. _____ ARE YOU 18 YEARS OR OLDER?   Yes ☐   No ☐

ARE YOU PREVENTED FROM LAWFULLY BECOMING EMPLOYED
IN THIS COUNTRY BECAUSE OF VISA OR IMMIGRATION STATUS?   Yes ☐   No ☐

EMPLOYMENT DESIRED

POSITION _____

DATE YOU
CAN START _____

SALARY
DESIRED _____

ARE YOU EMPLOYED NOW? _____

IF SO MAY WE INQUIRE
OR YOUR PRESENT EMPLOYER? _____

APPLIED TO THIS COMPANY BEFORE? _____ WHERE? _____ WHEN? _____

REFERRED BY _____

EDUCATION

	NAME AND LOCATION	NO. OF YEARS ATTENDED	DID YOU GRADUATE?	SUBJECTS STUDIED
GRAMMAR SCHOOL				
HIGH SCHOOL (GED)				
COLLEGE				
OTHER				

(continued)

EXHIBIT 8.4 Continued

GENERAL

SUBJECTS OF SPECIAL STUDY

SPECIAL SKILLS

ACTIVITIES (CIVIC, ATHLETIC, ETC.)

| U.S. MILITARY | | PRESENT MEMBERSHIP IN |
| SERVICE | RANK | NATIONAL GUARD OR RESERVES |

FORMER EMPLOYERS (LIST BELOW LAST 3 EMPLOYERS, STARTING WITH THE MOST RECENT)

	DATE	NAME & ADDRESS	SALARY	POSITION	REASON FOR LEAVING
FROM					
TO					
FROM					
TO					
FROM					
TO					

REFERENCES (GIVE THE NAMES OF 3 PERSONS NOT RELATED TO YOU)

	NAME	ADDRESS	BUSINESS	YEARS ACQUAINTED
1				
2				
3				

"I certify that all the information submitted by me on this applicationis true and complete, and I understand that if any false information, omissions, or misrepresentations are discovered, my application may be rejected and, if I am employed, my employment may be terminated at any time. In consideration of my employment, I agree to conform to the company's rules and regulations, and I agree that my employment and compensation can be terminated, with or without cause, and with or without notice, at any time, at either my or the company's option. I also understand and agree that the terms and conditions of my employment may be changed, with or without cause, and with or without notice, at any time by the company. I understand that no company representative, other than its president, and only when in writing and signed by the president, has any authority to enter into any agreement for employment for any specific period of time, or to make any agreement contrary to the foregoing."

| DATE | SIGNATURE |

eschewing college is "almost a badge of honor" because individuals are more free-thinking and risk-taking.[47]

Proponents of degrees counter with data that the educated earn far more in their lifetime than those without degrees, and thus the Zuckerbergs and the Gateses of the world are the exception rather than the norm. For example, college graduates earn about 75% more ($30,000+) on average than high school graduates. Further-more, a study by the Center on Education and the Workforce at Georgetown University has found that the average return on investment for any college education is $107,000 10 years after enrollment, and $723,000 40 years after enrollment. In general, it is likely that changes in higher education are on the horizon, and defi-nitions of "level of education" may be altered as a result of those changes.[48] For example, the US economy lost nearly 7.5 million jobs that required a high school degree in 2007, a vacancy that has further decreased by about 1.3 million in 2016. The high school diploma as a minimum requirement also has the lowest projected growth, suggesting that what is considered a standard level of education may shift upward toward other forms of postsecondary education.[49]

Grade Point Average. Classroom grades are measured using a grade point average (GPA). Care should be exercised when using GPA data as predictors. For example, a GPA in one's major in college may be different (usually higher) from one's GPA for all their classes. Grades also vary widely by field (e.g., grades in engineering tend to be lower than in other fields). Further, a GPA of 3.5 may be good at one school but not at another. Research suggests that the validity of GPA in predicting job performance may be as high as the mid .30s. College grades are no more valid than high school grades, and grades are most valid in predicting early job performance. Although there is variability from employer to employer, evidence indicates that GPA does not play a large role in most recruiters' evalua-tions. GPAs tend to have high disparate impact against minorities, and as with all selection measures with disparate impact, the validity evidence must be balanced against disparate impact implications.[50]

Quality of School. Much has been said and written about the quality of vari-ous educational programs. For example, *U.S. News and World Report* annually publishes the results of a survey showing ratings of school quality (or prestige, depending on the faith you have in such ratings).[51] Although people traditionally place a premium on prestige, there is some evidence to suggest that this perception is shifting. For example, one study found that when you control for other factors that might make a graduate from a prestigious institution succeed (e.g., parental income), the prestige-relevant differences between earning potentials are not that stark. Another study of 7,000 college graduates suggests that although prestige might make a difference for some degrees, it makes little difference for science, technology, engineering, or math (STEM) majors. In general, the conclusion from the 2014 Gallup-Purdue index (a survey of 30,000 graduates) suggests that "it's not 'where' you go to college, but 'how' you go to college."[52]

Major Field of Study.   The more specialized the knowledge requirements of a particular position, the more important an applicant's major field of study is likely to be as a predictor. An English major may do very well as an editor but may be unsuccessful as a physician. It should also be noted that choice of major does not guarantee that a certain number or type of classes have been taken. The number and type of classes needed for a major or minor vary from school to school and need to be scrutinized to ensure comparability across majors. The relationship between field of study and job performance is very difficult to assess; therefore, no conclusive validity evidence is available.

Extracurricular Activities.   The usefulness of extracurricular activities as a predictor depends on the job. Being an ice hockey player may have little relevance to being a successful manager. However, being elected captain of a hockey team may indeed be a sign of leadership qualities needed to be a successful manager. Information about extracurricular activities taken from an application blank must be relevant to the job in question. Evidence suggests that participation in extracurricular activities leads to higher employability perceptions as well as hiring manager attributions of strong communication, time management skills, and the ability to learn.[53] Furthermore, for jobs in which cultural intelligence (CQ) is an important component, studying abroad, along with cultural boundary-expanding experiences, may be a good indicator of a heightened CQ.[54] Despite these potential benefits, the organization should be cautious when inquiring about and using this type of information. Guidance from the Equal Employment Opportunity Commission (EEOC) suggests that information about clubs, societies, and organizations that may indicate the applicant is a member of a protected class should be avoided during selection.[55]

Training and Experience Requirements

Many past experiences predictive of future performance do not take place in a classroom. Instead, they come from life experiences in other institutions that can also be captured on an application blank. A great deal of weight is often put on training and experience requirements on the theory that actions speak louder than words. For example, experienced surgeons tend to make better surgeons. One study found that the mortality rate of procedures was about twice as high for inexperienced surgeons as for experienced surgeons.[56] As with other jobs, though, the benefits of experience tend to plateau after a certain amount. Beyond a certain level, added experience does not help much. Furthermore, experience can be considered at a variety of levels of analysis (e.g., job, organization, occupation) along with characteristics (e.g., amount, time, type).[57] The drawback of putting too much emphasis on previous work experience, however, is that the amount of experience and training an applicant has may be overstated. Additionally, applicants with high potential may be overlooked because they have not had the opportunity to gain the training or experience needed.

Various methods can be used to measure training and experience. Since training and experience information is not directly equivalent across applicants, all methods require the judgment of selection decision makers. These decision makers render judgments about how to classify and weight different levels of experience. An approach termed the "behavioral consistency method" has shown the highest degree of validity because it focuses on determining the quality of an applicant's previous training and experience. One of the means by which the behavioral consistency method determines quality is by asking applicants to complete a supplemental application wherein they describe their most significant accomplishments relative to a list of key job behaviors. Due to their involved nature, however, behavioral consistency ratings are time-consuming and expensive to administer, and they require the applicant to possess some degree of analytical ability and writing skills. Thus, the choice of weighting methods rests on a trade-off between accuracy and ease and cost of administration.[58]

Despite the strong theoretical basis behind using work experience in selection decisions, meta-analytic data from over 10,000 applicants suggest that it is a relatively weak predictor of job performance ($\bar{r}_{xy} = .05$), even when the experience is relevant for the position ($\bar{r}_{xy} = .06$). However, prehire work experience does appear to predict performance in training to a greater extent. If being able to hit the ground running is important for the position, it may make sense to consider prior work experience. Otherwise, there is no guarantee that the experiences employees bring from a prior job (even when relevant) will translate to job performance in the new job.[59] When examining the validity of prehire work experience, it appears that one needs to take into account not only job relevance but also characteristics of the new firm (values, norms, experiences, etc.).[60]

Licensing, Certification, and Job Knowledge

Many occupations require or encourage people to demonstrate mastery of a certain body of knowledge. Such mastery is commonly measured by two distinct methods: licensure and certification. A license is required by law to perform an activity, whereas a certification is voluntary in the sense that it is not mandated by law (though an individual employer may require it). The purpose of a license is to protect the public interest, whereas the purpose of a certification is to identify an individual who has met a minimum standard of proficiency. Licensing exams and certification exams are usually developed by subject matter experts (SMEs) in conjunction with testing specialists. Licensure and certification are to be distinguished from job knowledge tests. While licensure and certification demonstrate mastery of a general body of knowledge applicable to many organizations, job knowledge tests assess a specific body of knowledge within a particular organization. Job knowledge tests are usually used in the public sector as an initial screening device.

In the private sector, they are used primarily for promotion purposes. Although mentioned here, job knowledge tests will be covered in detail in the next chapter.

Licensing and certification requirements can be used as either an initial or a contingent assessment method. As an initial method, licensing and certification requirements are used to eliminate applicants who fail to possess these credentials. For example, a car repair shop electing to hire only certified mechanics might initially screen out individuals who fail to have the proper certification. When licensing and certification requirements are used as a contingent method, the selection process proceeds on the assumption that the applicant has the requisite credentials (or will have them by the time of hire). This is then verified after an initial offer decision has been made. For example, rather than verifying that each applicant for a nursing position possesses a valid state license, a hospital may assess applicants on the assumption that they have a valid license and then verify this assumption after a contingent job offer has been made. Thus, the difference between using licensing and certification requirements as an initial assessment method and using them as a contingent assessment method depends on when the information is considered in the selection process. Choosing between using licensing and certification requirements as a contingent method and using them as an initial assessment method depends on several factors, including the size of the applicant pool, the difficulty in obtaining verification, and the selection plan.

Increasingly, organizations are using voluntary professional certification as a method of verifying competence in various occupations. There are thousands of professional certifications, including those in law, teaching, nursing, human resources, project management, sales, IT, and network engineering, as well as software certifications (e.g., Google suite).[61] Most of these voluntary certifications are issued based on additional experience and education. Most certifications also require examinations.

There are several practical problems or limitations in using licensing and certification requirements in selection. First, one cannot assume that an applicant is qualified for the position simply because they have a license or certification. That assumption places full confidence in the licensing and certification standards of the professional organization. Licensing and certification requirements vary greatly in their rigor, and one should not accept on faith that the fulfillment of those requirements ensures professional competency. Moreover, even if the requirements did perfectly measure professional competence, because licenses and certifications are issued to those passing some minimum threshold, they do not differentiate between the minimally qualified and the exceptionally qualified. In other words, licenses and certifications are like considering an applicant's college degree without looking at the applicant's GPA.

A second difficulty with licensing and certification requirements is that, as with job titles, there has been significant proliferation. For example, among financial advisors are certified financial planners (CFPs), certified financial analysts (CFAs), certified investment management analysts (CIMAs), chartered financial consultants (ChFCs), chartered retirement planning counselors (CRPCs), and so forth. Indeed, more than 100 such titles are used by financial professionals.[62] No central regulator monitors these titles, and the growth in financial services certifications seems to have done little to prevent the myriad mistakes and malfeasances that plague Wall Street and Main Street alike. If selection decision makers wish to require certification, they need to research the types and meanings of certifications that may exist for a job.

Finally, there are practice effects with repeated tries at a licensing or certification exam, and these effects may be quite strong. One study of medical professionals found that for one certification exam, second-time examinees improved their scores by .79 standard deviations.[63] This would mean that someone who scored at the 34th percentile the first time out would be expected to score at the 66th percentile on the second try. Unlike some standardized tests, where scores may be reported for each time the test is taken, there is generally no way for a selection decision maker to know how many times an applicant has taken a licensing or certification exam (nor can one determine a test taker's exact score). However, these changes may not be a bad thing: one review of over 100 years of retest research suggests that retest exam scores are more reliable and valid than the initial scores.[64]

We are not arguing that these issues and limitations discredit the use of licensure and certification for selection decisions. They are important—even necessary—for many jobs. However, selection decision makers need to be informed consumers and may need to supplement licensure and certification requirements with other information to make the best decisions.

Weighted Application Blanks

Not all the information contained on an application blank is of equal value to the organization in making selection decisions. Depending on the organization and job, some information predicts success on the job better than other information. Procedures have been developed that help weight application blank information by the degree to which the information differentiates between high- and low-performing individuals.[65] This scoring methodology is referred to as a weighted application blank and is useful in making selection decisions. The statistical procedures involved help the organization discern which application blanks should be weighted more heavily in selection decisions based on how well they predict performance.

Evaluation of Application Blanks

Evidence suggests that scored evaluations of the unweighted application blank are not particularly valid predictors of job performance (average validity ranges from $\bar{r}_{xy} = .10$ to $\bar{r}_{xy} = .20$).[66] This is not surprising given the rudimentary information collected in application blanks. Another factor that may undermine the validity of application blanks is distortion. As discussed earlier, distortion and impression management occur quite frequently in the use of résumés, cover letters, and applications alike. Some individuals even go beyond misrepresentation to outright invention during the application process. As some (easily caught) examples, one applicant listed the same dates for each job on their application, one applicant claimed to be an antiterrorism agent for the CIA (even though the applicant would have been in elementary school at the time), and one applicant even claimed to have studied under Friedrich Nietzsche (who died over 100 years before the application was submitted).[67] Thus, as with résumés, application information that is weighted heavily in selection decisions should be verified.

The validity evidence for weighted application blanks is more positive.[68] In a sense, this would almost have to be true since items in the weighted application blank are scored and weighted according to their ability to predict job performance. Is the validity worth the cost? A weighted application blank may be cost-effective because the employer is able to make use of information often included on standardized applications (although care should be taken to correctly develop and score them).[69] Unfortunately, there is little recent research on the weighted application blank to predict job performance, so answering this question is difficult.

The relatively poor validity of unweighted application blanks also should not be taken as an indication that they are useless in selection decisions. Unweighted application blanks are a very inexpensive means of collecting basic information on job applicants. Most organizations use unweighted application blanks only for initial screening decisions (to rule out applicants who are obviously unqualified for the job). If application blanks are used in this context and not relied on to a significant degree in making substantive hiring decisions, they can be useful for making initial decisions about applicants.

Biographical Information

Biographical information, often called biodata, is personal history information on an applicant's background and interests. The principal assumption behind the use of biodata is the axiom "The best predictor of future behavior is past behavior," and these past behaviors may reflect job-relevant predictors such as ability or motivation. Biographical information has some similarities to reference and background checks (see the section on reference and background checks). Biodata and background checks are similar in that both examine an applicant's past. However, they differ in their general purpose and measurement. First, whereas a background check is often used to turn up any "buried bones" in an applicant's background, biodata is used to predict future performance. Second, whereas reference checks are conducted through checks of records and conversations with references, biodata information is collected by survey. Thus, biodata inventories and reference and background checks are distinct methods of selection that must be considered separately. Although biographical information is as much a substantive assessment method as it is an initial assessment method, because it shares many similarities with application blanks, we have included it in this section. Nevertheless, it should also be considered in deliberations about which substantive assessment methods are to be used.

The type of biographical information collected varies a great deal from inventory to inventory and often depends on the job. A biographical survey for executives might focus on career aspirations, accomplishments, and disappointments. Many biodata surveys consider individual accomplishments, group accomplishments, disappointing experiences, and stressful situations. The domains in which these attributes are studied often vary from job to job but can range from childhood experiences to educational or early work experiences to current hobbies or family relations.[70] For example, Google developed a biodata inventory by first asking its employees 300 questions and then correlating employee responses to their job performance. Once it isolated items that predicted the job performance of current employees, Google asked applicants a smaller set of questions that ranged from the age when an applicant first got excited about computers to whether the applicant has ever turned a profit at their own side business.[71]

Typically, biodata is collected in a questionnaire that applicants complete. Exhibit 8.5 provides example biodata items. As can be seen, the items are quite diverse. It has been suggested that each biodata item can be classified according to 10 criteria:[72]

- *History*—Does the item describe an event that occurred in the past or a future or hypothetical event?
- *Externality*—Does the item address an observable event or an internal event such as values or judgments?
- *Objectivity*—Does the item focus on reporting factual information or subjective interpretations?
- *First-handedness*—Does the item seek information that is directly available to the applicant rather than an evaluation of the applicant's behavior by others?
- *Discreteness*—Does the item pertain to a single, unique behavior or a simple count of events as opposed to summary responses?
- *Verifiability*—Can the accuracy of the response to the item be confirmed?
- *Controllability*—Does the item address an event that the applicant controlled?
- *Equal accessibility*—Are the events or experiences expressed in the item equally accessible to all applicants?
- *Job relevance*—Does the item solicit information closely tied to the job?
- *Invasiveness*—Is the item sensitive to the applicant's right to privacy?

Evaluation of Biodata

Research conducted on the reliability and validity of biodata is quite positive. Responses tend to be reliable (test–retest coefficients range from .60 to .90).[73] More important, past research suggests that biodata inventories are valid predictors of

EXHIBIT 8.5 **Examples of Biodata Items**

1. In college, my grade point average was:
   a. I did not go to college or completed less than two years
   b. Less than 2.50
   c. 2.50 to 3.00
   d. 3.00 to 3.50
   e. 3.50 to 4.00

2. In the past five years, the number of different jobs I have held is:
   a. More than five
   b. Three to five
   c. Two
   d. One
   e. None

3. The kind of supervision I like best is:
   a. Very close supervision
   b. Fairly close supervision
   c. Moderate supervision
   d. Minimal supervision
   e. No supervision

4. When you are angry, which of the following behaviors most often describes your reaction:
   a. Reflect on the situation for a bit
   b. Talk to a friend or spouse
   c. Exercise or take a walk
   d. Physically release the anger on something
   e. Just try to forget about it

5. Over the past three years, how much have you enjoyed each of the following (use the scale at right):
   a. _____ Reading   1 = Very much
   b. _____ Watching TV   2 = Some
   c. _____ Home improvements   3 = Very little
   d. _____ Music   4 = Not at all
   e. _____ Outdoor recreation

6. In most ways is your life close to ideal?
   a. Yes
   b. No
   c. Undecided or neutral

job performance. Several meta-analyses have been conducted, and the average validity has ranged from $\bar{r}_{xy} = .26$ to $\bar{r}_{xy} = .32$.[74]

In addition to job performance, biodata scores appear to predict turnover (individuals with a history of job changes are more likely to turn over) and embeddedness (individuals with a history of long tenures are more likely to stay).[75]

Despite the quite positive validity evidence, biodata does have some important limitations. First, biodata inventories tend to be validated using concurrent validity designs with incumbents and not with predictive validity designs with applicants; the validity of biodata inventories for applicants might be lower.[76]

Second, there is some concern about faking. Not only might applicants be motivated to fake their responses to biodata questions, but also responses to many questions are impossible to verify (e.g., "Did you collect coins or stamps as a child?"). Research also suggests, though, that faking can be reduced through several strategies: (1) use items that are more objective and verifiable, (2) simply warn applicants against faking, and (3) ask applicants to elaborate on and justify their responses. For example, if applicants are asked, "In the past year, how often have you read about new marketing strategies?" (1 = never, 5 = very often), they would receive a follow-up question to elaborate on their response: "If you answered 2, 3, 4, or 5, briefly list the strategies and the sources that you read."[77]

Third, applicants and managers do not react positively to biodata. The inventories often comprise more than 100 items, and most research suggests that applicants do not see the questions as job related and can even see them as an invasion of privacy. Apparently, HR managers do not favorably perceive biodata either. A survey of 255 HR professionals revealed that, among various selection measures, biodata beat only a "personal hunch" in terms of its perceived validity. Indeed, biodata measures tend not to be used that often in practice, due to the negative reactions of applicants and HR managers alike.[78]

Finally, some evidence suggests that biodata can have moderately high disparate impact, with Whites often scoring more than a third of a standard deviation higher than Blacks. It is important to focus on reducing the cognitive complexity of the biodata items (which can lead to disparate impact) as well as removing items that by their nature can lead to disparate impact (e.g., specifically asking about academic experiences).[79]

Despite these limitations, it is important to keep in mind that biodata can have impressive validity and that its use is appropriate when it is carefully validated and when its limitations are addressed.

Reference and Background Checks

Background information about job applicants can come not only from the applicant but also from people familiar with the applicant (e.g., employers, creditors, and neighbors). Organizations often solicit this information on their own or use the services of agencies that specialize in investigating applicants. Background information solicited from others consists of letters of recommendation, reference checks, and background checks.

Letters of Recommendation

A very common reference check in some settings (e.g., academic institutions) is to ask applicants to have letters of recommendation written for them. A recent meta-analysis, however, showed that letters of recommendation were rather weakly correlated to performance in graduate school and medical school.[80]

There are two major problems with using letters of recommendation. First, these letters may do little to help the organization discern the more qualified applicants from the less qualified applicants. The reason for this is that only very poor applicants are unable to arrange for positive letters about their accomplishments. Furthermore, because applicants are able to recruit their own letter writers, they are more likely to recruit people who like them and will write them a positive letter of recommendation; studies have shown that this influences the quality and accuracy of the letters.[81] Second, most letters are not structured or standardized, meaning the data the organization receives from the letter writers are not consistent across organizations. For example, a letter about one applicant may concern the applicant's educational qualifications, whereas a letter about another applicant may focus on work experience. Comparing the qualifications of applicants A and B under these circumstances is like comparing apples and oranges.

The problem with letters of recommendation is demonstrated dramatically in one study that showed there was a stronger correlation between two letters written by one person for two applicants than between two people writing letters for the same applicant.[82] Letters of recommendation may have more to do with the letter writer than with the person being written about. In fact, one study revealed that letter writers who had a dispositional tendency to be positive wrote consistently more favorable letters than letter writers with a tendency to be critical or negative. Furthermore, the writer's own implicit biases may emerge when writing a letter for a minority or female applicant.[83]

In addition, a surprising number of letters of recommendation are written by the applicants themselves. Regarding graduate school admissions, the Association of International Graduate Admissions Consultants discovered that a whopping 38% of applicants were asked by their recommenders to write their own letters, which the recommenders would then later sign. And some applicants have confessed to bypassing their recommender altogether, especially if the recommender was not fluent in English.[84]

Such problems indicate that organizations should downplay the weight given to letters unless a great deal of accountability can be attached to the letter writer's comments. In addition, a structured form should be provided so that each writer provides the same information about each applicant. Relatedly, using a standardized scoring key, as shown in Exhibit 8.6, can improve comparability across appli-

EXHIBIT 8.6   Scoring Letters of Recommendation

Dear Human Resource Manager:

I am pleased to write this letter of recommendation for Jordan Jones for the position of general sales manager. Jordan has worked for five years as an assistant manager in our sales department. Jordan has been a valuable employee. He stands out as one of our brightest on the sales team. His detail-oriented, analytical approach to problem solving is one of his greatest strengths. He has a friendly and outgoing nature and is always helpful to others. He has been a reliable and trustworthy employee and I highly recommend Jordan for this position. Please do not hesitate to contact me if you have further questions.

GMA 2   C 3   E 2   A 1   O 0   ES 0

Dear Human Resource Manager:

I am pleased to write this letter of recommendation for Jordan Jones for the position of general sales manager. Jordan has worked for five years as an assistant manager in our sales department. Jordan is one of our most likable employees. He is outgoing by nature, but more importantly is kind and always willing to help others. His ability to take charge and adapt to various work situations demonstrates he has the leadership skills to excel in the position he is applying for. He is dependable and his work is generally flawless. I highly recommend Jordan for this position. Please do not hesitate to contact me if you have further questions.

GMA 0   C 2   E 3   A 3   O 1   ES 0

Key   GMA = general mental ability
C = conscientiousness
E = extroversion
A = agreeableness
O = openness
ES = emotional stability

cants. With this method, categories of KSAOs (in this case, individual differences such as cognitive ability and personality) are established and become the scoring key (shown at the bottom of the exhibit). The adjectives in the letter are underlined and classified into the appropriate category. The number of adjectives used in each category constitutes the applicant's score. A total score could be derived from summing the category scores.

Reference Checks

With reference checking, an applicant's background is investigated by contacting people who know the applicant well. Usually the person contacted is the immediate supervisor of the applicant or is in the HR department of previous organizations that employed the applicant. Surveys reveal that 95% of organizations conduct reference checks, and that 60% enjoy better-quality hires as a result.[85] The most common information sought is on criminal background and verification of employment eligibility, education, credentials, former employers, dates of previous employment, and former job titles.[86] Exhibit 8.7 provides a sample reference request. Although this reference request was developed for checking references by mail, the questions contained in the request could easily be adapted for use in checking references via telephone.[87]

Both problems that occur with letters of recommendation occur with reference checks as well. An even more significant concern, however, is the reluctance of organizations to give out the requested information because they fear a lawsuit on the grounds of invasion of privacy or defamation of character. One survey indicated that 93% of employers refuse to provide reference information for fear of being sued. Although better reference information is needed, organizations are usually willing to provide information only on dates of employment.[88] As a result of employers' reluctance to provide reference information, reference checkers claim to receive inadequate information much of the time. To a large degree, this concern over providing even rudimentary reference information is excessive: less than 3% of employers have had legal problems with reference checks (see "Legal Issues" at the end of this chapter). If every organization refused to provide useful reference information, a potentially important source of applicant information could lose its value. Collect relevant information if you can, but make sure you do it correctly.[89]

Most reference checks are still done over the telephone. A small number of employers (27%), however, are mining networking websites such as Facebook, Twitter, MySpace, and LinkedIn not only to find out more about an applicant but also to locate references to contact.[90] No matter the source or method used to gather the information, it is critical that the questions be job related and that the same information is asked about all applicants. When properly structured and job relevant, references can have moderate levels of validity.[91]

Background Checks

How would you feel if you found out that the organization you are hoping to join was investigating your traffic record and moral character? How would you feel if an organization did *not* investigate the backgrounds of guards to be selected for the gun storage depot of the US military base near your home? More and more organizations are thoroughly checking applicants' backgrounds even when security is not a particular issue.

Although background checking may seem to be a very invasive procedure, such checks have increased dramatically. A recent survey indicated that many organizations now perform background checks.[92] There are several reasons for this. First, after the September 11 terrorist attacks, more organizations became concerned about security issues. Second, some ethical lapses, and many instances of work-

EXHIBIT 8.7 Sample Reference Request

TO BE COMPLETED BY APPLICANT

NAME (PRINT): SOCIAL SEC. NUMBER

I have made an application for employment at this company. I request and authorize you to release all information requested below concerning my employment record, reason for leaving your employ, or my education. I hereby release my personal references, my former employers and schools, and all individuals connected therewith from all liability for any damage whatsoever for furnishing this information.

SIGNATURE _____ DATE _____

SCHOOL REFERENCE

DATES ATTENDED

FROM: TO: GRADUATED? YES ☐ NO ☐

DEGREE AWARDED:

EMPLOYMENT REFERENCE

POSITION HELD: EMPLOYMENT DATES:

IMMEDIATE SUPERVISOR'S NAME

REASON FOR LEAVING DISCHARGED ☐ RESIGNED ☐ LAID OFF ☐

FORMER EMPLOYER OR SCHOOL—Please complete the following. Thank you.

IS THE ABOVE INFORMATION CORRECT? YES ☐ NO ☐

If not, give correct information: _____

PLEASE CHECK

	EXCEL.	GOOD	FAIR	POOR	COMMENTS:
ATTITUDE	_____	_____	_____	_____	
QUALITY OF WORK	_____	_____	_____	_____	
COOPERATION	_____	_____	_____	_____	
ATTENDANCE	_____	_____	_____	_____	

WOULD YOU RECOMMEND FOR EMPLOYMENT? YES ☐ NO ☐

ADDITIONAL COMMENTS

SIGNATURE OF EMPLOYER OR SCHOOL REPRESENTATIVE TITLE

place violence, might be avoided by background checks. For example, consider the case of Wal-Mart. In two separate incidents in South Carolina, Wal-Mart employees were accused of sexually assaulting young girls. Both accused employees had past criminal convictions for sexually related offenses. In response, Wal-Mart instituted criminal background checks on all of its employees.[93] According to a current benchmarking report, 56% of users of background checks report more consistent safety and security in their organizations as a result of their use.[94] A third reason behind the growing use of background checks is legal protection against responsibility for malfeasance, and defense against claims of negligent hiring (which we review under "Reference Checks" in "Legal Issues" at the end of the chapter). A fourth, and perhaps the most important, reason underlying the increasing use of background checks is easier access to technology. As public records have become more accessible, both legally (with so-called Sunshine laws) and practically (many local and state governments post criminal records online), and as credit checking has increased, it has become far easier to perform background checks. Fama, for example, regularly mines "public" information on applicants' social media profile pages using machine learning as a part of its reference checking services. However, many question the validity of this technique as the algorithms may flag any controversial post or like without considering the context or reasons behind doing so.[95]

Background checks cost anywhere from $5 to $1,000 per hire, depending on the type of position and the information sought. Most background checks cost around $25 per applicant. However, not following the law can be expensive: several large corporations and background check vendors have shelled out more than $325 million in settlements of class action lawsuits.[96] Background checks are too costly to not do correctly: even though they can provide helpful information, care should be taken so that they are completed in a systematic, legally compliant way.

Background checks identify more problems than one might think: 71% of organizations uncovered issues they would have otherwise missed.[97] Additionally, the consequences of failing to conduct a background check are quite serious. Take, for example, Nick Leeson, the "rogue trader" responsible for the demise of Barings Bank. When hiring Leeson, Barings's Singapore branch never checked his background, nor was his history discovered by the Singapore stock exchange. At Barings's Singapore office, Leeson made unauthorized speculative trades and creatively hid his mounting losses. Eventually, Britain's Securities and Futures Authority discovered that Leeson had lied on his application. The losses eventually accumulated to $1.3 billion, bankrupting the oldest bank in London.[98]

Background checks do have limitations. First, the records can be wrong, can be misinterpreted, or can contain misleading information. For example, one client of Sharon Dietrich's, a labor lawyer in Philadelphia, had a 65-page criminal history report from a background check that was attributable to unrelated people with a similar name.[99] Second, because background checks have become more commonplace, they can place a seemingly permanent bar on the reemployment of reformed criminals. Peter Demain was sentenced to six years for possessing 21 pounds of marijuana. While in prison, he was so adept in the prison kitchen that he quickly rose to head baker. Once out of prison, though, Demain was unable to find a job at bagel shops, coffeehouses, grocery stores, and bakeries. Is it fair for reformed criminals, no matter how long ago or the nature of the offense, to be banned from employment?[100]

Such a question is difficult to answer. In response, however, many states have begun instituting what are called "Ban the Box" laws, in which background information on application blanks or background checking is regulated to ensure that ex-offenders will not be excluded from consideration on a de facto basis. The law itself is a reference to the check box on an application form (i.e., an application blank) that asks applicants if they have ever been convicted of a crime. These laws regulate what applicants can be asked before they are hired, when employers can inquire about criminal history (and how far back one can go), and when background checks can be used. Kevin Bachman, founder of the CRA Doctor, notes that this does not necessarily affect employment safety; "ban-the-box just prevents an employer from asking upfront and knocking out the candidate without determining whether they'd be a good fit for the job." In 2015, President Obama banned the box for federal government jobs. Since then, several states and employers have banned the box, although the specific laws vary from state to state. This has made it difficult for national organizations to maintain standardized application forms and hiring practices across states. Furthermore, as a part of a backlash to the movement, several states (e.g., Indiana and Michigan) have passed laws that limit the reach of the ban. Regardless, employers should take care to ensure that they are using background checks in a fashion that is legally defensible and compliant with federal and local regulations.[101]

Finally, many labor unions have historically resisted background checks. In 2007, Major League Baseball owners clashed with the Umpires Union about background checks. Conversely, in 2010, the Air Line Pilots Association, which represents UPS pilots, backed increased use of background checks.[102]

One way to ameliorate some of these problems is to limit background checks to information that is job related (it may be difficult to establish that a spotty credit history is important to jobs that mostly involve manual labor) and to use multiple sources to verify problems for exclusionary information (i.e., if an applicant is to be excluded because of what a background check uncovered, it would be prudent to independently verify the information).

Evaluation of Recommendations, References, and Background Checks

Empirical research suggests that it is difficult to assess the validity of references and background checks. Most reference and background checks are used on a pass-fail basis; those that have examined their validity have found mixed results that may not extrapolate to other samples. The one exception is the credit score, as a recent study found that those with higher credit scores were more conscientious and were rated as higher performers ($r = .57$) and "good organizational citizens" ($r = .30$) by their supervisors. Although these are subjective assessments, they do suggest that credit scores as one form of background check may demonstrate validity. Additional recent research suggests that credit checks can lead to substantially more disparate impact in hiring.[103] Reference checks and letters of recommendation, on the other hand, tend to display relatively low levels of disparate impact.[104]

To some degree, the validity depends on who is *providing* the information. If it is the personnel officer, a coworker, a relative, or even the applicant themself, the information is not very valid. On the other hand, reference reports from supervisors and acquaintances may be somewhat more valid. The information from personnel officers may be less valid because they are less knowledgeable about the applicant (their past employee); the reports of coworkers and relatives are likely less valid because these individuals are positively biased toward the applicant. To another extent, the validity depends on who is *analyzing* the information. HR managers are probably not well equipped to discern the nuances of credit situations, complex conviction situations, and how these may or may not be job relevant.

Although references do not have high validity, we need to take a cost-benefit approach. In general, the quality of the information may be low, but in the few cases where reference information changes a decision, the payoff can be significant. An executive with the US Postal Service once told one of the authors that many of the acts of violence by Postal Service employees would have been avoided if a thorough background check had been conducted. Thus, since references are a relatively cheap method of collecting information on applicants, learning something new and important about an applicant may make reference checks a good investment. As with unweighted application blanks, using reference checks requires employers to turn elsewhere to obtain suitable information for making final decisions about applicants. Overall, despite a general lack of evidence, background and reference checks likely possess some utility when done correctly and depending on the situation.

Initial Interview

The initial interview occurs very early in the initial assessment process and is often the applicant's first personal contact with the organization and its staffing system. At this point, applicants are relatively undifferentiated to the organization in terms of KSAOs. The initial interview begins the process of necessary differentiation, a sort of "rough cut." Some applicants may even be deciding whether to continue in the job application process.[105]

The purpose of the initial interview is, and should be, to screen out the most obvious cases of person/job mismatches. To do this, the interview should focus on an assessment of KSAOs that are absolute requirements for the applicant. Examples of such minimum levels of qualifications for the job include certification and licensure requirements and necessary (not just preferred) training and experience requirements. Care should be taken to ensure that the interviewer focuses only on this information as a basis for decision making. Evaluations of personal characteristics of the applicant (e.g., race or sex), as well as judgments about an applicant's personality (e.g., "She seems very outgoing and just right for this job"), are to be avoided. However, that may be easier said than done. For example, one study found that applicants with facial stigmas (e.g., face tattoos) were rated lower by interviewers, who were distracted by the stigma and recalled fewer details about the interview, compared with applicants without a facial stigma.[106] Furthermore, there is evidence that supports the power of initial impressions on immediate and future job-related outcomes, including interview callbacks, interview scores, and position offers, although decreasing in effect over time.[107] Indeed, to avoid evaluations of personal characteristics, some organizations (e.g., civil service agencies) have eliminated the initial interview altogether and make the initial assessment from the written information provided by the applicant.

One of the limitations of the initial interview is that it is perhaps the most expensive method of initial assessment. One way to reduce costs dramatically is to conduct video or computer interviews, which we cover next.

Video and Computer Interviews

With the growth of videoconferencing software, it has become increasingly easy—and inexpensive—to conduct initial screening interviews from any location with Internet access. Skype, which has more than 500 million registered accounts, has become a common platform for conducting computer-based initial interviews. Larger companies often use a more customized platform to conduct initial interviews. HireVue, a Salt Lake City online video interview company, counts Urban Outfitters, the Boston Red Sox, and Cathay Pacific among its customers. The advantage of providers such as HireVue is that they allow interviews to be securely stored, shared with others in the organization, and accompanied by ratings and comments.[108]

Video-based interviews can dramatically lower the cost of initial interviews. This is particularly true for employers that wish to interview only a few applicants at a time. Another advantage is that the interviews can be arranged on short notice (no travel and no schedule rearrangements). Of course, the disadvantages of these interviews are that they do not permit face-to-face contact and that the quality of the video connection can, at times, be poor. Indeed, applicants tend to react more favorably to face-to-face interviews than to either phone or videoconferencing interviews: they perceive face-to-face interviews as fairer, leading to better outcomes, and even are more likely to accept a job offer if they receive one.[109]

Another form of video interview takes the process a step further. Digital interviews completely automate the interview process by removing the need for an interviewer, presenting questions (e.g., "Have you ever been terminated for stealing?") or realistic scenarios (e.g., an irate customer on the screen) to applicants, and recording applicants' responses.[110] These responses (and other metrics, such as how long it takes you to answer the question) are forwarded to selection decision makers for use in initial screening, without requiring the use (or judgments) of an interviewer. HireVue's digital interviewing platform even leverages artificial intelligence by using the camera on the applicant's device to analyze facial movements, diction, and speaking tone, and then creates an "employability score."[111] Retailers are beginning to use digital interviews on-site, where applicants walk into a store, enter a kiosk, and submit information about their work habits and experiences. The accuracy of digital interviews as compared with that of the old standby, the person-to-person variety, is unclear. However, anecdotes from the popular press suggest that applicants react quite negatively to these relatively impersonal methods. One applicant noted that her digital interview was horrible and cut her off completely after a minute of talking—without any follow-up questions or interaction.[112] Another applicant was frustrated by how single-sided the interchange seemed. After not being able to ask follow-up questions about the nature of the job or the organization for several minutes, she said, "At that point I hit 9 and just ended it."[113]

Evaluation of Initial Interview

Whether high-tech or traditional, the interview has its own benefits and limitations. Nearly all the research evaluating the interview in selection has considered it a substantive method (see "Structured Interview" in the next chapter). Thus, there is little evidence about the usefulness of the initial interview. However, organizations using the initial interview in selection are likely to find it more useful by following a few guidelines:

1. Ask questions that assess the most basic KSAOs identified by job analysis. This requires separating what is required from what is preferred.

2. Stick to basic, qualifying questions suitable for making rough cuts (e.g., "Have you completed the minimum certification requirements to qualify for this job?") rather than subtle, subjective questions more suitable for substantive decisions (e.g., "How would this job fit within your overall career goals?"). Remember, the purpose of the initial interview is closer to cutting with a saw than operating with a scalpel. Ask only the most fundamental questions now and leave the fine-tuning for later.

3. Keep interviews brief. Most interviewers make up their minds quickly, and given the limited usefulness and the type of information collected, a long interview (45–60 minutes) is unlikely to add much over a shorter one (15–30 minutes).

4. As with all interviews, ask all applicants the same questions and monitor equal employment opportunity (EEO) compliance.

Choice of Initial Assessment Methods

As described, a wide range of initial assessment methods are available to organizations to help reduce the applicant pool. Fortunately, with so many choices available to organizations, research can help guide the organization in choosing a method. This research is summarized in Exhibit 8.8. In the exhibit, each initial assessment method is rated according to several criteria. Each of these criteria will be discussed in turn.

Use

Use refers to how frequently organizations use each predictor. Use is probably an overused criterion in deciding which selection measures to adopt. Benchmarking— basing HR decisions on what other companies are doing—is a predominant method of decision making in all areas of HR, including staffing. However, is this a good way to make decisions about selection methods? Although it is always comforting to know what other organizations are doing, relying on information from other organizations assumes that they know what they are doing. Just because many organizations use a selection measure does not necessarily make it a good idea for any particular organization. Circumstances differ from organization to organization. In addition, at a time when many organizations are trying to differentiate themselves from their competitors, rigorous innovation in selection, rather than imitation, may be more effective in acquiring a talented workforce.

Perhaps more importantly, many organizational decision makers (and HR consultants) either lack knowledge about the latest findings in HR research or have decided that such findings are not applicable to their organization.[114] It is also difficult to determine whether a successful organization that uses a particular selection method is successful because it uses this method or because of some other reason. Thus, from a research standpoint, there may be a real strategic advantage in relying on "effectiveness" criteria (e.g., validity, utility, and disparate impact) rather than worrying about the practices of other organizations.

Another reason to have a healthy degree of skepticism about the use criterion is that there is a severe lack of timely and broad surveys of selection practices (i.e., coverage of many industries and regions in the United States). Since 2014, the North American Talent Board has conducted a candidate experience benchmark report, which includes usage statistics on several selection methods. However, this report includes only a handful of broadly defined constructs, competencies, and methods.[115] Other surveys of selection practices are available, but they generally cover only a single selection practice (e.g., drug testing) or lack adequate scope or breadth. In providing conclusions about the use of various selection methods in organizations, we are forced to make judgment calls concerning which survey to rely on. In the case of some selection measures (e.g., application blanks), there is little reason to believe the figures have changed much. With other predictors, the

EXHIBIT 8.8 Evaluation of Initial Assessment Methods

Predictor	Use	Cost	Reliability	Validity	Utility	Applicant Reactions	Disparate Impact
Résumé and cover letter	High	Low	Low	Low	?	Positive	Moderate
Level of education	High	Low	Moderate	Low	Low	?	High
Grade point average	Low	Low	Moderate	Moderate	?	?	High
Quality of school	?	Low	?	Low	?	?	?
Major field of study	?	Low	Moderate	?	?	?	Low
Extracurricular activity	?	Low	?	Moderate	?	?	Low
Training and experience	High	Low	High	Low	Low	?	Moderate
Licensing and certification	Moderate	Low	Moderate	Moderate	?	?	?
Weighted application blanks	Moderate	Moderate	Moderate	Moderate	High	Mixed	Moderate
Biographical data	Low	Moderate	High	Moderate	High	Mixed	Moderate
Letters of recommendation	Low	Low	Low	Low	?	?	Low
Reference check	High	Moderate	Low	Moderate	Moderate	Mixed	Low
Background check	Low	High	?	High	?	Negative	Moderate
Initial interview	High	High	Low	?	?	Positive	Moderate

use figures have shown a fair degree of volatility and change from year to year. Thus, in classifying the use of assessment methods, we rely on the most recent surveys that achieve some degree of breadth. For purposes of classifying the predictors, high use refers to use by more than two-thirds of organizations, moderate use is use by one-third to two-thirds of organizations, and low use refers to use by less than one-third of organizations.

Now that we have issued these caveats about the use criterion, Exhibit 8.8 reveals clear differences in the use of various methods of initial assessment. The most frequently used methods of initial assessment are the résumé and cover letter, education level, training and experience, reference check, and initial interview. These methods are considered, to some degree, in selection decisions for most types of positions. Licensing and certification requirements, as well as application blanks, have moderate levels of use. These methods are widely used in filling some types of positions but infrequently used in filling many others. The least widely used initial assessment methods are biographical data, letters of recommendation, and background checks. It is relatively unusual for organizations to use these methods for initial screening decisions (although letters of recommendation are more frequently used in some industries, like academia). There are no reliable figures on the use of quality of school, major field of study, and extracurricular activity in initial selection decisions; thus, their use could not be estimated.

Cost

Cost refers to expenses incurred in using the predictor. Although most of the initial assessment methods may seem relatively cost-free since the applicant provides the information on their own time, this is not entirely accurate. For most initial assessment methods, the major cost associated with each selection measure is administration. Consider an application blank. It is true that applicants complete application blanks on their own time, but someone must be present to hand out applications (or guide applicants to the relevant application website), answer inquiries in person and over the phone about possible openings, and collect, sort, and forward applications to the appropriate person. Then the selection decision maker must read each application, perhaps make notes about an applicant, weed out the clearly unacceptable applicants, and then make decisions about candidates. Although some of this process can be automated, there is still clearly a human element involved. Thus, even for the least expensive methods of initial assessment, costs associated with their use are far from trivial.

On the other hand, utility research has suggested that costs do not play a large part in evaluating the financial benefit of using particular selection methods. This becomes clear when one considers the costs of hiring a poor performer. For example, an administrative assistant who performs one standard deviation below average (16th percentile, if performance is normally distributed) may cost the organization $8,000 in lost productivity per year. This person is likely to remain on the job for more than one year, multiplying the costs. Considered in this light, spending an extra few hundred dollars to accurately identify good administrative assistants is an excellent investment. Thus, although costs need to be considered in evaluating assessment methods, more consideration should be given to the fact that valid selection measures pay off handsomely and will return many times their cost.

As can be seen in Exhibit 8.8, the least costly initial assessment methods include information that can be obtained from application blanks (level of education, grade point average, quality of school, major field of study, extracurricular activity, training and experience, and licensing and certification) and information provided by the applicant (letters of recommendation, résumés, and cover letters). Initial assessment methods of moderate cost include weighted application blanks, biographical data, and reference checks. Initial interviews and background checks are relatively expensive assessment methods; although video-based interviews may be less expensive.

Reliability

Reliability refers to consistency of measurement. As was noted in the measurement chapter, reliability is a requirement for validity, so it would be very difficult for a predictor with low reliability to have high validity. Similarly, it is unlikely that a valid predictor would have low reliability. Unfortunately, the reliability information on many initial assessment methods is lacking in the literature. However, given the frequency with which individuals distort their résumés, it is probably reasonable to infer that applicant-supplied information in application blanks and résumés is of moderate reliability. The reliability of reference checks appears to be relatively low. In terms of training and experience evaluations, while distortion can occur if the applicant supplies training and experience information, interrater agreement in evaluating this information is quite high.[116] Biographical information also generally has high reliability. The initial interview, like most unstructured interviews, has a relatively low level of reliability.

Validity

Validity refers to the strength of the relationship between the predictor and job performance. Low validity ranges from about .00 to .15, moderate validity ranges from about .16 to .30, and high validity is .31 and above. As might be expected, most initial assessment methods have moderate to low validity because they are used only for making rough cuts among applicants rather than for final decisions.

Utility

Utility refers to the monetary return associated with using the predictor, relative to its cost. According to researchers and decision makers, when comparing the utility of selection methods, validity appears to be the most important consideration.[117] In short, it would be very unusual for a valid selection method to have low utility.

Thus, as can be seen in Exhibit 8.8, predictors with low validity usually have lower utility. Based on the argument that validity should be related to utility, it is likely that high validity methods will also realize large financial benefits to organizations that choose to use them. However, it is also true that organizations can benefit from even moderate levels of validity, if the predictor is easy-to-implement, cost-effective, and provides incremental returns relative to their cost. For example, the validity (compared with cost) for biodata and weighted application blanks results in high utility levels, despite moderate validity levels. Question marks predominate this column in the exhibit because relatively few studies have directly investigated the utility of these methods.

Applicant Reactions

The applicant reactions column refers to how favorably individuals feel about a given selection practice. Applicant reactions have been suggested as an important criterion because applicants who feel positively about selection methods and the selection process might be more inclined to join or recommend an organization, and they have more positive attitudes toward the organization once hired. Some have argued, however, there is little evidence suggesting that applicant reactions matter for actual behavioral outcomes.[118]

Research suggests that whatever their centrality to the selection process, selection measures that are perceived as job related, that present applicants with an opportunity to perform, that are administered consistently, and that provide applicants with feedback about their performance are likely to generate favorable applicant reactions. Moreover, comprehensive meta-analyses have revealed that explanations justifying the use of selection measures shape applicant perceptions of justice and fairness of the selection process, perceived fit with the job and organization, their affective reactions to the organization, and job acceptance behavioral intentions.[119] Although research on applicants' reactions to specific selection procedures is lacking, evidence has been accumulating and suggests that applicants react more positively to some initial assessment methods, such as interviews, résumés, and cover letters, than to others, such as biodata or reference checks.[120] Given the "Ban the Box" movement we discussed earlier, as well as numerous concerns with privacy, applicants also tend to react negatively to background checks.

Disparate Impact

As reviewed previously, disparate impact refers to the possibility that a disproportionate number of protected-class members may be rejected using a given predictor. Several initial assessment methods have moderate degrees of disparate impact against protected classes, including the résumé and cover letter, training and experience, biographical data, background checks, and initial interview. Letters of recommendation and reference checks tend to display relatively low levels of disparate impact, whereas GPA and level of education tend to display the highest disparate impact out of the initial selection methods.

LEGAL ISSUES

Initial assessment methods are subject to numerous laws, regulations, and other legal considerations. Six major matters of concern pertain to using disclaimers, conducting reference checks, using social media screening, conducting background (credit and criminal) checks, making preemployment inquiries, and making BFOQ claims.

Disclaimers

During the initial stages of contact with job applicants, it is important for the organization to protect itself legally by clearly identifying the rights it wants to maintain. This involves the use of disclaimers, which are statements (usually written) that provide or confer explicit rights to the employer as part of the job seekers' submission of an application. The organization needs to decide (or reevaluate) which rights it wants to retain and how these will be communicated to job applicants.

Three areas of rights are usually suggested for possible inclusion in a disclaimer policy: (1) employment-at-will (right to terminate the employment relationship at any time, for any reason), (2) verification consent (right to verify information provided by the applicant), and (3) false statement warning (right to not hire, terminate, or discipline prospective employee for providing false information to the employer). An example of a disclaimer statement covering these three areas is shown at the bottom of the application blank in Exhibit 8.4. Disclaimer language must be clear, understandable, and conspicuous to the applicant or employee.[121]

Reference Checks

Reference checking creates a legal quagmire for organizations. Current or former employers of the job applicant may be reluctant to provide a reference (especially one with negative information about the applicant) because they fear the applicant may file a defamation suit against them. On the other hand, failure to conduct a reference check opens the organization to the possibility of a negligent hiring suit. To deal with such problems and obtain thorough, accurate information, the following suggestions are offered.

First, gather as much information as possible directly from the applicant, along with a verification consent. This will minimize the use of reference providers and the information demands on them. If you do request reference checks for applicants, make sure the request is made of all applicants and that you are treating everyone equally.

Second, be sure to obtain written authorization from the applicant to check references. The applicant should sign a blanket consent form for this purpose. In addition, the organization could prepare a request-for-reference form that the applicant would give to the person(s) being asked to provide a reference (see Exhibit 8.7).

Third, specify the type of information being requested and obtain the information in writing. The information should be specific, factual, and job related in content; do not seek medical, genetic, or disability information.

Fourth, be wary of (or even prohibit) information obtained from online social networking websites; information provided about applicants by other individuals on these sites should not be treated as a reference. Questions about accuracy, job relatedness, and confidentiality abound for such information. Also, develop a policy about whether your own employees can make recommendations about their current or former colleagues on these sites.

Fifth, limit access to reference information to those making selection decisions. Finally, check relevant state laws about permissible and impermissible reference-check practices. Always be sure that you are complying with EEOC and Federal Trade Commission (FTC) regulations, including record-keeping requirements.[122] Also, determine whether your organization is covered by state reference immunity laws, which provide some degree of immunity from civil liability to organizations that in good faith provide information about the job performance and professional conduct of former or current employees. Organizations in these states (currently 42) may be more willing to request and provide reference information.[123]

Social Media Screening

The scope of social media is broad. Social media includes information shared on social and professional networking sites (e.g., Facebook, LinkedIn, and Twitter), such as personal accounts, photos, video clips, résumés, blogs, podcasts, text messages, and e-mails, and on profiles. They can provide an incredible array of information about job applicants not typically obtained via a carefully constructed selection process. But use of this information can lead to problems, ones that go beyond those that can occur in recruitment via social media.

Legally protected characteristics may be readily available and visible, such as demographics, pregnancy, citizenship, and so on. People with identical names can cause obvious confusion. Information may not be accurate or job related, and it might even be maliciously planted (e.g., a fake account made to defame an individual). Information may depict questionable behavior. Finally, there might be depictions of off-duty conduct that may be legally protected by state and local statutes from being used in assessing applicants, such as smoking, drinking, medical marijuana use, and political activity.

So how might the organization tread in this new and evolving legal selection path? While there are no clear-cut laws or regulations yet, certain suggestions are appropriate. To start, the organization should decide whether to permit the collection and use of social media information in selection. Given the problems noted above, prohibiting such usage could save a lot of potential trouble, and many organizations are taking this option. One study found that only 22% of HR professionals were using social media for screening, and 74% of organizations were abstaining primarily because of legal risks.[124]

If social media is to be used for selection in a food-for-thought sense, what safeguards could be implemented? They include the following:

1. Get applicants' consent to search for social media information (do not ask for username or password) or give applicants a heads-up that such information will be searched for.
2. Decide for which specific positions social media information will be sought and used, and why.
3. Gather and evaluate only job-related, KSAO information for these specific positions.
4. Gather the information late in the process and only for finalists; it could also be gathered post-job offer, as part of a formal background check.
5. Be consistent and standardize the process—get the same information from each applicant at the same stage in the selection process.
6. Focus only on information posted by the applicant, not by others.
7. Allow only HR professionals or other trained people to gather and evaluate the information.
8. Document hiring decisions, especially rejections (including the reason(s)). Be sure to include what information was evaluated in the selection process and any social media information used. Keep a written record of all documentation.
9. Follow all laws, including the Fair Credit Reporting Act (discussed below), and ensure that any third-party vendor used to conduct a social media search follows all laws.

The above suggestions seem daunting and constraining on those who just want to do a "quick check" on applicants. But while these checks may be quick, easy, and seemingly revealing, they may also lead to erroneous and possibly illegal selection decisions. It is thus best to either avoid social media screening altogether or do it appropriately in line with these suggestions.[125]

Background Checks: Credit and Criminal

Credit Checks

Credit checking is coming under heightened legal scrutiny and regulation. Reasons for this include (1) credit report errors, (2) blanket usage of hiring bars for applicants with credit problems, regardless of type of job and job requirements, (3) lack of evidence supporting credit checks as a valid predictor of job performance or theft and embezzlement, and (4) possible disparate impact, especially against minorities. What should the organization do?

The first legal requirement for the organization is to comply with the federal Fair Credit Reporting Act (FCRA). The FCRA governs the gathering and use of background information on applicants and employees. Its requirements apply to both consumer reports and investigative consumer reports. Consumer reports are prepared from accessible databases by a consumer reporting agency and bear on the person's creditworthiness and standing, character, general reputation, personal information, and mode of living. Investigative consumer reports are a subset of consumer reports; they obtain information about the applicant's or employee's general reputation, character, personal characteristics, and mode of living via personal interviews with friends, neighbors, or business associates.

Before obtaining a consumer report, the organization must (1) give the applicant clear notice in writing that a report may be obtained and used in hiring or promotion procedures, and (2) obtain the applicant's written authorization to seek the report. Before taking any adverse action, such as denial of employment, based in whole or part on the report received, the organization must wait a reasonable amount of time and then provide the applicant with a copy of the report and a written description of their consumer rights put forth by the Consumer Financial Protection Bureau. After taking an adverse action, the organization must (1) notify (by written, oral, or electronic means) the applicant of the adverse action, (2) provide the name, address, and phone number of the consumer reporting agency to the applicant, (3) provide notice of the applicant's right to obtain a free copy of the report from the agency and to dispute the accuracy and completeness of the report, and (4) inform the applicant that the agency had no part in the decision.

Another legal requirement is to comply with the state and local laws that govern background checks. This should include the state/locale in which the individual being investigated resides, the reporting agency conducts business, and the requesting organization is incorporated and conducts business.[126]

Several other suggestions are offered for navigating these difficult legal waters. Consider credit checks only for jobs with financial and legal responsibilities, such as tellers, auditors, senior executives, and law enforcement. Be able to explain exactly why a credit check is necessary for the job and allow applicants to explain any unfavorable credit information. Be sure to watch for the development of new credit checking laws and regulations, especially at the state and local levels. Eleven states limit the use of credit information in employment. The Illinois Employer Credit Privacy Act, for example, prohibits employers from inquiring about or using a credit history or report from applicants and employees, except for certain positions, as does New York City.[127]

Criminal Checks

Criminal background checks are generally an attempt to head off potential problems of workplace violence, theft, fraud, and negligent hiring. The collection and use of criminal history (convictions) information is governed by numerous laws and regulations. The need for these protections is the result of several factors: (1) disparate treatment and impact against minorities (especially Blacks and Hispanics) in screening decisions based on the information, (2) the questionable relevance and validity of criminal information for many jobs, (3) use of blanket "no felon" hiring practices, and (4) the inaccuracy of criminal history information in databases and elsewhere.[128] Although there are laws and regulations that guide the use of convictions in employment decisions, an arrest itself does not establish that criminal conduct has occurred. Because of this, state and local preemployment inquiry laws and regulations generally prohibit the collection and use of arrest information, as does the EEOC guidance on preemployment inquiries.

The EEOC enforcement guidance on conviction records warns that collection and the use of conviction records could result in disparate treatment, in which case the organization must be prepared to either defend the impact as job related and consistent with business necessity or take steps to eliminate its occurrence.

For disparate impact the guidance is that there are two ways to meet this defense requirement. The first defense is providing validation evidence about the criminal history screening procedure, based on the Uniform Guidelines on Employee Selection Procedures (discussed in the next chapter). The evidence must show that the screening procedure is predictive of important employment outcomes, such as job performance or theft.

The second defense is for the organization to have a targeted screening procedure. The procedure must consider three factors in showing how specific criminal conduct may be linked to important employment outcomes for a specific position:

1. The nature and severity of the offense or conduct
2. The time that has passed since the offense, conduct, or sentence completion
3. The nature of the job held or sought

Moreover, in the procedure, the organization must conduct an individualized assessment for those who may be rejected for the job. In that assessment, the organization should tell the person a rejection may occur, let the person show reasons why the rejection should not occur, and consider whether a rejection would be job related and consistent with business necessity.

Finally, the enforcement guidelines do not preempt federal restrictions on hiring persons with convictions for certain jobs (e.g., airport security screener, law enforcement officer, child-care worker, bank employee, or port worker) or federal occupation and licensing requirements.

At the state and local levels, there is a wide variety of requirements and prohibitions on gathering and using criminal background information. Some states and localities prohibit asking about criminal history until after an interview or a conditional job offer. As mentioned earlier, this is sometimes called "Ban the Box," and these types of prohibitions are increasing. However, states may also provide exceptions that legally require criminal history information right away, much like the federal restrictions, for certain jobs.

Usage of criminal history information is also regulated. In New York, for example, refusal to hire must consider job responsibilities, time since the crime was committed, an applicant's age at the time of the crime, and seriousness of the offense. There may also be exemptions for conviction usage. Washington, for example, exempts law enforcement agencies, state agencies, school districts, and organizations that have a direct responsibility for the supervision, care, or treatment of children, mentally ill persons, or other vulnerable adults.[129]

If the organization uses a third-party vendor to conduct criminal background checks, the vendor must comply with the legal requirements described above. The organization should carefully choose vendors that practice compliance, and it should be wary of vendors that promise to provide "instant check" services, since such rapid service may well violate EEOC guidance and the FCRA.

Preemployment Inquiries

The term "preemployment inquiry" (PI) pertains to eliciting information through any selection method, such as an application blank or interview question, about applicants' personal and background data, such as demographics (race, color, religion, sex, national origin, and age), physical characteristics (disability, height, and weight), family and associates, residence, economic status, and education. At times, PIs may also occur as part of an unstructured interview.

PIs have been singled out for legal (equal employment opportunity and affirmative action [EEO/AA]) attention at both the federal and state levels. The reason for this is that PIs have great potential for use in a discriminatory manner early in the selection process. Moreover, research continually finds that organizations make inappropriate and illegal PIs. One study, for example, found that out of 48 categories of application blank items, employers used an average of 5.4 inadvisable items on their application blanks for customer service jobs.[130] It is thus critical to understand the laws and regulations surrounding the use of PIs.

Federal Laws and Regulations

The laws and their interpretation indicate that it is illegal to use PI information that has a disparate impact based on a protected characteristic (race, color, etc.), unless such disparate impact can be shown to be job related and consistent with business necessity. The emphasis here is on the potentially illegal use of the information rather than on its collection per se.

EEOC Guide to Preemployment Inquiries. The EEOC guide provides the principles given above, along with specific guidance (dos and don'ts) on PIs regarding race, color, religion, sex, national origin, age, height and weight, marital status, number of children, provisions for child care, English language skill, educational requirements, friends or relatives working for the employer, arrest records, conviction records, discharge from military service, citizenship, economic status, and availability for work on weekends or holidays.

Americans With Disabilities Act Regulations.   There appears to be a fine line between permissible and impermissible information that may be gathered, and between appropriate and inappropriate methods for gathering it, under the Americans With Disabilities Act (ADA). To help employers, the EEOC has developed specific enforcement guidance on these matters.

The general thrust of the guidance is that the organization may not ask disability-related questions and may not conduct medical examinations until after it makes a conditional job offer to a person. Once that offer is made, however, the organization may ask disability-related questions and conduct medical examinations so long as this is done for all entering employees in the job category. When such questions or exams screen out a person with a disability, the reason for rejection must be job related and consistent with business necessity. A person who provides a direct threat of substantial harm to themselves or others may be rejected for safety reasons. We will have more to say about the legality of medical examinations in the next chapter.

More specific guidance is provided for the pre-offer stage as follows. Disability-related questions cannot be asked, meaning questions that (1) inquire whether a person has a disability, (2) are likely to elicit information about a disability, or (3) are closely related to asking about a disability. Along with these general prohibitions, it is impermissible to ask applicants whether they will need reasonable accommodation to perform the functions of the job or can perform major life activities (e.g., lifting, walking), to ask about lawful use of drugs, to ask about workers' compensation history, or to ask third parties (e.g., former employers, references) questions that cannot be asked of the applicant.

Alternatively, before the offer is made, it is permissible to ask:

- Whether the applicant can perform the job, with or without reasonable accommodation
- Whether the applicant can meet the organization's attendance requirement
- Whether the applicant will need reasonable accommodation for the hiring process (unless there is an obvious disability or the applicant discloses a disability)
- The applicant to provide documentation of a disability if requesting reasonable accommodation for the hiring process
- The applicant to describe or demonstrate how they would perform the job (including any needed reasonable accommodation)
- The applicant for certifications and licenses

- About the applicant's current illegal use of drugs (but not past addiction)
- About the applicant's drinking habits (but not alcoholism)

State Laws and Regulations

There is a vast cache of state laws and regulations pertaining to PIs. These requirements vary substantially among the states and are often more stringent and inclusive than federal laws and regulations. The organization thus must become familiar with and adhere to the laws for each state in which it is located. An example of Ohio state law regarding PIs is shown in Exhibit 8.9. Notice how the example points out both lawful and unlawful ways of gathering PI information.

EXHIBIT 8.9 **Ohio Employment Guide—Questioning Applicants**

Inquiry	Lawful	Unlawful
Name	Name	Inquiry into any title that would indicate race, color, religion, sex, national origin, disability, age, or ancestry
Address	Inquiry into place and length of time at current address	Inquiry into any foreign addresses that would indicate national origin
Age	Any inquiry limited to establishing that applicant meets any minimum age requirement that may be established by law	A. Requirement of birth certificate or baptismal record B. Any inquiry that would reveal the date of high school graduation C. Any other inquiry that would reveal whether applicant is at least 40 years of age
Race, color, religion		Any inquiry that would indicate applicant's race, color, or religion
Sex		Any inquiry that would indicate the applicant's sex
Height and weight	Inquiries as to a person's ability to perform actual job duties and responsibilities	A requirement of a certain height or weight, unless the employer can show that no employee with the ineligible height or weight could do the work
Birthplace, national origin, ancestry		A. Any inquiry into place of birth B. Any inquiry into place of birth of parents, grandparents, or spouse C. Any other inquiry into national origin or ancestry

(continued)

EXHIBIT 8.9 **Continued**

Inquiry	Lawful	Unlawful
Citizenship	A. Whether a US citizen B. If not, whether applicant intends to become one C. If US residence is legal D. If spouse is citizen E. A requirement of proof of citizenship after hire F. Any other requirement mandated by the Immigration Reform and Control Act of 1986, as amended	A. Any inquiry that would indicate whether the applicant is native-born or naturalized B. A requirement of proof of citizenship before hire C. Any inquiry that would indicate whether the applicant's parents or spouse are native-born or naturalized
Disability	Inquiries necessary to determine applicant's ability to substantially perform a specific job without significant hazard	A. Any inquiry into past or current medical conditions B. Any inquiry into workers' compensation or similar claims
Work schedules	Inquiry into the job applicant's willingness to work a required schedule	Any inquiry into the job applicant's willingness to work any particular religious holidays
References	General, personal, and work references that do not reveal the race, color, religion, sex, national origin, disability, ancestry, or age of the applicant	Request for references specifically from clergy or any other persons that might reflect the race, color, religion, sex, national origin, disability, ancestry, or age of the applicant
Organizations	Inquiry into membership in organizations excluding those that reveal the race, color, religion, sex, national origin, disability, ancestry, or age of its members	Inquiry into every club and organization where membership is held, including those that reveal the race, color, religion, sex, national origin, disability, ancestry, or age of its members
Other	Any questions required to reveal qualifications for the job for which the applicant applied	Any non-job-related inquiry that may elicit information concerning race, color, religion, sex, national origin, disability, age, or ancestry of applicant

NOTE: The above is not a complete definition of what can and cannot be asked of applicants. It attempts to answer the questions most frequently asked concerning the law. The document specifically pertains to Ohio law and not the laws of any other state or any federal laws.
SOURCE: Ohio Civil Rights Commission, 2013.

One common PI that has been receiving increased attention at the city, county, and state levels is salary history inquiries. Many localities are banning salary history PIs as they are believed to perpetuate gender pay disparities. Currently, seven states and many cities and counties have outlawed salary history PIs.[131]

Bona Fide Occupational Qualifications (BFOQs)

Title VII of the Civil Rights Act explicitly permits the use of sex (including sexual orientation and gender identity), religion, or national origin (but not other protected class information) if it can be shown to be a BFOQ "reasonably necessary to the normal operation" of the business. The Age Discrimination in Employment Act (ADEA) contains a similar provision regarding age. These provisions thus permit the rejection of applicants because of their sex, religion, national origin, or age, if the rejection can be justified under the "reasonably necessary" standard.

Exactly how have BFOQ claims by employers fared? When are BFOQ claims upheld as legitimate? Several points are relevant to understanding the BFOQ issue. The burden of proof is on the employer to justify any BFOQ claim, and the BFOQ exception is narrowly construed.

To successfully defend a BFOQ claim, the organization must show that only (or just about only) people with the protected class characteristic can do the job, and that the job is integral to the essence and operation of the business. The bar for showing this sanctioned discrimination is very high. A classic case of usually not meeting the bar is a BFOQ claim based on customer, client, or coworker preferences. Examples include women customers preferring only women salespeople, or a refusal to hire people who wear turbans or hijabs due to a fear that customers or coworkers will not want to interact with them. Such preference claims usually cannot be successfully defended by the employer.[132]

BFOQ claims that might exceed the bar have involved rationale relating to authenticity (e.g., male actors for male roles), public safety (e.g., age requirements for transportation employees such as drivers or pilots), and privacy (e.g., female guards only for female prisoners). But even these examples are not clear cut. The success of a claim for female guards only might depend on how inhospitable and dangerous the work environment is (e.g., maximum versus minimum security prison). As another example, BFOQ claims based on privacy concerns may be justified when personal contact is required, such as jobs involving personal hygiene, health care, and rape victims. As a final example involving safety issues, an employer's fetal protection policy that excluded women from certain jobs leading to exposure to lead in the manufacture of batteries was held not to be a permissible BFOQ.

The discussion and examples here should make clear that BFOQ claims involve complex situations and considerations. The burden of proof to defend BFOQ claims lies with the organization. BFOQ provisions in the law are and continue to be construed very narrowly. The employer thus must have an overwhelming preponderance of evidence on its side in order to make and successfully defend a BFOQ claim.

SUMMARY

This chapter reviewed the processes involved in external selection and focused specifically on methods of initial assessment. Before candidates are assessed, it is important to base assessment methods on the logic of prediction and to use a selection plan. The logic of prediction focuses on the correspondence between elements in applicants' past situations and KSAOs critical to success on the job in question. The selection plan involves the process of detailing the required KSAOs and indicating which selection methods will be used to assess each KSAO, as well as their content and form. The selection sequence is the means by which the selection process is used to narrow the initial applicant pool to candidates, then finalists, and, eventually, job offer receivers.

Initial assessment methods are used during the early stages of the selection sequence to reduce the applicant pool to candidates for further assessment. The methods of initial assessment were reviewed in some detail; they include résumés and cover letters, application blanks, biographical information, reference and background checks, and initial interviews. Initial assessment methods differ widely in their usefulness. How these methods can be evaluated for potential use include frequency of use, cost, reliability, validity, utility, applicant reactions, and disparate impact.

Legal issues need to be considered in making initial assessments about applicants. The use of disclaimers as a protective mechanism is critical. Also, three areas of initial assessment that require special attention are reference and background checking, PIs, and BFOQs.

DISCUSSION QUESTIONS

1. A selection plan describes the predictor(s) that will be used to assess the KSAOs required to perform the job. What are the three steps to follow in establishing a selection plan?
2. In what ways are the initial assessment methods discussed similar and in what ways are they different?
3. Describe the criteria by which initial assessment methods are evaluated. Are some of these criteria more important than others?
4. Some methods of initial assessment appear to be more useful than others. If you were starting your own business, which initial assessment methods would you use and why?
5. How can organizations avoid legal difficulties in the use of preemployment inquiries in initial selection decisions?

ETHICAL ISSUES

1. Is it wrong to pad one's résumé with information that, while not an outright lie, is an enhancement? For example, would it be wrong to term one's job "maintenance coordinator" when in fact one simply emptied garbage cans?

2. Do you think employers have a right to check applicants' backgrounds? Even if there is no suspicion of misbehavior? Even if the job poses no security or sensitivity risks? Even if the background check includes driving offenses and credit histories?

APPLICATIONS

Reference Reports and Initial Assessment in a Start-Up Company

Stanley Jausneister owns a small high-tech start-up company called BioServer-Systems (BSS). Stanley's company specializes in selling web server space to clients (e.g., dedicated server hosting). The server space that Stanley markets runs from a network of computers. This networked configuration allows BSS to manage its server space more efficiently and provides greater flexibility to its customers, who often want weekly or even daily updates of their websites. The other innovation Stanley brought to BSS is special security encryption software protocols that make the BSS server space nearly impossible for hackers to access. This flexibility is particularly attractive to organizations that need to manage large, security-protected databases with multiple points of access. Stanley has even been contacted by the government, which is interested in using BSS's systems for some of its classified intelligence.

Due to its niche, BSS has experienced rapid growth. In the past year, BSS hired 12 programmers and 2 marketers, as well as a general manager, an HR manager, and other support personnel. Before starting BSS, Stanley was a manager with a large pharmaceutical firm. Because of his industry connections, most of BSS's business has been with drug and chemical companies.

Yesterday, Stanley received a phone call from Lee Rogers, head of biotechnology for Mercelle-Poulet, one of BSS's largest customers. Lee is an old friend, and he was one of BSS's first customers. Lee had called to express concern about BSS's security. One area of Mercelle-Poulet's biotech division is responsible for research and development on vaccines for various bioterrorist chemical weapons. Because the research and development on these vaccines require the company to develop cultures of the biological weapons themselves, Lee has used BSS to house information for this area. A great deal of sensitive information is housed on BSS's servers, including in some cases the formulas used in developing the cultures.

Despite the sensitivity of the information on BSS's servers, given BSS's advanced software, Stanley was very surprised to hear Lee's concern about security. "It's not your software that worries me," Lee commented, "it's the people running it." Lee explained that last week a Mercelle-Poulet researcher was arrested for attempting to sell certain cultures to an overseas client. This individual had been dismissed from a previous pharmaceutical company for unethical behavior, but this information did not surface during the individual's background check. This incident not only caused Lee to reexamine Mercelle-Poulet's background checks, but also made him think of BSS, as certain BSS employees have access to Mercelle-Poulet's information.

Instantly after hearing Lee's concern, Stanley realized he had a problem. Like many small employers, BSS did not do thorough background checks on its employees. It assumed that the information provided on the application was accurate and generally only called the applicant's previous employer (often with ineffective results). Stanley realized he needed to do more, not only to keep Lee's business but also to protect his company and customers.

1. What sort of background testing should BSS conduct on its applicants?
2. Is there any information BSS should avoid obtaining for legal or EEO reasons?
3. How can BSS know that its background testing programs are effective?
4. In the past, BSS has used the following initial assessment methods: application blank, interviews with Stanley and other BSS managers, and a follow-up with the applicant's former employer. Beyond changes to its background testing program, would you suggest any other alterations to BSS's initial assessment process?

Developing a Lawful Application Blank

Consolidated Trucking Corporation, Inc. (CTCI) is a rapidly growing short-haul (local) firm within the greater Columbus, Ohio, area. It has grown primarily through the acquisition of numerous small, family-owned trucking companies. Currently it has a fleet of 150 trucks and over 250 full-time drivers. Most of the drivers were hired initially by the firms that CTCI acquired, and they accepted generous offers to become members of the CTCI team. CTCI's expansion plans are very ambitious, but they will be fulfilled primarily from internal growth rather than additional acquisitions. Consequently, CTCI is now faced with the need to develop an external staffing system that will be geared to hire 75 new truckers within the next two years.

Terry Tailgater is a former truck driver for CTCI who was promoted to truck maintenance supervisor, a position he has held for the past five years. Once CTCI's internal expansion plans were finalized, the firm's HR director (and sole member of the HR department), Harold Hornblower, decided he needed a new person to handle staffing and employment law duties. Harold promoted Terry Tailgater to the job of staffing manager. One of Terry's major assignments was to develop a new staffing system for truck drivers.

One of the first projects Terry undertook was to develop a new, standardized application blank for the job of truck driver. To do this, Terry looked at the many different application blanks the current drivers had completed for their former companies. (These records were given to CTCI at the time of acquisition.) The application blanks showed that a large amount of information was requested and that the specific information sought varied among the application forms. Terry scanned the various forms and made a list of all the questions the forms contained. He then decided to evaluate each question in terms of its probable lawfulness under federal and state (Ohio) laws. Terry wanted to identify and use only lawful questions on the new form he is developing.

The following is the list of questions Terry developed, along with columns labeled "probably lawful" and "probably unlawful." Assume that you are Terry and are deciding on the lawfulness of each question. Place a check mark in the appropriate column for each question and prepare a justification for its mark as "probably lawful" or "probably unlawful."

Questions Terry Is Considering Including on Application Blank

Question About	Probably Lawful	Probably Unlawful
Birthplace	_____	_____
Previous arrests	_____	_____
Previous felony convictions	_____	_____
Distance between work and residence	_____	_____
Domestic responsibilities	_____	_____
Height	_____	_____
Weight	_____	_____
Previous work experience	_____	_____
Educational attainment	_____	_____
Favorite high school subjects	_____	_____
Grade point average	_____	_____
Received workers' compensation in past	_____	_____
Currently receiving workers' compensation	_____	_____
Child-care arrangements	_____	_____
Length of time on previous job	_____	_____
Reason for leaving previous job	_____	_____
Age	_____	_____
Sex	_____	_____
Home ownership	_____	_____
Any current medical problems	_____	_____
History of mental illness	_____	_____
OK to seek references from previous employer?	_____	_____
Have you provided complete/truthful information?	_____	_____
Native language	_____	_____
Willing to work on Easter and Christmas	_____	_____
Get recommendation from pastor/priest	_____	_____

ENDNOTES

1. R. Gillett and A. Cain, "38 Things You Should Never Include on Your Resume," *Business Insider*, Mar. 14, 2018 (*www.businessinsider.com/dont-put-these-things-on-your-resume-2015-75*); M. Tarpey, "5 Things to Leave Off Your Resume," *Career Builder*, Feb. 9, 2018 (*www.careerbuilder.com/advice /5-things-to-leave-off-your-resume*).

2. Gillet and Cain, "38 Things You Should Never Include on Your Resume."

3. D. T. Maurath, C. W. Wright, D. E. Wittorp, and D. Hardtke, "Volunteer Experience May Not Bridge Gaps in Employment," *International Journal of Selection and Assessment*, 2015, 23, pp. 284–294; C. L. Wilkin and C. E. Connelly, "Do I Look Like Someone Who Cares? Recruiters' Ratings of Applicants' Paid and Volunteer Experience," *International Journal of Selection and Assessment*, 2012, 20, pp. 308–318.

4. D. S. Chapman, K. L. Uggerslev, S. A. Carroll, K. A. Piasentin, and D. A. Jones, "Applicant Attraction to Organizations and Job Choice: A Meta-Analytic Review of the Correlates of Recruiting Outcomes," *Journal of Applied Psychology*, 2005, 90, pp. 928–944; J. W. Smither, R. R. Reilly, R. E. Millsap, K. Pearlman, and R. W. Stoffey, "Applicant Reactions to Selection Procedures," *Personnel Psychology*, 1993, 46, pp. 49–76; K. L. Uggerslev, N. E. Fassina, and D. Kraichy, "Recruiting Through the Stages: A Meta-Analytic Test of Predictors of Applicant Attraction at Different Stages of the Recruiting Process," *Personnel Psychology*, 2012, 65, pp. 597–660.

5. P. F. Wernimont and J. P. Campbell, "Signs, Samples, and Criteria," *Journal of Applied Psychology*, 1968, 52, pp. 372–376.

6. F. Lievens, W. De Corte, and L. Westerveld, "Understanding the Building Blocks of Selection Procedures: Effects of Response Fidelity on Performance and Validity," *Journal of Management*, 2015, 41, pp. 1604–1627.

7. M. C. Campion, M. A. Campion, E. D. Campion, and M. H. Reider, "Initial Investigation Into Computer Scoring of Candidate Essays for Personnel Selection," *Journal of Applied Psychology*, 2016, 101(7), pp. 958–975.

8. S. W. J. Kozlowski and R. P. DeShon, "A Psychological Fidelity Approach to Simulation-Based Training: Theory, Research, and Principles," in E. Salas, L. R. Elliott, S. G. Schflett, and M. D. Coovert (eds.), *Scaled Worlds: Development, Validation, and Applications* (Burlington, VT: Ashgate, 2004), pp. 75–99; E. L. Thorndike and R. S. Woodworth, "The Influence of Improvement in One Mental Function Upon the Efficiency of Other Functions," *Psychological Review*, 1901, 8, pp. 247–261.

9. S. Sajjadiani, A. J. Sojourner, J. D. Kammeyer-Mueller, and E. Mykerezi, "Using Machine Learning to Translate Applicant Work History Into Predictors of Performance and Turnover," *Journal of Applied Psychology*, 2019, 104(10), pp. 1207–1225.

10. C. A. Henle, B. R. Dineen, and M. K. Duffy, "Assessing Intentional Resume Deception: Development and Nomological Network of a Resume Fraud Measure," *Journal of Business and Psychology*, 2019, 34, pp. 87–106; M. Waung, P. McAuslan, J. M. DiMambro, and N. Miȩgoć, "Impression Management Use in Resumes and Cover Letters," *Journal of Business and Psychology*, 2017, 32, pp. 727–746.

11. A. Bibby, "Why Video Resumes Are on the Rise," *FlexJobs* (blog), Oct. 14, 2017 (*www.flexjobs .com/blog/post/video-resumes-rise/*); Z. Ihsan and A. Furnham, "The New Technologies in Personality Assessment: A Review," *Consulting Psychology Journal: Practice and Research*, 2018, 70(2), pp. 147–166.

12. V. Luckerson, "Finding a Job in 2012: Real-Life Success Stories," *Time*, June 21, 2012 (*http:// business.time.com/2012/06/21/finding-a-job-in-2012-real-life-success-stories/*).

13. Robert Half, "Best Resume Format: Traditional Trumps Trendy," *Robert Half* (blog), May 5, 2016 (*www.roberthalf.com/blog/writing-a-resume/best-resume-format*).

14. A. Ellin, "Lights! Camera! It's Time to Make a Résumé," *New York Times*, Apr. 21, 2007, pp. B1, B6; K. Gurchiek, "Video Résumé Use Rises, but So Do Big Questions," *SHRM Online*, Apr. 12, 2007, pp. 1–2.

15. C. Apers and E. Derous, "Are They Accurate? Recruiters' Personality Judgments in Paper Versus Video Resumes," *Computers in Human Behavior*, 2017, 73, pp. 9–19; M. S. Cole, H. S. Field, W. F. Giles, and S. G. Harris, "Recruiters' Inferences of Applicant Personality Based on Résumé Screening: Do Paper People Have a Personality?" *Journal of Business and Psychology*, 2009, 24, pp. 5–18; Ihsan and Furnham, "The New Technologies in Personality Assessment: A Review"; M. Waung, R. W. Hymes, and J. E. Beatty, "The Effects of Video and Paper Résumés on Assessments of Personality, Applied Social Skills, Mental Capability, and Résumé Outcomes," *Basic and Applied Social Psychology*, 2014, 36, pp. 238–251.

16. M. Waung, R. W. Hymes, J. E. Beatty, and P. McAuslan, "Self-Promotion Statements in Video Résumés: Frequency, Intensity, and Gender Effects on Job Applicant Evaluation," *International Journal of Selection and Assessment*, 2015, 23, pp. 345–360.

17. A. M. F. Hiemstra and E. Derous, "Video Resumes Portrayed: Findings and Challenges," in I. Nikolaou and J. K. Oostrom (eds.), *Employee Recruitment, Selection, and Assessment: Contemporary Issues for Theory and Practice* (East Sussex, UK: Psychology Press, 2015), pp. 44–60.

18. A. M. F. Hiemstra, E. Derous, A. W. Serlie, and M. P. Born, "Fairness Perceptions of Video Résumés Among Ethnically Diverse Applicants," *International Journal of Selection and Assessment*, 2012, 20, pp. 423–433.

19. M. J. de la Merced, "Student's Video Résumé Gets Attention (Some of It Unwanted)," *New York Times*, Oct. 21, 2006, pp. B1, B6.

20. C. Benz, "How to Make a Video Resume," *Glassdoor* (blog), Oct. 14, 2014 (*www.glassdoor.com/blog/how-to-make-a-video-resume/*).

21. A. Doyle, "How to Use Your LinkedIn Profile as a Resume," *The Balance Careers* (blog), Sept. 30, 2019 (*www.thebalancecareers.com/how-to-use-your-linkedin-profile-as-a-resume-2062598*); D. Meigs, "Can You Land a Job With 140 Characters?" *CNN*, Apr. 22, 2013 (*www.cnn.com/2013/04/22/business/twitter-resume-cv-job/index.html*).

22. B. Horovitz, "Forget Résumés, Tweet for the Job," *USA Today*, Feb. 18, 2013, p. 3A.

23. P. Yang, "Resume Study: How LinkedIn Affects the Interview Chances of Job Applicants," Mar. 17, 2019 (*www.resumego.net/research/linkedin-interview-chances/*).

24. J. Zide, B. Elman, and C. Shahani-Denning, "LinkedIn and Recruitment: How Profiles Differ Across Occupations," *Employee Relations*, 2014, 36(5), pp. 583–604.

25. Waung et al., "Impression Management Use in Resumes and Cover Letters."

26. Career Builder, "Employers Share Their Most Outrageous Resume Mistakes and Instant Deal Breakers in a New CareerBuilder Study" (press release), Aug. 24, 2018 (*http://press.careerbuilder.com/2018-08-24-Employers-Share-Their-Most-Outrageous-Resume-Mistakes-and-Instant-Deal-Breakers-in-a-New-CareerBuilder-Study?_ga=2.75816541.919593277.1535129260-116826127.1535129260*); HireRight, *2019 Employment Screening Benchmark Report* (Irvine, CA: author, 2019).

27. N. L. Pesce, "These Are the Most Outrageous Lies People Have Put on Their Résumés," *MarketWatch*, Aug. 30, 2019 (*www.marketwatch.com/story/these-are-the-most-hilarious-lies-people-have-put-on-their-resumes-2018-08-24*).

28. Pesce, "These Are the Most Outrageous Lies People Have Put on Their Résumés"; H. Restle and J. Smith, "17 Successful Executives Who Have Lied on Their Resumes," *Business Insider*, July 15, 2015 (*www.businessinsider.com/successful-executives-who-have-lied-on-their-resumes-2015-7*).

29. K. M. Kuhn, T. R. Johnson, and D. Miller, "Applicant Desirability Influences Reactions to Discovered Résumé Embellishments," *International Journal of Selection and Assessment*, 2013, 21, pp. 111–120.

30. K. Maher, "Job Seekers Use Imagination When Creating Their Resumes," *Wall Street Journal*, May 6, 2003 (*www.wsj.com/articles/SB105216957258592200*).

31. D. Papandrea, "The Biggest Resume Lies to Avoid," *Monster* (*www.monster.com/career-advice/article /the-truth-about-resume-lies-hot-jobs*), accessed Feb. 3, 2020; Monster, "Despite Recruiter Confidence, Exaggeration and Skills Gaps Plague the Hiring Process" (press release), Oct. 22, 2019 (*www.monster.com/about/a/State-of-the-Recruiter-2019*).

32. S. M. Heathfield, "Do You Know Who You're Hiring?" *The Balance Careers* (blog), June 25, 2019 (*www.thebalancecareers.com/do-you-know-who-you-re-hiring-1919148*).

33. A. Fennell, "Spelling Mistakes Won't Ruin Your Resume, but These Things Will," *Fast Company*, Oct. 29, 2018 (*www.fastcompany.com/90257859/spelling-mistakes-wont-ruin-your-resume-but-these -things-will*); A. Gannett, "Do Resume Typos Matter? Here's What Hundreds of LinkedIn Users Say," *Fast Company*, Feb. 28, 2018 (*www.fastcompany.com/40536077/do-resume-typos-matter-heres -what-hundreds-of-linkedin-users-say*); H. Hamilton, "5 Resume Mistakes That Will Cost You the Job," *Monster* (blog) (*www.monster.com/career-advice/article/resume-mistakes-that-will-cost-you-the-job*), accessed Feb. 3, 2020.

34. M. Abadi, "482 Hiring Managers Looked at Nearly 20,000 Résumés and Found the Classic Advice to Limit Your Résumé to One Page Might Be Wrong After All," *Business Insider*, Nov. 14, 2018 (*www.businessinsider.com/resume-length-two-pages-or-one-2018-11*); P. Yang, "Settling the Debate: One or Two Page Resumes," *ResumeGo* (blog), Nov. 10, 2018 (*www.resumego.net /research/one-or-two-page-resumes/*).

35. Waung et al., "Impression Management Use in Resumes and Cover Letters."

36. J. K. Arnulf, L. Tegner, and Ø. Larssen, "Impression Making by Résumé Layout: Its Impact on the Probability of Being Shortlisted," *European Journal of Work and Organizational Psychology*, 2010, 19, pp. 221–230; M. Singletary, "Beefing Up a Résumé," *Washington Post*, Aug. 1, 2013 (*www.washingtonpost.com/business/beefing-up-a-resume/2013/08/01/97614b3a-f9fd-11e2-8752 -b41d7ed1f685_story.html*).

37. J. Shields, "Wordsmithing Your Resume: Tenses, Plurals, and Optimized Keywords," *Jobscan* (blog), Oct. 11, 2017 (*www.jobscan.co/blog/resume-tenses-plurals-keywords/*).

38. S. B. Knouse, R. A. Giacalone, and H. Pollard, "Impression Management in the Résumé and Its Cover Letter," *Journal of Business and Psychology*, 1988, 3(2), pp. 242–249; A. Varma, S. M. Toh, and S. Pichler, "Ingratiation in Job Applicants: Impact on Selection Decisions," *Journal of Managerial Psychology*, 2006, 21(3), pp. 200–210.

39. A. Bleske-Rechek, K. Paulich, P. Shafer, and C. Kofman, "Grammar Matters: The Tainting Effect of Grammar Usage Errors on Judgments of Competence and Character," *Personality and Individual Differences*, 2019, 141, pp. 47–50.

40. M. S. Cole, R. S. Rubin, H. S. Feild, and W. F. Giles, "Recruiters' Perceptions and Use of Applicant Résumé Information: Screening the Recent Graduate," *Applied Psychology: An International Review*, 2007, 56(2), pp. 319–343.

41. Cole et al., "Recruiters' Inferences of Applicant Personality Based on Résumé Screening: Do Paper People Have a Personality?"; W.-C. Tsai, N.-W. Chi, T.-C. Huang, and A.-J. Hsu, "The Effects of Applicant Résumé Contents on Recruiters' Hiring Recommendations: The Mediating Roles of Recruiter Fit Perceptions," *Applied Psychology: An International Review*, 2011, 60(2), pp. 231–254.

42. E. Derous, A. M. Ryan, and H. D. Nguyen, "Multiple Categorization in Résumé Screening: Examining Effects on Hiring Discrimination Against Arab Applicants in Field and Lab Settings," *Journal of Organizational Behavior*, 2012, 33, pp. 544–570; E. Derous, A. M. Ryan, and A. W. Serlie, "Double Jeopardy Upon Résumé Screening: When Achmed Is Less Employable Than Aïsha," *Personnel Psychology*, 2015, 68, pp. 659–696; L. R. Martinez, C. D. White, J. R. Shapiro,

and M. R. Hebl, "Selection BIAS: Stereotypes and Discrimination Related to Having a History of Cancer," *Journal of Applied Psychology*, 2016, 11, pp. 122–128; A. M. F. Hiemstra, E. Derous, A. W. Serlie, and M. P. Born, "Ethnicity Effects in Graduates' Résumé Content," *Applied Psychology: An International Review*, 2013, 62, pp. 427–453.

43. A. M. Saks, J. D. Leck, and D. M. Saunders, "Effects of Application Blanks and Employment Equity on Applicant Reactions and Job Pursuit Intentions," *Journal of Organizational Behavior*, 1995, 16, pp. 415–430; J. C. Wallace, E. E. Page, and M. Lippstreu, "Applicant Reactions to Pre-employment Application Blanks: A Legal and Procedural Justice Perspective," *Journal of Business and Psychology*, 2006, 20(4), pp. 467–488.

44. A. Howard, "College Experiences and Managerial Performance," *Journal of Applied Psychology*, 1986, 71, pp. 530–552; R. Merritt-Halston and K. N. Wexley, "Educational Requirements: Legality and Validity," *Personnel Psychology*, 1983, 36, pp. 743–753.

45. C. Murray, *Real Education: Four Simple Truths for Bringing America's Schools Back to Reality* (New York: Crown Forum, 2008); T. W. H. Ng and D. C. Feldman, "How Broadly Does Education Contribute to Job Performance?" *Personnel Psychology*, 2009, 62, pp. 89–134.

46. College Board, *Trends in College Pricing 2019: Published Charges Over Time* (*https://research.collegeboard.org/pdf/2019-trendsincp-table-2.pdf*), accessed Feb. 3, 2020.

47. J. Barrett, "What's the Value of a College Education? It Depends," *CNBC* (Debt by Degree), June 19, 2015 (*www.cnbc.com/2015/06/19/is-a-college-degree-overvalued.html*); W. J. Bennett and D. Wilezol, *Is College Worth It? A Former United States Secretary of Education and a Liberal Arts Graduate Expose the Broken Promise of Higher Education* (Nashville, TN: Thomas Nelson, 2013); A. Williams, "Saying No to College," *New York Times*, Nov. 30, 2012 (*www.nytimes.com/2012/12/02/fashion/saying-no-to-college.html?pagewanted=all&_r=0*), accessed Aug. 9, 2013.

48. J. R. Abel and R. Deitz, "Despite Rising Costs, College Is Still a Good Investment," *Federal Reserve Bank of New York*, June 5, 2019 (*https://libertystreeteconomics.newyorkfed.org/2019/06/despite-rising-costs-college-is-still-a-good-investment.html*); A. P. Carnevale, B. Cheah, and M. Van der Werf, *A First Try at ROI: Ranking 4,500 Colleges* (Washington, DC: Center on Education and the Workforce, Georgetown University, 2019); E. Kerr, "Is College Worth the Cost?" *U.S. News & World Report*, June 17, 2019 (*www.usnews.com/education/best-colleges/paying-for-college/articles/2019-06-17/is-college-worth-the-cost*).

49. A. L. Watson, "Employment Trends by Typical Entry-Level Education Requirement," *Monthly Labor Review*, Sept. 2017, pp. 1–22.

50. A. E. McKinney, K. D. Carlson, R. L. Meachum, N. C. D'Angelo, and M. L. Connerley, "Recruiters' Use of GPA in Initial Screening Decisions: Higher GPAs Don't Always Make the Cut," *Personnel Psychology*, 2003, 56, pp. 823–845; P. L. Roth, C. A. BeVier, F. S. Switzer, and J. S. Schippman, "Meta-Analyzing the Relationship Between Grades and Job Performance," *Journal of Applied Psychology*, 1996, 81, pp. 548–556; P. L. Roth and P. Bobko, "College Grade Point Average as a Personnel Selection Device: Ethnic Group Differences and Potential Adverse Impact," *Journal of Applied Psychology*, 2000, 85, pp. 399–406.

51. U.S. News & World Report, "U.S. News Education Rankings: Colleges," 2020 (*www.usnews.com/best-colleges/rankings*), accessed February 3, 2020.

52. G. Daugherty, "Is University Prestige Really That Important?" *Investopedia*, June 25, 2019 (*www.investopedia.com/articles/personal-finance/051915/university-prestige-really-important.asp*); E. R. Eide and M. J. Hilmer, "Do Elite Colleges Lead to Higher Salaries? Only for Some Professions," *Wall Street Journal*, Jan. 31, 2016 (*www.wsj.com/articles/do-elite-colleges-lead-to-higher-salaries-only-for-some-professions-1454295674*); S. Jaschik, "College Selectivity and Income," *Inside Higher Ed*, Aug. 22, 2016 (*www.insidehighered.com/news/2016/08/22/study-finds-graduates-most-selective-colleges-enjoy-earnings-payoff*).

53. L. H. Pinto and D. C. Ramalheira, "Perceived Employability of Business Graduates: The Effect of Academic Performance and Extracurricular Activities," *Journal of Vocational Behavior*, 2017, 99, pp. 165–178; R. S. Robin, W. H. Bommer, and T. T. Baldwin, "Using Extracurricular Activity as an Indicator of Interpersonal Skill: Prudent Evaluation or Recruiting Malpractice?" *Human Resource Management*, 2002, 41(4), pp. 441–454.

54. D. Holtbrügge and F. Engelhard, "Study Abroad Programs: Individual Motivations, Cultural Intelligence, and the Mediating Role of Cultural Boundary Spanning," *Academy of Management Learning & Education*, 2016, 15, pp. 435–455.

55. US Equal Employment Opportunity Commission, "Prohibited Employment Policies/Practices" (*www.eeoc.gov/laws/practices/index.cfm*), accessed Feb. 5, 2020.

56. R. Tomsho, "Busy Surgeons Are Good for Patients," *Wall Street Journal*, Nov. 28, 2003, p. B3.

57. P. E. Tesluk and R. R. Jacobs, "Toward an Integrated Model of Work Experience," *Personnel Psychology*, 1998, 51, pp. 321–355.

58. R. A. Ash, "A Comparative Study of Behavioral Consistency and Holistic Judgment Methods of Job Applicant Training and Work Experience Evaluation," *Public Personnel Management*, 1984, 13, pp. 157–172; M. A. McDaniel, F. L. Schmidt, and J. E. Hunter, "A Meta-Analysis of the Validity of Methods for Rating Training and Experience in Personnel Selection," *Personnel Psychology*, 1988, 41, pp. 283–314.

59. C. H. Van Iddekinge, J. D. Arnold, R. E. Frieder, and P. L. Roth, "A Meta-Analysis of the Criterion-Related Validity of Prehire Work Experience," *Personnel Psychology*, 2019, 72, pp. 571–598.

60. G. Dokko, S. L. Wilk, and N. P. Rothbard, "Unpacking Prior Experience: How Career History Affects Job Performance," *Organization Science*, 2009, 20(1), pp. 51–68.

61. E. Moore, "8 Certifications That Actually Impress Recruiters," *Glassdoor*, Nov. 13, 2019 (*www.glassdoor.com/blog/certifications-impress-recruiters/*); E. Torpey, "Will I Need a License or Certification for My Job," *US Bureau of Labor Statistics: Career Outlook* (blog), Sept. 2016 (*www.bls.gov/careeroutlook/2016/article/will-i-need-a-license-or-certification.htm*); US Department of Labor, *Career One Stop* (*www.careeronestop.org/*), accessed Feb. 4, 2020.

62. Financial Management Association, "Finance Certifications" (*www.fma.org/finance-certifications*), accessed Feb. 4, 2020; Investopedia, "The Alphabet Soup of Financial Certifications," June 25, 2019 (*www.investopedia.com/articles/01/101001.asp*).

63. M. R. Raymond, S. Neustel, and D. Anderson, "Retest Effects on Identical and Parallel Forms in Certification and Licensure Testing," *Personnel Psychology*, 2007, 60, pp. 367–396.

64. J. McKillip and J. Owens, "Voluntary Professional Certifications: Requirements and Validation Activities," *Industrial-Organizational Psychologist*, July 2000, 38, pp. 50–57; C. H. Van Iddekinge and J. D. Arnold, "Retaking Employment Tests: What We Know and What We Still Need to Know," *Annual Review of Organizational Psychology & Organizational Behavior*, 2017, 4, pp. 445–471.

65. G. W. England, *Development and Use of Weighted Application Blanks* (Dubuque, IA: William C. Brown, 1961).

66. J. E. Hunter and R. F. Hunter, "Validity and Utility of Alternative Predictors of Job Performance," *Psychological Bulletin*, 1984, 96, pp. 72–98.

67. Pesce, "These Are the Most Outrageous Lies People Have Put on Their Resumes."

68. G. W. England, *Development and Use of Weighted Application Blanks*, rev. ed. (Minneapolis: University of Minnesota Industrial Relations Center, 1971).

69. S. R. Kaak, H. S. Field, W. F. Giles, and D. R. Norris, "The Weighted Application Blank: A Cost-Effective Tool That Can Reduce Employee Turnover," *Cornell Hotel & Restaurant Administration Quarterly*, Apr. 1998, pp. 18–24.

70. J. S. Breaugh, "The Use of Biodata for Employee Selection: Past Research and Future Directions," *Human Resource Management Review*, 2009, 19, pp. 219–231.

71. S. Hansell, "Google Answer to Filling Jobs Is an Algorithm," *New York Times*, Jan. 3, 2007, pp. A1, C9.

72. F. A. Mael, "A Conceptual Rationale for the Domain and Attributes of Biodata Items," *Personnel Psychology*, 1991, 44, pp. 763–792.

73. Breaugh, "The Use of Biodata for Employee Selection: Past Research and Future Directions"; K. D. Carlson, S. Sculten, F. L. Schmidt, H. Rothstein, and F. Erwin, "Generalizable Biographical Data Validity Can Be Achieved Without Multi-organizational Development and Keying," *Personnel Psychology*, 1999, 52, pp. 731–755; H. R. Rothstein, F. L. Schmidt, F. W. Erwin, W. A. Owens, and C. P. Sparks, "Biographical Data in Employment Selection: Can Validities Be Made Generalizable?" *Journal of Applied Psychology*, 1990, 75(2), pp. 175–184.

74. P. Bobko, P. L. Roth, and D. Potosky, "Derivation and Implications of a Meta-Analytic Matrix Incorporating Cognitive Ability, Alternative Predictors and Job Performance," *Personnel Psychology*, 1999, 52, pp. 561–589.

75. M. R. Barrick and R. D. Zimmerman, "Reducing Voluntary, Avoidable Turnover Through Selection," *Journal of Applied Psychology*, 2005, 90(1), pp. 159–166; A. L. Rubenstein, J. D. Kammeyer-Mueller, M. Wang, and T. G. Thundiyil, "'Embedded at Hire?' Predicting the Voluntary and Involuntary Turnover of New Employees," *Journal of Organizational Behavior*, 2019, 40, pp. 342–359.

76. Breaugh, "The Use of Biodata for Employee Selection: Past Research and Future Directions."

77. N. Schmitt, F. L. Oswald, B. H. Kim, M. A. Gillespie, L. J. Ramsay, and T. Yoo, "Impact of Elaboration on Socially Desirable Responding and the Validity of Biodata Measures," *Journal of Applied Psychology*, 2003, 88, pp. 979–988; J. Levashina, F. P. Morgeson, and M. A. Campion, "Tell Me Some More: Exploring How Verbal Ability and Item Verifiability Influence Responses to Biodata Questions in a High-Stakes Selection Context," *Personnel Psychology*, 2012, 65, pp. 359–383.

78. N. Anderson, J. F. Salgado, and U. R. Hülsheger, "Applicant Reactions in Selection: Comprehensive Meta-Analysis Into Reaction Generalization Versus Situational Specificity," *International Journal of Selection and Assessment*, 2010, 18, pp. 291–304; A. Furnham, "HR Professionals' Beliefs About, and Knowledge of, Assessment Techniques and Psychometric Tests," *International Journal of Selection and Assessment*, 2008, 16, pp. 300–305; J. M. Cucina, P. M. Caputo, H. F. Thibodeaux, and C. N. Maclane, "Unlocking the Key to Biodata Scoring: A Comparison of Empirical, Rational, and Hybrid Approaches at Different Sample Sizes," *Personnel Psychology*, 2012, 65, pp. 385–428.

79. P. Bobko and P. L. Roth, "Reviewing, Categorizing, and Analyzing the Literature on Black-White Mean Differences for Predictors of Job Performance: Verifying Some Perceptions and Updating/Correcting Others," *Personnel Psychology*, 2013, 66, pp. 91–126; P. Bobko, P. L. Roth, and D. Potosky, "Derivation and Implications of a Meta-Analytic Matrix Incorporating Cognitive Ability, Alternative Predictors and Job Performance," *Personnel Psychology*, 1999, 52, pp. 561–589; M. A. Dean, "Examination of Ethnic Group Differential Responding on a Biodata Instrument," *Journal of Applied Social Psychology*, 2013, 43, pp. 1905–1917.

80. N. R. Kuncel, R. J. Kochevar, and D. S. Ones, "A Meta-Analysis of Letters of Recommendation in College and Graduate Admissions: Reasons for Hope," *International Journal of Selection and Assessment*, 2014, 22, pp. 101–107.

81. D. Leising, J. Erbs, and U. Fritz, "The Letter of Recommendation Effect in Informant Ratings of Personality," *Journal of Personality and Social Psychology*, 2010, 98(4), pp. 668–682.

82. J. C. Baxter, B. Brock, P. C. Hill, and R. M. Rozelle, "Letters of Recommendation: A Question of Value," *Journal of Applied Psychology*, 1981, 66, pp. 296–301.

83. T. A. Judge and C. A. Higgins, "Affective Disposition and the Letter of Reference," *Organizational Behavior and Human Decision Processes*, 1998, 75, pp. 207–221; J. M. Madera, M. R. Hebl,

and R. C. Martin, "Gender and Letters of Recommendation for Academia: Agentic and Communal Differences," *Journal of Applied Psychology*, 2009, 94(6), pp. 1591–1599.

84. L. Everitt, "Why MBAs Are Writing Their Own Recommendation Letters," *Fortune*, July 15, 2013 (*http://fortune.com/2013/07/15/why-mbas-are-writing-their-own-recommendation-letters/*), accessed Aug. 9, 2013.

85. HireRight, *2019 Employment Screening Benchmark Report*, 2019 (*www.hireright.com/assets/uploads /files/2019-Benchmark-Report_US_Core_WEB.pdf*); Society for Human Resource Management, "Conducting Background Investigations and Reference Checks" (*www.shrm.org/resourcesandtools /tools-and-samples/toolkits/pages/conductingbackgroundinvestigations.aspx*), accessed Feb. 4, 2020.

86. M. E. Burke, *2004 Reference Check and Background Testing Survey Report* (Washington, DC: Society for Human Resource Management, 2005).

87. See, for example, P. J. Taylor, K. Pajo, G. W. Cheung, and P. Stringfield, "Dimensionality and Validity of a Structured Telephone Reference Check Procedure," *Personnel Psychology*, 2004, 57, pp. 745–772.

88. J. Click, "SHRM Survey Highlights Dilemmas of Reference Checks," *HR News*, July 1995, p. 13; B. Miller, "Pros and Cons of Checking Employee References," *HR Daily Advisor*, Aug. 27, 2019 (*https://hrdailyadvisor.blr.com/2019/08/27/pros-and-cons-of-checking-employee-references/*).

89. J. Greenwald, "Legal Issues With Background Checks," *Forbes*, July 10, 2015 (*www.forbes.com /sites/entrepreneursorganization/2015/07/10/legal-issues-with-background-checks/#5741ed744ef7*).

90. Society for Human Resource Management, "Conducting Background Investigations and Reference Checks."

91. Taylor et al., "Dimensionality and Validity of a Structured Telephone Reference Check Procedure."

92. HireRight, *2019 Employment Screening Benchmark Report*.

93. A. Zimmerman, "Wal-Mart to Probe Job Applicants," *Wall Street Journal*, Aug. 12, 2004, pp. A3, B6.

94. HireRight, *2019 Employment Screening Benchmark Report*.

95. M. Aspan, "AI Is Transforming the Job Interview—and Everything After," *Fortune*, Jan. 20, 2020 (*https://fortune.com/longform/hr-technology-ai-hiring-recruitment/*); Society for Human Resource Management, "Conducting Background Investigations and Reference Checks"; J. Sullivan, "The Top 10 Reasons Why Social Media Background Checks Are a Dumb Idea," *ERE Media* (blog), Aug. 20, 2018 (*www.ere.net/the-top-10-reasons-why-social-media-background-checks-are-a-dumb-idea/*).

96. M. Cerullo, "What Everyone Should Know About Employer Background Checks," *CBS News*, June 28, 2019 (*www.cbsnews.com/news/what-job-candidates-should-know-about-employer-background -checks/*).

97. HireRight, *2019 Employment Screening Benchmark Report*.

98. H. Drummond, *The Dynamics of Organizational Collapse: The Case of Barings Bank* (London: Routledge, 2007).

99. S. Melendez, "When Background Checks Go Wrong," *Fast Company*, Nov. 17, 2016 (*www.fast company.com/3065577/when-background-checks-go-wrong*).

100. A. Zimmerman and K. Stringer, "As Background Checks Proliferate, Ex-Cons Face Jobs Lock," *Wall Street Journal*, Aug. 26, 2004, pp. B1, B3.

101. K. M. Kuhn, "What We Overlook: Background Checks and Their Implications for Discrimination," *Industrial and Organizational Psychology: Perspectives on Science and Practice*, 2013, 6, pp. 419–423; R. Maurer, "'Ban the Box' Turns 20: What Employers Need to Know," *Society for Human Resource Management* (blog), Nov. 12, 2018 (*www.shrm.org/resourcesandtools/hr -topics/talent-acquisition/pages/ban-the-box-turns-20-what-employers-need-to-know.aspx*); E. McLean, "Ban the Box," *GoodHire* (blog), Sept. 4, 2019 (*www.goodhire.com/blog/ban-the-box/*); National Employment Law Project, "Maryland Becomes Latest State to 'Ban the Box,'" Apr. 4, 2013 (*www .nelp.org/page/-/Press-Releases/2013/PR-Ban-the-Box-Maryland.pdf?nocdn=1*).

102. L. Schwarz, "Baseball and Umpires Clash Over Background Checks," *New York Times*, Aug. 7, 2007, p. C15; A. Levin, "Unions: Safety Bar Set Lower for Cargo Planes," *USA Today*, Nov. 5, 2010, p. 1A.

103. J. B. Bernerth, S. G. Taylor, H. J. Walker, and D. S. Whitman, "An Empirical Investigation of Dispositional Antecedents and Performance-Related Outcomes of Credit Scores," *Journal of Applied Psychology*, 2012, 97, pp. 469–478; K. M. Kuhn, "What We Overlook: Background Checks and Their Implications for Discrimination," *Industrial & Organizational Psychology: Perspectives on Science & Practice*, 2013, 6(4), pp. 419–423; S. D. Volpone, S. Tonidandel, D. R. Avery, and S. Castel, "Exploring the Use of Credit Scores in Selection Processes: Beware of Adverse Impact," *Journal of Business Psychology*, 2015, 30, pp. 357–372; A. Weaver, "Is Credit Status a Good Signal of Productivity?" *Industrial Labor Relations Review*, 2015, 68(4), pp. 742–770.

104. M. G. Aamodt and F. Williams, "Reliability, Validity, and Adverse Impact of References and Letters of Recommendation," paper presented at the 20th annual meeting of the Society for Industrial and Organizational Psychology, Los Angeles, CA, Apr. 2005.

105. B. Schreurs, E. Derous, K. De Witte, K. Proost, M. Andriessen, and K. Glabeke, "Attracting Potential Applicants to the Military: The Effects of Initial Face-to-Face Contacts," *Human Performance*, 2005, 18(2), pp. 105–122.

106. J. M. Madera and M. R. Hebl, "Discrimination Against Facially Stigmatized Applicants in Interviews: An Eye-Tracking and Face-to-Face Investigation," *Journal of Applied Psychology*, 2012, 97, pp. 317–330.

107. M. R. Barrick, S. L. Dustin, T. L. Giluk, G. L. Stewart, J. A. Shaffer, and B. W. Swider, "Candidate Characteristics Driving Initial Impressions During Rapport Building: Implications for Employment Interview Validity," *Journal of Occupational and Organizational Psychology*, 2012, 85, pp. 330–352; M. R. Barrick, B. W. Swider, and G. L. Stewart, "Initial Evaluations in the Interview: Relationships With Subsequent Interviewer Evaluations and Employment Offers," *Journal of Applied Psychology*, 2010, 95, pp. 1163–1172; B. W. Swider, M. R. Barrick, and T. B. Harris, "Initial Impressions: What They Are, What They Are Not, and How They Influence Structured Interview Outcomes," *Journal of Applied Psychology*, 2016, 101, pp. 625–638.

108. M. Harding, "Companies Turning to Web Conferencing for Employment Interviews," *Pittsburgh Tribune Review*, Apr. 20, 2010, p. 1.

109. D. S. Chapman, K. L. Uggerslev, and J. Webster, "Applicant Reactions to Face-to-Face Technology-Mediated Interviews: A Field Investigation," *Journal of Applied Psychology*, 2003, 88(5), pp. 944–953.

110. N. Yang, "How to Ace a Job Interview With No Interviewer," *Monster* (*www.monster.com/career-advice/article/ace-recorded-job-interview-0916*), accessed Feb. 4, 2020.

111. D. Harwell, "A Face-Scanning Algorithm Increasingly Decides Whether You Deserve the Job," *Washington Post*, Nov. 6, 2019 (*www.washingtonpost.com/technology/2019/10/22/ai-hiring-face-scanning-algorithm-increasingly-decides-whether-you-deserve-job/*).

112. A. Kalish, "How to Nail Your Digital Interview (and Actually Get to Meet the Hiring Manager in Person)," *The Muse* (*www.themuse.com/advice/how-to-nail-your-video-assessment-and-actually-get-to-meet-the-hiring-manager-in-person*), accessed Feb. 4, 2020.

113. C. Cutter, "Your Next Job Interview May Be With a Robot," *Wall Street Journal*, Nov. 28, 2018 (*www.wsj.com/articles/its-time-for-your-job-interview-youll-be-talking-to-yourself-1543418495*).

114. D. J. R. Jackson, C. Dewberry, J. Gallagher, and L. Close, "A Comparative Study of Practitioner Perceptions of Selection Methods in the United Kingdom," *Journal of Occupational and Organizational Psychology*, 2018, 91, pp. 33–56; S. D. Risavy, P. A. Fisher, C. Robie, and C. J. König, "Selection Tool Use: A Focus on Personality Testing in Canada, the United States, and Germany," *Personnel Assessment and Decisions*, 2019, 5(1), pp. 62–72.

115. Talent Board, *2019 North American Candidate Experience Research Report* (Los Angeles, CA: author, 2019).

116. R. A. Ash and E. L. Levine, "Job Applicant Training and Work Experience Evaluation: An Empirical Comparison of Four Methods," *Journal of Applied Psychology*, 1985, 70, pp. 572–576.

117. G. P. Latham and G. Whyte, "The Futility of Utility Analysis," *Personnel Psychology*, 1994, 47, pp. 31–46.

118. P. R. Sackett and F. Lievens, "Personnel Selection," *Annual Review of Psychology*, 2008, 59, pp. 419–450; U. R. Hülsheger and N. Anderson, "Applicant Perspectives in Selection: Going Beyond Preference Reactions," *International Journal of Selection and Assessment*, 2009, 17, pp. 335–345; F. P. Morgeson and A. M. Ryan, "Reacting to Applicant Perspectives Research: What's Next?" *International Journal of Selection and Assessment*, 2009, 17, pp. 431–437.

119. J. P. Hausknecht, D. V. Day, and S. C. Thomas, "Applicant Reactions to Selection Procedures: An Updated Model and Meta-Analysis," *Personnel Psychology*, 2004, 57, pp. 639–683; D. S. Chapman, K. L. Uggerslev, S. A. Carroll, K. A. Piasentin, and D. A. Jones, "Applicant Attraction to Organizations and Job Choice: A Meta-Analytic Review of the Correlates of Recruiting Outcomes," *Journal of Applied Psychology*, 2005, 90, pp. 928–944; D. M. Truxillo, T. E. Bodner, M. Bertolino, T. N. Bauer, and C. A. Yonce, "Effects of Explanations on Applicant Reactions: A Meta-Analytic Review," *International Journal of Selection and Assessment*, 2009, 17, pp. 346–361; Uggerslev, Fassina, and Kraichy, "Recruiting Through the Stages: A Meta-Analytic Test of Predictors of Applicant Attraction at Different Stages of the Recruiting Process."

120. Anderson, Salgado, and Hülsheger, "Applicant Reactions in Selection: Comprehensive Meta-Analysis Into Reaction Generalization Versus Situational Specificity."

121. M. G. Danaher, "Handbook Disclaimer Dissected," *HR Magazine*, Feb. 2007, p. 116; D. J. Walsh, *Employment Law for Human Resource Practice*, 5th ed. (Mason, OH: Cengage Learning, 2016), pp. 674–676.

122. Equal Employment Opportunity Commission and Federal Trade Commission, *Background Checks: What Employers Need to Know* (*www.eeoc.gov/eeoc/publications/background_checks_employers.cfm*), accessed Feb. 4, 2020.

123. D. D. Bennett-Alexander and C. P. Hartman, *Employment Law for Business*, 8th ed. (New York: McGraw-Hill Education, 2015), pp. 148–158; M. E. Burke and L. A. Weatherly, *Getting to Know the Candidate: Providing Reference Checks* (Alexandria, VA: Society for Human Resource Management, 2005); S. Z. Hable, "The Trouble With Online References," *Workforce Management Online*, Feb. 2010 (*www.workforce.com/articles/the-trouble-with-online-references*), accessed June 22, 2010; L. S. Rosen, *The Safe Hiring Manual*, 2nd ed. (Tempe, AZ: 13RP Publications, 2012), pp. 173–192.

124. J. A. Segal, "Social Media Use in Hiring: Assessing the Risks," *HR Magazine*, Sept. 2014 (*www.shrm.org/hr-today/news/hr-magazine/pages/0914-social-media-hiring.aspx*).

125. S. Bates, "Use Social Media Smartly When Hiring," *Society for Human Resource Management*, 2013 (*www.shrm.org/resourcesandtools/hr-topics/technology/pages/be-smart-when-using-social-media-for-hiring.aspx*); J. A. Segal, "The Law and Social Media in Hiring," *HR Magazine*, Sept. 2014, pp. 70–72; J. A. Segal, "Should Employers Use Social Media to Screen New Applicants?" *HR Magazine*, Nov. 2014, p. 20; L. Rosen, *Ten Potential Dangers When Using Social Media Background Checks* (Novato, CA: Employment Screening Resources, 2016, *www.esr-dev.com.php56-17.ord1-1.websitetestlink.com/Tools-Resources/Whitepaper-Library/Social-Media-Background-Checks/index.php*), accessed February 5, 2016.

126. T. B. Stivarius, J. Skonberg, R. Fliegel, R. Blumberg, R. Jones, and K. Mones, "Background Checks: Four Steps to Basic Compliance in a Multistate Environment," *Legal Report*, Society for Human Resource Management, Mar.–Apr. 2003.

127. K. McNamera, "Bad Credit Derails Job Search," *Wall Street Journal*, Mar. 16, 2010, p. D6; R. Maurer, "Federal Lawmakers, Enforcers Set Sights on Background Screening," *Society for Human Resource Management*, Mar. 9, 2010 (*http://true-hire.com/industry-news/federal-lawmakers-enforcers-set-sights-on-background-screening/*); Employment Screening Resources, *ESR Newsletter and Legal Update*, Oct. 2009, pp. 1–2; Employment Screening Resources, *ESR Newsletter and Legal Update*, Aug. 2010, pp. 1–2; R. Lally, "Don't Ask About Credit History in New York City," *HR Magazine*, July–Aug. 2015, p. 14.

128. Walsh, *Employment Law for Human Resource Practice*, pp. 149–166; M. G. Aamodt, *Conducting Background Checks for Employee Selection*, Nov. 8, 2016 (*www.shrm.org/hr-today/trends-and-forecasting/special-reports-and-expert-views/Documents/SHRM-SIOP%20Background%20Checks.pdf*).

129. J. P. Hoag, "New 'Ban the Box' Laws in Washington Take Effect June 2018," *Davis Wright Tremaine* (blog), May 24, 2018 (*www.dwt.com/blogs/employment-labor-and-benefits/2018/05/new-ban-the-box-laws-in-washington-take-effect-jun*).

130. J. C. Wallace and S. J. Vadanovich, "Personal Application Blanks: Persistence and Knowledge of Legally Inadvisable Application Blank Items," *Public Personnel Management*, 2004, 33, pp. 331–349.

131. J. Janove, "More Jurisdictions Are Banning Salary-History Inquiries," *Society for Human Resource Management*, Apr. 4, 2019 (*www.shrm.org/resourcesandtools/legal-and-compliance/state-and-local-updates/pages/more-jurisdictions-are-banning-salary-history-inquiries.aspx*).

132. Bennett-Alexander and Hartman, *Employment Law for Business*, pp. 66–68; Walsh, *Employment Law for Human Resource Practice*, pp. 223–230; C. R. Miaskoff, *Title VII/Sex/BFOQ/Caregiver* (Washington, DC: EEOC, 2013).

CHAPTER NINE

External Selection II

Learning Objectives and Introduction
    Learning Objectives
    Introduction

Substantive Assessment Methods
    Performance Tests, Work Samples, and Simulations
    Situational Judgment Tests
    Structured Interviews
    Ability Tests
    Emotional Intelligence Tests
    Personality Tests
    Integrity Tests
    Interest, Values, and Preference Inventories
    Selection for Team Environments
    Selection of Leaders
    Choice of Substantive Assessment Methods

Discretionary Assessment Methods

Contingent Assessment Methods
    Drug Testing
    Medical Exams

Legal Issues
    Uniform Guidelines on Employee Selection Procedures
    Selection Under the Americans With Disabilities Act
    Marijuana and Other Drug Testing

Summary

Discussion Questions

Ethical Issues

Applications
    Assessment Methods for the Job of Human Resources Director
    Choosing Among Finalists for the Job of Human Resources Director

Endnotes

LEARNING OBJECTIVES AND INTRODUCTION

Learning Objectives

- Distinguish among initial, substantive, and contingent selection
- Review the advantages and disadvantages of personality and cognitive ability tests
- Compare and contrast work sample and situational judgment tests
- Understand the advantages of interviews and how interviews can be structured
- Review the logic behind contingent assessment methods and how they are administrated
- Understand the ways in which substantive and contingent assessment methods are subject to various legal rules and restrictions

Introduction

The previous chapter reviewed preliminary issues surrounding external staffing decisions made in organizations, including the use of initial assessment methods. This chapter continues the discussion of external selection by discussing in some detail substantive assessment methods. The use of discretionary and contingent assessment methods, collection of assessment data, and legal issues will be considered. Substantive and contingent assessment are at the heart of staffing decisions because they serve as the basis of actual hiring decisions. Done well, the stage is set for effective staffing. Done poorly, it is difficult, if not impossible, to staff successfully.

Whereas initial assessment methods are used to reduce the job applicant pool to candidates, substantive assessment methods are used to reduce the candidate pool to finalists. Thus, the use of substantive methods is often more involved than the use of initial methods. Numerous substantive assessment methods will be discussed in depth, including various tests (personality, ability, emotional intelligence, performance/work samples, situational judgment, and integrity); interest, values, and preference inventories; structured interviews; as well as assessments for leaders and team environments. The average validity (i.e., $\bar{r}_{xy}$) of each method and the criteria used to choose among methods will be reviewed.

Discretionary assessment methods are used in some circumstances to separate those who receive job offers from the finalists. The finalist characteristics that are assessed when using discretionary methods are sometimes very subjective. Several of the characteristics most assessed by discretionary methods will be reviewed.

Contingent assessment methods are used to make sure that tentative offer recipients meet remaining qualifications for the job. Although any assessment method can be used as a contingent method (e.g., licensing/certification requirements, background checks), drug tests and medical exams are perhaps the two most common methods. The procedures for these methods will be reviewed.

All forms of assessment decisions require the collection of data. The procedures used to make sure this process is properly conducted will be reviewed. Several issues will be discussed, including support services, training requirements in using various predictors, maintaining security and confidentiality, and the importance of standardized procedures.

Finally, many important legal issues surround the use of substantive, discretionary, and contingent methods of selection. The most important of these issues will be reviewed. Particular attention will be given to the Uniform Guidelines on Employee Selection Procedures (UGESP) and staffing requirements under the Americans With Disabilities Act (ADA).

SUBSTANTIVE ASSESSMENT METHODS

Organizations use initial assessment methods to make rough cuts among applicants, weeding out those who are obviously unqualified. Conversely, substantive assessment methods are used to make more precise decisions about candidates. These methods are generally used to answer the following question: Among those who meet the minimum qualifications for the job, who are the most likely to be high performers if hired? In other words, these methods are used to predict which candidates, if hired, will be the best performers. For that reason, the validity of substantive assessment methods is critical. Like initial assessment methods, substantive assessment methods are developed using the logic of prediction outlined in Exhibit 8.1 and the selection plan shown in Exhibit 8.2, and they are implemented at the appropriate stage of the applicant flow as outlined in Exhibit 8.3.

We discuss the substantive predictors in the following order. Working backward from the criterion the staffing professional is most likely seeking to predict, job performance, we first discuss performance tests and work samples (which most directly sample job performance), along with the closely related situational judgment tests (SJTs). Next, we discuss the structured interview, given its ubiquitous use in staffing. Another reason we discuss these three methods early on is that they can be targeted toward measuring several different constructs. For example, SJTs and structured interviews can be designed in such a way as to assess ability, emotional intelligence, personality, and integrity. After discussing structured interviews, we move to discuss ability, emotional intelligence, and personality. These are three of the most common construct-oriented predictors and are commonly measured by tests and surveys (although they can also be measured via SJTs and other methods mentioned earlier). Next, we talk about predictors that are generally directed toward assessing person/organization fit, reducing deviant behavior (e.g., theft, absenteeism), and improving motivation. These predictors include interest, values, and preference inventories and integrity tests. Finally, we discuss the application of these predictors toward staffing in context, such as selecting members of a team or selecting leaders.

Performance Tests, Work Samples, and Simulations

Performance tests and work samples assess actual performance rather than underlying abilities, personality traits, or other characteristics. Therefore, they are more akin to samples rather than signs of work performance. For example, Chrysler asks candidates for its assembly-line jobs to physically assemble auto parts, precisely mirroring a task that would be done on the job.[1] Exhibit 9.1 provides examples of performance tests and work samples for a variety of jobs. As can be seen in the exhibit, the potential uses of these selection measures are quite broad in terms of job content and skill level. However, performance tests and work samples are not to be confused with simulations, which will be discussed more thoroughly in

---

EXHIBIT 9.1   Examples of Performance Tests and Work Samples

Professor
   Teaching a class while on a campus interview
   Presenting research while on a campus interview

Mechanic
   Repairing a problem on a car
   Reading a blueprint

Clerical Worker
   Typing test
   Proofreading

Cashier
   Operating a cash register
   Counting money and totaling a balance sheet

TV Repair Person
   Repairing a broken television
   Finger and tweezer dexterity test

Police Officer
   Check police reports for errors
   Shooting accuracy test

Computer Programmer
   Programming and debugging test
   Hardware replacement test

SOURCE: *International Personality Item Pool* (*ipip.ori.org*).

the internal selection chapter. The former exactly reproduce tasks that one would encounter on the job; simulations, on the other hand, mimic the work environment without completely reproducing it.[2]

Types of Tests

Performance Test Versus Work Sample. A performance test directly measures what the person does on the job. The best examples of performance tests are those encountered in internships, in job tryouts, and during probationary periods. Although probationary periods have their uses when one cannot be completely confident in a new hire's ability to perform a job, they are no substitute for a valid prehire selection process. Discharging a probationary employee and finding a replacement is expensive and has numerous legal issues.[3] One interesting performance test that resembled a job tryout involved a promising applicant who looked perfect on paper but when taken on a sales call revealed troubling aspects of her behavior and was therefore not hired.[4] A work sample, on the other hand, is designed to capture *a part* of the job—for example, a drill press test for machine operators or a programming test for computer programmers.[5] A complete performance test is costlier to implement than a work sample, but it is usually a better predictor of job performance.

Motor Versus Verbal Work Samples. A motor work sample test involves the physical manipulation of things. Examples include installing a satellite dish or repairing a garage door. A verbal work sample test involves a problem situation requiring language skills and interaction with people. Examples include an actor following a script during a tryout or a bank teller interacting with a customer.

High- Versus Low-Fidelity Tests. A high-fidelity test uses realistic equipment and scenarios to simulate the actual tasks of the job. Therefore, it elicits actual responses encountered in performing the task.[6] A level of high fidelity is often a hallmark characteristic of performance tests and work samples.[7] An example of a high-fidelity test would be one in which a truck driver candidate goes through all of the steps to load and unload fuel from a tanker to a fuel reservoir at a fuel station. You may be thinking about the potential ramifications of having a candidate "actually" complete a job task: What if it's dangerous? What are the consequences of an error? Could we lose money?

Simulations and other mid- to low-fidelity tests simulate the task and elicit a response that mimics what one would find on the job rather than an actual response.[8] Extending our example for the high-fidelity test, a fuel-unloading simulation could be performed in a realistic setting (e.g., a site intended to look like a gas station) or through a virtual reality headset and mimic all the steps taken to load and unload fuel from a tanker to a fuel reservoir at a service station. It is not a test of perfect high fidelity, because fuel is not actually unloaded. It is, however, a much safer test because the dangerous process of fuel transfer is simulated rather than performed.[9] An example of an even lower fidelity test would be describing a work situation to job candidates and asking them what they would do in that situation. Low-fidelity work samples bear many similarities to some types of structured interview questions and SJTs, and in some cases they may be indistinguishable (see the "Structured Interviews" and "Situational Judgment Tests" sections).

Simulations and other low-fidelity tests can be used as substantive assessments during the selection process (see also our discussion of simulations as an integral part of assessment centers in the internal selection chapter). These tests are becoming more innovative and are drawing increasingly on technological advancements. For example, Employment Technologies has developed a simulation called the EASy Simulation for Contact Center Agents, in which candidates assume the role of a customer service specialist. In the simulation, the candidate takes phone calls, responds to e-mails, and completes other call center tasks. The test provides scores on rapport, problem solving, communication, sales orientation, and adaptation. Royal Caribbean Cruises successfully utilized the simulation as a part of its staffing efforts and realized a 57% decrease in turnover as a result.[10]

Evaluation

Earlier research indicated that performance or work sample tests have a moderately high degree of validity in predicting job performance. One meta-analysis suggests that the average validity is much lower but still quite moderate in size ($\bar{r} = .26$).[11] Because performance tests measure the entire job and work samples measure part of the job, they also have a high degree of content validity. Thus, when one considers the substantial degree of empirical and content validity, work samples are perhaps the most valid method of selection for many types of jobs. Work sample tests have also been found to be reliable, in terms of performance judgments by trained observers and consistency across sampled tasks.[12]

Performance tests and work samples have other advantages as well. Research indicates that these measures are widely accepted by candidates as being job related. One early study found that no candidates complained about performance tests but that 10%–20% complained about other selection procedures.[13] Confirming the results from this earlier study, a meta-analysis comparing candidates' favorability of selection methods found that work samples were the most highly favored selection method, across dozens of studies and thousands of candidates.[14] Another possible advantage of performance tests and work samples is that they tend to have low degrees of disparate impact, though some evidence suggests that they may have more disparate impact than is commonly thought, as dependent on the psychological constructs assessed with the work sample.[15]

Performance tests and work samples do have several limitations. The costs of the realism embedded in work samples are high. The closer a predictor comes to simulating actual job performance, the more expensive it is to use it. Having people perform the job, as with an internship, may require paying a wage. Using technology may also add costs. Thus, performance tests and work samples are among the most expensive means of selecting workers.

Their costs are amplified when one considers the lack of generalizability of such measures. More than any other selection method, performance tests and work samples are tied to the specific job at hand. This means that a different test, based on a thorough job analysis, will need to be developed for each job. While their validity may well be worth the cost, the costs of work samples may be prohibitive. One means of mitigating the administrative expense associated with performance tests or work samples is to use a two-stage selection process whereby the full set of applicants is reduced using relatively inexpensive tests (e.g., initial methods or less expensive substantive methods). Once the initial cut is made, performance tests or work samples can be administered to the smaller group of candidates who demonstrated minimum competency levels on the first-round tests.[16]

Finally, most performance tests and work samples assume that the candidate already possesses the knowledge, skill, ability, and other characteristics (KSAOs) necessary to do the job. If substantial training is involved, candidates will not be able to perform the work sample effectively, even though with adequate training they could be high performers. In such situations, work samples simply will not be feasible.

In the next section, we discuss the situational judgment test, which is very similar to a low-fidelity simulation and is less expensive and resource intensive than a performance test or work sample.

Situational Judgment Tests

A situational judgment test (SJT) presents the candidate with a hypothetical work-related situation and then elicits a response of what the candidate should or would do in that situation, usually from a selection of several alternatives.[17] For example, candidates for a 911 operator position may be presented with a situation involving a distress call, then are asked to choose the best response from a series of multiple-choice alternatives. Exhibit 9.2 provides two examples of SJT items.

As one can see, SJTs are very similar to low-fidelity work samples. SJTs can also be distinguished from typical job knowledge tests and work samples. A job knowledge test more explicitly taps the content of the job (areas that candidates are expected to know immediately upon hire), whereas SJTs are more likely to deal with relevant hypothetical job situations. SJTs differ from work samples and performance tests in that the former presents candidates with multiple-choice responses to the scenarios, whereas in the latter, candidates engage in behavior that is observed by others.

The principal argument in favor of SJTs is to capture the validity of work samples and performance tests in a way that is cheaper and that has potentially less disparate impact than cognitive ability tests. How well are these aims achieved? A meta-analysis of the validity of SJTs indicated that such tests are reasonably valid

---

EXHIBIT 9.2 Examples of Situational Judgment Test Items

Retail Industry Manager

You are the assistant manager of a large department store. One weekend day while you are in charge of the store, a customer seeks to return a pair of tennis shoes. The employee in charge of the customer service department has refused to accept the return. The customer has asked to speak to the manager, and so the employee has paged you. Upon meeting the customer—who is clearly agitated—you learn that the customer does not have a receipt, and, moreover, you see that the shoes are clearly well worn. When you ask the customer why she is returning the shoes, she tells you that she has bought many pairs of shoes from your store, and in the past they have "held up much better over time than these." You recognize the shoes as a brand that your store has stocked, so you have no reason to believe the customer is lying when she says that she bought them from your store. Still, the shoes have clearly been worn for a long time. Should you:

a. Issue a refund to the customer
b. Check with your boss—the store manager—when he is at the store on Monday
c. Deny a refund to the customer, explaining that the shoes are simply too worn to be returned
d. Inform the customer of the current sale prices on comparable tennis shoes

Park Ranger

You are a park ranger with the National Park Service, stationed in Yellowstone National Park. One of your current duties is to scout some of the park's more obscure trails to look for signs of lost hikers, to detect any malfeasance, and to inspect the conditions of the trails. It is mid-September, and you're inspecting one of the more remote trails in the Mount Washburn area to determine whether it should be closed for the season. When you first set out on your hike, the forecast called for only a slight chance of snow, but midway through your hike, an early fall blizzard struck. For a time you persisted on, but later you took refuge under a large lodgepole pine tree. Although the storm is now abating, it is near dark. Which of the following would be your best course of action?

a. Stay put until help comes
b. Reverse course and hike back to the ranger station
c. Once the clouds clear, locate the North Star, and hike north to the nearest ranger station
d. Use your matches to build a fire, and hike back in the morning

correlates of job performance ($\bar{r}_{xy} = .20$), although their validity depends on what they are assessing (from $\bar{r}_{xy} = .15$ for job knowledge to $\bar{r}_{xy} = .30$ for personality traits).[18] Research also suggests that SJTs have low disparate impact against minorities, although this clearly depends on what is being measured and how it is being measured: SJTs that assess cognitive abilities or knowledge or that are written in a cognitively complex way can actually demonstrate high levels of disparate impact.[19] Despite demonstrating reasonable criterion-related validity, content validity, and disparate impact (depending on the construct assessed), SJTs are not reliable in the traditional sense and do not display strong construct validity evidence.[20]

The poor reliability and construct validity evidence, however, is likely because SJTs are "methods" and not "constructs." As mentioned earlier, SJTs can be used to *measure* multiple types of *constructs*, so their construct validity and reliability evidence vary as a function of what is being assessed. Furthermore, there are many sources of error and differences in a SJT: the response instructions, format, what is being assessed, the candidates being assessed, the situations, and the response options and their format all contribute to differences in responses. Because of this, establishing reliability and construct validity is challenging.[21]

Surprisingly, removing the situation altogether seems to have little impact on the responses people choose. For example, across several studies, researchers found that people selected response options in consistent ways, regardless of whether or not they were required to read a situation first. This suggests that people are able to select the option which "looks" best to them, even if there is no situation to set the context and background. Another group of studies showed that including explicit assessments of the situation itself (rather than a behavioral response of what would be the most appropriate) added to the prediction of performance even above and beyond the traditional response judgment items.[22] The results from these studies pose an interesting dilemma: How "situational" are SJTs? Is the validity of SJTs in general harmed when we can remove the situation altogether and still obtain the same results? Or even when we can remove response options and obtain higher validities by candidates' assessment of the situation?

Regardless, if SJTs are used, three important decisions must be made. First, there is the issue of format. Some evidence suggests that video-based SJTs have less disparate impact than written ones and may have higher levels of validity.[23] Video-based SJTs (i.e., the situations are displayed as videos) appear to generate positive candidate reactions.[24] Response formats of SJTs also matter: a study of over 30,000 job candidates showed that of rating, ranking, and most/least judgments made in a SJT, the rating response format appears to be the best choice given its reduction in disparate impact and stronger construct validity evidence, although it is more subject to response distortions.[25] The instruction format matters as well: if you are trying to assess ability or knowledge, you should ask candidates what they *should* do; if you are trying to assess personality traits or behavioral tendencies, you should ask candidates what they *would* do.[26]

Second, there is the issue of scoring. Unfortunately, the way in which the scoring key is developed matters, and keys that were created in different ways may not always agree. For example, you may score a SJT by having a small group of subject matter experts (SMEs; see the measurement chapter) indicate what they think is the best answer. You could also score the same SJT by giving it to all the incumbents who hold the position you are hiring for (the most common response for each situation would be treated as the best answer). There is no guarantee that these two approaches will correspond completely. Generally, the best keys will be the ones that minimize measurement error the most, capture the construct as accurately as possible, and maximize predictive validity.[27]

Finally, the third issue is which constructs should be measured. Of course, job analysis should be the guide here: constructs that job analysis has suggested are important to perform the job should be assessed. They can be designed to assess several constructs, including general ability, social skills, job knowledge, and personality traits.[28] Specifically, research indicates that SJTs that measure leadership, personality traits, and teamwork skills tend to predict job performance best. That may be because these constructs are not well measured by other means (i.e., SJTs measure these important aspects particularly well).[29]

In the next section, we describe the structured interview. Like the SJT, the structured interview is a method and can be designed to assess several different constructs. The interview is also the most frequently used of all the selection methods discussed in this chapter, despite often being conducted in an unstructured way.

Structured Interviews

"It is rare, even unthinkable, for someone to be hired without some type of interview."[30] Thinking back to your prior employment experiences, chances are you had an interview at some point during the hiring process. You have probably been exposed to unstructured interviews more often than structured interviews. A typical unstructured interview has the following characteristics:[31]

- It is informal.
- Questions are often based on interviewer "hunches" or "pet questions" to determine candidate suitability.
- It may consist of casual, open-ended, or subjective questioning (e.g., "Tell me a little bit about yourself").
- It may consist of obtuse questions with questionable job relevance (e.g., "What type of animal would you most like to be, and why?").
- It may consist of highly speculative questions (e.g., "Where do you see yourself 10 years from now?").
- The interviewer may make a quick, and final, evaluation of the candidate (often in the first couple of minutes). Or, if a rating scale is involved, it may be focused on a global evaluation rather than specific dimensions.

The interview remains the most widely used substantive selection procedure. Research shows that organizations clearly pay a price for using unstructured interviews, and a large number of studies have shown that unstructured interviews have worse reliability and validity evidence than structured interviews.[32] Over the years, research has unraveled the reasons why the unstructured interview does not work well and what factors need to be changed to improve reliability and validity. Sources of error or bias in the unstructured interview include the following:

- Interviewers base their evaluations on different factors and have different standards.[33] Overall, the average interrater reliability estimates for employment interviews in general are fair ($\bar{r} = .68$), although the interrater reliability is moderated by level of structure (the greater the structure in place for both questions and responses, the higher the reliability) and by format (reliability is higher for panel interviews as opposed to separate interviews with each interviewer).[34] In general, unstructured interviews might reflect interviewers' own "theories" of what it means to be successful on the job rather than actual job requirements or qualifications.[35]
- Unstructured interviews are more prone to disparate impact against protected classes, as meta-analytic evidence suggests.[36] Unstructured interviews result in the exchange of information that is not relevant to the job, and as a result, this information may lead to biased decisions.[37]
- Evaluations from unstructured interviews are particularly affected by candidate impression management and nonverbal behavior.[38]
- Using unstructured interview information to make selection decisions may harm hiring decisions more than it helps, as hiring managers tend to be overconfident in the quality of information they obtain from these interviews, despite it leading to a worse selection decision.[39]

Thus, the unstructured interview is not very valid, and research has identified the reasons why. So why is it so prevalent? First, as mentioned above, individuals often believe that they are better at "people reading" than they are, and thus are unaware of the biases that distort evaluations during unstructured interviews. Second, interviewers with certain personality traits (e.g., conscientiousness) and who feel accountable for the results of the interview are more likely to use structured interviews.[40] Third, interviewers are often not trained in the use of or are otherwise not aware of the benefits of structured interviews.[41] Finally, an unstructured interview requires less advance preparation than a structured interview. All in all, staffing professionals have a responsibility to use methods that are reliable and valid, and more professionals should consider using a structured interview format.

Characteristics of Structured Interviews

There are numerous hallmarks of structured interviews. Some of the more prominent characteristics are the following: (1) questions are based on job analysis, (2) the same questions are asked of each candidate, (3) the response to each question is numerically evaluated, (4) detailed anchored rating scales are used to score each response, and (5) multiple well-trained interviewers are used to rate interviewees' behaviors.[42]

There are two types of structured interview questions: situational and experience based.[43] Situational interview questions assess what a candidate would do in relevant hypothetical situations, similar to the SJT discussed previously. The assumption behind the use of the situational interview is that the goals or intentions individuals set for themselves are good predictors of what they will do in the future. For example, one might ask a candidate: "You are applying for a customer service position in a cable television company. If a technician visits a home to make a repair and afterward you receive a call from the customer telling you that the technician left muddy footprints on her new carpeting, how would you respond?"[44]

On the other hand, experience-based or past behavioral interview questions assess past behaviors that are linked to the prospective job. The assumption behind the use of experience-based questions is the same as that for the use of biodata: past behavior is a good predictor of future behavior. For example, a related question for a customer service position in a cable company might ask the candidate to "describe a situation in which you were able to use persuasion to successfully convince someone to see things your way."[45]

Situational and experience-based questions have many similarities. Generally, both are based on the critical incidents approach to job analysis, where job behaviors especially important to (as opposed to typically descriptive of) job performance are considered. In addition, both approaches attempt to assess candidate *behaviors* rather than feelings, motives, values, or other psychological states. Finally, both methods have substantial reliability and validity evidence in their favor.[46]

Situational and experience-based questions also have important differences. The most obvious difference is that situational interviews are future oriented ("what *would* you do if?"), whereas experience-based interviews are past oriented ("what *did* you do when?"). Prior research has demonstrated that, despite being designed to assess behavior, situational questions (like SJTs) tend to assess knowledge and ability, whereas experience-based questions tend to assess experience, personality traits, and dispositions.[47] In other words, it appears that knowing how you *should* behave is what drives situational question performance, and doing what you *should* do is what drives experience-based question performance.[48] Although the two question types are strongly correlated ($\bar{r} = .40$), they are not interchangeable.[49] We agree with prior research that suggests that the question type should be guided by the purpose of the interview, the type of constructs to be assessed, and the specific interview context.[50] For example, it does not make much sense to ask candidates what they did in a situation if they have never been in that situation. Also, organizations should look for ways in which to draw on both types of questions, as they may complement one another.[51]

Structured Video Interviews.   In order to reduce costs and reach more candidates, some organizations are turning to video-mediated interviews, in which the interviewer meets with the candidate electronically to administer the structured interview.[52] A benchmarking report (of thousands of human resource [HR] professionals) from the Society for Human Resource Management (SHRM) found that generally 15%–29% of HR professionals use video interviews to assess candidates.[53] On the one hand, it may be easier for job hunters—especially those who are already employed—to squeeze in interviews after normal work hours. On the other hand, candidates may view the organization as impersonal, and the lack of face-to-face interaction, as well as an on-site visit, may make it difficult to assess person/organization fit. A recent meta-analysis on video-mediated interviews suggested that this type of interview had a pronounced and moderately sized negative effect on both ratings and candidate reactions. Thus, organizations may be better off using these types of interviews sparingly or as an initial screen.[54]

As mentioned in the previous chapter, some organizations are abandoning face-to-face interaction altogether by presenting candidates with a scripted set of questions and recording their responses for later scoring in a completely automated, digital format. For example, HireVue conducts 12-minute interviews consisting of one practice question and four actual questions. Candidates are given 30 seconds to read each question and consider their response, which is limited to about 3 minutes. HireVue provides a set of stock questions (e.g., "Tell us about a time you had to cope with a high-pressure or stressful work situation"), or companies can provide their own questions. The recorded interviews are then provided to the hiring employer, who will rate the answers to the interview questions.[55] Although digital interviews such as these offer several benefits to organizations, including increased efficiency, less bias, and greater standardization across interviews, some research suggests that candidates view digital interviews as less personal, an infringement on their privacy, and even creepy (leaving some to abandon the hiring process as a result).[56]

Constructing a Structured Interview

The structured interview, by design and conduct, standardizes and controls for sources of influence on the interview process and the interviewer. Doing so requires proceeding through each of the following steps: consult the job requirements matrix, develop the selection plan, develop the structured interview plan, select and train interviewers, and evaluate effectiveness. Each of these steps is elaborated next in a demonstration of constructing a situational interview.

The Job Requirements Matrix and Selection Plan

The starting point for the structured interview is the job requirements matrix. It identifies the tasks and KSAOs that define the job requirements around which the structured interview is constructed and conducted.

Because the selection plan flows from the KSAOs identified in the job requirements matrix, it helps identify which KSAOs are necessary to assess during selection and whether the structured interview is the preferred method of assessing them.

Is the KSAO Necessary?   The candidate must bring some KSAOs to the job, although others can be acquired on the job (through training and/or job experience). The bring-it/acquire-it decision must be made for each KSAO, and it should be guided by the importance indicator(s) for the KSAOs in the job requirements matrix.

Is the Structured Interview the Preferred Method?   Several factors should be considered when determining whether the structured interview is the preferred method of assessing each KSAO necessary for selection. The structured interview is probably best suited for assessing face-to-face skills and abilities, such as communication and other interpersonal skills. An example of a selection plan for the job of sales associate in a retail clothing store is shown in Exhibit 9.3. While there are five task dimensions for the job in the job requirements matrix, the selection plan shows only the dimension of customer service. Note in the exhibit that the customer service dimension has several required KSAOs. However, not all the KSAOs will be assessed during selection, and only some of them will be assessed by the structured interview. The method of assessment is thus carefully targeted to the KSAO to be assessed.

The Structured Interview Plan

Development of the structured interview plan proceeds along three sequential steps: construction of interview questions, construction of benchmark responses for the questions, and weighting of the importance of the questions. The output of this process for the sales associate job is shown in Exhibit 9.4 and is referred to in the discussion that follows.

Constructing Questions.   One or more questions must be constructed for each KSAO targeted for assessment by the structured interview. Care must be taken to

---

EXHIBIT 9.3   Partial Selection Plan for Job of Retail Store Sales Associate

Task Dimension: Customer Service		
KSAO	**Necessary for Selection?**	**Method of Assessment**
1. Ability to make customer feel welcome	Yes	Interview
2. Knowledge of merchandise to be sold	Yes	Written test
3. Knowledge of location of merchandise in store	No	None
4. Skill in being cordial with customers	Yes	Interview
5. Ability to create and convey ideas to customers ...	Yes	Interview

ensure that the questions reflect a sampling of the candidate's behavior, as revealed by past situations (behavioral description) or what the candidate reports would be their behavior in future situations (situational). The key to constructing both types of questions is to create a scenario relevant to the KSAO in question.

Exhibit 9.4 shows three questions for the KSAOs to be assessed by the interview, as determined by the initial selection plan for the job of sales associate in a retail store. As can be seen, all three questions present very specific situations that a sales associate is likely to encounter. The content of all three questions is clearly job relevant, a logical outgrowth of the process that began with the development of the job requirements matrix.

Although one can certainly write questions that directly reflect KSAOs, another approach (which is used more frequently) is to base the questions on critical incidents, or examples of poor and excellent performance episodes encountered by actual employees on the job.[57] Incumbents who are familiar with the job can either take part in a workshop where they brainstorm about these incidents or take part in a survey where they provide these incidents. These critical incidents can then be made into interview questions and even mapped onto the KSAOs identified in a job analysis. For example, a movie theater ticket booth operator may recall a time when a coworker was so frustrated with a customer that they threw off their headset and stormed away from the booth on a busy Saturday night. This incident might serve as the basis for a past-behavior question (e.g., "Think of a time when you were really frustrated with a customer; what did you do?"). A benefit of using the critical incidents approach is that it maximizes content validity: the questions are directly sourced from incumbents and tied to successful job performance.

Developing Benchmark Responses and Rating Scales. The interviewer must evaluate or judge the quality of the candidate's responses to the interview questions. Prior development of benchmark responses and rating scales will provide firm guidance to the interviewer in doing this task. Benchmark responses represent qualitative examples of the types of candidate responses that the interviewer may encounter. They are located on a rating scale (usually 1–5 or 1–7 rating scale points) to represent the level or "goodness" of the response. Referring to the ticket booth operator example, the "throwing off the headset" and "storming away" could serve as examples of poor performance (e.g., a 1 on a 1–5 scale). Exhibit 9.4 contains benchmark responses, positioned on a 1–5 rating scale, for each of the three interview questions. Note that all the responses are quite specific and that some answers are better than others.

Weighting Responses. Because each candidate will receive a total score, one must decide whether the questions should be weighted equally in contributing to the total score. If so, the candidate's total interview score is simply the sum of the scores on the individual rating scales. If some questions are more important

EXHIBIT 9.4   Structured Interview Questions, Benchmark Responses, Rating Scale, and Question Weights

Job: Sales Associate
Task Dimension: Customer Service

	Rating Scale					Rating	×	Weight	=	Score
	1	2	3	4	5					
Question No. One (KSAO 1) A customer walks into the store. No other salespeople are around to help the person, and you are busy arranging merchandise. What would you do if you were in this situation?	Keep on arranging merchandise		Keep working, but greet customer		Stop working, greet customer, offer to provide assistance	5		1		5
Question No. Two (KSAO 4) A customer is in the fitting room and asks you to bring her some shirts to try on. You do so, but by accident bring the wrong size. The customer becomes irate and starts shouting at you. What would you do if you were in this situation?	Tell customer to "keep her cool"		Go get correct size		Apologize, go get correct size	3		1		3
Question No. Three (KSAO 5) A customer is shopping for the "right" shirt for her 17-year-old granddaughter. She asks you to show her shirts that you think would be "right" for her. You do this, but the customer doesn't like any of them. What would you do if you were in this situation?	Tell customer to go look elsewhere		Explain why you think your choices are good ones		Explain your choices, suggest gift certificate as alternative	5		2		10
										18

than others, those questions should receive greater weight. The more important the question, the greater its weight relative to the other questions.

Exhibit 9.4 shows the weighting for the three interview questions. The candidate's assigned ratings for the questions are multiplied by their weights and then summed to determine a total score for this task dimension. In the exhibit, the candidate receives a score of 18 (5 + 3 + 10 = 18) for customer service. The candidate's total interview score would be the sum of the scores on all the dimensions.

Selection and Training of Interviewers

Some interviewers are more accurate in their judgments than others. Several studies have found differences in interviewer validity and that many interviewers form lasting early impressions even in structured interviews.[58] The selection of interviewers with characteristics that will enable them to make accurate decisions about candidates is important. Perhaps not surprisingly, cognitive ability (and more specifically, dispositional reasoning) has been linked to accuracy in evaluating others. Interviewer traits like positive and negative affectivity predict how well they can be swayed by interviewee impression management.[59]

The candidate's perception of the interviewer also matters—some research suggests that perceived warmth, job knowledge, general competence, humor, and unfriendliness significantly affect interviewee job choice intentions, candidate attraction, and interview anxiety.[60] Furthermore, *interviewer* impression management also makes a difference and is a fine balance to strike—the interviewer struggles to create a positive, friendly, and welcoming experience while at the same time being an impartial evaluator of the candidate's suitability for the job.[61]

Interviewers will probably need training in the structured interview process, as it may be quite different from what they have encountered and/or used. Training is a way of introducing them to the process, and it is another means of increasing the validity of structured interviews. Logical program content areas to be covered as part of the training are the following:

- Problems with the unstructured interview
- Advantages of the structured interview
- Development of the structured interview
- Use of note taking and elimination of rating errors
- Actual practice in conducting the structured interview

Research on various forms of interviewer training suggests that it is effective, in no small part because it increased the degree to which a structured format was followed. This research suggests that frame-of-reference training (i.e., where interviewers learn to use the same standards of evaluation and to share an understanding of how to rate the candidates appropriately) combined with behaviorally anchored rating scales and opportunities for practice improves the quality of interviewer ratings.[62]

Evaluation

Evidence for the validity of structured interviews has been positive. For example, one study found that it took three or four unstructured interviews to achieve the same validity as a single structured interview, which is a huge difference in time and resources.[63] In addition, meta-analyses have suggested the following conclusions:[64]

1. The average validity of interviews is $\bar{r} = .20$.
2. Structured interviews are more valid ($\bar{r} = .57$) than unstructured interviews ($\bar{r} = .20$).
3. Situational questions are slightly less valid ($\bar{r} = .26$) than experience-based questions ($\bar{r} = .31$), although the validities are similar in magnitude.
4. Panel interviews may be *less* valid ($\bar{r} = .17$) than individual interviews ($\bar{r} = .24$) and may have a detrimental effect on selection decisions, although they are more reliable than having separate interviewers conduct separate interviews with each candidate.
5. Interviewer training ($\bar{r} = .33$), interview standardization ($\bar{r} = .25$), and note taking ($\bar{r} = .29$) all moderately and significantly affect the validity of the interview (although each makes a modest contribution above and beyond structure). The length of the interview has no effect on validity.
6. Regardless of the construct being assessed by the interview or interview question, the validities are moderate in size, but especially for those used to assess job knowledge ($\bar{r} = .35$), creativity ($\bar{r} = .32$), agreeableness ($\bar{r} = .28$), job experience ($\bar{r} = .27$), and values fit ($\bar{r} = .27$).

There is some evidence to suggest that structured interviews are being used more frequently, at least among HR professionals who affiliate with professional organizations such as SHRM (and who, we assume, seek out information on how to conduct effective interviews). Notably, according to benchmarking data from SHRM-affiliated HR professionals, roughly twice as many report using structured interviews as report using unstructured interviews.[65]

Candidates tend to react very favorably to the interview, whether it is structured or not. Research suggests that most candidates believe the interview is an essential component of the selection process, and most view the interview as the most suitable measure of their relevant abilities. As a result, candidates have rated the interview as more job related than any other selection procedure, and it is second only to work sample tests, as mentioned earlier.[66]

The interview appears to have moderate disparate impact against minorities—more than personality tests but considerably less than cognitive ability tests (see the following sections for a discussion).[67] Factors such as candidate ethnicity, accent, and even weight can have not-so-subtle influences on the interview process and outcomes.[68] The extent of disparate impact appears to be moderated by the structure of the interview and constructs assessed. The more structure there is, the less disparate impact is likely to emerge in interviewer ratings.

In the sections that follow, we will move from our discussion of methods of assessing performance potential in candidates (e.g., performance tests, work samples, SJTs), as well as general methods of assessing various constructs (e.g., structured interviews and SJTs), toward specific candidate characteristics. We begin this shift by discussing ability and personality.

Ability Tests

Ability tests assess an individual's capacity to function in a certain way. A 2019 benchmarking study in North America revealed that 46% of organizations use some sort of ability test in selection decisions, down by 23% since 2014.[69] Organizations that use ability tests do so because they assume the tests assess a key determinant of employee performance. Without a certain level of ability, performance is unlikely to be acceptable, regardless of motivation. Students, for example, may try extremely hard to do well in a very difficult class (e.g., calculus) but will probably not be successful unless they have the ability to do so (e.g., mathematical aptitude).

There are four major classes of ability tests: cognitive, psychomotor, physical, and sensory/perceptual.[70] As these ability tests are quite distinct, each will be considered separately below. Because most of the research attention—and public controversy—has focused on cognitive ability tests, they are discussed in considerable detail.

Cognitive Ability Tests

Cognitive ability tests refer to measures that assess thinking (including perception), memory, reasoning, verbal, and mathematical abilities, as well as the expression of ideas. Although the benchmarking study described above reports that nearly half of organizations use ability tests in general, a much smaller number uses cognitive ability tests. A SHRM benchmarking report from 2017 suggests that only 16%–18% of organizations use cognitive ability tests to assess candidates.[71]

Is cognitive ability a general construct, or does it have many specific aspects? The answer is both: general intelligence causes individuals to have similar scores on measures of specific abilities, which are themselves useful.[72] Research shows that measures of specific cognitive abilities, such as verbal, quantitative, reasoning, and so on, appear to reflect general intelligence (sometimes referred to as general mental ability, IQ, or "g"). Someone who scores well on a measure of one specific ability is likely to score well on measures of other specific abilities.

Measures of Cognitive Ability.   Many cognitive ability tests measure both specific cognitive abilities and general mental ability. For example, items representing spatial, quantitative, and reasoning abilities are often used in cognitive ability tests in combination to assess both specific and general mental ability. To illustrate, sample items from the International Cognitive Ability Resource (ICAR) are presented in Exhibit 9.5. ICAR was developed as a public domain resource to make it easier for

---

EXHIBIT 9.5   Sample Cognitive Ability Test Items

1. In the following alphanumeric series, what letter comes next? I J L O S
   (1) T (2) U (3) V (4) X (5) Y (6) Z

2. If the day after tomorrow is two days before Thursday, then what day is it today?
   (1) Friday (2) Monday (3) Wednesday (4) Saturday (5) Tuesday (6) Sunday

3. What follows in the sequence 10, 19, 29, 40, 52?
   Your answer: _____

4.

5.

NOTE: Items 1–2 represent verbal reasoning; item 3 represents quantitative reasoning; items 4 and 5 represent spatial ability.
SOURCE: *International Cognitive Ability Resource Catalogue* [Version 1.0], June 2017, *https://icar-project .com/ICAR_Catalogue.pdf*.

researchers and practitioners to access and use cognitive ability tests. Many test publishers offer an array of tests. An example is the *Wonderlic Contemporary Cognitive Ability Test*, perhaps the most widely used test of general mental ability for selection decisions. Items range in type from spatial relations to numerical problems to analogies. The Wonderlic is not only a speed (timed) test but also a power test: the items get harder as the test progresses (very few individuals complete all items). The Wonderlic has been administered to millions of candidates from over 10,000 organizations. One prominent organization that has used the Wonderlic for more than 30 years is the NFL. Each year, potential recruits are given the Wonderlic, and although scores are supposedly confidential, they inevitably are leaked to the press. Much is then made about top prospects who "bomb" the Wonderlic versus those who "ace" it, although it seems that players' scores often do not play a major role in their performance.[73]

As another example, Pymetrics is a newcomer to the cognitive ability assessment scene. The company's CEO, Frida Polli, who was a neuroscientist at Harvard and MIT, came up with the idea for Pymetrics while studying toward her MBA at Harvard. The idea was to create an assessment that uses neuroscience-backed games to assess cognitive abilities and machine learning to maximize prediction and reduce bias. Pymetrics aims to improve the candidate experience by using gaming principles to make the assessment entertaining, while then using a Netflix-like matching algorithm to predict which candidates would be the best fit for the jobs.

Costs of cognitive ability tests usually vary per candidate, and usually depend on whether the organization scores the test. Before deciding which test to use, organizations should seek a reputable testing firm. The Association of Test Publishers was formed to help ensure that the testing community engages in professional and fair testing practices. It is also advisable to seek the advice of researchers or testing specialists, many of whom are members of the American Psychological Association.

Evaluation of Cognitive Ability Tests. The findings regarding general intelligence have had profound implications for personnel selection. Many meta-analyses have been conducted on the validity of cognitive ability tests. The most comprehensive reviews have estimated the "true" validity of measures of general cognitive ability to be roughly $\bar{r}_{xy} = .51$.[74] The conclusions from these meta-analyses are dramatic:

1. Cognitive ability tests are among the most valid methods of selection.
2. The validity of cognitive ability tests appears to generalize across organizations, job types, and all types of candidates.
3. Organizations using cognitive ability tests in selection enjoy large economic gains compared with organizations that do not use them.
4. Cognitive ability tests appear to generalize across cultures.
5. Beyond job performance, cognitive ability predicts other important criteria, including health-conscious behaviors (such as exercise), occupational prestige, income, steeper career success trajectories, citizenship and helping behaviors, and lower turnover.[75]

These conclusions are based on hundreds of studies of hundreds of organizations employing thousands of workers. Thus, whether an organization is selecting engineers, customer service representatives, or meat cutters, general mental ability is likely the single most valid method of selecting candidates. A large-scale review of multiple meta-analyses suggested relatively high average validities for many occupational groups:[76]

- Computer programmer, $\bar{r}_{xy} = .73$
- Manager, $\bar{r}_{xy} = .64$
- Clerical worker, $\bar{r}_{xy} =$ between .52 and .67
- Enlisted military personnel, $\bar{r}_{xy} =$ between .45 and .65
- Salesperson, $\bar{r}_{xy} = .40$
- Law enforcement officer, $\bar{r}_{xy} = .38$
- Refinery worker, $\bar{r}_{xy} = .31$

Cognitive ability tests are also more valid for jobs of medium complexity (e.g., technicians, administrators) and high complexity (e.g., computer programmers, managers), but they are also valid for jobs of relatively low complexity (e.g., refinery workers).[77] These results show that cognitive ability tests have at least a moderate degree of validity for all types of jobs. The same review also revealed that cognitive ability tests generally have very high degrees of validity in predicting training success ($\bar{r}_{xy} = .57$), and the validity may be even higher for certain occupations (e.g., $\bar{r}_{xy} = .76$ for law enforcement officers). Why do cognitive ability tests work so well in predicting job performance and training performance? This is due to the substantial learning component required during training; smart people tend to be able to learn more in a shorter amount of time and can adapt more quickly to changing circumstances.[78] Because intelligent employees learn more on the job, they are able to quickly acquire and retain job knowledge.[79]

Another important issue in understanding the validity of cognitive ability tests is the nature of specific versus general abilities. Researchers argue that specific abilities are sometimes more important than general mental abilities, and one study suggested that specific cognitive abilities may matter to certain narrow criteria (e.g., perceptual accuracy may predict the degree to which an editor spots errors).[80] Thus, while general mental ability is the most important predictor of job performance in nearly every situation, there may be situations in which specific abilities are important.

Potential Limitations.   If cognitive ability tests are so valid and useful, why don't more organizations use them? One of the main reasons is concern over the disparate impact and fairness of these tests. In terms of disparate impact, regardless of the type of measure used, cognitive ability tests have severe disparate impact against minorities. Specifically, Blacks on average have scored .72 standard deviations below Whites on cognitive ability tests on moderate complexity jobs, and the validities for cognitive ability tests are much lower for Blacks ($\overline{r}_{xy} = .24$) and slightly lower for Hispanics ($\overline{r}_{xy} = .30$) than for Whites ($\overline{r}_{xy} = .33$), with similar findings even after accounting for restriction of range.[81] These discrepant scores and validities have led to close scrutiny—and sometimes rejection—of cognitive ability tests by the courts (see the measurement chapter).

Thus, the dilemma is a real one for the organization. It must decide whether to (1) use the cognitive ability test and experience the positive benefits of using a valid predictor, (2) not use the cognitive ability test, to avoid disparate impact, and substitute a different measure or group of measures that has less disparate impact, or (3) use the cognitive ability test in conjunction with other predictors that do not have disparate impact, thus lessening disparate impact overall. Research suggests that while using other selection measures in conjunction with cognitive ability tests reduces the disparate impact of cognitive ability tests, it by no means eliminates it.[82] Because disparate impact is a concern for all selection predictors, it was discussed in more detail in the measurement chapter. Several other possible ways for reducing disparate impact are included within that chapter.

Candidate reactions present another concern over using cognitive ability tests in selection. In general, candidates perceive cognitive ability tests to be favorable, although less so than work samples, interviews, and résumés. However, some research suggests that potential "star employees," or candidates who are exceptional in quality, may become offended and potentially drop out of the candidate pool if required to take a cognitive ability test. Research also suggests that candidate reactions to cognitive ability tests are largely a function of how well candidates think they did on the test, as people who perform poorly are more likely to question the fairness of the test.[83]

Conclusion.   In sum, cognitive ability tests are one of the most valid selection measures across jobs; they also predict both learning and training success and retention. But they also have some troubling side effects, notably that the tests have substantial disparate impact against minorities. Given such prominent advantages and disadvantages, cognitive ability tests are here to stay, as is the controversy over their use.

Other Types of Ability Tests

Following the earlier classification of abilities into cognitive, psychomotor, physical, and sensory/perceptual, and having just reviewed cognitive ability tests, we now consider the other types of ability tests.

Psychomotor Ability Tests.   Psychomotor ability tests measure the link between thought and bodily movement. Psychomotor ability involves processes such as reaction time, arm-hand steadiness, control precision, and manual and digit dexterity.

An example of testing for psychomotor abilities can be found in the Test of Basic Aviation Skills (TBAS), which is used to select pilot candidates in the US Air Force. For example, the airplane tracking test (a TBAS subtest) requires candidates to use a joystick to keep a sight on an airplane that moves at a constant rate but randomly changes direction (this test assesses control precision).[84]

Physical Abilities Tests.   Physical abilities tests measure muscular strength, cardiovascular endurance, and movement quality.[85] An example of a test that requires all three is the test given to firefighters in the city of Milwaukee, Wisconsin. The test measures upper-body strength (bench press, a lateral pulldown, and grip strength pressure), abdominal strength (sit-ups), aerobic endurance (five-minute step tests), and physical mobility (roof ladder placement).[86]

Physical abilities tests are becoming increasingly common to screen out individuals susceptible to repetitive stress injuries, such as carpal tunnel syndrome. Physical abilities tests may also be necessary for equal employment opportunity (EEO) reasons.[87] Despite little to no race-related disparate impact, meta-analytic estimates suggest that there may be differences between men and women. For example, although they score equally on movement quality tests, female candidates typically score nearly two standard deviations lower than male candidates on muscular strength and cardiovascular endurance tests. However, the scores overlap considerably and vary depending on body region. Therefore, all candidates must be given a chance to pass the requirements and not be judged as a class. Physical fitness training is another way in which the disparate impact of physical abilities tests can be reduced, although modestly.[88]

Another reason to use physical abilities tests for appropriate jobs is to avoid injuries on the job. Well-designed tests will screen out candidates who have applied for positions that are poorly suited to their physical abilities. Thus, fewer injuries should result. In fact, one study using a concurrent validation approach on a sample of railroad workers found that physical ability testing reduced the injury incidence rate by 18.5%, a return on investment of $18 for every $1 spent on physical abilities testing.[89]

When carefully conducted for appropriate jobs, physical abilities tests can be highly valid. One comprehensive study of strength tests reported average validities from $\bar{r} = .39$ for warehouse workers to $\bar{r} = .87$ for enlisted army men. Although the candidate reactions to physical abilities tests have not been thoroughly examined, one study suggested that firefighters tended to perceive most physical abilities tests as fair and job related.[90]

Sensory/Perceptual Abilities Tests.   Sensory/perceptual abilities tests assess the ability to detect and recognize environmental stimuli. Referring to the TBAS used in the US Air Force, several of the tests included in the battery are sensory ability tests. For example, in one subtest, candidates are played a recording of several spoken letters and numbers, and each time they hear a specific letter or number they are instructed to squeeze a trigger.

Job Knowledge Tests. Job knowledge tests attempt to directly assess a candidate's ability to comprehend job requirements. Not surprisingly, job knowledge test scores tend to correlate highly with cognitive ability test scores (recall the link between cognitive ability and acquisition of job knowledge discussed earlier).[91] There are two types of job knowledge tests. One type asks questions that directly assess knowledge of the duties involved in a job. For example, an item from a job knowledge test for an oncology nurse might be, "Describe the five oncological emergencies in cancer patients." The other type of job knowledge test focuses on the level of experience with, and corresponding knowledge about, critical job tasks and tools necessary to perform the job. The state of Wisconsin uses the *Objective Inventory Questionnaire* to evaluate candidates based on their experience with tasks, duties, tools, technologies, and equipment that are relevant to a job.[92]

There has been less research on the validity of job knowledge tests than on other ability tests. One study, however, provided relatively strong support for the validity of job knowledge tests. A meta-analytic review of 502 studies indicated that the validity of job knowledge tests in predicting job performance is .48. These validities were found to be higher for complex jobs and when job and test content were similar.[93]

In the following section, we discuss another form of ability: emotional intelligence. Emotional intelligence deserves its own section, positioned in between abilities and personality tests as it shares characteristics of both types of predictors.

Emotional Intelligence Tests

Increasingly, researchers argue that measures of ability miss an important piece of the puzzle, namely, emotional intelligence or emotional competence.[94] More and more, organizations are using measures of emotional intelligence (EI) in selection decisions. We consider EI by answering four questions: (1) What is EI? (2) How is EI measured? (3) How valid is EI? and (4) What are the criticisms of EI?

What Is Emotional Intelligence?

Researchers have framed the study of EI in one of two ways: first, several researchers have classified EI as a set of individual differences and personality traits that are important for meeting the emotional and social demands of life (an approach that has been labeled as emotional or social competence, trait EI, or mixed EI; we will refer to it as the latter).[95] Although the examination of EI as a set of personality traits and individual differences is an approach in its own right, we focus solely on the second approach as we cover many of these personality traits in the next section. The second approach defines EI explicitly as a form of intelligence: EI is a

---

EXHIBIT 9.6 Sample Items Measuring Emotional Intelligence

Self-awareness

I have a good sense of why I have certain feelings most of the time.

I have good understanding of my own emotions.

Other Awareness

I am sensitive to the feelings and emotions of others.

I have good understanding of the emotions of people around me.

Emotion Regulation

I am quite capable of controlling my own emotions.

I have good control of my own emotions.

SOURCE: C-S. Wong and K. S. Law, "The Effects of Leader and Follower Emotional Intelligence on Performance and Attitude: An Exploratory Study," *Leadership Quarterly*, 2002, 13(3), pp. 243–274.

broad ability concerning how well one processes emotions and emotional information as well as how well one responds to emotional events. Thus, EI may be broken down into the following components:[96]

- *Self-awareness:* Ability to recognize and understand one's own emotions
- *Other awareness:* Ability to recognize and understand others' emotions
- *Emotion regulation:* Ability to make use of or manage this awareness

It is easy to see that this concept is important. Wouldn't nearly every employee be more effective if they could readily sense what they were feeling (and why), sense what others were feeling, and manage their own (and others') emotions?

How Is Emotional Intelligence Measured?

Although there are many variants, EI has mainly been measured in three ways. First, some EI measures are very similar to items contained in a self-report personality test (using the mixed EI approach defined above). Indeed, several reviews found that such EI items are strongly related to personality traits, especially emotional stability, extraversion, and conscientiousness (see the next section for a discussion of these traits).[97] Although some of these self-report tests were designed to assess mixed EI, others were designed to assess ability EI. Given this mismatch, there are issues with their construct validity, as they tend to be more easily faked, are only weakly related to cognitive ability, and are more related to personality traits than abilities.[98]

Second, other EI measures appear to be similar to cognitive ability tests. For example, some measures involve describing the emotional qualities of certain sounds and images. While these measures bear less similarity to the structure of personality measures, they have been criticized for having poor reliability and content validity. For example, one such item may have you select the emotion that is being displayed by a person in a picture without context. However, these tests do demonstrate more construct validity evidence, as these EI measures tend to be more strongly related to cognitive ability and readily fit into intelligence frameworks.[99] A third promising avenue for EI measurement can be found in SJTs (see earlier section) or performance-based measures. These measures, such as the *Situational Test of Emotional Understanding*, the *Situational Test of Emotion Management*, and the *Geneva Emotional Competence Test (GECo)*, present respondents with social situations and ask them to choose the response that the person in the situation would most likely feel or what they would do in that situation. For example, an item asking which emotion someone is most likely to feel when receiving a gift should most appropriately be answered with happy.[100]

Of the three types of EI measures, the personality-like variety is most common. Exhibit 9.6 contains items from one such EI measure.

How Valid Is Emotional Intelligence?

Evidence suggests that EI is modestly to moderately related to job performance, depending on how one defines and measures EI. The ability EI approach tends to have a slightly lower validity (when predicting supervisor ratings of performance) than the mixed EI approach ($\bar{r}_{xy} = .17$ vs. $\bar{r}_{xy} = .23$). The mixed EI measures appear to add little above and beyond a common set of personality traits (and can even be considered redundant with them). Ability EI, on the other hand, appears to predict job performance over and above cognitive ability. Thus, although ability EI may have a relatively small effect on job performance, mixed EI merely replicates the validity of common personality traits (perhaps it is "old wine in new bottles"). Some evidence also suggests that EI may be most important for jobs that are emotionally demanding.[101]

EI might be more critical for discretionary work behaviors, as mixed EI demonstrates a stronger effect on "citizenship" behaviors like helping coworkers and "deviant" behaviors like being rude to coworkers, even after cognitive ability and personality are controlled. Ability EI measures had a similar, albeit smaller, effect. The greater importance of EI for these behaviors (compared with job performance) may be due to the increased importance for interpersonal interactions in, for example, the health care and service industries.[102]

What Are the Criticisms of Emotional Intelligence?

It is safe to say that EI has been controversial—many criticisms and issues have risen over the past several decades.[103] First, many researchers have focused on measuring EI, or seeing how well EI predicts performance (often to disappointing effect), without paying sufficient attention to what EI might uniquely predict. To understand this, one must work from the criterion backward. Shouldn't EI better predict empathetic behavior on the part of social workers than predict whether a bank teller's cash drawer will balance?[104] Second, for many researchers, it is not clear what EI is. Is it really a form of intelligence? Beyond this definitional ambiguity, different EI researchers (especially those that take the mixed EI approach) have studied a dizzying array of concepts—including emotion recognition, self-awareness, empathy, self-control, interpersonal skills, stress management, well-being, and self-discipline. Some researchers have noted that there have been so many different conceptions of what EI is composed of, that it is no longer an intelligible concept.[105] Finally, some critics argue that because EI is so closely related to other constructs, once you control for these factors, EI has nothing unique to offer. For example, we noted in a previous section that mixed EI has little to add above and beyond personality (although this is not true for the ability-based approach).[106]

Furthermore, little research has examined the candidate reactions to and disparate impact of EI. One study found that although the disparate impact of a self-report measure of EI was low in general, the dimension associated with recognizing others' emotions was not. This suggests that there is some potential for disparate impact with EI tests, although the risks may be lower than other measures.[107] In the same study, candidates perceived the EI measure to represent the content of the job and to not be "too personal or invasive"; however, the candidates did not believe doing well on the assessment was important for job performance.[108] In a separate study of candidate reactions to more ability-oriented measures (e.g., those that resemble cognitive ability tests), the fairness and face validity of the measure depended on the dimension of EI that was assessed.[109] As a final concern that warrants more research attention, the potential for EI measures to discriminate against protected classes under the ADA has been discussed as a possibility, given the emotional content of such tests that could adversely affect candidates with Autism Spectrum Disorder.[110] Clearly, the findings from these initial studies suggest that there are causes for concern in EI measures with regard to disparate impact and candidate reactions.

Still, among consulting firms and in the popular press, EI is wildly popular. For example, one organization's promotional materials for an EI measure claim that its measure accounts for more than 85% of performance in its top leadership.[111] It is hard to validate this statement with the research literature.

Summary

Although few would deny that EI is important for many jobs, EI has proved difficult to assess and capture in practice.[112] It *is* clear, though, that more and more organizations are considering EI as a valuable characteristic of potential employees; in fact, one survey of over 2,500 HR professionals suggests that 71% would value EI more than a candidate's cognitive ability.[113] If an organization wishes to use an EI measure in selection decisions, we urge a certain amount of caution. At the very least, it should be restricted to jobs with exceptional interpersonal and emotional demands, and the construct and empirical validity of the EI measure should be investigated before it is used in actual selection decisions.[114]

Personality Tests

Most researchers have reached positive conclusions about the role of personality tests in predicting job performance.[115] Mainly, this is due to the widespread acceptance of a major taxonomy of personality, often called the Big Five. The Big Five are used to describe behavioral (as opposed to emotional or cognitive) traits that may capture most of an individual's personality.[116]

The Big Five factors are *extraversion* (tendency to be sociable, assertive, active, upbeat, and talkative), *agreeableness* (tendency to be altruistic, trusting, sympathetic, and cooperative), *conscientiousness* (tendency to be purposeful, determined, dependable, and attentive to detail), *emotional stability* (tendency to be calm, optimistic, and well adjusted), and *openness to experience* (tendency to be imaginative, attentive to feelings, intellectually curious, and independent). The Big Five are incredibly stable over time, a finding that has been consistently replicated over the past several decades. Controlling for various sources of error, the average population test–retest correlation for any given 15-year period for a given trait is about .60—and is much higher for shorter time intervals (.82).[117]

Measures of Personality

Although personality can be measured in many ways, for personnel selection, the most common measures are self-report surveys. Several survey measures of the Big Five traits are used in selection. The *International Personality Item Pool* (IPIP), which can be found online and used freely, contains several Big Five measures. Exhibit 9.7 provides sample items from the IPIP. Another commonly used measure of the Big Five is the *NEO Personality Inventory*, of which there are several versions that have been translated into numerous languages. A third alternative is the *Hogan Personality Inventory* (HPI), which is also based on the Big Five typology. Responses to the HPI can be scored to yield measures of employee reliability and service orientation, among other occupation-relevant scales. Evidence of validity in predicting job performance in various occupations for all these measures has been demonstrated.[118]

Surveys are often administered online, which is cheaper for the organization and more convenient for the candidate. However, because most online testing is unmonitored, there are three potential problems: (1) test security might be compromised (e.g., test items posted on a blog), (2) candidates may find it easier to cheat or be more motivated to cheat online, and (3) candidates may not tolerate long online personality tests (which may be needed to circumvent faking).[119] Although few differences have been found between paper-and-pencil and proctored Internet tests for undergraduate students,[120] these differences have been shown in a

---

EXHIBIT 9.7   Sample Items Measuring Big Five Personality Dimensions

Please rate how accurately each statement describes you on a scale from 1 = "to no extent" to 5 = "to a very great extent."

Extraversion

Am quiet around strangers. (reverse-scored)

Take charge.

Am skilled in handling social situations.

Agreeableness

Have a soft heart.

Insult people. (reverse-scored)

Have a good word for everyone.

Conscientiousness

Am always prepared.

Pay attention to details.

Am exacting in my work.

Emotional Stability

Am relaxed most of the time.

Seldom feel blue.

Have frequent mood swings. (reverse-scored)

Openness to Experience

Have a vivid imagination.

Love to think up new ways of doing things.

Try to avoid complex people. (reverse-scored)

SOURCE: *International Personality Item Pool (ipip.ori.org).*

number of meta-analyses to be much larger for job candidates, resulting in deflated validity coefficients.[121] For example, the Internet is rife with posts and blogs about Wal-Mart's preemployment test, which includes personality questions. Some posts include the items themselves, whereas others provide tips on how to game the test. Thus, even when companies attempt to keep their personality inventories as private as possible, word often leaks out.[122] There are no silver bullet remedies to these problems.

Several steps can be taken to ameliorate the problems with online testing. First, experts recommend keeping online personality tests as brief as possible, yet long enough to obtain quality information. If the test takes more than 20 minutes, candidates may grow impatient. Second, it is important to assign candidates identification codes, to collect basic background data, and to break the test into sections. These steps increase accountability (lessening the odds of faking) and ensure that if the candidate loses the Internet connection while taking the test, the portions completed will not be lost. Third, strategies designed to reduce faking by candidates should be implemented. As some examples, HR professionals should include measures to detect faking and screen these responses, examine the reliability and standard error of measurement every time a personality assessment is used for selection, and consider using forced-choice measures of personality (e.g., a personality assessment that forces candidates to choose between similarly desirable options).[123] We will discuss these and other faking mitigation methods later in this section. Finally, many experts recommend the use of "item banking" (variation in specific items used to measure each trait) to enhance test security.[124]

Evaluation of Personality Tests

Many comprehensive reviews of the validity of personality tests have been published.[125] Although there are some inconsistencies across reviews, the results can be summarized in Exhibit 9.8. As the exhibit shows, each of the Big Five traits has advantages and disadvantages. However, the traits differ in the degree to which they are a mixed blessing. Specifically, whereas the disadvantages of agreeableness and openness appear to offset their advantages, the advantages of conscientiousness, emotional stability, and extraversion outweigh the disadvantages.[126] These three traits also happen to have the strongest correlates with overall job performance. Thus, they also appear to be the most useful for selection contexts. Of course, in certain situations—such as where adaptability or creativity may be highly valued, or where cooperative relations are crucial—openness and agreeableness may be important to assess as well.[127]

Although there do not appear to be any direct disadvantages to conscientiousness, recent research suggests that when an employee's level of conscientiousness is "too" high, some disadvantages may arise. For example, drawing on the theory that you can have too much of a good thing, extremely conscientious employees have been found to experience greater negative affect, engage in perfectionist tendencies, react poorly to feedback, react adversely to negative life events, and perform poorly at work. The "too much of a good thing" theory does not stop at conscientiousness, however: some studies suggest it extends to the other four dimensions of the Big Five.[128]

Today there is widespread acceptance regarding the validity and utility of personality tests in personnel selection. This does not mean that the area is free of its critics, however. Some researchers have argued that personality traits are not useful selection tools.[129] Here we evaluate three of the most important criticisms of the use of personality tests in selection decisions: the validities are trivial, faking undermines their usefulness, and candidates react negatively to them.

EXHIBIT 9.8   Implications of Big Five Personality Traits at Work

Big Five Trait	Advantages	Disadvantages
Conscientiousness	• Better overall job performers • Perform better in sales • Better career decisions • Higher levels of job satisfaction • More engaged • More likely to emerge as leaders • More likely to be active in job search • Fewer "deviant" work behaviors • Higher retention (lower turnover)	• Lower flexibility and adaptability • Can be "too much of a good thing"
Emotional stability	• Better overall job performers • Better career decisions • Higher levels of job satisfaction • More effective leaders • More motivated • Higher retention (lower turnover) • Less prone to burnout • Less likely to experience work-non-work conflict	• Less able to identify threats • More likely to engage in high-risk behaviors • More likely to appear that they lack concern for others
Extraversion	• Perform better in sales • More likely to emerge as leaders • Higher levels of job satisfaction • More committed to their organization • More engaged • Higher self-efficacy • More likely to be active in job search • More likely to experience positive spillover between work and non-work experiences	• May spend less time on tasks (less productive) • May be dominating or may not give others a chance to share
Agreeableness	• More committed to their organization • More valued as team members • More "helping" behaviors • Fewer "deviant" work behaviors	• Lower career success • Less motivated to set goals • Less able to cope with conflict and stress • Give more lenient ratings • Focus too much on appeasing others
Openness	• Higher creativity • More "helping" behaviors • More effective leaders • More adaptable	• Less committed to employer • More varied "deviant" work behaviors

Trivial Validities.   One set of critics has argued that the validities of personality traits are so small as to border on the trivial, rendering them of limited usefulness as selection devices. While this is an extreme position, it does contain a grain of truth: the validities are far from perfect. For example, our best estimate of the raw validity of conscientiousness in predicting overall job performance is $\bar{r}_{xy} = .13$.[130] By no means would this be labeled a strong validity (though, in fairness, we are not aware of any personality researchers who have done so).

Does this mean that the validities of personality measures, though, are trivial? We do not believe so.[131] It is important to look at the multiple correlations between the set of Big Five traits as a whole and criteria such as job performance. For example, the multiple correlations between the Big Five and overall job performance is roughly $\bar{r}_{xy} = .32$ (moderately sized), and is even stronger for withdrawal, $\bar{r}_{xy} = .66$ (a very strong correlation).[132] Furthermore, there is usefulness in "splitting up" constructs assessed by the Big Five and performance outcomes. For example, the NEO-PI-R (NEO-Personality Inventory-Revised) splits each of the Big Five dimensions into six facets. Thus, extraversion could be split up into activity, assertiveness, excitement seeking, gregariousness, positive emotionality, and warmth. Combining the predictive power of these facets increases the validity of the Big Five. In fact, taking this approach results in validities for overall job performance that range from .19 to .41.[133] These validities are hardly trivial. Meta-analytic research suggests that the validity of personality measures can be improved by asking others to provide the ratings: the validities can be improved to as high as .28 for conscientiousness by having others who know the candidate well complete the assessment as an outside observer.[134]

Also, the Big Five do not exhaust the set of potentially relevant personality traits. Meta-analytic evidence suggests that a variety of other personality traits can be relevant for workplace outcomes.[135] As a first example, the Big Five Factor model framework has been extended and refined to include an honesty/humility factor as a sixth dimension. Some research suggests that this variable predicts deviant behavior above and beyond the Big Five, including unethical business decisions and sexual harassment proclivity.[136] Another trait, termed core self-evaluations (a reflection of an individual's self-confidence and self-worth), has also been linked to job performance. Research indicates that core self-evaluations are predictive of job performance, and the Core Self-Evaluations Scale (shown in Exhibit 9.9) appears to have validity equivalent to that of conscientiousness. A further advantage of this measure is that it is nonproprietary (i.e., free).[137] Research also suggests that additional traits are relevant for the work context: proactive personality (degree to which people take action) predicts performance, innovation, personal initiative behaviors, and job attitudes even after controlling for the Big Five;[138] hardiness or resilience (the degree to which people bounce back after hardship) reduces the experience of job burnout;[139] and the Dark Triad (a complex of narcissistic, Machiavellian, and psychopathic traits) predicts counterproductive work behavior.[140] However,

---

EXHIBIT 9.9 The Core Self-Evaluations Scale

Instructions: Below are several statements about you with which you may agree or disagree. Using the response scale below, indicate your agreement or disagreement with each item by placing the appropriate number on the line preceding that item.

1	2	3	4	5
Strongly Disagree	Disagree	Neutral	Agree	Strongly Agree

1. _____ I am confident I get the success I deserve in life.
2. _____ Sometimes I feel depressed. (r)
3. _____ When I try, I generally succeed.
4. _____ Sometimes when I fail, I feel worthless. (r)
5. _____ I complete tasks successfully.
6. _____ Sometimes I do not feel in control of my work. (r)
7. _____ Overall, I am satisfied with myself.
8. _____ I am filled with doubts about my competence. (r)
9. _____ I determine what will happen in my life.
10. _____ I do not feel in control of my success in my career. (r)
11. _____ I am capable of coping with most of my problems.
12. _____ There are times when things look pretty bleak and hopeless to me. (r)

Note: r = reverse-scored (for these items, 5 is scored 1, 4 is scored 2, 2 is scored 4, and 1 is scored 5).

SOURCE: T. A. Judge, A. Erez, J. E. Bono, and C. J. Thoresen, "The Core Self-Evaluations Scale: Development of a Measure," *Personnel Psychology*, 2003, 56, pp. 303–331.

regardless of the predictive validity of these additional personality traits, meta-analytic evidence has been emerging that suggests that these additional personality traits share a lot of conceptual and empirical overlap with the Big Five. This does not mean, however, that these personality traits are not useful—especially when the personality traits provide additional or incremental validity above and beyond that of the Big Five or when they are strongly predictive of important narrow criteria.

Finally, there is evidence that the validities of the Big Five may be improved by contextualizing the measures. Most personality inventories ask about behaviors in general, ignoring the context in which those behaviors occur. Researchers argue that tailoring items to ask about behaviors specific to the workplace, or asking candidates to report on how they behave at work only, will strengthen the validities of the Big Five.[141] A recent meta-analysis found support for this notion, demonstrating that the validity of each of the Big Five traits increased when the measures were contextualized. Specifically, for four of the Big Five traits—extraversion, agreeableness, emotional stability, and openness to experience—the validity of contextualized measures was twice as high as the validity of more traditional, decontextualized measures. Although measures of conscientiousness specific to the workplace also improved validities, those improvements were not as strong as the others, presumably because traditional measures of conscientiousness already reference people's work behaviors.[142]

Faking.   Another frequent criticism of personality measures is that they are "fakeable," meaning candidates may distort their responses to increase their odds of being hired. This concern is apparent when one considers personality items (see Exhibits 9.7 and 9.9) and the nature of the traits. Few individuals would want to describe themselves as disagreeable, neurotic, unconscientious, and unconfident. Because answers to these questions are nearly impossible to verify (e.g., imagine trying to verify whether a candidate prefers reading a book to watching television), the possibility of "faking good" is quite real.

There has been much research done on faking. The results of this literature can be summarized as follows. First, there is little doubt that some faking or enhancement does occur. Meta-analytic research suggests that candidates consistently score higher than current employees on socially desirable personality traits like conscientiousness, emotional stability, and agreeableness. Candidates can score nearly one-half of a standard deviation higher than non-candidates on emotional stability and conscientiousness. In most situations, there is no reason to believe that candidates should score more favorably on personality tests than employees—if anything, the reverse would be expected. Also, when individuals are informed that their scores matter (i.e., the scores might be used in selection decisions), their scores on personality tests increase.[143]

But what is the outcome of faking? Interestingly, the answer to this question is not as clear as it seems. In short, though candidates do try to look good by enhancing their responses to personality tests, this enhancement does not significantly detract from the validity of the tests in all cases. Why might this be the case? Evidence suggests that socially desirable responding, or presenting oneself in a favorable light, does not end once someone takes a job. Therefore, the same tendencies that cause someone to present themself in a somewhat favorable light on a personality test also help them do better on the job. As an example, consider the job of customer service representative. An individual in that occupation needs to be able to assess a customer's needs, deal with potential problems, and interact with that customer in a way that will result in the customer being satisfied. An employee who can assess a situation and determine the socially desirable response should be more adept at achieving customer satisfaction than an employee who is less skilled in this area. Thus, socially desirable responding may very well be desired in many cases.[144]

However, there are as many cases in which socially desirable behavior and responding would not be desirable on the job. For example, overestimation of competence, overclaiming of knowledge, or other socially desirable distortion of one's personality may lead one to take on tasks for which they are not well suited and cause the employee to be resented by their coworkers. In further support of why social desirability may not always be desirable, a meta-analysis found that individuals who craft positive impressions on personality surveys tend to not perform well on the job and at school.[145]

Because it is unclear whether faking undermines personality validities across contexts and situations, some of the proposed solutions to faking may be unnecessary or may cause more problems than they solve. For example, some have proposed correcting candidate scores for faking. However, the literature is quite clear that such corrections do not improve the validity of personality measures.[146] Another proposed solution is to use forced-choice personality measures, although these measures have some scoring issues that may prove tricky.[147] A third possible method of reducing faking involves warning candidates that their scores will be verified. Typically, this warning is presented to candidates before they begin the test. Although warning messages can reduce faking, they may also increase perceptions of testing unfairness. Overall, while warning candidates against faking has both pros and cons, studies have shown that such warnings can reduce faking (by as much as 30%) without undermining validities.[148]

A final possibility is to use other reports of personality. Individuals who have worked with a candidate could report on the candidate's personality. However, it is important to attend to information security concerns, as observer reports of candidates can also be faked. One should ensure that the observer nominated by the candidate completes the assessment and that the observer is asked to be objective in the assessment. In addition, to the extent possible, multiple observer ratings should be used, as this greatly improves reliability and, thus, validity.[149]

Candidate Reactions. Although their validity can be moderate to large in size, and their disparate impact can be near zero, it is important to understand how candidates react to personality tests. From a candidate's standpoint, the subjective and personal nature of the questions asked in these tests may raise questions about their validity and concerns about invasiveness. In fact, the available evidence concerning candidates' perceptions of personality tests suggests that they are viewed relatively negatively compared with other selection measures (although they are still perceived more favorably than measures such as honesty tests, handwriting analysis, and reaching out to personal contacts). To some degree, candidates who react the most negatively are those who believe they have scored the worst. In general, though, candidates do not perceive personality measures to be as face-valid as other selection measures. Thus, while personality tests—when used properly—do have validity, this validity does not seem to translate into favorable candidate perceptions. More research is needed into the ways that these tests could be made more acceptable to candidates.[150]

Although candidates prefer other selection methods, about 44% of organizations use some form of personality assessment (making it the third most frequently used assessment, according to the Talent Board, although lower estimates were found by SHRM [17%–32%]). Furthermore, there appear to be large gaps between what HR professionals do and what is supported by science. Notably, many practitioners still use personality typologies such as the Myers-Briggs Type Indicator (MBTI), despite most of the research community embracing the Five Factor Model. In general, it appears that perspectives need to change on the part of HR professionals and candidates, after which personality assessment may be effectively incorporated into staffing systems.[151]

In the next section we describe integrity testing. Often, these tests take the form of personality tests with the intention of predicting whether candidates will be deceptive or steal while on the job.

Integrity Tests

When asked to identify the qualities desired in ideal job candidates, employers routinely put integrity at the top of their lists. In one survey conducted by the National Association of Colleges and Employers (NACE), employers were asked to rate the importance of various job candidate qualities on a scale from 1 to 5, where 1 = not essential and 5 = absolutely essential. The following eight skills/qualities were the most highly rated:[152]

1. Critical thinking/problem solving   4.66
2. Teamwork/collaboration   4.48
3. Professionalism/integrity   4.41
4. Oral/written communication   4.30
5. Digital technology   3.84
6. Leadership   3.65
7. Career management   3.38
8. Global/multicultural fluency   2.78

The third category states that an "ability to demonstrate integrity, ethical behavior, act responsibly with the interest of the larger community in mind, and ability to learn from mistakes" is an important characteristic for employees to possess. Clearly, integrity is a quality that employers deem important for candidates, and integrity tests are designed to assess this attribute.

Integrity tests attempt to assess a candidate's propensity to engage in unethical behavior (e.g., dishonesty, theft).[153] They are alternatives to other methods that attempt to ascertain a candidate's honesty and morality, such as the polygraph (i.e., a "lie detector") test or deception detection in structured interviews. For most employers, polygraph tests are prohibited by law.[154] Even if they were legal, polygraphs are so invasive that negative candidate reactions would weigh against their use in most situations. Polygraph tests have poor validity evidence and relatively high false-positive rates.[155] Of course, interviewer evaluations of candidate integrity are not illegal, but they are unreliable as a method of detecting dishonesty as it is very hard to detect.[156] Even experts such as FBI agents, judges, and psychologists scarcely perform above chance in detecting lying. A review of 108 studies revealed that people detect lies at a rate that is only 4.2% better than chance.[157]

For these reasons, integrity tests are a superior alternative to polygraph tests and interviews. Although some surveys of HR professionals in the United States and Canada suggest that only 10%–15% of organizations use integrity tests, they are used much more frequently in positions of public trust (e.g., military, security).[158] The tests are especially likely to be used where theft, safety, or malfeasance is an important concern. For example, retail organizations lose an estimated $15.5 billion per year to employee theft; and it might surprise you to learn that theft due to employees accounts for roughly one-third (33.2%) of all inventory shrinkage, about on par with that attributed to shoplifting (35.7%).[159] On average, each *case* of employee dishonesty results in a loss of $1,264.10.[160]

The promise of integrity testing is that it will weed out those most prone to these counterproductive work behaviors. Indeed, in one study with a total sample of over 30,000 employees across four industries, when integrity tests were not used, employees made more workers' compensation claims and claimed a higher dollar value than those who were screened (the underlying assumption is that many who were not screened with integrity tests overclaimed workers' compensation that they were not entitled to).[161]

Measures

There are two major types of integrity tests: clear purpose (sometimes called overt) and general purpose (sometimes called veiled purpose or personality-oriented). Exhibit 9.10 provides examples of items from both types of measures. Clear purpose tests directly assess employee attitudes toward theft. Such tests often consist of two sections: (1) questions of antitheft attitudes (see items 1 and 2 in Exhibit 9.10) and (2) questions about the frequency and degree of involvement in theft or other counterproductive activities (see items 3 and 4 in Exhibit 9.10).[162] General or veiled purpose integrity tests assess employee personality with the idea that personality influences dishonest behavior (see items 5–8 in Exhibit 9.10). Examples of clear purpose or overt integrity tests are the *Personnel Selection Inventory*, the *Reid Report*, and the *Stanton Survey*. Examples of general or veiled purpose tests are the *PDI Employment Inventory, the Workplace Productivity Profile,* and the *Reliability Scale of the Hogan Employment Inventory*. Notably, integrity tests can be administered via paper and pencil, unproctored on the Internet, and on mobile devices. One recent study found few differences among computer-, tablet-, and smartphone-based integrity assessments.[163]

EXHIBIT 9.10   Sample Integrity Test Questions

Clear Purpose or Overt Test Questions

1. Do you think most people would cheat if they thought they could get away with it?
2. Do you believe a person has a right to steal from an employer if he or she is unfairly treated?
3. Did you ever write a check knowing there was not enough money in your bank account?
4. Have you ever stolen anything?

Veiled Purpose or Personality-Based Test Questions

5. Would you rather go to a party than read a newspaper?
6. How often do you blush?
7. Do you almost always make your bed?
8. Do you like to take chances?

As mentioned in the previous section, some have suggested that honesty (or, perhaps, integrity) represents a sixth personality factor, something unique from the Big Five traits.[164] However, most researchers believe that scores on integrity tests reflect a broad or "compound" personality trait that is a combination of several Big Five personality traits. Specifically, integrity test scores appear to reflect conscientiousness, agreeableness, and emotional stability.[165] Regardless of which aspects of personality integrity tests measure, it appears that they predict workplace deviance or counterproductive behaviors better than any of the individual Big Five traits.[166]

Validity of Integrity Tests

Over the years, several meta-analyses have been published attempting to evaluate the validity of integrity tests. These meta-analyses have suggested that there is criterion-related validity for integrity tests. For example, the average validities range from .10 to .18 for overt tests and from .14 to .22 for personality-oriented tests. The validities are much higher for predicting CWB (counterproductive work behaviors): .30 to .39 for overt tests and .22 to .23 for personality-oriented tests. Interestingly, one meta-analysis found that validities were stronger when they came from studies authored by publishers of integrity tests.[167]

In any event, although integrity tests do have some validity and very little disparate impact,[168] the prior meta-analyses varied in terms of the *size* of that validity. In the newest meta-analysis, when restricting the frame of studies to *only* candidate samples that used a predictive validation design with non-self-report performance ratings, the validity shrinks to between .09 and .11 for *both* performance and CWBs. Although organizations would likely benefit from using integrity tests for a wide array of jobs, given the findings reviewed above, we recommend that

HR professionals considering the use of integrity tests scrutinize the variability in validity estimates reported above and make their own determination of whether to use an integrity test based on a sound job analysis. HR professionals should also consider the importance of integrity to the occupation, industry, and even country. Recent research suggests that integrity tests may be less fake-able and more valid in countries where corruption and higher crime rates are more prevalent.[169]

Criticisms and Concerns

Faking. One of the most significant concerns with the use of integrity tests is the obvious possibility that candidates might fake their responses. Consider answering the questions in Exhibit 9.10. Now consider answering those questions in the context of applying for a job that you want. It seems more than plausible that candidates might distort their responses in such a context (particularly given that most of the answers would be impossible to verify). This possibility becomes a real concern when one considers the prospect that the individuals most likely to "fake good" (people behaving dishonestly) are exactly the type of candidates organizations would want to weed out.[170]

Embedded within the issue of faking are three questions: (1) Can integrity tests be faked? (2) Do candidates fake or enhance their responses to integrity tests? and (3) Does faking harm the validity of the tests, such that a "perverse inversion" occurs where those who get high scores are those who have the least integrity (i.e., fake the most)?

First, candidates can fake their scores when instructed or otherwise sufficiently motivated to do so, just as they can with personality tests. Studies that compare individuals who are asked to respond honestly with those who are told to "fake good" reveal that, unsurprisingly, integrity test scores in the "fake condition" situation are higher—especially for overt tests (candidate scores of those who fake are roughly 1 standard deviation higher than the scores of those who did not) but less so for personality-based tests.[171]

Second, a problem with interpreting whether candidates *can* fake is that it does not tell us whether they indeed *do* fake. After all, job candidates certainly are not told to "fake good" when completing employment tests, and many candidates do not purposely enhance their responses for moral reasons (they feel it would be wrong to enhance) or practical reasons (they believe enhancements would be detected). Unfortunately, there is much less evidence on this second question. Notably, some recent strides have been made in detecting integrity test faking by looking at item-level response times, which on average detect 26% more cases of faking and have 53% less false positives than traditional faking detection methods (those instructed to fake an integrity test generally take half of a standard deviation longer to answer each item).[172]

Finally, in terms of whether faking matters, if faking was pervasive, integrity test scores would either have no validity in predicting performance from candidate scores or have *negative* validity (honest candidates reporting worse scores than dishonest candidates). The fact that validity was positive for candidate samples suggests that if faking does occur, it does not severely impair the predictive validity of integrity tests. Regardless of the reason, it does seem clear that if faking is a problem, it is not enough to undermine the validity of the tests.

Misclassification and Stigmatization. Some object to integrity tests because of candidates being misclassified as dishonest.[173] We think the larger issue is the possible stigmatization of candidates who are thought to be dishonest due to their test scores and the gravity of being labeled as dishonest. These problems can be avoided with proper procedures for maintaining the security and confidentiality of test scores (which, of course, should be done in any case).

Negative Candidate Reactions. A meta-analysis compared candidate reactions to 10 selection procedures, including interviews, work samples, cognitive ability tests, and integrity tests. The results revealed that candidates react negatively to integrity tests—indeed, they rated integrity tests lower than all other methods except graphology (handwriting analysis) and reference checks.[174] It is likely that candidates react quite differently to various kinds of integrity test questions (e.g., candidates react most negatively to overt items),[175] and that candidates' negative reactions might be mollified with explanations and administrative instructions.

In the next section, we discuss predictors that are more in line with the motivational and cultural fit aspects of staffing. Interests, values, and preferences tend to be most relevant when determining whether a candidate would be a good fit for the job, team, or organization as a function of similar interests, values, or preferences.

Interest, Values, and Preference Inventories

Interest, values, and preference inventories attempt to assess the activities individuals *prefer* to do both on and off the job, rather than assess whether the person *can* do the job. Just because a person can do a job does not guarantee success on the job. If the person does not want to do the job, that individual will fail, regardless of ability.

Interests

Although interests seem important, they have not been used very much in HR selection. There are, however, firms that sell interest assessments. For example, Prevue's interests assessment evaluates whether candidates are interested in working with people, data, or things.[176] Many of these assessments measure vocational interests (e.g., the type of career that would motivate and satisfy someone) rather than organizational interests (e.g., the type of job or organization that would motivate and satisfy someone). Example interest inventory items are provided in Exhibit 9.11.

EXHIBIT 9.11   Sample Items From Interest Inventory

Instructions: This inventory contains a list of activities that you might be interested in doing. Please indicate how much you would like to do each activity by placing the appropriate number on the line preceding that item.

1	2	3	4	5
Strongly Dislike	Dislike	Neutral	Like	Strongly Like

1._____ Direct all sales activities for a company.
2._____ Be an administrator for city government.
3._____ Serve as a president of a university.
4._____ Direct and coordinate the work activities of subordinates.
5._____ Direct the operations of a medium-size company.
6._____ Coordinate the activities of all departments in a bank.
7._____ Plan and direct training and staff development for a business.
8._____ Plan and coordinate a convention for a professional association.
9._____ Direct the business affairs of a university.

SOURCE: Adapted from J. Rounds, *The Basic Interest Markers: Management Subscale* (measure), from the Interest Item Pool (IIP), Oct. 15, 2018.

Past research has suggested that interest inventories are not valid predictors of job performance, but this conclusion appears to be premature. There has been a renewed interest in using vocational interests for selection purposes: the results of a large validation study suggested that interests not only predict job performance but also contribute uniquely above the effects of cognitive ability and the Big Five.[177] Furthermore, recent meta-analyses of the criterion-related validity and disparate impact potential of vocational interests have been positive.[178] For example, vocational interest composites have been shown to be moderate predictors of job performance ($\bar{r} = .28$) and turnover ($\bar{r} = -.25$), although these estimates are slightly weaker in applicant samples. Moreover, individual vocational interests (e.g., an interest in artistic occupations) appear to be more predictive of performance when the interest itself is relevant for the job (e.g., a job opening for a graphic design artist).[179] Relatedly, another stream of research in this area has examined the extent to which candidates' interests match those fulfilled by the job. In a separate series of meta-analyses, the interest congruence was found to predict task performance and motivational persistence with validities ranging from .20 to .30.[180] These positive effects may be due to a motivational benefit of candidates being in jobs and careers that fulfill their aspirations and allow them to do work that they want to do; conversely, being in an unfulfilling job can make you lose motivation and even engage in CWBs.[181]

Although specific interests do not appear to predict job performance on their own, the alignment between a candidate's interests and what the job provides is predictive. Undoubtedly, one of the reasons why vocational interests are not *more* predictive of job performance is because the interests are tied to the occupation rather than the organization or the job.

Values

Research suggests that while interest inventories play an important role in candidate fit for the job, a more promising way of considering fit with the organization during the staffing process is to focus on values and value congruence.[182] As was discussed in the staffing models and strategy chapter, person/organization fit argues that it is not the candidate's characteristics alone that influence performance but rather the congruence between the candidate's characteristics and those of the organization. For example, an individual who values continuous learning may perform well in an organization that emphasizes professional development, trying new things, and innovating but do poorly in an organization whose culture is characterized by tradition and convention. Thus, value inventories may be more valid when they consider the match between candidate values and organizational values (person/organization fit).

Indeed, one meta-analysis of nearly 100 studies conducted around the world found that there was a positive relationship between values congruence and performance that ranged from .10 to .17. However, the numbers were much stronger for job satisfaction and commitment, suggesting that values congruence may be more important for employee satisfaction than performance.[183] However, not much work has been done on the disparate impact or candidate reactions to value congruence fit assessment.

How might organizations measure fit in practice? One way is through the structured interview: one study suggested that interviewers can successfully make judgments regarding whether candidates fit with the values of the organization.[184] Another way is through assessment: a number of vendors offer organizational culture assessments (e.g., Denison Consulting, Twegos) that could be used to measure the congruence between employee/applicant values and the organization's espoused values.[185]

Selection for Team Environments

Many managers have recognized the importance of selecting employees who will work well in teams (if, of course, teamwork is a job requirement).[186] For example, Alex Milling, vice president of client and merchant services at Eved (an event commerce software company), notes: "Being a good manager and building a great team culture starts before people officially join your team or company. I now invest a lot more time in the hiring process to ensure new team members are set up for success and the position is a good fit for both parties."[187] If you have worked with the same team for a long period of time and then lost a member (e.g., the team member moved away or joined a different team), you may have witnessed just how much of an impact one person can have on the effectiveness of a team.[188]

Selection in team environments is a function of team-related tasks, KSAOs, and team member roles. To understand the proper steps for selection in team-based environments, one must first understand the requirements of the job. This involves determining the team tasks and the knowledge, skills, and abilities (KSAs) required for teamwork. As some examples, team tasks and activities could require planning, distributing resources, coordinating, motivating, monitoring systems and resources, and monitoring and evaluating performance.[189] Depending on the task or activity, to be effective in a teamwork assignment, an employee may need to demonstrate *interpersonal KSAs* (consisting of conflict resolution, collaborative problem solving, and communication skills), *self-management KSAs* (consisting of goal setting and performance management skills, or planning and task coordination skills), or *boundary-spanning KSAs* (consisting of networking skills and ability in identifying opportunities).[190] In virtual teams, technology knowledge, professional skills, and intercultural knowledge (and cultural intelligence) can be especially useful in navigating unique challenges.[191] Sometimes, it is useful to divide the team tasks and their requisite KSAs into particular team roles; other times it might be important for team members to take on multiple roles that require different KSAs.

To better predict team performance in a selection context, the Teamwork Knowledge, Skills, and Ability test was developed.[192] Exhibit 9.12 provides some sample items from the 35-item SJT. This test has been validated against multiple criteria (including teamwork, OCB (organizational citizenship behavior), and overall performance; its average criterion-related validity across nine validation studies is .20), and it predicts team member performance and OCB above and beyond social skills and the Big Five.[193] However, more recent validations of the measure have noted issues with its reliability and construct validity. Recall from the section on SJTs that since there are so many facets to a SJT (candidates, situations, items, dimensions, etc.), it is very difficult to demonstrate reliability and validity evidence for these types of measures.[194] It should be noted that tests are not the only method of measuring teamwork KSAs. Other methods of assessment that some leading companies have used in selecting team members include structured interviews, personality tests, and biodata.[195] Another aspect important to team selection is the determination of person/group fit. Earlier we discussed a person's value congruence with the organization. In a similar way, the fit between the candidate and the group could be assessed.[196]

There are many important decisions to make in selecting for team environments. Beyond considering candidates' ability to meet job requirements, another focus is on value creation and forming a competitive advantage. For example, some considerations in team staffing include creating market opportunities (e.g., hiring innovative, creative team members who work well together), reducing costs (e.g., team

---

EXHIBIT 9.12 Example Items Assessing Teamwork KSAs

1. Suppose that you find yourself in an argument with several coworkers about who should do a very disagreeable but routine task. Which of the following would likely be the most effective way to resolve this situation?
   A. Have your supervisor decide, because this would avoid any personal bias.
   B. Arrange for a rotating schedule so everyone shares the chore.
   C. Let the workers who show up earliest choose on a first-come, first-served basis.
   D. Randomly assign a person to do the task and don't change it.

2. Your team wants to improve the quality and flow of the conversations among its members. Your team should:
   A. Use comments that build on and connect to what others have said.
   B. Set up a specific order for everyone to speak and then follow it.
   C. Let team members with more to say determine the direction and topic of conversation.
   D. Do all of the above.

3. Suppose you are presented with the following types of goals. You are asked to pick one for your team to work on. Which would you choose?
   A. An easy goal to ensure the team reaches it, thus creating a feeling of success.
   B. A goal of average difficulty so the team will be somewhat challenged, but successful without too much effort.
   C. A difficult and challenging goal that will stretch the team to perform at a high level, but attainable so that effort will not be seen as futile.
   D. A very difficult, or even impossible, goal so that even if the team falls short, it will at least have a very high target to aim for.

SOURCE: M. J. Stevens and M. A. Campion, "Staffing Work Teams: Development and Validation of a Selection Test for Teamwork Settings," *Journal of Management*, 1999, 25(2), pp. 207–228.

players are less likely to leave and may even inspire others to stay), and enhancing competitive advantage (e.g., treating team members as assets who could defect to competing organizations or who understand the market well [having been with other organizations]).[197] Another important decision in team member selection is who should make the hiring decisions. In many cases, team assessments are made by members of the self-directed work team in deciding who becomes a member of the group. Some organizations also consult external experts when making decisions in selecting team members. However, there can be differences between what is important to "insiders" and what is important to "outsiders" in these instances—for example, a study examining prior job performance, citizenship, and deviant behaviors demonstrated that citizenship was valued more by insiders than by outsiders, although it was predictive of performance in the NFL.[198]

Selection of Leaders

Over the past several decades, the HR landscape has witnessed a surge of interest in identifying individuals with "high potential" for leadership—across benchmarking studies, the number of organizations with these programs has increased by 35% (from 42% in 1994 to 77% in 2018). It has been deemed one of the greatest challenges in HR today, with only 18% of HR professionals satisfied with their current leadership strength.[199] Although most of these "high-potential" programs are relevant for internal selection (see the next chapter), many organizations choose to examine specific predictors of leadership potential when selecting external candidates. For example, Development Dimensions International (DDI) has developed several assessments geared toward identifying leadership potential, including the Early Identifier, the Leadership Insight Inventory, and the Leadership Readiness Assessment. As another example, research has shown that senior executives' perceptions of fit of newly hired junior executives are important for performance.[200]

As with the method for selecting teammates, one should first consider the tasks expected of managers and leaders as well as the KSAOs needed to fulfill these requirements. Managerial work role requirements have been identified to focus on conceptual aspects (e.g., decision making, strategy, and innovation), interpersonal aspects (e.g., managing people and managing the demands and resources of the work environment), and technical aspects (e.g., managing the logistics, technological aspects, administration, and control of the work environment).[201] Leadership, however, goes beyond management: it involves influencing others to accomplish goals.[202] Thus, these activities, or expected behaviors, focus on influence. These activities can be task oriented (e.g., enhancing understanding and helping employees put vision into action) or relationship oriented (e.g., fostering and promoting coordination among employees, motivating employees, and developing an engaging work environment).[203] Emotional intelligence, cognitive ability, personality traits, and an ability to grow and learn have been identified as important leader KSAOs that predict leader success and failure.[204]

Regardless of the method one chooses to assess leadership potential, one should be careful of disparate impact. Differences in the selection of leaders have been found across men and women, as well as for other protected classes. For example, women are less likely to be selected as leaders, as are individuals of certain races or ethnicities (e.g., Asian Americans and Blacks).[205] Research has demonstrated that these differences are a function of unfair stereotypes in leader categorization. Therefore, one should take care to avoid this bias seeping into the leader selection process—especially during the interview (see earlier section on structured interviews). Beyond disparate impact, leader evaluations are further influenced by irrelevant physical characteristics, which can be more salient during the interview: research suggests physical height and even facial features influence leader categorization.[206]

Choice of Substantive Assessment Methods

As with the choice of initial assessment methods, a large amount of research has been conducted on substantive assessment methods that can help guide organizations in the appropriate methods to use. Reviews of this research, using the same criteria that were used to evaluate initial assessment methods, are shown in Exhibit 9.13. Specifically, the criteria are use, cost, reliability, validity, utility, candidate reactions, and disparate impact.

Use

As can be seen in Exhibit 9.13, only leader potential assessments appear to be used frequently in organizations (i.e., methods that are used by at least two-thirds of all organizations). Personality tests and emotional intelligence tests have moderate degrees of use. Although not reflected in the chart, some subforms (e.g., work samples, values inventories, and cognitive ability tests) have moderate use in some benchmarking surveys. The other substantive methods are only occasionally or infrequently used by organizations.

Cost

The costs of substantive assessment methods vary. Some methods can be purchased from vendors quite inexpensively (personality tests; emotional intelligence tests; interest, values, and preference inventories; integrity tests; leader potential assessments); of course, the costs of administering and scoring the tests must be factored in. Some methods, such as team assessments, can vary in price depending on whether the organization develops the measure itself or purchases it from a vendor. But these still tend to be expensive given the degree of customization required for teams (e.g., selecting individuals who will be the right fit for a specific team) and the complexity in team placement decisions. Other methods, such as structured interviews, performance tests and work samples, and SJTs, generally require extensive time and resources to develop; thus, these measures are the most expensive of the substantive assessment methods.

Reliability

The reliability of most of the substantive assessment methods is moderate or high. This is because many of these methods have undergone extensive development efforts by vendors. However, whether an organization purchases an assessment tool from a vendor or develops it independently, the reliability of the method must be investigated. Just because a vendor claims a method is reliable does not necessarily mean it will be so within a particular organization. Also, due to development challenges with SJTs, their reliability in a traditional sense is low (although there are other ways of demonstrating reliability and validity). For these reasons, the SJT and team assessments categories were labeled as low.

EXHIBIT 9.13   Evaluation of Substantive Assessment Methods

Predictors	Use	Cost	Reliability	Validity	Utility	Applicant Reactions	Disparate Impact
Personality tests	Low	Low	High	Moderate	?	Negative	Low
Ability tests	Low	Low	High	High	High	Negative	High
Emotional intelligence tests	Moderate	Low	High	Low	?	?	Low
Performance tests and work samples	Moderate	High	High	High	High	Positive	Low
Situational judgment tests	Low	High	Moderate	Moderate	?	Positive	Moderate
Integrity tests	Low	Low	High	High	High	Negative	Low
Interest, values, and preference inventories	Low	Low	High	Low	?	?	Low
Structured interviews	Moderate	High	Moderate	High	?	Positive	Mixed
Team assessments	Low	Moderate	?	?	?	Positive	?

Validity

Like cost, the validity of substantive assessment methods varies a great deal. Some methods, such as integrity tests, have demonstrated little validity in predicting job performance. However, integrity tests are moderately to strongly predictive of counterproductive work behaviors such as theft; if it is important to prevent theft in the position, an integrity test may be a useful predictor to collect. Most of the methods have moderate levels of validity. As was noted when reviewing these measures, however, steps can be taken to increase their validity through design decisions and careful selection of constructs. Ability tests, performance tests, and work samples have high levels of validity.

Utility

As with initial assessment methods, the utility of most substantive assessment methods is surprisingly high, if the KSAOs assessed are relevant for the job. The utility for interest, values, and preference inventories is low according to the most recent evidence. However, since this evidence was collected quite some time ago, more work is needed to verify whether this is still true. Finally, there is not enough information on the utility of team and leader potential assessments and more research is needed.

Candidate Reactions

Research shows that candidates' reactions to substantive assessment methods appear to depend on the method. Relatively abstract methods that require a candidate to answer questions not directly tied to the job (e.g., questions on personality tests, most ability tests, and integrity tests) seem to generate negative reactions from candidates. Thus, research tends to suggest that candidates view personality, ability, and integrity tests unfavorably. Methods that are manifestly related to the job for which candidates are applying appear to generate positive reactions. Research suggests that candidates view performance tests, work samples, and structured interviews favorably. The remaining methods tend to have mixed evidence, and candidates' reactions depend on their construction. Little is known about candidate reactions to team and leader potential assessments, as well as interest, values, and preference inventories.

Disparate Impact

A considerable amount of research has been conducted on disparate impact of some substantive assessment methods. Research suggests that personality tests, performance tests and work samples, and integrity tests have little disparate impact against protected classes. In the past, interest inventories had substantial disparate impact against women, but this problem has been corrected. In general, however, there is not enough information on the disparate impact of interest, values, and preference inventories to be definitive. Conversely, ability tests have a high degree of disparate impact. Cognitive ability tests have substantial disparate impact against certain racial minorities, while physical ability tests have significant disparate impact against women. The disparate impact of structured interviews was denoted as moderate. Since even structured interviews have an element of subjectivity, the potential always exists for interviewer bias to enter the process.

A comparison of Exhibits 8.8 and 9.13 is instructive. In general, both the validity and the cost of substantive assessment procedures are higher than those of initial assessment procedures. As with the initial assessment procedures, the economic and social impacts of substantive assessment procedures are not well understood. Many initial assessment methods are widely used, whereas most substantive assessment methods have moderate or low degrees of use. Thus, many organizations rely on initial assessment methods to make substantive assessment decisions. This is unfortunate, because the validity of substantive assessment methods is almost always higher. This is especially true of the unstructured interview relative to the structured interview. At a minimum, organizations need to add more structure to their interview process (for both initial and substantive assessments). Better yet, organizations should strongly consider using assessments such as performance tests and work samples (if feasible) as well as personality tests along with either type of interview.

DISCRETIONARY ASSESSMENT METHODS

Discretionary assessment methods are used to separate those who receive job offers from the list of finalists. Sometimes discretionary methods are not used, because all finalists may receive job offers. When used, discretionary assessment methods are typically highly subjective and rely heavily on the intuition of the decision maker. Thus, factors other than KSAOs may be assessed. For example, organizations intent on maintaining strong cultures may wish to consider assessing the person/organization match at this stage of the selection process (e.g., using a values inventory).

Staffing professionals should be careful in choosing who receives a job offer among their set of finalists. Although also an issue at the recruitment phase of staffing, staffing manager preference or bias can easily trickle in at this stage. For example, there is a long history of *favoritism* (hiring favorites without regard to other finalists' suitability), *cronyism* (hiring friends or personal connections), and *nepotism* (hiring family members or relatives) in staffing decisions.[207] Although cultures in China and India may view the practice of hiring family members or social ties more favorably,[208] in other cultures, such as the United States or United Kingdom, it is viewed less favorably (and even illegal in public employment for many states) despite being fairly common.[209] In the United States, for example, approximately 13%–22% of children will share the same employer as their father by the time they reach age 30.[210] In general, research shows that nepotism and cronyism can have a negative effect on current employees' perceptions of fairness and lead to negative attitudes toward the employee that persist long after they are hired.[211]

Beyond cautiously approaching favoritism, nepotism, and cronyism, staffing professionals should also be aware of the political context that may influence the discretionary decision. For example, one case study of a fire chief and HR manager revealed that they were pressured by city council members and key city political figures to provide job offers to three candidates who failed integrity tests and admitted to crimes of theft and drug use (see earlier section on integrity tests and note their common use in public safety hiring).[212] Similarly, rumors can be spread about finalists that may affect their chances of being hired, even though staffing professionals may deny such rumors have an influence on their decisions.[213]

Despite political influences on discretionary assessment, the subjective nature of the selection decision can be affected by several biases. As some examples, decisions can be affected by staffing professionals' motivation (should we hire the safe finalist who will uphold the status quo or the finalist with innovative ideas who can transform the company?).[214] Furthermore, information that is obtained from different sources (e.g., a job at Goldman Sachs that is listed on a résumé and a description of experience at a less prestigious firm from the structured interview) may be viewed less favorably than information obtained from one source. In other words, staffing professionals may discount mildly favorable information across multiple sources, even when it is job relevant.[215] Finally, staffing professionals can be prone to consider most finalists at this stage to be "above average" (even when they may not be) and overestimate their competence compared with that of current employees.[216]

Staffing professionals should try to minimize subjective biases during this phase of the hiring process. First, as noted in the measurement chapter, subjectivity leads to poor decisions. One recent meta-analysis concluded that (a) subjective, holistic judgments (even by experts!) performed worse than algorithm or formula when compiling results from substantive assessment methods, and (b) the algorithm or formula approach improved prediction by more than 50% when compared with the subjective approach.[217] Second, using a decision aid (e.g., structured decision process, data ranking or comparing finalists) may be helpful in making decisions less subjective.[218] Although research shows that these approaches may be more effective, managers are reluctant to use them, react negatively to them, and believe that they are able to make better decisions.[219] Third, discretionary assessments should follow the organization's staffing philosophy regarding equal employment opportunity and affirmative action (EEO/AA) commitments. Here, the commitment may be to enhance the representation of minorities and women in the organization's workforce—for example, as part of affirmative action plans and programs (AAPs). Regardless of how the organization chooses to make its discretionary assessments, they should never be used without being preceded by initial and substantive methods.

CONTINGENT ASSESSMENT METHODS

As shown in Exhibit 8.3, contingent methods are not always used, depending on the nature of the job and legal mandates. Virtually any selection method can be used as a contingent method. For example, a health clinic may verify that a finalist for a nursing position possesses a valid license after a tentative offer has been made. Similarly, a defense contractor may perform a security clearance check on offer receivers once initial, substantive, and discretionary methods have been exhausted. Depending on the preferences of the organization, two selection methods—drug testing and medical exams—should be used exclusively as contingent assessment methods for legal compliance. When drug testing and medical exams are used, considerable care must be taken in their administration and evaluation.

Drug Testing

More than 70% of substance abusers hold jobs, and substance abuse has been identified as a major cause of lost productivity in the workplace, absenteeism, and increased health care costs totaling $81 billion every year.[220] A workplace study revealed that the average drug user was 3.6 times more likely than a nonuser to be involved in an accident, received 3 times the average level of sick benefits, was 5 times more likely than a nonuser to file a workers' compensation claim, and missed 10 times as many work days as a nonuser.[221]

As a result of the manifold problems caused by drug use, many employers have drug-testing programs to screen out drug users. A variety of tests may be used to ascertain substance abuse. The major categories of tests for preemployment screening include the analysis of hair, blood, or urine.[222] A survey of over 600 organizations by the Society for Human Resource Management found that 57% conducted preemployment drug testing on all job finalists. Drug testing was more likely in larger organizations (those employing more than 2,500 employees) and in publicly owned, for-profit organizations. On average, each drug test cost the company between $30 and $40.[223] These figures are much lower than they were in 1996, when drug testing peaked and 81% of employers screened workers and finalists.[224] Indeed, drug-testing programs are used less and less, and some HR practitioners have even gone so far as to say that they are now "obsolete" (despite being used for positions of public trust, similar to integrity tests).[225]

One of the reasons drug testing has declined is because traditional (urine-based) drug tests do not catch many people; in fact, a popular drug-testing firm (Quest Diagnostics) annually reports positivity rates across the US workforce and consistently finds that the positivity rate is between 3.5% and 4.5% (since 2004). Far and away the highest positive test rate is for marijuana, and in 2018 it was only 2.3% in the combined US workforce (federal/sensitive and non-federal employees), meaning that only 2.3% of those tested in the workplace tested positive for marijuana. Nearly every other drug tested resulted in a positivity rate of a fraction of a percent.

Worthy of noting, this includes *all employees taking drug tests for any reason*, including random, periodic, and follow-up tests; post-accident tests; preemployment tests; return-to-duty tests; and even those tested for "just cause." Although marijuana has the highest positivity rates, legislatures in the United States are beginning to bar preemployment drug testing for marijuana, and many "employers appear to be treating marijuana use like alcohol use" by tolerating or ignoring off-duty use for recreational purposes.[226]

Overall, only about 5% of employees tested positive for any type of drug. This means that if an organization tested 100 finalists, only about 5 would fail the test (i.e., test positive).[227] These low rates may be due to the insensitivity of drug-testing measurement to reliably capture the underlying drug usage within the workforce. It may also reflect finalists gaming the tests (diluting, adulterating, or substituting samples); though, as we note shortly, if properly conducted, drug tests are difficult to fake.

The Other Drugs: Smoking and Alcohol

Increasingly, employers are banning smokers from hiring consideration. World-renowned Cleveland Clinic, for example, bans hiring of smokers (about half of US states prohibit rejecting candidates based on smoking). Union Pacific, a railroad that operates in 23 states, screens job candidates for smoking not by a nicotine test but by not processing applications of people who identify as smokers. Because smoking has been linked to higher health care costs, increased accident claims, and absenteeism, such policies may be justified. On the other hand, employers need to have arguments and evidence to support such policies: you should "make the business case," as one expert noted. U-Haul recently made a statement that it will not hire anyone who uses nicotine (in the states where this practice is permitted). Individuals who apply to work at U-Haul will be aware of this policy through a disclaimer on the application, will be questioned about nicotine usage in the structured interview, and will have to submit to nicotine screening after an offer is made. U-Haul notes that it has taken these steps because of the serious health risks of nicotine and because it wants to establish a culture of wellness.[228] Employers that screen out smokers need to ensure that their policies comply with federal, state, and local regulations.[229] Regardless, being a smoker can hurt your employment chances: one study found that employers that find out about job seekers' smoking habits are more likely to have unfavorable impressions of them.[230]

As for alcohol, few employers test candidates for alcohol use for two reasons. First, because alcohol use is legal, and far more socially accepted than use of other mood-altering drugs, most employers have no desire to test candidates for alcohol; doing so would exclude large numbers of candidates. A second reason alcohol testing is infrequently used is because alcohol remains in the system for only a day. Some organizations that do test for alcohol use a test called ethyl glucuronide (EtG) testing. The advantage of this test is that rather than scanning for the presence of alcohol, a scan is done for EtG, a by-product of the metabolization of alcohol that remains in the system for about 80 hours. Currently, the only organizations using the EtG test are those that prohibit or restrict alcohol use in certain jobs (e.g., some health care positions, transportation jobs).[231] Like smoking, heavy alcohol usage can affect employment prospects: one study of over 800 graduating college seniors found that continued heavy drinking resulted in a 10% reduction in the odds of employment.[232]

Evaluation

It is commonly believed that drug testing results in a large number of false positives. Nevertheless, if the proper procedures are followed, drug test results are extremely accurate and error rates are very low. Accuracy of the test, however, is not the same as its validity in predicting important job criteria. The most accurate drug test in the world will be a poor investment if it cannot be established that substance abuse is related to employee behaviors such as accidents, absenteeism, tardiness, impaired job performance, and so on.

Although more research on the validity of drug-testing programs is needed, some organizations are conducting research on the deleterious effects of substance abuse. The US Postal Service conducted an evaluation of its drug-testing program using candidates who applied for positions in 21 sites over a six-month period.[233] A quality control process revealed that the drug-testing program was 100% accurate (zero false positives and false negatives). Ten percent of candidates tested positive for drug use (for the purposes of the study, candidates were hired without regard to their test results). Of those positive tests, 65% were for marijuana, 24% were for cocaine, and 11% were for other drugs. The evaluation revealed higher absenteeism for drug users and higher dismissal rates for cocaine users. Drug use was not related to accidents or injuries. A cost-benefit analysis suggested that full implementation of the program would save the Postal Service several million dollars per year in lower absenteeism and turnover rates.

Some organizations have also developed psychological scales to assess attitudes toward substance use and to determine whether they predict performance. In one meta-analysis across dozens of validation studies (of over 4,000 candidates), the validity was moderate in size ($\bar{r} = .25$).[234] However, of organizations that drug test, few rely on psychological tests. Regardless of this positive evidence, the validity of performance and psychological drug tests is not well established (very little research exists). As with integrity tests, a major concern is faking, but an advantage of psychological drug tests is that candidates are likely to perceive them as less intrusive. However, those that are drug users may be more likely to perceive them as intrusive and unfair.

In considering the validity of drug tests, one should not assume that the logical criterion against which the tests are validated is job performance. Typically, the criterion of job performance is central to evaluating the validity of most selection measures, yet drug tests have not been entirely validated against job performance.

Thus, it is far from clear that drug tests do a good job of discerning good performers from poor performers. Drug tests do appear to predict other work behaviors, however, including absenteeism, accidents, and other counterproductive behavior. For the purposes for which they are suited, then, drug tests can be concluded to have high validity.

Finally, as with other assessment methods, two other criteria against which drug testing should be evaluated are disparate impact and candidate reactions. The disparate impact of drug testing is not universally accepted, but the Postal Service study indicated that drug-testing programs have a moderate to high degree of disparate impact against Black and Hispanic candidates. Research on candidate reactions to drug tests shows that if candidates perceive a need for drug testing, they are more likely to find such a program acceptable.[235] Thus, organizations that do a good job of explaining the reasons for the tests to candidates are more likely to find that candidates react favorably to the program.

Recommendations for Effective Drug-Testing Programs

For the results of drug tests to be accurate, precautions must be taken in their administration. The US Department of Health and Human Services has established specific guidelines that must be followed by federal agencies (and are good guidelines to follow in the private sector as well).[236] First, care must be taken in the selection of a reputable drug-testing firm. Various certification programs, such as those of the College of American Pathologists and the National Institute for Drug Abuse (NIDA), exist to ensure that accurate procedures are followed. Dozens of drug-testing laboratories have been certified by NIDA. Second, positive drug tests should always be verified by a second test to ensure reliability.

What does a well-conducted drug-testing program look like?[237] Samples are first submitted to screening tests, which are relatively inexpensive ($30–$50 per candidate) but yield many false positives (test indicates drug use when none occurred, for reasons such as drug interactions, sample contamination, etc.). Confirmatory tests are then used, which are extremely accurate but more expensive. Error rates for confirmatory tests with reputable labs are very low. To avoid false positives, most organizations have nonzero cutoff levels for most drugs. Thus, if a mistake does occur, it is much more likely to be a false negative (testing negative when in fact drug use did occur) than a false positive. Thus, some candidates who occasionally use drugs may pass a test, but it is very rare for an individual who has never used drugs to fail the test, assuming the two-step process described above is followed. Exhibit 9.14 outlines the steps involved in a well-designed drug-testing program. In this example:

- Candidates are advised in advance of testing.
- All candidates are screened by urine testing.
- Prescreening is done in-house; positives are referred to an independent lab.
- A strict chain of custody is followed.

EXHIBIT 9.14   Example of an Organizational Drug-Testing Program

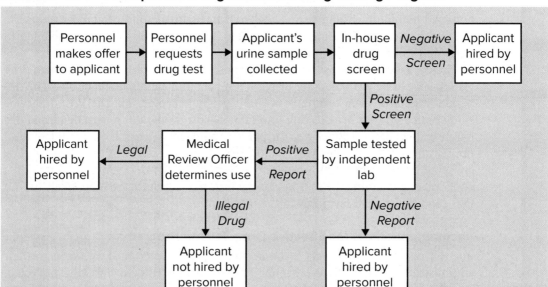

- Verified positive candidates are disqualified.
- Disqualified candidates cannot reapply for two years.

Though fewer organizations are using drug testing as a preemployment screen, it is likely to continue as a contingent assessment method among positions of public safety and large employers. To make organizations' drug-testing programs as accurate and effective as possible, six recommendations are outlined as follows:

1. Emphasize drug testing in safety-sensitive jobs as well as in positions where the link between substance abuse and negative outcomes has been documented.
2. Use only reputable testing laboratories and ensure that a strict chain of custody is maintained.
3. Ask candidates for their consent and inform them of test results; provide rejected candidates an opportunity to appeal.
4. Use retesting to validate positive samples from the initial screening test.
5. Ensure that proper procedures are followed to maintain the candidate's right to privacy.
6. Review the program and validate the results against relevant criteria (accidents, absenteeism, CWB, turnover, and job performance); conduct a cost-benefit analysis of the program, as a very small number of detections may cause the program to have low utility.

Medical Exams

Medical exams are often used to identify potential health risks in job candidates. Care must be taken to ensure that medical exams are used only when there is a compelling reason to do so. This is to ensure that individuals with disabilities unrelated to job performance are not screened out. Because of these sorts of potential abuses, the use of medical exams is strictly regulated by the Americans With Disabilities Act (ADA; discussed later in this chapter).

Although many organizations use medical exams, they are not particularly valid and are not always job related.[238] Finally, the emphasis is usually on short-term rather than long-term health. One way to make medical exams more reliable, and therefore more valid, is to ensure that the exam is based on job-related medical standards (i.e., the exam focuses on the specific diseases and health conditions that prohibit adequate functioning on specific jobs or clusters of tasks). Such an approach should improve not only content validity (because it is job related) but also reliability because it standardizes the diagnosis across physicians.

LEGAL ISSUES

This section discusses three major legal issues. The first of these is the UGESP, a document that addresses the need to determine whether a selection procedure is causing disparate impact, and if so, the validation requirements for the procedure. The second issue is selection in conformance with the ADA as pertains to reasonable accommodation to job candidates and the use of medical tests. The final issue is that of marijuana and other drug testing for job candidates.

Uniform Guidelines on Employee Selection Procedures

The UGESP are a comprehensive set of federal regulations specifying requirements for the selection systems of organizations covered under the Civil Rights Acts and under E.O. 11246. The regulations apply to virtually all selection measures (those covered in this chapter as well as those in the previous chapter) used as a selection procedure. They also apply to all employment decisions—hire, promote, transfer, demote, and retain.[239] The general requirements of the UGESP are as follows:

1. Keep candidate flow data (candidate and hire statistics) for each job category and protected group on the EEO-1 form (see the staffing system management chapter).
2. Conduct disparate impact analysis, using the 80% rule, for each group in each job category (see the measurement chapter).
3. Where disparate impact is found, either provide validity evidence for the selection procedure or take steps to eliminate the disparate impact by using an alternative procedure that causes less disparate impact.

4. Use content, criterion, or construct validation procedures (see the measurement chapter).

5. For each job or job category, keep detailed records of disparate impact; where disparate impact is found, provide evidence of validity.

6. Keep in mind that compliance with the UGESP does not relieve the organization of any affirmative action obligation it has.

There are two important exceptions to these general requirements. First, a small employer (fewer than 100 employees) does not have to keep separate records for each job category, but only for its total selection process across all jobs. Second, records for race or national origin do not have to be kept for groups constituting less than 2% of the labor force in the relevant labor area.

The UGESP make substantial demands on an organization and its staffing systems. Those demands exist to ensure organizational awareness of the possibility of disparate impact in employment decisions. When disparate impact is found, the UGESP provide mechanisms (requirements) for addressing the issues. The UGESP thus should occupy a prominent place in any covered organization's EEO/AA policies and practices.

Selection Under the Americans With Disabilities Act

The ADA, as interpreted by the Equal Employment Opportunity Commission (EEOC), creates substantial requirements and suggestions for compliance pertaining to external selection.[240] The general nature of these is identified and commented on next.

General Principles

Two major, overarching principles pertain to selection. The first principle is that it is unlawful to screen out individuals with disabilities, unless the selection procedure is job related and consistent with business necessity. The second principle is that a selection procedure must accurately reflect the KSAOs being measured, and not impaired sensory, manual, or speaking skills, unless those impaired skills are the ones being measured by the procedure.

The first principle is obviously very similar to principles governing selection generally under federal laws and regulations. The second principle is important because it cautions the organization to be sure that its selection procedures do not inadvertently and unnecessarily screen out candidates with disabilities.

Access to Job Application Process

The organization's job application process must be accessible to individuals with disabilities. Reasonable accommodation must be provided to enable all persons to apply, and candidates should be provided assistance (if needed) in completing the application process. Candidates should also be told about the nature and content of the selection process. This allows them to request reasonable accommodation to testing, if needed, in advance.

Reasonable Accommodation to Testing

In general, the organization may use any kind of test in assessing job candidates. These tests must be administered consistently to all job candidates for any particular job. A very important provision of testing pertains to the requirement to provide reasonable accommodation if requested by a candidate to take the test. The purpose of this requirement is to ensure that the test accurately reflects the KSAO being measured, rather than an impairment of the candidate. Reasonable accommodation, however, is not required for a person with an impaired skill if the purpose of the test is to measure that skill. For example, the organization does not have to provide reasonable accommodation on a manual dexterity test to a person with arthritis in the fingers and hands if the purpose of the test is to measure manual dexterity.

Numerous types of reasonable accommodation can be made. Examples include substituting an oral test for a written one (or vice versa); providing extra time to complete a test; scheduling rest breaks during a test; administering tests in large print, in Braille, or by reader; and using assistive technologies to adapt computers, such as a special mouse or screen magnifier.

Inquiries About Disabilities

Virtually all assessment tools and questions are affected by the ADA. A summary of permissible and impermissible practices is shown in Exhibit 9.15. Note that permissibility depends on the assessment tool, whether the tool is being used for an external candidate or employee, and whether the tool is being used prehire (like most selection procedures) or after a conditional offer has been made. Also note the many stipulations governing usage.

Medical Examinations: Offer Receivers

Substantial regulations surround medical exams, both before and after a job offer is made. Prior to the offer, the organization may not make medical inquiries or require medical exams of a candidate. The job offer, however, may be conditional, pending the results of a medical exam.

After an offer has been extended, the organization may conduct a medical exam. The exam must be given to all offer receivers for a particular job, not just individuals with a known or suspected disability. Whereas the content of the exam is not restricted to being only job related, the reasons for rejecting an offer receiver based on the exam must be job related. A person may also be rejected if exam results indicate a direct threat to the health and safety of the finalist or others such as employees or customers. This rejection must be based on reasonable medical judgment,

EXHIBIT 9.15 **What Inquiries About Disabilities Can Be Made at Each Staffing Stage?**

Predictor or Assessment	Staffing Stage		
	Pre-Offer Stage	Post-Offer Stage	Current Employee
Drug testing	—	—	—
• Drug tests (e.g., urinalysis)	Y	Y	Y
• Alcohol tests, surveys, or oral questions	N	Y[b,d]	Y[b,e]
• Smoking survey or oral questions	Y	Y	Y
• Illegal drug use history survey	N	Y[b,d]	Y[b,e]
• Request to provide evidence of drug abstinence	Y	Y	Y
Physical abilities testing	-	-	-
• Physical exam	N	Y[c,d]	Y[b,e]
• Physical agility test	Y[a,c]	Y[a,c]	Y[a,c]
Psychological testing	N	Y[c,d]	Y[b,e]
Medical/health history survey	N	Y[c,d]	Y[b,e]
Worker's compensation history survey	N	Y[c,d]	Y[b,e]
Structured interview or applications	-	-	-
• Questions about ability to perform work	Y	Y	Y
• Questions about disability or its nature	Y	Y[a,c]	Y[b,e]
• Questions about how individual would perform work with (or without) reasonable accommodation	Y[d,f]	Y[c,d]	Y[b,e]

NOTE: Y=Yes / Permissible N=No;
Conditions to Permissibility are indicated by the following superscripts: [a]*Standardized Administration—*Must be administered to all applicants/employees; [b]*Job-related—*Must be consistent with business necessity; [c]*Reasonable Accommodation—*Should be Considered; [d]*Unified Standards—*All employees or applicants are subject to the same standards; [e]*Compliance—*Permissible to determine fitness for duty, reasonable accommodation, direct threat, or to meet legal requirements; [f]*Post-Disclosure—*Permissible if disability is known and may interfere with performance.
SOURCE: Adapted from S. K. Willman, "Tips for Minimizing Abuses Under the Americans With Disabilities Act," *Legal Report,* Society for Human Resource Management, Jan.–Feb. 2003, p. 8.

not a simple judgment that the offer receiver might or could cause harm. Each offer receiver must be assessed individually in order to determine whether an impairment creates a significant risk of harm and cannot be accommodated through reasonable means. Results of medical exams are to be kept confidential, held separate from the employee's personnel file, and released only under very specific circumstances.

It may be difficult to determine whether something is a medical examination and thus subject to the above requirements surrounding its use. The EEOC defines a medical examination as "a procedure or test that seeks information about an individual's physical or mental impairments or health."[241] The following factors are suggestive of a selection procedure that would be considered a medical examination:

- It is administered by a health care professional and/or someone trained by such a professional.
- It is designed to reveal an impairment of physical or mental health.
- It is invasive (e.g., requires drawing blood, urine, or breath).
- It measures the candidate's physiological responses to performing a task.
- It is normally given in a medical setting and/or medical equipment is used.
- It tests for alcohol consumption.

Though closely allied with medical examinations, several types of tests fall outside the bounds of medical examinations. These tests may be used pre-offer and include physical agility tests, physical fitness tests, vision tests, and tests that measure honesty, tastes, and habits.

A gray area involves the use of psychological tests, such as personality tests. They are considered medical if they lead to identifying a medically recognized mental disorder or impairment, such as those in the American Psychiatric Association's *Diagnostic and Statistical Manual of Mental Disorders*. Future regulations and court rulings may help clarify which types of psychological tests are medical exams.

Medical Examinations: Current Employees

This enforcement guidance applies to employees generally, not just employees with disabilities.[242] An employee who applies for a new (different) job with the same employer should be treated as a candidate for a new job and thus subject to the provisions described above for job candidates. An individual is not a candidate where she or he is entitled to another position with the same employer (e.g., because of seniority or satisfactory performance in their current position) or when returning to a regular job after being on temporary assignment in another job. Instead, these individuals are considered employees.

For employees, the employer may make disability-related inquiries and require medical examinations only if they are job related and consistent with business necessity. Any information obtained, or voluntarily provided by the employee, is a confidential medical record. The record may only be shared in limited circumstances with managers, supervisors, first aid and safety personnel, and government officials investigating ADA compliance. Generally, a disability-related inquiry or medical examination is job related and consistent with business necessity when the employer has a reasonable belief, based on objective evidence, that (1) an employee's ability to perform essential job functions will be impaired by a medical condition or (2) an employee will pose a direct threat due to a medical condition.

A medical examination for employees is defined the same way as for job candidates. Examples of disability-related inquiries include the following:

- Asking an employee whether they are disabled (or ever had a disability) or how they became disabled, or asking about the nature or severity of an employee's disability
- Asking an employee to provide medical documentation regarding their disability
- Asking an employee's coworkers, family members, doctor, or another person about the employee's disability
- Asking about an employee's genetic information
- Asking about an employee's prior workers' compensation history
- Asking if an employee is taking any medication or drugs or has done so in the past
- Asking an employee broad information that is likely to elicit information about a disability

UGESP

The UGESP do not apply to the ADA or its regulations. This means that the guidance and requirements for employers' selection systems under the Civil Rights Act may or may not be the same as those required for compliance with the ADA.

Marijuana and Other Drug Testing

Candidate and employee usage of marijuana and other drugs presents special legal challenges. The organization not only must comply with a host of laws and regulations, but also must fashion specific policies and practices that will create such compliance within the operation of its staffing systems.[243]

For marijuana compliance there is new and ever-evolving terrain to navigate. Federal law (the Controlled Substances Act) makes marijuana possession and use illegal. But under the ADA, a candidate or employee with a covered disability that is being treated with medical marijuana may require a reasonable accommodation to that use.[244]

Marijuana laws vary a lot at the state level. Most states have now legalized marijuana usage, primarily for medical purposes, but some states (e.g., Colorado) also permit recreational usage. These laws do not require the organization to permit or tolerate marijuana use at work, with the occasional exception of requiring an accommodation for medical usage (e.g., Nevada). State laws also usually allow the organization to have a blanket ban on marijuana use for safety-sensitive positions or in order to comply with federal or other contract requirements.[245]

Testing for other drugs is also surrounded by an amalgam of laws and regulations at the federal and state levels. Special law for the Department of Transportation, Department of Defense, and Nuclear Regulatory Commission requires (or requires in certain situations) alcohol and drug testing for transportation workers in safety-sensitive jobs.[246] The organization should seek legal and medical advice to determine whether it should do drug testing and, if so, what the nature of the drug-testing program should be. Beyond that, the organization should require and administer drug tests on a contingency (post-offer) basis only, to avoid the possibility of obtaining and using medical information illegally. For example, positive drug test results may occur because of the presence of a legal drug and using these results pre-offer to reject a person would be a violation of the ADA. The organization could also learn about other organizations' testing policies and practices to inform its own decisions.[247]

SUMMARY

This chapter continued the discussion of proper methods and processes to be used in external selection. Specifically, substantive, discretionary, and contingent assessment methods were discussed, as well as collection of assessment data and pertinent legal issues.

Most of the chapter discussed various substantive methods, which are used to separate finalists from candidates. Like initial assessment methods, substantive assessment methods should always be based on the logic of prediction and the use of selection plans. The substantive methods that were reviewed include personality tests; ability tests; emotional intelligence tests; performance tests and work samples; situational judgment tests; integrity tests; interest, values, and preference inventories; and structured interviews. Special applications for substantive assessment, such as selecting leaders and team members, were also discussed. As with initial assessment methods, the criteria used to evaluate the effectiveness of substantive assessment methods are frequency of use, cost, reliability, validity, utility, candidate reactions, and disparate impact. In general, substantive assessment methods show a marked improvement in reliability and validity over initial assessment methods. This is probably due to the stronger relationship between the sampling of the candidate's previous situations and the requirements for success on the job.

Discretionary selection methods are somewhat less formal and more subjective than other selection methods. When discretionary methods are used, it is important to minimize subjectivity as much as possible, consider the political environment, and use decision aids in order to maximize the validity of the decision.

Though discretionary methods are subjective, contingent assessment methods typically involve decisions about whether candidates meet certain objective requirements for the job. The two most common contingent methods are drug testing and medical exams. Particularly in the case of drug testing, the use of contingent methods is relatively complex from an administrative and legal standpoint.

Regardless of predictor type, attention must be given to the proper collection and use of predictor information. Support services need to be established, administrators with the appropriate credentials need to be hired, data need to be kept private and confidential, and administration procedures must be standardized.

Along with administrative issues, legal issues need to be considered as well. Attention must be paid to regulations that govern permissible activities by organizations. Regulations include those in the UGESP and the ADA.

DISCUSSION QUESTIONS

1. Describe the similarities and differences between personality tests and integrity tests. When is each warranted in the selection process?
2. How would you advise an organization considering adopting a cognitive ability test for selection?
3. Describe the structured interview. What are the characteristics of structured interviews that improve on the shortcomings of unstructured interviews?
4. Compare and contrast the ability and mixed approaches to EI—how are they similar, how are they different?
5. What issues surround discretionary assessment methods? What would you do to mitigate these issues as a staffing professional?
6. What is the best way to collect and use drug-testing data in selection decisions?
7. How should organizations apply the general principles of the UGESP to practical selection decisions?

ETHICAL ISSUES

1. Do you think it is unethical for employers to select candidates on the basis of measures such as "Dislike loud music" and "Enjoy wild flights of fancy" even if the scales that such items measure have been shown to predict job performance? Explain.
2. Cognitive ability tests are one of the best predictors of job performance, yet they have substantial disparate impact against minorities. Do you think it is fair to use such tests? Why or why not?

APPLICATIONS

Assessment Methods for the Job of Human Resources Director

Nairduwel, Inoalot, and Imslo (NII) is a law firm specializing in business law. Among other areas, it deals in equal employment opportunity law, business litigation, and workplace torts. The firm has more than 50 partners and approximately 120 employees. It does business in three states and has law offices in two major metropolitan areas. The firm has no federal contracts.

NII plans to expand into two additional states, opening offices in two major metropolitan areas. One of the primary challenges accompanying this ambitious expansion plan is how to staff the new offices. Accordingly, the firm wishes to hire an HR director to oversee employee recruitment, selection, training, performance appraisal, and compensation activities accompanying the business expansion, as well as supervise the HR activities in the existing NII offices. The newly created job description for the HR director is listed in the accompanying exhibit.

The firm wishes to design and then use a selection system for assessing candidates that will achieve two objectives: (1) create a valid and useful system that will do a good job of matching candidate KSAOs to job requirements, and (2) be in compliance with all relevant federal and state employment laws.

The firm is considering numerous selection techniques for possible use. For each method listed below, decide whether you would or would not use it in the selection process and state why.

1. A job knowledge test specifically designed for HR professionals that focuses on a candidate's general knowledge of HR management
2. A medical examination and drug test at the beginning of the selection process in order to determine whether candidates can cope with the high level of stress and frequent travel requirements of the job and to ensure they are drug-free
3. An overt integrity test
4. An online management simulation
5. A structured behavioral interview that would be specially designed for use in filling only this job
6. An emotional intelligence situational judgment test
7. A general cognitive ability test
8. A vocational interest inventory
9. A personality test
10. A set of interview questions that the firm typically uses for filling any position:
    a. Tell me about a problem you solved on a previous job.
    b. Do you have any physical impairments that would make it difficult for you to travel on business?
    c. Have you ever been tested for AIDS?
    d. Are you currently unemployed, and if so, why?
    e. This position requires fresh ideas and energy. Do you think you have those qualities?
    f. What is your definition of success?
    g. What kind of sports do you like?
    h. How well do you work under pressure? Give me some examples.

If you could choose up to three substantive assessments for this position, which three assessments would you choose and why? Describe in detail issues pertaining to balancing their cost, reliability/validity evidence, applicant reactions, projected utility, and potential disparate impact.

Exhibit

Job Description for Human Resources Director

JOB SUMMARY

Performs responsible administrative work managing personnel activities. Work involves responsibility for the planning and administration of HRM programs, including recruitment, selection, evaluation, appointment, promotion, compensation, and recommended change of status of employees, and a system of communication for disseminating information to workers. Works under general supervision, exercising initiative and independent judgment in the performance of assigned tasks.

TASKS

1. Participates in overall planning and policy making to provide effective and uniform personnel services.
2. Communicates policy through organization levels by bulletin, meetings, and personal contact.
3. Supervises recruitment and screening of job candidates to fill vacancies. Supervises interviewing of candidates, evaluation of qualifications, and classification of applications.
4. Supervises administration of tests to candidates.
5. Confers with supervisors on personnel matters, including placement problems, retention or release of probationary employees, transfers, demotions, and dismissals of permanent employees.
6. Initiates personnel training activities and coordinates these activities with work of officials and supervisors.
7. Establishes effective service rating system and trains unit supervisors in making employee evaluations.
8. Supervises maintenance of employee personnel files.
9. Supervises a group of employees directly and through subordinates.
10. Performs related work as assigned.

JOB SPECIFICATIONS

1. *Experience and Training*
   Should have considerable experience in area of HRM administration. Six years minimum.

2. *Education*
   Graduation from a four-year college or university, with major work in human resources, business administration, or industrial psychology. Master's degree in one of these areas is preferable.

3. *Knowledge, Skills, and Abilities*
   Considerable knowledge of principles and practices of HRM, including staffing, compensation, training, and performance evaluation.

4. *Responsibility*
   Supervises the human resource activities of six office managers, one clerk, and one assistant.

Choosing Among Finalists for the Job of Human Resources Director

Assume that NII, after weighing its options, decided to use the following selection methods to assess candidates for the HR director job: cognitive ability test, job knowledge test, structured interview, and questions (f) and (g) from the list of generic interview questions.

NII advertised for the position extensively, and out of a pool of 23 initial candidates, three finalists were chosen. Shown in the accompanying exhibit are the results from the assessment of the three finalists using the various selection methods. In addition, information from an earlier résumé screen is included for possible consideration. For each finalist, decide whether you would hire the person and why.

Exhibit

Results of Assessment of Finalists for Human Resources Director Position

	Finalist 1— Lola Vega	Finalist 2— Sam Fein	Finalist 3— Shawanda Jackson
Résumé	GPA 3.9/Cornell University B.S. Human Resource Mgmt. 5 years' experience in HRM • 4 years in recruiting	GPA 2.8/SUNY Binghamton B.B.A. Finance 20 years' experience in HRM • Numerous HR assignments • Certified HR professional	GPA 3.2/Auburn University B.B.A. Business and English 8 years' experience in HRM • 3 years HR generalist • 4 years compensation analyst
	No supervisory experience	15 years' supervisory experience	5 years' supervisory experience
Cognitive ability test	90% correct	78% correct	84% correct
Knowledge test	94% correct	98% correct	91% correct
Structured int. (out of 100 pts.)	85	68	75
Question (f)	Ability to influence others	To do things you want to do	Promotions and earnings
Question (g)	Golf, shuffleboard	Spectator sports	Basketball, tennis

ENDNOTES

1. E. White, "Walking a Mile in Another's Shoes," *Wall Street Journal*, Jan. 16, 2006, p. B3.
2. G. C. Thornton III and R. A. Mueller-Hanson, *Developing Organizational Simulations: A Guide for Practitioners and Students* (New York: Lawrence Erlbaum, 2004).
3. R. Miller, "The Legal Minefield of Employment Probation," *Benefits and Compensation Solutions*, 1998, 21, pp. 40–43; I. S. Wolfe, "Why Employment Probation Periods Are Ineffective," *Rework* (blog), May 28, 2018 (*www.cornerstoneondemand.com/rework/why-employment-probation -periods-are-ineffective*).
4. P. Thomas, "Not Sure of a New Hire? Put Her to a Road Test," *Wall Street Journal*, Jan. 2003, p. B7.
5. P. R. Sackett and F. Lievens, "Personnel Selection," *Annual Review of Psychology*, 2008, 59, pp. 419–450.
6. P. L. Roth, P. Bobko, and L. A. McFarland, "A Meta-Analysis of Work Sample Test Validity: Updating and Integrating Some Classic Literature," *Personnel Psychology*, 2005, 58, pp. 1009–1037.
7. R. M. Guion, *Assessment, Measurement, and Prediction for Personnel Decisions*, 2nd ed. (New York: Routledge, 2011); G. C. Thornton III and U. Kedharnath, "Work Sample Tests," in K. F. Geisinger, B. A. Bracken, J. F. Carlson, J-I. C. Hansen, N. R. Kuncel, S. P. Reise, and M. C. Rodriguez (eds.), *APA Handbook of Testing and Assessment in Psychology*, Vol. 1 (Washington, DC: American Psychological Association, 2013).
8. S. J. Motowidlo, M. D. Dunnette, and G. W. Carter, "An Alternative Selection Procedure: The Low-Fidelity Simulation," *Journal of Applied Psychology*, 1990, 75, pp. 640–647.
9. W. Arthur, Jr., G. V. Barrett, and D. Doverspike, "Validation of an Information Processing-Based Test Battery Among Petroleum-Product Transport Drivers," *Journal of Applied Psychology*, 1990, 75, pp. 621–628.
10. Employment Technologies, "Royal Caribbean Cruises" (*https://employmenttechnologies.com /success-stories/royal-caribbean-cruises/*), accessed Feb. 7, 2020.
11. P. L. Roth, P. Bobko, and L. A. McFarland, "A Meta-Analysis of Work Sample Test Validity: Updating and Integrating Some Classic Literature," *Personnel Psychology*, 2005, 58, pp. 1009–1037.
12. W. C. Borman and G. L. Hallam, "Observation Accuracy for Assessors of Work-Sample Performance: Consistency Across Task and Individual-Difference Correlates," *Journal of Applied Psychology*, 1991, 76(1), pp. 11–18; C. E. Lance, C. D. Johnson, S. S. Douthitt, W. Bennett, Jr., and D. L. Harville, "Good News: Work Sample Administrators' Global Performance Judgments Are (About) as Valid as We've Suspected," *Human Performance*, 2000, 13(3), pp. 253–277.
13. W. Cascio and W. Phillips, "Performance Testing: A Rose Among Thorns?" *Personnel Psychology*, 1979, 32, pp. 751–766.
14. N. Anderson, J. F. Salgado, and U. R. Hülsheger, "Applicant Reactions in Selection: Comprehensive Meta-Analysis Into Reaction Generalization Versus Situational Specificity," *International Journal of Selection and Assessment*, 2010, 18, pp. 291–304.
15. P. Bobko and P. L. Roth, "Reviewing, Categorizing, and Analyzing the Literature on Black-White Mean Differences for Predictors of Job Performance: Verifying Some Perceptions and Updating/ Correcting Others," *Personnel Psychology*, 2013, 66, pp. 91–126; P. Bobko, P. L. Roth, and M. A. Buster, "Work Sample Selection Tests and Expected Reduction in Adverse Impact: A Cautionary Note," *International Journal of Selection and Assessment*, 2005, 13, pp. 1–24.
16. K. A. Hanisch and C. L. Hulin, "Two-Stage Sequential Selection Procedures Using Ability and Training Performance: Incremental Validity of Behavioral Consistency Measures," *Personnel Psychology*, 1994, 47, pp. 767–785.
17. M. C. Campion, R. E. Ployhart, and W. I. MacKenzie, Jr., "The State of Research on Situational Judgment Tests: A Content Analysis and Directions for Future Research," *Human Performance*,

2014, 27(4), pp. 283–310; D. L. Whetzel and M. A. McDaniel, "Situational Judgment Tests: An Overview of Current Research," *Human Resource Management Review*, 2009, 19, pp. 188–202.

18. M. S. Christian, B. D. Edwards, and J. C. Bradley, "Situational Judgment Tests: Constructs Assessed and a Meta-Analysis of Their Criterion-Related Validities," *Personnel Psychology*, 2010, 63, pp. 83–117; M. A. McDaniel, N. S. Hartman, D. L. Whetzel, and W. L. Grubb, "Situational Judgment Tests, Response Instructions, and Validity: A Meta-Analysis," *Personnel Psychology*, 2007, 60, pp. 63–91.

19. Bobko and Roth, "Reviewing, Categorizing, and Analyzing the Literature on Black-White Mean Differences for Predictors of Job Performance: Verifying Some Perceptions and Updating/Correcting Others"; P. L. Roth, P. Bobko, and M. A. Buster, "Situational Judgment Tests: The Influence and Importance of Applicant Status and Targeted Constructs on Estimates of Black-White Subgroup Differences," *Journal of Occupational and Organizational Psychology*, 2013, 86, 394–409; D. L. Whetzel, M. A. McDaniel, and N. T. Nguyen, "Subgroup Differences in Situational Judgment Test Performance: A Meta-Analysis," *Human Performance*, 2008, 21, pp. 291–309.

20. D. J. R. Jackson, A. C. LoPilato, D. Hughes, N. Guenole, and A. Shalfrooshan, "The Internal Structure of Situational Judgment Tests Reflects Candidate Main Effects: Not Dimensions or Situations," *Journal of Occupational and Organizational Psychology*, 2017, 90, pp. 1–27; N. Kasten and P. A. Freund, "A Meta-Analytical Multilevel Reliability Generalization of Situational Judgment Tests (SJTs)," *European Journal of Psychological Assessment*, 2016, 32(3), pp. 230–240; W. I. MacKenzie, Jr., R. E. Ployhart, J. A. Weekley, and C. Ehlers, "Contextual Effects on SJT Responses: An Examination of Construct Validity and Mean Differences Across Applicant and Incumbent Contexts," *Human Performance*, 2010, 23, pp. 1–21.

21. Campion, Ployhart, and MacKenzie, "The State of Research on Situational Judgment Tests: A Content Analysis and Directions for Future Research"; M. A. McDaniel and N. T. Nguyen, "Situational Judgment Tests: A Review of Practice and Constructs Assessed," *International Journal of Selection and Assessment*, 2001, 9, pp. 103–113; Whetzel and McDaniel, "Situational Judgment Tests: An Overview of Current Research."

22. S. Krumm, F. Lievens, J. Hüffmeier, A. A. Lipnevich, H. Bendels, and G. Hertel, "How 'Situational' Is Judgment in Situational Judgment Tests?" *Journal of Applied Psychology*, 2015, 100, pp. 399–416; T. Rockstuhl, S. Ang, K.-Y. Ng, F. Lievens, and L. Van Dyne, "Putting Judging Situations Into Situational Judgment Tests: Evidence From Intercultural Multimedia SJTs," *Journal of Applied Psychology*, 2015, 100, pp. 464–480; P. Schäpers, P. Mussel, F. Lievens, C. J. König, J-P. Freudenstein, and S. Krumm, "The Role of Situations in Situational Judgment Tests: Effects on Construct Saturation, Predictive Validity, and Applicant Perceptions," *Journal of Applied Psychology*, in press; P. Schäpers, F. Lievens, J-P. Freudenstein, J. Hüffmeier, C. J. König, and S. Krumm, "Removing Situation Descriptions From Situational Judgment Test Items: Does the Impact Differ for Video-Based Versus Text-Based Formats," *Journal of Occupational and Organizational Psychology*, in press.

23. F. Lievens and P. R. Sackett, "Video-Based Versus Written Situational Judgment Tests: A Comparison in Terms of Predictive Validity," *Journal of Applied Psychology*, 2006, 91, pp. 1181–1188.

24. Ibid.

25. W. Arthur, Jr., R. M. Glaze, S. M. Jarrett, C. D. White, I. Schurig, and J. E. Taylor, "Comparative Evaluation of Three Situational Judgment Test Formats in Terms of Construct-Related Validity, Subgroup D and Susceptibility to Response Distortion," *Journal of Applied Psychology*, 2014, 99, pp. 535–545.

26. McDaniel et al., "Situational Judgment Tests, Response Instructions, and Validity: A Meta-Analysis."

27. M. E. Bergman, F. Drasgow, M. A. Donovan, J. B. Henning, and S. E. Juraska, "Scoring Situational Judgment Tests: Once You Get the Data, Your Troubles Begin," *International Journal of*

Selection and Assessment, 2006, 14(3), pp. 223–235; C. St-Sauveur, S. Girouard, and V. Goyette, "Use of Situational Judgment Tests in Personnel Selection: Are the Different Methods for Scoring the Response Options Equivalent?" *International Journal of Selection and Assessment*, 2014, 22(3), pp. 225–239; Q. Weng, H. Yang, F. Lievens, and M. A. McDaniel, "Optimizing the Validity of Situational Judgment Tests: The Importance of Scoring Methods," *Journal of Vocational Behavior*, 2018, 104, pp. 199–209.

28. M. S. Christian, B. D. Edwards, and J. C. Bradley, "Situational Judgment Tests: Constructs Assessed and a Meta-Analysis of Their Criterion-Related Validities," *Personnel Psychology*, 2010, 63, pp. 83–117; M. A. McDaniel and N. T. Nguyen, "Situational Judgment Tests: A Review of Practice and Constructs Assessed," *International Journal of Selection and Assessment*, 2001, 9(1/2), pp. 103–113; M. A. McDaniel and D. L. Whetzel, "Situational Judgement Test Research: Informing the Debate on Practical Intelligence Theory," *Intelligence*, 2005, 33, pp. 515–525.

29. Christian, Edwards, and Bradley, "Situational Judgment Tests: Constructs Assessed and a Meta-Analysis of Their Criterion-Related Validities."

30. A. I. Huffcutt and S. S. Culbertson, "Interviews," in S. Zedeck (ed.), *APA Handbook of Industrial and Organizational Psychology* (Washington, DC: APA, 2010), p. 185.

31. Ibid.

32. J. Levashina, C. J. Hartwell, F. P. Morgeson, and M. A. Campion, "The Structured Employment Interview: Narrative and Quantitative Review of the Research Literature," *Personnel Psychology*, 2014, 67, pp. 241–293.

33. M. A. Campion, D. K. Palmer, and J. E. Campion, "A Review of Structure in the Selection Interview," *Personnel Psychology*, 1997, 50, pp. 655–702.

34. A. I. Huffcutt, S. S. Culbertson, and W. S. Weyhrauch, "Employment Interview Reliability: New Meta-Analytic Estimates by Structure and Format," *International Journal of Selection and Assessment*, 2013, 21, pp. 264–276.

35. Levashina et al., "The Structured Employment Interview: Narrative and Quantitative Review of the Research Literature."

36. Ibid.

37. E. Erous, A. Buijsrogge, N. Roulin, and W. Duyck, "Why Your Stigma Isn't Hired: A Dual-Process Framework of Interview Bias," *Human Resource Management Review*, 2016, 26, pp. 90–111.

38. M. R. Barrick, J. A. Shaffer, and S. W. DeGrassi, "What You See May Not Be What You Get: Relationships Among Self-Presentation Tactics and Ratings of Interview and Job Performance," *Journal of Applied Psychology*, 2009, 94, pp. 1394–1411.

39. E. E. Kausel, S. S. Culbertson, and H. P. Madrid, "Overconfidence in Personnel Selection: When and Why Unstructured Interview Information Can Hurt Hiring Decisions," *Organizational Behavior and Human Decision Processes*, 2016, 137, pp. 27–44; F. Lievens, S. Highhouse, and W. De Corte, "The Importance of Traits and Abilities in Supervisors' Hirability Decisions as a Function of Method of Assessment," *Journal of Occupational and Organizational Psychology*, 2005, 78, pp. 453–470.

40. W-C. Tsai, F. H. Chen, H-Y. Chen, and K-Y. Tseng, "When Will Interviewers Be Willing to Use High-Structured Job Interviews? The Role of Personality," *International Journal of Selection and Assessment*, 2016, 24(1), pp. 92–105.

41. N. Roulin and A. Bangerter, "Understanding the Academic-Practitioner Gap for Structured Interviews: 'Behavioral' Interviews Diffuse, 'Structured' Interviews Do Not," *International Journal of Selection and Assessment*, 2012, 20(2), pp. 149–158.

42. Campion, Palmer, and Campion, "A Review of Structure in the Selection Interview"; D. S. Chapman and D. I. Zweig, "Developing a Nomological Network for Interview Structure: Antecedents and Consequences of the Structured Selection Interview," *Personnel Psychology*, 2005, 58, pp. 673–702; Levashina et al., "The Structured Employment Interview: Narrative and Quantitative Review of the Research Literature."

43. T. Janz, "Initial Comparison of Patterned Behavior Description Interviews Versus Unstructured Interviews," *Journal of Applied Psychology*, 1982, 67, pp. 577–580; G. P. Latham, L. M. Saari, E. D. Pursell, and M. A. Campion, "The Situational Interview," *Journal of Applied Psychology*, 1980, 65, pp. 422–427.

44. Society for Human Resource Management, "Interviewing Candidates for Employment," *SHRM* (Toolkits) (*www.shrm.org/resourcesandtools/tools-and-samples/toolkits/pages/interviewingcandidates foremployment.aspx*), accessed Feb. 8, 2020.

45. Ibid.

46. Levashina et al., "The Structured Employment Interview: Narrative and Quantitative Review of the Research Literature."

47. Ibid.

48. P. V. Ingold, M. Kleinmann, C. J. König, K. G. Melchers, and C. H. Van Iddekinge, "Why Do Situational Interviews Predict Job Performance? The Role of Interviewees' Ability to Identify Criteria," *Journal of Business and Psychology*, 2015, 30, pp. 387–398; J. K. Oostrom, K. G. Melchers, P. V. Ingold, and M. Kleinmann, "Why Do Situational Interviews Predict Performance? Is It Saying How You Would Behave or Knowing How You Should Behave?" *Journal of Business and Psychology*, 2016, 31, pp. 279–291.

49. S. S. Culbertson, W. S. Weyhrauch, and A. I. Huffcutt, "A Tale of Two Formats: Direct Comparison of Matching Situational and Behavior Description Interview Questions," *Human Resource Management Review*, 2017, 27, pp. 167–177.

50. Levashina et al., "The Structured Employment Interview: Narrative and Quantitative Review of the Research Literature."

51. Huffcutt and Culbertson, "Interviews"; Levashina et al., "The Structured Employment Interview: Narrative and Quantitative Review of the Research Literature."

52. N. Blacksmith, J. C. Willford, and T. S. Behrend, "Technology in the Employment Interview: A Meta-Analysis and Future Research Agenda," *Personnel Assessment and Decisions*, 2016, 2(1), pp. 12–20.

53. Society for Human Resource Management, *Talent Acquisition Benchmarking Report* (Alexandria, VA: author, 2017).

54. Blacksmith, Willford, and Behrend, "Technology in the Employment Interview: A Meta-Analysis and Future Research Agenda"; J. R. Castro and R. H. Gramzow, "Rose Colored Webcam: Discrepancies in Personality Estimates and Interview Performance Ratings," *Personality and Individual Differences*, 2015, 74, pp. 202–207.

55. S. Adams, "The Innovation That Could Make Most Job Interviews Obsolete," *Forbes*, Aug. 8, 2012 (*www.forbes.com/sites/susanadams/2012/08/28/the-innovation-that-could-make-most-job-interviews-obsolete/*), accessed Aug. 12, 2013.

56. M. Langer, C. J. König, and K. Krause, "Examining Digital Interviews for Personnel Selection: Applicant Reactions and Interviewer Ratings," *International Journal of Selection and Assessment*, 2017, 25, pp. 371–382.

57. Huffcutt and Culbertson, "Interviews"; S. J. Motowidlo, G. W. Carter, M. D. Dunnette, N. Tippins, S. Werner, J. R. Burnett, and M. J. Vaughan, "Studies of the Structured Behavioral Interview," *Journal of Applied Psychology*, 1992, 77, pp. 571–587.

58. C. H. Van Iddekinge, C. E. Sager, J. L. Burnfield, and T. S. Heffner, "The Variability of Criterion-Related Validity Estimates Among Interviewers and Interview Panels," *International Journal of Selection and Assessment*, 2006, 14, pp. 193–205; M. R. Barrick, B. W. Swider, and G. L. Stewart, "Initial Evaluations in the Interview: Relationships With Subsequent Interviewer Evaluations and Employment Offers," *Journal of Applied Psychology*, 2010, 95, pp. 1163–1172.

59. F. S. De Kock, F. Lievens, and M. P. Born, "An In-Depth Look at Dispositional Reasoning and Interviewer Accuracy," *Human Performance*, 2015, 28, pp. 199–221; C.-C. Chen, I. W.-F. Yang, and

W.-C. Lin, "Applicant Impression Management in Job Interview: The Moderating Role of Interviewer Affectivity," *Journal of Occupational and Organizational Psychology*, 2010, 83, pp. 739–757.

60. S. A. Carless and A. Imber, "The Influence of Perceived Interviewer and Job and Organizational Characteristics on Applicant Attraction and Job Choice Intentions: The Role of Applicant Anxiety," *International Journal of Selection and Assessment*, 2007, 15, pp. 359–371; B. Farago, J. S. Zide, and C. Shahani-Denning, "Selection Interviews: Role of Interviewer Warmth, Interview Structure, and Interview Outcome in Applicants' Perceptions of Organizations," *Consulting Psychology Journal: Practice and Research*, 2013, 65(3), pp. 224–239.

61. J. C. Marr and D. M. Cable, "Do Interviewers Sell Themselves Short? The Effects of Selling Orientation on Interviewers' Judgments," *Academy of Management Journal*, 2014, 57(3), pp. 624–651; A. Wilhelmy, M. Kleinmann, C. J. König, K. G. Melchers, and D. M. Truxillo, "How and Why Do Interviewers Try to Make Impressions on Applicants? A Qualitative Study," *Journal of Applied Psychology*, 2016, 101(3), pp. 313–332.

62. D. S. Chapman and D. I. Zweig, "Developing a Nomological Network for Interview Structure: Antecedents and Consequences of the Structured Selection Interview," *Personnel Psychology*, 2005, 58, pp. 673–702; N. M. A. Hauenstein and M. E. McCusker, "Rater Training: Understanding Effects of Training Content, Practice Ratings, and Feedback," *International Journal of Selection and Assessment*, 2017, 25, pp. 253–266; K. G. Melchers, N. Lienhardt, M. Von Aarburg, and M. Kleinmann, "Is More Structure Really Better? A Comparison of Frame-of-Reference Training and Descriptively Anchored Rating Scales to Improve Interviewers' Rating Quality," *Personnel Psychology*, 2011, 64, pp. 53–87.

63. F. L. Schmidt and R. D. Zimmerman, "A Counterintuitive Hypothesis About Employment Interview Validity and Some Supporting Evidence," *Journal of Applied Psychology*, 2004, 89, pp. 553–561.

64. A. I. Huffcutt, "An Empirical Review of the Employment Interview Construct Literature," *International Journal of Selection and Assessment*, 2011, 19(1), pp. 62–81; A. I. Huffcutt and W. Arthur, Jr., "Hunter and Hunter (1984) Revisited: Interview Validity for Entry-Level Jobs," *Journal of Applied Psychology*, 1994, 79(2), pp. 184–190; A. I. Huffcutt, J. M. Conway, P. L. Roth, and N. J. Stone, "Identification and Meta-Analytic Assessment of Psychological Constructs Measured in Employment Interviews," *Journal of Applied Psychology*, 2001, 86, pp. 897–913; Huffcutt, Culbertson, and Weyhrauch, "Employment Interview Reliability: New Meta-Analytic Estimates by Structure and Format"; A. I. Huffcutt and D. J. Woehr, "Further Analysis of Employment Interview Validity: A Quantitative Evaluation of Interviewer-Related Structuring Methods," *Journal of Organizational Behavior*, 1999, 20, pp. 549–560; M. A. McDaniel, D. L. Whetzel, F. L. Schmidt, and S. D. Maurer, "The Validity of Employment Interviews: A Comprehensive Review and Meta-Analysis," *Journal of Applied Psychology*, 1994, 79, pp. 599–616; Schmidt and Zimmerman, "A Counterintuitive Hypothesis About Employment Interview Validity and Some Supporting Evidence"; T. J. Thorsteinson, "A Meta-Analysis of Interview Length on Reliability and Validity," *Journal of Occupational and Organizational Psychology*, 2018, 91, pp. 1–32.

65. Society for Human Resource Management, *Talent Acquisition Benchmarking Report*; K. I. van der Zee, A. B. Bakker, and P. Bakker, "Why Are Structured Interviews So Rarely Used in Personnel Selection?" *Journal of Applied Psychology*, 2002, 87, pp. 176–184.

66. Anderson, Salgado, and Hülsheger, "Applicant Reactions in Selection: Comprehensive Meta-Analysis Into Reaction Generalization Versus Situational Specificity"; J. P. Hausknecht, D. V. Day, and S. C. Thomas, "Applicant Reactions to Selection Procedures: An Updated Model and Meta-Analysis," *Personnel Psychology*, 2004, 57(3), pp. 639–683.

67. Bobko and Roth, "Reviewing, Categorizing, and Analyzing the Literature on Black-White Mean Differences for Predictors of Job Performance: Verifying Some Perceptions and Updating/Correcting Others."

68. S. Merritt, C. Gardner, K. Huber, B. Wexler, C. Banister, and A. Staley, "Imagine Me and You, I Do: Effects of Imagined Intergroup Contact on Anti-fat Bias in the Context of Job Interviews," *Journal of Applied Social Psychology*, 2018, 48, pp. 80–89; S. L. Segrest Purkiss, P. L. Perrewé, T. L. Gillespie, B. T. Mayes, and G. R. Ferris, "Implicit Sources of Bias in Employment Interview Judgments and Decisions," *Organizational Behavior and Human Decision Processes*, 2006, 101, pp. 152–167; S. Wolgast, F. Björklund, and M. Bäckström, "Applicant Ethnicity Affects Which Questions Are Asked in a Job Interview: The Role of Expected Fit," *Journal of Personnel Psychology*, 2018, 17(2), pp. 66–74.

69. Talent Board, *2019 North American Candidate Experience Research Report* (Los Angeles: author, 2019).

70. J. B. Carroll, *Human Cognitive Abilities: A Survey of Factor-Analytic Studies* (New York: Cambridge University Press, 1993); E. A. Fleishman and M. E. Reilly, *Handbook of Human Abilities* (Palo Alto, CA: Consulting Psychologists Press, 1992); P. R. Sackett, F. Lievens, C. H. Van Iddekinge, and N. R. Kuncel, "Individual Differences and Their Measurement: A Review of 100 Years of Research," *Journal of Applied Psychology*, 2017, 102(3), pp. 254–273.

71. Society for Human Resource Management, *Talent Acquisition Benchmarking Report*.

72. C. L. Reeve and N. Blacksmith, "Identifying g: A Review of Current Factor Analytic Practices in the Science of Mental Abilities," *Intelligence*, 2009, 37(5), pp. 487–494; W. J. Schneider and D. A. Newman, "Intelligence Is Multidimensional: Theoretical Review and Implications of Specific Cognitive Abilities," *Human Resource Management Review*, 2015, 25, pp. 12–27.

73. B. D. Lyons, B. J. Hoffman, and J. W. Michel, "Not Much More Than g? An Examination of the Impact of Intelligence on NFL Performance," *Human Performance*, 2009, 22(3), pp. 225–245.

74. F. L. Schmidt and J. E. Hunter, "The Validity and Utility of Selection Methods in Personnel Psychology: Practical and Theoretical Implications of 85 Years of Research Findings," *Psychological Bulletin*, 1998, 124, pp. 262–274; J. F. Salgado, N. Anderson, S. Moscoso, C. Bertua, F. de Fruyt, and J. P. Rolland, "A Meta-Analytic Study of General Mental Ability Validity for Different Occupations in the European Community," *Journal of Applied Psychology*, 2003, 88, pp. 1068–1081; F. L. Schmidt and J. Hunter, "General Mental Ability in the World of Work: Occupational Attainment and Job Performance," *Journal of Personality and Social Psychology*, 2004, 86, pp. 162–173.

75. T. A. Judge, R. Ilies, and N. Dimotakis, "Are Health and Happiness the Product of Wisdom? The Relationship of General Mental Ability to Educational and Occupational Attainment, Health, and Well-Being," *Journal of Applied Psychology*, 2010, 95(3), pp. 454–468; M. A. Maltarich, A. J. Nyberg, and G. A. Reilly, "A Conceptual and Empirical Analysis of the Cognitive Ability-Voluntary Turnover Relationship," *Journal of Applied Psychology*, 2010, 95(6), pp. 1058–1070; E. Gonzalez-Mulé, M. K. Mount, and I.-S. Oh, "A Meta-Analysis of the Relationship Between General Mental Ability and Nontask Performance," *Journal of Applied Psychology*, 2014, 99, pp. 1222–1243.

76. Schmidt and Hunter, "The Validity and Utility of Selection Methods in Personnel Psychology: Practical and Theoretical Implications of 85 Years of Research Findings"; A. J. Vinchur, J. S. Schippmann, F. S. Switzer III, and P. L. Roth, "A Meta-Analytic Review of Predictors of Job Performance for Salespeople," *Journal of Applied Psychology*, 1998, 83(4), pp. 586–597.

77. Schmidt and Hunter, "The Validity and Utility of Selection Methods in Personnel Psychology: Practical and Theoretical Implications of 85 Years of Research Findings."

78. J. W. B. Lang and P. D. Bliese, "General Mental Ability and Two Types of Adaptation to Unforeseen Change: Applying Discontinuous Growth Models to the Task-Change Paradigm," *Journal of Applied Psychology*, 2009, 94(2), pp. 411–428; M. J. Ree and J. A. Earles, "Predicting Training Success: Not Much More Than g," *Personnel Psychology*, 1991, 44, pp. 321–332; Schmidt and Hunter, "The Validity and Utility of Selection Methods in Personnel Psychology: Practical and Theoretical Implications of 85 Years of Research Findings."

79. F. L. Schmidt and J. E. Hunter, "Development of a Causal Model of Processes Determining Job Performance," *Current Directions in Psychological Science*, 1992, 1, pp. 89–92; Schmidt and Hunter, "The Validity and Utility of Selection Methods in Personnel Psychology: Practical and Theoretical Implications of 85 Years of Research Findings."

80. J. W. B. Lang, M. Kersting, U. R. Hülsheger, and J. Lang, "General Mental Ability, Narrower Cognitive Abilities, and Job Performance: The Perspective of the Nested-Factors Model of Cognitive Abilities," *Personnel Psychology*, 2010, 63(3), pp. 595–640; M. K. Mount, I. Oh, and M. Burns, "Incremental Validity of Perceptual Speed and Accuracy Over General Mental Ability," *Personnel Psychology*, 2008, 61(1), pp. 113–139; Schneider and Newman, "Intelligence Is Multidimensional: Theoretical Review and Implications of Specific Cognitive Abilities."

81. Bobko and Roth, "Reviewing, Categorizing, and Analyzing the Literature on Black-White Mean Differences for Predictors of Job Performance: Verifying Some Perceptions and Updating/ Correcting Others"; C. M. Berry, "Differential Validity and Differential Prediction of Cognitive Ability Tests: Understanding Test Bias in the Employment Context," *Annual Review of Organizational Psychology and Organizational Behavior*, 2015, 2, pp. 435–463; C. M. Berry, M. A. Clark, and T. K. McClure, "Racial/Ethnic Differences in the Criterion-Related Validity of Cognitive Ability Tests: A Qualitative and Quantitative Review," *Journal of Applied Psychology*, 2011, 96, pp. 881–906; C. M. Berry, M. J. Cullen, and J. M. Meyer, "Racial/Ethnic Subgroup Differences in Cognitive Ability Test Range Restriction: Implications for Differential Validity," *Journal of Applied Psychology*, 2014, 99, pp. 21–37.

82. W. F. Cascio, R. Jacobs, and J. Silva, "Validity, Utility, and Adverse Impact: Practical Implications From 30 Years of Data," in J. L. Outtz (ed.), *Adverse Impact: Implications for Organizational Staffing and High Stakes Selection* (New York: Routledge/Taylor & Francis, 2010), pp. 271–288; D. Potosky, P. Bobko, and P. L. Roth, "Forming Composites of Cognitive Ability and Alternative Measures to Predict Job Performance and Reduce Adverse Impact: Corrected Estimates and Realistic Expectations," *International Journal of Selection and Assessment*, 2005, 13, pp. 304–315; R. E. Ployhart and B. C. Holtz, "The Diversity-Validity Dilemma: Strategies for Reducing Racioethnic and Sex Subgroup Differences and Adverse Impact in Selection," *Personnel Psychology*, 2008, 61, pp. 153–172.

83. Anderson, Salgado, and Hülsheger, "Applicant Reactions in Selection: Comprehensive Meta-Analysis Into Reaction Generalization Versus Situational Specificity"; Hausknecht, Day, and Thomas, "Applicant Reactions to Selection Procedures: An Updated Model and Meta-Analysis"; J. K. Oostrom and B. De Soete, "Ethnic Differences in Perceptions of Cognitive Ability Tests: The Explanatory Role of Self-Serving Attributions," *International Journal of Selection and Assessment*, 2016, 24(1), pp. 14–23; J. J. Sumanth and D. M. Cable, "Status and Organizational Entry: How Organizational and Individual Status Affect Justice Perceptions of Hiring Systems," *Personnel Psychology*, 2011, 64, pp. 963–1000.

84. T. R. Caretta, *Development and Validation of the Test of Basic Aviation Skills (TBAS)*, Report No. 0172 (Wright-Patterson Air Force Base, Dayton, OH: Air Force Research Laboratory, 2005).

85. J. Hogan, "Physical Abilities," in M. D. Dunnette and L. M. Hough (eds.), *Handbook of Industrial and Organizational Psychology*, Vol. 2 (Palo Alto, CA: Consulting Psychologists Press, 1991), pp. 753–831.

86. N. Henderson, M. W. Berry, and T. Malic, "Field Measures of Strength and Fitness Predict Firefighter Performance on Physically Demanding Tasks," *Personnel Psychology*, 2007, 60, pp. 431–473.

87. M. A. Campion, "Personnel Selection for Physically Demanding Jobs: Review and Recommendations," *Personnel Psychology*, 1987, 36, pp. 527–550; S. H. Courtright, B. W. McCormick, B. E. Postlethwaite, C. J. Reeves, and M. K. Mount, "A Meta-Analysis of Sex Differences in Physical Ability: Revised Estimates and Strategies for Reducing Differences in Selection Contexts," *Journal of Applied Psychology*, 2013, 98, pp. 623–641.

88. M. A. Campion, "Personnel Selection for Physically Demanding Jobs: Review and Recommendations," *Personnel Psychology*, 1987, 36, pp. 527–550; S. H. Courtright, B. W. McCormick, B. E. Postlethwaite, C. J. Reeves, and M. K. Mount, "A Meta-Analysis of Sex Differences in Physical Ability: Revised Estimates and Strategies for Reducing Differences in Selection Contexts," *Journal of Applied Psychology*, 2013, 98, pp. 623–641; P. L. Roth, C. H. Van Iddekinge, P. S. DeOrtentiis, K. J. Hackney, L. Zhang, and M. A. Buster, "Hispanic and Asian Performance on Selection Procedures: A Narrative and Meta-Analytic Review of 12 Common Predictors," *Journal of Applied Psychology*, 2017, 102(8), pp. 1178–1202.

89. ErgoScience, "Physical Abilities Testing Causes Legal Problems? Overruled!" *ErgoScience News* (blog), Mar. 15, 2017 (*http://info.ergoscience.com/news/physical-abilities-testing-causes-legal-problems-overruled*); D. Lechner, "Physical Ability Testing: Worth It or Not in Reducing Workplace Injuries?" *The Well Workplace* (blog), June 17, 2015 (*http://info.ergoscience.com/employer-blog/physical-ability-testing-worth-it-or-not-in-reducing-workplace-injuries*); M. Littleton, "Cost-Effectiveness of a Prework Screening Program for the University of Illinois at Chicago Physical Plant," *Work*, 2003, 21, pp. 243–250.

90. A. M. Ryan, G. J. Greguras, and R. E. Ployhart, "Perceived Job Relatedness of Physical Ability Testing for Firefighters: Exploring Variations in Reactions," *Human Performance*, 1996, 9(3), pp. 219–240.

91. D. DuBois, V. L. Shalin, K. R. Levi, and W. C. Borman, *Job Knowledge Test Design: A Cognitively-Oriented Approach*, Report No. 241 (Minneapolis, MN: Personnel Decisions Research Institutes, 1993).

92. Wisconsin Department of Employment Relations, *Developing Wisconsin State Civil Service Examinations and Assessment Procedures* (Madison, WI: author, 1994).

93. D. M. Dye, M. Reck, and M. A. McDaniel, "The Validity of Job Knowledge Measures," *International Journal of Selection and Assessment*, 1993, 1, pp. 153–157; Schmidt and Hunter, "The Validity and Utility of Selection Methods in Personnel Psychology: Practical and Theoretical Implications of 85 Years of Research Findings."

94. S. Côté, "Emotional Intelligence in Organizations," *Annual Review of Organizational Psychology and Organizational Behavior*, 2014, 1, pp. 459–488.

95. C. Cherniss, "Emotional Intelligence: Toward Clarification of a Concept," *Industrial and Organizational Psychology*, 2010, 3, pp. 110–126; K. V. Petrides, M. Mikolajczak, S. Mavroveli, M-J. Sanchez-Ruiz, A. Furnham, and J-C. Pérez-González, "Developments in Trait Emotional Intelligence Research," *Emotion Review*, 2016, 8(4), pp. 335–341.

96. Côté, "Emotional Intelligence in Organizations"; H. A. Elfenbein and C. MacCann, "A Closer Look at Ability Emotional Intelligence (EI): What Are Its Component Parts, and How Do They Relate to Each Other?" *Social and Personality Psychology Compass*, 2017, 11(7), pp. 1–13; J. D. Mayer, D. R. Caruso, and P. Salovey, "The Ability Model of Emotional Intelligence: Principles and Updates," *Emotion Review*, 2016, 8(4), pp. 290–300; J. M. Mestre, C. MacCann, R. Guil, and R. D. Roberts, "Models of Cognitive Ability and Emotion Can Better Inform Contemporary Emotional Intelligence Frameworks," *Emotion Review*, 2016, 8(4), pp. 322–330.

97. D. L. Joseph, J. Jin, D. A. Newman, and E. H. O'Boyle, "Why Does Self-Reported Emotional Intelligence Predict Job Performance? A Meta-Analytic Investigation of Mixed EI," *Journal of Applied Psychology*, 2015, 100, pp. 298–342; D. van der Linden, K. A. Pekaar, A. B. Bakker, J. A. Schermer, P. A. Vernon, C. S. Dunkel, and K. V. Petrides, "Overlap Between the General Factor of Personality and Emotional Intelligence: A Meta-Analysis," *Psychological Bulletin*, 2017, 143(1), pp. 36–52.

98. M. T. Brannick, M. M. Wahi, M. Arce, H-A. Johnson, S. Nazian, and S. B. Goldin, "Comparison of Trait and Ability Measures of Emotional Intelligence in Medical Students," *Medical Education*, 2009, 43, pp. 1062–1068; D. L. Joseph and D. A. Newman, "Discriminant Validity of

Self-Reported Emotional Intelligence: A Multitrait-Multisource Study," *Educational and Psychological Measurement*, 2010, 70(4), pp. 672–694; H. A. Livingstone and A. L. Day, "Comparing the Construct and Criterion-Related Validity of Ability-Based and Mixed-Model Measures of Emotional Intelligence," *Educational and Psychological Measurement*, 2005, 65(5), pp. 757–779; C. A. Webb, Z. J. Schwab, M. Weber, S. DelDonno, M. Kipman, M. R. Weiner, and W. D. S. Killgore, "Convergent and Divergent Validity of Integrative Versus Mixed Model Measures of Emotional Intelligence," *Intelligence*, 2013, 41, pp. 149–156; D. S. Whitman, D. L. Van Rooy, C. Viswesvaran, and A. Alonso, "The Susceptibility of a Mixed Model Measure of Emotional Intelligence to Faking: A Solomon Four-Group Design," *Psychology Science Quarterly*, 2008, 58(1), pp. 44–63.

99. T. R. Evans, D. J. Hughes, and G. Steptoe-Warren, "A Conceptual Replication of Emotional Intelligence as a Second-Stratum Factor of Intelligence," *Emotion*, in press; C. MacCann, D. L. Joseph, D. A. Newman, and R. D. Roberts, "Emotional Intelligence Is a Second-Stratum Factor of Intelligence: Evidence From Hierarchical and Bifactor Models," *Emotion*, 2014, 14(2), pp. 358–374.

100. V. D. Allen, A. Weissman, S. Hellwig, C. MacCann, and R. D. Roberts, "Development of the Situational Test of Emotional Understanding—Brief (STEU-B) Using Item Response Theory," *Personality and Individual Differences*, 2014, 65, pp. 3–7; N. Libbrecht and F. Lievens, "Validity Evidence for the Situational Judgment Test Paradigm in Emotional Intelligence Measurement," *International Journal of Psychology*, 2012, 47(6), pp. 438–447; C. MacCann and R. D. Roberts, "New Paradigms for Assessing Emotional Intelligence: Theory and Data," *Emotion*, 2008, 8(4), pp. 540–551; K. Schlegel and M. Mortillaro, "The Geneva Emotional Competence Test (GECo): An Ability Measure of Workplace Emotional Intelligence," *Journal of Applied Psychology*, 2019, 104(4), pp. 559–580.

101. Joseph et al., "Why Does Self-Reported Emotional Intelligence Predict Job Performance? A Meta-Analytic Investigation of Mixed EI"; D. L. Joseph and D. A. Newman, "Emotional Intelligence: An Integrative Meta-Analysis and Cascading Model," *Journal of Applied Psychology*, 2010, 95(1), pp. 54–78.

102. D. H. Kluemper, T. DeGroot, and S. Choi, "Emotion Management Ability: Predicting Task Performance, Citizenship, and Deviance," *Journal of Management*, 2013, 39, pp. 878–905; C. Miao, R. H. Humphrey, and S. Qian, "Are the Emotionally Intelligent Good Citizens or Counterproductive? A Meta-Analysis of Emotional Intelligence and Its Relationships With Organizational Citizenship Behavior and Counterproductive Work Behavior," *Personality and Individual Differences*, 2017, 116, pp. 144–156.

103. Côté, "Emotional Intelligence in Organizations"; M. Zeidner, G. Matthews, and R. D. Roberts, "Emotional Intelligence in the Workplace: A Critical Review," *Applied Psychology: An International Review*, 2004, 53, pp. 371–399.

104. S. Kaplan, J. Cortina, and G. A. Ruark, "Oops . . . We Did It Again: Industrial-Organizational's Focus on Emotional Intelligence Instead of on Its Relationships to Work Outcomes," *Industrial and Organizational Psychology*, 2010, 3(2), pp. 171–177.

105. E. A. Locke, "Why Emotional Intelligence Is an Invalid Concept," *Journal of Organizational Behavior*, 2005, 26, p. 426.

106. Joseph et al., "Why Does Self-Reported Emotional Intelligence Predict Job Performance? A Meta-Analytic Investigation of Mixed EI."

107. D. S. Whitman, E. Kraus, and D. L. Van Rooy, "Emotional Intelligence Among Black and White Job Applicants: Examining Differences in Test Performance and Test Reactions," *International Journal of Selection and Assessment*, 2014, 22(2), pp. 199–210.

108. Ibid.

109. D. Iliescu, A. Ilie, D. Ispas, and A. Ion, "Emotional Intelligence in Personnel Selection: Applicant Reactions, Criterion, and Incremental Validity," *International Journal of Selection and Assessment*, 2012, 20(3), pp. 347–358.

110. M. J. Carley, "Autism Without Fear: Is Corporate Use of 'Emotional Intelligence' Grounds for Discrimination Under the ADA?" *Huffington Post*, Aug. 26, 2014 (*www.huffpost.com/entry/autism -without-fear-is-co_b_5697890*).

111. F. J. Landy, "Some Historical and Scientific Issues Related to Research on Emotional Intelligence," *Journal of Organizational Behavior*, 2005, 26, p. 421.

112. P. N. Lopes, "Emotional Intelligence in Organizations: Bridging Research and Practice," *Emotion Review*, 2016, 8(4), pp. 316–321.

113. CareerBuilder, "Seventy-One Percent of Employers Say They Value Emotional Intelligence Over IQ" (press release), Aug. 18, 2011 (*www.careerbuilder.ca/share/aboutus/pressreleasesdetail.aspx ?id=pr652&sd=8%2f18%2f2011&ed=8%2f18%2f2099*).

114. See, for example, C. T. H. Miners, S. Côté, and F. Lievens, "Assessing the Validity of Emotional Intelligence Measures," *Emotion Review*, 2018, 10(1), pp. 87–95.

115. L. M. Hough, F. L. Oswald, and J. Ock, "Beyond the Big Five: New Directions for Personality Research and Practice in Organizations," *Annual Review of Organizational Psychology and Organizational Behavior*, 2015, 2, pp. 183–209; T. A. Judge, R. Klinger, L. S. Simon, and I. W. F. Yang, "The Contributions of Personality to Organizational Behavior and Psychology: Findings, Criticisms, and Future Research Directions," *Social and Personality Psychology Compass*, 2008, 2, pp. 1982–2000; P. R. Sackett and P. T. Walmsley, "Which Personality Attributes Are Most Important in the Workplace?" *Perspectives on Psychological Science*, 2014, 9(5), pp. 538–551.

116. O. P. John, L. P. Naumann, and C. J. Soto, "Paradigm Shift to the Integrative Big Five Trait Taxonomy: History, Measurement, and Conceptual Issues," in O. P. John, R. W. Robins, and L. A. Pervin (eds.), *Handbook of Personality: Theory and Research*, 3rd ed. (New York: Guilford, 2008), pp. 114–158.

117. I. Anusic and U. Schimmack, "Stability and Change of Personality Traits, Self-Esteem, and Well-Being: Introducing the Meta-Analytic Stability and Change Model of Retest Correlations," *Journal of Personality and Social Psychology*, 2016, 110(5), pp. 766–781; P. T. Costa, R. R. McCrae, and C. E. Löckenhoff, "Personality Across the Lifespan," *Annual Review of Psychology*, 2019, 70, pp. 423–448; T. Gnambs, "A Meta-Analysis of Dependability Coefficients (Test-Retest Reliabilities) for Measures of the Big Five," *Journal of Research in Personality*, 2014, 52, pp. 20–28.

118. P. T. Costa and R. R. McCrae, "NEO Personality Inventory-Revised," *Psychological Assessment Resources* (*www.parinc.com/Products/Pkey/276*), accessed Feb. 11, 2020; Hogan, *Hogan Personality Inventory* (HPI) (*www.hoganassessments.com/assessment/hogan-personality-inventory*), accessed Feb. 11, 2020; *International Personality Item Pool* (*https://ipip.ori.org/*), accessed Feb. 11, 2020.

119. N. Blacksmith and T. Poeppelman, "The Realities of Internet Testing: Security Considerations and Best Practices," *Industrial-Organizational Psychologist*, 2015, 53(2), pp. 54–59.

120. Y. Le Corff, V. Gingras, and M. Busque-Carrier, "Equivalence of Unproctored Internet Testing and Proctored Paper-and-Pencil Testing of the Big Five," *International Journal of Selection and Assessment*, 2017, 25, pp. 154–160.

121. S. A. Birkeland, T. M. Manson, J. L. Kisamore, M. T. Brannick, and M. A. Smith, "A Meta-Analytic Investigation of Job Applicant Faking on Personality Measures," *International Journal of Selection and Assessment*, 2006, 14(4), pp. 317–335; J. F. Salgado, "A Theoretical Model of Psychometric Effects of Faking on Assessment Procedures: Empirical Findings and Implications for Personality at Work," *International Journal of Selection and Assessment*, 2016, 24(3), pp. 209–228.

122. See, for example, A. Doyle, "Walmart Job Application and Pre-Employment Assessment Test" (*www.thebalance.com/walmart-job-application-tips-2061582*), accessed Dec. 2, 2016.

123. A. J. Berinsky, M. F. Margolis, and M. W. Sances, "Can We Turn Shirkers Into Workers?" *Journal of Experimental Social Psychology*, 2016, 66, pp. 20–28; Salgado, "A Theoretical Model of Psychometric Effects of Faking on Assessment Procedures: Empirical Findings and Implications for Personality at Work"; J. F. Salgado, N. Anderson, and G. Tauriz, "The Validity of Ipsative and Quasi-Ipsative Forced-Choice Personality Inventories for Different Occupational Groups: A Comprehensive Meta-Analysis," *Journal of Occupational and Organizational Psychology*, 2015, 88, pp. 797–834.

124. N. T. Tippins, J. Beaty, F. Drasgow, W. M. Gibson, K. Pearlman, D. O. Segall, and W. Shepherd, "Unproctored Internet Testing in Employment Settings," *Personnel Psychology*, 2006, 59, pp. 189–225; S. Overman, "Online Screening Saves Time and Money," *Staffing Management*, July–Sept. 2005, pp. 18–22.

125. Exhibit 9.8 and the review here are based on G. Alarcon, K. J. Eschleman, and N. A. Bowling, "Relationships Between Personality Variables and Burnout: A Meta-Analysis," *Work & Stress*, 2009, 23(3), pp. 244–263; C. M. Berry, D. S. Ones, and P. R. Sackett, "Interpersonal Deviance, Organizational Deviance, and Their Common Correlates: A Review and Meta-Analysis," *Journal of Applied Psychology*, 2007, 92, pp. 410–424; D. S. Chiaburu, I.-S. Oh, C. M. Berry, N. Li, and R. G. Gardner, "The Five-Factor Model of Personality Traits and Organizational Citizenship Behaviors: A Meta-Analysis," *Journal of Applied Psychology*, 2011, 96, pp. 1140–1166; D. Choi, I.-S. Oh, and A. E. Colbert, "Understanding Organizational Commitment: A Meta-Analytic Examination of the Roles of the Five-Factor Model of Personality and Culture," *Journal of Applied Psychology*, 2015, 100, pp. 1542–1567; M. M. Hammond, N. L. Neff, J. L. Farr, A. R. Schwall, and X. Zhao, "Predictors of Individual-Level Innovation at Work: A Meta-Analysis," *Psychology of Aesthetics, Creativity, and the Arts*, 2011, 5, pp. 90–105; T. A. Judge, D. Heller, and M. K. Mount, "Five-Factor Model of Personality and Job Satisfaction: A Meta-Analysis," *Journal of Applied Psychology*, 2002, 87(3), pp. 530–541; T. A. Judge and R. Ilies, "Relationship of Personality to Performance Motivation: A Meta-Analytic Review," *Journal of Applied Psychology*, 2002, 87, pp. 797–807; R. Kanfer, C. R. Wanberg, and T. M. Kantrowitz, "Job Search and Employment: A Personality-Motivational Analysis and Meta-Analytic Review," *Journal of Applied Psychology*, 2001, 86(5), pp. 837–855; K. M. Martincin and G. B. Stead, "Five-Factor Model and Difficulties in Career Decision Making: A Meta-Analysis," *Journal of Career Assessment*, 2015, 23(1), pp. 3–19; J. S. Michel, M. A. Clark, and D. Jaramillo, "The Role of the Five Factor Model of Personality in the Perceptions of Negative Positive Forms of Work–Nonwork Spillover: A Meta-Analytic Review," *Journal of Vocational Behavior*, 2011, 79, pp. 191–203; M. B. Smith, A. D. Hill, J. C. Wallace, T. Recendes, and T. A. Judge, "Upsides to Dark and Downsides to Bright Personality: A Multidomain Review and Future Research Agenda," *Journal of Management*, 2018, 44(1), pp. 191–217; Vinchur et al., "A Meta-Analytic Review of Predictors of Job Performance for Salespeople"; H. R. Young, D. R. Glerum, W. Wang, and D. L. Joseph, "Who Are the Most Engaged at Work? A Meta-Analysis of Personality and Employee Engagement," *Journal of Organizational Behavior*, 2018, 39, pp. 1330–1346.

126. P. R. Sackett and P. T. Walmsley, "Which Personality Attributes Are Most Important in the Workplace?" *Perspectives on Psychological Science*, 2014, 95(5), pp. 538–551.

127. M. R. Barrick and M. K. Mount, "Autonomy as a Moderator of the Relationships Between the Big Five Personality Dimensions and Job Performance," *Journal of Applied Psychology*, 1993, 78, pp. 111–118; T. A. Judge and C. P. Zapata, "The Person-Situation Debate Revisited: Effect of Situation Strength and Trait Activation on the Validity of the Big Five Personality Traits in Predicting Job Performance," *Academy of Management Journal*, 2015, 58, pp. 1149–1179.

128. N. T. Carter, D. K. Dalal, A. S. Boyce, M. S. O'Connell, M.-C. Kung, and K. M. Delgado, "Uncovering Curvilinear Relationships Between Conscientiousness and Job Performance: How Theoretically Appropriate Measurement Makes an Empirical Difference," *Journal of Applied Psychology*,

2014, 99, pp. 564–586; N. T. Carter, L. Guan, J. L. Maples, R. L. Williamson, and J. D. Miller, "The Downsides of Extreme Conscientiousness for Psychological Well-Being: The Role of Obsessive Compulsive Tendencies," *Journal of Personality*, 2016, 84, pp. 510–522; N. T. Carter, J. D. Miller, and T. A. Widiger, "Extreme Personalities at Work and in Life," *Current Directions in Psychological Science*, 2018, 27(6), pp. 429–436; J. R. Pierce and H. Aguinis, "The Too-Much-of-a-Good-Thing Effect in Management," *Journal of Management*, 2013, 39, pp. 313–338.

129. For a review of these criticisms and responses to them, see F. P. Morgeson, M. A. Campion, R. L. Dipboye, J. R. Hollenbeck, K. Murphy, and N. Schmitt, "Reconsidering the Use of Personality Tests in Personnel Selection Contexts," *Personnel Psychology*, 2007, 60, pp. 683–729; F. P. Morgeson, M. A. Campion, R. L. Dipboye, J. R. Hollenbeck, K. Murphy, and N. Schmitt, "Are We Getting Fooled Again? Coming to Terms With Limitations in the Use of Personality Tests for Personnel Selection," *Personnel Psychology*, 2007, 60, pp. 1029–1049; D. S. Ones, S. Dilchert, C. Viswesvaran, and T. A. Judge, "In Support of Personality Assessments in Organizational Settings," *Personnel Psychology*, 2007, 60, pp. 995–1027; R. P. Tett and N. D. Christiansen, "Personality Tests at the Crossroads: A Response to Morgeson, Campion, Dipboye, Hollenbeck, Murphy, and Schmitt (2007)," *Personnel Psychology*, 2007, 60, pp. 967–993.

130. M. R. Barrick and M. K. Mount, "The Big Five Personality Dimensions and Job Performance: A Meta-Analysis," *Personnel Psychology*, 1991, 44, pp. 1–26; M. R. Barrick, M. K. Mount, and T. A. Judge, "Personality and Performance at the Beginning of the New Millennium: What Do We Know and Where Do We Go Next?" *International Journal of Selection & Assessment*, 2001, 9, pp. 9–30.

131. Morgeson et al., "Reconsidering the Use of Personality Tests in Personnel Selection Contexts," p. 694; validity estimate from T. A. Judge, J. B. Rodell, R. L. Klinger, L. S. Simon, and E. R. Crawford, "Hierarchical Representations of the Five-Factor Model of Personality in Predicting Job Performance: Integrating Three Organizing Frameworks With Two Theoretical Perspectives," *Journal of Applied Psychology*, 2013, 98, pp. 875–925.

132. N. Li, M. R. Barrick, R. D. Zimmerman, and D. S. Chiaburu, "Retaining the Productive Employee: The Role of Personality," *Academy of Management Annals*, 2014, 8, pp. 347–395.

133. Judge et al., "Hierarchical Representations of the Five-Factor Model of Personality in Predicting Job Performance."

134. I-S. Oh, G. Wang, and M. K. Mount, "Validity of Observer Ratings of the Five-Factor Model of Personality Traits," *Journal of Applied Psychology*, 2011, 96(4), pp. 762–773.

135. Hough, Oswald, and Ock, "Beyond the Big Five: New Directions for Personality Research and Practice in Organizations."

136. M. C. Ashton and K. Lee, "The Prediction of Honesty-Humility-Related Criteria by the HEXACO and Five-Factor Models of Personality," *Journal of Research in Personality*, 2008, 42, pp. 1216–1228; M. C. Ashton, K. Lee, and R. E. de Vries, "The HEXACO Honesty-Humility, Agreeableness, and Emotionality Factors: A Review of Research and Theory," *Personality and Social Psychology Review*, 2014, 18, pp. 139–152.

137. C-H. Chang, D. L. Ferris, R. E. Johnson, C. C. Rosen, and J. A. Tan, "Core Self-Evaluations: A Review and Evaluation of the Literature," *Journal of Management*, 2012, 38(1), pp. 81–128; T. A. Judge and J. E. Bono, "Relationship of Core Self-Evaluations Traits—Self-Esteem, Generalized Self-Efficacy, Locus of Control, and Emotional Stability—With Job Satisfaction and Job Performance: A Meta-Analysis," *Journal of Applied Psychology*, 2001, 86, pp. 80–92; T. A. Judge, A. Erez, J. E. Bono, and C. J. Thoresen, "The Core Self-Evaluations Scale: Development of a Measure," *Personnel Psychology*, 2003, 56, pp. 303–331.

138. S. V. Marinova, C. Peng, N. Lorinkova, L. Van Dyne, and D. Chiaburu, "Change-Oriented Behavior: A Meta-Analysis of Individual and Job Design Predictors," *Journal of Vocational Behavior*, 2015, 88, pp. 104–120; J. P. Thomas, D. S. Whitman, and C. Viswesvaran, "Employee Proactivity in Organizations: A Comparative Meta-Analysis of Emergent Proactive Constructs," *Journal of*

Occupational and Organizational Psychology, 2010, 83, pp. 275–300; K. Tornau and M. Frese, "Construct Clean-Up in Proactivity Research: A Meta-Analysis on the Nomological Net of Work-Related Proactivity Concepts and Their Incremental Validity," *Applied Psychology: An International Review*, 2013, 62(1), pp. 44–96.

139. K. J. Eschleman, N. A. Bowling, and G. M. Alarcon, "A Meta-Analytic Examination of Hardiness," *International Journal of Stress Management*, 2010, 17, pp. 277–307.

140. J. M. LeBreton, L. K. Shiverdecker, and E. M. Grimaldi, "The Dark Triad and Workplace Behavior," *Annual Review of Organizational Psychology and Organizational Behavior*, 2018, 5, pp. 387–414; E. H. O'Boyle, Jr., D. R. Forsyth, G. C. Banks, and M. A. McDaniel, "A Meta-Analysis of the Dark Triad and Work Behavior: A Social Exchange Perspective," *Journal of Applied Psychology*, 2012, 97, pp. 557–579.

141. D. M. Fisher, S. Cunningham, A. J. Kerr, and S. P. Allscheid, "Contextualized Personality Measures in Employee Selection: Extending Frame-of-Reference Research With Job Applicant Samples," *International Journal of Selection and Assessment*, 2017, 25, pp. 18–35; S. Highhouse, M. J. Zickar, M. E. Brooks, C. L. Reeve, S. T. Sarkar-Barney, and R. M. Guion, "A Public-Domain Personality Item Bank for Use With the Raymark, Schmit, and Guion (1997) PPRF," *Personnel Assessment and Decisions*, 2016, 2(1), pp. 48–56; C. Robie, S. D. Risavy, D. Holtrop, and M. P. Born, "Fully Contextualized, Frequency-Based Personality Measurement: A Replication and Extension," *Journal of Research in Personality*, 2017, 70, pp. 56–65.

142. J. A. Shaffer and B. E. Postlethwaite, "A Matter of Context: A Meta-Analytic Investigation of the Relative Validity of Contextualized and Noncontextualized Personality Measures," *Personnel Psychology*, 2012, 65, pp. 445–494.

143. Birkeland et al., "A Meta-Analytic Investigation of Job Applicant Faking on Personality Measures."

144. J. E. Ellingson, D. B. Smith, and P. R. Sackett, "Investigating the Influence of Social Desirability on Personality Factor Structure," *Journal of Applied Psychology*, 2001, 86, pp. 122–133; D. S. Ones, C. Viswesvaran, and A. D. Reiss, "Role of Social Desirability in Personality Testing for Personnel Selection: The Red Herring," *Journal of Applied Psychology*, 1996, 81(6), pp. 660–679; D. B. Smith and J. E. Ellingson, "Substance Versus Style: A New Look at Social Desirability in Motivating Contexts," *Journal of Applied Psychology*, 2002, 87, pp. 211–219.

145. M. N. Bing, D. Kluemper, H. Kristl Davison, S. Taylor, and M. Novicevic, "Overclaiming as a Measure of Faking," *Organizational Behavior and Human Decision Processes*, 2011, 116, pp. 148–162; L. Chang, B. S. Connelly, and A. A. Geeza, "Separating Method Factors and Higher-Order Traits of the Big Five: A Meta-Analytic Multi-Trait Multi-Method Approach," *Journal of Personality and Social Psychology*, 2012, 102, pp. 408–426; B. S. Connelly and U. R. Hülsheger, "A Narrower Scope or a Clearer Lens? Examining the Validity of Personality Ratings From Observers Outside the Workplace," *Journal of Personality*, 2012, 80, pp. 603–631; B. S. Connelly and L. Chang, "A Meta-Analytic Multitrait Multirater Separation of Substance and Style in Social Desirability Scales," *Journal of Personality*, 2016, 84, pp. 319–334.

146. N. Schmitt and F. L. Oswald, "The Impact of Corrections for Faking on the Validity of Noncognitive Measures in Selection Settings," *Journal of Applied Psychology*, 2006, 91, pp. 613–621.

147. E. D. Heggestad, M. Morrison, C. L. Reeve, and R. A. McCloy, "Forced-Choice Assessments of Personality for Selection: Evaluating Issues of Normative Assessment and Faking Resistance," *Journal of Applied Psychology*, 2006, 91, pp. 9–24; S. Dilchert, D. S. Ones, C. Viswesvaran, and J. Deller, "Response Distortion in Personality Measurement: Born to Deceive, yet Capable of Providing Valid Self-Assessments?" *Psychology Science*, 2006, 48, pp. 209–225; Salgado, Anderson, and Tauriz, "The Validity of Ipsative and Quasi-Ipsative Forced-Choice Personality Inventories for Different Occupational Groups: A Comprehensive Meta-Analysis."

148. S. A. Dwight and J. J. Donovan, "Do Warnings Not to Fake Reduce Faking?" *Human Performance*, 2003, 16, pp. 1–23; J. Hogan, P. Barrett, and R. Hogan, "Personality Measurement, Faking, and Employment Selection," *Journal of Applied Psychology*, 2007, 92, pp. 1270–1285; J. E. Ellingson, P. R. Sackett, and B. S. Connelly, "Personality Assessment Across Selection and Development Contexts: Insights Into Response Distortion," *Journal of Applied Psychology*, 2007, 92, pp. 386–395; E. A. J. van Hooft and M. P. Born, "Intentional Response Distortion on Personality Tests: Using Eye-Tracking to Understand Response Processes When Faking," *Journal of Applied Psychology*, 2012, 97(2), pp. 301–316; J. Fan, D. Gao, S. A. Carroll, F. J. Lopez, T. S. Tian, and H. Meng, "Testing the Efficacy of a New Procedure for Reducing Faking on Personality Tests Within Selection Contexts," *Journal of Applied Psychology*, 2012, 97, pp. 866–880.

149. C. J. König, L. A. Steiner Thommen, A-M. Wittwer, and M. Kleinmann, "Are Observer Ratings of Applicants' Personality Also Faked? Yes, but Less Than Self-Reports," *International Journal of Selection and Assessment*, 2017, 25, pp. 183–192; I. Oh and C. M. Berry, "The Five-Factor Model of Personality and Managerial Performance: Validity Gains Through the Use of 360 Degree Performance Ratings," *Journal of Applied Psychology*, 2009, 94(6), pp. 1498–1513; R. D. Zimmerman, M. Triana, and M. R. Barrick, "Predictive Criterion-Related Validity of Observer Ratings of Personality and Job-Related Competencies Using Multiple Raters and Multiple Performance Criteria," *Human Performance*, 2010, 23(4), pp. 361–378.

150. Anderson, Salgado, and Hülsheger, "Applicant Reactions in Selection: Comprehensive Meta-Analysis Into Reaction Generalization Versus Situational Specificity"; Hausknecht, Day, and Thomas, "Applicant Reactions to Selection Procedures: An Updated Model and Meta-Analysis."

151. S. D. Risavy, P. A. Fisher, C. Robie, and C. J. König, "Selection Tool Use: A Focus on Personality Testing in Canada, the United States, and Germany," *Personnel Assessment and Decisions*, 2019, 5(1), pp. 62–72; Society for Human Resource Management, *Talent Acquisition Benchmarking Report*; Talent Board, *2019 North American Candidate Experience Research Report*.

152. NACE, "The Four Career Competencies Employers Value Most," Mar. 29, 2019 (*www.naceweb .org/career-readiness/competencies/the-four-career-competencies-employers-value-most/*).

153. C. M. Berry, P. R. Sackett, and S. Wiemann, "A Review of Recent Developments in Integrity Test Research," *Personnel Psychology*, 2007, 60, pp. 271–301.

154. Wage and Hour Division, US Department of Labor, *Employee Polygraph Protection Act of 1988* (Fact Sheet #36), (Washington, DC: US Department of Labor, 2008).

155. R. Adelson, "The Polygraph in Doubt," *APA Monitor*, 2004, 35, p. 71 (*www.apa.org/monitor/julaug04 /polygraph.aspx*); D. T. Lykken, "Polygraphic Interrogation," *Nature*, 1984, 307, pp. 681–684; and W. G. Iacono and D. T. Lykken, "The Validity of the Lie Detector: Two Surveys of Scientific Opinion," *Journal of Applied Psychology*, 1997, 82(3), pp. 426–433.

156. A-M. Leach, R. C. L. Lindsay, R. Koehler, J. L. Beaudry, N. C. Bala, K. Lee, and V. Talwar, "The Reliability of Lie Detection Performance," *Law & Human Behavior*, 2009, 33, pp. 96–109.

157. M. G. Aamodt and H. Custer, "Who Can Best Catch a Liar? A Meta-Analysis of Individual Differences in Detecting Deception," *Forensic Examiner*, Spring 2006, pp. 6–11.

158. S. Fine, J. Goldenberg, and Y. Noam, "Integrity Testing and the Prediction of Counterproductive Behaviours in the Military," *Journal of Occupational and Organizational Psychology*, 2016, 89, pp. 198–218; Risavy et al., "Selection Tool Use: A Focus on Personality Testing in Canada, the United States, and Germany."

159. National Retail Federation, *2018 National Retail Security Survey* (Washington, DC: author, 2018).

160. National Retail Federation, *2019 National Retail Security Survey* (Washington, DC: author, 2019).

161. C. Oliver, M. Shafiro, P. Bullard, and J. C. Thomas, "Use of Integrity Tests May Reduce Workers' Compensation Losses," *Journal of Business Psychology*, 2012, 27, pp. 115–122.

162. P. R. Sackett and J. E. Wanek, "New Developments in the Use of Measures of Honesty, Integrity, Conscientiousness, Dependability, Trustworthiness, and Reliability for Personnel Selection," *Personnel Psychology*, 1996, 49, pp. 787–829.

163. K. D. Dages, S. Zimmer, and J. W. Jones, "Pre-employment Risk Screening: Comparability of Integrity Assessment Technology Platforms," *International Journal of Selection and Assessment*, 2017, 25, pp. 390–400.

164. B. Marcus, K. Lee, and M. C. Ashton, "Personality Dimensions Explaining Relations Between Integrity Tests and Counterproductive Behavior: Big Five, or One in Addition?" *Personnel Psychology*, 2007, 60, pp. 1–34.

165. Berry, Sackett, and Wiemann, "A Review of Recent Developments in Integrity Test Research"; Sackett and Wanek, "New Developments in the Use of Measures of Honesty, Integrity, Conscientiousness, Dependability, Trustworthiness, and Reliability for Personnel Selection."

166. V. M. Catano, D. F. O'Keefe, R. E. Francis, and S. M. Owens, "Construct-Based Approach to Developing a Short, Personality-Based Measure of Integrity," *International Journal of Selection and Assessment*, 2018, 26, pp. 75–92; D. S. Ones, C. Viswesvaran, and S. Dilchert, "Personality at Work: Raising Awareness and Correcting Misconceptions," *Human Performance*, 2005, 18(4), pp. 389–404.

167. D. S. Ones, C. Viswesvaran, and F. L. Schmidt, "Comprehensive Meta-Analysis of Integrity Test Validities: Findings and Implications for Personnel Selection and Theories of Job Performance," *Journal of Applied Psychology* (monograph), 1993, 78, pp. 531–537; C. H. Van Iddekinge, P. L. Roth, P. H. Raymark, and H. N. Odle-Dusseau, "The Criterion-Related Validity of Integrity Tests: An Updated Meta-Analysis," *Journal of Applied Psychology*, 2012, 97, pp. 499–530. For commentaries, see P. R. Sackett and N. Schmitt, "On Reconciling Conflicting Meta-Analytic Findings Regarding Integrity Test Validity," *Journal of Applied Psychology*, 2012, 97, pp. 550–556; D. S. Ones, C. Viswesvaran, and F. L. Schmidt, "Integrity Tests Predict Counterproductive Work Behaviors and Job Performance Well: Comment on Van Iddekinge, Roth, Raymark, and Odle-Dusseau (2012)," *Journal of Applied Psychology*, 2012, 97, pp. 537–542.

168. Berry, Sackett, and Wiemann, "A Review of Recent Developments in Integrity Test Research"; S. Fine, "A Look at Cross-Cultural Integrity Testing in Three Banks," *Personnel Review*, 2013, 42(3), pp. 266–280; D. S. Ones and C. Viswesvaran, "Gender, Age, and Race Differences on Overt Integrity Tests: Results Across Four Large-Scale Job Applicant Data Sets," *Journal of Applied Psychology*, 1998, 83(1), pp. 35–42.

169. S. W. Billings and K. D. Dages, "Cross-Cultural Validity of Integrity Assessments for Lower-Level and Higher-Level Jobs," *International Journal of Selection and Assessment*, 2018, 26, pp. 66–74.

170. R. J. Karren and L. Zacharias, "Integrity Tests: Critical Issues," *Human Resource Management Review*, 2007, 17, pp. 221–234.

171. G. M. Alliger and S. A. Dwight, "A Meta-Analytic Investigation of the Susceptibility of Integrity Tests to Faking and Coaching," *Educational and Psychological Measurement*, 2000, 60(1), pp. 59–72.

172. Berry, Sackett, and Wiemann, "A Review of Recent Developments in Integrity Test Research"; S. Fine and M. Pirak, "Faking Fast and Slow: Within-Person Response Time Latencies for Measuring Faking in Personnel Testing," *Journal of Business Psychology*, 2016, 31, pp. 51–64.

173. Karren and Zacharias, "Integrity Tests: Critical Issues."

174. Anderson, Salgado, and Hülsheger, "Applicant Reactions in Selection: Comprehensive Meta-Analysis Into Reaction Generalization Versus Situational Specificity"; Hausknecht, Day, and Thomas, "Applicant Reactions to Selection Procedures: An Updated Model and Meta-Analysis."

175. S. A. Dwight and G. M. Alliger, "Reactions to Overt Integrity Test Items," *Educational and Psychological Measurement*, 1997, 57(6), pp. 937–948.

176. Prevue HR, "Hire People Who Actually Think Their Job Is Cool" (*www.prevuehr.com/products /motivations-assessment/*), accessed Feb. 12, 2020.

177. J. E. Hunter and R. F. Hunter, "Validity and Utility of Alternative Predictors of Job Performance," *Psychological Bulletin*, 1984, 96, pp. 72–98; C. H. Van Iddekinge, D. J. Putka, and J. P. Campbell, "Reconsidering Vocational Interests for Personnel Selection: The Validity of an Interest-Based Selection Test in Relation to Job Knowledge, Job Performance, and Continuance Intentions," *Journal of Applied Psychology*, 2011, 96(1), pp. 13–33.

178. Roth et al., "Hispanic and Asian Performance on Selection Procedures."

179. C. H. Van Iddekinge, P. L. Roth, D. J. Putka, and S. E. Lanivich, "Are You Interested? A Meta-Analysis of Relations Between Vocational Interests and Employee Performance and Turnover," *Journal of Applied Psychology*, 2011, 96(6), pp. 1167–1194.

180. C. D. Nye, R. Su, J. Rounds, and F. Drasgow, "Vocational Interests and Performance: A Quantitative Summary of Over 60 Years of Research," *Perspectives on Psychological Science*, 2012, 7, pp. 384–403; C. D. Nye, R. Su, J. Rounds, and F. Drasgow, "Interest Congruence and Performance: Revisiting Recent Meta-Analytic Findings," *Journal of Vocational Behavior*, 2017, 98, pp. 138–151.

181. D. Ilescu, D. Ispas, C. Sulea, and A. Ilie, "Vocational Fit and Counterproductive Work Behaviors: A Self-Regulation Perspective," *Journal of Applied Psychology*, 2015, 100(1), pp. 21–39; B. Marcus and U. Wagner, "What Do You Want to Be? Criterion-Related Validity of Attained Vocational Aspirations Versus Inventoried Person-Vocation Fit," *Journal of Business Psychology*, 2015, 30, pp. 51–62.

182. J. R. Edwards and D. M. Cable, "The Value of Value Congruence," *Journal of Applied Psychology*, 2009, 94(3), pp. 654–677; A. L. Kristof-Brown, R. D. Zimmerman, and E. C. Johnson, "Consequences of Individuals' Fit at Work: A Meta-Analysis of Person-Job, Person-Organization, Person-Group, and Person-Supervisor Fit," *Personnel Psychology*, 2005, 58, pp. 281–342; A. E. M. van Vianen, "Person-Environment Fit: A Review of Its Basic Tenets," *Annual Review of Organizational Psychology and Organizational Behavior*, 2018, 5, pp. 75–101.

183. G. J. Greguras and J. M. Diefendorff, "Different Fits Satisfy Different Needs: Linking Person-Environment Fit to Employee Commitment and Performance Using Self-Determination Theory," *Journal of Applied Psychology*, 2009, 94(2), pp. 465–477; I-S. Oh, R. P. Guay, K. Kim, C. M. Harold, J-H. Lee, C-G. Heo, and K-H. Shin, "Fit Happens Globally: A Meta-Analytic Comparison of the Relationships of Person-Environment Fit Dimensions With Work Attitudes and Performance Across East Asia, Europe, and North America," *Personnel Psychology*, 2014, 67, pp. 99–152.

184. D. M. Cable and T. A. Judge, "Interviewers' Perceptions of Person-Organization Fit and Organizational Selection Decisions," *Journal of Applied Psychology*, 1997, 82(4), pp. 546–561.

185. K. Bouton, "Recruiting for Cultural Fit," *Harvard Business Review*, July 17, 2015 (*https://hbr.org /2015/07/recruiting-for-cultural-fit*).

186. F. P. Morgeson, S. E. Humphrey, and M. C. Reeder, "Team Selection," in N. Schmitt (ed.), *The Oxford Handbook of Personnel Assessment and Selection* (Oxford: Oxford University Press, 2012), pp. 1–30.

187. A. Zenon III, "9 Women in Tech Share Their Best Advice for Managing a Team," *Built in Chicago* (blog), Feb. 13, 2020 (*www.builtinchicago.org/2020/02/13/chicago-women-managing-teams*).

188. See, for example, J. Li and J. M. P. Gevers, "Dynamics Between the Member Replacement and Team Performance: The Role of Members' Relative Attributes," *Applied Psychology: An International Review*, 2018, 67(1), pp. 61–90; F. Rink and N. Ellemers, "The Pernicious Effects of Unstable Work Group Membership: How Work Group Changes Undermine Unique Task Contributions and Newcomer Acceptance," *Group Processes & Intergroup Relations*, 2015, 18(1), pp. 6–23.

189. E. A. Fleishman and S. J. Zaccaro, "Toward a Taxonomy of Team Performance Functions," in R. W. Swezey and E. Salas (eds.), *Teams: Their Training and Performance* (Norwood, NJ: Ablex, 1992), pp. 31–56).

190. T. V. Mumfor, M. A. Campion, and F. P. Morgeson, "Situational Judgment in Work Teams: A Team Role Typology," in J. A. Weekley and R. E. Ployhart (eds.), *Situational Judgment Tests: Theory, Measurement, and Application* (Mahwah, NJ: Lawrence Erlbaum, 2006), pp. 319–343.

191. G. Hertel, U. Konradt, and K. Voss, "Competencies for Virtual Teamwork: Development and Validation of a Web-Based Selection Tool for Members of Distributed Teams," *European Journal of Work and Organizational Psychology*, 2006, 15(4), pp. 477–504; S. Krumm, J. Kanthak, K. Hartmann, and G. Hertel, "What Does It Take to Be a Virtual Team Player? The Knowledge, Skills, Abilities, and Other Characteristics Required in Virtual Teams," *Human Performance*, 2016, 29(2), pp. 123–142; J. Schulze and S. Krumm, "The 'Virtual Team Player': A Review and Initial Model of Knowledge, Skills, Abilities, and Other Characteristics for Virtual Collaboration," *Organizational Psychology Review*, 2017, 7(1), pp. 66–95.

192. M. J. Stevens and M. A. Campion, "Staffing Work Teams: Development and Validation of a Selection Test for Teamwork Settings," *Journal of Management*, 1999, 25(2), pp. 207–228.

193. A. C. McClough and S. G. Rogelberg, "Selection in Teams: An Exploration of the Teamwork Knowledge, Skills, and Ability Test," *International Journal of Selection and Assessment*, 2003, 11, pp. 56–65; F. P. Morgeson, M. H. Reider, and M. A. Campion, "Selecting Individuals in Team Settings: The Importance of Social Skills, Personality Characteristics, and Teamwork Knowledge," *Personnel Psychology*, 2005, 58, pp. 583–611; T. A. O'Neill, R. D. Goffin, and I. R. Gellatly, "The Knowledge, Skill, and Ability Requirements for Teamwork: Revisiting the Teamwork-KSA Test's Validity," *International Journal of Selection and Assessment*, 2012, 20(1), pp. 36–52.

194. K. A. French, J. L. Kottke, and R. J. Kirchner, "Evaluating the Psychometric Properties of the Teamwork KSA Test," *International Journal of Selection and Assessment*, 2015, 23(4), pp. 307–315; O'Neill, Goffin, and Gellatly, "The Knowledge, Skill, and Ability Requirements for Teamwork: Revisiting the Teamwork-KSA Test's Validity."

195. Morgeson, Humphrey, and Reeder, "Team Selection."

196. J. Y. Seong, A. L. Kristof-Brown, W-W. Park, D-S. Hong, and Y. Shin, "Person-Group Fit: Diversity Antecedents, Proximal Outcomes, and Performance at the Group Level," *Journal of Management*, 2015, 41(4), pp. 1184–1213; J. D. Werbel and D. J. Johnson, "The Use of Person-Group Fit for Employment Selection: A Missing Link in Person-Environment Fit," *Human Resource Management*, 2001, 40(3), pp. 227–240.

197. T. P. Munyon, J. K. Summers, and G. R. Ferris, "Team Staffing Modes in Organizations: Strategic Considerations on Individual and Cluster Hiring Approaches," *Human Resource Management Review*, 2011, 21, pp. 228–242.

198. S. W. Whiting and T. D. Maynes, "Selecting Team Players: Considering the Impact of Contextual Performance and Workplace Deviance on Selection Decisions in the National Football League," *Journal of Applied Psychology*, 2016, 101, pp. 484–497.

199. R. Y. Prager, A. H. Church, R. Silzer, and J. Scott, "Getting the Best From Your High Potential Leadership: Spotlight on the 2018 Leading Edge Consortium," *Society for Industrial and Organizational Psychology: Leading Edge Consortium*, Sept. 28, 2018 (*www.siop.org/Research-Publications/Items-of-Interest/ArtMID/19366/ArticleID/1341/Getting-the-Best-From-Your-High-Potential-Leadership-Spotlight-on-the-2018-Leading-Edge-Consortium*).

200. J. Hu, S. J. Wayne, T. N. Bauer, B. Erdogan, and R. C. Liden, "Self and Senior Executive Perceptions of Fit and Performance: A Time-Lagged Examination of Newly Hired Executives," *Human Relations*, 2016, 69(6), pp. 1259–1286.

201. E. C. Dierdorff, R. S. Rubin, and F. P. Morgeson, "The Milieu of Managerial Work: An Integrative Framework Linking Work Context to Role Requirements," *Journal of Applied Psychology*, 2009, 94(4), pp. 972–988.

202. D. R. Glerum, "The Power of Words: Uncovering Trends in Leadership Perceptions, Research and Interest," *Lead Read Today*, Dec. 2018 (*https://fisher.osu.edu/blogs/leadreadtoday/blog/the-power-of-words/*).

203. P. Behrendt, S. Matz, and A. S. Göritz, "An Integrative Model of Leadership Behavior," *Leadership Quarterly*, 2017, 28, pp. 229–244; G. Yukl, "Effective Leadership Behavior: What We Know and What Questions Need More Attention," *Academy of Management Perspectives*, 2012, 26(4), pp. 66–85.

204. N. Dries and R. Pepermans, "How to Identify Leadership Potential: Development and Testing of a Consensus Model," *Human Resource Management*, 2012, 51(3), pp. 361–385; L. M. Finkelstein, D. P. Costanza, and G. F. Goodwin, "Do Your High Potentials Have Potential? The Impact of Individual Differences and Designation on Leader Success," *Personnel Psychology*, 2018, 71, pp. 3–22; K. S. Nei, J. L. Foster, A. M. Ness, and D. S. Nei, "Rule Breakers and Attention Seekers: Personality Predictors of Integrity and Accountability in Leaders," *International Journal of Selection and Assessment*, 2018, 26, pp. 17–26.

205. K. L. Badura, E. Grijalva, D. A. Newman, T. T. Yan, and G. Jeon, "Gender and Leadership Emergence: A Meta-Analysis and Explanatory Model," *Personnel Psychology*, 2018, 71, pp. 335–367; S. Gündemir, A. M. Carton, and A. C. Homan, "The Impact of Organizational Performance on the Emergence of Asian American Leaders," *Journal of Applied Psychology*, 2019, 104(1), pp. 107–122; A. S. Rosette, C. Z. Koval, A. Ma, and R. Livingston, "Race Matters for Women Leaders: Intersectional Effects on Agentic Deficiencies and Penalties," *Leadership Quarterly*, 2016, 27(3), pp. 429–445.

206. T. A. Judge and D. M. Cable, "The Effect of Physical Height on Workplace Success and Income: Preliminary Test of a Theoretical Model," *Journal of Applied Psychology*, 2004, 89(3), pp. 428–441; D. E. Re and N. Rule, "Distinctive Facial Cues Predict Leadership Rank and Selection," *Personality and Social Psychology Bulletin*, 2017, 43(9), pp. 1311–1322; A. Todorov, C. Y. Olivola, R. Dotsch, and P. Mende-Siedlecki, "Social Attributions Form Faces: Determinants, Consequences, Accuracy, and Functional Significance," *Annual Review of Psychology*, 2015, 66, pp. 519–545.

207. J. Nadler and M. Schulman, "Favoritism, Cronyism, and Nepotism," *Markkula Center for Applied Ethics, Santa Clara University*, Oct. 23, 2015 (*www.scu.edu/government-ethics/resources/what-is-government-ethics/favoritism-cronyism-and-nepotism/*).

208. X-X. Liu, J. Keller, and Y-Y. Hong, "Hiring of Personal Ties: A Cultural Consensus Analysis of China and the United States," *Management and Organization Review*, 2015, 11(1), pp. 145–169; C. Sun, "5 Simple Ways to Handle Nepotism in the Workplace," *Entrepreneur*, May 16, 2019 (*www.entrepreneur.com/slideshow/302245*).

209. National Conference of State Legislatures, "Nepotism Restrictions," Dec. 17, 2019 (*www.ncsl.org/research/ethics/50-state-table-nepotism-restrictions.aspx*).

210. M. Stinson and C. Wignall, "Fathers, Children, and the Intergenerational Transmission of Employers," *The Survey of Income and Program Participation*, Report No. 265 (Washington, DC: US Census Bureau, 2014).

211. R. Derfler-Rozin, B. Baker, and F. Gino, "Compromised Ethics in Hiring Processes? How Referrers' Power Affects Employees' Reactions to Referral Practices," *Academy of Management Journal*, 2018, 61(2), pp. 615–636; M. Y. Padgett, R. J. Padgett, and K. A. Morris, "Perceptions of Nepotism Beneficiaries: The Hidden Price of Using a Family Connection to Obtain a Job," *Journal of Business and Psychology*, 2015, 30, pp. 283–298.

212. W. M. Haraway III and J. C. Kunselman, "Ethical Leadership and Administrative Discretion: The Fire Chief's Hiring Dilemma," *Public Personnel Management*, 2006, 35(1), pp. 1-14.

213. D. K. Dalal, D. L. Diab, and R. S. Tindale, "I Heard That...: Do Rumors Affect Hiring Decisions?" *International Journal of Selection and Assessment*, 2015, 23(3), pp. 224-236.

214. K. M. Kuhn, "Selecting the Good vs. Rejecting the Bad: Regulatory Focus Effects on Staffing Decision Making," *Human Resource Management*, 2015, 54(1), pp. 131-150.

215. K. Weaver and S. M. Garcia, "The Adding-and-Averaging Effect in Bundles of Information: Preference Reversals Across Joint and Separate Evaluation," *Journal of Experimental Psychology: Applied*, 2018, 24(3), pp. 296-305.

216. A. H. Riege and K. H. Teigen, "Everybody Will Win, and All Must Be Hired: Comparing Additivity Neglect With the Nonselective Superiority Bias," *Journal of Behavioral Decision Making,* 2017, 30, pp. 95-106.

217. N. R. Kuncel, D. M. Klieger, B. S. Connelly, and D. S. Ones, "Mechanical Versus Clinical Data Combination in Selection and Admissions Decisions: A Meta-Analysis," *Journal of Applied Psychology*, 98(6), 2013, pp. 1060-1072.

218. A. T. Jackson, M. E. Young, S. S. Howes, P. A. Knight, and S. L. Reichin, "Examining Factors Influencing Use of a Decision Aid in Personnel Selection," *Personnel Assessment and Decisions*, 2019, 5(1), pp. 1-36.

219. K. P. Nolan and S. Highhouse, "Need for Autonomy and Resistance to Standardized Employee Selection Practices," *Human Performance*, 2014, 27, pp. 328-346.

220. J. Juergens, "Addiction in the Workplace," *Addiction Center* (resource page), Dec. 5, 2019 (*www.addictioncenter.com/addiction/workplace/*).

221. "Why Worry About Drugs and Alcohol in the Workplace?" Facts for Employers, American Council for Drug Education, 2007.

222. L. Paik, "Organizational Interpretations of Drug Test Results," *Law & Society Review*, Dec. 2006, 40, pp. 1-28.

223. "SHRM Poll: Drug Testing Efficacy," *Society for Human Resource Management*, Sept. 7, 2011 (*www.shrm.org/research/surveyfindings/articles/pages/ldrugtestingefficacy.aspx*).

224. "U.S. Corporations Reduce Levels of Medical, Drug and Psychological Testing of Employees," *American Management Association*, 2007 (*www.amanet.org*).

225. L. DePillis, "Companies Drug Test a Lot Less Than They Used to—Because It Doesn't Really Work," *Washington Post*, March 10, 2015 (*www.washingtonpost.com/news/wonk/wp/2015/03/10/companies-drug-test-a-lot-less-than-they-used-to-because-it-doesnt-really-work/*); J. Reidy and D. Hewick, "Are Employer Drug-Testing Programs Obsolete? Two Experts Debate the Issue," *HR Magazine*, May 23, 2018 (*www.shrm.org/hr-today/news/hr-magazine/0618/pages/are-employer-drug-testing-programs-obsolete.aspx*).

226. L. Nagele-Piazza, "Workplace Drug Testing: Can Employers Still Screen for Marijuana?" *Society for Human Resource Management*, Jan. 21, 2020 (*www.shrm.org/resourcesandtools/legal-and-compliance/state-and-local-updates/pages/can-employers-still-test-for-marijuana.aspx*).

227. Quest Diagnostics, *Drug Testing Index: A Comprehensive Analysis of Workplace Drug Use Trends, Employer Solutions Annual Report*, Spring 2019 (*www.questdiagnostics.com/dms/Documents/Employer-Solutions/DTI-2019/quest-drug-testing-index-brochure-2019.pdf*).

228. C. Isidore, "Do You Smoke? Then You Can't Get Hired at U-Haul in These States," *CNN Business,* Jan. 6, 2020 (*www.cnn.com/2020/01/02/business/uhaul-smokers/index.html*).

229. S. Overman, "Wanted: Non-Smokers," *Staffing Management*, 2008, 4(1), pp. 29-34.

230. N. Roulin and N. Bhatnagar, "Smoking as a Job Killer: Reactions to Smokers in Personnel Selection," *Journal of Business Ethics*, 2018, 149, pp. 959-972.

231. K. Helliker, "A Test for Alcohol—and Its Flaws," *Wall Street Journal*, Aug. 12, 2006, pp. A1, A6.

232. P. A. Bamberger, J. Koopmann, M. Wang, M. Larimer, I. Nahum-Shani, I. Geisner, and S. B. Bacharach, "Does College Alcohol Consumption Impact Employment Upon Graduation? Findings From a Prospective Study," *Journal of Applied Psychology*, 2018, 103(1), pp. 111–121.

233. J. Normand, S. D. Salyards, and J. J. Mahoney, "An Evaluation of Preemployment Drug Testing," *Journal of Applied Psychology*, 1990, 75, pp. 629–639.

234. S. L. Martin and C. Godsey, "Assessing the Validity of a Theoretically-Based Substance Abuse Scale for Personnel Selection," *Journal of Business and Psychology*, 1999, 13(3), pp. 323–337.

235. J. M. Crant and T. S. Bateman, "An Experimental Test of the Impact of Drug-Testing Programs on Potential Job Applicants' Attitudes and Intentions," *Journal of Applied Psychology*, 1990, 75, pp. 127–131; K. R. Murphy, G. C. Thornton III, and D. H. Reynolds, "College Students' Attitudes Toward Employee Drug Testing Programs," *Personnel Psychology*, 1990, 43, pp. 615–631.

236. *Mandatory Guidelines and Proposed Revisions to Mandatory Guidelines for Federal Workplace Drug Testing Programs*, Department of Health and Human Services, Substance Abuse and Mental Health Services Administration, 2004.

237. S. Overman, "Debating Drug Test ROI," *Staffing Management*, Oct.–Dec. 2005, pp. 19–22.

238. M. A. Campion, "Personnel Selection for Physically Demanding Jobs: Review and Recommendations," *Personnel Psychology*, 1983, 36, pp. 527–550; E. A. Fleishman, "Some New Frontiers in Personnel Selection Research," *Personnel Psychology*, 1988, 41, pp. 679–701.

239. Equal Employment Opportunity Commission, "Uniform Guidelines on Employee Selection Procedures (1978)," *Code of Federal Regulations*, Title 29, Part 1607, Aug. 25, 1978; D. J. Walsh, *Employment Law for Human Resource Practice*, 5th ed. (Boston: Cengage Learning, 2016), pp. 204–215; Equal Employment Opportunity Commission, "Employment Tests and Selection Procedures" (*www.eeoc.gov/policy/docs/factemployment_procedures.html*), accessed Feb. 12, 2016; W. F. Cascio and H. Aquinis, "The Federal Uniform Guidelines on Employee Selection Procedures: An Update on Selected Issues," *Review of Public Personnel Administration*, 2001, 21, pp. 200–218; C. Daniel, "Separating Law and Professional Practice From Politics: The Uniform Guidelines Then and Now," *Review of Public Personnel Administration*, 2001, 21, pp. 175–184; A. I. E. Ewoh and J. S. Guseh, "The Status of the Uniform Guidelines on Employee Selection Procedures: Legal Developments and Future Prospects," *Review of Public Personnel Administration*, 2001, 21, pp. 185–199; G. P. Panaro, *Employment Law Manual*, 2nd ed. (Boston: Warren Gorham Lamont, 1993), pp. 3-28 to 3-82.

240. Equal Employment Opportunity Commission, "Regulations to Implement the Equal Employment Provisions of the Americans With Disabilities Act, as Amended," *Code of Federal Regulations*, Title 29, Part 1630, July 1, 2011; Equal Employment Opportunity Commission, "The ADA: Your Responsibilities as an Employer," 2008 (*www.eeoc.gov/facts/ada17.html*), accessed Feb. 8, 2016; A. Lyer and S. Mashing, *Recruiting, Hiring, Retaining, and Promoting People With Disabilities*, Equal Employment Opportunity Commission, 2015 (*https://obamawhitehouse.archives.gov/sites/default/files/docs/employing_people_with_disabilities_toolkit_february_3_2015_v4.pdf*); D. D. Bennett-Alexander and L. P. Hartman, *Employment Law for Business*, 8th ed. (New York: McGraw-Hill Education, 2015), pp. 584–653; Walsh, *Employment Law for Human Resource Practice*, pp. 193–216.

241. Equal Employment Opportunity Commission, "Employment Tests and Selection Procedures."

242. Equal Employment Opportunity Commission, *Enforcement Guidance on Disability-Related Inquiries and Medical Examinations of Employees Under the Americans With Disabilities Act* (Washington, DC: author, 2001).

243. Walsh, *Employment Law for Human Resource Practice*, pp. 187–193.

244. J. Schramm, "Reefer Madness," *HR Magazine*, Feb. 2016, p. 64; S. Lan, "Medical Marijuana," *HR Magazine*, Oct. 2016, p. 21; L. Nagele-Piazza, "Marijuana at the Polls and in the Workplace," Oct. 12, 2016 (*www.shrm.org/resourcesandtools/legal-and-compliance/state-and-local-updates/pages/marijuana-ballot-initiatives-2016.aspx*).

245. J. Gantt and K. Wessels, *Policies for Marijuana Use in the Workplace* (Alexandria, VA: Society for Human Resource Management, 2015); I. Hentze, *Cannabis and Employment: Medical and Recreational Policies in the States* (Washington, DC: National Conference of State Legislatures, 2019).

246. *Considerations for Safety- and Security-Sensitive Industries* (Rockville, MD: Substance Abuse and Mental Health Services Administration, 2019).

247. Gantt and Wessels, *Policies for Marijuana Use in the Workplace*.

CHAPTER TEN

Internal Selection

Learning Objectives and Introduction
Learning Objectives
Introduction

Preliminary Issues
The Logic of Prediction
Types of Predictors
Selection Plan

Initial Assessment Methods
Talent Management Systems
Peer Assessments
Self-Assessments
Managerial Sponsorship
Informal Discussions and Recommendations
Choice of Initial Assessment Methods

Substantive Assessment Methods
Seniority
Job Knowledge Tests
Performance Appraisal
Promotability Ratings
Assessment Centers
Interview Exercises
Promotion Panels and Review Boards
Choice of Substantive Assessment Methods

Discretionary Assessment Methods

Legal Issues
Uniform Guidelines on Employee Selection Procedures
The Glass Ceiling and the Glass Cliff

Summary

Discussion Questions

Ethical Issues

Applications
Changing a Promotion System
Promotion From Within at Citrus Glen

Endnotes

LEARNING OBJECTIVES AND INTRODUCTION

Learning Objectives

- Compare how the logic of prediction applies to internal selection decisions with how it applies to external selection decisions
- Evaluate the relative advantages and disadvantages of the five initial assessment methods used in internal selection
- Consider the merits and pitfalls of using seniority for internal selection decisions
- Describe the main features of assessment centers
- Understand the advantages and disadvantages of using assessment centers for internal selection decisions
- Evaluate the relative advantages and disadvantages of the seven substantive assessment methods used in internal selection

Introduction

Internal selection refers to the assessment and evaluation of employees from within the organization as they move between jobs via transfer and promotion systems. Internal selection is of considerable practical value to an organization because one nearly always knows one's own employees better than external applicants, and effective internal selection decisions can motivate valued employees in any organization. One study of a US investment banking firm found that promoted employees were better performers and less likely to leave the organization or be terminated than those externally hired. However, this does not mean external selection is without benefit: external hires tend to have higher levels of experience and education, are promoted faster, and tend to be paid more.[1] As another example, a comparison between thousands of internally and externally hired quick-service retail managers found that the internally hired managers performed better, commanded lower salaries, and had stores that had higher levels of customer service performance, compared with external hires.[2]

Preliminary issues we will discuss to guide the use of assessment methods include the logic of prediction, the nature of predictors, and the development of a selection plan. Initial assessment methods are used to select candidates from among the internal applicants. Methods that will be reviewed include talent management systems, peer assessments and self-assessments, managerial sponsorship, and informal discussions and recommendations. The criteria used to choose among these methods will be discussed.

Substantive assessment methods are used to select finalists from among the internal candidates. Various methods will be reviewed, including seniority, job knowledge tests, performance appraisals, promotability ratings, assessment centers, interview exercises, and promotion panels and review boards. The criteria used to choose among the substantive assessment methods will also be discussed.

Discretionary assessment methods are used to select offer recipients from among the finalists. The factors on which these decisions are based will also be considered, including equal employment opportunity and affirmative action (EEO/AA) concerns, whether the finalist had previously been a finalist, and second opinions about the finalist by others in the organization.

All these assessment methods require a large amount of data to be collected. Accordingly, attention must be given to support services; the required expertise needed to administer and interpret predictors; security, privacy, and confidentiality; and the standardization of procedures. Also, the use of internal selection methods requires a clear understanding of legal issues.

PRELIMINARY ISSUES

The Logic of Prediction

The logic of prediction, described in the external selection chapters, is equally relevant to the case of internal selection. Specifically, indicators of internal applicants' degree of success in past situations should be predictive of their likely success in new situations. Importantly, past situations include not only the current job but also previous jobs held by the applicant within the organization. The new situation is the internal vacancy the applicant is seeking via the organization's transfer or promotion system.

There may also be similarities between internal and external selection in terms of the effectiveness of selection methods. As you may recall from the chapters covering external selection, two of the most valid external selection measures are cognitive ability tests and personality tests. These methods also have validity in internal selection decisions. Personality measures have been found to be a valid predictor of promotion, with conscientious, extraverted, proactive, and emotionally stable employees receiving promotions more often. Research indicates that cognitive ability is predictive of promotion and career advancement. Although they are not very valid as an initial assessment method, training and skill development experiences, education, and experience with the organization are also moderate predictors of promotion.[3] In this chapter we focus on processes and methods of selection that are unique to promotion and transfer decisions. However, in considering these methods and processes, it should be remembered that many of the techniques of external selection might be relevant as well.

Although the logic of prediction and the likely effectiveness of selection methods are similar for external and internal selection, internal selection has several potential advantages over external selection in practice. In particular, the data collected on internal applicants in their previous jobs often provide greater depth, relevance, and verifiability than the data collected on external applicants. This is because organizations usually have much more detailed and in-depth information about internal candidates' previous job experiences.

Along with depth and relevance, another positive aspect of the nature of predictors for internal selection is variability. Rather than simply relying on the opinion of one person as to the suitability of an internal candidate for the job, multiple assessments may be solicited from other supervisors and peers. By pooling opinions, it is possible to get a more complete and accurate picture of a candidate's qualifications.

While internal selection has important advantages over external selection, three factors can derail the logic of prediction. First, impression management and organizational politics can play important roles in who gets promoted in organizations. Although impression management also plays a role in external hiring (especially in employment interviews), internal "apple polishers" have a much greater opportunity to work their magic, with more targets for their influence and over a longer period, than external candidates. On this point, one study found that those who are politically skilled were more likely to be viewed as promotable by not only their bosses but also their peers and direct reports.[4] On the staffing professionals' side, one meta-analysis of nearly 60,000 employees found that the performance appraisal ratings used for promotion or other staffing decisions were one-third of a standard deviation higher than those used for employee development or research purposes.[5] Thus, decision makers selecting internal candidates need to make sure they are selecting candidates for the right reasons. A second factor that can undermine the logic of prediction for internal selection is title inflation. One study revealed that the job responsibilities of nearly half (46%) of recently promoted executives remained roughly the same after their new titles. Although such title inflation may not be harmful, the newly promoted, with no corresponding change in pay or responsibilities, should see these "promotions" for what they are. Being given a title of "process change manager" may mean little more than words.[6] Finally, restriction of range can deflate correlations obtained from internal predictor validation studies (see the measurement chapter). If you are trying to develop a predictor assessment for promotion (e.g., a value fit assessment), the internal candidates are already a part of the organization (and perhaps selected on these predictors before being hired). If the internal candidates already exhibit high levels on the predictor (e.g., they all share the same organizational values), there would be little variation in their scores, and thus lower validity coefficients. Although this is certainly a limitation of internal selection, special forms of the correlation coefficient can be calculated that predict what the correlation would be if there were no restriction of range.[7]

Types of Predictors

The distinctions made between the types of predictors used in external selection are also applicable to the different types of internal predictors. One important difference to note between internal and external predictors pertains to the content. There is usually greater depth and relevance to the data available on internal candidates. That is, the organization can go to its own files or managers to get reports on the applicants' previous experiences.

Selection Plan

Often it seems that internal selection is based on "who you know" rather than on relevant knowledge, skill, ability, and other characteristics (KSAOs). Managers tend to rely heavily on the subjective opinions of previous managers who supervised the internal candidate. When asked why they rely on these subjective assessments, the answer is often, "because the candidate has worked here for a long time, and I trust the supervisor's opinion of the candidate."

Decision errors often occur when relying on subjective feelings for internal selection decisions. For example, in selecting managers to oversee engineering and scientific personnel in organizations, it is sometimes felt that those internal job candidates with the best technical skills will be the best managers. This is not always the case.[8] Some technical wizards are poor managers and vice versa. As another example, because internal candidates have spent some time in the organization, feelings and friendships that have developed over time may create barriers to effective selection. Such "feelings" about job applicants may result in lowered hiring standards for some employees, discrimination against protected-class employees, and decisions with low validity. Sound internal selection procedures need to be followed to guard against these errors. A sound job analysis may show that *both* technical and managerial skills need to be assessed with well-crafted predictors, while at the same time leaving irrelevant factors off the table. Therefore, it is imperative that a selection plan be used for internal as well as external selection. As described in the first chapter on external selection, a selection plan lists the predictors to be used for assessment of each KSAO.

INITIAL ASSESSMENT METHODS

The internal recruitment process may generate many applications for vacant positions. This is especially true when an open recruitment system (where jobs are posted for employees to apply) rather than a closed recruitment system is used. Given the time and cost of rigorous selection procedures, organizations use initial assessment methods to screen out applicants who do not meet the minimum qualifications needed to become a candidate.[9] Initial assessment methods for internal recruitment typically include the following predictors: talent management systems, peer evaluations, self-assessments, managerial sponsorship, and informal discussions and recommendations. Each of these predictors will be discussed in turn, followed by a general evaluation of all predictors.

Talent Management Systems

Most organizations have a desire to internally select (or promote from within) for both informational and motivational reasons. Respectively, the reasons are that one knows one's employees better than external applicants and that valued employees may be motivated and retained based on an expectation of future promotions.[10] For example, nearly all managers at Enterprise Rent-A-Car, including its CEO, began in the company's management trainee program. Based on their performance, employees move up the ranks from management trainee, to assistant manager, to branch manager, to area and city manager, and so forth—all from within the company. Though internal selection is attractive to employees, a major problem for organizations (especially medium-sized and large ones) is finding out which employees have the desired skills. This is where talent management (TM) systems come into play.

TM systems, despite being defined in several different ways,[11] are generally designed to enable organizations to strategically anticipate and meet talent needs, especially for critical positions. Although TM has expanded to include external selection, most of the traditional practices are directed toward existing employees. Broadly speaking, TM systems focus on sourcing, identifying, managing, and retaining the organization's talent pool. To further these aims, TM systems often involve routinely keeping an organizational record of the skills, talents, and capabilities of an organization's employees to inform human resource (HR) decisions. TM systems can be used to attain many goals, including performance management, succession and replacement planning, recruitment needs analysis, employee development, retention, compensation, and career management. However, one of the primary goals of such systems is to facilitate internal selection decisions by keeping an organized, up-to-date record of employee skills, talents, and capabilities.[12]

As logical as TM systems seem, recent surveys and benchmarking reports reveal that between roughly 20% and 30% of employers have such a system in place. Organizations may not use a TM system for three reasons. First, it may be perceived as too costly. However, the cost of a TM system should be considered against the cost of not using a system: what are the costs of making selection decisions based on incomplete knowledge of the skills and capabilities of current employees? Second, the expertise to develop a system may not be available. This problem can be mitigated by working with a vendor that specializes in TM software. According to one recent estimate, the TM software market will continue to grow by 16% over the next several years.[13] TM software is often integrated within a vendor's human resource information systems (HRISs). For example, the two largest HRIS providers—SAP and Oracle/PeopleSoft—include TM systems in the HRIS packages they market to organizations. The third and most likely reason is due to increases in labor demand uncertainty. Demand uncertainty has led to difficulties in forecasting KSAOs needed, turnover, and consumer demand (which leads to the creation of positions). This has led to external selection becoming a default option for many organizations (despite limitations associated with this practice, such as being at the mercy of the labor market). Considering these relatively modern challenges, organizations should realize that these are not either-or decisions, and the staffing approach should consider costs and predictable aspects of market demand to make staffing decisions.[14]

One of the problems with TM systems is that they often quickly become outdated. For the system to be useful (rather than simply another bureaucratic procedure to complete), managers must systematically update the database with the latest skills acquired by employees. On the other hand, the market changes frequently—and so do the KSAOs needed for effective performance. TM systems, according to some staffing professionals, should have processes in place to determine market changes and how to adapt to them.[15] Another limitation is that the KSAOs are often rather general or generic. For a TM system to be successful, it must be specific, actively maintained and updated, aligned with an organization's strategies (so as to anticipate future talent needs), and used when internal selection decisions are made.[16]

Another problem with TM systems is that some approaches do not consider their effect on employees or employee reactions to these systems. TM systems can cause negative reactions, especially when they are secretive, communicate ambiguous or inconsistent messages to employees (e.g., saying that one competency is valued but observing people without that competency being hired), or result in high-potential employees receiving a greater allocation of resources needed to succeed. Even those who are identified as high potentials or talent can react negatively: they may become stressed, may perceive more demands and higher expectations, or may experience job insecurity or identity struggles.[17] Furthermore TM systems may not recognize the role proactive employees have in influencing or leveraging the systems themselves. For example, proactive personality traits have been shown to enable employees to "gain access" to TM systems and shape what is valued or how it is assessed. They also enable employees, despite their qualifications, to "figure out" what is desired by management and signal these KSAOs through informal means, even if they do not possess those characteristics.[18]

Whether developed internally or purchased from a vendor, a good TM system includes the KSAOs held by each employee in the organization. The KSAOs are organized by skill categories such as education/experience, intangible talents such as leadership accomplishments and potential, and ratings of managerial competencies or talents. An effective TM system also includes the employee's current position, along with any future positions that the employee is capable of occupying. Additionally, a good TM system also summarizes the data so that a skills audit can be generated to ascertain unit- or organization-wide talent shortages. The Subway fast-casual chain, for example, utilizes a TM system to immediately generate reports for recruitment, internal selection, and performance management purposes.[19]

Peer Assessments

Assessments by peers or coworkers can be used to evaluate the promotability of an internal applicant. A variety of methods can be used, including peer ratings, peer nominations, and peer rankings.[20] Examples of all three are shown in Exhibit 10.1.

As can be seen in Exhibit 10.1, whereas peers are used to make promotion decisions in all three methods of peer assessments, the format of each is different. With

EXHIBIT 10.1 Peer Assessment Methods

Peer Rating

On a scale of 1–5, please rate the following employees for the position of manager as described in the job requirements matrix:

	Not Promotable		Promotable in One Year		Promotable Now
	1	**2**	**3**	**4**	**5**
Jean	1	2	3	4	5
John	1	2	3	4	5
Andy	1	2	3	4	5
Herb	1	2	3	4	5

Peer Nomination

Please place an X next to the employee who is most promotable to the position of manager as described in the job requirements matrix:

Joe _____
Nishant _____
Carlos _____
Suraphon _____
Renee _____

Peer Ranking

Please rank the following employees from the most promotable (1) to the least promotable (5) for the position of manager as described in the job requirements matrix:

Ila _____
Karen _____
Phillip _____
Yi-Chan _____
Kimlang _____

peer ratings, readiness to be promoted is assessed using a rating scale for each peer. The person with the highest rating is deemed most promotable. Peer nominations rely on voting for the most promotable candidates. Peers receiving the greatest number of votes are the most promotable. Finally, peer rankings rely on a rank ordering of peers. Those peers with the highest rankings are the most promotable.

Peer assessments have been used extensively in the military over the years and to a lesser degree in industry. A virtue of peer assessments is that they rely on raters who presumably are very knowledgeable of the applicants' KSAOs due to their day-to-day contact with them. A possible downside to peer assessments, however, is that they may encourage friendship bias and may undermine morale in a work group by fostering a competitive environment.[21]

Another possible problem is that the criteria by which assessments are made are not always made clear. For peer assessments to work, the KSAOs needed for successful performance in the position the peer is being considered for should be outlined in advance. To do so, a job requirements matrix should be used. In addition, research on peer nominations specifically suggests that examining not only nominations but also the candidate's social networks (e.g., how long the peers have known the focal individual, the strength of their relationship) can help improve the validity of peer assessment. Of course, that increased accuracy comes with increased complexity and time.[22]

A probable virtue of peer assessments is that peers are more likely to feel that the decisions reached are fair since they had input into the process; thus, it is not seen as a "behind the back" maneuver by management. Peer assessments are used more often with open rather than closed systems of internal recruitment.

Self-Assessments

Job incumbents can be asked to evaluate their own skills as a basis for determining promotability. This procedure is sometimes used with open recruitment systems. Caution must be exercised in using this process for selection, as it may raise the expectations of those rating themselves that they will be selected. As one VP of HR noted, "Some people think a lot more highly of their skills and talent" than is warranted. Employees' supervisors should encourage upward mobility (not "hoard" talent), but they also need to ensure that employees are realistic in their self-assessments.[23] Further caution is also warranted given that even the inclusion of self-assessments may result in biased promotion judgments by HR experts and novices alike.[24] However, combining self-assessments with peer assessments may help staffing professionals triangulate on the employees' KSAOs. For example, in a study of nearly 800 managers considered for leadership positions in a succession planning system, agreement between peer assessments and self-assessments on leadership dimensions positively predicted promotions and deterred voluntary turnover.[25]

Managerial Sponsorship

Increasingly, organizations are relying on higher-ups to identify and develop the KSAOs of those at lower levels in the organization. Historically, the higher-up has been the person's immediate supervisor. Today, however, the higher-up may be a person at a higher level of the organization who does not have direct responsibility for the person being rated. Meta-analytic research suggests that supervisor support does not have a very strong effect on promotion ($\bar{r}_{xy} = .02$), although higher-up sponsorship does have a weak effect ($\bar{r}_{xy} = .12$).[26]

These individuals may sometimes be labeled as coaches, sponsors, or mentors, depending on the role they fulfill (as defined in Exhibit 10.2). Some organizations have formal programs where employees are assigned coaches, sponsors, or mentors. In other organizations, these matches may naturally occur, often progressing from supervisor to sponsor or mentor as the relationship matures. When these relationships are informal, employees will sometimes engage in influence tactics (such as ingratiation) to increase their likelihood of being sponsored or mentored.[27] Regardless of the formality of the relationship, these sponsoring individuals often have considerable influence in promotion decisions.

Important, too, is the developmental nature of these relationships. Sponsors are able to not only internally select candidates to sponsor but also give these

---

EXHIBIT 10.2 Employee Advocates

Coach

- Provides task-related and professional support (e.g., understanding problems, clarifying goals).
- May recommend specific developmental opportunities that may be instrumental to promotion.
- No reciprocity required; a coach is usually a trained role (e.g., an executive or career coach).

Sponsor

- Provides task-related and professional support (e.g., actively promotes person for advancement opportunities).
- Guides person's career rather than simply informing them of opportunities; creates opportunities to develop the skills of the employee (e.g., lead a task force).
- Moderate-to-high degree of reciprocity. A sponsor who chooses to advocate for an employee likely has built an effective exchange relationship with that employee.

Mentor

- Provides task-related, professional, and personal support (e.g., provides emotional support when faced with career challenges).
- Can be informal or formally appointed.
- Usually time-bound (e.g., a formal mentorship program might end after a year or so).
- Moderate-to-high degree of reciprocity. Mentors and protégés are expected to help each other, and the mentorship experience may be similar to a friendship.

SOURCE: G. T. Chao, "Challenging Research in Mentoring," *Human Resource Development Quarterly,* 1998, 9(4), pp. 333–338; L. T. Eby, "Mentoring," in S. Zedeck (ed.), *APA Handbook of Industrial and Organizational Psychology* (Washington, DC: APA, 2011), pp. 505–525; K. E. Kram, *Mentoring at Work* (Glenview, IL: Foresman, 1985).

individuals valuable developmental experiences that make them viable candidates in the future. Research shows that employees working with sponsors who provide them with challenging developmental experiences earn higher promotability ratings after those experiences.[28] Mentors, too, may provide "psychosocial" support for employees—by being a sounding board, a source of interpersonal support, or a confidant—and, indeed, this form of support may be the clearest consequence of mentoring.[29]

Research also has shown that protégés are not the only ones who benefit from mentoring relationships. Mentors do as well. A meta-analysis found that those who mentored others had higher levels of job satisfaction, commitment to the organization, and job performance than those not in mentoring roles. Thus, rather than being just a one-sided relationship, effective mentoring can be reciprocally rewarding for both parties.[30]

Informal Discussions and Recommendations

Not all promotion decisions are made based on formal HR policy and procedures. For many promotions, much or all of the decision process occurs outside normal channels, through informal discussions and recommendations.[31] For example, Kathy Caprino, a career coach, recalls a time working with a senior director at an international sales organization who was up for a promotion. The leadership team was seeking to promote the senior director and terminate the individual currently in the role. Kathy noted it "was a very messy situation, with potentially a great deal of fall out affecting . . . the entire team." The leadership, informally and behind "closed doors," planned everything in order to minimize disruptions to meeting key deadlines.[32] Although such informal discussions are common in internal selection decisions, especially in small companies, they may have limited validity because they are quite subjective. The personal and subjective nature of these conversations may compromise the ability of leadership to make internal selection decisions relative to "cold and hard" data such as skills, accomplishments, abilities, and so forth. Such is the case with many, if not most, informal approaches to selection.

Choice of Initial Assessment Methods

As was discussed, there are several formal and informal methods of initial assessment available to screen internal applicants to produce a list of candidates. Research has been conducted on the effectiveness of each method, which will now be presented to help determine which initial assessment methods should be used. The reviews of this research are summarized in Exhibit 10.3.

In Exhibit 10.3, the same criteria are applied to evaluate the effectiveness of these predictors as were used to evaluate the effectiveness of predictors for external

EXHIBIT 10.3 Evaluation of Initial Assessment Methods

Predictor	Use	Cost	Reliability	Validity	Utility	Employee Applicant Reactions	Disparate impact
Talent management systems	Low	High	Moderate	Moderate	High	Negative	?
Peer assessments	Low	Low	Moderate	Moderate	?	Positive	?
Self-assessments	Low	Low	Low	Low	?	?	?
Managerial sponsorship	Moderate	Moderate	?	Moderate	?	Positive	Low
Informal discussions & recommendations	High	Low	?	?	?	Mixed	?

selection. Use refers to how much or how often the predictor is utilized. Cost refers to expenses incurred in using the predictor. Reliability refers to the consistency of measurement. Validity refers to the strength of the relationship between the predictor and job performance. Low validity ranges from about .00 to .30, moderate validity ranges from about .31 to .50, and high validity is .51 and above. Utility refers to the monetary return, minus costs, associated with using the predictor. Employee applicant reactions refers to whether employees are expected to react positively or negatively to the predictor. Finally, disparate impact refers to the possibility that a disproportionate number of women and minorities will be rejected using this predictor.

Two points should be made about the effectiveness of initial internal selection methods. First, managerial sponsorship and informal methods are used most extensively, suggesting that many organizations continue to rely on closed rather than open internal recruitment systems. Certainly this is a positive procedure when administrative ease is of importance. However, it must be noted that talented applicants may be overlooked in these approaches. Also, there may be minor disparate impact on women and minorities.

The second point is that peer assessment methods are very promising in terms of reliability and validity (especially when combined with self-assessments). They are not frequently used, but more organizations should consider using them as a screening device. Perhaps this will take place as organizations continue to decentralize decision making and empower employees to make business decisions historically made only by the supervisor.

SUBSTANTIVE ASSESSMENT METHODS

The internal applicant pool is narrowed down to candidates using the initial assessment methods. The following substantive assessment methods are used to determine which internal candidates will become finalists: seniority, job knowledge tests, performance appraisal, promotability ratings, assessment centers, interview exercises, and promotion panels and review boards. Each of these methods is discussed, followed by a general evaluation of all methods.

Seniority

Initially, the concepts of seniority and experience (as introduced in the external selection chapters) may seem the same. However, they are quite different. Seniority typically refers to length of service or tenure with the organization, department, or job. For example, organizational seniority is measured as length of continuous employment in an organization—the difference between the present date of employment and the date of hire. Thus, seniority is a purely quantitative measure that has nothing to do with the type or quality of job experiences; it represents how long you have been in your position, been with your team, or been at the company.

Conversely, experience generally has a broader meaning. While seniority may be one aspect of experience, experience itself encompasses a broader range. As an example, two employees working at the same company for 20 years may have the same level of seniority but very different levels of experience if one of them has performed a number of different jobs, worked in different areas of the organization, and enrolled in various training programs. So, although seniority and experience are often considered synonymous, the example shows that they are quite different. And as we will see in the following discussion, these differences have real implications for internal selection decisions.

Use and Evaluation

Seniority is becoming less common as a method for internal selection.[33] However, most unionized companies still place heavy reliance on seniority over other KSAOs for advancement, and most union contracts stipulate that seniority be considered in promotion decisions. Indeed, research suggests that seniority matters more to the wages and advancement of union workers than nonunion workers.[34] In policy, nonunion organizations claim to place less weight on seniority than on other factors in making advancement decisions. In practice, however, at least one study showed that regardless of the wording in policy statements, heavy emphasis is still placed on seniority in nonunion settings. Research has shown that seniority is more likely to be used for promotions in small, unionized, and capital-intensive companies.[35]

Seniority is often used in internal selection for many reasons. First, organizations believe that direct experience with an organization reflects an accumulated stock of KSAOs necessary to perform the job (as well as knowledge of other jobs). Second, seniority data are easily obtained. Furthermore, unions believe that reliance on objective measures such as seniority protects the employee from capricious treatment and favoritism. Finally, promoting senior individuals is socially acceptable because it is seen as rewarding loyalty. Due to these reasons, moving from a seniority-based system is not easy, particularly in union environments. When former Washington, DC, mayor Adrian Fenty and former schools chancellor Michelle Rhee attempted to reduce the weight placed on seniority in teacher hiring, promotion, and pay decisions, they were met with fierce resistance from teachers and teachers' unions.[36]

In evaluating seniority as a method of internal selection, meta-analyses have revealed that while seniority (organizational tenure) was rather moderately related to promotions (suggesting that employers may use it in promotion decisions; $\bar{r}_{xy} = .24$), it tends to be weakly related to task performance ($\bar{r}_{xy} = .09$) and OCB (organizational citizenship behavior) ($\bar{r}_{xy} = .08$).[37]

Several conclusions drawn from the research evidence about the use of seniority in internal selection decisions seem appropriate:

1. As discussed in the external selection chapters, experience is a more valid method of internal selection than seniority (although unionized employers may have little choice but to use seniority). It is also better suited to predict short-term rather than long-term potential.

2. Employees might expect that promotions will go to the most senior or experienced employee, so using seniority or experience for promotions may yield positive reactions from some employees. Other employees, however, may feel demotivated if they work harder and smarter than a more senior employee and yet are not eligible for a promotion.[38]

3. Seniority (as well as experience), regardless of how many promotions have been awarded during tenure, seems to lead employees to feel as if they have "plateaued" in the organization and are not able to move up. Such feelings may cause otherwise well-qualified employees to seek other organizations where they may have more opportunities for growth. This may be evidence that awarding a promotion to senior, well-qualified candidates may help foster their engagement and prevent them from stagnating.[39]

Job Knowledge Tests

Job knowledge, which was also described as a substantive predictor in the external selection chapters, measures one's mastery of the concepts needed to perform a given job. A job knowledge test, given to a current employee in an internal selection context, reflects both ability (the capacity to learn from job experiences) and seniority (what the employee has learned from their time in the position and with the organization). For example, a job knowledge test used to select sales managers from salespeople must identify the specific knowledge necessary for being a successful sales manager (e.g., critical aspects of the salesperson job).

Job knowledge tests are often used in occupations where specific job knowledge is needed immediately on the first day of the job. Accordingly, they are often used for jobs that require technical or specialized knowledge that cannot be quickly acquired or learned. Job knowledge tests are very specific to the occupation for which candidates are being selected. For example, a job knowledge test for an information technology analyst in the health care industry might ask about knowledge of specific software used in that industry, such as Epic and NextGen.

Although job knowledge is not as well researched as other substantive methods of either internal or external employee selection, it is a strong predictor of job performance. This is because it may reflect a combination of previous experiences of an applicant and cognitive ability, an important KSAO (see also the external selection chapters).[40] In a promotion context, allowing candidates to retake job knowledge tests can lessen the threat of disparate impact (which tends to be large for job knowledge tests) and can even lead to more valid scores, especially for younger candidates and females.[41] Job knowledge tests are also likely to be viewed favorably by candidates, so long as they see the link between the knowledge being tested and the knowledge required to perform the job.[42]

Performance Appraisal

One possible predictor of future job performance is past job performance. This assumes, of course, that elements of the future job are similar to those of the past job. Data on employees' previous performance may be routinely collected as part of the performance appraisal process and thus available for use in internal selection.[43]

One advantage of performance appraisals over other internal assessment methods is that they are readily available in many organizations. Another desirable feature is that they likely capture both ability and motivation. Hence, they can offer a complete look at the person's qualifications for the job. Care must be taken in using performance appraisals, because there is not always a direct correspondence between the requirements of the current job and the requirements of the position applied for.[44] Performance appraisals should only be used as predictors when job analysis indicates a close relationship between the current job and the position applied for.

For example, performance in a highly technical position (e.g., scientist, engineer) may require certain skills (e.g., quantitative skills) that are required in both junior- and senior-level positions. Thus, using the results of the performance appraisal of the junior position is appropriate in predicting performance in the senior position. It is not, however, appropriate to use the results of the performance appraisal for the junior-level technical job to predict performance in a job requiring a different set of skills (e.g., planning, organizing, and staffing), such as that of manager.

Although there are some advantages to using performance appraisal results for internal selection, they are far from perfect predictors. They are subject to many influences that have nothing to do with the likelihood of success in a future job.[45] For example, using performance evaluation data to make promotion decisions may lead to disparate treatment of women when they are not perceived to be a good "fit" for the upper-level job because of stereotypes or because past displays of competence misalign with traditional gender stereotypes.[46] Therefore, staffing professionals should take care in ensuring that promotion decisions made from performance appraisal data are made in an unbiased way.

In addition, decision makers appear to be swayed not only by a person's level of performance but also by their trajectory, that is, whether the person's performance has increased or decreased over time. One study found that NBA players whose performance was on a positive trajectory received higher levels of compensation than those whose trajectory was not as positive, even controlling for their average level of performance. Presumably, those with positive trajectories were viewed as "rising stars," despite those views being overly optimistic.[47] One implication is that employees viewed as rising stars, when their initial performance is low, may be promoted more quickly than they deserve as they are perceived to be harder workers.[48]

The well-known Peter Principle—that individuals rise to their lowest level of incompetence—illustrates another limitation of using the performance appraisal as a method for internal staffing decisions.[49] The argument behind the Peter Principle is that if organizations promote individuals on the basis of their past performance, the only time people stop being promoted is when they perform poorly in the job into which they were last promoted. Thus, over time, organizations will have internally staffed positions with incompetent individuals. In fact, the authors have data from a Fortune 100 company showing that less than one-fifth of the variance in an employee's current performance rating can be explained by the performance ratings of the previous three years. Thus, although past performance may have some validity in predicting future performance, the relationship may not be overly strong. As an additional (albeit strong) limitation, there is some evidence to suggest that using relative performance appraisal results for promotion decisions can lead employees to engage in CWBs (counterproductive work behaviors) in order to "get ahead."[50]

This is not to suggest that organizations should abandon using performance ratings as a factor in internal staffing decisions. Rather, the validity of using performance appraisals as an internal selection method may depend on several considerations. Exhibit 10.4 provides several questions that should be asked in deciding how much weight to place on performance appraisals as a means of making internal selection decisions. Answering yes to these questions suggests that past performance may be valid for making internal selection decisions.

If organizations do rely on performance appraisals to make internal staffing decisions, a challenge is to ensure that performance measures are interpreted similarly by raters. This is especially the case when ratings from multiple sources (e.g., supervisors, peers, and direct reports) are obtained. Evidence suggests that providing raters with an explicit frame of reference can increase rating accuracy. An explicit frame of reference is achieved by including definitions and specific behavioral exam-

---

EXHIBIT 10.4 Questions to Ask in Using Performance Appraisal as a Method of Making Internal Staffing Decisions

- Is the performance appraisal process reliable and unbiased?
- Is the present job content representative of future job content?
- Have the KSAOs required for performance in the future job(s) been acquired and demonstrated in the previous job(s)?
- Is the organizational or job environment stable such that what led to past job success will lead to future job success?

ples of performance on the measure itself and using multiple behavioral indicators for each competency assessed. The overall goal of this approach is to reduce idiosyncratic scoring tendencies between different raters (e.g., being consistently lenient or harsh) by providing raters with an unambiguous frame of reference. For example, if "ability to work in teams" is a performance dimension being assessed, the rating scale itself would have an explicit definition of high versus low levels of performance, as well as multiple examples of behaviors exemplifying high performance.[51]

An advance over the simple use of performance ratings is to review past performance records more thoroughly, including evaluating various dimensions of performance that are particularly relevant to job performance (where the dimensions are based on job analysis results). For example, a study of police officer promotions showed that a pool of six supervisors was used to score officers on four job-relevant police officer performance dimensions—supervisory-related education and experience, disciplined behavior, commendatory behavior, and reliability—with the goal of predicting future performance. Results of the study indicated that using ratings of past performance records was an effective method of promoting officers.[52] A similar system was implemented in the Royal Canadian Mounted Police with success: both candidates and supervisors reacted positively to the performance appraisal system.[53] Such a method might be adapted to other positions and provide a useful means of incorporating past performance data into a more valid prediction of future potential. Additional advancements have been made in using various types of past behaviors (as recorded on performance appraisals) for promotion purposes. As some examples, research has examined ratings and records of CWBs such as absence and OCBs such as helping behaviors.[54] Technology has even enabled staffing professionals to quantify and analyze supervisors' text comments about their subordinates, a practice that might be enhanced by machine learning.[55]

Promotability Ratings

In many organizations, an assessment of promotability (assessment of potential for a higher level job) is made at the same time that performance appraisals are conducted. Replacement and succession planning frequently use both types of assessments (see the planning chapter).

Promotability ratings are useful not only from a selection perspective but also from a recruitment perspective. By discussing what is needed to be promotable, employee development may be encouraged as well as coupled with organizational sponsorship of the opportunities needed to develop. In turn, the development of new skills in employees increases the internal recruitment pool for promotions.

Caution must be exercised in using promotability ratings. If employees receive separate evaluations for purposes of performance appraisal, promotability, and pay, they may receive mixed messages. For example, it would be difficult to understand why one received an excellent performance rating and a solid pay raise, but at the same time was rated as not promotable. Care must be taken to show employees the relevant judgments being made in each assessment. In this example, it must be clearly indicated that promotion is based not only on past performance but also on skill acquisition and opportunities for advancement.

Assessment Centers

An assessment center is an elaborate method that is primarily used in internal selection for higher-level jobs. It consists of a collection of behavioral predictors (performance tests, work samples, simulations, and other exercises) used to forecast success. Assessment centers are used for higher-level jobs because of the high costs involved in conducting the center. The assessment center can be used to select employees for lower-level jobs as well, though this is not as common as their use for higher-level jobs (and even training).[56]

The theory behind assessment centers is relatively straightforward: the main concern is with predicting an individual's effectiveness in critical roles, such as management positions. Since these roles require complex behaviors, multiple KSAOs will be required to predict those behaviors. Hence, there is a need to carefully identify and assess multiple KSAOs, using multiple methods and multiple assessors. The use of multiple methods and assessors to measure a number of important KSAOs results in a higher validity than could be obtained from a single method or assessor.[57]

As with any sound selection procedure, the assessment center predictors are based on a job analysis that results in the identification of relevant KSAOs as well as aids in the construction of content-valid methods of assessment for those KSAOs.[58] As a result, a selection plan must be developed when using assessment centers. An example of such a selection plan is shown in Exhibit 10.5.

Characteristics of Assessment Centers

Whereas some characteristics of assessment centers vary from situation to situation, they generally follow a similar format. Candidates usually participate in an assessment center for a period of days rather than hours. The length of the assessment center depends on the number of candidates to be tested and the number of exercises (usually four or five). As we describe shortly, a big part of assessment centers is the behavioral exercises (such as simulations, like those discussed earlier in the external selection chapters), where employees participate in exercises that mimic, but do not exactly reproduce, working conditions.

The participants in the center are usually managers who are being assessed for mid- to high-level managerial jobs. Normally, they are nominated to participate (either self-nominations or supervisor nominations). Selection may also be based on an employee's current level of job performance (e.g., performance appraisal ratings tracked through a TM system).[59]

The trained assessors are usually line managers who know the focal job in question well, although sometimes external psychologists are used as well. The ratio of

EXHIBIT 10.5   Selection Plan for an Assessment Center

KSAO	Writing Exercise	Speech Exercise	Problem Analysis	In-Basket Tent.	In-Basket Final	Leaderless Group Discussion Management Problems	Leaderless Group Discussion City Council
Oral communications					X	X	X
Oral presentation		X			X	X	
Written communications	X		X	X	X	X	X
Stress tolerance				X	X	X	
Leadership			X	X	X	X	X
Sensitivity				X	X	X	X
Tenacity				X	X	X	
Risk taking			X	X	X	X	X
Initiative			X	X	X	X	X
Planning & organization			X	X	X	X	X
Management control			X	X	X		
Delegation				X	X		
Problem analysis			X	X	X	X	X
Decision making			X	X	X	X	X
Decisiveness			X	X	X	X	X
Responsiveness			X	X	X	X	X

SOURCE: Department of Employment Relations, State of Wisconsin.

assessors to participants ranges from 1:1 to 4:1 (2:1 is the average). The assessors observe and take note of the participant behaviors, focusing on the candidates they have been assigned. After each exercise, the assessors review their observations and notes, and may make initial ratings.[60]

At the conclusion of the assessment center, the participants are evaluated by the assessors over a period of several hours. Typically, this involves the assessor examining all the information gathered about each participant. The information is then translated into a series of ratings on several dimensions of KSAOs. Typical dimensions assessed include communication (written and oral), problem solving and decision making, organizing and planning, leadership and influence, and consideration (or awareness of others).[61] A meta-analysis found that these dimensions cluster into three broad factors: administrative skills, relational skills, and drive.[62] In order to reliably and accurately evaluate these dimensions, assessors are trained (often over a period of several days) to observe, record, and classify critical behaviors that represent highly effective or ineffective responses to the exercises; know the exercises and their dynamics inside and out; interact with the candidates in a professional manner; and recognize and prevent judgment errors and bias.[63] There may also be an overall assessment rating that represents the bottom-line evaluation for each participant.[64] Assessment center dimensions are relatively highly correlated with one another, though evidence suggests that the dimensions do add to the prediction of performance beyond the overall score.[65] Exhibit 10.6 provides a sample rating form.

A variety of exercises are used with the assessment center method. Although many assessment centers can be combined with written tests and interviews (such as those discussed in the external selection chapters) as a part of the selection plan, the behavioral predictors (e.g., simulations) are the heart of the assessment center. Some of the most frequently used exercises are the role play, in-basket exercise, and leaderless group discussion. Each of these exercises will be briefly described.

Role Play. The most used assessment center exercise is the role play. Of a number of US organizations that use the assessment center method, 76% included a role-play exercise.[66] For example, an exercise for an assessment center for promotion to a sales manager position might have the participant imagine being in a situation where they need to persuade a skeptical client to purchase an enterprise-level software system. The participant would role-play the sales manager (often with a trained actor playing the client), and an assessor would observe the participant's behavior during the role play.[67] Introducing a role player, however, adds a whole new level of complexity: research shows that the role player and their portrayed personality have an effect on the reliability and accuracy of role-play performance ratings.[68] Thus, staffing professionals should make sure to properly train role players (just as intensively as assessors) so that they know the exercise instructions and role-play prompts thoroughly.[69] Darden Restaurants (the company behind Red Lobster, Olive Garden, and a number of other full-service restaurant brands), for

EXHIBIT 10.6 Sample Assessment Center Rating Form

Participant Name: _____

Personal Qualities
    1. Energy   _____
    2. Risk taking   _____
    3. Tolerance for ambiguity   _____
    4. Objectivity   _____
    5. Reliability   _____

Communication Skills
    6. Oral   _____
    7. Written   _____
    8. Persuasion   _____

Human Relations
    9. Teamwork   _____
    10. Flexibility   _____
    11. Awareness of social environment   _____

Leadership Skills
    12. Impact   _____
    13. Autonomy   _____

Decision-Making Skills
    14. Decisiveness   _____
    15. Organizing   _____
    16. Planning   _____

Problem Solving Skills
    17. Fact finding   _____
    18. Interpreting information   _____

Overall Assessment Rating
Indication of potential to perform
effectively at the next level is:
    Excellent   _____
    Good   _____
    Moderate   _____
    Low   _____

example, utilizes the assessment center method for its managers for both promotion and development purposes.[70] Management participants often take part in a role-play exercise in which they interact with an unhappy customer. Clearly, the "unhappy customer" should be trained to properly play the role and to standardize the experience across participants.

In-Basket Exercise.   Another common assessment center exercise is the in-basket (according to one study, 57% of assessment centers use it).[71] The in-basket (sometimes called "inbox") usually contains memoranda, reports, e-mails, phone messages, and letters that require a response. These materials are presented to a candidate, and they are asked to respond to the items by prioritizing them, drafting responses, scheduling meetings, and so forth. It is a timed exercise, and the candidate usually has two to three hours to complete it. Even when used alone, the in-basket exercise seems to predict performance and is reacted to favorably by candidates.[72] However, staffing professionals should exercise caution to avoid disparate impact with in-basket exercises, as they are the most highly correlated with cognitive ability of all assessment center exercises.[73]

Leaderless Group Discussion.   In a leaderless group discussion, a small group of candidates is given a problem to solve. The problem is one they would likely encounter in the higher-level position for which they are applying. As the candidates work on the problem, assessors observe the group and evaluate how each candidate behaves in an unstructured setting. They focus primarily on communication skills and leadership emergence.[74] Roughly 43% of assessment centers include a leaderless group discussion.[75] Although less common, some group discussion exercises assign candidates specific roles to play, but most are leaderless in that no one is assigned a particular role (and so leader emergence can be assessed). An example of the former is where participants are part of a project team and each participant assumes a role (IT, HR, marketing, etc.). An example of the latter is a "lost in the wilderness" exercise, where a group of individuals is presented a scenario in which they are lost and have few resources on which they can survive and find their way home. Both forms of group discussions assess the skills of persuasion and influence, teamwork, and interpersonal sensitivity. Prior validation studies have found that leaderless group discussions are reliable and valid exercises that explain additional variance in performance beyond cognitive ability and personality tests.[76] However, other research has found that performance in leaderless group discussions does assess personality traits to some degree, such as conscientiousness, extraversion, and individualism.[77]

Validity and Effective Practices

Meta-analyses of validity studies (drawing on data from thousands of candidates) revealed that the correlation between the assessment center overall assessment rating (OAR) and job performance was moderate and positive ($\bar{r}_{xy} = .28$).[78] Another advantage of assessment centers is that they appear to have little to no disparate impact against protected classes, even when the assessors are predominantly White men.[79] However, this depends on the constructs and exercises included in the assessment center: as mentioned earlier, the more the exercise requires cognitive ability, the higher the potential for disparate impact. Finally, analyses based on meta-analytic data suggest that assessment centers add incremental validity over personality and cognitive ability—and may even be stronger predictors of performance in the promotion context.[80]

On the other hand, research has uncovered several problems with assessment centers. First, the construct validity of assessment center evaluations is often questioned.[81] Research has shown that there are much stronger exercise and assessor effects than there are dimension effects, meaning that more consistent findings are found using the exercises and assessor scores as predictors than are found using the dimension, or KSAO scores they are intended to assess. Recent research illuminates that reliability of assessment center ratings is a complex interaction between assessors, exercises, and dimensions and recommends separating ratings into finer categories as opposed to simply aggregating ratings into one score. However, it is unclear whether the construct validity improvements are substantial enough to warrant the increased complexity that would result from such separation.[82] In short, assessment center dimensions do not show much construct validity, calling into question the content of what is being assessed. As one reviewer of the literature noted, "Assessment centers (ACs), as they are often designed and implemented, do not work as they are intended to work and probably never will." Two reasons why dimensional effects tend to be weak are (1) halo effects in assessors' ratings (if an assessor thinks an assessee is a strong candidate, it spills over to ratings on other dimensions), and (2) assessee behavior tends to be inconsistent across situations (and thus across exercises and dimensions) but consistent within exercises (blurring distinctions between multiple dimensions). These pieces of evidence do not mean assessment centers utterly lack construct validity, but they do suggest that more research is needed as to what constructs are uniquely captured with assessment centers.[83]

One proposed solution suggests that although error and exercise-specific variance appears to dominate on the surface, relevant dimension variance (e.g., the various KSAOs across exercises) tends to accumulate with the addition of more exercises, and criterion-related validity tends to improve with exercises that impose substantively different demands.[84] However, a recent comprehensive study of the specific sources of variance related to exercises and dimensions across assessment center ratings found that less than 1.12% of the variance in assessment center ratings is attributable to dimensions. Notably, the variation was mostly attributable to exercise factors and the general performance factor.[85]

Another way of approaching the construct validity of assessment centers impasse is by adopting the lens of trait activation theory.[86] When there is an opportunity to observe trait-relevant behavior in any given exercise, the construct validity evidence of assessment center ratings may improve (e.g., the exercises themselves do not offer the same opportunities to observe traits, which may be why they do not converge across exercises). Drawing on 30 separate studies of assessment center ratings, one review found support for the application of trait activation theory to assessment centers, observing improvements in construct validity when exercises provided opportunities to observe trait-relevant behavior.[87]

So what assessment center design features can make a difference in increasing the chances to observe trait-relevant behaviors? Making sure the targeted dimensions are masked (or not transparent) to applicants is one way to potentially prevent them from acting in a socially desirable way (or do what they think raters are looking for).[88] In addition, some research suggests that impression management, along with being able to identify what is required of you/the situational demands in an assessment center exercise, is related to on-the-job performance, further bolstering the argument to mask dimensions (although problematic for construct validity and trait assessment).[89] Overall, a focus on design for trait activation combined with a focus on improving measurement accuracy probably holds the most promise for improving assessment center behavioral ratings.[90]

One of the biggest limitations of assessment centers is their cost. The nature of the individualized assessment and the requirement of multiple assessors make them cost-prohibitive for many organizations. One way some organizations are mitigating the costs is through other related assessments. For example, the organization can videotape an assessee's performance so that assessors can evaluate it when convenient. This saves coordination and travel costs. A practice that results in even greater cost savings is to use situational judgment tests, where assessees are given various exercises in written, video, or computerized form. A meta-analysis of 45 studies suggested that the validity of a situational judgment test composite score ($\bar{r}_{xy} = .28$) was identical to the validity of assessment centers.[91]

Another way to reduce the costs of the assessment center is to use computerized assessments.[92] One research study reported favorable results for a computerized assessment center simulation that asked assessees to prioritize information, formulate e-mail correspondences, make decisions about hypothetical simulations, and engage in strategic planning.[93] Another means of reducing costs is to use off-the-shelf assessments provided by vendors (22% of organizations go this route).[94] For example, Business Training Systems (BTS) is a Swedish company that offers an assessment center solution for organizations to purchase. The simulations, role plays, and in-basket exercises (among others) are integrated, allowing the assessment center to represent "a day in the life" of an employee in the focal position (e.g., a sales manager).[95]

While using off-the-shelf products may save money, it is critical that assessors have proper training. Without the right training, the resulting assessment or score derived from the assessment may be so scattershot as to be useless. One recent study uncovered several dysfunctional aspects of the assessment center method that happen in practice (see Exhibit 10.7). These dysfunctional aspects reveal that

EXHIBIT 10.7 Dysfunctional Aspects of Assessment Centers

Relevant for Designers
- Ask assessors to work long hours without breaks
- Do not offer training and practice opportunities to assessors
- Ask assessors to take part in assessment center evaluations at the last minute, with no time to prepare
- Do not standardize or randomize candidate or exercise order (which can lead to order effects)

Relevant for Assessors
- Do not have enough observation opportunities or scores per candidate (due to rushed exercise experience)
- Receive insufficient time to evaluate and score candidates
- Are rushed in post-exercise meetings with other assessors
- Are under pressure to quickly make dimension ratings
- Have less time to discuss candidates at the end of the post-exercise meeting than those discussed at the beginning of the meeting
- Engage in unnecessary and unproductive discussion during post-exercise meetings

Relevant for Candidates
- Receive unclear guidance on exercise instructions and, potentially, what they will be scored on (if transparent)
- Receive insufficient feedback during the assessment center exercises
- Have negative reactions to poorly designed exercises

SOURCE: Adapted from C. Dewberry and D. J. R. Jackson, "The Perceived Nature and Incidence of Dysfunctional Assessment Center Features and Processes," *International Journal of Selection and Assessment*, 2016, 24(2), pp. 189–196.

although assessment center procedures may look good on paper, a great deal of care and effort needs to be put into ensuring that they are run properly.

There is little research that has examined participant reactions to assessment centers, although some reviews suggest that they are more face valid than paper-and-pencil tests (they allow participants to directly demonstrate their skills on job-relevant exercises) and are reacted to positively in selection and promotion contexts, and that these reactions hold across countries.[96] However, it is commonly noted that assessment centers are stressful to participants, and the unfavorable feedback that often results from participation is particularly taxing to assessees. Those with low self-esteem and self-efficacy are particularly sensitive to assessment center feedback. This does not mean, however, that assessment centers always or even generally generate negative reactions from assessees, and assessees quickly recover from either positive or negative initial reactions from assessment center participation. Perhaps more important is what happens *after* the assessment center experience (whether the assessee was promoted and whether the feedback proved helpful) than what happened *during* the assessment center experience.[97]

Interview Exercises

Interview exercises mimic the oral communication required on the job. They may be included as predictors within an assessment center. They may also be used as a predictor separate from the assessment center (this is true of any of the previously discussed exercises). There are several different forms of interview exercises, which vary in their degree of usage. The most frequently used interview exercise (and the second most frequently used exercise in assessment centers, with 64% of organizations adopting it) is the presentation. Situational interviews (48%), background interviews (35%), and fact-finding interviews (29%) are also used to a lesser extent.[98]

Given the importance of interpersonal skills in many jobs, it is fortunate that more organizations are using interview exercises. This is especially true with internal selection, where the organization knows whether the person has the right credentials (e.g., company experiences, education, and training) but may not know whether the person has the right communication or influence skills to be successful in a higher-level position. To be effective, these interviews need to be structured and evaluated according to observable behaviors identified in the job analysis as necessary for successful performance.

In this section, we will discuss presentations and fact-finding interviews. Situational and background interviews most closely align with the structured interview methods discussed in the external selection chapter. Furthermore, although these types of structured interviews are included as exercises in assessment centers, current guidelines dissuade against this practice as they (a) do not necessarily match the behavioral predictor definition of assessment center exercises and (b) have been shown to be empirically distinct from other assessment center exercises (e.g., the behaviors assessed by interviews appear to be conceptually different from those assessed by other exercises).[99] Beyond presentations and fact-finding interviews, we discuss performance interviews as one interview exercise that shows promise for internal selection.

Oral Presentations

In many jobs, presentations need to be made to customers, clients, or even boards of directors. To select someone to perform this role, an oral presentation can be required. This approach would be useful, for example, for seeing what sort of "sales pitch" a consultant might make or for seeing how an executive would present their proposed strategic plan to a board of directors. One study of the use of presentations for sales managers, however, found relatively weak correlations (ranging from

.06 to .13) between the presentation and sales performance.[100] As with the role play discussed earlier, introverts and candidates who are apprehensive about communication may do poorly in presentations.[101] Furthermore, presentation scores may be influenced by the degree to which the candidate engages in impression management.[102] However, some argue that impression management might be a desired KSAO in certain positions; thus, this may not be as large an issue for some roles.

Fact Finding

In a fact-finding interview, the job candidate is presented with a case or problem with incomplete information. The candidate's job is to solicit from the interviewer or a resource person the additional facts needed to resolve the case. A candidate for the position of EEO manager, for example, might be presented with a case where disparate impact is suggested. The candidate would be evaluated by the interviewer according to the data they solicit to confirm or disconfirm disparate impact.

Performance Interviews

Although, to our knowledge, the performance interview has not been used much in practice, we believe that it holds promise for internal selection. A performance interview for skill-based jobs follows a format similar to that of a structured interview (see the chapter on external selection). The structured interview questions are based on a job analysis or competency model and follow the logic of behavioral consistency, outlining basic, advanced, and expert-level tasks that reflect real skill differences. The interview questions, like a job knowledge test, are designed to elicit the candidate's declarative (e.g., facts, rules, principles) and procedural (e.g., knowing what to do and how to do it) knowledge and proficiency. The interviewer asks the candidate a series of questions, and the candidate either describes the principles and procedures behind the task or physically shows the interviewer how to do them. For example, in a sample of 230 auto parts manufacturing employees who were vying for a promotion, the interviewer asked questions about specific machines, such as "How do you set up this machine?" "What adjustments are made to this machine?" and "How do you insert the pins?" The candidates responded with what to do or physically showed the interviewer how to set up or use the machines. Candidates are then rated on their overall skill and knowledge levels for that skill. Notably, this procedure showed very promising validity evidence ($\bar{r}_{xy} = .47$), excellent face validity, and no disparate impact. The performance interview method may have potential value for certain positions and could also be positioned as a part of an assessment center.[103]

Promotion Panels and Review Boards

In the public sector, it is a common practice to use a panel or board of people to review the qualifications of candidates.[104] Frequently, both internal and external candidates are assessed (see external selection chapters for how panel interviews stack up against individual interviews). The panel or board typically consists of job experts, HR professionals, and representatives from constituencies in the community that the board represents. Having a board to hire public servants, such as school superintendents or fire and police officials, offers two advantages. First, as with assessment centers, there are multiple assessors with which to ensure a complete and accurate assessment of the candidate's qualifications. Second, by participating in the selection process, constituents are likely to be more committed to the decision reached. This buy-in is particularly important for community representatives with whom the job candidate will interact. It is hoped that by having a say in the process, they will be less likely to voice objections once the candidate is hired.

Despite the fairness benefits, promotion panels have limitations that are similar to those of interview exercises in that they tend to be sensitive to introversion and impression management.[105] More importantly, however, panel interviews may result in disparate impact that is a function of not only the race of the candidate but also the racial composition of the panel interviewers.[106]

Choice of Substantive Assessment Methods

Along with research on initial assessment methods, research has also been conducted on substantive assessment methods. The reviews of this research are summarized in Exhibit 10.8. The same criteria are applied to evaluating the effectiveness of these predictors as were used to evaluate the effectiveness of initial assessment methods.

An examination of Exhibit 10.8 indicates that there is no single best method of narrowing down the candidate list to finalists. What is suggested, however, is that some predictors are more likely to be effective than others. Job knowledge tests, performance appraisal, promotability ratings, and assessment centers have compelling records in terms of reliability and validity in choosing candidates. A very promising development for internal selection is the use of job knowledge tests. The validity of these tests appears to be substantial, but unfortunately, few organizations use them for internal selection purposes (perhaps due to disparate treatment concerns). Seniority, although it might lead to positive employee reactions depending on the case and context, is generally not related to performance despite its common use in the public sector. Interview exercises appear to be a promising technique for jobs requiring public contact skills, although they tend not to be as valid as other predictors. The exception is the performance interview, which does not appear to be used that often in practice and may only be appropriate for certain jobs and industries. All these techniques need additional research, especially regarding the utility, applicant reactions, and disparate impact associated with substantive assessment methods. The areas that need the most additional research are perhaps the promotability ratings, interview exercises, and promotion panels, although the panels' low validity evidence may be one reason that they do not attract additional research attention.

EXHIBIT 10.8 **Evaluation of Substantive Assessment Methods**

Predictor	Use	Cost	Reliability	Validity	Utility	Employee Applicant Reactions	Disparate Impact
Seniority	Moderate	Low	High	Low	?	Mixed	Low
Job knowledge tests	Low	Moderate	High	High	High	Positive	High
Performance appraisal	Moderate	Moderate	Moderate	Moderate	?	Mixed	High
Promotability ratings	Low	Low	High	Moderate	?	Mixed	?
Assessment centers	Low	High	Moderate	Moderate	High	Mixed	Low
Interview exercises	Low	High	Moderate	Moderate	?	Mixed	Low
Promotion panels and review boards	Moderate	High	Moderate	Low	?	Positive	Moderate

DISCRETIONARY ASSESSMENT METHODS

Discretionary methods are used to narrow down the list of finalists to those who will receive job offers. Sometimes all finalists will receive offers, but other times there may not be enough positions to fill for each finalist to receive an offer. As with external selection, the same issues of favoritism, cronyism, nepotism, and various political influences apply—and perhaps even more so, given that the finalists have a "history" with the organization.

Two areas of discretionary assessment differ from external selection and need to be considered in deciding job offers.

First, multiple assessors, who may personally know the candidates up for the promotion, are generally used with internal selection. Thus, not only can the hiring manager's opinion be used to select who will receive a job offer but so can the opinions of others (e.g., previous manager, top management) who are knowledgeable about the candidate's profile and the requirements of the current position. As a result, in deciding which candidates will receive job offers, evaluations by people other than the hiring manager may be accorded substantial weight. Depending on the political context and relationships among the manager, assessors, and the candidate, this may pave the way for nepotism, cronyism, or favoritism to creep into the decision.

Second, previous finalists who do not receive job offers do not simply disappear. They *might* remain with the organization in hopes of securing an offer the next time the position is open, although meta-analytic research suggests that they are slightly more likely to leave than stay.[107] At the margin, this may be a factor in decision making because being bypassed a second time may create a disgruntled employee. Indeed, "left behind" employees who feel that the promotion decisions were unjust may experience diminished mental and physical health outcomes, a lowered self-concept, poorer job attitudes, less of a desire to engage in OCBs, and perhaps even motivation to engage in CWBs.[108]

Many may consider these "left behind" employees to be a fact of organizational life. However, the organization can employ several measures to show that the promotion decisions are fair. For example, research shows that transparent, equitable, standardized, and job-related promotion procedures (and the predictors that inform those decisions) improve perceptions of fairness.[109] Furthermore, it is likely that opportunities for retesting, offering appeals, explanatory and developmental feedback, and opening two-way communication between those "left behind" and upper management are ways in which fairness reactions can be improved.[110] One approach that shows promise is all in the framing: focus more on the career growth and goals of the employee and less on the more mechanical aspects of job and vacancy.[111] It may be that when employees view the denied promotion as a challenge or opportunity for growth, they become more engaged in their work, become more proactive about their career, and even develop resilience in their career, even if the new framing results in them leaving the job.[112]

LEGAL ISSUES

From a legal perspective, methods and processes of internal selection are to be viewed in the same way as those of external selection. The laws and regulations do not distinguish between internal and external selection. Consequently, most of the legal influences on internal selection have already been treated in the external selection chapters. There are, however, some brief comments to be made about the internal selection legal influences of the Uniform Guidelines on Employee Selection Procedures (UGESP) and the glass ceiling.

Uniform Guidelines on Employee Selection Procedures

The UGESP define a "selection procedure" in such a way that virtually any selection method, be it used in an external or internal context, is covered by the requirements of the UGESP. Moreover, the UGESP apply to any "employment decision," which explicitly includes promotion decisions.

When there is disparate impact in promotions, the organization is given the opportunity to justify the use of the predictor or the selection system by providing validation evidence. This evidence is usually from criterion-related or content validity studies. Ideally, criterion-related studies with predictive validation designs will be used, as has been done in the case of assessment centers. Unfortunately, these place substantial administrative and research demands on the organization that are often difficult to fulfill. Many of the methods of assessment used in internal selection attempt to gauge KSAOs and behaviors directly associated with a current job that are felt to be related to success in higher-level jobs. Examples include seniority, performance appraisals, and promotability ratings. These are based on current as well as past job content. Validation of these methods, if legally necessary, may necessitate content validity evidence (e.g., the content of the predictors matches the higher-level job). Therefore, the organization should pay close attention to the validation and documentation requirements for content validation in the UGESP.

The Glass Ceiling and the Glass Cliff

In the internal recruitment chapter, the nature of the glass ceiling was discussed, as well as staffing steps to remove it from organizational promotion systems. Most of that discussion centered on internal recruitment and supporting activities that could be undertaken. Surprisingly, selection methods used for promotion assessment are rarely mentioned in literature on the glass ceiling.

This is a major oversight. Whereas the internal recruitment practices recommended may enhance the identification and attraction of minority and women candidates for promotion, effectively matching them to their new jobs requires applying internal selection processes and methods. One early study documenting the glass ceiling in a sample of nearly 31,000 financial service managers found that the glass ceiling is more prominent for women in external selection than in internal selection. However, there was evidence that women were passed up more often for promotions to higher-level management positions than for promotions to lower-level management positions.[113] This suggests that the glass ceiling phenomenon may manifest in internal selection at higher levels of the organization. When candidates perceive a glass ceiling in an internal selection context, this can lead to negative justice perceptions and turnover.[114]

The trouble does not stop when underrepresented groups *do* break through the glass ceiling. First, evidence for the "queen bee" phenomenon suggests that some women who are promoted into leadership positions do not support the advancement of junior women into leadership positions, and thus they end up "reinforcing" the glass ceiling.[115] Second, sometimes underrepresented groups may be promoted into positions that are more risky, precarious, or "set up to fail."[116] For example, women may be promoted into these positions because of a "think crisis–think female" stereotype: when teams or the organization is in crisis, women are seen as better "people managers" or are more willing to take the blame for organizational failure.[117] Finally, even without a glass cliff, underrepresented groups can face discrimination in their new position: a study of NBA head coaches from 2003 to 2015 found that minority coaches were less likely to be nominated for awards and more likely to be terminated than their White counterparts.[118]

The policy of the Equal Employment Opportunity Commission (EEOC) on nondiscriminatory promotions is (1) the KSAOs to be assessed must be job related and consistent with business necessity, and (2) there must be uniform and consistently applied standards across all promotion candidates.[119] How might the organization operate its internal selection system to comply with EEOC policy?

The first possibility is for greater use of selection plans. As discussed in the external selection chapters, these plans lay out the KSAOs required for a job, which KSAOs are necessary to bring to the job (as opposed to being acquired on the job), and, of those necessary, the most appropriate method of assessment for each. Such a plan forces an organization to conduct job analysis, construct career ladders or KSAO lattices, and consider alternatives to many of the traditional methods of assessment used in promotion systems.

A second suggestion is for the organization to back away from use of the traditional methods of assessment as much as possible, in ways that are consistent with the selection plan. This means a move away from casual, subjective methods such as supervisory recommendation, typical promotability ratings, quick reviews of personnel files, and informal recommendations. In their place should be more formal, standardized, and job-related assessment methods. Examples here include assessment centers and interview exercises.

A final suggestion is for the organization to pay close attention to the types of KSAOs necessary for advancement and undertake programs to impart these KSAOs to aspiring employees. These developmental actions might include key job and committee assignments, participation in conferences and other networking opportunities, mentoring and coaching programs, and skill acquisition in formal training programs. Internal selection methods would then be used to assess proficiency on these newly acquired KSAOs, in accordance with the selection plan.[120]

SUMMARY

The selection of internal candidates follows a process very similar to the selection of external candidates. The logic of prediction is applied, and a selection plan is developed and implemented.

One important area where internal and external selection methods differ is in the nature of the predictors. Predictors used for internal selection tend to have greater depth, tend to have more relevance, and are better suited for verification. As a result, the types of predictors used for internal selection decisions are different from those used for external selection decisions.

Initial assessment methods are used to narrow down the applicant pool to a set of qualified candidates. Approaches used are talent management systems, peer assessments, self-assessments, managerial sponsorship, and informal discussions and recommendations. Of these approaches, none is particularly strong in predicting future performance. Hence, consideration should be given to using multiple predictors to verify the accuracy of any one method. These results also point to the need to use substantive as well as initial assessment methods in making internal selection decisions.

Substantive assessment methods are used to select finalists from the list of candidates. Predictors used to make these decisions are seniority, job knowledge tests, performance appraisals, promotability ratings, assessment centers, interview exercises, and panels and review boards. Of this set of predictors, job knowledge tests, performance appraisals, promotability ratings, and assessment centers work well (when designed properly). Organizations need to give greater consideration to these predictors in replacement of, or combination with, more commonly used predictors such as seniority and promotion panels.

Although very costly, the assessment center seems to be very effective. This is because it is grounded in behavioral science theory and the logic of prediction. Samples of behavior are analyzed, multiple assessors and predictors are used, and predictors are developed based on job analysis. Despite issues with construct validity, well-designed assessment centers can be an invaluable, although expensive, internal selection predictor.

Due to their physical proximity to the data, internal job applicants potentially have greater access to selection data than external job applicants. As a result, procedures must be implemented to ensure that manual and computer files with sensitive data are kept private and confidential.

Two areas of legal concern for internal selection decisions are the UGESP and the glass ceiling. In terms of the UGESP, particular care must be taken to ensure that internal selection methods are valid if disparate impact is occurring. To minimize glass ceiling and cliff effects, organizations should make greater use of selection plans and more objective internal assessment methods, as well as help impart the KSAOs necessary for advancement.

DISCUSSION QUESTIONS

1. Explain how internal selection decisions differ from external selection decisions.
2. What are the differences between peer ratings, peer nominations, and peer rankings?
3. Explain the theory behind assessment centers.
4. Describe three different types of interview exercises.
5. Evaluate the effectiveness of seniority, assessment centers, and job knowledge as substantive internal selection procedures.
6. What steps should be taken by an organization that is committed to shattering the glass ceiling?

ETHICAL ISSUES

1. Given that seniority is not a particularly valid predictor of job performance, do you think it is ethical for a company to use it as a basis for promotion? Why or why not?
2. Vincent and Peter are sales associates and are up for promotion to sales manager. In the past five years, on a scale of 1–5 (where 1 = poor and 5 = excellent), Vincent's average performance rating was 4.7 and Peter's was 4.2. In an assessment center that was meant to simulate the job of sales manager, on a scale of 1–10 (where 1 = very poor and 10 = outstanding), Vincent's average score was 8.2 and Peter's was 9.2. Other things being equal, who should be promoted? Why?
3. As a member of a promotion board, you have been confronted with a difficult decision. The board is fairly split on who to promote into the vacant manager position, and results from several valid predictors have not differentiated very well among the few candidates for the position: there is not a candidate that is clearly outperforming the others. Although you tried to avoid it, several board members have political reasons for preferring one finalist over the rest (this person is not the best choice, according to the predictor data). Furthermore, the results of this promotion decision (a vacancy that the company has not seen in years) are likely to reverberate throughout the

organization—all the finalists are key internal players who exercise immense influence and command the loyalty of their subordinates. If one of the finalists were to leave or become disgruntled, it would be devastating for the organization. Many of the board members believe that the finalists should not have the privilege of knowing what went into the decision; they believe the board's say is final, regardless of how it affects the finalists. As a key board member overseeing the promotion process, how would you go about making a decision?

APPLICATIONS

Changing a Promotion System

Bioglass, Inc. specializes in sales of a wide array of glass products. One area of the company, the commercial sales division (CSD), specializes in selling high-tech mirrors, microscopes, and photographic lenses. Sales associates in CSD are responsible for selling the glass products to corporate clients. CSD has four levels of sales associates, ranging in pay from $28,000 to $76,000 per year. There are also four levels of managerial positions; those positions range in pay from $76,000 to $110,000 per year.

Tom Caldwell has been a very effective sales associate. He has consistently demonstrated good sales techniques in his 17 years with Bioglass and has a large and loyal client base. Over the years, Tom has risen from the lowest level of sales associate to the highest. He has proved himself successful at each stage. An entry-level management position in CSD opened last year, and Tom was a natural candidate. Although several other candidates were considered, Tom was the clear choice for the position.

However, once in the position, Tom had a great deal of difficulty being a manager. He was not accustomed to delegating and rarely provided feedback or guidance to the people he supervised. Although he set goals for himself, he never set performance goals for his workers. Morale in Tom's group was low, and group performance suffered. The company felt that demoting Tom back to sales would be disastrous for him and present the wrong image to other employees; firing such a loyal employee was considered unacceptable. Therefore, Bioglass decided to keep Tom where he was but not consider him for future promotions. It was also considering enrolling Tom in some expensive managerial development programs to enhance his management skills.

Meanwhile, Tom's replacement, although successful at the lower three levels of sales associate positions, was struggling with the large corporate contracts that the highest-level sales associates must service. Two of Tom's biggest clients had recently left Bioglass for a competitor. CSD was confused about how such a disastrous situation had developed when they seemed to make all the right decisions.

Based on this application and your reading of this chapter, answer the following questions:

1. What is the likely cause of CSD's problems?
2. How might CSD, and Bioglass more generally, make better promotion decisions in the future? Be specific.
3. In general, what role should performance appraisals play in internal selection decisions? Are there some cases in which they are more relevant than others? Explain.

Promotion From Within at Citrus Glen

Mandarine "Mandy" Pamplemousse is vice president of HR for Citrus Glen, a juice producer based in south Florida that supplies orange and grapefruit juice to grocery stores, convenience stores, restaurants, and food processors throughout the United States. Citrus Glen has been growing rapidly over the last few years, leading Mandy to worry about how to hire and promote enough qualified individuals to staff the ever-expanding array of positions within the company.

One of the ways Mandy has been able to staff positions internally is by contracting with Staffing Systems International (SSI), a management consulting firm based in Charlotte, North Carolina. When positions open at Citrus Glen that are appropriate to staff internally, Mandy sends a group of candidates for the position up to SSI to participate in its assessment center. The candidates return from SSI three days later, and a few days after that, SSI sends Mandy the results of the assessment with a recommendation. Though Mandy has never formally evaluated the accuracy of the promotions, she feels that the process is accurate. Of course, for $5,500 per candidate, Mandy thought, it *should* be accurate.

A few days ago, Mandy was hosting Thanksgiving, and her brother-in-law, Vin Pomme, joined them. Vin is a doctoral student in industrial psychology at Ohio International University. After Thanksgiving dinner, while Mandy, Vin, and their family were relaxing on her lanai and enjoying the warm Florida sunshine, Mandy began telling Vin about her worries in promoting from within and the cost of SSI's assessment process. Vin quickly realized that SSI was using an assessment center. He was also aware of research suggesting that although assessment centers predict performance, they have poor construct validity evidence. Given the high cost of assessment centers, he reasoned, one must wonder whether the assessment center used by Citrus Glen predicts performance. After Vin conveyed these impressions to Mandy, she decided that after the holidays she would reexamine Citrus Glen's internal selection processes.

1. Drawing from concepts presented in the measurement chapter, how can Mandy more formally evaluate SSI's assessment process and, as Vin suggests, determine whether the assessment process adds anything above and beyond other selection measures she uses, such as personality and cognitive ability tests.

2. Construct a scenario in which you think Mandy should continue her business relationship with SSI. On the other hand, if Mandy decides on an alternative assessment process, what would that process be? How would she evaluate whether that process was effective?

3. Citrus Glen has considered expanding its operations into the Caribbean and Latin America. One of Mandy's concerns is how to staff such positions. If Citrus Glen does expand its operations to different cultures, how should Mandy go about staffing such positions? Be specific.

ENDNOTES

1. M. Bidwell, "Paying More to Get Less: The Effects of External Hiring Versus Internal Mobility," *Administrative Science Quarterly*, 2011, 56(3), pp. 369–407.

2. P. S. DeOertentiis, C. H. Van Iddekinge, R. E. Ployhart, and T. D. Heetderks, "Build or Buy? The Individual and Unit-Level Performance of Internally Versus Externally Selected Managers Over Time," *Journal of Applied Psychology*, 2018, 103(8), pp. 916–928.

3. T. W. H. Ng, L. T. Eby, K. L. Sorensen, and D. C. Feldman, "Predictors of Objective and Subjective Career Success: A Meta-Analysis," *Personnel Psychology*, 2005, 58, pp. 367–408; T. W. H. Ng and D. C. Feldman, "Human Capital and Objective Indicators of Career Success: The Mediating Effects of Cognitive Ability and Conscientiousness," *Journal of Occupational and Organizational Psychology*, 2010, 83, pp. 207–235.

4. W. Gentry, D. C. Gilmore, M. L. Shuffler, and J. B. Leslie, "Political Skill as an Indicator of Promotability Among Multiple Rater Sources," *Journal of Organizational Behavior*, 2012, 33, pp. 89–104.

5. I. M. Jawahar and C. R. Williams, "Where All the Children Are Above Average: The Performance Appraisal Purpose Effect," *Personnel Psychology*, 1997, 50, pp. 905–926.

6. A. D. Martinez, M. D. Laird, J. A. Martin, and G. R. Ferris, "Job Title Inflation," *Human Resource Management Review*, 2008, 18, pp. 19–27; "Nearly Half of Newly-Promoted Executives Say Their Responsibilities Are the Same," *IPMA-HR Bulletin*, Dec. 22, 2006, p. 1.

7. P. L. Roth, H. Le, I-S. Oh, C. H. Van Iddekinge, and S. B. Robbins, "Who R U? On the (In)accuracy of Incumbent-Based Estimates of Range Restriction in Criterion-Related and Differential Validity Research," *Journal of Applied Psychology*, 2017, 102(5), pp. 802–828.

8. J. T. Austin, L. G. Humphreys, and C. L. Hulin, "Another View of Dynamic Criteria: A Critical Reanalysis of Barrett, Caldwell, and Alexander," *Personnel Psychology*, 1989, 42, pp. 583–596; J. A. Dahlke, J. W. Kostal, P. R. Sackett, and N. R. Kuncel, "Changing Abilities vs. Changing Tasks: Examining Validity Degradation With Test Scores and College Performance Criteria Both Assessed Longitudinally," *Journal of Applied Psychology*, 2018, 103(9), pp. 980–1000; E. E. Ghiselli, "Dimensional Problems of Criteria," *Journal of Applied Psychology*, 1956, 40, pp. 1–4.

9. See, for instance, N. Benit, A. Mojzisch, and R. Soellner, "Preselection Methods Prior to the Internal Assessment Center for Personnel Selection in German Companies," *International Journal of Selection and Assessment*, 2014, 22(3), pp. 253–260.

10. J. A. Griffith, J. E. Baur, and M. R. Buckley, "Creating Comprehensive Leadership Pipelines: Applying the Real Options Approach to Organizational Leadership Development," *Human Resource Management Review*, 2019, 29, pp. 305–315.

11. J. W. Boudreau, "Appreciating and 'Retooling' Diversity in Talent Management Conceptual Models: A Commentary on 'The Psychology of Talent Management: A Review and Research

Agenda,'" *Human Resource Management Review*, 2013, 23, pp. 286–289; E. Gallardo-Gallardo, N. Dries, and T. F. González-Cruz, "What Is the Meaning of 'Talent' in the World of Work?" *Human Resource Management Review*, 2013, 23, pp. 290–300.

12. P. Cappelli and J. R. Keller, "Talent Management: Conceptual Approaches and Practical Challenges," *Annual Review of Organizational Psychology and Organizational Behavior*, 2014, 1, pp. 305–331; D. G. Collings and K. Mellahi, "Strategic Talent Management: A Review and Research Agenda," *Human Resource Management Review*, 2009, 19, pp. 304–313; N. Dries, "The Psychology of Talent Management: A Review and Research Agenda," *Human Resource Management Review*, 2013, 23, pp. 272–285; R. E. Lewis and R. J. Heckman, "Talent Management: A Critical Review," *Human Resource Management Review*, 2006, 16, pp. 139–154.

13. *Talent Management Software Market Research Report - Global Forecast 2023*, No. MRFR/ICT/ 2641-HCR (Maharashtra, India: Market Research Future, 2020).

14. Cappelli and Keller, "Talent Management: Conceptual Approaches and Practical Challenges"; Collings and Mellahi, "Strategic Talent Management: A Review and Research Agenda"; S. E. Khilji, I. Tarique, and R. S. Schuler, "Incorporating the Macro View in Global Talent Management," *Human Resource Management Review*, 2015, 25, pp. 236–248.

15. P. Cappelli and A. Tavis, "HR Goes Agile," *Harvard Business Review*, Mar.–Apr. 2018 (*https:// hbr.org/2018/03/the-new-rules-of-talent-management*); K. Harsch and M. Festing, "Dynamic Talent Management Capabilities and Organizational Agility—a Qualitative Exploration," *Human Resource Management*, 2020, 59, pp. 43–61; T. N. Krishnan and H. Scullion, "Talent Management and Dynamic View of Talent in Small and Medium Enterprises," *Human Resource Management*, 2017, 27, pp. 431–441.

16. E. E. Lawler III, "Make Human Capital a Source of Competitive Advantage," *Organizational Dynamics*, 2009, 38(1), pp. 1–7; R. Burbach and T. Royle, "Talent on Demand? Talent Management in the German and Irish Subsidiaries of a US Multinational Corporation," *Personnel Review*, 2010, 39(4), pp. 414–431; A. McDonnell, R. Lamare, and P. Gunnigle, "Developing Tomorrow's Leaders—Evidence of Global Talent Management in Multinational Enterprises," *Journal of World Business*, 2010, 45(2), pp. 150–160.

17. G. De Boeck, M. C. Meyers, and N. Dries, "Employee Reactions to Talent Management: Assumptions Versus Evidence," *Journal of Organizational Behavior*, 2018, 39, pp. 199–213; J. Gelens, N. Dries, J. Hofmans, and R. Pepermans, "The Role of Perceived Organizational Justice in Shaping the Outcomes of Talent Management: A Research Agenda," *Human Resource Management Review*, 2013, 23, pp. 341–353.

18. M. C. Meyers, "The Neglected Role of Talent Proactivity: Integrating Proactive Behavior Into Talent-Management Theorizing," *Human Resource Management Review*, in press.

19. "Subway Elevates Business Strategy With Ultipro's Cloud Platform," *UltiPro* (*www.ultimatesoftware .com/UltiPro-Case-Study/SUBWAY*), accessed Feb. 24, 2020.

20. J. J. Kane and E. E. Lawler, "Methods of Peer Assessment," *Psychological Bulletin*, 1978, 85, pp. 555–586.

21. W. A. Gentry, D. C. Gilmore, M. L. Shuffler, and J. B. Leslie, "Political Skill as an Indicator of Promotability Among Multiple Rater Sources," *Journal of Organizational Behavior*, 2012, 33, pp. 89–104; W. A. Gentry and J. J. Sosik, "Developmental Relationships and Managerial Promotability in Organizations: A Multisource Study," *Journal of Vocational Behavior*, 2010, 77, pp. 266–278; S. Gurbuz, O. S. Habiboglu, and D. Bingol, "Who Is Being Judged Promotable: Good Actors, High Performers, Highly Committed or Birds of a Feather?," *International Journal of Selection and Assessment*, 2016, 24(2), pp. 197–208; S. Sonnentag, "Identifying High Performers: Do Peer Nominations Suffer From a Likeability Bias?" *European Journal of Work and Organizational Psychology*, 2010, 1(4), pp. 501–515.

22. G. Luria and Y. Kalish, "A Social Network Approach to Peer Assessment: Improving Predictive Validity," *Human Resource Management*, 2013, 52, pp. 537–560.

23. L. Grensing-Pophal, "Internal Selections," *HR Magazine*, Dec. 2006, p. 75.

24. Z. Chen and S. Kemp, "Lie Hard: The Effect of Self-Assessments on Academic Promotion Decisions," *Journal of Economic Psychology*, 2012, 33, pp. 578–589.

25. K. M. Carter, E. Gonzalez-Mulé, M. K. Mount, I-S. Oh, and L. Sinclair Zachar, "Managers Moving on Up (or Out): Linking Self-Other Agreement on Leadership Behaviors to Succession Planning and Voluntary Turnover," *Journal of Vocational Behavior*, in press.

26. Ng et al., "Predictors of Objective and Subjective Career Success: A Meta-Analysis."

27. H. Sibunruang, P. R. J. M. Garcia, and L. R. Tolentino, "Ingratiation as an Adapting Strategy: Its Relationship With Career Adaptability, Career Sponsorship, and Promotability," *Journal of Vocational Behavior*, 2016, 92, pp. 135–144.

28. S. J. Wayne, R. C. Liden, M. L. Kraimer, and I. K. Graf, "The Role of Human Capital, Motivation and Supervisor Sponsorship in Predicting Career Success," *Journal of Organizational Behavior*, 1999, 20, pp. 577–595.

29. T. D. Allen, L. T. Eby, M. L. Poteet, E. Lentz, and L. Lima, "Career Benefits Associated With Mentoring for Proteges: A Meta-Analysis," *Journal of Applied Psychology*, 2004, 89(1), pp. 127–136; J. D. Kammeyer-Mueller and T. A. Judge, "A Quantitative Review of Mentoring Research: Test of a Model," *Journal of Vocational Behavior*, 2008, 72, pp. 269–283.

30. R. Ghosh and T. G. Reio, Jr., "Career Benefits Associated With Mentoring for Mentors: A Meta-Analysis," *Journal of Vocational Behavior*, 2013, 83, pp. 106–116.

31. D. Krackhardt and J. R. Hanson, "Informal Networks: The Company Behind the Chart," *Harvard Business Review*, July-Aug. 1993 (*https://hbr.org/1993/07/informal-networks-the-company-behind-the-chart*); P. Tharenou, "Going Up? Do Traits and Informal Social Processes Predict Advancing in Management?" *Academy of Management Journal*, 2001, 44(5), pp. 1005–1017.

32. K. Caprino, "How to Ask for a Promotion in the Most Compelling and Convincing Way," *Forbes*, Mar. 11, 2019 (*www.forbes.com/sites/kathycaprino/2019/03/11/how-to-ask-for-a-promotion-in-the-most-compelling-and-convincing-way/#1e58b2a84835*).

33. "Seniority," *Inc.* (*www.inc.com/encyclopedia/seniority.html*), accessed Feb. 24, 2020.

34. S. M. Heathfield, "What Seniority Means at Work: Seniority Means More in the Public Sector Than in the Private Sector," *The Balance Careers*, Nov. 27, 2019 (*www.thebalancecareers.com/what-seniority-means-at-work-1919372*).

35. N. Williams, "Seniority, Experience, and Wages in the UK," *Labour Economics*, 2009, 16, pp. 272–283.

36. B. Turque, "Top Teachers Have Uneven Reach in District," *Washington Post*, Nov. 14, 2010, pp. M1–M2.

37. Ng et al., "Predictors of Objective and Subjective Career Success: A Meta-Analysis"; Ng and Feldman, "Human Capital and Objective Indicators of Career Success: The Mediating Effects of Cognitive Ability and Conscientiousness."

38. J. Haden, "Why You Should Never Promote an Employee Based on Seniority," *Inc.*, Oct. 19, 2017 (*www.inc.com/jeff-haden/why-seniority-is-worst-reason-to-promote-an-employee.html*).

39. T. D. Allen, J. E. A. Russell, M. L. Poteet, and G. H. Dobbins, "Learning and Development Factors Related to Perceptions of Job Content and Hierarchical Plateauing," *Journal of Organizational Behavior*, 1999, 20, pp. 1113–1137.

40. F. L. Schmidt and J. E. Hunter, "Development of a Causal Model of Processes Determining Job Performance," *Current Directions in Psychological Science*, 1992, 1, pp. 89–92.

41. P. L. Roth, C. H. Van Iddekinge, P. S. DeOrtentiis, K. J. Hackney, L. Zhang, and M. A. Buster, "Hispanic and Asian Performance on Selection Procedures: A Narrative and Meta-Analytic Review of 12 Common Predictors," *Journal of Applied Psychology*, 2017, 102(8), pp. 1178–1202;

C. H. Van Iddekinge, F. P. Morgeson, D. J. Schleicher, and M. A. Campion, "Can I Retake It? Exploring Subgroup Differences and Criterion-Related Validity in Promotion Retesting," *Journal of Applied Psychology*, 2011, 96(5), pp. 941–955.

42. J. B. Becton, H. S. Feild, W. F. Giles, and A. Jones-Farmer, "Racial Differences in Promotion Candidate Performance and Reactions to Selection Procedures: A Field Study in a Diverse Top-Management Context," *Journal of Organizational Behavior*, 2008, 29, pp. 265–285.

43. P. Cappelli and M. J. Conyon, "What Do Performance Appraisals Do?" *ILR Review*, 2018, 71(1), pp. 88–116; A. Denisi and C. E. Smith, "Performance Appraisal, Performance Management, and Firm-Level Performance," *Academy of Management Annals*, 2014, 8(1), pp. 127–179; D. J. Schleicher, H. M. Baumann, D. W. Sullivan, P. E. Levy, D. C. Hargrove, and B. A. Barros-Rivera, "Putting the *System* Into Performance Management Systems: A Review and Agenda for Performance Management Research," *Journal of Management*, 2018, 44(6), pp. 2209–2245.

44. Austin et al., "Another View of Dynamic Criteria"; Dahlke et al., "Changing Abilities vs. Changing Tasks: Examining Validity Degradation With Test Scores and College Performance Criteria Both Assessed Longitudinally"; Ghiselli, "Dimensional Problems of Criteria."

45. N. Sirola and M. Pitesa, "The Macroeconomic Environment and the Psychology of Work Evaluation," *Organizational Behavior and Human Decision Processes*, 2018, 144, pp. 11–24; J. R. Spence and L. Keeping, "Conscious Rating Distortion in Performance Appraisal: A Review, Commentary, and Proposed Framework for Research," *Human Resource Management Review*, 2011, 21, pp. 85–95; X. M. Wang, K. F. Ellick Wong, and J. Y. Y. Kwong, "The Roles of Rater Goals and Ratee Performance Levels in the Distortion of Performance Ratings," *Journal of Applied Psychology*, 2010, 95(3), pp. 546–561.

46. J. M. Hoobler, S. J. Wayne, and G. Lemmon, "Bosses' Perceptions of Family-Work Conflict and Women's Promotability: Glass Ceiling Effects," *Academy of Management Journal*, 2009, 52(5), pp. 939–957; M. E. Inesi and D. M. Cable, "When Accomplishments Come Back to Haunt You: The Negative Effect of Competence Signals on Women's Performance Evaluations," *Personnel Psychology*, 2015, 68, pp. 615–657; K. S. Lyness and M. E. Heilman, "When Fit Is Fundamental: Performance Evaluations and Promotions of Upper-Level Female and Male Managers," *Journal of Applied Psychology*, 2006, 91(4), pp. 777–785.

47. C. M. Barnes, J. Reb, and D. Ang, "More Than Just the Mean: Moving to a Dynamic View of Performance-Based Compensation," *Journal of Applied Psychology*, 2012, 97, pp. 711–718.

48. M. Soliman and R. Buehler, "Why Improvement Can Trump Consistent Strong Performance: The Role of Effort Perceptions," *Journal of Behavioral Decision Making*, 2018, 31, pp. 52–64.

49. L. J. Peter and R. Hull, *The Peter Principle* (New York: William Morrow, 1969); J. Romaine, "The Peter Principle Resuscitated: Are Promotion Systems Useless?" *Human Resource Management Journal*, 2014, 24(4), pp. 410–423.

50. K. Tzini and K. Jain, "Unethical Behavior Under Relative Performance Evaluation: Evidence and Remedy," *Human Resource Management*, 2018, 57, pp. 1399–1413; J. Werbel and D. B. Balkin, "Are Human Resource Practices Linked to Employee Misconduct? A Rational Choice Perspective," *Human Resource Management Review*, 2010, 20, pp. 317–326.

51. B. J. Hoffman, C. A. Gorman, C. A. Blair, J. P. Meriac, B. Overstreet, and E. K. Atchley, "Evidence for the Effectiveness of an Alternative Multisource Performance Rating Methodology," *Personnel Psychology*, 2012, 65, pp. 531–563.

52. G. C. Thornton III and D. M. Morris, "The Application of Assessment Center Technology to the Evaluation of Personnel Records," *Public Personnel Management*, 2001, 30, pp. 55–66.

53. V. M. Catano, W. Darr, and C. A. Campbell, "Performance Appraisal of Behavior-Based Competencies: A Reliable and Valid Procedure," *Personnel Psychology*, 2007, 60, pp. 201–230.

54. C. Hui, S. S. K. Lam, and K. K. S. Law, "Instrumental Values of Organizational Citizenship Behavior for Promotion: A Field Quasi-Experiment," *Journal of Applied Psychology*, 2000, 85(5),

pp. 822–828; M. K. Judiesch and K. S. Lyness, "Left Behind? The Impact of Leaves of Absence on Managers' Career Success," *Academy of Management Journal*, 1999, 42(6), pp. 641–651.

55. A. B. Speer, "Quantifying With Words: An Investigation of the Validity of Narrative-Derived Performance Scores," *Personnel Psychology*, 2018, 71, pp. 299–333.

56. T. L. Eurich, D. E. Krause, K. Cigularov, and G. C. Thornton III, "Assessment Centers: Current Practices in the United States," *Journal of Business and Psychology*, 2009, 24(4), pp. 387–407; International Taskforce on Assessment Center Guidelines, "Guidelines and Ethical Considerations for Assessment Center Operations," *Journal of Management*, 2015, 41(4), pp. 1244–1273; M. Kleinmann and P. V. Ingold, "Toward a Better Understanding of Assessment Centers: A Conceptual Review," *Annual Review of Organizational Psychology and Organizational Behavior*, 2019, 6, pp. 349–372.

57. W. Arthur, Jr., and E. A. Day, "Assessment Centers," in S. Zedeck (ed.), *APA Handbook of Industrial and Organizational Psychology* (Washington, DC: APA, 2011), pp. 205–235.

58. Eurich et al., "Assessment Centers: Current Practices in the United States"; International Taskforce on Assessment Center Guidelines, "Guidelines and Ethical Considerations for Assessment Center Operations."

59. Arthur and Day, "Assessment Centers"; Eurich et al., "Assessment Centers: Current Practices in the United States."

60. Arthur and Day, "Assessment Centers."

61. Arthur and Day, "Assessment Centers"; Eurich et al., "Assessment Centers: Current Practices in the United States."

62. J. P. Meriac, B. J. Hoffman, and D. J. Woehr, "A Conceptual and Empirical Review of the Structure of Assessment Center Dimensions," *Journal of Management*, 2014, 40, pp. 1269–1296.

63. Eurich et al., "Assessment Centers: Current Practices in the United States"; C. A. Gorman and J. R. Rentsch, "Retention of Assessment Center Rater Training," *Journal of Personnel Psychology*, 2017, 16(1), pp. 1–11.

64. Arthur and Day, "Assessment Centers."

65. W. Arthur, Jr., E. A. Day, T. L. McNelly, and P. S. Edens, "A Meta-Analysis of the Criterion-Related Validity of Assessment Center Dimensions," *Personnel Psychology*, 2003, 56, pp. 125–154; M. C. Bowler and D. J. Woehr, "A Meta-Analytic Evaluation of the Impact of Dimension and Exercise Factors on Assessment Center Ratings," *Journal of Applied Psychology*, 2006, 91(5), pp. 1114–1124; D. J. Woehr and W. Arthur, Jr., "The Construct-Related Validity of Assessment Center Ratings: A Review and Meta-Analysis of the Role of Methodological Factors," *Journal of Management*, 2003, 29(2), pp. 231–258.

66. Eurich et al., "Assessment Centers: Current Practices in the United States."

67. Kleinmann and Ingold, "Toward a Better Understanding of Assessment Centers: A Conceptual Review."

68. F. Lievens, E. Schollaert, and G. Keen, "The Interplay of Elicitation and Evaluation of Trait-Expressive Behavior: Evidence in Assessment Center Exercises," *Journal of Applied Psychology*, 2015, 100(4), pp. 1169–1188; T. Oliver, P. Hausdorf, F. Lievens, and P. Conlon, "Interpersonal Dynamics in Assessment Center Exercises: Effects of Role Player Portrayed Disposition," *Journal of Management*, 2016, 42(7), pp. 1992–2017.

69. E. Schollaert and F. Lievens, "The Use of Role-Player Prompts in Assessment Center Exercises," *International Journal of Selection and Assessment*, 2011, 19(2), pp. 190–197; E. Schollaert and F. Lievens, "Building Situational Stimuli in Assessment Center Exercises: Do Specific Exercise Instructions and Role-Player Prompts Increase the Observability of Behavior?" *Human Performance*, 2012, 25, pp. 255–271.

70. Darden Restaurants, *Sustainability Report* (Orlando, FL: author, 2012).

71. Eurich et al., "Assessment Centers: Current Practices in the United States."

72. J. K. Oostrom, L. Bos-Broekema, A. W. Serlie, M. Ph. Born, and H. T. van der Molen, "A Field Study of Pretest and Posttest Reactions to a Paper-and-Pencil and a Computerized In-Basket Exercise," *Human Performance*, 2012, 25, pp. 95–113; J. S. Schippmann, E. P. Prien, and J. A. Katz, "Reliability and Validity of In-Basket Performance Measures," *Personnel Psychology*, 1990, 43, pp. 837–859; D. L. Whetzel, P. F. Rotenberry, and M. A. McDaniel, "In-Basket Validity: A Systematic Review," *International Journal of Selection and Assessment*, 2014, 22(1), pp. 62–79.

73. Kleinmann and Ingold, "Toward a Better Understanding of Assessment Centers: A Conceptual Review"; Whetzel, Rotenberry, and McDaniel, "In-Basket Validity: A Systematic Review."

74. Arthur and Day, "Assessment Centers."

75. Eurich et al., "Assessment Centers: Current Practices in the United States."

76. X. Borteyrou, F. Lievens, M. Bruchon-Schweitzer, A. Congard, and N. Rascle, "Incremental Validity of Leaderless Group Discussion Ratings Over and Above General Mental Ability and Personality in Predicting Promotion," *International Journal of Selection and Assessment*, 2015, 23(4), pp. 373–381; R. Gatewood, G. C. Thornton III, and H. W. Hennessey, Jr., "Reliability of Exercise Ratings in the Leaderless Group Discussion," *Journal of Occupational Psychology*, 1990, 63, pp. 331–342.

77. D. L. Paulhus and K. L. Morgan, "Perceptions of Intelligence in Leaderless Groups: The Dynamic Effects of Shyness and Acquaintance," *Journal of Personality and Social Psychology*, 1997, 72(3), pp. 581–591; D. A. Waldman, L. E. Atwater, and R. A. Davidson, "The Role of Individualism and the Five-Factor Model in the Prediction of Performance in a Leaderless Group Discussion," *Journal of Personality*, 2004, 72(1), pp. 1–28.

78. Arthur et al., "A Meta-Analysis of the Criterion-Related Validity of Assessment Center Dimensions"; E. Hermelin, F. Lievens, and I. T. Robertson, "The Validity of Assessment Centres for the Prediction of Supervisory Performance Ratings: A Meta-Analysis," *International Journal of Selection and Assessment*, 2007, 15, pp. 405–411.

79. P. Bobko and P. L. Roth, "Reviewing, Categorizing, and Analyzing the Literature on Black-White Mean Differences for Predictors of Job Performance: Verifying Some Perceptions and Updating/Correcting Others," *Personnel Psychology*, 2013, 66, pp. 91–126; Roth et al., "Hispanic and Asian Performance on Selection Procedures: A Narrative and Meta-Analytic Review of 12 Common Predictors"; G. C. Thornton III, D. E. Rupp, A. M. Gibbons, and A. J. Vanhove, "Same-Gender and Same-Race Bias in Assessment Center Ratings: A Rating Error Approach to Understanding Subgroup Differences," *International Journal of Selection and Assessment*, 2019, 27, pp. 54–71.

80. S. Dilchert and D. S. Ones, "Assessment Center Dimensions: Individual Differences Correlates and Meta-Analytic Incremental Validity," *International Journal of Selection and Assessment*, 2009, 17(3), pp. 254–270; B. J. Hoffman, C. L. Kennedy, A. C. LoPilato, E. L. Monahan, and C. E. Lance, "A Review of the Content, Criterion-Related, and Construct-Related Validity of Assessment Center Exercises," *Journal of Applied Psychology*, 2015, 100, pp. 1143–1168; J. P. Meriac, B. J. Hoffman, D. J. Woehr, and M. S. Fleisher, "Further Evidence for the Validity of Assessment Center Dimensions: A Meta-Analysis of the Incremental Criterion-Related Validity of Dimension Ratings," *Journal of Applied Psychology*, 2008, 93(5), pp. 1042–1052; P. R. Sackett, O. R. Shewach, and H. N. Keiser, "Assessment Center Versus Cognitive Ability Tests: Challenging the Conventional Wisdom on Criterion-Related Validity," *Journal of Applied Psychology*, 2017, 102(10), pp. 1435–1447.

81. Hoffman et al., "A Review of the Content, Criterion-Related, and Construct-Related Validity of Assessment Center Exercises"; Kleinmann and Ingold, "Toward a Better Understanding of Assessment Centers: A Conceptual Review."

82. D. J. Putka and B. J. Hoffman, "Clarifying the Contribution of Assessee-, Dimension-, Exercise-, and Assessor-Related Effects to Reliable and Unreliable Variance in Assessment Center Ratings," *Journal of Applied Psychology*, 2013, 98, pp. 114–133.

83. A. M. Gibbons and D. E. Rupp, "Dimension Consistency as an Individual Difference: A New (Old) Perspective on the Assessment Center Construct Validity Debate," *Journal of Management*, 2009, 35(5), pp. 1154–1180; C. E. Lance, "Why Assessment Centers Do Not Work the Way They Are Supposed To," *Industrial and Organizational Psychology*, 2008, 1, pp. 84–97; B. S. Connelly, D. S. Ones, A. Ramesh, and M. Goff, "A Pragmatic View of Assessment Center Exercises and Dimensions," *Industrial and Organizational Psychology*, 2008, 1, pp. 121–124.

84. B. J. Hoffman, K. G. Melchers, C. A. Blair, M. Kleinmann, and R. T. Ladd, "Exercises and Dimensions Are the Currency of Assessment Centers," *Personnel Psychology*, 2011, 64, pp. 351–395; N. R. Kuncel and P. R. Sackett, "Resolving the Assessment Center Construct Validity Problem (as We Know It)," *Journal of Applied Psychology*, 2014, 99, pp. 38–47; N. Merkulova, K. G. Melchers, M. Kleinmann, H. Annen, and T. Szvircsev Tresch, "A Test of the Generalizability of a Recently Suggested Conceptual Model for Assessment Center Ratings," *Human Performance*, 2016, 29(3), pp. 226–250; A. B. Speer, N. D. Christiansen, R. D. Goffin, and M. Goff, "Situational Bandwidth and the Criterion-Related Validity of Assessment Center Ratings: Is Cross-Exercise Convergence Always Desirable?" *Journal of Applied Psychology*, 2014, 99, pp. 282–295.

85. D. J. R. Jackson, G. Michaelides, C. Dewberry, and Y.-J. Kim, "Everything That You Have Ever Been Told About Assessment Center Ratings Is Confounded," *Journal of Applied Psychology*, 2016, 101, pp. 976–994.

86. S. Haaland and N. D. Christiansen, "Implications of Trait-Activation Theory for Evaluating the Construct Validity of Assessment Center Ratings," *Personnel Psychology*, 2002, 55, pp. 137–163; R. P. Tett and H. A. Guterman, "Situation Trait Relevance, Trait Expression, and Cross-Situational Consistency: Testing a Principle of Trait Activation," *Journal of Research in Personality*, 2000, 34, pp. 397–423.

87. F. Lievens, C. S. Chasteen, E. A. Day, and N. D. Christiansen, "Large-Scale Investigation of the Role of Trait Activation Theory for Understanding Assessment Center Convergent and Discriminant Validity," *Journal of Applied Psychology*, 2006, 91(2), pp. 247–258.

88. P. V. Ingold, M. Kleinmann, C. J. König, and K. G. Melchers, "Transparency of Assessment Centers: Lower Criterion-Related Validity but Greater Opportunity to Perform?" *Personnel Psychology*, 2016, 69, pp. 467–497; K. A. Smith-Jentsch, "The Impact of Making Targeted Dimensions Transparent on Relations With Typical Performance Predictors," *Human Performance*, 2007, 20(3), pp. 187–203.

89. A. Jansen, K. G. Melchers, F. Lievens, M. Kleinmann, M. Brändli, L. Fraefel, and C. J. König, "Situation Assessment as an Ignored Factor in the Behavioral Consistency Paradigm Underlying the Validity of Personnel Selection Procedures," *Journal of Applied Psychology*, 2013, 98(2), pp. 326–341; U.-C. Klehe, M. Kleinmann, C. Nieß, and J. Grazi, "Impression Management Behavior in Assessment Centers: Artificial Behavior or Much Ado About Nothing?" *Human Performance*, 2014, 27, pp. 1–24; A. B. Speer, N. D. Christiansen, K. G. Melchers, C. J. König, and M. Kleinmann, "Establishing the Cross-Situational Convergence of the Ability to Identify Criteria: Consistency and Prediction Across Similar and Dissimilar Assessment Center Exercises," *Human Performance*, 2014, 27, pp. 44–60.

90. Lievens, Schollaert, and Keen, "The Interplay of Elicitation and Evaluation of Trait-Expressive Behavior: Evidence in Assessment Center Exercises."

91. M. S. Christian, B. D. Edwards, and J. C. Bradley, "Situational Judgment Tests: Constructs Assessed and a Meta-Analysis of Their Criterion-Related Validities," *Personnel Psychology*, 2010, 63(1), pp. 83–117.

92. See, for instance, A. C. Howland, R. Rembisz, T. S. Wang-Jones, S. R. Heise, and S. Brown, "Developing a Virtual Assessment Center," *Consulting Psychology Journal: Practice and Research*, 2015, 67(2), pp. 110–126.

93. F. Lievens, E. Van Keer, and E. Volckaert, "Gathering Behavioral Samples Through a Computerized and Standardized Assessment Center Exercise: Yes, It Is Possible," *Journal of Personnel Psychology*, 2010, 9(2), pp. 94–98.

94. Eurich et al., "Assessment Centers: Current Practices in the United States."

95. BTS, "Assessment Centers: Expertise and Impact" (*www.bts.com/assessments/expertise-impact*), accessed Feb. 25, 2020.

96. Arthur and Day, "Assessment Centers"; C. J. König, C. B. Fell, V. Steffen, and S. Vanderveken, "Applicant Reactions Are Similar Across Countries: A Refined Replication With Assessment Center Data From the European Union," *Journal of Personnel Psychology*, 2015, 14(4), pp. 213–217.

97. D. E. Krause and G. C. Thornton III, "A Cross-Cultural Look at Assessment Center Practices: Survey Results From Western Europe and North America," *Applied Psychology: An International Review*, 2009, 58(4), pp. 557–585; N. Merkulova, K. G. Melchers, M. Kleinmann, H. Annen, and T. S. Tresch, "Effects of Individual Differences on Applicant Perceptions of an Operational Assessment Center," *International Journal of Selection and Assessment*, 2014, 22, pp. 356–370; I. J. van Emmerik, A. B. Bakker, and M. C. Euwema, "What Happens After the Developmental Assessment Center? Employees' Reactions to Unfavorable Performance Feedback," *Journal of Management Development*, 2008, 27(5), pp. 513–527; N. Anderson and V. Goltsi, "Negative Psychological Effects of Selection Methods: Construct Formulation and an Empirical Investigation Into an Assessment Center," *International Journal of Selection and Assessment*, 2006, 14(3), pp. 236–255.

98. Eurich et al., "Assessment Centers: Current Practices in the United States."

99. International Taskforce on Assessment Center Guidelines, "Guidelines and Ethical Considerations for Assessment Center Operations"; J. Lee, B. S. Connelly, M. Goff, and J. F. Hazucha, "Are Assessment Center Behaviors' Meanings Consistent Across Exercises? A Measurement Invariance Approach," *International Journal of Selection and Assessment*, 2017, 25, pp. 317–332.

100. W. A. Burroughs and L. L. White, "Predicting Sales Performance," *Journal of Business and Psychology*, 1996, 11(1), pp. 73–84.

101. B. D. Blume, G. F. Dreher, and T. T. Baldwin, "Examining the Effects of Communication Apprehension Within Assessment Centres," *Journal of Occupational and Organizational Psychology*, 2010, 83, pp. 663–671.

102. L. A. McFarland, G. J. Yun, C. M. Harold, L. Viera, Jr., and L. G. Moore, "An Examination of Impression Management Use and Effectiveness Across Assessment Center Exercises: The Role of Competency Demands," *Personnel Psychology*, 2005, 58, pp. 949–980.

103. F. P. Morgeson, M. A. Campion, and J. Levashina, "Why Don't You Just Show Me? Performance Interviews for Skill-Based Promotions," *International Journal of Selection and Assessment*, 2009, 17(2), pp. 203–218.

104. See, for instance, P. L. Roth and J. E. Campion, "An Analysis of the Predictive Power of the Panel Interview and Pre-employment Tests," *Journal of Occupational and Organizational Psychology*, 1992, 65, pp. 51–60.

105. S. M. Osborn, H. S. Feild, and J. G. Veres, "Introversion-Extraversion, Self-Monitoring, and Applicant Performance in a Situational Panel Interview: A Field Study," *Journal of Business and Psychology*, 1998, 13(2), pp. 143–156.

106. M. R. Buckley, K. A. Jackson, M. C. Bolino, J. G. Veres III, and H. S. Feild, "The Influence of Relational Demography on Panel Interview Ratings: A Field Experiment," *Personnel Psychology*, 2007, 60, pp. 627–646; L. A. McFarland, A. M. Ryan, J. M. Sacco, and S. D. Kriska,

"Examination of the Structured Interview Ratings Across Time: The Effects of Applicant Race, Rater Race, and Panel Composition," *Journal of Management*, 2004, 30(4), pp. 435–452; A. J. Prewett-Livingston, H. S. Feild, J. G. Veres III, and P. M. Lewis, "Effects of Race on Interview Ratings in a Situational Panel Interview," *Journal of Applied Psychology*, 1996, 81(2), pp. 178–186.

107. P. P. Carson, K. D. Carson, R. W. Griffeth, and R. P. Steel, "Promotion and Employee Turnover: Critique, Meta-Analysis, and Implications," *Journal of Business and Psychology*, 1994, 8(4), pp. 455–466.

108. D. K. Ford, D. M. Truxillo, and T. N. Bauer, "Rejected but Still There: Shifting the Focus in Applicant Reactions to the Promotional Context," *International Journal of Selection and Assessment*, 2009, 17(4), pp. 402–416.

109. T. A. Beehr, V. N. Nair, D. M. Gudanowski, and M. Such, "Perceptions of Reasons for Promotion of Self and Others," *Human Relations*, 2004, 57(4), pp. 413–438; A. L. García-Izquierdo, S. Moscoso, and P. J. Ramos-Villagrasa, "Reactions to the Fairness of Promotion Methods: Procedural Justice and Job Satisfaction," *International Journal of Selection and Assessment*, 2012, 20(4), pp. 394–403.

110. Ford, Truxillo, and Bauer, "Rejected but Still There: Shifting the Focus in Applicant Reactions to the Promotional Context."

111. J. B. Prince, "Career-Focused Employee Transfer Process," *Career Development International*, 2005, 10(4), pp. 293–309; H. C. Vough and B. B. Caza, "Where Do I Go From Here? Sensemaking and the Construction of Growth-Based Stories in the Wake of Denied Promotions," *Academy of Management Review*, 2017, 42(1), pp. 103–128.

112. Vough and Caza, "Where Do I Go From Here? Sensemaking and the Construction of Growth-Based Stories in the Wake of Denied Promotions."

113. K. S. Lyness and M. K. Judiesch, "Are Women More Likely to Be Hired or Promoted Into Management Positions?" *Journal of Vocational Behavior*, 1999, 54, pp. 158–173.

114. S. Foley, D. L. Kidder, and G. N. Powell, "The Perceived Glass Ceiling and Justice Perceptions: An Investigation of Hispanic Law Associates," *Journal of Management*, 2002, 28(4), pp. 471–496.

115. K. Faniko, N. Ellemers, B. Derks, and F. Lorenzi-Cioldi, "Nothing Changes, Really: Why Women Who Break Through the Glass Ceiling End Up Reinforcing It," *Personality and Social Psychology Bulletin*, 2017, 43(5), pp. 638–651.

116. C. Glass and A. Cook, "Leading at the Top: Understanding Women's Challenges Above the Glass Ceiling," *Leadership Quarterly*, 2016, 27, pp. 51–63; M. K. Ryan, S. Alexander Haslam, T. Morgenroth, F. Rink, J. Stoker, and K. Peters, "Getting on Top of the Glass Cliff: Reviewing a Decade of Evidence, Explanations, and Impact," *Leadership Quarterly*, 2016, 27, pp. 446–455.

117. S. Alexander Haslam and M. K. Ryan, "The Road to the Glass Cliff: Differences in the Perceived Suitability of Men and Women for Leadership Positions in Succeeding and Failing Organizations," *Leadership Quarterly*, 2008, 19, pp. 530–546; M. K. Ryan, S. Alexander Haslam, M. D. Hersby, and R. Bongiorno, "Think Crisis—Think Female: The Glass Cliff and Contextual Variation in the Think Manager—Think Male Stereotype," *Journal of Applied Psychology*, 2011, 96(3), pp. 470–484.

118. W. G. Obenauer and N. Langer, "Inclusion Is Not a Slam Dunk: A Study of Differential Leadership Outcomes in the Absence of a Glass Cliff," *Leadership Quarterly*, in press.

119. Equal Employment Opportunity Commission, EEOC Compliance Manual-Section 15: Race and Color Discrimination, 2006 (*www.eeoc.gov/policy/docs/race-color.html*); J. A. Segal, "Land Executives, Not Lawsuits," *HR Magazine*, Oct. 2006, pp. 123–130.

120. D. J. Walsh, *Employment Law for Human Resource Practice*, 5th ed. (Boston: Cengage Learning, 2016), pp. 250–255.

The Staffing Organizations Model

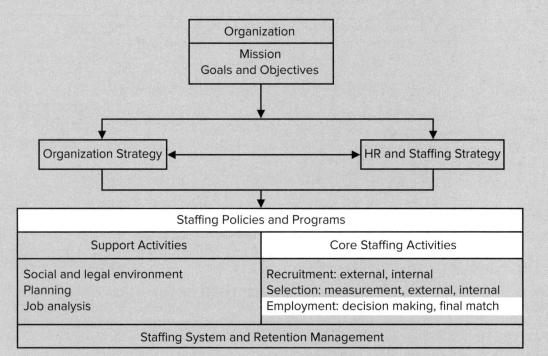

PART FIVE

Staffing Activities: Employment

CHAPTER ELEVEN

Decision Making

Learning Objectives and Introduction
    Learning Objectives
    Introduction

Choice of Assessment Method
    Validity Coefficient
    Validity for Multiple Criteria
    Workforce Diversity
    Correlation With Other Predictors
    Hiring Success Gain
    Economic Gain

Determining Assessment Scores
    Single Predictor
    Multiple Predictors

Hiring Standards and Cut Scores
    Description of the Process
    Consequences of Cut Scores
    Methods to Determine Cut Scores

Methods of Final Choice
    Random Selection
    Ranking
    Grouping and Banding
    Differential Weighting
    Incorporating Diversity

Decision Makers
    Organizational Leaders
    Human Resource Professionals
    Managers
    Coworkers

Legal Issues
    Uniform Guidelines on Employee Selection Procedures
    Diversity and Hiring Decisions

Summary

Discussion Questions

Ethical Issues

Applications
    Utility Concerns in Choosing an Assessment Method
    Choosing Entrants Into a Management Training Program

Endnotes

LEARNING OBJECTIVES AND INTRODUCTION

Learning Objectives

- Be able to interpret validity coefficients
- Evaluate diversity implications of various decision processes
- Evaluate the utility of selection systems
- Learn about methods for combining multiple predictors
- Establish hiring standards and cut scores
- Compare methods of making a final selection choice
- Understand the roles of decision makers in the staffing process

Introduction

The preceding chapters described a variety of techniques that organizations can use to assess candidates. However, collecting data on applicants does not ultimately lead to a straightforward conclusion about who should be selected. Should interviews take precedence over standardized ability tests? Should job experience be the primary focus of selection decisions, or will organizations make better choices if experience ratings are supplemented with data on personality? What role should experience and education have in selection? This chapter describes how this information can be used to make decisions about who will ultimately be hired. As we will see, subjective factors often enter into the decision process. Having methods to resolve any disputes that arise in the process of evaluating candidates in advance can greatly facilitate efficient decision making and reduce conflict among members of the hiring committee.

When it comes to making final decisions about candidates, it is necessary to understand the nature of the organization and the jobs being staffed. Organizations that have strong cultures and heavy needs for customer service might put a stronger emphasis on candidate personality and values. For jobs with a stronger technical emphasis, it makes more sense to evaluate candidates on the basis of demonstrated knowledge and skills. Throughout this chapter, you will want to consider how your own organization's strategic goals factor into staffing decision making.

The process of translating predictor scores into assessment scores is broken down into a series of subtopics. First, techniques for using single predictors and multiple predictors are discussed. The process and methods used to determine minimum standards (a.k.a. "cut scores") will be described, as well as the consequences of cut scores. Methods of final choice must be considered to determine who from among the finalists will receive a job offer. For all the preceding decisions, consideration must be given to who should be involved in the decision process. Finally, legal issues should also guide decision making. Particular consideration will be given to the Uniform Guidelines on Employee Selection Procedures (UGESP) and to the role of diversity considerations in hiring decisions.

CHOICE OF ASSESSMENT METHOD

In our discussions of external and internal selection methods, we listed multiple criteria to consider when deciding which method(s) to use. In this section, we will consider a variety of techniques managers can use to assess how well various selection methods predict future performance, and which should therefore be retained in the measurement process.

Our discussion of how to choose an assessment method is based on the material we have already presented regarding the value of standardization, objectivity, and statistical decision tools. Despite a great deal of evidence supporting the use of these decision aids, managers often prefer to use their intuition when making important decisions. Although it is tempting to conclude that one's own subjective feeling and intuition will perform better than a mathematical formula for decision making, a very large body of research shows that experts seldom are as good as the mathematical models they develop when it comes to combining information and assessing across specific alternatives.[1] Put differently, experts are very good at designing systems for decision rules, and are usually better off relying on these systems in practice, rather than making specific choices on the fly. Intuitive decision making tends to rely on relatively little information, stories about past events that may not represent the current situation, and personal biases. One study that involved recording panels of managers making hiring decisions found that the managers often completely departed from the standardized information they were provided. They used very minor cues, like inferring intellectual ability from the speed of answering one question, and attempted to read complex motives or personality traits from the subtle wording of answers to interview questions. Decision makers are strongly encouraged to focus their attention on objective, standardized assessment tools and decision-making aids as much as possible for important decisions like hiring.

Validity Coefficient

Validity refers to the relationship between predictor and criterion scores. Often this relationship is assessed using a correlation (see the measurement chapter). The correlation between predictor and criterion scores is known as a validity coefficient. The usefulness of a predictor is determined on the basis of the practical significance and statistical significance of its validity coefficient. As was noted in the measurement chapter, reliability is a necessary condition for validity. Selection measures with questionable reliability will have questionable validity.

Practical Significance

Practical significance represents the extent to which the predictor adds value to the prediction of job success. It is assessed by examining the magnitude of the validity coefficient. The magnitude of the validity coefficient refers to the absolute value, ranging from 0 (no prediction) to 1.0 (perfect prediction). The closer the validity coefficient is to 1.00, the greater the magnitude, and the more helpful the predictor will be in identifying strong job applicants. As shown in the previous chapters, validity coefficients for current assessment methods range from 0 to about .60. Any validity coefficient above 0 is better than random selection and may be somewhat useful. Validities above .15 are moderately useful, and validities above .30 are highly useful.

Statistical Significance

Statistical significance, as assessed by probability or p values (see the measurement chapter), is another factor that should be used to interpret the validity coefficient. A low p value indicates that it is likely that the method of prediction is better than random chance. Convention has it that a reasonable level of significance is $p < .05$. This means there are fewer than 5 chances in 100 of mistakenly concluding there is a relationship in the population of job applicants.

Statistical significance does not always gauge the usefulness of a predictor. Nonsignificant validity coefficients may simply be due to the small samples of employees used to calculate the validity coefficients. Alternatively, in very large samples it is possible to obtain statistical significance with very small practical significance. These concerns over significance testing have led some researchers to recommend the use of "confidence intervals," for example, showing that one can be 90% confident that the true validity is no less than .30 and no greater than .40.[2]

Validity for Multiple Criteria

Although we have been discussing validity as if it were a single number assessing prediction of overall job performance up to this point, hiring tools differ in which types of performance they might predict. The preceding chapters described how selection tools that measure different characteristics are useful for predicting different outcomes. For example, cognitive ability tests are very useful for identifying future performance in core job tasks. Looking at job analysis KSAO (knowledge, skills, abilities, and other characteristics) categories, cognitive ability will improve acquiring knowledge, knowing when to use skills, and facility in using skills. Conscientiousness, on the other hand, influences the degree to which individuals are organized in doing job tasks and are goal directed. Unlike cognitive ability, conscientiousness also predicts attendance and attention to detail. Agreeableness is not consistently related to task performance but is related to cooperating and group facilitation. Openness to experience is also not related to core task performance but is related to creativity. Considering multiple criteria means considering which forms of performance are most important for a given role and then picking measures that assess KSAOs associated with success.

Workforce Diversity

In addition to assessing relationships between predictors and outcomes, the diversity of the workforce is also a concern when evaluating selection tools. In many cases, potential screening tools may have disparate impact as a result of factors not related to performance on the job. Educational credentials are easier to obtain for people with more family wealth, so using education as a screening tool may work against hiring underrepresented groups who have less access to financial resources.[3] Rating interviewees on specific leadership behaviors that are more typical of men than of women may similarly reduce diversity while failing to recognize the value of alternative modes of leadership.

A very difficult judgment call arises when one predictor has high validity and high disparate impact while another predictor has low validity and low disparate impact.[4] Balancing the trade-offs is difficult and requires use of the organization's staffing philosophy regarding equal employment opportunity and affirmative action (EEO/AA). Later in this chapter we consider some possible solutions to this important problem. The research literature on selection and diversity shows that using a variety of different selection tools together can maintain high validity while maintaining comparatively lower disparate impact.[5] In fact, breaking down cognitive ability into component subtests with differential disparate impact, and putting greater weight on lower disparate impact sections of the test can greatly increase diversity with little decrease in validity.[6] Techniques to statistically adjust selection based on a small number of predictors can reduce, but not eliminate, the validity/ diversity paradox. Adding measures with lower disparate impact can improve diversity without sacrificing validity.

Correlation With Other Predictors

If a predictor is to be considered useful, it must add value to the prediction of job success, which is to say that it must add to the prediction of success above and beyond the forecasting powers of current predictors. In general, a predictor is more useful if it has a *smaller* correlation with other predictors and a higher correlation with the criterion. Predictors are likely to be highly correlated with one another when their content domain is similar.

To assess whether the predictor adds anything new to forecasting, a matrix showing all of the correlations between the predictors and the criteria should always be generated. If the correlations between the new predictor and the existing predictors are high, the new predictor is not adding much. Multiple regression takes the correlation among predictors into account and can estimate the incremental validity of adding a new predictor.

Exhibit 11.1 shows an example of a (hypothetical) incremental validity assessment for predicting performance among operations managers for an electronics manufacturer. The organization has previously relied on unstructured interviews, years of work experience in a similar field, and college grade point average (GPA). Because unstructured interviews and years of work experience do not predict performance well, the organization is considering supplementing its current selection methods with cognitive ability tests, situational judgment tests, and structured

EXHIBIT 11.1 Incremental Validity Assessment

	Task Performance		Innovation	
	Validity	**Increment**	**Validity**	**Increment**
Cognitive ability	0.35	0.27	0.28	0.20
Conscientiousness	0.18	0.12	0.08	0.02
Situational judgment	0.43	0.13	0.35	0.14
Structure interview	0.22	0.18	0.39	0.33

interviews. In the exhibit, the validity column shows good prediction from cognitive ability (r = .35) and situational judgment (r = .43). However, college GPA is highly correlated with situational judgment for this job, since the material on the situational judgment test is very similar to that encountered in operations classes. As a result, cognitive ability adds more predictive power to the existing system (increment = .27), while situational judgment tests add less (increment = .13). Similarly, situational judgment has a good individual validity in predicting innovation (r = .35) but adds little incremental value relative to the existing selection on GPA (increment = .14). The structured interview is a better additional measure for this outcome (increment = .33). It seems that using a combination of cognitive ability and structured interview scores is the best option, since the existing selection system does not assess these constructs very well.

Hiring Success Gain

Hiring success refers to the proportion of new hires who turn out to be successful on the job. Hiring success *gain* refers to the increase in the proportion of successful new hires that is expected to occur as a result of adding a new predictor to the selection system. This is closely related to incremental prediction, except rather than just describing changes in validity, the results take the applicant pool and job difficulty into account. Thus, gain is influenced not only by the validity of the new predictor but also by the selection ratio and base rate.

Selection Ratio

The selection ratio is the number of people hired divided by the number of applicants (sr = number hired / number of applicants). When the company has a large number of applicants for an opening, the selection ratio is low, and the company can freely pick its most preferred applicants from a large pool. On the other hand, when the selection ratio is high, there are few applicants for openings, and the company needs to hire nearly every applicant. On an operational level, the more successful a company's recruiting methods, the higher the selection ratio.

Base Rate

The base rate is the proportion of current employees who are successful (br = number of successful employees / number of employees). When nearly everyone an organization hires can do the job at an acceptable level, the base rate is very high. On the other hand, when many employees are not minimally acceptable, the base rate tends to be lower. On an operation level, the lower the base rate, the more difficult the job is for the average applicant.

Taylor-Russell Tables

Taylor-Russell tables combine information on selection ratios, base rates, and predictor validity coefficients. An excerpt is shown in Exhibit 11.2. As our discussion will show, when the base rate is high and the selection ratio is high, it means that most applicants are successful and you have to hire all of them. In this case, an expensive, time-consuming selection system is probably not helpful. On the other hand, when the base rate is low and the selection ratio is low, it means that only a select few applicants are successful and that there are a lot of applicants for the position. In this case, spending extra time and effort in recruiting is a good idea.

The cells show the percentages of new hires who will be successful. The top matrix (A) shows the percentages of successful new hires when the base rate is low (.30), the validity coefficient is low (.20) or high (.60), and the selection ratio is low (.10) or high (.70). The bottom matrix (B) shows the percentages of successful new hires when the base rate is high (.80), the validity coefficient is low (.20) or high (.60), and the selection ratio is low (.10) or high (.70).

Two illustrations show how these tables may be used.

The first illustration has to do with the decision of whether to use a new test to select computer programmers. The current test has a validity coefficient of .20. A consulting firm has approached the organization with a new test that has a validity coefficient of .60. Should the organization purchase and use the new test?

At first blush, the answer might seem to be yes, because the new test has a substantially higher level of validity. This initial reaction, however, must be gauged in the context of the selection ratio and the current base rate. If the current base rate is .80 and the current selection ratio is .70, then, as can be seen in matrix B of Exhibit 11.2, the new selection procedure will only result in a hiring success gain from 83% to 90%. The organization may already have a very high base rate due to other facets of human resource (HR) management it does quite well (e.g., training, rewards). When most employees are successful, careful selection will not improve success much.

On the other hand, if the existing base rate is .30 and the existing selection ratio is .10, the organization should strongly consider the new test. Few current

---

EXHIBIT 11.2   Excerpt From the Taylor-Russell Tables

A.

	Base Rate = .30	
	Selection Ratio	
Validity	**.10**	**.70**
.20	43%	33
.60	77	40

B.

	Base Rate = .80	
	Selection Ratio	
Validity	**.10**	**.70**
.20	89%	83
.60	99	90

employees are successful, so being able to predict performance can make major improvements. As shown in matrix A of Exhibit 11.2, the hiring success gain will go from 43% to 77% with the addition of the new test.

A second illustration using the Taylor-Russell tables has to do with recruitment in conjunction with selection. Consider the case where the organization's current hiring method, combining a structured job interview and simulation, has a validity of .60. A new college recruitment program has been very aggressive. As a result, there is a large swell in the number of applicants, and the selection ratio has decreased from .70 to .10. Given this, the organization must decide whether to continue the college recruitment program.

An initial reaction may be that the program should be continued because of the large increase in applicants generated. As shown in matrix A of Exhibit 11.2, this answer would be correct if the current base rate is .30. By decreasing the selection ratio from .70 to .10, the hiring success gain increases from 40% to 77%. On the other hand, if the current base rate is .80 (most new hires are already successful), continuing the program probably is not worth it. The hiring success increases from 90% to 99%, which may not justify the very large expense associated with aggressive college recruitment campaigns.

The point of these illustrations is that the decision of whether to use a new predictor depends on the validity coefficient, base rate, and selection ratio. They should not be considered independent of one another. When organizational leaders ask whether they should invest more money in recruiting or in using a new predictor, HR professionals can give a more meaningful answer when considering all of these issues.

Economic Gain

Economic gain refers to the bottom-line or monetary impact of a predictor on the organization. The greater the economic gain the predictor produces, the more useful the predictor. Considerable work has been done over the years in assessing the economic gain associated with predictors. Exhibit 11.3 describes three techniques that have been developed over time and in a variety of disciplines to facilitate predictions of economic gain from using selection tools.[7] The exhibit reviews the sources of information to derive each estimate of economic gain, the economic outcome that is predicted, and links to other areas of the business. This final component is crucial for enhancing the strategic relevance of HR practices, as HR managers are continually urged to put the value of interventions, like staffing, into terms that are well understood by those in finance, marketing, operations, and other functional areas.

Utility Analysis

The first of these procedures is utility analysis. Originally developed by industrial psychologists as a complement to Taylor-Russell tables, this procedure combines the improvement in selection accuracy with information on the financial returns of job performance. In essence, this model multiplies the improved validity from

---

EXHIBIT 11.3   Assessment of Economic Impact

Technique	Sources of Information	What Is Evaluated?	Links to Other Areas
Utility analysis	Data on predictor validity, applicant test scores, and estimated dollar value of performance variability	Expected value of improved job performance if a new selection tool is implemented	Line manager judgments of employee value, expected financial returns for investing in selection
Predictive analytics	Historical information on performance outcomes for business units	Contribution of different characteristics of the workforce to performance outcomes	Existing "hard" data from organizational records for valued outcomes
Kano analysis	Line manager and director descriptions of strategic impact of performance across domains	Changes in economic performance from enhanced levels of different types of employee skills	Tools from marketing, manager judgments regarding critical competencies are incorporated

a new selection tool by the average standardized score of the new hires to show improvement in performance. This improvement in performance is then multiplied by the dollar value of an additional standard deviation in performance over a year, which gives an estimate of the increased revenue for a single individual over that year. Then this value is multiplied by the number of individuals to be hired. Other adjustments can be incorporated, such as taking the costs of recruiting and selection tools into account when assessing economic returns.

The utility approach is highly useful for communication purposes because it takes raw validity and hiring success information and converts it into a dollar metric. Utility analysis has been criticized because of the inherent difficulty in estimating how much additional revenue is produced by a worker who is one standard deviation above the average. However, the same criticism could be put forward for nearly every financial accounting model commonly employed in industry. Ultimately, the utility approach provides a starting point for considering how much financial performance might increase in a job role for a given time period if a new selection procedure is employed.

Predictive Analytics

The planning chapter described how tools like multiple regression could be used to assess future labor demand by determining which variables in previous time periods were associated with higher and lower demand. Predictive analytics uses similar statistical tools, except that different performance metrics become the focus of prediction. For example, an organization might use existing data to predict turnover rates for different departments based on the percentage of employees who had family and friends in the organization, the average level of conscientiousness in each group, and the average level of experience in each group. A regression analysis might show that turnover rates are 10% lower in groups where a majority of employees learned about the job from family members or friends, and that conscientiousness is also negatively related to turnover rates. Or perhaps sales data could be predicted by different levels of employee competence or skill in relationship management, so the organization should hire based on this trait. From this information, the organization can learn which characteristics of new hires or staffing procedures are directly related to economically valued outcomes of interest.

The use of existing operational data on financially valued outcomes in predictive models is the major contribution of predictive analytics approaches. In the past, there may have been some difficulty in collecting enough data to make these predictions, but most contemporary organizations have ample information on performance across employees or groups of employees to easily create predictive analytic models for a variety of KSAOs.

Kano Analysis

Kano analysis, named after Professor Noriaki Kano, was originally designed as a technique to evaluate how customers of a business react to changes in product attributes. The essential insight from this technique is that in some cases, small improvements in certain features of a product can result in a substantial increase in customer interest, whereas in other cases even large improvements will not create much change. To perform these analyses, curves are drawn showing how the level of an outcome relates to changes in the product, usually illustrating points of diminishing returns or increasing returns.

The same logic has been applied to the job performance domain. For example, perhaps sales managers at an online store find that when customer service representatives have high levels of product knowledge and the ability to discuss product features, they are able to significantly increase sales. On the other hand, as long as the individual is at least minimally polite, increases in friendliness produce very small sales gains. This suggests that, for this organization, a minimum bar for politeness is all that is needed, whereas product market knowledge and communication skills should receive more careful attention in selection. Other organizations have found that expertise in production serves as a useful base for performance in operations, and that there is a greater payoff for enhancing expertise in global sourcing.

This comparison of payoffs across performance areas is the essential point that differentiates Kano analysis from other techniques. Kano analysis highlights areas where maximum strategic impact from performance is possible, rather than assuming that all increments in job performance have comparable increments in financial performance. In any of these cases, manager judgments related to critical competencies for economic performance are required, but data from predictive analytics models can be incorporated into these estimates as well. While Kano analysis is not especially useful for quantifying how much economic gain can occur from a change in focus, it is very useful for assessing areas where existing assessment and selection tools are performing adequately, and identifying areas where increased rigor in selection will yield larger improvements in performance.

DETERMINING ASSESSMENT SCORES

Once the predictors for final decision making have been selected, it is necessary to develop procedures for comparing candidates. This process will assign numerical scores to each candidate. These methods vary in complexity, from using a single predictor, to combining information from multiple predictors simultaneously, to sequentially eliminating candidates from consideration at each stage.

Single Predictor

Using a single predictor in selection decisions simplifies the process of determining scores. In fact, scores on the single predictor *are* the final assessment scores. Thus, concerns over how to combine assessment scores are not relevant when a single predictor is used in selection decisions. Although using a single predictor has the advantage of simplicity, there are some obvious drawbacks. First, few employers would feel comfortable hiring applicants on the basis of a single attribute. In fact, almost all employers use multiple methods in selection decisions. A second and related reason for using multiple predictors is that utility increases as the number of valid predictors used in selection decisions increases. In most cases, using two valid selection methods results in more effective selection decisions than using a sole predictor. Unfortunately, in many cases, organizations rely entirely on an unstructured interview, which has already been described as less than desirable because it is inconsistent, low in validity, and potentially difficult to defend in a lawsuit. For these reasons, basing selection decisions on a single predictor is rarely the best way to make decisions.

Multiple Predictors

Given the less-than-perfect validities of predictors, most organizations use multiple predictors in making selection decisions. With multiple predictors, decisions must be made about combining the resultant scores. These decisions can be addressed through compensatory, multiple hurdles, and combined approaches.

Compensatory Model

With a compensatory model, scores on one predictor are simply added to scores on another predictor to yield a total score. This means that high scores on one predictor can compensate for low scores on another. For example, if an employer is using an interview and GPA to select a person, an applicant with a low GPA who does well in the interview may still get the job.

The advantage of a compensatory model is that it recognizes that people have multiple talents and that many different constellations of talents may produce success on the job. The disadvantage of a compensatory model is that, at least for some jobs, the level of proficiency for specific talents cannot be compensated for by other proficiencies. For example, a firefighter requires a certain level of strength that cannot be compensated for by intelligence.

In terms of using the compensatory model to make decisions, four procedures may be followed: clinical prediction, unit weighting, rational weighting, and multiple regression. The four methods differ from one another in terms of the manner in which predictor scores are weighted before being added together for a total or composite score.

Exhibit 11.4 illustrates these procedures. Differences in weighting methods are shown in the bottom part of Exhibit 11.4, and a selection system consisting of interviews, application blanks, and recommendations is shown in the top part. For simplicity, assume that scores on each predictor have been standardized to fit in a range from 1 to 5. Scores on these three predictors are shown for three applicants.

EXHIBIT 11.4   Raw Scores for Applicants on Three Predictors

	Predictor		
Applicant	Interview	Application Blank	Recommendation
A	3	5	2
B	4	3	4
C	5	4	3

Clinical Prediction
$P_1, P_2, P_3 \rightarrow$ Subjective assessment of qualifications
Example: Select applicant A based on "gut feeling" for overall qualification level.

Unit Weighting
$P_1 + P_2 + P_3$ = Total score
Example: All predictor scores are added together.
Applicant A = 3 + 5 + 2 = 10
Applicant B = 4 + 3 + 4 = 11
Applicant C = 5 + 4 + 3 = 12

Rational Weighting
$w_1P_1 + w_2P_2 + w_3P_3$ = Total score
Example: Weights are set by manager judgment at w_1 = .5, w_2 = .3, w_3 = .2
Applicant A = (.5 × 3) + (.3 × 5) + (.2 × 2) = 3.4
Applicant B = (.5 × 4) + (.3 × 3) + (.2 × 4) = 3.7
Applicant C = (.5 × 5) + (.3 × 4) + (.2 × 3) = 4.3

Multiple Regression
$a + b_1P_1 + b_2P_2 + b_3P_3$ = Total score
Example: Weights are set by statistical procedures at a = .09, b_1 = .9, b_2 = .6, b_3 = .2
Applicant A = .09 + (.9 × 3) + (.6 × 5) + (.2 × 2) = 6.19
Applicant B = .09 + (.9 × 4) + (.6 × 3) + (.2 × 4) = 6.29
Applicant C = .09 + (.9 × 5) + (.6 × 4) + (.2 × 3) = 7.59

Clinical Prediction.   In the clinical prediction approach in Exhibit 11.4, managers use their expert judgment to arrive at a total score for each applicant. That final score may or may not be a simple addition of the three predictor scores shown in the exhibit. Hence, applicant A may be given a higher total score than applicant B even though simple addition shows that applicant B had one more point (4 + 3 + 4 = 11) than applicant A (3 + 5 + 2 = 10).

Frequently, clinical prediction is done by initial screening interviewers or hiring managers. These decision makers may or may not have "scores" per se, but they have multiple pieces of information on each applicant, and they make a decision on the applicant by taking everything into account. For example, when making an initial screening decision on an applicant, a manager at a fast-food restaurant might subjectively combine their impressions of various bits of information about the applicant on the application form and a quick interview. A hiring manager for a professional position might focus on a finalist's résumé and answers to the manager's interview questions to decide whether to extend an offer to the finalist.

The advantage of the clinical prediction approach is that it draws on the expertise of managers to weight and combine predictor scores. In turn, managers may be more likely to accept the selection decisions. Unfortunately, this preference usually is embedded in overconfidence. Many managers believe that basing decisions on their experiences, rather than on mechanical scoring, makes them better at judging which applicants will be successful.[8] The problem is that the reasons for the weightings are known only to the manager. In addition, clinical predictions have been consistently shown to be less accurate than mechanical decisions. Research has shown again and again that experts who rely on intuition are less capable of accurately combining information compared with using a standardized system based on mathematical tools for combining information. This finding has been replicated in domains such as picking stocks, making medical diagnoses, granting university admission to students, and hiring employees.[9]

Unit Weighting. With unit weighting, each predictor is weighted the same at a value of 1.00. As shown in Exhibit 11.4, the predictor scores are simply added together to generate a total score. Therefore, the total scores for applicants A, B, and C are 10, 11, and 12, respectively. The advantage of unit weighting is that it is a simple and straightforward process and makes the importance of each predictor explicit to decision makers. The problem with this approach is that it assumes each predictor contributes equally to the prediction of job success, which is often not the case.

Rational Weighting. With rational weighting, each predictor receives a differential rather than equal weighting. Managers and other subject matter experts (SMEs) establish the weights for each predictor according to the degree to which each is believed to predict job success. These weights (w) are then multiplied by each raw score (P) to yield a total score, as shown in Exhibit 11.4.

For example, the predictors are weighted .5, .3, and .2 for the interview, application blank, and recommendation, respectively. This means managers think interviews are the most important predictors, followed by application blanks, and then recommendations. Each applicant's raw score is multiplied by the appropriate weight to yield a total score. For example, the total score for applicant A is $(.5)3 + (.3)5 + (.2)2 = 3.4$.

The advantage of this approach is that it considers the relative importance of each predictor and makes this assessment explicit. The downside, however, is that it is an elaborate procedure that requires managers and SMEs to agree on the differential weights to be applied.

Multiple Regression.   Multiple regression is similar to rational weighting in that the predictors receive different weights. With multiple regression, however, the weights are established on the basis of statistical procedures rather than on judgments by managers or other SMEs. The statistical weights are developed from (1) the correlation of each predictor with the criterion, and (2) the correlations among the predictors. As a result, regression weights provide optimal weights in the sense that they will yield the highest total validity.

The calculations result in a multiple regression formula like the one shown in Exhibit 11.4. A total score for each applicant is obtained by multiplying the statistical weight (b) for each predictor by the predictor (P) score and summing these along with the intercept value (a). As an example, assume the statistical weights are .9, .6, and .2 for the interview, application blank, and recommendation, respectively, and that the intercept is .09. Using these values, the total score for applicant A is $.09 + (.9)3 + (.6)5 + (.2)2 = 6.19$.

Multiple regression offers the possibility of a higher degree of precision in the prediction of criterion scores than do the other methods of weighting. Unfortunately, this level of precision is realized only under a certain set of circumstances. In particular, for multiple regression to be more precise than unit weighting, there must be a small number of predictors, low correlations between predictor variables, and a large sample that is similar to the population that will be tested.[10] Many selection settings do not meet these criteria, so in these cases consideration should be given either to unit or rational weighting or to alternative regression-based weighting schemes that have been developed, such as general dominance weights or relative importance weights.[11] In situations where these conditions are met, however, multiple regression weights can produce higher validity and utility than the other weighting schemes.

Choosing Among Weighting Schemes.   The choice of the best weighting scheme is consequential and likely depends on answers to the most important questions about clinical, unit, rational, and multiple regression schemes:

- For clinical weighting: Do selection decision makers have considerable experience and insight into selection decisions, and is managerial acceptance of the selection process important?
- For unit weighting: Is there reason to believe that each predictor contributes relatively equally to job success?
- For rational weighting: Are there differences in importance across predictor areas, and can these be better assessed through judgment rather than through statistical tools?
- For regression weighting: Are the conditions under which multiple regression is superior (relatively small number of predictors, low correlations among predictors, and large sample) satisfied?

Answers to these questions will go a long way toward deciding which weighting scheme to use. We should also note that while statistical weighting is more valid than clinical weighting, the combination of both methods may yield the highest validity. One study indicated that regression-weighted predictors were more valid than clinical judgments, but that clinical judgments contributed uniquely to performance after controlling for regression-weighted predictors. Other work shows that when there are high levels of uncertainty, an expert-guided decision process can take context into account and result in better selection decisions than a raw regression analysis using prior data. Finally, managers are more accepting of statistically based decision rules if they are able to have input into the process. This suggests that both statistical tools and clinical judgments have contributions to make. In other words, the weighting schemes are not necessarily mutually exclusive and may be complementary.[12]

Multiple Hurdles Model

With a multiple hurdles approach, an applicant must earn a passing score on each predictor before advancing in the selection process. Such an approach is taken when each requirement measured by a predictor is critical to job success. The decision to move a candidate forward is based on either a top-down selection from early predictor scores (or through the use of cut scores at some stages) or a top-down selection for later stages (discussed in the next section). Unlike the compensatory model, the multiple hurdles model does not allow a high score on one predictor to compensate for a low score on another predictor, because some individuals have no scores on some predictors.

Many organizations use multiple hurdles selection systems to both reduce the cost of selecting applicants and make the decision-making process more tractable in the final selection stage. It would be very inefficient to process all the possible information the organization might collect on a large number of candidates, so some candidates are screened out relatively early in the process. Typically, the first stage of a selection process screens the applicant pool down to those who meet some minimal educational or years-of-experience requirement. Collecting information on such requirements is fairly inexpensive for organizations and can usually be readily quantified. After this stage, the pool of remaining applicants might be further reduced by administering relatively inexpensive standardized tests to those who passed the initial screen. Further reducing the pool of potential candidates allows the organization to devote more resources to interviewing finalists and having them meet with managers at the organization's headquarters. This is the selection stage. There are many variations in how the multiple hurdles model can be implemented, and the exact nature of the "screen" versus "select" measures will vary based on the job requirements.

Combined Model

For jobs where some but not all requirements are critical to job success, a combined method involving both the compensatory and the multiple hurdles models may be used. The process starts with the multiple hurdles model and ends with the compensatory method.

EXHIBIT 11.5 Combined Model for Recruitment Manager

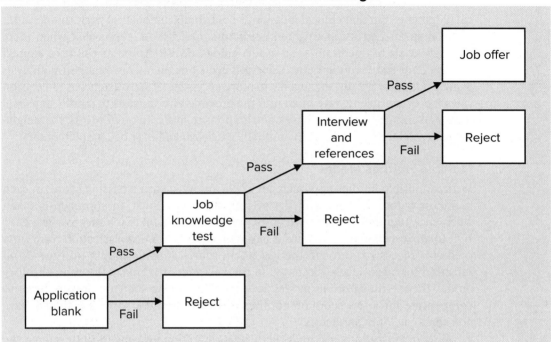

An example of the combined approach for the position of recruitment manager is shown in Exhibit 11.5. The selection process starts with two hurdles that applicants must pass in succession: the application blank and the job knowledge test. Failure to clear either hurdle results in rejection. Applicants who pass receive an interview and have their references checked. Information from the interview and the references is combined in a compensatory manner. Those who pass are offered jobs, and those who do not pass are rejected.

HIRING STANDARDS AND CUT SCORES

Hiring standards or cut scores address the issue of what constitutes a minimally qualified candidate. The purpose of establishing cut scores is twofold. First, selection decision makers can eliminate individuals below the cut from further consideration and focus their attention on evaluating and attracting the most qualified candidates. Second, legal compliance requires defining what constitutes a minimally qualified candidate. Cut scores rigorously establish what constitutes these minimal qualifications.

Description of the Process

Once one or more predictors have been chosen, a decision must be made as to who advances in the selection process. This decision requires that one or more cut scores be established. A cut score is the score that separates those who advance in the process (e.g., applicants who become candidates) from those who are rejected. For example, assume a test is used on which scores range from 0 to 100 points. A cut score of 70 means that those applicants with a 70 or higher would advance, while all others would be rejected for employment purposes. A cut score also needs to be established for jobs where there will be ongoing hiring needs. For example, even when a compensatory model is used, there might be a minimum standard on one predictor that would completely rule out a candidate no matter how well he or she performed on other parts of the process. In some cases, legal requirements mandating minimum hiring standards must be considered, such as a passing score on a nursing licensure exam.

Consequences of Cut Scores

Setting a cut score is a very important process, as it has consequences for the organization and the applicant. The consequences of cut scores are shown in Exhibit 11.6, which contains a summary of a scatter diagram of predictor and criterion scores. The horizontal line shows the criterion score at which the organization has determined whether an employee is successful or unsuccessful—for example, a 3 on a 5-point performance appraisal scale where 1 is low performance and 5 is high performance. The vertical line is the cut score for the predictor—for example, a 3 on a 5-point interview rating scale where 1 reveals no chance of success and 5 a high chance of success.

The consequences of setting the cut score at a particular level are shown in each of the quadrants. Quadrants A and C represent correct decisions, which have positive consequences for the organization. Quadrant A applicants are called true positives because they were assessed as having a high chance of success using the predictor and would have succeeded if hired. Quadrant C applicants are called true negatives because they were assessed as having little chance for success and, indeed, would not be successful if hired.

Quadrants D and B represent incorrect decisions, which have negative consequences for the organization and affected applicants. Quadrant D applicants are called false negatives because they were assessed as not being likely to succeed, but had they been hired, they would have been successful. Not only was an incorrect decision reached, but a person who would have done well was not hired. Quadrant B applicants are called false positives. They were assessed as being likely to succeed, but would have ended up being unsuccessful performers. Eventually, these people would need to receive remedial training, be transferred to a new job, or even be terminated.

EXHIBIT 11.6   Consequences of Cut Scores

Criterion	Predictor Cut Score	
	D	A
Successful	False negatives	True positives
	C	B
Unsuccessful	True negatives	False positives
	No hire	Hire

Predictor

How high or low a cut score is set has a large impact on the consequences shown in Exhibit 11.6, and trade-offs are always involved. Compared with the moderate cut score in the exhibit, a high cut score results in fewer false positives but a larger number of false negatives. Is this a good, bad, or inconsequential set of outcomes for the organization? The answer depends on the job open for selection and the costs involved. If the job is an astronaut position for NASA, it is essential that there be no false positives. The cost of a false positive may be the loss of human life.

Now consider the consequences of a low cut score, relative to the one shown in Exhibit 11.6. There are fewer false negatives and more true positives, but more false positives are hired. In organizations that gain competitive advantage in their industry by hiring the very best, this set of consequences may be unacceptable. Alternatively, for EEO/AA purposes it may be desirable to have a low cut score so that the number of false negatives for underrepresented groups is minimized.

Methods to Determine Cut Scores

The setting of ideal cut scores for proficiency has received a great deal of attention in educational psychology, occupational licensure, and organizational practice.[13] Although there are complex analytic techniques that can be brought to bear in solving an ideal cut score, the core ideas can be boiled down into compensatory minimum standards, conjunctive minimum standards, and maximum standards. Each of these is described below, along with professional guidelines for setting cut scores. As shown in Exhibit 11.7, the example organization has evaluated applicant

EXHIBIT 11.7   Use of Cut Scores in Selection Decisions

| | Evaluation Scores | | | | Cut Score Methods | | | | | |
| | | | | | | | Conjunctive | | | |
Applicant	Exp	Jknow	Int	Total	Compensatory	Jknow	Exp	Int	Maximum
Black	6	4	3	13	Fail	Pass	Fail	Fail	Pass
Boseman	1	4	2	7	Fail	Fail	Fail	Fail	Pass
Nguyen	10	7	8	25	Pass	Pass	Pass	Pass	Pass
Garcia	9	4	8	21	Pass	Pass	Fail	Pass	Pass
Gurira	8	4	4	16	Fail	Pass	Fail	Fail	Pass
Jones	4	4	3	11	Fail	Fail	Fail	Fail	Pass
Kaluuya	10	8	9	27	Pass	Pass	Pass	Pass	Fail
Chang	8	2	4	14	Fail	Pass	Fail	Fail	Pass
Patil	5	8	4	17	Pass	Pass	Pass	Fail	Pass
Perez	2	8	3	13	Fail	Fail	Fail	Fail	Pass
Shah	9	8	10	27	Pass	Pass	Pass	Pass	Fail
Smith	8	7	8	23	Pass	Pass	Pass	Pass	Pass
Steel	4	8	9	21	Pass	Fail	Pass	Pass	Pass
Wang	8	9	7	24	Pass	Pass	Pass	Pass	Pass
Weasley	8	3	3	14	Fail	Pass	Fail	Fail	Pass

Minimum total for compensatory cut = 17
Minimum for each predictor in conjunctive cut = 5
Maximum total for maximum cut = 27

job knowledge, experience, and interview scores. All of these numbers have been converted into a standardized metric so they can be combined sensibly.

The Angoff method is a rigorous approach to establishing cut points based on a consensus of SMEs.[14] In this approach, SMEs review the content of the predictor (e.g., test items) and determine the proportion of individuals with a minimum level of competence who would answer each item correctly. For example, experts might estimate that at least 75% of minimally qualified electricians would be able to define the term "ampacity" on a quiz. The experts might estimate that only 25% would be able to identify a bonding jumper. These ratings can then be summed together to obtain a minimal cut score for a compensatory cut score, or evaluated as distinct for a set of conjunctive cut scores. The results of this procedure are dependent on the SMEs. It is very difficult to get members of the organization to agree on who "the" SMEs are. Which SMEs are selected may have a bearing on the actual cut scores developed. There may also be judgmental errors and biases in how cut scores are set. If the Angoff method is used, it is important that SMEs be provided with a common definition of minimally competent test takers and encouraged to discuss their estimates. Each of these steps has been found to increase the reliability of the SME scores.[15] Standards for these minimum scores established through the Angoff method can take the form of either a compensatory or a conjunctive model.

Minimum Competency

Using the minimum competency method, the cut score is set on the basis of the minimum qualifications deemed necessary to perform the job across multiple dimensions. This approach is often needed in situations where the first step in the hiring process is the demonstration of minimum skill requirements. Exhibit 11.7 illustrates the use of cut scores in selection. The scores of 15 applicants on a qualification method are listed. The cut score for each minimum qualification method is set at the level at which applicants who score below the line are deemed unqualified for the job.

Compensatory Cut Scores.   We have already mentioned compensatory scoring in our discussion of determining assessment scores. This same approach can be used for setting cut scores. In this model, a single aggregate measure of performance is used to select the cut score for applicants. Thus, in Exhibit 11.7, all applicants who scored below the minimum total score of 17 are deemed unqualified and are rejected, and all applicants who scored 17 or above are deemed at least minimally qualified. Hiring managers in this organization believe that strong job knowledge test scores, for example, can offset a lack of experience, or a candidate who had a great interview may have what it takes to learn the job. The shaded cells indicate that several candidates meet this minimum threshold (Garcia, Kaluuya, Nguyen, Patil, Shah, Smith, Steel, and Wang).

Conjunctive Cut Scores.   The compensatory method looks to some aggregate model of minimum qualifications. In practice, many organizations have multiple sets of cut points that must be independently satisfied. In this case, the preference changes to conjunctive scoring. As shown in Exhibit 11.7, the organization developed minimum acceptable scores on applicant job knowledge, a minimum level of experience, and a minimum score on person-group fit from an interview. These are all very different types of predictors, and the hiring managers in the organization think that applicants who are below standards on any of these cannot do the job adequately. The shaded cells demonstrate that several candidates who would have been hired under the compensatory model (Garcia, Patil, and Steel) would not be hired through the conjunctive model because of individual scores below 5.

Maximum Competency

One variant on the minimum competency approach is to impose a maximum competency to identify overqualified applicants. The assumption here is that the job will not be sufficiently rewarding and the overqualified employee will quickly quit. In Exhibit 11.7, the unshaded cells in the maximum competency column indicate that Kaluuya and Shah might be rejected for being *too* qualified, since their total scores were at or above the threshold of 27.

Evidence suggests that employees who perceive themselves to be overqualified for their jobs report lower levels of job satisfaction and higher intentions to leave.[16] This may be because individuals who feel that they are overqualified believe that they deserve a better job and that their present work does not sufficiently challenge them. Employers can use tactics like increasing employee empowerment to alleviate these feelings among overqualified employees and therefore allow the organization to retain individuals who have exceptional levels of skills.[17] Managers should exercise caution before automatically rejecting individuals who appear to be overqualified. Sometimes people are interested in a job for reasons unknown to the hiring manager. There are also legal dangers, as many apparently overqualified applicants are over the age of 40. As one manager said, "I think it's a huge mistake not to take a second look at overqualified candidates. Certainly there are valid reasons to reject some candidates, but it shouldn't be a blanket response."[18]

METHODS OF FINAL CHOICE

The discussion thus far has been on decision rules that can be used to narrow down the list of people to successively smaller groups that advance in the selection process from applicant to candidate to finalist. How does the organization determine which finalists will receive job offers? Discretionary assessments about the finalists must be converted into final choice decisions. The methods of final choice are the mechanisms by which discretionary assessments are translated into job offer decisions.

Methods of final choice include random selection, ranking, and grouping. Examples of each of these methods are shown in Exhibit 11.8, continuing with the applicants who passed the initial screen in Exhibit 11.7.

Random Selection

With random selection, each finalist has an equal chance of being selected. The only rationale for selecting a person is the "luck of the draw." For example, the eight names from Exhibit 11.8 could be put in a hat and the finalist drawn out and tendered a job offer. This approach has the advantage of being quick. In addition, with random selection, one cannot be accused of favoritism, because everyone has an equal chance of being selected. The disadvantage of this approach is that discretionary assessments are simply ignored.

Although hiring at random from available candidates is obviously inferior to methods that use selection measures to identify the best candidates, many organizations end up hiring somewhat randomly when they are forced to hire the first acceptable candidate. When the hiring process is continuous, there is never a final list of candidates to choose from. Instead, ongoing needs might require continuously collecting résumés from interested parties, and then when positions open up, calling in everyone who passes the minimum qualifications for open jobs for interviews. This means hiring managers never see a total pool of candidates from which to choose the finalists. Hiring based on the first acceptable candidate is also used when the organization, because of staffing shortages, needs to hire anyone who meets the minimum competency level. Jobs with very high turnover rates, like entry-level retail and food service positions, are typically staffed in this way. While hiring the first acceptable candidate may seem necessary, it is far from an ideal hiring strategy and the costs may not be revealed until it is too late.

Ranking

With ranking, finalists are ordered from the most desirable to the least desirable based on results of discretionary assessments. As shown in Exhibit 11.8, Kaluuya and Shah are tied for first in terms of preferences, whereas Patil is the least preferred. It is important to note that desirability should be viewed in the context of the entire selection process. In this case, persons with lower levels of desirability should not be viewed necessarily as unacceptable. All of the remaining applicants have passed the minimum cut score for qualifications. Job offers are extended to people on the basis of their rank ordering, with the top-ranked person receiving the first offer. Should that person turn down the job offer or withdraw from the selection process, finalist number 2 receives the offer, and so on.

The advantage of ranking is that it indicates the relative worth of each finalist for the job. Using all selection measures is the best way to obtain maximum validity. All the information available on candidates is used in the same way, so the rules

EXHIBIT 11.8 Methods of Final Choice

| Applicant | Evaluation Scores | | | | | Selection Choices | | | |
	Exp	Jknow	Int	Total	Weight	Random	Ranking	Grouping	Weighted
Nguyen	10	7	8	25	7.7	2	3	1st round	5
Garcia	9	4	8	21	6.1	1	6 (tie)	Wait list	7 (tie)
Kaluuya	10	8	9	27	8.6	5	1 (tie)	1st round	2
Patil	5	8	4	17	6.1	7	8	Wait list	7 (tie)
Shah	9	8	10	27	8.9	8	1 (tie)	1st round	1
Smith	8	7	8	23	7.5	4	5	Wait list	6
Steel	4	8	9	21	8	6	6 (tie)	Wait list	4
Wang	8	9	7	24	8.1	3	4	1st round	3

are fair and the process is transparent. It also provides a set of backups should one or more of the finalists withdraw from the process.

Grouping and Banding

For both external hiring and internal promotions, the top-down method will yield the highest validity and utility. This method has been criticized, however, for ignoring the possibility that small differences between scores are due to measurement error. The top-down method also makes it hard to incorporate other outcomes, like diversity or a sense of cultural fit. With the grouping method, more flexibility in use of managerial discretion is maintained as finalists are banded together into rank-ordered categories. In Exhibit 11.8, the finalists are grouped according to whether they are top choices or on the wait list. The advantage of this method is that it permits ties among finalists, thus avoiding the need to assign a different rank to each person. In other words, grouping means applicants who score within a certain score range or band are considered to have scored equivalently. A simple grouping procedure is provided in Exhibit 11.8. In this case, a group of top applicants available for first-round selection were identified based on having a total score of 23 or higher. Hiring within bands could then be done based on a variety of other factors, including workforce composition, perceived fit, or likelihood of accepting a job offer. In practice, band widths are usually calculated on the basis of the standard error of measurement.

Differential Weighting

A differential weighting approach to hiring is very similar to the ranking approach but allows for approaches like rational or multiple regression weights for the most important predictors. In Exhibit 11.8, this is represented in the column of "weight" scores. The organization decided that experience was relatively unimportant for performance, so it received a weight of 0.1; job knowledge was very important, so it received a weight of 0.5; and interview performance was moderately important, so it received a weight of 0.4. The results of the weighting procedure do change some of the conclusions in this case. Note that Wang, who did exceptionally well on the job knowledge test, moves from fourth in the raw score ranking to third in the weighted ranking, whereas Kaluuya, who is exceptionally experienced, moves from a tie for first to second place.

Incorporating Diversity

We noted earlier that there are multiple techniques to evaluate whether predictors have disparate impact, and evaluate whether to replace those with disparate impact with those that are more likely to maintain diversity. However, there are also methods that have been developed to address diversity goals after administration of selection measures.[19]

The application of the technique of grouping scores, as described earlier, and then selecting from these groups to foster inclusion of underrepresented groups is called "banding." This should not be confused with group-based scoring (i.e., one set of standards for one demographic group and different standards for another), which is prohibited. Rather, when there are multiple candidates with similar scores, preference is given to those who belong to underrepresented groups. For example, in Exhibit 11.8, we might note that the applicant Nguyen, who is from a group that is underrepresented in the organization, is in the first round (based on qualifications) and might be preferred for selection.

Research suggests that banding procedures result in substantial decreases in the disparate impact of cognitive ability tests. The major limitation with banding is that it sacrifices validity. Obviously, taking scores on a 100-point test and lumping applicants into only two groups wastes a great deal of important information on applicants. There is also evidence that typical banding procedures overestimate the width of bands, which of course exacerbates the problem.[20] Organizations considering the use of banding in personnel selection decisions must weigh the pros and cons carefully, including the legal issues. A review of lawsuits concerning banding found that it was generally upheld by the courts.[21] In the end, however, a values choice may need to be made: to optimize validity (to some detriment to diversity) or to optimize diversity (with some sacrifice in validity).

In an effort to resolve this somewhat pessimistic trade-off between validity and diversity goals, alternative techniques closer to the differential weighting approach have been proposed. One advantage of these alternatives is that most retain the decision-making logic of top-down selection, which is generally perceived as fairer by members of both majority and underrepresented groups. Some researchers have developed differential weighting schemes that attempt to find optimal solutions that maximize validity and diversity. One effort produced a statistical algorithm that attempts to achieve an optimal trade-off between validity and disparate impact by giving more weight to predictors that have less disparate impact. Such algorithms allow decision makers to more clearly see the trade-offs for different choices, and do tend to produce some solutions with lower disparate impact and comparable validity to unit weighting predictors.[22]

Other work has evaluated the use of multistage selection procedures, as we described previously.[23] Most evidence suggests that using lower disparate impact predictors, such as integrity tests, structured interviews, and conscientiousness tests, early in selection, and then incorporating higher disparate impact predictors, such as ability tests, later in the process tends to have the effect of lowering disparate impact earlier in the process. Validity levels are comparable. Simply put, the early screen should minimize disparate impact.

DECISION MAKERS

A final consideration in decision making for selection is who should participate in the decisions. That is, who should determine the process to be followed (e.g., establishing cut scores), and who should determine the outcome (e.g., who gets the job offer)? The answer is that organizational leaders, HR professionals, and line managers must play a role.[24] Employees may play certain roles as well. Each of these parties has its own specialized knowledge and outlook that can greatly facilitate the successful implementation of the selection system. Exhibit 11.9 demonstrates the level of involvement in the decision-making process in staffing of each of these parties.

Organizational Leaders

Selection systems can have a huge impact on organizational capabilities and performance, so leaders of the organization, including executives and directors, will have some input into decision making. Leaders have a uniquely valuable, holistic understanding of the purpose of a selection system. Having buy-in from organizational

EXHIBIT 11.9   Decision Makers in Selection

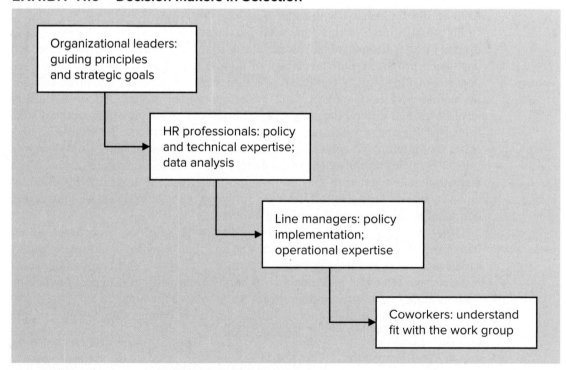

leaders also greatly enhances the success of any policy initiative.[25] This support will be far greater when leaders are able to describe the goals of the selection system.

Organizational leaders can serve several functions in the design and implementation of selection systems. First, they can develop a philosophy of staffing systems that links to the organization's strategy and is compelling for line managers. Second, leaders are in a good position to develop policies and procedures for the entire organization that fit with the organization's culture overall. Third, besides articulating an overall philosophy of the selection system, leaders can coordinate competency modeling with organizational plans and goals from the top down. This means specific attributes to be measured are determined based on input from organizational leaders. Finally, leaders can ensure that the metrics gathered through the staffing process are relevant for organizational success, so the efficacy of the system in meeting relevant goals is ensured. This can help HR professionals communicate effectively in terms that matter to leaders. Except in the smallest organizations, leaders will not participate in most day-to-day hiring, but as this discussion shows, their guidance in structuring the selection system should not be overlooked.

Human Resource Professionals

HR professionals should be consulted in matters such as which predictors to use and how to best use them. In particular, they need to orchestrate the development of policies and procedures to ensure the best selection outcomes. These professionals have, or know where to find, the technical expertise needed to develop sound selection decisions. They also have access to quantitative information from HR information systems that can be used to quantify predictor-outcome relationships within the organization. Finally, they can represent the interests and concerns of employees to management.

Although the primary role HR professionals should play is in terms of the process, they should also have some involvement in determining who receives job offers. HR professionals may be able to provide an external perspective on applicants. For example, they may be able to offer some insight on the applicants' fit with the broader set of competencies across the organization. They may have more fine-grained data to contribute to the process as a result of their screening interviews, knowledge of how to interpret standard selection instruments (e.g., personality tests), and interactions with internal candidates (e.g., serving on task forces with the candidates).

The other area where HR professionals may contribute to outcomes is in terms of initial assessment methods. Many times, HR professionals are empowered to make initial screening decisions, such as who gets invited into the organization for administration of the next round of selection. Doing so saves managers time and allows them to concentrate their efforts on the most promising candidates. In addition, HR professionals can ensure the overall diversity of the applicant pool.

Managers

As a general rule, a manager's primary involvement in staffing is in determining who is selected for employment. Managers are the SMEs for their business areas, and they are thus held accountable for the success of the people hired. They are far less involved in determining the processes followed to staff the organization, because they often do not have the time or expertise to do so. The average manager also is unlikely to have extensive knowledge regarding the more technical details of designing and implementing selection systems.[26]

Although they may not play a direct role in establishing processes, managers should be periodically consulted on process issues. They will be in a good position to identify critical needs in the selection system that might not be addressed, and can also identify areas where the policies and procedures are too complex or burdensome to be effective. Their work with new hires can also identify characteristics that are important for getting up to speed quickly in specific roles.

An additional benefit of allowing management a role in process issues is that, as a result of their involvement, managers may develop a better understanding of why HR professionals prescribe certain practices. When they are not invited to be part of the process to establish staffing policy and procedures, line managers may view HR professionals as obstacles to hiring the right person for the job. In this case, it is likely that managers will not make an effort to implement the selection system effectively.[27] And as a final concern, the more managers participate in the process of selecting specific individuals to work under them, the more likely it is that they will find the new hire acceptable and will support their development.

Coworkers

Traditionally, coworkers of the new hire have not been considered part of the decision-making process in staffing, but this tradition is slowly changing. For example, in team assessment approaches, coworkers may have a voice in both the staffing process and its outcomes. That is, they may have ideas about how selection procedures are established, and they may make decisions about, or provide input into, who gets hired. Involvement in the team approach is encouraged because it may give group members a sense of ownership of the work process and help them better identify with organizational goals. Also, it may result in selecting members who are more compatible with the goals of the work team. Google includes line managers and peers in its hiring process. Its consensus-based hiring process is seen as a valuable way to get a variety of perspectives on the fit between applicants and the organization.[28] In order for employee involvement to be effective, employees need to be provided with staffing training just as managers are.

LEGAL ISSUES

One of the most important legal issues in decision making is that of establishing cut scores or hiring standards. These scores or standards regulate the flow of individuals from applicant to candidate to finalist to new hire. Throughout this flow, disparate impact may occur. When it does, the UGESP come into play. In addition, the organization could form a multipronged strategy for increasing workforce diversity.

Uniform Guidelines on Employee Selection Procedures

If the use of cut scores does not lead to disparate impact in decision making, the UGESP are essentially silent on the issue of cut scores. The discretion exercised by the organization as it makes its selection decisions is thus unconstrained legally. If disparate impact is occurring, the UGESP become directly applicable to decision making.

Under conditions of disparate impact, the UGESP require the organization to either eliminate its occurrence or justify it by conducting validity studies and carefully setting cut scores:

> Where cutoff scores are used, they should normally be set as to be reasonable and consistent with normal expectations of acceptable proficiency within the workforce. Where applicants are ranked on the basis of properly validated selection procedures and those applicants scoring below a higher cutoff score than appropriate in light of such expectations have little or no chance of being selected for employment, the higher cutoff score may be appropriate, but the degree of adverse impact should be considered.

This provision suggests that the organization should be cautious in general about setting cut scores that are above those necessary to achieve acceptable proficiency among those hired. In other words, even with a valid predictor, the organization should be cautious that its hiring standards are not so high that they create needless disparate impact. This is particularly true with ranking systems. Use of random methods—or to a lesser extent, grouping methods—would help overcome this particular objection to ranking systems.

Whatever cut score procedure is used, the UGESP also require that the organization be able to document its establishment and operation. Specifically, the UGESP say that "if the selection procedure is used with a cutoff score, the user should describe the way in which normal expectations of proficiency within the workforce were determined and the way in which the cutoff score was determined."

The UGESP also suggest two options to eliminate disparate impact rather than to justify it as in the validation and cut score approach. One option is use of "alternative procedures." Here, the organization uses an alternative selection procedure that causes less disparate impact (e.g., work sample instead of a written test) but has roughly the same validity as the procedure it replaces.

The other option is that of affirmative action. The UGESP do not relieve the organization of any affirmative action obligations it may have. Also, the UGESP strive to "encourage the adoption and implementation of voluntary affirmative action programs" for organizations that do not have any affirmative action obligations.

Diversity and Hiring Decisions

There has been considerable controversy and litigation over the issue of whether it is permissible for a legally protected characteristic such as race or gender to enter into a staffing decision, and if so, under exactly what circumstances. At the crux of the matter is whether staffing decisions should be based solely on a person's qualifications or on qualifications along with the protected characteristic. It is argued that allowing the protected characteristic to receive some weight in the decision would serve to create a more diverse workforce, which many public and private organizations claim is something they have a compelling interest in and responsibility to do (refer back to the planning chapter and the discussion of affirmative action).

It can be concluded that unless the organization is under a formal affirmative action plan (AAP), protected characteristics (e.g., race, sex, and religion) should not be considered in selection decision making. This conclusion is consistent with Equal Employment Opportunity Commission (EEOC) policy: the organization should use job-related hiring standards, and the same selection techniques and weights must be used for all people.[29]

How should the organization proceed, especially if it wants to not only comply with the law but also increase the diversity of its workforce? Several things might be done. First, carefully establish KSAOs for jobs so that they are truly job related; as part of that process, establish some job-related KSAOs that correlate with protected characteristics, such as diversity in experience and customer contacts. For example, a KSAO for the job of marketing manager might be "substantial contacts within diverse racial and ethnic communities." Both White and nonWhite applicants could potentially meet this requirement, increasing the chances of recruiting and selecting a person of color for the job. Second, use recruitment (both external and internal) as a tool for attracting a more qualified and diverse applicant pool. Third, use valid methods of KSAO assessment derived from a formal selection plan. Fourth, avoid clinical or excessively subjective prediction in making the assessment and deriving a total assessment or score for candidates. Instead, establish and use the same set of predictors and weights for them to arrive at the final assessment. Fifth, provide training in selection decision making for hiring managers and staffing managers. Content of the training should focus on overcoming the use of stereotypes, learning how to gather and weight predictor information consistently for all candidates, and looking for red flags about acceptance or rejection based on vague judgments about the candidate being a "good fit." Sixth, use a diverse group of hiring and staffing managers to gather and evaluate KSAO information, including a diverse team to conduct interviews. Finally, monitor selection decision making and challenge those decision makers who reject candidates who would enhance diversity to demonstrate that the reasons for rejection are job related.

When the organization is under an AAP, either voluntary or court imposed, the above recommendations are still appropriate. Attempts to go even further and provide a specific "plus" to protected characteristics should not be undertaken without a careful examination and opinion of whether this would be legally permissible.

SUMMARY

The selection component of a staffing system requires that decisions be made in several areas. The critical concerns are deciding which predictors (assessment methods) to use, determining assessment scores and setting cut scores, making final decisions about applicants, considering who within the organization should help make selection decisions, and legal compliance.

In deciding which assessment methods to use, consideration should be given to validity coefficients, incremental validity, multiple criteria, workforce diversity, and economic utility. Ideally, predictors a) have large magnitude validity coefficients, b) predict multiple work-relevant outcomes, c) have low correlations with other predictors, d) maintain or enhance diversity, and e) have high utility. In practice, this ideal situation is hard to achieve, so decisions about trade-offs are necessary.

How assessment scores are determined depends on whether a single predictor or multiple predictors are used. In the case of a single predictor, assessment scores are simply the scores on the predictor. With multiple predictors, a compensatory, multiple hurdles, or combined model must be used. A compensatory model allows a person to compensate for a low score on one predictor with a high score on another predictor. A multiple hurdles model requires that a person achieve a passing score on each successive predictor. A combined model uses elements of both the compensatory and the multiple hurdles models.

In deciding who earns a passing score on a predictor or a combination of predictors, cut scores must be set. When doing so, the consequences of setting different levels of cut scores should be considered, especially those of assessing some applicants as false positives or false negatives. Approaches to determining cut scores include compensatory, conjunctive, and maximum competence (for overqualification).

Methods of final choice involve determining who will receive job offers from among those who have passed the initial hurdles. Several methods of making these decisions were reviewed, including random selection, ranking, and grouping. Each has advantages and disadvantages.

Multiple individuals may be involved in selection decision making. HR professionals play a role primarily in determining the selection process to be used and in making selection decisions based on initial assessment results. Managers play a role primarily in deciding whom to select during the final choice stage. Employees are becoming part of the decision-making process, especially in team assessment approaches.

A basic legal issue is conformance with the UGESP, which provide guidance on how to set cut scores in ways that help minimize disparate impact and allow the organization to fulfill its EEO/AA obligations. In the absence of an AAP, protected class characteristics must not enter into selection decision making. That prohibition notwithstanding, organizations can take numerous steps to increase workforce diversity.

DISCUSSION QUESTIONS

1. Your boss is considering using a new predictor. The base rate is high, the selection ratio is low, and the validity coefficient is high for the current predictor. What would you advise your boss and why?
2. What are the positive consequences associated with a high predictor cut score? What are the negative consequences?
3. Under what circumstances should a compensatory model be used? When should a multiple hurdles model be used?
4. What are the advantages of ranking as a method of final choice over random selection?
5. What roles should HR professionals play in staffing decisions? Why?
6. What guidelines do the UGESP offer to organizations when it comes to setting cut scores?

ETHICAL ISSUES

1. Do you think companies should use banding and related methods to enhance diversity in selection decisions? Defend your position.
2. Is clinical prediction the fairest way to combine assessment information about job applicants, or are statistically based weighting methods fairer? Why?

APPLICATIONS

Utility Concerns in Choosing an Assessment Method

Randy May is a 32-year-old airplane mechanic for a small airline based on Nantucket Island, Massachusetts. Recently, Randy won $2 million in the New England lottery. Because Randy is relatively young, he decided to invest his winnings in a business to create a future stream of earnings. After weighing many investment options, Randy chose to open up a chain of ice cream shops in the Cape Cod area. (As it turns out, Cape Cod and the nearby islands are short of ice cream shops.) Randy reviewed his budget and figured he had enough cash to open shops on each of the two islands (Nantucket and Martha's Vineyard) and two shops in small towns on the Cape (Falmouth and Buzzards Bay). Randy contracted with a local builder, and the construction/renovation of the four shops is well under way.

The task that is occupying Randy's attention now is how to staff the shops. Two weeks ago, he placed advertisements in three area newspapers. So far, he has received 100 applications. Randy has done some informal HR planning and figures he needs to hire 50 employees to staff the four shops. Being a novice at this, Randy is unsure how to select the 50 people he needs to hire. Randy consulted his friend Mary, who owns the lunch counter at the airport. Mary told Randy that she used interviews to get "the most knowledgeable people possible" and recommended it to Randy because her people had "generally worked out well." While Randy greatly respected Mary's advice, on reflection some questions came to mind. Does Mary's use of the interview mean that it meets Randy's requirements? How can Randy determine whether his chosen method of selecting employees is effective or ineffective?

Confused, Randy also sought the advice of Professor Ray Higgins, from whom Randy took an HR management course while getting his business degree. After learning of the situation and offering his consulting services, Professor Higgins suggested that Randy choose one of two selection methods (after paying Professor Higgins's consulting fees, he cannot afford to use both methods). The two methods Professor Higgins recommended are the interview (as Mary recommended) and a work sample test that entails scooping ice cream and serving it to a customer. Randy estimates that it would cost $100 to interview an applicant and $150 per applicant to administer the work sample. Professor Higgins told Randy that the validity of the interview in predicting overall job performance for customer service employees is $r = .30$, while the validity of the work sample in predicting overall job performance is $r = .50$. Professor Higgins also informed Randy that the selection ratio is probably fairly high because there are not a lot of job seekers and because the minimum wage he plans on paying is not likely to attract people in this area.

Randy would really appreciate it if you could help him answer the following questions:

1. What parts of this information seem most important for the choice of selection measures? How does each piece of information fit with the "choice of assessment method" discussion?
2. If Randy can use only one method, which should he use?

3. If the number of applicants for these jobs increases dramatically (more applications are coming in than Randy expected), how will your answers to questions 1 and 2 change?
4. What are some additional pieces of information you would like to have before committing to any of these options? What other criteria might be relevant?

Choosing Entrants Into a Management Training Program

Come As You Are, a convenience store chain headquartered in Fayetteville, Arkansas, has developed an assessment program to promote nonexempt employees into its management training program. The minimum entrance requirements for the program are five years of company experience, a college degree from an accredited university, and a minimum acceptable job performance rating (3 or higher on a 1–5 scale). Anyone interested in applying for the management program can enroll in the half-day assessment program, where the following assessments are made:

1. Cognitive ability test
2. Integrity test
3. Signed permission for background test
4. Brief (30-minute) interview by various members of the management team
5. Drug test

At the Hot Springs store, 11 employees have applied for openings in the management training program. The selection information on the candidates is provided in the following exhibit. (The scoring key is provided at the bottom of the exhibit.) It is estimated that three slots in the program are available for qualified candidates from the Hot Springs location. Given this information and what you know about external and internal selection, as well as staffing decision making, answer the following questions:

1. How would you go about deciding whom to select for the openings? In other words, without providing your decisions for the individual candidates, describe how you would weigh the various selection information to reach a decision.
2. Using the decision-making process from the previous question, which three applicants would you select for the training program? Explain your decision.
3. Although the data provided in the exhibit reveal that all selection measures were given to all 11 candidates, would you advise Come As You Are to continue to administer all the predictors at one time during the half-day assessment program? Alternatively, should the predictors be given in a sequence so that a multiple hurdles or combined approach could be used? Explain your recommendation.

Exhibit
Predictor Scores for 11 Applicants to Management Training Program

Name	Company Experience	College Degree	Performance Rating	Cognitive Ability Test	Integrity Test	Background Test	Interview Rating	Drug Test
Radhu	4	Yes	4	9	6	OK	6	P
Merv	12	Yes	3	3	6	OK	8	P
Marianne	9	Yes	4	8	5	Arrest '95	4	P
Helmut	5	Yes	4	5	5	OK	4	P
Siobhan	14	Yes	5	7	8	OK	8	P
Galina	7	No	3	3	4	OK	6	P
Raul	6	Yes	4	7	8	OK	2	P
Frank	9	Yes	5	2	5	OK	7	P
Osvaldo	10	Yes	4	10	9	OK	3	P
Byron	18	Yes	3	3	7	OK	6	P
Aletha	11	Yes	4	7	6	OK	5	P
Scale	Years	Yes–No	1–5	1–10	1–10	OK–Other	1–10	P–F

ENDNOTES

1. R. Hastie and R. M. Dawes, *Rational Choice in an Uncertain World*, 2nd ed. (Thousand Oaks, CA: Sage, 2010); D. Kahneman, *Thinking, Fast and Slow* (New York: Farrar, Straus, and Giroux, 2011); P. Bolander and J. Sandberg, "How Employee Selection Decisions Are Made in Practice," *Organization Studies*, 2013, 34, pp. 285–311.

2. R. B. Kline, *Beyond Significance Testing: Statistics Reform in the Behavioral Sciences*, 2nd ed. (Washington, DC: American Psychological Association, 2013).

3. C. L. Ryan and K. Bauman, *Educational Attainment in the United States: 2015. Population Characteristics* (Current Population Reports, No. P20-578) (Washington, DC: US Census Bureau, 2016); D. H. Autor, "Skills, Education, and the Rise of Earnings Inequality Among the Other 99 Percent," *Science*, 2014, 344, pp. 843–851.

4. W. De Corte, P. R. Sackett, and F. Lievens, "Selecting Predictor Subsets: Considering Validity and Adverse Impact," *International Journal of Selection and Assessment*, 2010, 18, pp. 260–270; W. De Corte, F. Lievens, and P. R. Sackett, "Combining Predictors to Achieve Optimal Trade-Offs Between Selection Quality and Adverse Impact," *Journal of Applied Psychology*, 2007, 92, pp. 1380–1393.

5. R. E. Ployhart and B. C. Holtz, "The Diversity-Validity Dilemma: Strategies for Reducing Racio-ethnic and Sex Subgroup Differences and Adverse Impact in Selection," *Personnel Psychology*, 2008, 61, pp. 153–172; J. Bradburn and N. Schmitt, "Combining Cognitive and Noncognitive Predictors and Impact on Selected Individual Demographics: An Illustration," *International Journal of Selection and Assessment*, 2019, 27, pp. 21–30.

6. S. Wee, D. A. Newman, and D. L. Joseph, "More Than g: Selection Quality and Adverse Impact Implications of Considering Second-Stratum Cognitive Abilities," *Journal of Applied Psychology*, 2014, 99, pp. 547–563; Ployhart and Holtz, "The Diversity-Validity Dilemma: Strategies for Reducing Racioethnic and Sex Subgroup Differences and Adverse Impact in Selection."

7. I. S. Fulmer and R. E. Ployhart, "Our Most Important Asset: A Multidisciplinary/Multilevel Review of Human Capital Valuation for Research and Practice," *Journal of Management*, 2014, 40, pp. 161–192; J. W. Boudreau, *Retooling HR: Using Proven Business Tools to Make Better Decisions About Talent* (Boston: Harvard Business School Press, 2010); J. Fitz-Enz and J. R. Mattox, *Predictive Analytics for Human Resources* (Hoboken, NJ: Wiley, 2014); J. W. Boudreau, "'Retooling' Evidence-Based Staffing: Extending the Validation Paradigm Using Management Mental Models," in N. Schmitt (ed.), *Oxford Handbook of Personnel Assessment and Selection* (New York: Oxford University Press, 2012), pp. 793–813.

8. S. Highhouse, "Stubborn Reliance on Intuition and Subjectivity in Employee Selection," *Industrial and Organizational Psychology*, 2008, 1, pp. 333–342; D. L. Diab, S-Y Pui, M. Yankelevich, and S. Highhouse, "Lay Perceptions of Selection Decision Aids in US and Non-US Samples," *International Journal of Selection and Assessment*, 2011, 19, pp. 209–216.

9. E. E. Kausel, S. S. Culbertson, and H. P. Madrid, "Overconfidence in Personnel Selection: When and Why Unstructured Interview Information Can Hurt Hiring Decisions," *Organizational Behavior and Human Decision Processes*, 2016, 137, pp. 27–44; Hastie and Dawes, *Rational Choice in an Uncertain World*; Kahneman, *Thinking, Fast and Slow*.

10. R. E. McGrath, "Predictor Combination in Binary Decision-Making Scenarios," *Psychological Assessment*, 2008, 20, pp. 195–205.

11. J. M. LeBreton, M. B. Hargis, B. Griepentrog, F. L. Oswald, and R. E. Ployhart, "A Multidimensional Approach for Evaluating Variables in Organizational Research and Practice," *Personnel Psychology*, 2007, 60, pp. 475–498.

12. S. Luan, J. Reb, and G. Gigerenzer, "Ecological Rationality: Fast-and-Frugal Heuristics for Managerial Decision Making Under Uncertainty," *Academy of Management Journal*, 2019, 62,

pp. 1735–1759; B. J. Dietvorst, J. P. Simmons, and C. Massey, "Overcoming Algorithm Aversion: People Will Use Imperfect Algorithms If They Can (Even Slightly) Modify Them," *Management Science*, 2016, 64, pp. 1155–1170; Y. Ganzach, A. N. Kluger, and N. Klayman, "Making Decisions From an Interview: Expert Measurement and Mechanical Combination," *Personnel Psychology*, 2000, 53, pp. 1–20.

13. M. R. Peabody and S. A. Wind, "Exploring the Influence of Judge Proficiency on Standard-Setting Judgments," *Journal of Educational Measurement*, 2019, 56, pp. 101–120.

14. R. J. Tannenbaum and I. R. Katz, "Standard Setting," in *APA Handbook of Testing and Assessment in Psychology*, Vol. 3, *Testing and Assessment in School Psychology and Education* (Washington, DC: American Psychological Association, 2013), pp. 455–477.

15. G. M. Hurtz and M. A. Auerbach, "A Meta-Analysis of the Effects of Modifications to the Angoff Method on Cutoff and Judgment Consensus," *Educational and Psychological Measurement*, 2003, 63, pp. 584–601.

16. M. B. Harari, A. Manapragada, and C. Viswesvaran, "Who Thinks They're a Big Fish in a Small Pond and Why Does It Matter? A Meta-Analysis of Perceived Overqualification," *Journal of Vocational Behavior*, 2017, 102, pp. 28–47; P. G. Martinez, M. L. Lengnick-Hall, and M. Kulkarni, "Overqualified? A Conceptual Model of Managers' Perceptions of Overqualification in Selection Decisions," *Personnel Review*, 2014, 43, pp. 957–974; L. S. Simon, T. N. Bauer, B. Erdogan, and W. Shepherd, "Built to Last: Interactive Effects of Perceived Overqualification and Proactive Personality on New Employee Adjustment," *Personnel Psychology*, 2019, 72, pp. 213–240.

17. B. Erdogan and T. N. Bauer, "Perceived Overqualification and Its Outcomes: The Moderating Role of Empowerment," *Journal of Applied Psychology*, 2009, 94, pp. 557–565.

18. S. J. Wells, "Too Good to Hire?" *HR Magazine*, Oct. 2004, pp. 48–54.

19. P. R. Sackett, N. Schmitt, J. E. Ellingson, and M. B. Kabin, "High-Stakes Testing in Employment, Credentialing, and Higher Education," *American Psychologist*, 2001, 56, pp. 302–318; Ployhart and Holtz, "The Diversity-Validity Dilemma: Strategies for Reducing Racioethnic and Sex Subgroup Differences and Adverse Impact in Selection."

20. S. M. Gasperson, M. C. Bowler, K. L. Wuensch, and J. L. Bowler, "A Statistical Correction to 20 Years of Banding," *International Journal of Selection and Assessment*, 2013, 21, pp. 46–56.

21. C. A. Henle, "Case Review of the Legal Status of Banding," *Human Performance*, 2004, 17, pp. 415–432.

22. Q. C. Song, S. Wee, and D. A. Newman, "Diversity Shrinkage: Cross-Validating Pareto-Optimal Weights to Enhance Diversity via Hiring Practices," *Journal of Applied Psychology*, 2017, 102, pp. 1636–1657; H. Aguinis and M. A. Smith, "Understanding the Impact of Test Validity and Bias on Selection Errors and Adverse Impact in Human Resource Selection," *Personnel Psychology*, 2007, 60, pp. 165–190.

23. D. M. Finch, B. D. Edwards, and J. C. Wallace, "Multistage Selection Strategies: Simulating the Effects on Adverse Impact and Expected Performance for Various Predictor Combinations," *Journal of Applied Psychology*, 2009, 94, pp. 318–340.

24. C. Chadwick, J. F. Super, and K. Kwon, "Resource Orchestration in Practice: CEO Emphasis on SHRM, Commitment-Based HR Systems, and Firm Performance," *Strategic Management Journal*, 2015, 36, pp. 360–367; D. Ulrich, J. Allen, W. Brockbanck, J. Younger, and M. Nyman, *HR Transformation: Building Human Resources From the Outside In* (Chicago: McGraw-Hill, 2009); T. Henneman, "Is HR at Its Breaking Point?" *Workforce*, Mar. 22, 2013 (*www.workforce.com*).

25. D. G. Sirmon, M. A. Hitt, R. D. Ireland, and B. A. Gilbert, "Resource Orchestration to Create Competitive Advantage: Breadth, Depth, and Life Cycle Effects," *Journal of Management*, 2011, 37, pp. 1390–1412; P. Stanton, S. Young, T. Bartram, and S. G. Leggat, "Singing the Same Song: Translating HRM Messages Across Management Hierarchies in Australian Hospitals," *International Journal of Human Resource Management*, 2010, 21, pp. 567–581.

26. M. D. Nowicki and J. G. Rosse, "Managers' Views of How to Hire: Building Bridges Between Science and Practice," *Journal of Business and Psychology*, 2002, 17, pp. 157–170.

27. D. M. Sikora and G. R. Ferris, "Strategic Human Resource Practice Implementation: The Critical Role of Line Management," *Human Resource Management Review*, 2014, 24, pp. 271–281.

28. "Google Goes for Consensus in Hiring," *Recruiter*, Apr. 28, 2010, p. 5.

29. D. D. Bennett-Alexander and L. P. Hartman, *Employment Law for Business*, 8th ed. (New York: McGraw-Hill-Education, 2015), pp. 224–237; R. K. Robinson, G. M. Franklin, and R. E. Wayland, *Employment Regulation in the Workplace* (Armonk, NY: M. E. Sharpe, 2010), pp. 182–212; US Equal Employment Opportunity Commission, "EEOC Compliance Manual," 2006 (*www.eeoc.gov/policy/docs/race-color.html*), accessed July 27, 2010; D. Walsh, *Employment Law for Human Resource Practice*, 5th ed. (Boston: Cengage Learning, 2016), pp. 212–218 and 240–255.

CHAPTER TWELVE

Final Match

Learning Objectives and Introduction
Learning Objectives
Introduction

Employment Relationships
Setting Expectations
Parties to the Relationship
Starting Date and Duration
Disclaimers and Contingencies

Job Offer Content
Strategic Approach to Job Offers
Compensation and Benefits
Signing Bonuses and Relocation Assistance
Idiosyncratic Deals
Restrictions on Employees

Job Offer Process
Formulation of the Job Offer
Timing of the Offer
Presentation of the Job Offer
Job Offer Negotiation
Job Offer Acceptance, Rejection, and Revoking

New Employee Orientation and Socialization
Orientation
Socialization
Long-Term Adjustment

Legal Issues
Contractual Obligations
Employment Eligibility Verification
Negligent Hiring
Employment-at-Will

Summary

Discussion Questions

Ethical Issues

Applications
    Making a Job Offer
    Evaluating a Hiring and Variable-Pay Plan

Endnotes

LEARNING OBJECTIVES AND INTRODUCTION

Learning Objectives

- Learn about the importance of matching expectations in the employment relationship
- Understand how to make strategic job offers
- Plan for the steps of formulating and presenting a job offer
- Consider policies for negotiating job offers
- Develop effective plans for new employee orientation and socialization
- Understand how communications might create formal employment obligations

Introduction

In the decision-making chapter, we described how to reduce the initial applicant pool to a smaller set of candidates and identify one or more job finalists. In this chapter we move to the next stage—the process of actually hiring the individuals who have been selected. A final match occurs when the offer receiver and the organization have determined that there is sufficient overlap between the person's knowledge, skill, ability, and other characteristics (KSAOs) and the job's requirements and rewards. Once the decision to enter the employment relationship has been made, the organization and the candidate establish mutual agreements on the terms and conditions of employment.

The initial theme of this chapter is setting the stage for a sound employment relationship. Establishing accurate expectations and developing lines of communication are especially vital as the relationship first develops. Human resource (HR) professionals need to ensure that offer receivers know about job responsibilities, pay and benefits, working hours, and other role expectations before accepting the offer. Details about the nature of the relationship and the time frame for the relationship should also be very clear before an offer is formulated.

The discussion proceeds to the process of convincing promising job finalists to take the job offer, and developing the grounds of the relationship that will persist throughout this individual's employment through onboarding or socialization activities. A strategic approach to job offers is presented, followed by a discussion of the major components of a job offer. Through the job offer process, terms and conditions are proposed, discussed, negotiated, modified, and, ultimately, agreed on. Once agreement on the terms and conditions of employment has been reached, the final match process is completed, and the formal employment relationship is established. To phase the new hire into their job, appropriate techniques for orienting and socializing the newcomer must be developed.

The chapter concludes with a discussion of specific legal issues that pertain not only to the establishment of the employment relationship but also to potential long-term consequences of the relationship that must be considered at the time it is established. Organizations often get into legal trouble when they fail to understand the contractual nature of many employment relationships. As we show, careless promises or guarantees made during the job offer can come back to haunt an organization when it needs to alter the employment relationship at a later time.

EMPLOYMENT RELATIONSHIPS

Since the staffing process in general, and the job offer process in particular, involves communicating terms and conditions of employment, it is important to establish a solid relationship from the start. This involves setting expectations, determining the parties to the relationship, establishing disclaimers and contingencies on offers, and establishing the time frame (start date and duration) for the relationship.

Setting Expectations

When creating a job offer, the organization should (1) clarify what job offer receivers can expect or not expect in a new job, and (2) be sure that actions are taken to ensure that promises or expectations are met whenever possible. Fulfilled expectations can foster an environment of trust and build lasting relationships. Unfulfilled expectations may spur the disappointed person to become dissatisfied, complain about the organization online or to friends, or pursue legal action against the organization. Although not formally part of the job offer itself, this conversation is also a key opportunity to reinforce the culture and facilitate person/ organization fit.

A considerable body of research has looked into the antecedents and consequences of new hire expectations. Early interactions with the organization as a whole, supervisors, and coworkers set the stage for the future of relationships. Accurate, honest communication during the job offer process about what to expect at work can foster engagement and commitment. Inaccuracies and violated expectations, on the other hand, appear to be one of the strongest factors driving distrust. Several studies have examined violations of perceived promises (termed "psychological contract breach") across a variety of organizations. Outcomes of these psychological contract breaches include lower levels of job satisfaction, perceptions of job insecurity, and higher levels of stress.[1]

As reviewed in other chapters describing the social and legal environment for employment, many of the statements made by employers can become legally binding.[2] On the other hand, employees have considerably more leverage in the agreements and their own statements are less likely to be held as enforceable in court. Employers should be aware of this one-way contractual tie and ground their communication and interpretation of employee communication accordingly. We cover the specific legal issues in greater detail at the end of the chapter.

HR professionals have identified several key job offer features that should be clarified up front before the relationship starts.[3] Many of these features can be identified through the job analysis process. Offer receivers should be aware of the most important job tasks, expectations for performance, and the ways work goals are accomplished. Reporting relationships and the flow of work should also be clarified. This information can come from a job requirements analysis. The contribution of the job to the organization's goals, and the capabilities that span multiple roles should be addressed. This information is derived from competency modeling. Compensation and benefits plans are also areas to address. Finally, potential career growth paths should be very clear, and every effort needs to be directed toward being detailed and not overpromising the rate at which career advancement will occur. This information is derived from a job rewards analysis.

There are bound to be questions and areas that need clarifying during the job offer process. Adequate communication at this phase sends a strong signal to the offer receiver about the future relationship. Employees and employers need to have a mutual flow of information. Assumptions about what the other party to the agreement expects should always be questioned. Current employees should be surveyed to determine whether their own expectations were violated when they started.

Parties to the Relationship

Two issues arise regarding the parties to the relationship: whether the employer is entering into a relationship with an employee or an independent contractor, and whether an outsider or third party can execute or otherwise play a role in the employment relationship.

Employee or Independent Contractor

Individuals are hired by the organization as either employees or independent contractors.[4] Both of these terms have definite legal meanings that the organization should review (see the social and legal environment chapter) before entering into a relationship. The organization should be clear in its offer whether the relationship being sought is that of employer–employee or employer–independent contractor.

Companies increasingly claim that individuals who should be classified as employees are being reported as independent contractors.[5] As a result, the Department of Labor has been working to identify organizations that are misclassifying employees. This push has resulted in the collection of millions of dollars in unpaid taxes, as well as payouts of millions of additional dollars due to underpayments and insufficient provision of benefits. Violations typically involve situations in which the employment relationship is too long to be considered contingent, or when the organization is overstepping the level of managerial authority that can be exercised over independent contractors. The rise of the "gig economy" creates further areas of concern, as company rules for conduct and work hours at rideshare companies and delivery services have been scrutinized.

Third Parties

Often, someone other than the employer or the offer receiver speaks on their behalf in the establishment or modification of an employment relationship. For the employer, this may mean the use of outsiders such as staffing agencies, executive recruiters, or search consultants; it also usually means the use of one or more employees, such as the HR department representative, the hiring manager, and other managers within the organization. For the offer receiver, it may mean the use of a special representative, such as a professional agent for an athlete or an executive. It should be very clear who speaks for the offer receiver and what limits are placed on this person by the offer receiver. Employers have to be especially careful, because virtually any employee could suggest and agree to contract terms, knowingly or unknowingly. This means that the employer should formulate and enforce explicit policies as to who is authorized to speak on its behalf and what the spokesperson is authorized to discuss and agree to.

Starting Date and Duration

In addition to clarifying expectations about what the job will be like and the parties to the relationship, the time frame for the relationship is also a key consideration. In the initial discussion of a job offer, the start and duration of the relationship should be stated explicitly and frequently.

Starting Date

Normally, the organization controls when the employment relationship begins. To do so, it must provide a definite starting date in its offer. If it does not, acceptance and consideration of the offer occur at the time the new hire actually begins work. Oftentimes, the starting date is one that allows the offer receiver at least two weeks to provide notification of resignation to a current employer. Start dates are sometimes negotiable—offer receivers should be told when there is flexibility. Companies are more accommodating with schedules when looking to hire in tight labor markets or when offer receivers have especially valuable KSAOs.

Starting dates are not always straightforward. For example, many employers will bring on a new hire with a specific probationary period or training period. Formal training periods are considered employment by the courts, so any differences in wages or benefits for trainees need to be elaborated. Specific guidelines for training compensation terms communicated in advance can also ensure that new hires do not assume they will receive their full wages and benefits right away. Internships are also a form of trial employment. In both cases, setting aside a specific early period of time helps establish expectations about the degree of mutual commitment for both employer and employee. Of course, with employment-at-will, either party can end the relationship at any time for any legally permissible reason. However, it is both socially and legally easier to terminate an employment relationship when both parties recognize in advance that the relationship is still in a trial phase.

Duration of Relationships

Employment relationships may be of a fixed term (i.e., have a definite ending date) or an indeterminate term (i.e., have no definite ending date). The decision about duration is intimately related to the employment-at-will issue.

A fixed-term contract provides certainty to both the new hire and the organization regarding the length of the employment relationship. Both parties decide on the term of employment and must abide by it. The organization can then (according to common law) terminate the contract prior to its expiration date for "just cause" only. Determination and demonstration of just cause can be a complicated legal problem for the organization.

Most organizations are unwilling to provide such employment guarantees. They much prefer an employment-at-will relationship, in which either party may terminate the employment relationship at any time without having to demonstrate just cause.[6] Should the organization decide to have indeterminate-term employment contracts, it should carefully state in its written offer that the duration is indeterminate and that it may be terminated by either party at any time, for any reason. Because of the overriding importance of this issue, all wording should be approved at the highest organizational level.

Although employers can request that employees give advance notice (e.g., two weeks' notice) before quitting, employment-at-will generally does not allow employers to compel employees to give advance notice. Some employers specify in their policies that employees who do not give notice will be ineligible for rehire or will be denied accumulated vacation time, but some state laws prohibit these actions.[7]

Disclaimers and Contingencies

Part of the initial formation of an employment relationship is clarifying what the organization is not providing. These statements take the form of disclaimers and contingencies.

Disclaimers

A disclaimer is a statement (oral or written) that explicitly limits an employee's right and reserves that right for the employer.[8] Disclaimers are often used in letters of appointment, job application blanks, and employee handbooks.

A common employee "right" that is being limited by a disclaimer is that of job security. Here, through its policy of employment-at-will, the employer explicitly makes no promise of any job security and reserves the right to terminate the employment relationship at its own will. The following is an example of such a disclaimer suggested by the Society for Human Resource Management:

> Your employment with [company name] is a voluntary one and is subject to termination by you or [company name] at will, with or without cause, and with or without notice, at any time. Nothing in these policies shall be interpreted to be in conflict with or to eliminate or modify in any way the employment-at-will status of [company name] employees. This policy of employment-at-will may not be modified by any officer or employee and shall not be modified in any publication or document.[9]

An employment-at-will disclaimer should appear in the job offer letter. It should also appear on the application blank, along with two other disclaimers. First, there should be a statement of consent by the applicant for the organization to check provided references, along with a waiver of the right to make claims against them for anything they say. Second, there should be a so-called false statement warning, indicating that any false statement, misleading statement, or material omission may be grounds for dismissal.

In the case of disclaimers in employee handbooks, the employer must consider whether these statements are legally enforceable or merely informational. While there is legal opinion on both sides of this question, handbooks are increasingly being considered as a legally enforceable part of the employment contract. To avoid this occurrence, the employer may wish to place an explicit disclaimer in the handbook that states the intent is to provide only information to employees and that the employer will not be bound by any of the statements contained in the handbook.

Disclaimers are generally enforceable. They can thus serve as an important component of employment contracts. Their use should be guided by the following set of recommendations:[10]

1. They should be clearly stated and conspicuously placed in appropriate documents.
2. The employee should acknowledge receipt and review of the document and the disclaimer.
3. The disclaimer should state that it may be modified only in writing and by whom.
4. The terms and conditions of employment, including the disclaimer, as well as limits on their enforceability, should be reviewed with offer receivers and employees.

Contingencies

The employer may wish to make a job offer that is contingent on certain other conditions being fulfilled by the offer receiver.[11] Examples of such contingencies include (1) passage of a particular test, such as a licensure exam (e.g., CPA or bar exam), (2) passage of a medical exam, including alcohol/drug screening tests,

(3) satisfactory background and reference checks, and (4) proof of employability under the Immigration Reform and Control Act (IRCA).

Though contingencies are generally enforceable, contingencies to an employment contract (especially those involving any of the preceding examples) are exceedingly complex and may be made only within defined limits. For this reason, contingencies should not be used in employment contracts without prior legal counsel.

JOB OFFER CONTENT

A job offer is an attempt by the organization to induce the offer receiver into the establishment of an employment relationship. The agreement signifies that the person/job match is about to become a reality. That reality, in turn, becomes the start of, and foundation for, subsequent employee effectiveness on various HR outcomes. For these reasons, the content and extension of the job offer become critical final parts of the overall staffing process.

Strategic Approach to Job Offers

The strategic approach to job offers is grounded in a careful analysis of all the factors that contribute to striking a compelling offer. Rather than hastily crafting job offers in the heat of the hiring moment and with a desire to fill the vacancy now, it is better to think strategically about job offer content in advance. A job rewards analysis can help identify the aspects of the job that are most likely to be desired by offer receivers.

Exhibit 12.1 indicates that labor market conditions, organization needs, applicant needs, and legal issues are forces to consider in the creation of job offers. This exhibit shows the strategic approach to job offers, or the employee value proposition (EVP). The EVP is the total package of extrinsic and intrinsic rewards that the position will provide to the finalist if the job offer is accepted. First and foremost, the job offer must be an EVP the finalist will find more enticing than alternatives.[12] The offer thus must present a package of rewards with the right combination of magnitude, mix, and distinctiveness to be compelling to the offer receiver. At the same time, the offer should correspond to the value of the job to the organization, the quality of the offer receiver, and alternatives to hiring any one person.

Labor Markets

The simple availability of potential offer receivers needs to be considered. If there are few individuals with the required KSAOs, offers may need to be more generous than if the skills are easily acquired. Similarly, in a tight labor market in which there are few applicants per opening, job offers need to have a stronger EVP communicated compared with the situation when many job seekers can be found. Having

EXHIBIT 12.1 Strategic Approach to Job Offers

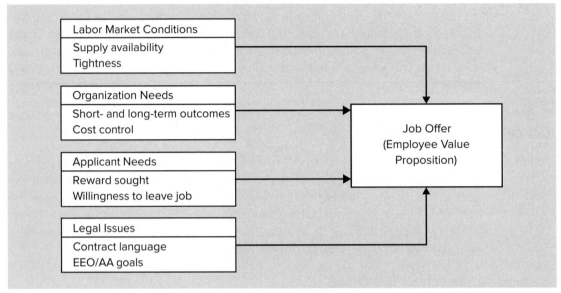

said that, no matter how few alternatives exist, there is never an operational or ethical case to be made for overselling a position. No matter how easily alternative candidates may be found, there is never an operational or ethical case to be made for the employer's striking a deal that disfavors the applicant. If the process is successful, the offer receiver will be entering into an enduring relationship with the organization, so a good foundation should be established early.

Organization Needs

The organization has both short- and long-term goals for hiring. Short-term objectives include getting someone in the position and ready to perform quickly. Such objectives produce pressure for hiring bonuses and high starting pay. Long-term outcomes such as the extent to which the employee fits in with the organization and work unit, the promotability of the employee, and expected retention suggest correspondingly long-term offer components like deferred compensation and development plans. Finally, cost control must come into play. All job offers will cost the organization if accepted, so how much is it willing to spend?

Applicant Needs

In terms of applicant needs, the organization must seek to identify the rewards likely sought by applicants. Many of the principles related to applicant attraction that were covered in the discussion of job rewards analysis and the recruiting strategy are still relevant during the offer stage. The best offers are differentiated from those of competitors, building from the branding strategy described in the recruiting chapter. For example, Red Frog Events emphasizes factors that set it apart from alternative employers. The extrinsic features of the EVP include not just competitive pay and benefits but also unlimited vacation days and a four-week, all-expenses-paid sabbatical for travel after five years of service. Unique intrinsic features of the EVP include a casual environment, energized and motivated teams, and one-on-one job coaching.[13] The EVP should also be tailored to the types of employees being sought. One study of over 1,000 individuals in the United States demonstrated some of the different types of employee preference sets.[14] About a third of respondents were identified as stabilizers and preferred team-based rewards, communication, and work-value balance. A quarter of respondents were pioneers who were more intrinsically motivated and most valued work that allowed them to learn and contribute. Drivers, who made up about a quarter of respondents, valued achievement and success and so preferred work with a clear track to promotions. Finally, the remaining respondents were most interested in social work environments in which they could make a positive impact on others.

Finalists' willingness to leave their current jobs is a major concern. If the finalist is relatively willing, or even eager, to leave, the job offer may not need to be very compelling in magnitude, mix, or distinctiveness. On the other hand, if the finalist is satisfied with the current job and current geographic location, the need to craft a compelling offer rises dramatically. Essentially, such offers must provide an EVP that boosts the willingness to change locations, both by pointing out positive features of the new location and by minimizing the costs of making the move. These considerations are at least as important for internal recruiting as they are for external recruiting. Knowledge and skill development opportunities, performance-related incentives, and visible promotion chains all help induce a future-oriented perspective among internal applicants, which can then prompt them to accept offers for new internal positions.[15]

Legal Issues

The job offer process is one of the most legally fraught parts of the staffing process, so all individuals who are involved need to be trained on the organization's policies and procedures. The issue of contract language is discussed at length in the "Legal Issues" section of this chapter.

Compensation and Benefits

Although recent research suggests that organizational characteristics and perceived working conditions are the strongest predictors of applicant attraction in the final stages of the job choice process, compensation remains a powerful predictor of employee interest at the point of a job offer.[16] Compensation is a multi-faceted set of rewards that may be presented to the offer receiver in many forms. Sometimes it consists of a standard pay rate and benefits package, which must be simply accepted or rejected. Other times the offer may be more tailor-made, often negotiated in advance.

Job seekers carry with them a set of pay preferences and expectations that shape how they respond to the compensation components of the job offer. This means that rates of pay should be carefully and accurately communicated. Policies around pay variability should also be described. Misrepresentation of organizational policy is likely to result in employees quitting or taking the company to court.

Base Pay

Base pay is the guaranteed rate of compensation for a given job. This comes in the form of either an hourly rate of pay or a salaried amount, depending on job level. Most job offers indicate that base compensation rates are variable, depending on the employee's qualifications. The exact nature of which qualifications are associated with starting base pay is often not specified in the advertisement, but at the point of hire, the elements of the system used in determining variation should be noted. It should also be clear whether pay is hourly or salaried. There are legal constraints on when an employer can offer a salary rather than hourly wages, so legal compliance always dictates which method is appropriate.

For civil service jobs and those under collective bargaining agreements, the system is well specified, available to new hires, and consistently applied. Usually in these cases, objective information on educational status and years of work experience in the field is used to set wages. Education and experience enter into base pay for the broader labor market as well. Science and technology majors make more than humanities majors, and the returns on a science or technology degree are even greater for individuals with higher levels of cognitive ability.[17] Sometimes the starting pay rate for any particular job may need to vary because of average pay differentials across geographic areas. For example, for the job of HR manager, which had an average national rate of $113,300 in 2018, pay varied from $85,290 in Idaho to $169,040 in New Jersey.[18] For internal markets, promotions, seniority systems, and completion of specific training programs are used in a formulaic manner to set wages. For all systems, the basis for well-specified wage policies should be communicated as preset during the job offer process.

In other cases, employers preserve flexibility for negotiation in wages (this topic is covered in more detail in our discussions of negotiation and idiosyncratic deals). Sometimes organizations are more willing to adjust wages in the job offer process when the organization is under intense pressure to acquire new employees and fill vacancies promptly. To accomplish these outcomes, flexibility in starting pay offers is used to respond to finalists' demands and demonstrate a willingness to accommodate their needs.

Despite its advantages, use of differential starting pay rates requires attention to several potential problems.[19] Issues of fairness and internal equity among employees may arise when there is too much discretion in the range of starting salaries. Naturally, similarly qualified employees receiving wide differences in starting pay is a guaranteed recipe for perceived pay inequities, and paying new hires starting salaries that exceed those of longer-tenured employees also fuels perceived inequity.

A large and growing body of evidence shows that women and other underrepresented groups are less likely to negotiate and that their efforts to negotiate are often penalized, leading to discriminatory outcomes and undermining efforts to create an inclusive culture.[20] For these reasons, whenever differential rates of starting pay are used, the organization must carefully consider what is permissible and within bounds. Attention should be paid to demographic differences in negotiation outcomes. One way to address this issue is by clearly communicating whether negotiation is appropriate and what parts of the compensation package can be negotiated.[21] These constraints may specify when differential starting pay offers may be made and where within a pay range starting pay rates must fall. Exhibit 12.2 contains an example of such starting pay policies.

Variable Pay

The organization should also communicate policies related to variable pay (pay that is contingent on performance) during the job offer process. Individual commission-based pay used in sales is highly attractive to ambitious employees and can serve as an advantage in getting offer receivers to accept. Conversely, such individual incentives may be unattractive for offer receivers who have many fixed expenses or who prefer to work on teams. They should know about pay policies in advance of the job offer, so that they can select out of a job with an unattractive pay policy; avoiding this poor person/job fit is to the advantage of both the potential employee

---

EXHIBIT 12.2   **Example of Starting Pay Policies**

The Wright Company

The following policies regarding starting pay must be adhered to:

1. No person is to be offered a salary that is below the minimum, or above the midpoint, of the salary range for the job.

2. Generally, persons with reasonable qualifications should be offered a salary within the first quartile (bottom 25%) of the salary range for the job.

3. Salary offers above the first quartile, but not exceeding the midpoint, may be made for exceptionally well-qualified persons, or when market conditions dictate.

4. Salary offers should be fair in relation to other offers made and to the salaries paid to current employees.

5. Salary offers below the first quartile may be made without approval; offers at or above the first quartile must be approved in advance by the manager of compensation.

6. Counteroffers may not be accepted without approval of the manager of compensation.

and the organization. Bonuses for landing new clients in consulting, piece rates for manufacturing, and incentives for volume of patients treated in medicine should be similarly clarified for the same reasons. Employees should also be made aware of differences in pay related to supervisor evaluations of performance.

Job offer receivers should be thoroughly informed about the policies that go into setting variable pay. The job offer should emphasize that specific levels of earnings are contingent on performance and that incumbents differ in how much they earn. Most people tend to overestimate how much they will earn, so it is best to set realistic expectations early to avoid disappointment.

Benefits

A job is usually accompanied by a fixed benefits package that is offered to all offer receivers. Components of a benefits package may include health insurance, retirement plans, child care, on site health and wellness programs, and work/life plans. Employers often are able to get these benefits at a premium rate relative to an individual employee, and there are tax-shielding benefits for both employee and employer when providing nonmonetary rewards. Because of this, benefits are less expensive for the employer and sometimes more attractive to applicants than pure wage increases. Specific benefits packages can help reinforce the organization's employment brand, and so are a feature to emphasize in the job offer process.

When a fixed or standard benefits package is offered, the offer letter should not spell out all of the specific benefit provisions. Rather, it should state that the employee would be eligible to participate in the benefit plans maintained by the organization, as provided in written descriptions of these plans. In this way, the job offer letter does not inadvertently make statements or promises that contradict or go beyond the organization's actual benefits plan.

Severance Packages

Severance packages include terms and conditions that the organization states the employee is entitled to upon departure from the organization. Content of the package typically includes one or two weeks of pay for every year of service, earned vacation and holiday pay, extended health insurance coverage and premium payment, and outplacement assistance in finding a new job.[22]

Severance packages for top executives are usually expected and provided. Other organizational leaders and high-level technical experts can also be promised severance pay. For new hires, the severance package can offset the risk they are taking with the new job. Executives are often leaving a high-paying, high-quality job and are reluctant to make such a major decision unless there is some cushion if they are terminated. These risks are likely front-of-mind for executives who have an especially high risk of termination early in their tenure. Employers sometimes use severance packages as a way to minimize the reputation as a high-risk employer that could arise from terminations. However, both internal and external organizational members may complain about high-profile severance packages, as they are sometimes seen as a "reward for failure." In sum, while severance packages have their merits, they are not without their critics.

Signing Bonuses and Relocation Assistance

In addition to the terms associated with long-term employment, organizations will often provide immediate inducements for high-value employees. Signing bonuses and relocation assistance are two of the most common onetime rewards that feature in the job offer process.

Signing Bonuses

Signing bonuses are onetime payments offered and subsequently paid upon acceptance of the offer. Typically, the bonus is in the form of an outright cash grant; the bonus may also be in the form of a cash advance against future expected earnings. New college graduates can also be promised full or partial repayment of student loans upon signing up. Top executives are likely to receive not only a cash bonus but also restricted stock and/or stock options. Use of short-term incentives is continually increasing, with one study finding that over half of surveyed companies offer hiring bonuses.[23]

Although hiring bonuses can be a powerful tool in landing offer receivers in a competitive market, it is necessary to carefully monitor them so that they do not get out of control. Avoid getting into overly spirited hiring bonus bidding wars with competitors—the other rewards of the job need to be emphasized in addition to the bonus. As with other conditions set for specific new hires, hiring bonuses might give rise to feelings of jealousy and inequity, necessitating retention bonuses if existing employees learn of the bonuses given to new hires. Another potential problem is that bonus recipients may be tempted to take the money and run, by either leaving soon after receiving the bonus or putting forth minimal effort after being hired because their bonus money is not contingent on their job performance.

To address these problems, the organization may place restrictions on the bonus payment, paying half up front and the other half after some designated time period, such as 6 or 12 months; another option is to make payment of a portion or all of the bonus contingent on meeting certain performance goals within a designated time period.[24] Such payment arrangements should encourage only serious and committed offer receivers to accept the offer. Although such "clawbacks" are awkward, and some employers have had difficulties enforcing such agreements, they are generally necessary in some form because the labor markets in which bonuses are most likely to be used (tight labor markets) are the same markets in which alternative jobs are plentiful.

Relocation Assistance

Acceptance of the offer may require a geographic move and entail relocation costs for the offer receiver.[25] Moving expenses are usually covered for both new hires to the organization and internal transfers. The organization may want to provide assistance to conduct the move, as well as totally or partially defray moving costs. Thus, a relocation package may include assistance with house hunting, guaranteed purchase of the applicant's home, a mortgage subsidy, actual moving cost reimbursement, and a cost-of-living adjustment if the move is to a higher-cost area. Managers should be especially attentive to the potential needs of dual-career couples and may find offering job search assistance as part of the package a valuable enticement.[26] An increasing number of companies are giving employees relocation counseling prior to a formal job offer, to ensure that applicants know all the costs and benefits of moving in advance. If applicants are well informed about the likely outcome of a move, those who might drop out of the process can be eliminated from consideration before an expensive investment in selection and hiring is made.[27]

Idiosyncratic Deals

While most of our discussion up to this point has centered around negotiating common contract terms, with an emphasis on salary and benefits, many organizations find that employees wish to engage in a discussion of unique terms that go beyond the traditional menu. The results of these negotiations are "idiosyncratic deals," and they can have important consequences.[28]

What makes a deal idiosyncratic? The most important features are that it is individually negotiated, concerns issues unique to the specific employee, is mutually beneficial for the employee and the employer, and varies in its scope. The main goal here is to strike an integrative or win–win arrangement in which both the employer and the employee expand the terms of the negotiation process to capture positive outcomes that benefit both parties.[29] Unlike traditional negotiation, which asks "how much" employees get from a job (e.g., how much money), idiosyncratic negotiations are about "what" employees get (e.g., a variety of different work and benefit items).

Four broad categories cover the content of most idiosyncratic deals.[30] They are described in Exhibit 12.3, along with examples of each category. Because of the nature of idiosyncratic deals, it is impossible to list all the possible elements of these deals; each situation is unique.

Idiosyncratic deals have resulted in a number of unique positive outcomes. Research has shown that employees who have negotiated tasks, work responsibilities, and schedule flexibility to fit their needs are particularly satisfied, committed to their employers, and engaged in their work.[31] Because we know that satisfied and committed employees are less likely to quit, employers should definitely take these deals into account during the negotiation process. Other research has shown that employees who have idiosyncratic deals are less cynical, help their coworkers, and pitch in with extra effort above and beyond what is generally required.[32] These

---

EXHIBIT 12.3   Elements and Examples of Idiosyncratic Deals

Category	Examples
Tasks and work responsibilities that are specially tailored to the employee's unique KSAOs	• Allow an engineer with an interest and background in marketing to participate in marketing meetings • Give a salesperson who is especially familiar with a certain product line paid time to share expertise with other workers • Give a customer service provider who is interested in management paid time to attend skill development workshops
Flexible schedules to accommodate individual employee needs	• Allow an employee to come in later in the day and leave later to accommodate child care needs • Allow an employee whose spouse works a nonstandard workweek to work a Tuesday to Saturday schedule • Allow a nonexempt employee to work variable hours from week to week
The ability to work outside the main office	• Use a virtual private network or cloud-based servers to allow employees to access work data remotely • Provide a mobile device like a tablet computer or smartphone and pay for connectivity fees for an employee who travels frequently with family
Financial incentives that are particular to the employee and match their unique contribution to the organization	• Compensate an especially productive research developer based on patent applications • Designate an employee with well-developed social networks a "rainmaker" and pay him a bonus for each new client he brings in • Pay a bonus to a manager with strong developmental skills for each person successfully mentored

findings further demonstrate the importance of taking a broader perspective of the job negotiation process.

Restrictions on Employees

In some situations, the organization may want to place certain restrictions on employees to protect its own interests. These restrictions should be known, and agreed to, by the new employee at the time of hire. Thus, they should be incorporated into the job offer and resultant employment relationship. Because of the potential complexities in these restrictions and because they are subject to state contract laws, legal counsel should be sought to guide the organization in drafting appropriate contract language. Several types of restrictions are possible.

Confidentiality Agreement

One form of restriction involves confidentiality or nondisclosure clauses that prohibit current or departing employees from the unauthorized use or disclosure of confidential information during or after employment.[33] Confidential information is any information not made public and that gives the organization an advantage over its competitors. Examples of such information include trade secrets, customer lists, secret formulas, manufacturing processes, marketing and pricing plans, and business forecasts. It will be necessary to spell out, to some degree, exactly what information the organization considers confidential, as well as the time period after employment for which confidentiality must be maintained. These agreements can also indicate when and where employees are authorized to speak for the organization or use organizational logos, with specific consequences for violating the agreement terms. There are limits to confidentiality agreements. Following from labor law, confidentiality agreements cannot include provisions that prohibit employees from discussing wages, hours, or conditions of employment (employers cannot enforce wage secrecy!). Employees also cannot be prohibited from pursuing discrimination claims or disclosing illegal behavior conducted by the employer.

Noncompete Agreement

Another restriction, known as a noncompete agreement, seeks to keep departed employees from taking a job with a competing organization.[34] Such agreements have traditionally been invoked for individuals employed in the science or technology field who have specialized knowledge of trade secrets or new technologies. Noncompetes are also frequently used for consultants, lawyers, doctors, or financial advisors who have established relationships with clients. More generally, noncompete agreements cannot keep departed employees from practicing their trade or profession completely or indefinitely, for this would in essence restrict the person from earning a living in a chosen field. Accordingly, the noncompete agreement must be carefully crafted in order to be enforceable. The agreement should probably not be a blanket statement that applies to all employees; rather, the agreement should apply to those employees who truly could turn into competitors, such as high-level managers, scientists, and technical staff. Additionally, the agreement must be limited in time and geography. The time should be of short duration (less than two years), and the area should be limited to the geographic area of the organization's competitive market. For example, the VP of sales for an insurance agency with locations in two counties of a state might have a noncompete agreement that prohibits working with any other agencies within the two counties, and the solicitation of the agency's policyholders, for one year. Noncompete agreements are very controversial, and as they have become more widespread in organizations, they have also faced increased scrutiny from the legal system. Some courts have completely voided noncompetes, so organizations should not rely too heavily on them.

Arbitration Agreement

Arbitration agreements are restrictions that require employees to resolve employment disputes through an arbitration process rather than through the courts.[35] Arbitration of disputes is conducted by a neutral private-citizen third party, such as a retired judge, and the determination of the arbitrator is binding on both parties. By circumventing jury trials, both the employee and the employer can avoid the time and public exposure involved in a full courtroom procedure. These agreements can be binding, but only if they are very specific, provide for a neutral arbitrator, describe the types of claims that can be brought to arbitration, and hold for both the employer and the employee. Like noncompetes, arbitration agreements are both common and controversial.

Payback Agreement

A final type of restriction is a payback agreement. The intent of this restriction is to retain new hires for some period of time and to financially discourage them from leaving the organization, particularly soon after they have joined. A typical payback agreement requires the employee to repay (in full or pro rata) the organization for any up-front payments made at the time of hire if the employee departs within the first year of employment. These payments might include hiring bonuses, relocation expenses, tuition reimbursements, or any other financial hiring lures. Executive pay packages might contain even more restrictions designed to tie the executive to the organization for an extended period of time. Annual bonuses might be deferred for two or three years and be contingent on the executive not leaving during that time, or an executive may forfeit accrued pension benefits if they depart before a particular date.

Sample Job Offer Letter

A sample job offer letter that summarizes and illustrates the previous discussion and recommendations regarding job offers is shown in Exhibit 12.4. This letter should be read and analyzed for purposes of becoming familiar with job offer letters, as well as gaining an appreciation for the many points that need to be addressed in such a letter. Remember that, normally, whatever is put in the job offer letter, once accepted by the receiver, becomes a binding employment contract. Examples of more complex job offer letters, more relevant to executives, might also be consulted.

EXHIBIT 12.4 Example of Job Offer Letter

The Wright Company

Mr. Vern Markowski
152 Legion Lane
Clearwater, Minnesota

Dear Mr. Markowski:

We are pleased to offer you the position of Human Resource Specialist, beginning March 1, 2020. Your office will be located here in our main facility at Silver Creek, Minnesota.

This offer is for full-time employment, meaning you will be expected to work a minimum of 40 hours per week. Weekend work is also expected, especially during peak production periods.

You will receive a signing bonus of $2,500, half payable on March 1, 2020, and the other half on August 1, 2020, if you are still an employee of the company. Your starting pay will be $3,100 per month. Should you complete one year of employment, you will then participate in our managerial performance review and merit pay process. You will be eligible to participate in our benefit plans as provided in our written descriptions of those plans.

Should you choose to relocate to the Silver Creek area, we will reimburse you for one house/apartment hunting trip for up to $1,000. We will also pay reasonable and normal moving expenses up to $7,500, with receipts required.

It should be emphasized that we are an employment-at-will employer. This means that we, or you, may terminate our employment relationship at any time, for any reason. Only the president of the Wright Company is authorized to provide any modification to this arrangement.

We must have your response to this offer by February 1, 2020, at which time the offer will lapse. If you wish to accept our offer as specified in this letter, please sign and date at the bottom of the letter and return it to me (a copy is enclosed for you). Should you wish to discuss these or any other terms prior to February 1, 2020, please feel free to contact me.

Sincerely yours,

Mary Kaiser
Senior Vice President, Human Resources

I accept the employment offer, and its terms, contained in this letter. I have received no promises other than those contained in this letter.

_____   _____
Signed   Date

JOB OFFER PROCESS

Besides knowing the types of issues to address in a job offer, it is equally important to understand the total job offer process. The content of any specific job offer must be formulated within a broad context of considerations. Once these have been taken into account, the specific offer must be developed and presented to the finalist. Following this, there will be matters to address in terms of either acceptance or rejection of the offer. Finally, there will be an occasional need to deal with the unfortunate issue of revoking, either by the organization or by the offer receiver.

Formulation of the Job Offer

When the organization puts together a specific job offer, several factors should be explicitly considered: knowledge of the terms and conditions offered by competitors, applicant truthfulness about KSAOs and reward information provided, the receiver's likely reaction to the offer, and policies on negotiation of job offer content with the offer receiver.

Knowledge of Competitors

The organization competes for labor within labor markets. The job offer must be sensitive to the labor demand and supply forces operating, for these forces set the overall parameters for job offers to be extended.

On the demand side, this requires becoming knowledgeable about the terms and conditions of job contracts offered by competitors. Here, the organization must confront two issues: exactly who are the competitors, and exactly what terms and conditions are they offering for the type of job for which the hiring organization is staffing?

Assume the hiring organization is a national discount retailer, and it is hiring recent or soon-to-be college graduates for the job of management trainee. It may identify as competitors other retailers at the national level, as well as regional discount retailers. There may be fairly direct competitors in other industries as well (e.g., banking, insurance) that typically place new college graduates in training programs.

Once such competitors are identified, the organization needs to determine what terms and conditions they are offering, if possible. This may be done through formal mechanisms such as performing salary surveys, viewing competitors' ads and websites, or consulting with trade associations. Information may be gathered informally as well, such as through telephone contacts with competitors and conversations with actual job applicants, who have firsthand knowledge of competitors' terms.

The organization may quickly acquire salary information through the use of free online salary sites or ones that charge fees. Salary information is also available through O*NET, Glassdoor, Indeed, and other sources. Generally, the user should be cautious in the use of these data, being careful to assess salary survey character-istics such as sample nature and size, currency of data, definitions of terms and job descriptions, and data presentation. The organization should remember that a job seeker can and will access these data, making this individual a very knowledgeable "shopper" and negotiator.

Through all of the above mechanisms, the organization becomes "marketwise" regarding its competitors. Invariably, however, the organization will discover that for any given term or condition, a range of values will be offered. For example, starting pay might range from $50,000 to $70,000 per year, and the length of the training program may vary from three months to two years. The organization will thus need to determine where within these ranges it wishes to position itself in general, as well as for each particular offer receiver.

On the labor supply side, the organization will need to consider its needs con-cerning both labor quantity and quality (KSAOs and motivation). In general, offers need to be attractive enough that they yield the head count required. Moreover, offers need to take into account the KSAOs each specific receiver possesses and what these specific KSAOs are worth in terms and conditions offered the person. This is illustrated in Exhibit 12.2, which shows an example of an organization's policies regarding differential starting pay offers among offer receivers. Such differ-ential treatment, and all the issues and questions it raises, applies to virtually any other term or condition as well.

Applicant Truthfulness

Throughout the recruitment and selection process, the applicant provides infor-mation about KSAOs and other factors (e.g., current salary). Initially, this infor-mation is gathered as part of the assessment process, the purpose of which is to determine which applicants are most likely to provide a good fit with the job requirements and rewards. For applicants who pass the hurdles and are to receive job offers, the information that has been gathered may very well be used to decide the specific terms and conditions included in the job offer. Just how truthful or believable is this information? The content and cost of job offers depend on how the organization answers this question.

Indications are that deceit may be common. One estimate suggests that over 80% of organizations that institute background screening systems find evidence of résumé fraud. Applicants may be tempted to embellish or enhance not only their reported salaries but also their KSAOs to provide an artificially high base or start-ing point for the organization as it prepares its job offer. Some companies special-ize in providing job applicants with tips and assistance in fabricating educational qualifications, embellishing prior work tasks and responsibilities, and overstating previous salaries; they even provide contacts who will "verify" that an applicant performed well at a job they may have never held.[36]

To combat such deceit by applicants, organizations are increasingly verifying all applicant information, including salary. Integrated applicant tracking systems with reference check databases allow the process of fraud detection to continue from application through the post-hire period. This continual updating is crucial as new information may come online. At the executive level, some organizations even require people to provide copies of their W-2 income forms. The organization should not act on finalist-provided information in the preparation of job offers unless it is willing to assume, or has verified, that the information is accurate.

Likely Reactions of Offer Receivers

Naturally, the terms and conditions presented in an offer should be based on some assessment of the receiver's likely reaction to it. Will the receiver jump at it, laugh at it, or respond somewhere in between?

One way to gauge likely reactions to the offer is to gather information about various preferences from the offer receiver during the recruitment/selection process. Such preliminary discussions and communications will help the organization construct an offer that is likely to be acceptable. At the extreme, the process may lead to almost simultaneous presentation and acceptance of the offer. Another way to assess likely reactions to offers from offer receivers is to conduct research on reward importance to employees and applicants.

Initial Offer Strategies

Once the organization determines its posture regarding the presentation of the initial offer to the receiver there are three strategies to choose from: lowball, market-matching, and best-shot. None of these initial offer strategies is inherently best, with each being appropriate for specific situations. The organization could also choose to tailor a strategy to fit the finalist pursued, as well as other circumstances.

Lowball.   The lowball strategy involves offering the lower bounds of terms and conditions to the receiver. Advantages of this strategy include getting acceptances from desperate or unknowledgeable receivers, minimizing initial employment costs, and leaving plenty of room to negotiate upward. Dangers of the lowball strategy include failing to get any acceptances, driving people away from and out of the finalist pool, developing an unsavory reputation among future potential applicants, and creating inequities and hard feelings that the reluctant accepter may carry into the organization, which may then influence postemployment attraction outcomes such as retention.

Market-Matching.   With a market-matching strategy, the organization prepares an offer that corresponds to the average salary for a given job based on salary survey information. The market-matching strategy should yield a sufficient number of job offer acceptances overall, though not all of the highest-quality (KSAO) applicants. This strategy leaves room for subsequent negotiation, should it be necessary. Market-matching offers are unlikely to offend or excite the receiver, and they probably will not have negative consequences for postemployment outcomes.

Best-Shot. With the best-shot strategy, the organization goes for broke and gives a high offer, one right at the upper bounds of feasible terms and conditions. Accompanying this offer is usually a statement to the receiver that this is indeed the organization's best shot, thus leaving little or no room for negotiation. The best-shot strategy may be chosen (1) for high-quality finalists, (2) when there is strong hiring pressure from competitors, (3) when the organization is pressured to fill vacancies quickly, and (4) as part of an aggressive equal employment opportunity and affirmative action (EEO/AA) recruitment program. A generous starting offer should enhance both preemployment attraction outcomes (e.g., filling vacancies quickly) and postemployment outcomes (e.g., job satisfaction). Best-shot offers obviously increase employment costs. They also leave little or no room for negotiation or for sweetening the offer. Finally, they may create feelings of inequity or jealousy among current employees.

Timing of the Offer

Another issue that must be considered in the process of presenting an offer is the timing of the offer. In general, organizations will want to deliver the offer as quickly as possible after a final decision has been reached. Post-interview delays in communication with candidates have been linked to negative perceptions of the organization.[37] Research has also demonstrated that organizations that make offers more quickly are more likely to have their offers accepted than organizations that wait to make an offer.[38] This same research has shown that individuals who accept these quicker offers have levels of performance and turnover similar to those of individuals who received later offers. In sum, it appears that organizations can increase acceptance rates and reduce vacancy times by making offers in a timely manner.

To extend offers quickly, a plan should be made even before the selection process starts. The results at the final stages of selection should be immediately communicated with decision makers so they can determine who will receive an offer. Job offer letter templates and plans for more personal contacts should be in place. Someone should also have accountability for checking in with offer receivers regularly to keep interest up.

Presentation of the Job Offer

Presentation of the offer may proceed along many different paths. The precise path chosen depends on the content of the offer, as well as factors considered in formulating the offer. To illustrate, two extreme approaches to presenting the job offer—the mechanical approach and the sales approach—are detailed.

Mechanical Approach

The mechanical approach relies on simple one-way communication from the organization to the offer receiver. Little more than a standard (or "form") written offer is sent to the person. The organization then awaits a response. Little or no input about the content of the offer is received from the person, and after the offer has been made, there is no further communication with the person. If the person rejects the offer, another form letter acknowledging receipt of the rejection is sent. Meanwhile, the offer process is repeated anew, without modification, for a different receiver. Although there are obvious disadvantages to such an approach, it is highly efficient and inexpensive. It also ensures that all offer receivers are treated in exactly the same manner, which may improve the legal defensibility of the process.

Sales Approach

The sales approach treats the job offer as a product that must be developed and sold to the customer (i.e., receiver). There is active interaction between the organization and the receiver as the terms and conditions are developed and incorporated into an offer package. Informal agreement unfolds between the receiver and the organization, and reduction of that agreement into an actual job offer is a mere formality. After the formal offer has been presented, the organization continues to have active communication with the receiver. In this way, the organization can be alert to possible glitches that occur in the offer process and can continue to sell the job to the receiver. The sales approach is much more expensive and time-consuming, but it may have a higher chance of the receiver accepting the offer. It is more likely to be employed for high-value employees who likely have more varied KSAO sets than entry-level employees.

Job Offer Negotiation

Before making job offers, the organization should decide whether it will negotiate on them. In essence, the organization must decide whether its first offer to a person will also be its final offer. If there will be room for negotiation, the style of negotiation should also be determined and communicated to applicants.[39]

In making this decision, it is helpful to consider what components of the salary and benefits part of the offer are considered open to negotiation by organizations. Exhibit 12.5 gives example components of a job offer, ranged from most to least likely to be negotiable. A few key principles underline this ordering. Companies prefer to negotiate one-time expenses or issues, like signing bonuses or start dates, rather than ongoing costs, like health benefits. These long-term expenses tend to be off the table because they end up costing the company much more over time. Salary is an obvious exception to this rule. Components like severance and health insurance can also be very legally complicated to change or hard to budget, both of which also add to time costs. Some components are commonly negotiated because the organization benefits from them. Working from home reduces office expenses, professional development opportunities increase performance and retention, and wellness lower insurance costs. Finally, components that fundamentally alter the workflow or structure of the job will seldom be negotiable. Variance in working

EXHIBIT 12.5   Negotiable Components of Job Offer

Very commonly negotiable	Salary
	Signing bonus
	Relocation expenses
	Start date
Commonly negotiable	Working from home
	Professional development opportunities
	Wellness benefits
Seldom negotiable	Hours worked per week
	Work schedules
Very seldom negotiable	Reporting relationships
	Core job responsibilities
	Severance packages
	Health insurance packages

hours or schedules, reporting, and job responsibilities create too much disruption, so few organizations allow for new hires to modify these. It should be acknowledged that the willingness of the company to negotiate will be contingent on their operating environment. In some jobs, scheduling or job tasks are more flexible, whereas in others, working from home is not possible. To understand what can be negotiated, the context needs to be taken into account.

Policies for how negotiations will be conducted should also be discussed in advance. The individual who makes the initial job offer—either lowball, market-matching, or best-shot—will have to know which style of negotiation is appropriate. Research has generally suggested that individuals are more satisfied with a give-and-take negotiation than a hardline "take it or leave it" approach.[40] In other words, offer receivers may be more satisfied with their offer if they feel as though they have a chance to move the initial figure somewhat. This argues against setting in stone all components of the job offer in advance. A nonconfrontational tone may also generate more positive outcomes down the road. Research also suggests that individuals who are more satisfied with the job negotiation process and outcomes are more satisfied with their subsequent compensation and jobs in general and have lower intentions to leave a year later.[41]

Several considerations should be kept in mind when formulating strategies and policies for making job offers. First, remember that job offers occur for both external and internal staffing. For external staffing, the job offer is intended to convert the offer receiver into a new hire. For internal staffing, the job offer is being made to induce the employee to accept a new job assignment or to attempt to retain the employee by making a counteroffer to an offer the employee has received from another organization.

Second, consider the costs of the offer receiver not accepting the job offer. Are other equally qualified individuals available as backup offer receivers? How long can the organization afford to let a position remain vacant? How will current employees feel about job offers being rejected—will they, too, feel rejected or will they feel that something they are unaware of is amiss in the organization? Will those next in line to receive an offer feel like second-class citizens or choices of desperation and last resort? Answers to such questions often suggest it may be desirable to negotiate (up to a point) with the offer receiver.

Finally, job seekers are often quite sophisticated in formulating and presenting their demands to the organization. They know what it will truly cost them to leave their current job and will frame their demands accordingly. They are aware of the particular KSAOs that they have to offer, will make these acutely known to the organization, and will demand a high price for them. The terms demanded (or more politely, proposed) may focus not only on salary but on myriad other possibilities, including vacation time, a flexible work schedule to help balance work and family pressures, guaranteed expenditures on training and development, higher employer matching to a 401(k) retirement plan, and so on. In short, unless it is illegal, it is negotiable, and the organization must be prepared to handle demands from job seekers on virtually every term and condition of employment.

Job Offer Acceptance, Rejection, and Revoking

Ultimately, of course, job offers are accepted or rejected. Throughout the chapter we have emphasized clear and frequent communication, and these factors are especially critical in the acceptance, rejection, and revoking processes.

Acceptance

When the offer receiver accepts a job offer, the organization should do two important things. First, it should check that the receiver has accepted the position as required in the offer. Thus, the acceptance should not come in the form of a counteroffer or with any other contingencies attached to it. Also, the acceptance should occur in the manner required (normally in writing), and it should arrive on or before the date specified.

Second, the organization must maintain contact with the new hire. Initially, this means acknowledging receipt of the acceptance. Additional communication may also be appropriate to further cement the deal and build commitment to the new job and organization. Examples of such continued communication include soon-to-be coworkers calling and offering congratulations to the new hire, sending work materials and reports to the new hire to help phase the person into the new job, and inviting the new hire to meetings and other activities prior to that person's starting date.

The final job offer should specify terms of acceptance required of the offer receiver. For reasons previously noted regarding informal contracts, acceptances should normally be formal. The receiver should be required to accept or reject the offer in total, without revision. Any other form of acceptance is not an acceptance, merely a counteroffer. Finally, the offer should specify the date, if any, by which it will lapse. A lapse date is recommended so that certainty and closure are brought to the offer process.

Rejection

The organization may reject the finalist, and the finalist may reject the organization.

By the Organization. Depending on the decision-making process used, the acceptance of an offer by one person means that the organization will have to reject others. This should be done promptly and courteously. Moreover, the organization should keep records of those it rejects. This is necessary for legal purposes (e.g., applicant flow statistics) and for purposes of building and maintaining a pool of potential applicants that the organization may wish to contact about future vacancies.

The content of the rejection message (usually a letter) is at the discretion of the organization. Most organizations opt for short and vague content that mentions a lack of fit between the applicant's KSAOs and the job's requirements. Providing more specific reasons for rejection should only be done with caution. The reasons provided should be candid and truthful, and they should match the reasons recorded and maintained on other documents by the organization.

By the Offer Receiver. When the receiver rejects the job offer, the organization must decide whether to accept the rejection or extend a new offer to the person. If the organization's position on negotiations has already been determined, as ideally it should, the organization simply needs to carry out its plan to either extend a new offer or move on to the next candidate.

The organization should accept the rejection in a prompt and courteous manner. Moreover, records should be kept of these rejections, for the same reasons they are kept when rejection by the organization occurs.

Revoking

Occasionally, and unfortunately, revoking occurs. Organizations rescind extended offers, and receivers rescind accepted offers. Sometimes revoking is unavoidable. The organization may experience a sudden downturn in business conditions, which causes planned-on jobs to evaporate, or the offer receiver may experience sudden changes in circumstances requiring revoking, such as a change in health status.

As an example of revoking, consider the case of Ford Motor Company, which extended offers of employment as assemblers to hundreds of individuals in its Oakville plant in Ontario, Canada.[42] A sudden drop in demand for vehicles led Ford to withdraw these job offers soon after they had been made. As a result, the individuals who had lost their offers brought a class-action lawsuit, claiming that they had faced considerable economic difficulties because of this repudiation of the employment agreement. Economic damages included lost wages for individuals who had terminated work at other employers in anticipation of these jobs with Ford. In addition to the legal concerns, there are also reputational concerns that come with revoking. As word of the Oakville plant problems spread, Ford could anticipate problems in staffing future positions because applicants might be worried about the company's tendency to not keep its word.

Exhibit 12.6 reviews methods to reduce revoking, as well as actions that can be taken to minimize the negative consequences of revoking. They represent attempts to be fair to the offer receiver while still representing the interests of the organization. It is also advisable to let receivers know exactly why an offer is being revoked, because they may sue if they are not given sufficient opportunity to contest the grounds on which the offer was withdrawn.[43]

For the offer receiver, high standards of fairness are also required. The receiver should not be frivolous and should not go through the application process just "for the experience." Nor should the receiver accept an offer as a way of extracting a counteroffer out of their current employer. Indeed, organizations should be aware that some people to whom they make job offers will receive such counteroffers, and this should be taken into account during the time the offer is initially formulated

---

EXHIBIT 12.6   Organization Actions to Deal With Revoking

A. To Lessen the Occurrence of Revoking

- Extend offers only for positions known to exist and be vacant
- Require top management approval of all revoking
- Conduct thorough assessments of finalists prior to job offer
- Honor outstanding offers but make no new ones
- Discourage offer receiver from accepting offer
- Defer starting date and provide partial pay in interim
- Keep offer open but renegotiate or reduce salary and other economic items
- Stagger new hire starting dates to smooth out additions to payroll

B. To Handle Revoking

- Communicate honestly and quickly with offer receiver
- Provide consolation or apology package (e.g., hiring bonus, three months' salary)
- Pay for any disruption costs (e.g., relocation)
- Hire as consultant (independent contractor), convert to employee later
- Guarantee priority over other applicants when future vacancies occur

and presented. Finally, the receiver should carefully assess the probable fit for the person/job match prior to accepting an offer.

NEW EMPLOYEE ORIENTATION AND SOCIALIZATION

Establishment of the employment relationship through final match activities does not end a concern with the person/job and person/organization match. Rather, that relationship must now be nurtured and maintained over time to ensure that the intended match becomes and remains effective. The new hires become newcomers, and their initial entry into the job and organization should be guided by orientation and socialization activities. Orientation and socialization may be concurrent, overlapping activities that occur for the newcomer. Orientation is typically more immediate, while socialization is more long term.

Despite the importance of a quality orientation program, many organizations do not invest substantial resources in helping new employees get on board.[44] A survey conducted by Harris Interactive found that only 29% of employers give managers training in techniques to facilitate orientation for newcomers, and 15% leave the process of getting new employees on board entirely in the hands of the hiring manager. Experts agree that this shortsighted approach can be very costly, as turnover rates for new hires tend to be much higher than those for established employees. Programs that continue to challenge and develop employees are an especially important element in effective orientation and socialization processes.

It should be remembered that the newcomer is likely entering a situation of uncertainties and unknowns. Research indicates that how the organization responds to the situation will have an important impact on how well the newcomer adapts to the job and remains with the organization. Several factors have been identified as influencing the likely effectiveness of orientation and socialization:[45]

- Providing realistic recruitment information about job requirements and rewards (orientation begins before the job does)
- Clarifying for the newcomer the job requirements, knowledge, and skills to be acquired
- Encouraging the newcomer to actively seek out information and build relationships
- Ensuring that managers and coworkers provide assistance to the newcomer
- Conducting active mentoring for the newcomer

Orientation

Orientation requires considerable advanced planning in terms of topics to cover, development of materials for the newcomer, and scheduling of the many activities that contribute to an effective program. Often, the HR department is responsible for the design and conduct of the orientation, and it will seek close coordination of actual orientation activities and schedules with the newcomer's supervisor. This is also the organization's first opportunity to welcome new hires and to emphasize the opportunities it can provide.

Exhibit 12.7 contains a far-ranging set of suggested topics of information for an orientation program, delivery of which is accomplished via written materials, online services, training programs, meetings with various people, and visual inspection. Note that these activities are spaced out rather than concentrated in just the first day of work for the newcomer. An effective orientation program will foster an understanding of the organization's culture and values, help the new employee understand their role and how they will fit into the total organization, and help the new employee achieve objectives and shorten the learning curve.

Some organizations see the orientation program as a crucial part of their culture formation process.[46] For example, Accenture Consulting puts new employees through a two-week orientation at headquarters, followed by an additional two-week New Joiner Orientation program. During the orientation program, new employees learn about the company's methods for interacting with clients, go through mock client engagement sessions, make presentations to clients, and implement systems to solve client problems. As a follow-up, each new hire has a career counselor who reinforces orientation materials in the workplace and helps the new employee

---

EXHIBIT 12.7   New Employee Orientation Guidelines

Before the Employee Arrives

- Notify everyone in your unit that a new person is starting and what the person's job will be; ask the other staff members to welcome the new employee and encourage their support
- Prepare interesting tasks for the employee's first day
- Provide the new employee with a copy of the job description, job performance standards, organization chart, and your department's organization chart
- Enroll the employee in any necessary training programs
- Make sure the employee's work location is available, clean, and organized
- Make sure a copy of the appropriate personnel policy manual or contract is available for the employee
- Have a benefits information package available
- If possible, identify a staff member to act as a peer mentor for the first week
- Put together a list of key people the employee should meet and interview to get a broader understanding of their roles
- Arrange for a building pass, parking pass, and IDs if necessary
- Draft a training plan for the new employee's first few months

(continued)

EXHIBIT 12.7 Continued

First Day on the Job

- Give a warm welcome and discuss the plan for the first day
- Tour the employee's assigned work space
- Explain where restrooms, vending machines, and break areas are located
- Provide required keys
- Arrange to have lunch with the new employee
- Tour the building and immediate area and introduce the new employee to other staff members
- Introduce the new employee to the person you've identified as a peer mentor (if appropriate)
- Review the job description
- Review the department's (or office's) organizational chart
- Review your office's policies and procedures involving working hours, telephone, e-mail and Internet use, office organization, office resources, and ethics

During the First Week

- Check the employee's work area to ensure needed equipment is in place
- Set up a brief meeting with the employee and the assigned peer mentor to review the first week's activities (if appropriate)
- Schedule a meeting with the human resources office to complete required paperwork, review personnel policies and procedures, learn about benefits, obtain credentials, and explain other policies and procedures

Within the First Month of Employment

- Meet with the employee to review:
  - ❑ Job description
  - ❑ Performance standards
  - ❑ Work rules
  - ❑ Organization structure
  - ❑ Health and safety
  - ❑ Benefits

Within Six Months of Starting

- Revisit performance standards and work rules
- Schedule a performance appraisal meeting

SOURCE: Based on "Guide to Managing Human Resources: New Employee Orientation," Human Resources, University of California, Berkeley (*http://hr.berkeley.edu/hr-network/central-guide -managing-hr/managing-hr/recruiting-staff/new-employee/checklist*).

throughout their career. Although this extensive orientation program is costly, representatives from the organization argue that it has helped create a unified culture among employees who work in offices around the world. Some experts argue that in addition to making sure the first few weeks are successful, organizations should conduct routine follow-up sessions with new employees throughout the first year of employment as a means of enhancing newcomer engagement and retention. This extended check-in period bridges the gap between orientation and socialization.

Socialization

Socialization of the newcomer is a natural extension of orientation activities. Like orientation, socialization aims to achieve effective person/job and person/ organization matches. Whereas orientation focuses on the initial and immediate aspects of newcomer adaptation, socialization emphasizes helping the newcomer fit into the job and organization over time. The emphasis is on the long haul, seeking to gain newcomers' adaptation in ways that will make them want to be successful, long-term contributors to the organization. Research has shown that when socialization programs are effective, they facilitate new employee adjustment by increasing employees' role clarity (clarify job duties and performance expectations), by enhancing their self-efficacy (their belief that they can do the job), and by fostering their social acceptance (making employees believe that they are valued members of the team).[47]

To increase new employees' role clarity, self-efficacy, and social acceptance, two key issues should be addressed in developing and conducting an effective socialization process. First, what are the major elements or contents of socialization that should occur? Second, how can the organization best deliver those elements to the newcomer?

Content

While the content of the socialization process should obviously be somewhat job- and organization-specific, several components are likely candidates for inclusion. From the newcomer's perspective, these components are the following:[48]

1. *People*—meeting and learning about coworkers, key contacts, informal groups and gatherings, and networks; becoming accepted and respected by these people as "one of the gang"
2. *Performance proficiency*—becoming very familiar with job requirements; mastering tasks; having an impact on performance results; and acquiring necessary KSAOs for proficiency in all aspects of the job
3. *Organization goals and values*—learning of the organization's goals; accepting these goals and incorporating them into the line of sight for performance proficiency; learning about values and norms of desirable behavior (e.g., working late and on weekends; making suggestions for improvements)

4. *Politics*—learning about how things really work; becoming familiar with key players and their quirks; taking acceptable shortcuts; schmoozing and networking

5. *Language*—learning special terms, buzzwords, and acronyms; knowing what not to say; learning the jargon of people in the trade or profession

6. *History*—learning about the origins and growth of the organization; becoming familiar with customs, rituals, and special events; understanding the origins of the work unit and the backgrounds of people in it

Many of these topics overlap with the possible content of an orientation program, suggesting that orientation and socialization programs be developed in tandem so that they are synchronized and seamless as the newcomer passes from orientation into socialization.

Delivery

Helping to socialize the newcomer should be the responsibility of several people. First, the newcomer's supervisor should be personally responsible for socializing the newcomer, particularly in terms of performance proficiency and organization goals and values. The supervisor is intimately familiar with and the "enforcer" of these key elements of socialization. It is important that the newcomer and the supervisor communicate directly, honestly, and formally about these elements.

Peers in the newcomer's work unit or team are promising candidates for assisting in socialization. They can be most helpful in terms of politics, language, and history, drawing on their own accumulated experiences and sharing them with the newcomer. They can also make their approachability and availability known to the newcomer when they want to ask questions or raise issues in an informal manner.

To provide a more formal information and support system to the newcomer, but one outside a chain of command, a mentor or sponsor may be assigned to (or chosen by) the newcomer. The mentor functions as an identifiable point of contact for the newcomer, as well as someone who actively interacts with the newcomer to provide the inside knowledge, savvy, and personal contacts that will help the newcomer settle into the current job and prepare for future job assignments. Mentors can also play a vital role in helping shatter the glass ceiling of the organization.

Given the advances in computer technology and the increasing geographic dispersion of an organization's employees, organizations might be tempted to conduct their orientation programs online. Web-based recruiting tools make it easy to track and monitor new hires, provide new hires with an online tour complete with streaming video, provide mandatory training, and automate processes like signing up for insurance, e-mail addresses, and security badges.[49] Though some of this may be necessary, depending on the job, research suggests that socialization programs are less effective when conducted entirely online—in the eyes of both the employees and their supervisors. As would be expected, when compared with in-person programs, online socialization programs do a particularly poor job of socializing employees to the personal aspects of the job and organization, such as organizational goals and values, politics, and how to work well with others.[50]

Finally, the HR department can be very useful to the socialization process. Its representatives can help establish formal, organization-wide socialization activities such as mentoring programs, special events, and informational presentations. Also, representatives may undertake development of training programs on socialization topics for supervisors and mentors. Representatives might also work closely, but informally, with supervisors and coach them in how to become successful socializers of their own newcomers.

Long-Term Adjustment

After an initial period of facilitating adjustment through socialization and orientation programs, many organizations opt for a more hands-off approach. This can be unintentional. Coworkers and supervisors become accustomed to the newcomer's presence and assume that all the necessary information has already been provided. At other times, the lower investment in a newcomer is part of a tacit assumption about how to get employees to be more independent. Help and guidance might be withdrawn, leaving a newcomer to sink or swim.

Unfortunately, this laissez-faire approach to longer-term adjustment is likely leading to lower levels of retention among established employees, and can diminish their interest in further advancement through internal recruiting drives. The assumption that employees become dependent if too much help is provided does not seem to be supported in research.[51] Employees who receive more help are actually found to be more proactive, making more efforts to learn and develop independently. Those who see less help over time, on the other hand, may exert less effort to learn and adapt, settling for a more passive and less engaged work style. Heavy levels of conflict further diminish newcomer proactivity in the socialization process. In sum, it seems that continued support provides an indication that the organization, supervisor, and coworkers want the newcomer to succeed, resulting in greater engagement among newcomers.

Another form of long-term adjustment concerns providing orientation and socialization for employees as they progress through an internal labor market. Sometimes a shift from an independent contributor to a leadership role can be an even more dramatic change in role expectations than starting work at a new organization.[52] Old habits and relationships within the organization will change, and some sort of formal socialization program may be needed to provide effective skills and knowledge to accommodate the change. Similarly, an employee accepting a job assignment overseas will need significant organizational support in the form of orientation and socialization for the new role. Providing sufficient support throughout the adjustment period helps alleviate stress, enhance performance, and limit turnover of expatriates.[53]

LEGAL ISSUES

In the process of establishing the employment relationship, the organization must deal with certain obligations and responsibilities pertaining to (1) meeting contractual obligations, (2) employing only those people who meet the employment requirements under the Immigration Reform and Control Act (IRCA), (3) avoiding negligent hiring, and (4) maintaining the organization's posture toward employment-at-will.

Contractual Obligations

Assuming that the offer is accepted, the organization and the offer receiver will have established a legally binding relationship. Legal obligations are not necessarily mutually binding on both sides, with the employer's promises being taken as more enforceable than the employee's promises.

Besides the social ramifications from informal expectations that are not met, described throughout the chapter, there are also potential legal consequences that arise when perceived promises are not met.[54] The first claim is that of breach of contract. This occurs when the candidate believes that an offer was made but was not fulfilled. This can happen even when an organizational representative makes an offhand comment like, "I'm sure you'll get this promotion that you applied for" or "You can expect a long career here." The second claim is that of promissory estoppel. Here, employees may claim that they relied on promises made by the organization, to their subsequent detriment, since the actual or presumed job offer was withdrawn (such withdrawal is known as revoking and was discussed earlier in this chapter). Examples of detrimental effects include resigning from one's current employer, passing up other job opportunities, relocating geographically, and incurring expenses associated with the job offer. The final claim is that of fraud, where the employee claims the organization made promises it had no intention of keeping. Employees may legally pursue fraud claims and seek both compensatory and punitive damages.

Communication regarding employment agreements may be formal, informal, or a combination of the two.[55] Either written or oral communication can serve as binding on the employer, and therefore HR should monitor policies around these promises and ensure that managers are not putting the organization at legal risk.

Formal Communication

Formal communications may take many forms, and all may be legally enforceable as binding on the employer. Examples of a written document that may be construed as a contract include a letter of offer and acceptance (the usual example), a statement on a job application blank (such as an applicant voucher to the truthfulness of information provided), internal job posting notices, e-mail messages, and statements in employee handbooks or on websites. The more specific the information and statements in the documentation, the more likely they are to be considered employment contracts.

A company's desire to have a strictly at-will employment relationship may unintentionally become undercut by documentation that implies something else. For example, electronic correspondence with an applicant may talk of "continued employment after you complete your probationary period." This statement might be legally interpreted as creating something other than a strict at-will employment relationship.

Care must be taken to ensure that all communication accurately conveys only the intended meanings regarding terms and conditions of employment. To this end, the following suggestions should be heeded:[56]

- Before putting anything in writing, ask, Does the company mean to be held to this?
- Avoid using words that imply a binding commitment.
- Make sure all related documentation is internally consistent.
- Always have a second person, preferably a lawyer, review what has been written.
- Look at the entire hiring procedure, including recruiting and selection practices, and consider any and all written documentation within that context.

Informal Communication

Sources of informal communication include in-person communications, text messages, and e-mails. While informal contracts may be every bit as binding as written contracts, there are two notable exceptions that support placing greater importance on written contracts.

Generally, informal statements are more likely to be enforceable as employment contract terms in the following situations:[57]

- When there is some corroborating record of the communication, such as an audio recording, text message, saved e-mail, or oral statements witnessed by others
- When there is no written statement regarding the terms of employment in question
- When the terms in the informal statement are quite certain and specific
- When the person making the informal statement is in a position of authority to do so (e.g., the hiring manager as opposed to a coworker)
- When the informal statement is made under more formal circumstances

For example, if a supervisor (person in authority) says to a potential employee during a job interview (formal circumstance), "Your work schedule will only cover weekdays" (certain and specific terms), and there is no written evidence to the contrary, the oral statement may be seen as part of a contract. On the other hand, if a coworker (not in authority) says to a potential employee during a meet-and-greet event at a college recruiting fair (informal circumstance), "People don't usually work weekends, but it can vary" (uncertain and vague terms), and the actual written employment agreement specifies that weekend work is possible, the informal statement is far less likely to be seen as part of a contract.

Informal statements may present legal problems not only at the time of the initial employment contract but also throughout the course of the employment relationship. Such issues commonly arise in internal recruiting and selection processes, such as in promotion or professional development contexts. Of particular concern here are oral promises made to employees regarding future events, such as job security ("Don't worry, you will always have a place with us") or job assignments ("After training, you will be assigned as the assistant manager at our new store"). On the other hand, no matter how certain, specific, and formal, employee communications like "I plan to continue to work here for the next three years" seldom can be enforced. Even if such a statement is written by the employee as part of a formal professional development plan, courts frequently allow employees to revoke such promises (i.e., quit) whenever they want without repercussion.

Employment Eligibility Verification

Under the IRCA, the organization must verify each new employee's identity and employment eligibility (authorization).[58] The verification cannot begin until after the job offer has been accepted. Specific federal regulations detail the requirements and methods of compliance eligibility.

For each new employee, the employer must complete the newest I-9 form. Section One, seeking employee information, must be completed no later than the first day of employment. Section Two, requiring the employer to examine evidence of the employee's identity and employment authorization, must be completed within three business days of the date employment begins. Both identity and employment authorization must be verified. The I-9 form shows only those documents that may be used for verification. Some documents (e.g., US passport) verify both identity and authorization; other documents verify only identity (e.g., state-issued driver's license or ID card) or eligibility (e.g., original Social Security card or birth certificate). Section Three deals with reverification and rehires.

E-Verify is an Internet-based system that allows the employer to determine employment eligibility and the validity of Social Security numbers, based on I-9 information. The information is checked against federal databases, usually yielding results in a few seconds. E-Verify verifies only employment eligibility, not immigration status. Federal contractors and subcontractors, along with employers in some states, are required to use E-Verify. Other employers may voluntarily participate in E-Verify. Users must first complete an E-Verify tutorial and pass a mastery test. Employers may not use E-Verify to prescreen applicants or selectively verify only some new employees.

I-9 records should be retained for three years after the date of hire or one year after the date of employment ends, whichever is later. Use of paper or electronic systems or a combination of these is permitted, as are electronic signatures. Employees must be given a copy of the record if they request it.

Finally, since the IRCA prohibits national origin or citizenship discrimination, it is best not to ask for proof of employment eligibility before making the offer. The reason for this is that many of the identity and eligibility documents contain personal information that pertains to national origin and citizenship status, and such personal information might be used in a discriminatory manner. As a further matter of caution, the organization should not refuse to make a job offer to a person based on that person's foreign accent or appearance.

Negligent Hiring

Negligent hiring is a claim made by an injured party (coworker, customer, client, or the general public) against the employer. The claim is that an injury was the result of the employer hiring a person it knew, or should have known, was unfit and posed a threat of risk. In short, negligent hiring is a failure to exercise "due diligence" in the selection and hiring of employees. Injuries may include violence, physical damage, bodily or emotional injury, death, and financial loss. For example, elderly patients in a long-term care facility may suffer injury from a health care attendant due to overmedication or failure to provide adequate food and water, or an accountant might divert funds from a client's account into their own personal account.

The grounds for determining whether negligent hiring occurred are based on several factors. These include whether the organization had a duty (such as a legal or professional requirement) to try to avoid hiring an unfit employee, whether proper staffing steps and care were taken to avoid negligent hiring, whether the hired employee caused damage or injury, and whether the lack of care in hiring was the proximate cause of the harm that occurred.[59]

Notice the importance of the need for following proper and careful staffing steps for minimizing negligent hiring occurrences. What exactly are such steps? Several things could be done.[60] First, be sure to identify in advance, using a selection plan, the KSAOs that must be assessed as hiring requirements. Pay particular attention to the "Os," such as educational and licensure requirements, background and criminal history, references, employment gaps, and alcohol and illegal drug use. Second, follow through by actually using valid and legal selection techniques, and document their usage.

Third, obtain complete KSAO information from each applicant. Where information is lacking or questionable, fill in the gaps and questions rather than ignore or gloss over them. This includes verifying the information provided by the applicant. Unfortunately, there are often pressures to ignore this recommendation, based on claims such as the need for a quick hire, unfavorable applicant reactions to excessive and delaying probes, and the excessive cost of a thorough follow-through.

Fourth, require the applicant to sign a disclaimer statement allowing the employer to check references and otherwise conduct a background investigation. In addition, have the applicant sign a statement indicating that all provided information is true and that no requested information has been withheld.

Fifth, apply utility analysis to determine whether it is worthwhile to engage in the preceding recommendations to try to avoid the (usually slight) chance of a negligent hiring lawsuit. Such an analysis will undoubtedly indicate great variability among jobs in terms of how many resources the organization wishes to invest in negligent hiring prevention.

Finally, when in doubt about a finalist and whether to extend a job offer, do not proceed until those doubts have been resolved. Acquire more information from the finalist, verify existing information more thoroughly, and seek the opinions of others on whether to proceed with the job offer.

Employment-at-Will

As discussed in this chapter and in the social and legal environment chapter, employment-at-will involves the right of either the employer or the employee to unilaterally terminate the employment relationship at any time, for any legal reason. In general, the employment relationship is at-will, and usually the employer wishes it to remain that way. Hence, during the final match (and even before), the employer must take certain steps to ensure that its job offers clearly establish the at-will relationship. These steps are merely a compilation of points already made regarding employment contracts and employment-at-will.

First, ensure that job offers are for an indeterminate time period, meaning that they have no fixed term or specific ending date. Second, include in the job offer a specific disclaimer stating that the employment relationship is strictly at-will. Third, review all written documents (e.g., employee handbook, application blank) to ensure that they do not contain any language that implies anything but a strictly at-will relationship. Finally, take steps to ensure that organizational members do not make any oral statements or promises that would serve to create something other than a strictly at-will relationship.

SUMMARY

During the final match, the offer receiver and the organization move toward each other through the job offer and acceptance process. They seek to enter into the employment relationship that is mutually agreeable to both parties. Important principles in setting expectations need to be observed if a positive relationship is to be achieved. Other important principles focus on the identity of parties to the relationship, disclaimers by the employer, contingencies, other sources that may also specify terms and conditions of employment (e.g., employee handbooks), and unfulfilled promises.

Job offers are designed to induce the offer receiver to join the organization. Offers should be strategically viewed and used by the organization. In that strategy, labor market conditions, organization and applicant needs, and legal issues all converge to shape the job offer and EVP. Job offers may contain virtually any legal terms and conditions of employment. Generally, the offer addresses terms pertaining to compensation and benefits, signing bonuses and relocation assistance, idiosyncratic hiring inducements, and restrictions on employees.

The process of making job offers can be complicated, involving a need to think through multiple issues before making formal offers. Offers should take into account the content of competitors' offers, potential problems with applicant truthfulness, likely reactions of the offer receiver, and the organization's policies on negotiating offers. Presentation of the offer can range from a mechanical process all the way to a major sales approach. Policies and strategies for negotiation make a major difference in terms of the final deal that is struck. Ultimately, the offers are accepted and rejected, and all offer receivers should receive prompt and courteous attention during these events. Steps should be taken to minimize revoking by either the organization or the offer receiver.

Acceptance of the offer marks the beginning of the employment relationship. To help ensure that the initial person/job match starts out and continues to be effective, the organization should undertake both orientation and socialization activities for newcomers.

From a legal perspective, knowledge of employment contract principles is central to understanding the final match. The most important principle pertains to the requirements for a legally enforceable employment contract. The organization must be sure that the offer receiver is employable according to provisions of the IRCA. Both identity and authorization for employment must be verified. The potential negligent hiring of individuals who, once on the job, cause harm to others (employees or customers) is also of legal concern. Those so injured may bring suit against the organization. The organization can take steps to help minimize the occurrence of negligent hiring lawsuits. There are limits on these steps, however, such as the legal constraints on the gathering of background information about applicants. Finally, the organization should have its posture, policies, and practices regarding employment-at-will firmly developed and aligned.

DISCUSSION QUESTIONS

1. If you were the HR staffing manager for an organization, what guidelines might you recommend regarding oral and written communication with job applicants by members of the organization?

2. If the same job offer content is to be given to all offer receivers for a job, is there any need to use the strategic approach to job offers? Explain.

3. What are the advantages and disadvantages of the sales approach in the presentation of the job offer?

4. What are examples of orientation experiences you have had as a new hire that have been particularly effective (or ineffective) in helping to make the person/job match happen?

5. What steps should an employer take to develop and implement its policy regarding employment-at-will?

ETHICAL ISSUES

1. A large financial services organization is thinking of adopting a new staffing strategy for entry into its management training program. The program will provide the trainees all the knowledge and skills they need for their initial job assignment after training. The organization has therefore decided to do college recruiting at the end of the recruiting season. It will hire those who have not been fortunate enough to receive any job offers, pay them a salary 10% below market, and provide no other inducements such as a hiring bonus or relocation assistance. The organization figures this strategy and EVP will yield a high percentage of offers accepted, low cost per hire, and considerable labor cost savings due to below-market salaries. Evaluate this strategy from an ethical perspective.

2. An organization has a staffing strategy in which it hires 10% more employees than it actually needs in any job category in order to ensure its hiring needs are met. It reasons that some of the new hires will revoke the accepted offer and that the organization can revoke some of its offers, if need be, in order to end up with the right number of new hires. Evaluate this strategy from an ethical perspective.

APPLICATIONS

Making a Job Offer

Clean Car Care (3Cs) is located within a western city of 175,000 people. The company owns and operates four full-service car washes in the city. The owner of 3Cs, Arlan Autospritz, has strategically cornered the car wash market, with his only competition being two coin-operated car washes on the outskirts of the city. The unemployment rate in the city and surrounding area is 3.8%, and it is expected to dip even lower.

Arlan has staffed 3Cs by hiring locally and paying wage premiums (above-market wages) to induce people to accept job offers and to remain with 3Cs. Hiring occurs at the entry level only, for the job of washer. If they remain with 3Cs, washers have the opportunity to progress upward through the ranks, going from washer to shift lead person to assistant manager to manager of one of the four car wash facilities. Until recently, this staffing system worked well for Arlan. He was able to hire high-quality people, and a combination of continued wage premiums and promotion opportunities meant he had relatively little turnover (under 30% annually). Every manager at 3Cs, past or present, had come up through the ranks. This is now changing with the sustained low unemployment and the new hires, who just naturally seem more turnover-prone. The internal promotion pipeline is thus drying up, since few new hires are staying with 3Cs long enough to begin climbing the ladder.

Arlan has a vacancy for the job of manager at the north-side facility. Unfortunately, he does not think any of his assistant managers are qualified for the job, and he reluctantly concluded that he has to fill the job externally.

A vigorous three-county recruitment campaign netted Arlan a total of five applicants. Initial assessments resulted in four of those being candidates, and two candidates became finalists. Jane Roberts is the number-one finalist, and the one to whom Arlan has decided to extend the offer. Jane is excited about the job and told Arlan she will accept an offer if the terms are right. Arlan is quite certain Jane will get a counteroffer from her company. Jane has excellent supervisory experience in fast-food stores and a light manufacturing plant. She is willing to relocate, a move of about 45 miles. She will not be able to start for 45 days, due to preparing for the move and the need to give adequate notice to her present employer. As a single parent, Jane wants to avoid working weekends. The number-two finalist is Betts Cook. Though she lacks the supervisory experience that Jane has, Arlan views her as superior to Jane in customer service skills. Jane told Arlan she needs to know quickly if she is going to get the offer, since she is in line for a promotion at her current company and she wants to begin at 3Cs before being offered and accepting the promotion.

Arlan is mulling over what kind of offer to make to Jane. His three managers make between $38,000 and $48,000, with annual raises based on a merit review conducted by Arlan. The managers receive one week of vacation the first year, two weeks of vacation for the next four years, and three weeks of vacation after that. They also receive health insurance (with a 20% employee co-pay on the premium). The managers work five days each week, with work on both Saturday and Sunday frequently occurring during peak times. Jane currently makes $40,500, receives health insurance with no employee co-pay, and has one week of vacation (she is due to receive two weeks shortly, after completing her second year with the company). She works Monday through Friday, with occasional work on the weekends. Betts earns $47,500, receives health insurance fully paid by her employer, and has one week of vacation (she is eligible for two weeks in another year). Occasional weekend work is acceptable to her.

Arlan is seeking input from you on how to proceed. Specifically, he wants you to:

1. Recommend whether Jane should receive a best-shot, market-matching, or lowball offer, and why.
2. Recommend other inducements beyond salary, health insurance, vacation, and schedule that might be addressed in the job offer, and why.
3. Draft a proposed job offer letter to Jane, incorporating your recommendations from items 1 and 2 above, as well as other desired features that should be part of a job offer letter.

Evaluating a Hiring and Variable-Pay Plan

Effective Management Solutions (EMS) is a small, rapidly growing management consulting company. EMS has divided its practice into four areas: management systems, business process improvement, human resources, and quality improvement. Strategically, EMS has embarked on an aggressive revenue growth plan, seeking a 25% revenue increase in each of the next five years for each of the four practice areas. A key component of its plan involves staffing growth, since most of EMS's current entry-level consultants (associates) are at peak client loads and cannot take on additional clients; the associates are also at peak hours load, working an average of 2,500 billable hours per year.

Staffing strategy and planning have resulted in the following information and projections. Each practice area currently has 25 associates, the entry-level position and title. Each year, on average, each practice area has five associates promoted to senior associate within the area (there are no promotions or transfers across areas, due to differing KSAO requirements), and five associates leave EMS, mostly to go to other consulting firms. Replacement staffing thus averages 10 new associates in each practice area, for a total of 40 per year. To meet the revenue growth goals, each practice area will need to hire 15 new associates each year, for a total of 60. A total of 100 associate new hires will thus be needed each year (40 for replacement and 60 for growth).

Currently, EMS provides each job offer receiver with a generous benefits package plus what it deems to be a competitive salary that is nonnegotiable. About 50% of such offers are accepted. Most of those who reject the offer are the highest-quality applicants; they take jobs in larger, more established consulting firms that provide somewhat below-market salaries but high-upside monetary potential through various short-term variable-pay programs, plus rapid promotions.

Faced with these realities and projections, EMS recognizes that its current job offer practices need to be revamped. Accordingly, it has asked Manuel Rodriguez, who functions as a one-person HR "department" for EMS, to develop a job offer proposal for the EMS partners to consider at their next meeting. The partners tell Rodriguez they want a plan that will increase the job offer acceptance rate, slow down the outflow of associates to other firms, and not create dissatisfaction among the currently employed associates.

In response, Rodriguez developed the proposed hiring and variable pay (HVP) program. It has as its cornerstone varying monetary risk/reward packages through a combination of base and short-term variable (bonus) pay plans. The specifics of the HVP program are as follows:

- The offer receiver must choose one of three plans to be under, prior to receiving a formal job offer. The plans are high-risk, standard, and low-risk.
  - The high-risk plan provides a starting salary that is 10% to 30% below the market average and participation in the annual bonus plan, with a bonus range from 0% to 60% of current salary.
  - The standard plan provides a starting salary that is 10% below the market average and participation in the annual bonus plan, with a bonus range from 0% to 20% of current salary.
  - The low-risk plan provides a starting salary that is 5% above the market average and no participation in the annual bonus plan.
- The average market rate will be determined by salary survey data obtained by HR.
- The individual bonus amount will be determined by individual performance on three indicators: number of billable hours, number of new clients generated, and client-satisfaction survey results.
- The hiring manager will negotiate the starting salary for those in the high-risk and standard plans, based on likely person/job and person/organization fit and on need to fill the position.
- The hiring manager may also offer a skills premium of up to 10% of initial starting salary under all three plans—the premium will lapse after two years.
- Switching plans is permitted only once every two years.
- Current associates may opt into one of the new plans at their current salary.

Evaluate the HVP program as proposed, answering the following questions:

1. If you were an applicant, would the HVP program be attractive to you? Why or why not? If you were an offer receiver, which of the three plans would you choose, and why?
2. Will the HVP program likely increase the job offer acceptance rate? Why or why not?
3. Will the HVP program likely reduce turnover? Why or why not?
4. How will current associates react to the HVP program, and why?
5. What issues and problems will the HVP plan create for HR? For the hiring manager?
6. What changes would you make in the HVP program, and why?

ENDNOTES

1. L. Jiang, T. M. Probst, and W. L. Benson, "Organizational Context and Employee Reactions to Psychological Contract Breach: A Multilevel Test of Competing Theories," *Economic and Industrial Democracy*, 2017, 38, pp. 513–534; D. M. Rousseau, S. D. Hansen, and M. Tomprou, "A Dynamic Phase Model of Psychological Contract Processes," *Journal of Organizational Behavior*, 2018, 39, pp. 1081–1098; O. N. Solinger, J. Hofmans, P. M. Bal, and P. G. W. Jansen, "Bouncing Back From Psychological Contract Breach: How Commitment Recovers Over Time," *Journal of Organizational Behavior*, 2016, 37, pp. 494–514; M. Feffer, "Fixing Poor Engagement Starts With Understanding Its Cause," *Society for Human Resource Management Employee Relations*, Mar. 26, 2018 (*www.shrm.org*).

2. C. H. Fleischer, *The SHRM Essential Guide to Employment Law* (Alexandria, VA: Society for Human Resource Management, 2018); D. D. Bennett-Alexander and L. P. Hartman, *Employment Law for Business*, 9th ed. (New York: McGraw Hill-Education, 2019).

3. J. Mates, "14 Things Your Job Offer Letter Must Have to Be Effective," *Society for Human Resource Management Talent Acquisition*, June 6, 2017 (*www.shrm.org*).

4. M. W. Bennett, D. J. Polden, and H. J. Rubin, *Employment Relationships: Law and Practice (New York: Aspen, 2004); Society for Human Resource Management,* "Employing Independent Contractors," Dec. 19, 2019 (*www.shrm.org*).

5. M. A. Cherry and A. Aloisi, "Dependent Contractors in the Gig Economy: A Comparative Approach," *American University Law Review*, 2017, 66, pp. 635–690; S. Greenhouse, "U.S. Cracks Down on 'Contractors' as a Tax Dodge," *New York Times*, Feb. 17, 2010 (*www.nytimes.com*).

6. Bennett, Polden, and Rubin, *Employment Relationships: Law and Practice*.

7. R. Mayhew, "Can My Boss Keep My Last Paycheck If I Don't Put My Two Weeks Notice In?" *Houston Chronicle*, Aug. 15, 2013 (*http://work.chron.com/can-boss-keep-last-paycheck-dont-put-two-weeks-notice-in-8946.html*).

8. Bennett, Polden, and Rubin, *Employment Relationships: Law and Practice*.

9. Society for Human Resource Management, "At Will: Policy Statement," Mar. 2010 (*www.shrm.org*).

10. Fleischer, *The SHRM Essential Guide to Employment Law.*

11. Society for Human Resource Management, "Conditional Job Offer Letter" (*www.shrm.org*), accessed Mar. 9, 2020; Society for Human Resource Management, "Unconditional Job Offer Letter" (*www.shrm.org*), accessed Mar. 9, 2020.

12. G. Stahl, I. Björkman, E. Farndale, S. S. Morris, J. Paauwe, P. Stiles, J. Trevor, and P. Wright, "Six Principles of Effective Global Talent Management," *Sloan Management Review*, 2012, 53, pp. 25–42.

13. M. M. Breslin, "Why Companies Are Embracing the Employee Value Proposition," *Workforce*, Feb. 28, 2013 (*www.workforce.com*).

14. M. Pokorny, "Getting to Know Your Employees and What Motivates Them," *Employment Relations Today*, 2013, 39, pp. 45–52.

15. J. Korff, T. Biemann, and S. C. Voelpel, "Human Resource Management Systems and Work Attitudes: The Mediating Role of Future Time Perspective," *Journal of Organizational Behavior*, 2017, 38, pp. 45–67; Society for Human Resource Management, "Developing Employee Career Paths and Ladders" (*www.shrm.org*), accessed Mar. 11, 2020.

16. K. L. Uggerslev, N. E. Fassina, and D. Kraichy, "Recruiting Through the Stages: A Meta-Analytic Test of Predictors of Applicant Attraction at Different Stages of the Recruiting Process," *Personnel Psychology*, 2012, 65, pp. 597–660.

17. M. Hout, "Social and Economic Returns to College Education in the United States," *Annual Review of Sociology*, 2012, 38, pp. 379–400; L. Reisel, "Is More Always Better? Early Career Returns

to Education in the United States and Norway," *Research in Social Stratification and Mobility*, 2013, 31, pp. 49–68.

18. Bureau of Labor Statistics, "Annual Mean Wage of Human Resources Managers, by State, May 2018" (*bls.gov/oes*).

19. Y. Rofcanin, A. Berber, E. Marescaux, P. M. Bal, F. Mughal, and M. Afacan Findikli, "Human Resource Differentiation: A Theoretical Paper Integrating Co-workers' Perspective and Context," *Human Resource Management Journal*, 2019, 29, pp. 270–286.

20. F. D. Blau and L. M. Kahn, "The Gender Wage Gap: Extent, Trends, and Explanations," *Journal of Economic Literature*, 2017, 55, pp. 789–865; M. Hernandez, D. R. Avery, S. D. Volpone, and C. R. Kaiser, "Bargaining While Black: The Role of Race in Salary Negotiations," *Journal of Applied Psychology*, 2018, 104, pp. 581–592.

21. K. G. Kugler, J. A. M. Reif, T. Kaschner, and F. C. Brodbeck, "Gender Differences in the Initiation of Negotiations: A Meta-Analysis," *Psychological Bulletin*, 2017, 144, pp. 198–222; B. Artz, A. H. Goodall, and A. J. Oswald, "Do Women Ask?" *Industrial Relations: A Journal of Economy and Society*, 2018, 57, pp. 611–636.

22. A. P. Cowen, A. W. King, and J. J. Marcel, "CEO Severance Agreements: A Theoretical Examination and Research Agenda," *Academy of Management Review*, 2015, 41, pp. 151–169.

23. C. Connley, "13 Companies Offering Hiring Bonuses up to $20,000 Right Now," *CNBC*, July 28, 2019 (*www.cnbc.com*); Society for Human Resource Management, "Use of Short Term Incentives Up," *SHRM Online*, Nov. 9, 2012 (*www.shrm.org*).

24. C. Kirschbaum, "The Secret Danger in Your Signing Bonus and How It Can Trap You," *LinkedIn*, Oct. 6, 2017 (*www.linkedin.com*); B. Chappell, "U.S. Soldiers Told to Repay Thousands of Signing Bonuses From Height of War Effort," *National Public Radio*, Oct. 23, 2016 (*www.npr.org*).

25. Society for Human Resource Management, "Managing Employee Relocation" (*www.shrm.org*), accessed Mar. 11, 2020.

26. J. M. Vick and J. S. Furlong, "The Logistics of a Dual-Career Search," *Chronicle of Higher Education*, Mar. 14, 2012 (*http://chronicle.com/article/the-logistics-of-a-dual-career/131140/*).

27. H. O'Neill, "Relocation Benefits Are on the Move," *Workforce*, Feb. 6, 2012 (*www.workforce.com*).

28. D. M. Rousseau, V. T. Ho, and J. Greenberg, "I-Deals: Idiosyncratic Terms in Employment Relationships," *Academy of Management Review*, 2006, 31, pp. 977–994.

29. M. A. Wheeler, quoted in K. Johnston, "The Art of Haggling," *Harvard Business School: Working Knowledge*, May 7, 2012 (*http://hbswk.hbs.edu/item/6922.html*).

30. C. C. Rosen, D. J. Slater, C. Chang, and R. E. Johnson, "Let's Make a Deal: Development and Validation of the Ex Post I-Deals Scale," *Journal of Management*, 2013, 39, pp. 709–742.

31. Rosen et al., "Let's Make a Deal: Development and Validation of the Ex Post I-Deals Scale"; S. Hornung, D. M. Rousseau, J. Glaser, P. Angerer, and M. Weigel, "Beyond Top-Down and Bottom-Up Work Redesign: Customizing Job Content Through Idiosyncratic Deals," *Journal of Organizational Behavior*, 2010, 31, pp. 187–215.

32. M. Morf, A. B. Bakker, and A. Feierabend, "Bankers Closing Idiosyncratic Deals: Implications for Organisational Cynicism," *Human Resource Management Journal*, 2019, 29, pp. 585–599; S. Anand, P. R. Vidyarthi, R. C. Liden, and D. M. Rousseau, "Good Citizens in Poor-Quality Relationships: Idiosyncratic Deals as a Substitute for Relationship Quality," *Academy of Management Journal*, 2010, 53, pp. 970–988.

33. E. N. Bass, "Practical Guidance for Employers on Confidentiality Provisions That Survive NLRB Scrutiny," *A.B.A. Journal of Labor and Employment Law*, 2019, pp. 113–130; J. M. Pacella, "Silencing Whistleblowers by Contract," *American Business Law Journal*, 2018, 55, pp. 261–313.

34. R. Maurer, "Democrats Propose Bans on Noncompete, No-Poach Agreements," *Society for Human Resource Management Talent Acquisition*, May 10, 2018 (*www.shrm.org*); R. Zeidner, "Are

Noncompete Agreements Right for You?" *HR Magazine*, Nov. 29, 2017; J. J. Prescott, N. D. Bishara, and E. Starr, "Understanding Noncompetition Agreements: The 2014 Noncompete Survey Project," *Michigan State Law Review*, 2016, pp. 369–464.

35. Fleischer, *The SHRM Essential Guide to Employment Law*; J. M. Pacella, "Silencing Whistleblowers by Contract," *American Business Law Journal*, 2018, 55, pp. 261–313.

36. R. Maurer, "Background Screening Goes With the Workflow," *HR Magazine*, Oct. 1, 2016 (*www.shrm.org*).

37. D. S. Chapman and J. Webster, "Toward an Integrated Model of Applicant Reactions and Job Choice," *International Journal of Human Resource Management*, 2006, 17, pp. 1032–1057.

38. W. J. Becker, T. Connolly, and J. E. Slaughter, "The Effect of Job Offer Timing on Offer Acceptance, Performance, and Turnover," *Personnel Psychology*, 2010, 63, pp. 223–241.

39. J. Summer, "The Viability of Banning Salary Negotiations," *Society for Human Resource Management Compensation*, July 10, 2015 (*www.shrm.org*); S. A. O'Brien, "Reddit: You Can't Negotiate Your Salary" *CNN Business*, Apr. 7, 2015 (*money.cnn.com*).

40. S. Kwon and L. R. Weingart, "Unilateral Concessions From the Other Party: Concession Behavior, Attributions, and Negotiation Judgments," *Journal of Applied Psychology*, 2004, 89, pp. 263–278.

41. J. R. Curhan, H. A. Elfenbein, and G. J. Kilduff, "Getting Off on the Right Foot: Subjective Value Versus Economic Value in Predicting Longitudinal Job Outcomes From Job Offer Negotiations," *Journal of Applied Psychology*, 2009, 94, pp. 524–534.

42. T. Stefanik, "Ford Hit With Class-Action Lawsuit After Backing Out of 100s of Jobs," *Canadian HR Reporter*, Mar. 8, 2010, p. 5.

43. R. Maurer, "Employers Should Share All Background Check Reports Before Revoking Job Offers," *Society for Human Resource Management Talent Acquisition*, Oct. 20, 2017 (*www.shrm.org*)

44. K. Gurchiek, "Many Employers Wing Support of New Hires," *HR News*, Sept. 18, 2007 (*www.shrm.org*).

45. A. M. Saks and J. A. Gruman, "Getting Newcomers on Board: A Review of Socialization Practices and Introduction to Socialization Resources Theory," in C. R. Wanberg (ed.), *Oxford Handbook of Organizational Socialization* (New York: Oxford University Press, 2012), pp. 27–55; T. N. Bauer, T. Bodner, B. Erdogan, D. M. Truxillo, and J. S. Tucker, "Newcomer Adjustment During Organizational Socialization: A Meta-Analytic Review of Antecedents, Outcomes, and Methods," *Journal of Applied Psychology*, 2007, 92, pp. 707–721; H. J. Klein, B. Polin, and K. L. Sutton, "Specific Onboarding Practices for the Socialization of New Employees," *International Journal of Selection and Assessment*, 2015, 23, pp. 263–283.

46. J. Marquez, "Connecting a Virtual Workforce," *Workforce Management*, Sept. 22, 2008, pp. 23–25; F. Hansen, "Onboarding for Greater Engagement," *Workforce Management Online*, Oct. 2008 (*www.workforce.com*).

47. Bauer et al., "Newcomer Adjustment During Organizational Socialization: A Meta-Analytic Review of Antecedents, Outcomes, and Methods."

48. G. T. Chao, A. M. O'Leary-Kelly, S. Wolf, H. J. Klein, and P. D. Gardner, "Organizational Socialization: Its Content and Consequences," *Journal of Applied Psychology*, 1994, 79, pp. 730–743.

49. A. D. Wright, "Experts: Web-Based Onboarding Can Aid Employee Retention," July 14, 2008 (*www.shrm.org*).

50. M. J. Wesson and C. I. Gogus, "Shaking Hands With a Computer: An Examination of Two Methods of Organizational Newcomer Orientation," *Journal of Applied Psychology*, 2005, 90, pp. 1018–1026.

51. J. D. Kammeyer-Mueller, C. R. Wanberg, A. L. Rubenstein, and Z. Song, "Support, Undermining, and Newcomer Socialization: Fitting In During the First 90 Days," *Academy of Management*

Journal, 2013, 56, pp. 1104–1124; S. S. Nifadkar and T. N. Bauer, "Breach of Belongingness: New-comer Relationship Conflict, Information, and Task-Related Outcomes During Organizational Socialization," *Journal of Applied Psychology*, 2016, 101, pp. 1–13.

52. D. W. Johnston and W. Lee, "Extra Status and Extra Stress: Are Promotions Good for Us?" *Industrial and Labor Relations Review*, 2013, 66, pp. 32–54; T. J. Mauer and M. London, "From Individual Contributor to Leader: A Role Identity Shift Framework for Leader Development Within Organizations," *Journal of Management*, 2018, 4, pp. 1426–1452.

53. M. Kraimer, M. Bolino, and B. Mead, "Themes in Expatriate and Repatriate Research Over Four Decades: What Do We Know and What Do We Still Need to Learn?" *Annual Review of Organizational Psychology and Organizational Behavior*, 2016, 3, pp. 83–109; B. M. Firth, G. Chen, B. L. Kirkman, and K. Kim, "Newcomers Abroad: Expatriate Adaptation During Early Phases of International Assignments," *Academy of Management Journal*, 2013, 57, pp. 280–300.

54. M. W. Bennett, D. J. Polden, and H. J. Rubin, *Employment Relationships: Law and Practice* (New York: Aspen, 2019); R. Maurer, "Beware: Rescinding Job Offers Can Prompt Legal Consequences," *SHRM Talent Acquisition*, Aug. 25, 2016 (*www.shrm.org*).

55. Fleischer, *The SHRM Essential Guide to Employment Law*.

56. Society for Human Resource Management, "How to Create an Offer Letter Without Contractual Obligations" (*www.shrm.org*), accessed Mar. 9, 2020.

57. Fleischer, *The SHRM Essential Guide to Employment Law*; Society for Human Resource Management, "How to Create an Offer Letter Without Contractual Obligations."

58. Equal Employment Opportunity Commission, "Immigration Control and Reform Act" (*eeoc.gov /eeoc/history/35th/thelaw/irca.html*), retrieved Jan. 18, 2020.

59. R. K. Robinson, G. M. Franklin, and R. F. Wayland, *Employment Regulation in the Workplace* (Armonk, NY: M. E. Sharpe, 2010); Bennett-Alexander and Hartman, *Employment Law for Business*; D. J. Walsh, *Employment Law for Human Resource Practice*, 6th ed. (Boston: Cengage Learning, 2019), pp. 149–160.

60. F. Hansen, "Taking 'Reasonable Action' to Avoid Negligent Hiring Claims," *Workforce Management*, Dec. 11, 2006, pp. 31–33; Bennett-Alexander and Hartman, *Employment Law for Business*; Walsh, *Employment Law for Human Resource Practice*.

The Staffing Organizations Model

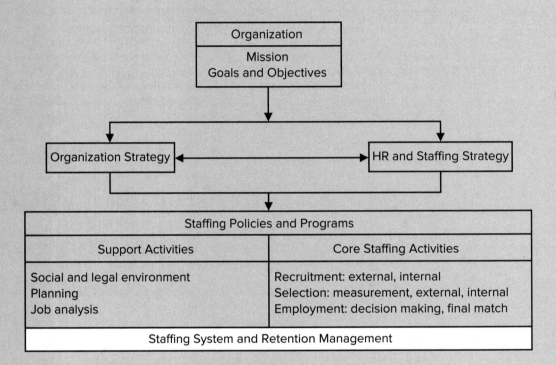

PART SIX

Staffing System and Retention Management

CHAPTER THIRTEEN

Staffing System Management

LEARNING OBJECTIVES AND INTRODUCTION

Learning Objectives

- Recognize the importance of effective policies and procedures for staffing
- Understand the importance of concrete, fair policies and procedures in selection
- Evaluate the advantages and disadvantages of outsourcing staffing processes
- Understand how to evaluate the various results of staffing processes
- Develop metrics for the measurement of staffing systems
- Understand different methods for analyzing the results of staffing systems
- Recognize the legal issues involving record keeping and applicant/employee privacy
- Plan for effective dispute resolution

Introduction

Up to this point, we have covered how organizations plan for effective staffing system implementation, recruit candidates, evaluate candidates, select from candidates, and make a final match. We now take a step back from these operational issues and evaluate whether the overall staffing system is functioning effectively. Staffing systems involve complex processes and decisions that require organizational direction, coordination, and evaluation.

The evaluation of the effectiveness of a staffing system as a whole has become a central issue for human resource (HR) managers. An increased push for accountability in all areas of HR that began over 20 years ago has become a permanent feature of the organizational landscape. Staffing managers who are successfully adapting to this environment focus on analytics, which demonstrate relationships between a variety of staffing functions and organizational performance.[1]

The chapter starts by describing how the staffing function operates within the HR department of many organizations. The role and nature of staffing policies and procedures in administering the staffing function are explained, as is the use of human resource information systems (HRISs) to enhance efficient operation of staffing systems. Next, a discussion of ways to evaluate the effectiveness of the staffing function is presented. Methods for analyzing the results of the staffing process are compared to gauge the effectiveness of staffing systems. Legal issues surrounding the management of staffing systems are discussed, including matters of compiling various records and reports and of conducting legal audits of staffing activities. Finally, training in employment law and compliance requirements for managers and employees, and mechanisms for dispute resolution are described.

DESIGN AND ADMINISTRATION OF STAFFING SYSTEMS

The preceding chapters have described some of the individual practices that make up a staffing system, including job analysis, internal and external recruiting, internal and external selection, job offers, and newcomer orientation and socialization. Staffing professionals need to have expertise in all of these areas. At this point, we move to a discussion of how these individual elements come together to form a more overarching system of interdependent parts.

Defining the Mission of Staffing

A well-defined mission statement and goals serve as a foundation for any staffing system. All other administrative decisions flow from this starting point. As we have seen throughout the book, a clear understanding of the organization's strategy and culture can help create the best solutions.

Experts emphasize that an effective HR function must be aware of organizational strategy, build capabilities to execute strategies, integrate talent and organizational practices, and advocate for the effective implementation of policies and procedures.[2] To develop a system of integrated practices that fits strategic considerations, organizational leaders analyze where the organization sits in the market and how it compares with other firms. Staffing experts should create metrics for the evaluation of staffing systems, and these metrics should have a direct relationship with strategic needs.

An increasing body of research supports the idea that the link between HR systems and organizational performance is contingent on a fit between these systems and strategy.[3] An organization that is primarily focused on creating customer value by providing the lowest-cost products and services will want a staffing system that is similarly frugal and efficient. In this case, fewer steps in the process, greater use of automated systems, and higher tolerance for lower levels of qualifications are called for. Conversely, an organization that emphasizes quality will seek the best employees, which entails a more rigorous and elaborate screening system. Organizations in rapidly changing environments will emphasize systems that can be rapidly modified and are flexible with more temporary and contingent workers, whereas more stable operating environments call for long-term and predictable selection and internal staffing systems.

Corporate culture will dictate other components of the staffing system. A staffing system that corresponds with the values, norms, and habits of organizational members will be accepted as well as implemented consistently and effectively. Some of the most significant issues related to culture, such as hierarchy versus participation, or competition versus cooperation, will create different sets of preferences for decision making that are reflected in organizational arrangements. For the operational and staffing functions to work well together in organizations, there must be frequent communication among all managers during the process. A successful staffing function will help site managers and line managers easily and quickly fill vacancies with qualified individuals. A failure in coordination and communication, on the other hand, can make the staffing function an administrative hurdle that managers will try to circumvent whenever possible.

In addition to integrating with organizational strategy, staffing systems must be integrated with other elements of the HR system as a whole. Taking a systematic, integrative view of HR practices has been consistently shown to enhance organizational performance.[4] Effective, consolidated HR systems are visible and understandable to employees, applied in a way that shows a consistent set of goals, and agreed upon by multiple layers of management. Staffing can contribute to organizational success only if it complements practices in the areas of compensation, training and development, and employee relations.[5] For example, staffing members must coordinate their activities with the compensation and benefits group in developing policies on the economic components of job offers, such as starting pay, hiring bonuses, and special perks. Staffing activities must also be closely coordinated with the training and development function to identify training needs for external, entry-level new hires and to plan transfer and promotion-enhancing training experiences for current employees. The director of employee relations will work with the staffing area to determine how policies and practices will be combined with corporate communications and other programs to improve employee morale and motivation.

Organizational Arrangements

An organizational arrangement refers to how the organization structures itself to conduct HR and staffing activities, often within the HR department. The specific form of these arrangements is derived from the goals described earlier under the strategic and cultural factors.

Culture clearly will have an impact on organizational arrangements. Organization-wide staffing systems improve operational outcomes through the actions of both central administration and direct supervisors.[6] An organization that has a hierarchical system for decision making will incorporate a greater degree of centralized authority to maintain this control, whereas a flat or participative culture is better matched with devolving staffing choices to individual managers, who would likely prefer to participate in staffing activities. An organization that seeks to build team consensus should implement systems that lead to the hiring of individuals with agreeable personality traits and that allow team members to evaluate applicants in person, whereas employees in a more competitive or aggressive organization might feel as though screening new hires is a waste of their work time or might even select applicants who seem like they will not be able to compete with them effectively. These are just some examples; many other cultural considerations can be taken into account when determining the organizational arrangements that best fit the organization's workforce.

Organizational arrangements are also dependent on logistical considerations. The size and resource base of organizations vary widely. The majority of organizations (about 11 million) in the United States have fewer than 100 employees, and employ slightly more than half of all working adults. A relatively smaller group of about 20,000 organizations have 500 or more employees, and employ about half of all working adults.[7] In small firms, staffing is most likely to be conducted by the owner, the president, or the work unit manager. Only a small percentage (13%) of these organizations have an HR department that is responsible for staffing. Among these small organizations, staffing activities are quite varied in terms of establishing job requirements, recruitment sources, recruitment communication techniques, selection methods, decision making, and job offers.

As organization size increases, so does the likelihood of there being an HR department and a unit within it that is responsible for staffing. But the exact configuration of the HR department and staffing activities will depend on whether the organization is composed of business units pursuing a common business product or service (an integrated business organization) or a diverse set of products or services (a multiple-business organization).[8] Because of its diversity, the multiple-business organization will likely not try to have a major, centralized corporate HR department. Rather, it will have a small corporate HR department, with a separate HR department within each business unit. In this arrangement, staffing activities will be quite decentralized, with some guidance and expertise from the corporate HR department.

An integrated business organization will likely have a highly centralized HR department at the corporate level, with a much smaller HR presence at the plant, store, or site level. As pertains to staffing, such centralization creates economies of scale and consistency in staffing policies and processes, as well as in hiring standards and new hire quality.

Exhibit 13.1 gives two examples of how staffing systems might be organized. Organization A has a hierarchical administrative arrangement. Such a system is marked by strong specialization of roles, with distinct chains of command for HR and operations. This is a good fit for large organizations in stable environments that have predictable production demands and a highly formal culture. The chief human resources officer receives information from top management regarding organizational strategy and goals, and then translates this into policies and procedures. Methods for tracking and evaluating success against standardized metrics are also developed. Talent management directors oversee the HR representatives, who implement recruiting drives and perform the initial screening of applicants. The director of operations, site managers, and line managers focus on their own areas of specialization, receiving detailed and standardized files of applicants who have been screened by HR representatives. This separation of roles is highly efficient and ensures that all systems function smoothly.

On the other hand, Organization B is far more decentralized and participative. This system is more characteristic of firms in which work is performed in teams and all employees have a role in determining how to best perform their tasks. This

EXHIBIT 13.1 **Examples of Staffing System Administrative Arrangements**

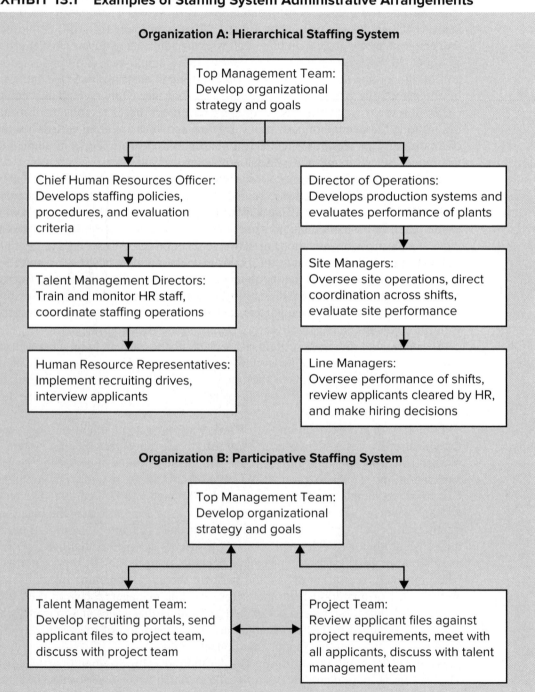

Organization A: Hierarchical Staffing System

Top Management Team:
Develop organizational
strategy and goals

Chief Human Resources Officer:
Develops staffing policies,
procedures, and evaluation
criteria

Director of Operations:
Develops production systems and
evaluates performance of plants

Talent Management Directors:
Train and monitor HR staff,
coordinate staffing operations

Site Managers:
Oversee site operations, direct
coordination across shifts,
evaluate site performance

Human Resource Representatives:
Implement recruiting drives,
interview applicants

Line Managers:
Oversee performance of shifts,
review applicants cleared by HR,
and make hiring decisions

Organization B: Participative Staffing System

Top Management Team:
Develop organizational
strategy and goals

Talent Management Team:
Develop recruiting portals, send
applicant files to project team,
discuss with project team

Project Team:
Review applicant files against
project requirements, meet with
all applicants, discuss with talent
management team

type of system is a good fit for rapidly changing environments where continual adaptation is the norm and the culture recognizes a need for employee voice. The top management team still develops organizational strategy and goals, but the talent management team and the project team continually interact with organizational leaders and have consultative meetings. Fitting with the lack of specialization, talent management team members sit on committees with project teams. During these meetings, project team managers discuss their needs for workplace competencies, as the talent management team members provide resources and guidance in how to acquire these competencies using internal and external staffing systems. The project team reviews all candidate files and participates in staffing decisions, while the talent management team informs project teams and top management teams what sorts of capabilities are available to meet each goal. This interactive approach may not possess the extreme efficiency of the hierarchical system, but it is uniquely adapted to the operational environment.

Organizations A and B are two examples of different configurations of HR systems within two fairly extreme situations. Most organizations find that they have a system that combines elements of both the hierarchical system and the participative system—for example, departments focused on manufacturing or routine customer service are hierarchical, while departments focused on research and development are configured in a more participative system.

Policies and Procedures

A policy is a selected course or guiding principle. It is an objective to be sought through appropriate actions. For example, the organization might have a promotion-from-within policy as follows: "It is the intent of XXX organization to fill from within all vacancies above the entry level, except in instances of critical, immediate need for a qualified person unavailable internally." This policy makes it clear that promotion from within is the desired objective; the only exception is in the absence of an immediately available, qualified current employee.

A procedure is a prescribed routine or way of acting in similar situations. It provides the rules that govern a particular course of action. To carry out the promotion-from-within policy, for example, the organization may follow specific procedures for listing and communicating the vacancy, identifying eligible applicants, and assessing the qualifications of the applicants.

Policies and procedures can improve the strategic focus of the staffing area.[9] Clearly articulated systems of policies and procedures make it possible to consider the meaning and function of the entire system at a strategic level. On the other hand, poorly thought out or inconsistent policies and procedures result in HR managers spending an inordinate amount of time playing catch-up or "putting out fires," as inconsistent behavior across organizational units inevitably leads to employee complaints. Without clear staffing policies, managers scramble to develop solutions to recruitment or selection needs at the last minute. Dealing with these routine breakdowns in procedures leaves less time to consult organizational goals or consider alternatives. The final result is inefficiency and wasted time.

Policies and procedures can also greatly enhance the perceived justice of staffing activities. Research conducted in a wide variety of organizations has consistently shown that employees perceive organizational decision making as most fair when decisions are based on facts rather than social influence or personal biases, when decision-making criteria are clearly communicated, and when the process is consistently followed across all affected individuals.[10] The use of well-articulated policies and procedures can increase perceived justice considerably. There are also bottom-line implications: employee perceptions of organizational justice have been linked to increased intention to pursue a job in the recruitment context, increased intention to accept a job in the selection context, increased satisfaction and commitment in job assignments, and decreased intention to sue a former employer in the layoff context.[11]

What are the keys to writing staffing policies and procedures that enhance organizational effectiveness? Exhibit 13.2 summarizes the most important principles.[12] A clear link between organizational goals and staffing policies and procedures underlies every one of these principles. The policy and procedure process is a cycle, in which existing practices are continually revised to match environmental demands. The plan is therefore based on identifying strategic goals, employing specific methods to achieve these goals, measuring the success of these methods, and responding to ongoing information.

The first stage is determining the overarching HR strategy, as described in the planning chapter. The second stage involves defining specific objectives for staffing policies and procedures. The third stage is communicating policies and procedures to employees and ensuring that they are implemented correctly. As we noted previously, major benefits of the policies and procedures are the clarity they provide to employees and the perceived justice that comes from explicit rules for decision making. Organizations that communicate the content of policies and procedures make the most of this benefit. The fourth stage is evaluating whether policies and procedures are effective in achieving goals. Based on this evidence, new policies and procedures will be implemented when HR strategy and priorities change (such as a shift toward a focus on competencies linked to innovation), when existing policies and procedures are not effective (such as finding that not enough qualified individuals are being recruited through current methods), or when new methods for achieving goals are developed (such as the development of more accurate or informative measures of employee knowledge, skill, ability, and other characteristics [KSAOs] levels).

Human Resource Information Systems

Staffing activities generate and use considerable information. Having the technical expertise to work with this information has become an essential tool for staffing managers.[13] Job descriptions, application materials, résumés, correspondence,

---

EXHIBIT 13.2 Guidelines for Creating Effective Staffing Policies and Procedures

Planning Process Stage	Example Elements of the Process
Stage 1: Determine the overarching HR strategy and priorities that guide all policies and procedures	• Align employee capabilities and efforts with annual strategic plans • Maintain diversity of employee expertise and perspectives • Deliver services in a timely and cost-effective manner
Stage 2: Define specific objectives for staffing policies and procedures	• Evaluate KSAOs and competencies that will guide the recruiting and selection process • Recruit highly qualified individuals from a variety of sources • Use standardized and validated selection processes and tools • Coordinate all facets of the staffing process with managers to ensure positions are filled quickly and effectively
Stage 3: Communicate policies and procedures to all employees and ensure their implementation	• Provide all employees with links to policy and procedure statements on the company intranet or through a policy and procedure manual • Train managers in techniques for implementing policies and procedures • Provide experts who can explain policies and procedures, answer questions, and take suggestions • Monitor ongoing compliance with policies and procedures
Stage 4: Evaluate and revise existing policies and procedures	• Analyze staffing metrics • Perform periodic reviews of manager opinions regarding policy and procedure outcomes • Review changes to organizational and HR strategy to determine new staffing strategy and priorities • Assess new technology and techniques for improving staffing outcomes

applicant profiles, applicant flow and tracking, and reports are examples of the types of information necessary for the operation of a staffing system. An HRIS can be a central repository to integrate recording, accessing, and using these huge quantities of data. By using a common framework within an HRIS, analytic techniques can assess how all elements of the staffing (and broader human resources) systems relate to one another. This process of integration and interpretation is covered in the evaluation of staffing systems later in this chapter.

Most organizations with a sufficient number of employees to warrant a dedicated HR department have integrated the staffing function with an HRIS. Many vendors have developed specialized HRIS interfaces that can track the critical processes and outcomes involved in staffing, as shown in Exhibit 13.3. The features

EXHIBIT 13.3 **Human Resource Information Systems for Staffing Tasks**

Staffing Task	HRIS Functionality
Legal compliance	EEO data analysis and reports Policy and procedure writing guides Statistical analysis for demonstrating job relatedness
Planning	Tracking historical demand for employees Forecasting workforce supply Replacement and succession planning
Job analysis	Database of job titles and responsibilities Database of competencies across jobs Comparing job descriptions with O*NET
External recruitment and selection	Job posting reports Time-to-fill hiring requisitions Applicant logs and status and tracking reports Recruitment source effectiveness Electronic résumé routing Keyword scanning of applications New hire reports (numbers, qualifications, assignments) Validation of selection systems
Internal recruitment and selection	Employee succession planning Intranet for job postings Skills databases Tracking progress through assessment centers Job performance reports Individual development plans
Final match	Tracking job acceptance rates Contract development Tracking employee socialization progress
Staffing system management	System cost reports Return on investments Record-keeping functions
Retention	Collection and analysis of job satisfaction data Tracking differences in turnover rates across locations and time Documenting performance management and/or progressive discipline

listed in the exhibit are meant to be illustrative rather than exhaustive; new functionality is continually being added to HRISs. Providing hard data on staffing system outcomes can increase the credibility of staffing services in organizations. The increased availability of data on staffing processes following from the use of HRISs means that organizations will also be able to track the efficacy of policies and procedures with accuracy. Staffing policies that do not show a return on investment can be eliminated, whereas those that show positive results can be expanded. Organizations that have outsourced staffing functions should also be aware of the information provided by HRISs and should ensure that they are receiving accurate and comprehensive reports from their vendor's HRIS database. Organizations considering outsourcing options should request historical data showing the efficacy of staffing systems in other organizations before committing resources toward any particular vendor. If an outsourcing service provider cannot provide these data, this may be a sign that it does not communicate well or may not be very rigorous about evaluating the quality of its services.

Web-based staffing management systems are also available from application service providers (ASPs) or software-as-a-service (SaaS) providers. With such systems, the vendor provides both the hardware (e.g., servers, scanners) and the software, as well as day-to-day management of the system. Recruiters and hiring managers access the system through a web browser. Designed to facilitate the management of all aspects of the selection system, this customizable set of staffing tools can be designed to work for a wide variety of organizations. For example, the system can link an organization with a variety of online and social media applications to advertise a position. Applicants can then enter their qualifications directly into the system. Other tools facilitate the management of recruiting events, like campus visits or job fairs, including rapid screening of applicants and interview schedules. Alternatively, for organizations that outsource recruiting, tools are available to manage information flow across multiple hiring agencies or consulting companies. Managers can then access these applications directly and use a variety of search criteria to identify applicants who best match the job requirements. Once individuals are in the system, screening tests can be performed prior to face-to-face interviews. Some modules are even able to facilitate the onboarding process by creating hiring checklists, online forms, and so forth.

Several trends continue to alter the landscape of HRISs.[14] Core staffing functions like recruitment and screening are now frequently integrated into even low-cost software solutions. Performance evaluations, workforce competency assessments, and succession planning processes within an HRIS are also increasingly used to facilitate management of internal staffing. Besides their use as tools in the staffing process, data gathered from these systems can be used to evaluate and improve policies and procedures. Many studies illustrate best practices in HR reporting and analytics based on reviews of results across a variety of organizations. We cover some of these possibilities later in the chapter.

Most HRISs allow frontline managers and employees to access their HR records and engage with the system directly rather than working through a centralized HR employee. These processes are implemented to facilitate internal staffing functions. Employees can use self-service pages to stay up to date with succession management plans, find training that will help them prepare for higher-level positions, and submit applications for openings. These self-service functions increase engagement and allow employees to take advantage of the organization's full range of options for personal development and career progression. Experts suggest that these self-service applications should create a consumer-friendly experience for employees, modeled on the digital commerce sites most workers are already familiar with.[15] The increased availability of web-based solutions also makes it easier for even small employers with limited resources to provide a full suite of automated HRIS solutions for staffing.

Social networking applications for information sharing, mirroring Facebook or Twitter, have become much more common in HRISs. They have been particularly popular elements of employee orientation or onboarding programs because they allow newcomers to interact with established employees quickly.

Effectiveness

When assessing HRISs for staffing tasks, HR managers must carefully consider their needs and goals for the entire HRIS today and in the future.[16] Some of the key factors that differentiate HRISs include whether the system is hosted on-site or as an SaaS on a remote server run by an HRIS provider, the degree and nature of custom reporting provided by the HRIS, the ability to generate reports that integrate a variety of HR functions, and the degree to which systems for recruitment, selection, record keeping, orientation, benefits, and compensation are integrated with one another. Other factors to consider include how long the service provider has been in business, how often it upgrades its system, how many other customers the provider has, who those clients are, and, of course, costs. The sheer complexity of deciding which HRIS to use means that the decision is seldom made by a single individual; rather, the decision is made by joint committees made up of executives, members of the HR staff, and information technology professionals.

Staffing technologies have a multitude of potential positive and negative effects. Many of these effects extend beyond process improvement (e.g., speed of staffing) and cost reduction. While these two potential advantages are very important, they need to be considered in the cultural context. A strong HRIS platform should also be supported by personal interactions. The digital marketing analogy can be considered here as well: companies that sell online are successful only when they have a strong support team of customer service agents. In organizations, leaders, supervisors, and individual contributors who have special requests or who have difficulty using the system should be able to contact HR professionals directly. Proceed with due diligence when deciding how to use new staffing technologies, evaluating products and vendors, establishing service agreements with vendors, and planning prior to implementation. After staffing technologies are implemented, monitoring and system improvement will need to be periodically undertaken.

Outsourcing

Outsourcing refers to contracting out work to a vendor or third-party administrator. In previous chapters we discussed outsourcing work for noncore organizational processes. Here, we consider the case of outsourcing certain staffing functions. Examples of specific staffing activities that are often outsourced include legal compliance audits, contingent staffing, executive search, skill testing, background checks, job fairs, employee relocation, assessment centers, and affirmative action planning. A number of factors that influence the decision of whether to outsource are reviewed in Exhibit 13.4. Outsourcing decisions require consideration of

EXHIBIT 13.4 Comparison of Outsourced and In-House Staffing

	Outsourced	In-House
Strategy	Staffing functions not linked to core organizational competencies	Staffing functions linked to core organizational competencies
Size	Small organizations, organizations without a centralized HR function, or organizations with continual hiring needs	Large organizations where economies of scale will pay off or for executive selection tasks where knowledge of the organization is crucial
Skills required	General human capital, such as that easily obtained through education	Firm-specific human capital, such as required knowledge of organizational policies or specific personality traits
Examples	• Recruiting packaging employees in a small warehouse • Screening registered nurses for a long-term care facility • Developing a website for automatically screening entry-level candidates • Providing temporary employees for a highly cyclical manufacturing organization	• Recruiting creative talent for an advertising firm • Selecting members of the organization's executive team • Providing employee orientation • Recruiting and selecting employees for a large retail organization • Recruiting and selecting individuals for an interdependent work team

organizational strategy, size of the organization, and the skills required. Thus, the decision of whether to outsource is not an all-or-nothing proposition. Some staffing functions are more easily outsourced, so many organizations use outsourcing for some tasks but not for others.

One of the benefits of outsourcing is that it frees the internal HR department from performing day-to-day administrative activities that could be more efficiently managed by an external organization. Reviews of best practices show that the major advantages of outsourcing include access to superior information from specialists, access to technology and services that are difficult to implement internally, and general cost reduction.[17] By eliminating the day-to-day work of routine staffing activities, it is possible to dedicate more energy to analyzing and improving the effectiveness of the staffing system as a whole. Because specialized staffing firms work with the same processes all the time, they can develop specialized, highly efficient systems that deliver results more quickly and more cheaply than an organization's in-house staffing services. An external staffing firm will have more resources to keep up with developments in its area. For example, a firm that specializes in equal employment opportunity compliance will always have the latest information regarding court decisions and changing precedents.

These advantages of outsourcing should always be weighed against the potential downfalls of outsourcing too many staffing functions or outsourcing functions too rapidly. Experts in this area warn that the expected benefits will not materialize if the decision to outsource is not accompanied by a complete transformation of the way HR is delivered.[18] Organizations that outsource need to hold external providers accountable by keeping track of staffing metrics, especially since specialized staffing firms have access to better systems for managing and reporting staffing data. Someone inside the organization needs to have final, bottom-line accountability for any outsourced services. In many organizations, there is resistance to outsourcing, and employees may feel that the company is treating them impersonally if questions or concerns about employment are directed to an external vendor. Thus, employees who have complaints or concerns about staffing services should be able to discuss their concerns with someone inside the organization who can respond to them.

A professional employer organization (PEO) is similar to a staffing firm, but unlike a staffing firm, a PEO provides a wider range of HR services and has a long-term commitment to the client. Under a typical arrangement, the client organization enters into a contractual relationship with a PEO to conduct some or all HR activities and functions. The client and the PEO are considered co-employers of record. A PEO is particularly appealing to small employers because it can provide special HR expertise and technical assistance, conduct the administrative activities and transactions of an HR department, provide more affordable employee benefits, meet legal obligations (payroll, withholding, workers' compensation, and unemployment insurance), and manage legal compliance. A survey of over 740 small businesses suggested that small businesses that used a PEO had higher levels of satisfaction with HR outcomes and more efficient implementation of HR processes relative to small businesses that did not use a PEO, and that the more functions the company outsourced to the PEO, the greater the results.[19]

The health care industry has often turned to outsourcing for staffing needs, with individual hospitals hoping to learn best practices that have worked in other facilities. For example, Fauquier Health, a small hospital in Virginia, was experiencing difficulty in finding and retaining qualified staff. It turned to three HR outsourcing firms that had expertise in the areas of situational assessments, standardized testing, and health care hiring practices. The firms worked in concert to develop a selection tool that incorporated simulations to assess interpersonal skills, cognitive ability and personality tests, and medical knowledge. These different selection tools, when used together, helped Fauquier achieve a 98% retention rate for the year. Representatives from Fauquier note that the previous experience these firms had in implementing staffing solutions across other organizations greatly facilitated the process.[20]

Another example of successful staffing outsourcing comes from Chequed, a firm that specializes in applicant assessment. By studying competencies required for hundreds of positions over time, it was able to create a standardized questionnaire that can assess qualifications quickly, with assessments tailor-made to specific job requirements. In addition to gathering information regarding which applicants are most qualified, it can also note competency gaps that might need to be addressed in the future. Because it has data across so many different jobs and companies—data that are much more comprehensive than the data of an in-house HR function—it can more easily identify which characteristics are associated with success. As with the previous example, the goal of using this deep knowledge of job fit is to allow the HR department to focus its attention on organization fit and its unique strategic needs.[21]

At the outset, it is important to remember that the agreement (often called a service-level agreement, or SLA) with the vendor is usually negotiable, and that flaws in the negotiating stage are often responsible for many problems that may subsequently occur in the relationship. Using some form of legal or consulting assistance might be desirable, especially for the organization that has little or no staffing outsourcing experience.

There are many issues to discuss and negotiate when working with a vendor. Awareness of these factors and advance preparation with regard to the organization's preferences and requirements are critical to a successful negotiation with a potential vendor. The factors include the actual staffing services sought and provided, client control rights (e.g., monitoring of the vendor's personnel and the software to be used), fees and other costs, guaranteed improvements in service levels and cost savings, benchmarking metrics and performance reviews, and willingness to hire the organization's own employees to provide expertise and coordination. On top of these factors, the choice of vendor should take into account the vendor's track record and familiarity with the organization's industry.

EVALUATION OF STAFFING SYSTEMS

The evaluation of staffing systems involves an examination of the effectiveness of the total system. This entails focusing on the operations of the staffing process, establishing metrics to assess the system and analyzing alternative processes.

Process Evaluation

The staffing process establishes and governs the flow of employees into, within, and out of the organization. Developing a process requires mapping the intended stages for the flow of employees and assigning areas of accountability for each stage. Well-constructed process maps ensure standardization of the staffing process, remove bottlenecks, and improve the speed of the operation.

Standardization refers to the operational consistency of the staffing system. The use of standardized staffing systems ensures that the same KSAO information is gathered from all job applicants, which in turn is a key requirement for reliably and validly measuring these KSAOs. Standardization will enhance applicants' perceptions of the procedural fairness of the staffing system and of the decisions made about them by the organization. Finally, standardized staffing systems are less likely to generate legal challenges and more likely to maintain diversity; both statutes and case law advocate for consistent treatment of all employees as a way to minimize the impact of biases.

Mapping out the staffing process involves constructing a staffing flowchart. The staffing flowchart shown in Exhibit 13.5 depicts the staffing system of a medium-sized (580 employees) graphic design company. It shows the actual flow of staffing activities and both organization and applicant decision points, from the time a vacancy occurs until the time it is filled with a new hire.

Using a flowchart like this can help supervisors, staffing services, and the organization's leadership team answer questions about the hiring sequence and evaluate who is responsible for each stage. The example shown here is a generic system that can be used for both entry-level and higher-level jobs. The sequence of stages is an outgrowth of the planning process. Supervisors know when a vacancy occurs in their workgroup, and the leadership team knows when changes in product demand, technology, or strategy mean a new position is needed. The supervisor, staffing services, and leadership team work collaboratively to determine HR needs and availabilities before making a decision about staffing needs. Staffing services handle the details of creating a requisition, but ultimate accountability for starting recruiting resides in the leadership team.

The staffing process now moves into operation. Supervisor knowledge of their field can help staffing services design and disseminate the recruiting message in a way that qualified applicants will find compelling. Staffing services use their specialized expertise to take care of the nuts and bolts of sourcing, processing, and screening applicants using the procedures described throughout the earlier chapters

EXHIBIT 13.5   Staffing Flowchart for Medium-Sized Graphic Design Company

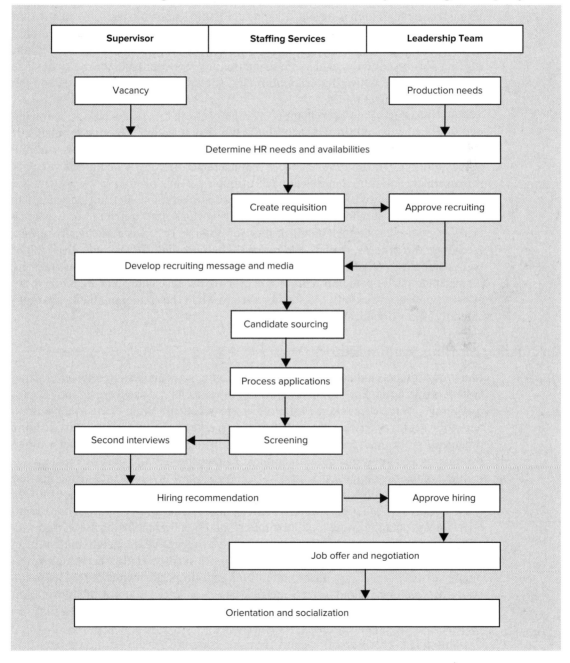

of this book. In this organization, the supervisor conducts a second round of interviews more focused on fit with the work team. Together with staffing services, a hiring recommendation is developed and sent to the leadership team. To ensure that offers are conducted within legal, policy, and strategic guidelines, the final offer and negotiation are handled through leadership and staffing services. The supervisor, staffing services, and the leadership team are jointly accountable for the final stage of developing and delivering orientation and socialization messages for person-job and person-organization fit.

After the process has been mapped, routinely check for any deviations. Knowing where and why deviations are occurring is the first stage in correcting problems. If managers simply do not know what the process is or how to implement it, training is the solution. On the other hand, if managers are actively resisting the process, it is useful to solicit manager feedback through surveys or interviews on why the process is not followed. If they find the process cumbersome, inefficient, or ineffective, the process should be changed. If staffing does not contribute to organizational effectiveness, it must adapt. If it is not possible or if it is strategically unwise to change the process, explain the rationale behind the process; incentives might be considered to align manager motivation with organizational interests. Getting managers to participate in the process is crucial, because managers are much more effective collaborators with the staffing system when they understand and are motivated to follow organizational plans.[22]

Calculating Staffing System Metrics

Many quantitative indicators can show how effectively and efficiently the staffing system is operating. For example, how many applicants does a given vacancy attract on average? What percentage of job offers are accepted? What is the average number of days it takes to fill a vacancy? What percentage of new hires remain with the organization for one year post hire? Answers to such questions can be determined by tracking and analyzing data on applicant flows through the staffing pipeline.

It is sometimes argued that most of the processes involved in staffing are too subjective or difficult to quantify. In the past, staffing managers could not provide representatives from operations, finance, and accounting with the hard cost-effectiveness data they were looking for. Fortunately, a dramatic increase in the availability and functionality of database software in recent years means that staffing system effectiveness can be assessed much more readily. HRISs can catalog and quickly display recruiting, hiring, retention, and job performance data. HR scholars have developed standardized metrics based on these sources of information that can help staffing managers communicate the business case for staffing services across the organization.[23]

Exhibit 13.6 provides a flowchart for using metrics to evaluate and update staffing processes. The first step is to collect and synthesize the objectives of the staffing process that were developed in stage 2 of policy and procedure creation (reviewed in

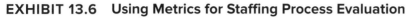

EXHIBIT 13.6 Using Metrics for Staffing Process Evaluation

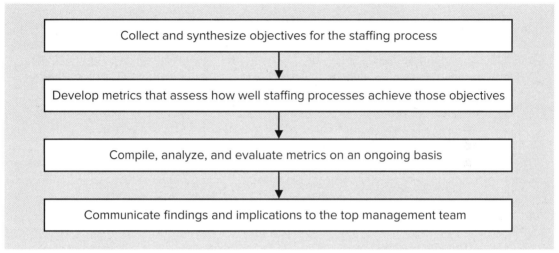

Collect and synthesize objectives for the staffing process

Develop metrics that assess how well staffing processes achieve those objectives

Compile, analyze, and evaluate metrics on an ongoing basis

Communicate findings and implications to the top management team

Exhibit 13.2). The second step is to develop metrics that are associated with those objectives. There should be a very close relationship between the objectives of the staffing process and the objectives that are selected. Simply because an HR-related outcome is readily available in the HRIS does not necessarily mean that assessing and analyzing it will be informative. The third step is to actually gather, analyze, and evaluate metrics. Both internal and external benchmarks can be useful here. An internal benchmark can evaluate whether some business units are in greater need of attention than others, and it can evaluate trends in HR outcomes over time. External benchmarks can evaluate whether your organization is achieving exceptional, average, or poor results relative to other organizations in your industry or area. Finally, it is essential that these findings be communicated effectively to top management teams. Develop concrete plans for correcting any problems identified in the process.

Common Staffing Metrics

In Exhibit 13.7 we offer some suggestions for the types of financial and process data that might be most useful for assessing the effectiveness of staffing systems overall. These suggestions are based on established research on best practices in the field.[24] Following from several other writers, we divided the outcomes into four key categories: cost, timeliness, outcomes, and reactions. For each category, we present some representative metrics that might be useful, and highlight ways that HR metrics can be used to help facilitate progress toward strategic goals.

These metrics are very useful barometers for gauging the pulse of the staffing flow. They have an objective, bottom-line nature that can be readily communicated

EXHIBIT 13.7 **Common Staffing Metrics**

	Cost	Timeliness	Outcomes	Reactions
Staffing system	Staffing budget Staffing-to-employee ratios Staffing expenses for full-time equivalents (FTEs)	Time to respond to requests	Evaluation of employee readiness for strategic goals	Communication Satisfaction with services provided
Recruiting	Advertising expenses Cost per applicant	Recruits per week	Number of recruits	Applicant quality
Selection	Test costs per candidate Interview expenses Cost per candidate	Time to hire Days to fill	Competence Workforce diversity	Candidate quality Satisfaction with tests
Final match	Training costs per hire Cost per hire	Days to start Time to perform	Number of positions filled Job performance	New employee satisfaction
Retention	Exit interview expenses Replacement costs	Timely response to external offers	Voluntary separation rate Involuntary separation rate	Employee job satisfaction

to managers and others in the organization. These types of data are also useful for comparative purposes, as described below. We have already outlined methods for assessing the costs and benefits of staffing policies and procedures. Below we present some common methods for calculating and interpreting these metrics. The number of positions filled is a straightforward count of the number of individuals who accepted positions during the fiscal year. These data are collected for both internal and external candidates. The time to fill openings is estimated by assessing the number of days it takes for a job requisition to result in a job acceptance by a candidate. Hiring cost estimates are the sum of advertising, agency fees, employee referrals, travel costs for applicants and staff, relocation costs, and pay and benefits for recruiters. Hiring cost estimates are often indexed by dividing by the number of positions filled. As we noted in the chapters on recruiting, these cost estimates may be subdivided in a number of ways to get a better idea of which portions of the staffing process are comparatively more expensive.

Turnover rates are also often used as staffing metrics. The annual turnover rate is estimated by dividing the number of separations per month by the average number of individuals employed each month and then taking the sum of these average monthly rates. Turnover rates are often differentiated based on whether they represent voluntary or involuntary turnover, which we cover in the next chapter. Other cost data, and how to calculate them, are also available.

Another staffing metric is the staffing cost or efficiency ratio. It takes into account the notion that recruiting applicants for jobs with a higher compensation level might cost more due to such costs as executive search fees, recruitment advertising, relocation, and so forth. The formula for the efficiency ratio is total staffing cost ratio = total staffing costs / total compensation recruited. Though the cost per hire may be greater for one job category than for another, their staffing cost ratios may be the same.

Comparative Uses of Staffing Metrics

Once staffing metrics have been collected, it is time to put them to use. Descriptive staffing metrics can be used for evaluating staffing systems.[25] Breakouts and tracking over time are two of the most common ways to examine metrics. The breakout method involves collecting and comparing data across different units of the organization. For example, simply knowing about differences in cost per hire across units can inform the budgeting process when staffing shortages need to be filled. In a more prescriptive sense, it might be found that the fit between applicant qualifications and job demands is very different across divisions. This may suggest that greater investment in targeted recruiting or screening is needed in some areas. In recruiting, the relative effectiveness and efficiency of staffing systems in two different units of the organization could also be assessed by comparing their respective yield ratios.

Tracking over time involves collecting and comparing data over multiple quarters or years. Such time-based comparisons are useful for tracking trends in effectiveness and efficiency. These comparisons are also used to help judge whether changes in staffing practices have improved staffing process performance. As with breakouts, changes in the costs of screening candidates per hire over time can be used for budgeting purposes, as indicators of changes in the labor market, or as a signal that the organization is being either more or less efficient in screening candidates over time.

External benchmarking is another way to assess whether metrics are in line with what is expected.[26] The Society for Human Resource Management (SHRM) provides a number of guidelines for developing and interpreting staffing metrics. Its website lists a number of benchmarking studies, including surveys that outline the use of benchmarking and perceived efficacies across a number of practices, such as retention initiatives, e-recruiting, and diversity management. More detailed metrics can also be obtained from SHRM surveys of human capital benchmarks. Learning what other organizations are doing may not always be especially informative for determining the effectiveness of these policies and procedures for the organization. Many practices that work in one context may not be as useful in another context, and the research on HR bundling suggests that policies need to be implemented into a comprehensive system rather than just implementing individual practices in isolation. Therefore, although it is helpful to have some external information, each organization faces unique strategic and cultural challenges that might explain why its own metrics differ from benchmarks.

Example Use of Staffing Metrics

Exhibit 13.8 shows the required layout for tracking staffing metrics. In Part A, the steps in the staffing process start with the announcement of a vacancy and run through a sequential flow of selection, job offer, offer acceptance, start as new hire, and retention. A timeline shows the average number of days to complete each step. In this illustration, 25 vacancies attracted 1,000 applicants who proceeded through the staffing process. Ultimately, all 25 vacancies were filled, and these new hires were tracked to see how many remained with the organization for six months and one year post hire.

Example aggregate staffing metrics can be found in Part B of Exhibit 13.8. The first indicator is applicants per vacancy, which averaged 40. This is an indication of the effectiveness of recruitment activities. The second indicator is the yield ratio; it indicates the percentage of people who moved on to one or more of the next steps in the staffing process. The percentage of applicants who became candidates is 20%; the percentage of job offers accepted is 83.3%. The third indicator, elapsed time (or cycle time), shows the average amount of time elapsed between each step in the staffing process. It can be seen that the average number of days to fill a vacancy is 44. The final indicator is retention rate; the six-month retention rate for new hires is 80% and the one-year rate is 52%.

Analysis of Staffing System Results

Compiling staffing system metrics and comparing them with benchmarks or tracking them over time can be informative, but these are only descriptive statistics. They can answer *whether* metrics are in line with goals, but they do not tell decision makers *how* to achieve goals with specific policies. We now turn our attention to methods to analyze the extent to which different staffing system procedures might influence these metrics. These methods fall under the umbrella of predictive and prescriptive analytics, meaning that they evaluate how systems are associated with positive outcomes and give guidance for staffing leaders looking to improve performance.[27] The strategies for analysis described below, and the inferences that can reasonably be developed from each method are based on the extensive literature on evidence-based management.[28] We note the shortcomings of these approaches as we go, but even with their limits, these methods of systematic

EXHIBIT 13.8   Evaluation of Staffing Process and Results: Example

A. Staffing Process Example

No. of vacancies filled = 25

Process step	Vacancy announced (1)	Applicants (2)	Candidates (3)	Finalists (4)	Offer receiver (5)	Offer acceptance (6)	Start as new hire (7)	On the job	
								Six months (8)	One year (9)
No. of people	0	1,000	200	125	30	25	25	20	13
Process time (avg. no. of days)	0	14	21	28	35	42	44		

B. Staffing Process Results

Applicants/Vacancy = 1,000/25 = 40

Yield ratio: candidates/applicant = 20%; new hires/applicant = 2.5%; offers accepted/received = 83.3%

Elapsed time: avg. no. of days to offer = 35; avg. no. of days to start = 44 (cycle time)

Retention rate: $\dfrac{\text{on job six months}}{\text{new hires}}$ = 80% for six months; $\dfrac{\text{on job one year}}{\text{new hires}}$ = 52% for first year analysis of staffing system results are all considerably superior to drawing conclusions about program effectiveness from guesswork and assumptions that would otherwise guide choices.

The pilot program and repeated measures techniques described below emphasize evaluating an alternative staffing system relative to the status quo. However, these techniques are not just useful for evaluating new programs; they can also assess the utility of an existing program. To assess the effectiveness of an existing program, the program in question can be discontinued. If the temporary elimination of a costly program does not appreciably alter business outcomes, it may be wise to eliminate the program permanently.

As you read through the descriptions of different methods for analyzing results, refer to Exhibit 13.9, which gives an example of how the methods would be implemented in the case of a school district working on a new recruiting technique. For each analysis type, there is a description of how the procedure is implemented and the inferences drawn from each technique. Procedures like analysis of variance (ANOVA) and multiple regression are used to assess statistical significance; the concept of statistical significance is addressed in the chapters on measurement and methods of final choice.

Pilot Program

Pilot programs are one common type of analysis used to establish a relationship between staffing system features and metrics. As with a classic experimental design, the organization's leaders choose some business units to use an alternative component of a staffing system, while other business units continue to use the current system. In the language of experiments, those that use the alternative system are the treatment group, and those that continue to use the current system are the control group. If the new procedures are truly randomly assigned, differences between the treatment and control groups are strong indicators that the new system is effective.

A pilot program is implemented as follows:

1. Establish methods to measure valid and operationally meaningful staffing metrics.
2. Develop alternative staffing system procedures with clear links to staffing metrics.
3. Assign some business units to start using the alternative staffing system while the other business units continue using the current system.
4. Calculate staffing metrics for each of the two systems and compare results.

Although the discussion to this point has emphasized a single contrast between treatment and control, it is also possible to test multiple systems at once by assigning one group of organization units to use one new method, another group to use a second new method, and a third group to continue using the current system. As an example, a pilot analysis might begin with the premise that an alternative

EXHIBIT 13.9   Examples of Methods to Analyze Staffing System Results

(A)   Pilot Program

This example involves a large school district that employs 3,184 paraprofessional and support staff across 113 buildings. A random sample of 30 buildings implemented an alternative integrated hiring system with applicant tracking, screening, and selection tools. The other 83 continued using the current application system. The results were as follows:

- Locations using current application system: average days to start = 24.1, standard deviation = 2.12
- Locations using alternative application system: average days to start = 22.9, standard deviation = 2.28
- New system is 1.2 days faster; ANOVA shows difference is statistically significant (F-value = 6.54)

(B)   Repeated Measures

In this example, the large school district described in (A) tracked days to start for six months. The alternative applicant tracking system was then implemented in all 113 locations, and the days-to-start measure was tracked for another six months. The results were as follows:

- Before change in application system: average days to start = 23.3, standard deviation = 1.93
- After change in application system: average days to start = 22.5, standard deviation = 1.97
- New system is 0.8 days faster; repeated-measures ANOVA shows difference is statistically significant (F-value = 9.30)

(C)   Observational Design

In this example, the large school district described in (A) collected data from each of the 113 locations on days to hire, HR-to-employee ratios, and annual advertising expenses. On average, each location had 1 HR representative for every 80 employees and spent about $200 a month posting advertisements. Advertising expenditures were expressed in hundreds for the analysis. Multiple regression was estimated to predict days to start. The unstandardized regression results were as follows:

days_to_start = 36.9 − 2.27 x (HR-to-employee ratio) − 0.43 (advertising)

- Adding additional staff would probably not decrease days to start; the coefficient of −2.27 is not statistically significant (p = .58)
- Increasing advertising by $100 per location would reduce days to start by −0.43; this is statistically significant (p < .01)
- If there are not any unmeasured confounding variables, spending just $300 per location could result in an average of over a day reduction in days to start

selection program will affect operational outcomes by identifying the most competent applicants, improving the organization's ability to focus its recruiting efforts on the most competent workers, thereby reducing costs while improving workforce performance. The specific metrics for this proposed program include measures of employee qualifications, manager ratings of candidate quality, and costs per candidate. The target employee population is split into three groups. A structured interview protocol is initiated with one group, a situational judgment test is initiated with a second group, and the third group, serving as the control, uses the current system. The different group outcomes would be compared with one another.

Pilot programs are useful for comparing across different staffing systems, but only if the business units that use the alternative system are similar to those that use the current system. If especially effective or ineffective units use the alternative system, then differences in metrics after the pilot could just be a reflection of how different the groups were before the pilot started. Two techniques are especially helpful for addressing the problem of nonequivalent pilot and control groups.[29] Random assignment to pilot and control groups means prior differences across units will cancel one another out, and differences between groups can be attributed to the difference in systems. When random assignment is not possible for logistical reasons, comparing baselines before the change can also be informative in assessing how much the pilot may change outcomes.

Repeated Measures Design

If it is not possible to use a pilot technique because the workforce does not have geographically or operationally distinct units, it is still possible to use metrics to assess the efficacy of proposed system changes. Staffing managers can compare long-run data on a single business unit's effectiveness before and after a change has been initiated. The same technique can be used in cases where the whole organization changes the staffing system simultaneously. This change from a baseline over time is called a repeated measures design, or simply put, a measure of change. To make valid inferences, take benchmark data over a long period of time before and after the alternative systems are in place so that changes in staffing metrics can be reliably attributed to the program implementation rather than just routine variability in organizational performance.

A repeated measures analysis is implemented as follows:

1. Establish methods to measure valid and operationally meaningful staffing metrics.
2. Track staffing metrics across multiple time periods.
3. Develop and implement an alternative staffing system across all units.
4. Calculate staffing metrics before and after the change.

One advantage of the repeated measures design is that the entire pre-change group serves as the baseline. In a sense, we can think of the pre-change measures as coming from a control group and the post-change measures as coming from the group adopting the alternative system. This means that the problem of nonequivalent alternative and control groups is avoided. The method does have disadvantages, though. It can be very expensive and risky to change staffing systems for the entire organization at once. If the alternative system does not have positive effects, significant financial and staff time resources will be needed to switch back. It is also difficult to be certain that the changes from one period to the next are because of the change in the staffing system rather than changes in the business environment. For example, if the economy goes into a recession around the same time that an alternative recruiting system is implemented across the organization, it might look like the new system is increasing the number of applicants when the real driving force is the increase in the number of job seekers. The best way to minimize these problems is being aware of these alternative explanations and using measures of them in the process of evaluating results.

Observational Design

Unlike the pilot program or repeated measures methods, observational designs do not start from a deliberate change in a staffing system. Observational designs use existing differences across organizational units as a basis for comparing staffing systems. Such differences often exist in decentralized organizations where units have discretion in how they implement policies. Some managers might resist the use of structured interviews, so there will be some units using structured interviews while others do not. Or some managers will prefer to use referrals for recruiting, while others rely on formal connections with universities and technical colleges. The observational method can even assess varying degrees of staffing system use across units rather than comparing one whole system with another. Continuing from the examples above, some business units may use totally unstructured interviews, some will use a mix of structured and unstructured, and others will use only structured. Or some units may use only referrals, a mix of referrals and formal sources, or all formal sources. Staffing metrics can be compared across these different levels of the policy implementation to see whether different systems' characteristics are associated with different outcomes.

An observational analysis is implemented as follows:

1. Establish methods to measure valid and operationally meaningful staffing metrics.
2. Measure staffing metrics across locations.
3. Measure differences across locations in system implementation procedures.
4. Use statistical software to estimate the influence of different procedures. The most common statistical technique for observational designs is multiple regression, which we covered in the discussion of multiple predictors in the chapter on final choice.

An observational design has one obvious advantage: nothing needs to be changed to evaluate differences across units. Instead, differences are based on administrative records already in existence. Because the data in question already exist in an HRIS, answers regarding which staffing system features are associated with superior outcomes can be found in a few hours rather than taking weeks or months for a new program to have effects. The biggest disadvantage of the observational method is that differences in staffing metrics across groups could be the result of factors that have nothing to do with staffing systems. Turnover in urban areas tends to be higher because employees have more immediate alternative job options, and urban areas also have greater impacts from media campaigns for the same reason. Many other factors that might be associated with program outcomes could similarly cause spurious conclusions about the effects of staffing programs.

Machine learning methods are a form of analysis of observational data. These methods represent a growing family of techniques that are coming into broader use within analytics in general, and in HR analytics more specifically.[30] A wide variety of techniques fall under the broader family of machine learning, but they have several features in common. Unlike the random samples, repeated measures, and regression-based approaches, machine learning systems use algorithms to build up predictive models. This means that both the questions being asked and the methods to answer these questions are developed by a system that effectively teaches itself. In other words, the machine learning tools look through data to identify patterns and then use these patterns to build up a predictive model. As noted earlier in the book, search engines and online retailers use these systems to recommend products and services to you every time you go online. These applications can facilitate combing through masses of HRIS and production data more quickly and efficiently than having an individual person perform this task. However, because machine learning is data driven, the models that are produced may not be especially informative for policy making. Like all the evaluation methods we have described, these systems are effective only when they are directed to solve a meaningful business problem.

LEGAL ISSUES

Record Keeping and Privacy

Numerous legal constraints and requirements surround staffing information, so staffing systems need to be designed to ensure adequate record keeping and privacy for job applicants and employees.

Record Keeping

The organization creates a wide range of information during staffing and other HR activities. Examples include personal data (name, address, date of birth, dependents, etc.), KSAO information (application blank, references, test scores, etc.), medical information, performance appraisal and promotability assessments, and changes in employment status (promotions, transfers, etc.). Why should records of such information be created?

Records must be created and maintained for two major legal purposes in staffing. First, they are necessary for legal compliance. Federal, state, and local laws specify what information to keep and for how long. Second, having records allows the organization to provide documentation to justify staffing decisions or to defend these decisions against legal challenge. For example, performance appraisal and promotability assessments might be used to explain to employees why they were or were not promoted. Or, these same records might be used as evidence in a legal proceeding to show that promotion decisions were job related and unbiased.

It is strongly recommended that two sets of records be created. These records can be kept in paper or electronic form. The first set should be the individual employee's personnel file. It will comprise only those documents that relate directly to the job and the employee's performance of it. To determine which documents to place in the personnel file, ask if it is a document on which the organization could legally base an employment decision. If the answer is "no," "probably no," or "unsure," do not place the document in the employee's personnel file. The second set of records contains documents that cannot be used in staffing decisions. Examples include documents pertaining to medical information (both physical and mental), equal employment opportunity (e.g., information about protected characteristics such as age, sex, religion, race, color, national origin, and disability), and information about authorization to work (e.g., I-9 forms).[31]

Any document that is to be placed in an employee's personnel file should be reviewed before it becomes part of that record. Examine the document for incomplete, inaccurate, or misleading information, as well as potentially damaging notations or comments about the employee. All such information should be completed, corrected, explained, or, if necessary, eliminated. Remember that any document in the personnel file is a potential court exhibit that may work either for or against the employer's defense of a legal challenge.

Federal equal employment opportunity and affirmative action (EEO/AA) laws contain general record-keeping requirements. Though the requirements vary somewhat from law to law, major subject areas for which records are to be kept (if created) are shown in Exhibit 13.10. Requirements by the Office of Federal Contract Compliance Programs (OFCCP) are broader than those shown, and records must be maintained for at least two years.

The various laws also have requirements about length of retention of records. As a general rule, most records must be kept for a minimum of one year from the date a document is made or a staffing action is taken, whichever is later. Exceptions to the one-year requirements all provide for even longer retention periods. If a charge of discrimination is filed, the records must be retained until the matter is resolved.

EXHIBIT 13.10   Federal Record-Keeping Requirements

Records that should be kept include the following:

- Applications for employment (hire, promote, or transfer)
- Reasons for refusal to hire, promote, or transfer
- Tests and test scores, plus other KSAO information
- Job orders submitted to labor unions and employment agencies
- Medical exam results
- Advertisements or other notices to the public or employees about job openings and promotion opportunities
- Requests for reasonable accommodation
- Impact of staffing decisions on protected groups (disparate impact statistics)
- Records related to filing of a discrimination charge

All records should be kept for a minimum of one year.

Privacy Concerns

The organization must observe legal requirements governing employees' and others' access to information in personnel files, as well as guard against unwarranted disclosure of the information to third-party requesters (e.g., other employers). Matters of information access and disclosure raise privacy concerns under both constitutional and statutory law.[32]

Several states have laws guaranteeing employees reasonable access to their personnel files. The laws generally allow the employee to review and copy pertinent documents; some documents such as letters of reference or promotion plans for the person may be excluded from access. The employee may also have a right to seek to correct erroneous information in the file. Where there is no state law permitting access, employees are usually allowed access to their personnel file only if the organization has a policy permitting it. Disclosure of information in a personnel file to third parties is often regulated as well and may require the employee's written consent.

At the federal level, numerous laws and regulations restrict access to and disclosure of employee personnel information. An example is the Americans With Disabilities Act (ADA) and its provisions regarding the confidentiality of medical information. There is, however, no general federal privacy law covering private employees. Public employees' privacy rights are protected by the Privacy Act of 1974.

EEO Report

The law requires many private employers and federal contractors to submit an annual EEO-1 (Standard Form 100) report, which has two components. Federal contractors with 50–99 employees must file Component 1; federal contractors and private employers with 100 or more employees must file Component 2.

Component 1 requires head-count employment data about employee ethnicity, race, and sex, by job category, as shown in Exhibit 13.11. The data may be gathered from organizational records, visual inspection, or self-report. Detailed instructions and guidance for completing the form are online (*eeoc.gov*).

Component 2 (not shown) contains 12 annual salary pay bands, ranging from $19,239 and lower (grade 1) to $208,000 and above (grade 12). For each job category shown in Exhibit 13.11 the ethnicity/race/sex data from Component 1 must be broken down into the 12 pay bands.

Legal Audits

It is highly desirable to periodically conduct audits or reviews of the organization's degree of compliance with laws and regulations pertaining to staffing.[33] The audit forces the organization to study and specify its staffing practices and to compare these current practices against legally desirable and required practices. Results can be used to identify potential legal trouble spots and to map out changes in staffing practices that will serve to minimize potential liability and reduce the risk of lawsuits being filed against the organization. Note that development of affirmative action plans (AAPs) and reports include a large audit and review component. They do not, however, cover the entire legal spectrum of staffing practices, nor do they require sufficient depth of analysis of staffing practices in some areas. For these reasons, AAPs and reports are not sufficient as legal audits, though they are immensely important and useful inputs to a legal audit.

The audit could be conducted by the organization's own legal counsel. Alternatively, the HR department might first conduct a self-audit and then review its findings with legal counsel. Conducting an audit after involvement in employment litigation is also recommended.

Training for Managers and Employees

Training in employment law and compliance requirements for managers and employees is not only a sound practice but also increasingly a defense point for the organization in employment litigation. The constantly changing employment law landscape reinforces the need for training. New laws, regulations, and court rulings can all redefine permissible and impermissible staffing practices.[34]

Though the requirements for employment law training are still being developed, several components should be incorporated: (1) the training should be for all members of the organization; (2) basic harassment and discrimination training should be given immediately to new employees, managers should receive additional training, and refresher training should occur periodically and when special circumstances arise, such as a significant change in policy or practice; (3) the trainers should have

EXHIBIT 13.11   Component 1 of the EEO-1 Form

Job Categories		Number of Employees (Report employees in only one category)														
		Race/Ethnicity														
		Hispanic or Latino		Not-Hispanic or Latino												
				Male							Female						Total Col A–N
		Male	Female	White	Black or African American	Native Hawaiian or other Pacific Islander	Asian	American Indian or Alaska Native	Two or more races	White	Black or African American	Native Hawaiian or other Pacific Islander	Asian	American Indian or Alaska Native	Two or more races	
		A	B	C	D	E	F	G	H	I	J	K	L	M	N	O
Executive/Senior Level Officials and Managers	1.1															
First/Mid-Level Officials and Managers	1.2															
Professionals	2															
Technicians	3															
Sales Workers	4															
Administrative Support Workers	5															
Craft Workers	6															
Operatives	7															
Laborers and Helpers	8															
Service Workers	9															
TOTAL	10															
PREVIOUS YEAR TOTAL	11															

SOURCE: EEO-1 Joint Reporting Committee, *Employer Information Report EEO-1*, n.d. (www.eeoc.gov/employers/eeo1survey/upload/instructions_form.pdf).

special expertise in employment law and practice; (4) the training content should be substantive and cover EEO practices in several staffing areas—such as recruitment, hiring, succession planning, and promotion—as pertains to the numerous EEO laws and regulations; training in other areas of HR, such as compensation and benefits, should also be provided; and (5) the training materials should also be substantive, incorporate the organization's specific harassment and discrimination policies, and allow for both information presentation and active practice by the participants.[35] Trainees should learn which EEO actions they can implement on their own and which actions should be referred to the HR department. Finally, the training should be matched with diversity initiatives to avoid an overly legalistic perspective.[36]

To help heighten trainee awareness and acceptance, the organization might blend material on implicit (hidden) biases into the training.[37] Such biases are deeply held at the unconscious level and could unknowingly enter into how individuals interact with others at work and make decisions about them (such as hiring, promoting, and terminating). The biases could include a wide array of personal characteristics (e.g., demographic) and information (e.g., political views).

The Implicit Association Test (IAT) may be used in training to help reveal each trainee's many possible hidden biases, including skin tone, disability, ethnicity, race, sexuality, weight, age, religion, gender-science, and gender-career. (The IAT for many of these biases can be accessed and taken at *https://implicit.harvard.edu/implicit /selectatest.html*).

Once hidden biases are revealed and acknowledged in a nonthreatening way, steps for avoiding or controlling their effects can be suggested and implemented. Organizations have addressed hidden biases by providing staffing decision makers with prompts or tip sheets about hidden bias during staffing activities, encouraging social interaction at work with people different from oneself, using objective scoring systems for evaluating applicants' résumés, and giving hiring managers specific interview questions to help gauge cultural fit of the applicant to the organization's culture.

Dispute Resolution

Employment laws naturally lead to claims of their violation by job applicants and employees. This sets in motion various ways to resolve the dispute externally or internally.

External Resolution

A complaint must be filed with the agency that administers the law in question, and that agency will have its own process for dealing with the complaint. For example, if the agency is the EEOC, it will assign an investigator to the case who will determine whether there is reasonable cause to assume a violation occurred.[38] The organization can conduct its own investigation (described below) to help figure out what to do next. The EEOC prefers that the organization seek mediation or settlement in order to resolve the dispute informally, voluntarily, and quickly (see Chapter 2). If the organization decides against this, a formal charge-handling process will be followed to investigate and determine whether there is reasonable cause. If reasonable cause is not found, the complaint is dismissed. But if reasonable cause is found, the informal process of conciliation will be used to seek voluntary settlement. If that fails, the EEOC can then file suit or give the charging party the right to file a lawsuit by providing it a right-to-sue letter. In short, the EEOC prefers an informal means of settlement.

Internal Resolution

A complaint filed internally by an employee should be promptly investigated, with appropriate corrective action following. Alternative dispute resolution (ADR) techniques might also be used.

Internal Investigation.   The goal is to conduct an investigation that could be shown to an external agency such as the EEOC or used in court. This will require careful planning and handling of many steps, which could include ensuring confidentiality, providing necessary protection to the person making the complaint, choosing a qualified and objective investigator (e.g., HR staff person, legal counsel, outside investigator), forming an investigation plan for gathering documents and interviewing people, developing interview questions, conducting the interviews, reviewing the documents and interview responses, making a decision about the validity of the complaint, making necessary corrective actions (e.g., promoting a rejected candidate, changing the promotion system), and making a final report.[39]

Alternative Dispute Resolution.   Along with conducting an internal investigation, or separately, the organization could use one of the forms of ADR shown in Exhibit 13.12. These approaches range from informal (e.g., joint decision making) to formal (e.g., a binding decision issued by a neutral arbitrator).

Sometimes new hires are required to sign a provision as part of an employment contract that waives their protected rights under civil rights laws to file or participate in a proceeding against the organization and to instead use only a specified ADR system to resolve complaints. As noted in the chapter on final match, these provisions are highly controversial and may not always be enforceable in court.

With arbitration as the ADR procedure, the employer and the job applicant or employee agree in advance to submit their dispute to a neutral third-party arbitrator, who will issue a final and binding decision. Such arbitration agreements usually include statutory discrimination claims, meaning that the employee agrees not to pursue charges of discrimination against the employer by any means (e.g., lawsuit) except arbitration. The courts have ruled that such arbitration agreements generally are legally permissible and enforceable. However, such agreements do not serve as a bar to pursuit by the EEOC of a discrimination claim seeking victim-specific relief. Legal counsel should be sought prior to use of arbitration agreements.

EXHIBIT 13.12 Alternative Dispute Resolution Approaches

Approach	Description
Negotiation	Employer and employee discuss complaint with goal of resolving complaint.
Fact finding	A neutral person from within or outside the organization investigates a complaint and develops findings that may be the basis for resolving the complaint.
Peer review	A panel of employees and managers work together to resolve the complaint.
Mediation	A neutral person (mediator) from within or outside the organization helps the parties negotiate a mutually acceptable agreement. Mediator is trained in mediation methods. Settlement is not imposed.
Arbitration	A neutral person (arbitrator) from within or outside the organization conducts a formal hearing and issues a decision that is binding on the parties.

SUMMARY

The multiple and complex set of activities collectively known as a staffing system must be integrated and coordinated throughout the organization. Such management of the staffing system requires both careful administration and evaluation, as well as compliance with legal mandates.

To manage the staffing system, the usual organizational arrangement in all but very small organizations is to create an identifiable staffing or employment function and place it within the HR department. That function then manages the staffing system at the corporate and/or plant and office levels.

The myriad staffing activities require staffing policies to establish general staffing principles and procedures to guide the conduct of those activities. Lack of clear policies and procedures can lead to misguided and inconsistent staffing practices, as well as potentially illegal ones. Staffing technology can help achieve these consistencies and aid in improving staffing system efficiency. Outsourcing of staffing activities is also being experimented with as a way of improving staffing system operation and results.

Evaluation of the effectiveness of the staffing system should proceed along several fronts. First is assessment of the staffing system from a process perspective. Here, it is desirable to examine the degree of standardization (consistency) of the process, as well as use a staffing flowchart to identify deviations in staffing practice and bottlenecks. Multiple metrics are available to assess the current status of the organization's staffing functions. Evidence-based procedures like pilot programs, repeated measures, and observational designs help transform the descriptive metrics into prescriptive tools that can improve the staffing system's functioning.

Various laws require maintenance of numerous records and protection of privacy. It is desirable to conduct a legal audit of all the organization's staffing activities periodically. This will help identify potential legal trouble spots that require attention. Employment law training for managers and employees is increasingly becoming necessary. Methods for addressing employment disputes, known as ADRs, should be explored.

DISCUSSION QUESTIONS

1. What are the advantages of having a centralized staffing function, as opposed to letting each manager be totally responsible for all staffing activities in their individual units?
2. What are the advantages and disadvantages of outsourcing an entire staffing system to a vendor?
3. In developing a report on the current status of a staffing process for entry-level jobs, what metrics would you address and why?
4. Which method of analyzing the results of staffing programs do you find most informative?
5. How would you encourage individual managers to be more aware of the legal requirements of staffing systems and to take steps to ensure that they themselves engage in legal staffing actions?

ETHICAL ISSUES

1. It has been suggested that the use of staffing technology dehumanizes the staffing experience, making it nothing but a mechanical process that treats applicants like digital widgets. Evaluate this assertion.
2. Since there are no standard ways of creating staffing process results and cost metrics, is there a need for some sort of oversight of how these data are calculated, reported, and used within the organization? Explain.

APPLICATIONS

Developing Staffing Policies and Procedures

Humanizing Cookware is a small 50-person firm that works to help small start-ups that make kitchen gadgets improve the design of their products. The name "Humanizing Cookware" is a reflection of the firm's unique approach to product development. Specifically, the company's designers, called kitchen lifestyle facilitators (KLFs), use tools and techniques from anthropology to study how people use kitchen gadgets in their homes. This means carefully observing how people cook, using ethnographic techniques to uncover what their cooking experience means to them, and then using these raw data in the creation of designs that appeal to the dreams and wishes of home cooks.

Although the company has avoided using standardized job descriptions, you have been able to determine that most employees spend their time either talking directly with client organizations to find out what their needs are or conducting the studies of cooks in kitchens. For example, a KLF might watch a cook peel carrots for a soup and ask them how and why they are using a specific technique, why they like carrots as an ingredient in soup, and why they cook rather than order from a restaurant. As home cooks talk, the facilitator might learn that products should focus less on convenience and more on giving the appearance of something handcrafted and personal. Then this information would be presented to a client organization that will then modify its products to bring them in line with the advice of the KLF.

As the description of Humanizing Cookware might suggest, this is a rather unusual company with an artistic and free-spirited orientation to its work. Company nature retreats and mindfulness meditation sessions are the norm. Structure and planning are not emphasized. But despite this unconventional approach, the company is quite successful. Few other companies can match the insights its unique anthropological approach is able to glean from home cooks.

The company has little in the way of hierarchy or formal rules. This is in keeping with the culture. However, the lax policies and procedures have resulted in some very poor hiring procedures and problems with meeting legal guidelines for documentation. The company's leadership team has asked you to help them develop a set of standardized policies and procedures that will make the process of hiring new KLFs more standardized.

They would like you to develop a staffing flowchart, something like the one shown in Exhibit 13.5. The process will be different, however, because there is no separate staffing services group; all responsibility is shared by the supervisors and the leadership team. They would also like to use fewer steps in the process if possible. You will also want to develop a set of policies and procedures that can help all members of the organization ensure that new hires are treated in a fair and consistent manner. Information for how to develop these policies can be found in Exhibit 13.2.

Once you have created a staffing flowchart and some policies, consider the following questions:

1. How does the small size and flat structure of the company impact the flowchart and policies you developed?

2. How does the organization's informal culture influence the types of policies and procedures you would implement? What are the advantages and

challenges such a culture poses for designing and implementing policies and procedures?

3. How would you get buy-in for a more standardized set of policies and procedures in this organization? What arguments could you make that would persuade employees to follow through with the new system?

Evaluating Staffing Process Results

The Keepon Trucking Company (KTC) is a manufacturer of custom-built trucks. It does not manufacture any particular truck lines, styles, or models. Rather, it builds trucks to customers' specifications; these trucks are used for specialty purposes such as snow removal, log hauling, and military cargo hauling. One year ago, KTC received a new, large order that would take three years to complete and required the external hiring of 100 new assemblers. To staff this particular job, the HR department manager of nonexempt employment hurriedly developed and implemented a special staffing process for filling these new vacancies. Applicants were recruited from three sources: newspaper ads, employee referrals, and a local employment agency. All applicants generated by these methods were subjected to a common selection and decision-making process. All offer receivers were given the same terms and conditions in their job offer letters and were told there was no room for any negotiation. All vacancies were eventually filled.

After the first year of the contract, the manager of nonexempt employment, Dexter Williams, decided to pull together some data to determine how well the staffing process for the assembler jobs had worked. Since he had not originally planned on doing any evaluation, Dexter was able to retrieve only the following data to help him with his evaluation:

Exhibit
Staffing Data for Filling the Job of Assembler

Recruitment Source	Applicants	Offer Receivers	Start as New Hires	Remaining at Six Months
Newspaper ads				
No. apps.	300	70	50	35
Avg. no. days	30	30	10	
Employee referral				
No. apps.	60	30	30	27
Avg. no. days	20	10	10	
Employment agency				
No. apps.	400	20	20	8
Avg. no. days	40	20	10	

1. Determine the yield ratios (offer receivers / applicants, new hires / applicants), elapsed time or cycle times (days to offer, days to start), and retention rates associated with each recruitment source.

2. What is the relative effectiveness of the three sources in terms of yield ratios, cycle times, and retention rates?

3. What are some possible reasons for the fact that the three sources differ in their relative effectiveness?

4. What would you recommend Dexter do differently in the future to improve his evaluation of the staffing process?

ENDNOTES

1. T. H. Davenport, J. Harris, and J. Shapiro, "Competing on Talent Analytics," *Harvard Business Review*, Oct. 2010, pp. 52–58.

2. C. Boon, R. Eckardt, D. P. Lepak, and P. Boselie, "Integrating Strategic Human Capital and Strategic Human Resource Management," *International Journal of Human Resource Management*, 2018, 29, pp. 34–67.

3. Y. Kim and R. E. Ployhart, "The Strategic Value of Selection Practices: Antecedents and Consequences of Firm-Level Selection Practice Usage," *Academy of Management Journal*, 2018, 61, pp. 46–66; A. J. Nyberg, J. R. Pieper, and C. O. Trevor, "Pay-for-Performance's Effect on Future Employee Performance: Integrating Psychological and Economic Principles Toward a Contingency Perspective," *Journal of Management*, 2016, 42, pp. 1753–1783; B. Okay-Somerville and D. Scholarios, "A Multilevel Examination of Skills-Oriented Human Resource Management and Perceived Skill Utilization During Recession: Implications for the Well-Being of All Workers," *Human Resource Management*, 2019, 58, pp. 139–154.

4. G. Saridakis, Y. Lai, and C. L. Cooper, "Exploring the Relationship Between HRM and Firm Performance: A Meta-Analysis of Longitudinal Studies," *Human Resource Management Review*, 2017, 27, pp. 87–96; C. Ostroff and D. E. Bowen, "Reflections on the 2014 Decade Award: Is There Strength in the Construct of HR System Strength?" *Academy of Management Review*, 2016, 41, pp. 196–214; R. A. Posthuma, M. C. Campion, M. Masimova, and M. A. Campion, "A High Performance Work Practices Taxonomy," *Journal of Management*, 2013, 39, pp. 1184–1220.

5. J. H. Marler and E. Parry, "Human Resource Management, Strategic Involvement and e-HRM Technology," *International Journal of Human Resource Management*, 2016, 27, pp. 2233–2253; S. T. Hunt, *Driving Business Execution Through Integrated Talent Management* (Brisbane, QLD, Australia: Success Factors, 2012).

6. S. Aryee, F. O. Walumbwa, E. Y. M. Seidu, and L. E. Otaye, "Impact of High Performance Work Systems on Individual- and Branch-Level Performance: Test of a Multilevel Model of Intermediate Linkages," *Journal of Applied Psychology*, 2012, 97, pp. 287–300; Y. Hong, H. Liao, J. Hu, and K. Jiang, "Missing Link in the Service Profit Chain: A Meta-Analytic Review of the Antecedents, Consequences, and Moderators of Service Climate," *Journal of Applied Psychology*, 2013, 98(2), pp. 237–267.

7. US Census Bureau, "2014 SUSB Annual Data Tables by Establishment Industry," Dec. 2016 (*www.census.gov/data/tables/2014/econ/susb/2014-susb-annual.html*), accessed Mar. 9, 2017.

8. E. E. Lawler III and A. A. Mohrman, *Creating a Strategic Human Resources Organization* (Stanford, CA: Stanford University Press, 2003), pp. 15–20.

9. M. Fiester, "Practicing Strategic Human Resources," *SHRM Templates and Toolkits*, Mar. 21, 2013 (*www.shrm.org*).

10. J. A. Colquitt, B. A. Scott, J. B. Rodell, D. M. Long, C. P. Zapata, D. E. Conlon, and M. J. Wesson, "Justice at the Millennium, a Decade Later: A Meta-Analytic Test of Social Exchange and Affect Based Perspective," *Journal of Applied Psychology*, 2013, 98, pp. 199–236.

11. J. M. McCarthy, T. N. Bauer, D. M. Truxillo, N. R. Anderson, A. C. Costa, and S. M. Ahmed, "Applicant Perspectives During Selection: A Review Addressing 'So What?,' 'What's New?,' and 'Where to Next?,'" *Journal of Management*, 2017, 43, pp. 1693–1725; K. L. Uggerslev, N. E. Fassina, and D. Kraichy, "Recruiting Through the Stages: A Meta-Analytic Test of Predictors of Applicant Reaction at Different Stages of the Recruiting Process," *Personnel Psychology*, 2012, 65, pp. 597–660; M. Richter, C. J. König, C. Koppermann, and M. Schilling, "Displaying Fairness While Delivering Bad News: Testing the Effectiveness of Organizational Bad News Training in the Layoff Context," *Journal of Applied Psychology*, 2016, 101, pp. 779–792.

12. D. Ulrich, J. Younger, W. Brockbank, and M. Ulrich, *HR From the Outside In* (New York: McGraw-Hill, 2012); S. A. Smith and R. Mazin, *The HR Answer Book* (New York: American Management Association, 2011).

13. S. Meisinger, "Aligning HR Tech to Strategy," *SHRM Special Reports and Expert Views*, Sept. 1, 2016 (*www.shrm.org*).

14. A. Tursunbayeva, R. Bunduchi, M. Franco, and C. Pagliari, "Human Resource Information Systems in Health Care: A Systematic Evidence Review," *Journal of the American Medical Informatics Association*, 2017, 24, pp. 633–654.

15. G. Selke and P. B. Soule, "Translating the HR Digital Revolution to Everyday Work," SAP White Paper, 2017 (*www.sap.com*).

16. B. Roberts, "How to Get Satisfaction From SAAS," *HR Magazine*, Apr. 2010 (*www.shrm.org*); E. Frauenheim, "Talent Tools Still Essential," *Workforce Management*, Apr. 2009, pp. 20–26.

17. A. Collis, "Outsourcing the HR Function," *SHRM Toolkits*, Mar. 2013 (*www.shrm.org*).

18. E. Van Slyke, "Laying the Groundwork for HR Outsourcing," *Workforce Management*, Jan. 2010 (*www.workforce.com*); P. Meskanik, "Critical Success Factors for Recruiting Process Outsourcing," *Oil and Gas Journal*, Jan. 1, 2009, pp. 8–11.

19. B. S. Klaas, H. Yang, T. Gainey, and J. A. McClendon, "HR in the Small Business Enterprise: Assessing the Impact of PEO Utilization," *Human Resource Management*, 2005, 44, pp. 433–448.

20. B. E. Rosenthal, "Coopitition Is an Rx for Success for Three HR Suppliers in the Healthcare Arena," *Outsourcing Center*, Jan. 2013 (*www.outsourcing-center.com*).

21. B. E. Rosenthal, "Employers Make Better Hiring Decisions Using an Online Reference Checking App That Uses Logic," *Outsourcing Center*, Jan. 2013 (*www.outsourcing-center.com*).

22. D. Ulrich, J. Younger, W. Brockbank, and M. Ulrich, *HR Transformation* (New York: McGraw-Hill, 2009); P. M. Wright, J. W. Boudreau, D. A. Pace, E. Sartain, P. McKinnon, and R. L. Antoine, *The Chief HR Officer: Defining the New Role of Human Resource Leaders* (San Francisco: Wiley, 2011).

23. J. Fitz-enz and J. R. Mattox, *Predictive Analytics for Human Resources* (Hoboken, NJ: John Wiley & Sons, 2014); M. A. Huselid, B. E. Becker, and R. W. Beatty, *The Workforce Scorecard: Managing Human Capital to Execute Strategy* (Boston: Harvard Business School Press, 2005); Society for Human Resource Management, *2017 Human Capital Benchmarking Report* (Alexandria, VA: author, 2017).

24. M. Feffer, "Beyond the Numbers," *HR Magazine*, Oct. 2017, pp. 60–64; L. Adler, "Metrics for Better Hires," *HR Magazine*, Mar. 2016, pp. 60–61.

25. Fitz-enz and Mattox, *Predictive Analytics for Human Resources*.

26. Society for Human Resource Management, *2017 Human Capital Benchmarking Report*; Society for Human Resource Management, *2017 Talent Acquisition Benchmarking Report* (Alexandria, VA: author, 2017).

27. Fitz-enz and Mattox, *Predictive Analytics for Human Resources*.

28. S. L. Rynes and J. M. Bartunek, "Evidence-Based Management: Foundations, Development, Controversies and Future," *Annual Review of Organizational Psychology and Organizational Behavior*, 2017, 4, pp. 235–261; A. Camuffo, A. Cordova, A. Gambardella, and C. Spina, "A Scientific Approach to Entrepreneurial Decision Making: Evidence From a Randomized Control Trial." *Management Science*, 2020, 66, pp. 564–586.

29. D. Eden, "Field Experiments in Organizations," *Annual Review of Organizational Psychology and Organizational Behavior*, 2017, 4, pp. 91–122.

30. D. J. Putka, A. S. Beatty, and M. C. Reeder, "Modern Prediction Methods: New Perspectives on a Common Problem," *Organizational Research Methods*, 2018, 21, pp. 689–732; M. S. Fleisher, "Creating a Human Capital Analytics Function in a Multinational Organization," *SHRM Special Reports and Expert Views*, n.d., retrieved Mar. 22, 2020 (*www.shrm.org*).

31. Nolo, "What to Keep in Personnel Files" (*www.nolo.com/legal-encyclopedia/what-keep-employee -personnel-files-30240.html*); Equal Employment Opportunity Commission, "Recordkeeping Requirements" (*www.eeoc.gov//employers/recordkeeping.cfm*).

32. M. W. Finkin, *Privacy in Employment Law*, 3rd ed. (Washington, DC: BNA Books, 2009), pp. 650–657.

33. Equal Employment Advisory Council, *Equal Employment Self-Audit Checklist* (Washington, DC: author, 2016); Equal Employment Advisory Council, *EEO Reference Manual* (Washington, DC: author, 2016); Society for Human Resource Management, *Employment Labor Law Audit* (Alexandria, VA: author, 2016); J. W. Janove, "It's Not Over, Even When It's Over," *HR Magazine*, Feb. 2004, pp. 123–131.

34. A. Smith, "Managerial Training Needed as Hiring Resumes" (*www.shrm.org*), accessed Mar. 16, 2010; D. G. Bower, "Don't Cut Legal Compliance Training," *Workforce Management*, Feb. 2009 (*www.workforce.com*).

35. S. K. Williams, "The New Law of Training," *HR Magazine*, May 2004, pp. 115–118.

36. J. A. Segal, "Unlimited Check-Writing Authority for Supervisors?" *HR Magazine*, Feb. 2007, pp. 119–124; J. C. Ramirez, "A Different Bias," *Human Resource Executive*, May 2006, pp. 37–40.

37. D. Wilkie, "Bringing Bias Into the Light," *HR Magazine*, Dec. 2014, pp. 22–27.

38. Equal Employment Opportunity Commission, "Resolving a Charge" (*www.eeoc.gov/employers /resolving.cfm*); Equal Employment Opportunity Commission, "What You Can Expect After a Charge Is Filed" (*www.eeoc.gov/employers/process.cfm*).

39. Society for Human Resource Management, "Investigations: How to Conduct an Investigation" (*www.shrm.org/templatestools/howtoguides/pages/default.aspx*).

CHAPTER FOURTEEN

Retention Management

Summary

Discussion Questions

Ethical Issues

Applications
Managerial Turnover: A Problem?
Retention: Deciding to Act

Endnotes

LEARNING OBJECTIVES AND INTRODUCTION

Learning Objectives

- Differentiate the types and causes of employee turnover
- Recognize the different reasons employees leave their jobs
- Evaluate the costs and benefits of turnover
- Learn about techniques companies use to limit turnover
- See how performance management and progressive discipline limit discharge turnover
- Understand how companies manage downsizing
- Recognize legal issues that affect separation policies and practices

Introduction

Even the best recruitment and selection system in the world will be of little value if employees leave their jobs soon after being hired. Retention management seeks to keep employees with needed knowledge, skill, ability, and other characteristics (KSAOs). High rates of turnover create significant recurring costs in recruiting, hiring, and training. Staff shortages reduce sales and productivity, and therefore decrease revenues. If a highly productive employee with unique skills leaves, both the costs of replacement and performance losses increase dramatically. In sum, turnover can severely limit the organization's ability to achieve strategic goals. However, retention management also involves terminating employment relationships that are not beneficial for the organization or the employee. When an employee who lacks the necessary competencies leaves, an opportunity arises to find a more suitable replacement. When overstaffing is an issue, selective layoffs may be required to keep the organization afloat. In light of these issues, throughout the chapter we highlight the complex positive and negative aspects of turnover.

The chapter begins with a look at three types of turnover—voluntary, discharge, and downsizing. Retention management must be based on a thorough analysis of these three types of turnover. Turnover analyses include measuring turnover, determining employees' reasons for leaving, and assessing the costs and benefits of turnover. Attention then turns to retention initiatives. As we will see, organizations often encourage retention by focusing on the extrinsic nature of jobs—by creating desirable compensation plans, matching offers from competitors, developing unique benefits programs, and providing incentives for long-term service. Organizations can also improve the intrinsic quality of jobs by providing more satisfying working conditions, improving the social nature of interactions with coworkers, and ensuring that supervisors engage in effective and motivational leadership behaviors.

Finally, involuntary turnover is addressed. We discuss how performance management and progressive discipline initiatives can help employees improve and can help ensure that discharge occurs only when truly necessary. Although most organizations avoid layoffs, downsizing is necessary at times. We therefore discuss strategies for effectively and ethically reducing head count. The chapter ends with a discussion of the myriad laws and regulations pertaining to employee separation.

TURNOVER AND ITS CAUSES

Nature of the Problem

At its core, a retention strategy focuses on maintaining a workforce with the KSAOs and motivation to perform key work tasks. Turnover works against this goal if a departing employee means a loss of KSAOs that were identified in the recruiting and selection process. Retention must be tackled realistically, however, since some amount of employee turnover is inevitable. The Department of Labor estimates that employees between the ages of 18 and 44 have held an average of 11 jobs, and among employees aged 33–38, 58% of jobs lasted less than two years. In some industries, high voluntary turnover is a continual fact of life and cost of doing business. Turnover among managers of sit-down restaurants, for example, hovers around 50% annually.[1]

Although turnover is often seen as a detriment to organizational performance, there may be several functional outcomes, including reduced labor costs and elimination of unqualified employees. Thus, an employee retention strategy should start by assessing retention costs and benefits. With this information, initiatives can be designed to balance retention benefits and costs. Moreover, retention strategies and tactics must focus on not only how many employees are retained but also what types of employees are retained. Some employees make greater contributions to job and organizational effectiveness than others. The retention agenda should make special efforts to retain these high-value employees.

When people voluntarily leave an organization, they do so for a variety of reasons, only some of which are potentially avoidable (controllable) by the organization. Sound retention management thus must be based on a gathering and analysis of employees' reasons for leaving. Specific retention initiatives must be tailor-made to address these reasons in a cost-effective way.

Types of Turnover

Exhibit 14.1 provides a basic classification of the different types of employee turnover.[2] Turnover is classified as either voluntary (initiated by the employee) or involuntary (initiated by the organization). This is something of an oversimplification,

EXHIBIT 14.1   Types of Employee Turnover

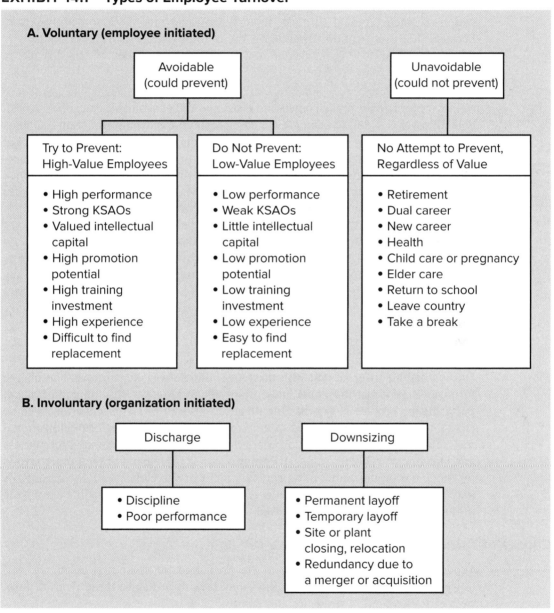

A. Voluntary (employee initiated)

Avoidable
(could prevent)

Unavoidable
(could not prevent)

Try to Prevent:
High-Value Employees

- High performance
- Strong KSAOs
- Valued intellectual capital
- High promotion potential
- High training investment
- High experience
- Difficult to find replacement

Do Not Prevent:
Low-Value Employees

- Low performance
- Weak KSAOs
- Little intellectual capital
- Low promotion potential
- Low training investment
- Low experience
- Easy to find replacement

No Attempt to Prevent,
Regardless of Value

- Retirement
- Dual career
- New career
- Health
- Child care or pregnancy
- Elder care
- Return to school
- Leave country
- Take a break

B. Involuntary (organization initiated)

Discharge

Downsizing

- Discipline
- Poor performance

- Permanent layoff
- Temporary layoff
- Site or plant closing, relocation
- Redundancy due to a merger or acquisition

because some employees "volunteer" to leave after being asked to resign, and sometimes the desire to end the employment relationship is mutual. The line of demarcation between types of turnover in organizational records is sometimes fuzzy because the classification depends on the opinions supervisors have about why turnover occurs.

Voluntary

Voluntary turnover is broken down into avoidable and unavoidable categories. Avoidable turnover could have been prevented by certain organizational actions, such as a pay raise or a new job assignment. Unavoidable turnover represents employee quits that the organization probably could not have prevented, such as when people retire, return to full-time schooling, pursue a different career path, experience health problems that require taking a different type of job, have child care and elder care responsibilities, or move away from the job location.

Organizations further differentiate avoidable turnover that they wish to prevent from avoidable turnover that they are willing to accept, or even encourage. As shown in Exhibit 14.1, the organization will try to prevent high-value employees from quitting—those employees with high job performance, strong KSAOs, key intellectual capital, high promotion potential, and high investments of training and development, and who are difficult to replace. The organization is less likely to try to retain low-value employees.

Involuntary

Involuntary turnover is split into discharge and downsizing turnover. Discharge turnover is aimed at the individual employee and is due to discipline and/or job performance problems. Downsizing turnover, also known as a reduction in force (RIF), typically involves groups of employees. It occurs as part of organizational restructuring or a cost-reduction program to improve organizational effectiveness and increase shareholder value. RIFs may occur as permanent or temporary layoffs for the entire organization, or as part of a plant or site closing or relocation. RIFs may also occur as the result of a merger or acquisition, in which some employees in the combined workforce are viewed as redundant.

Causes of Turnover

Separate models of turnover causes are presented for voluntary, discharge, and downsizing turnover. The organization may seek to influence these types of turnover with its retention strategies and tactics.

Voluntary Turnover

Models of voluntary turnover have been developed and tested through research by many individuals across many organizations over many years.[3] The model shown in Exhibit 14.2 is a distillation of that research. The employee's intention to quit

EXHIBIT 14.2   Causes (Drivers) of Voluntary Turnover

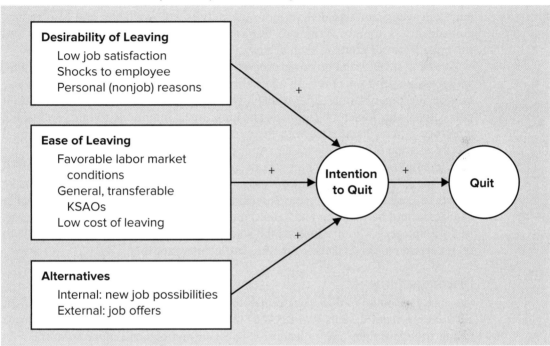

NOTE: The relative importance of the drivers and how they interact to determine the decision to quit varies across situations.

depends on three general factors: the perceived desirability of leaving, the perceived ease of leaving, and alternatives available to the employee. The model illustrates both avoidable and unavoidable turnover.

The perceived desirability of leaving is often an outgrowth of a poor person/job or person/organization fit. There may be a difference between what the employee wants and what the job provides. In addition to misfit, unexpected events or "shocks" may occur to the employee that trigger a more impulsive intention to quit, such as a dramatic fight with a coworker or a stressful interaction with a customer. Finally, employees may find it desirable to leave for personal, nonjob reasons that are unavoidable.

The perceived ease of leaving represents a high likelihood of finding a new job with minimal sacrifice for leaving. Employees believe the ease of leaving will be higher when the unemployment rate is low, or if the employee possesses KSAOs that they think will be desirable to other employers. Employees who are highly embedded in their jobs, organizations, and communities are less likely to leave. Some of the factors that increase embeddedness can be influenced by the organization, such as interpersonal relationships with supervisors and coworkers, or benefits that other employers cannot provide. On the other hand, the turnover of friends and colleagues can signal that good alternatives are available, and also reduce embeddedness, thereby leading to "turnover contagion." Other factors are beyond the organization's control, such as ties to the local community.[4]

The final stage of the turnover process is the formation of the intention to quit, which will depend on other job alternatives available to the employee within and outside the organization. The availability of promotion, transfer, and relocation alternatives may lessen or eliminate the employee's intentions to quit, even if the employee is very dissatisfied with the current job. In addition, actual or potential receipt of a job offer from another employer represents a clear external alternative for the employee. Job searching has been empirically identified as a close correlate of turnover; however, employers should not assume that it is too late to make efforts to keep an employee who is seeking another job. Directly addressing what changes would be necessary to keep the employee is a good strategy in this case. Many employees who are looking for an alternative would be willing to stay with their current employer if their job were sufficiently modified.

Discharge Turnover

Discharge turnover is due to extremely poor person/job fit, particularly a misfit between job requirements and KSAOs. One form of misfit involves the employee failing to follow rules and procedures. These infractions can range from the relatively minor (e.g., dress code violations, horseplay) to the very serious (e.g., bringing a firearm to work). Often it is the cumulative effect of multiple incidents that results in the discharge.

The other form of discharge turnover involves unacceptable job performance. Here, the KSAO/job requirements misfit is severe, and it is unlikely that either the employee's competencies or the job requirements are likely to change in a way that would create fit.

Downsizing Turnover

Downsizing turnover reflects a staffing level misfit in which the organization is, or is projected to be, overstaffed. In other words, the head count available exceeds the head count required. Overstaffing may be due to (1) a lack of forecasting and planning, (2) inaccuracies in forecasting and planning, or (3) unanticipated changes in labor demand and/or labor supply. For example, optimistic forecasts of demand for products and services that do not materialize may lead to overstaffing, as may unanticipated downturns in demand that create a sudden excess head count. Alternatively, a change in the labor market may reduce the ease of movement, causing fewer employees to leave the organization, an unanticipated decrease in the voluntary turnover rate, and thus a change in workforce head count available.

ANALYSIS OF TURNOVER

Several analytical tools can help organizations evaluate the magnitude of turnover and uncover the underlying reasons for turnover. These analyses require measures of the three types of turnover, identification of the reasons for turnover, and an assessment of the costs and benefits of each type of turnover.

Measurement

Turnover Rate and Employment Duration

Since turnover involves the discrete action of leaving or staying with the organization, it is expressed as the proportion or percentage of employees who leave the organization in some time period. Thus:

$$\text{turnover rate} = \frac{\text{number of employees leaving}}{\text{average number of employees}} \times 100$$

This estimate requires decisions about (1) the time period of interest (e.g., month, year), (2) the type of employee "counts" (e.g., full time only, part time, seasonal), and (3) a determination of how to calculate the average number of employees over the time period, such as a straight or weighted average.

An alternative metric, focused on retention, is assessing the average level of tenure possessed by employees. This information is often similar to the results from assessing turnover rates, with high turnover rates corresponding to low employment duration, and low turnover rates corresponding to high employment duration. However, employment duration frames the information on turnover differently by quantifying the retention of existing employees. At times, turnover rates can be quite different than just a mirror image of employment duration, such as in an organization that has rapid turnover of new hires, coupled with very long-term retention of employees who make it past this initial entry period. In this case, turnover rates might be quite high, and average employment duration might be high as well.

Benchmarks

Benchmark turnover data can aid in the interpretation of the turnover and retention rates. One type of benchmark is internal, looking at changes in the organization's own turnover data over time. Such trend analysis can identify whether retention is worsening or improving. Trends can also demonstrate the effectiveness of new retention initiatives.

Another form of benchmarking is external, in which the organization compares its own data with the current turnover rates and trends of other organizations. One major external benchmarking source is the data from the Job Openings and Labor Turnover Survey (JOLTS), collected and published by the US Department of Labor. The JOLTS is conducted monthly among 16,000 business establishments

---

EXHIBIT 14.3   Data From the JOLTS

	Hire Rates	Total Separations Rates	Quit Rates	Layoff and Discharge Rates	Other Separations Rates
Construction	60.6%	56.1%	21.5%	32.0%	3.8%
Manufacturing	25.7%	25.5%	13.3%	10.0%	2.6%
Retail trade	58.1%	56.2%	35.0%	15.5%	5.7%
Finance and insurance	26.3%	24.5%	13.5%	6.9%	4.1%
Health care and social assistance	34.2%	30.8%	21.0%	7.2%	2.6%
Accommodation and food services	74.4%	72.1%	50.3%	19.5%	2.3%
State and local education	17.5%	16.9%	8.6%	5.6%	2.8%

NOTE: Rates reflect hires, quits, layoffs and discharges, and other separations as a percentage of total employment in the industry.
SOURCE: Bureau of Labor Statistics, "Job Openings and Labor Turnover Survey," Mar. 17, 2016 (*www .bls.gov/jlt/*).

and provides data on total employment, job openings, hires, quits, layoffs and discharges, and other separations.

Exhibit 14.3 provides data from the JOLTS, summarizing mobility across a few representative industries for the year 2015. The differences across industries are helpful for understanding just where a company stands relative to its context. A company in the manufacturing industry, for example, would be quite concerned about a quit rate of 30% per year, because this is far above the industry average rate of 13.3%. Conversely, a company in the accommodation and food services industry would note that its quit rate of 30% per year is well below the industry average rate of 50.3%. The data are also useful for evaluating quits versus layoffs and discharge rates. For example, construction has a higher proportion of layoffs than quits, reflecting the strong project-based and seasonal nature of the industry. In finance and insurance, layoff rates are only about half of quit rates, reflecting less seasonal fluctuation.

Reasons for Leaving: Self-Report

Measuring turnover rates and benchmarks provides preliminary information on the scope of the turnover situation for an organization. To learn more about the specific reasons underlying exit decisions, however, more in-depth probing of employee motivation is necessary and can be obtained through exit interviews and post-exit surveys.[5]

Exit Interviews

Exit interviews are formally planned and conducted discussions with departing employees. Exhibit 14.4 contains examples of structured exit interview questions.

The following suggestions will hopefully elicit accurate information from the interviewee: (1) a structured interview format should be developed that contains questions about unavoidable and avoidable reasons for leaving; (2) the interviewer should be a neutral person (someone from the human resources department or an external consultant); (3) the interviewer should be trained in how to put the employee at ease and explain the purposes of the interview, how to take appropriate

---

EXHIBIT 14.4   Examples of Exit Interview Questions

1. Current job title _____ Department/work unit _____
2. Length of time in current job _____ Length of time with organization _____
3. Are you leaving for any of the following reasons?
   retirement _____ dual career _____ new career _____ health _____
   child care or pregnancy _____ elder care _____ return to school _____
   leave the country _____ take a break _____
4. Do you have another job lined up? _____ New employer _____
5. What aspects of your new job will be better than your current job? _____
6. Before deciding to leave did you check the possibility of:
   job transfer _____ promotion _____ relocation _____
7. Was it easy to find another job? _____ Why? _____
8. Do many of your current skills fit with your new job? _____
9. What aspects of your job have been most satisfying? _____
   least satisfying? _____
10. What could the company have done to improve your job satisfaction? _____
11. How satisfactory has your job performance been since your last review? _____
12. What are things the company or your manager could have done to help you improve
    your performance? _____
13. If you could have had a different manager, would you have been more likely to stay
    with the company? _____
14. Are you willing to recommend the company to others as a place to work? _____
15. Would you be willing to hire back with the company? _____
16. Is there anything else you would like to tell us about your decision to leave the
    company? _____

notes, and how to end the interview on a positive note; (4) the interviewer should prepare for each exit interview by reviewing the interview format and the interviewee's personnel file; (5) the interview should be conducted in a private place, before the employee's last day; and (6) the interviewee should be told that the interview is confidential and that only aggregate results will be used to help the organization better understand why employees leave. The best exit interview process starts well before the employee's last day. An ongoing pattern of communication and trust throughout the employment relationship will greatly increase the likelihood that a departing employee will give forthright and thoughtful information about why they are leaving.

In addition to providing an opportunity to learn the employee's reasons for leaving, exit interviews are used to explain such things as rehiring rights, benefits, and confidentiality agreements. Conducting the interview before an employee's last day can sometimes bring up issues that, if addressed, could prevent the employee from leaving. For example, if an exit interview reveals that an employee is only leaving for higher pay, the organization can make a counteroffer. An employee who is leaving on good terms may also provide suggestions or advice on how to improve the organization.

Post-Exit Surveys

To increase confidentiality and reduce the administrative burden of individual interviews, anonymous post-exit surveys might be used. It is recommended that the survey cover the same areas as an exit interview, and that the survey be sent shortly after the employee's last day. Open-ended surveys can be used to gather more detailed information from the employee's individual point of view, while surveys with specific questions and standardized response options make it easier to quickly compile and compare responses.

Employee Satisfaction Surveys

Conducting job satisfaction surveys is a good way to discover the types of job rewards that are most satisfying to employees, and might therefore enhance retention. Conversely, low levels of satisfaction with job features indicate areas for improvement. Conducting job satisfaction surveys has the advantage of learning from all employees who respond to the survey, rather than just those who have already left. Satisfaction survey results also give the organization information it can use to preempt turnover by making changes that will increase job satisfaction. Online surveys allow managers to quickly and conveniently collect information from geographically dispersed employees.

Reasons for Leaving: Predictive Analytics

While exit interviews and surveys can be informative, they are plagued by significant measurement issues, especially when former employees respond in a guarded manner for fear of creating a poor impression. Research suggests that there are differences between the reasons for turnover that employees provide in exit interviews and the reasons they provide in anonymous surveys.[6] Departing employees are reluctant to complain about their employer because they do not want to burn any bridges or jeopardize future references. It is also possible that employees do not have the appropriate insight into their own reactions to identify actions the organization might take to reduce turnover. For all of these reasons, predictive analytics are an important tool for evaluating turnover.

The simplest way to evaluate turnover using an analytical approach is by breaking out turnover rates across various employee and organizational characteristics. Factors that are relevant for breakouts include (1) type of turnover: voluntary (avoidable and unavoidable) or involuntary (discharge and downsizing), (2) type of employee (e.g., exempt/nonexempt, demographics, KSAOs, and performance level), (3) job category, and (4) geographic location. Such breakouts help identify how much variation in turnover there is around the overall average and pockets of the most and least severe turnover. Human resource information systems (HRISs) are designed to process and track employee departures, so data are often readily available regarding when, where, and even why employee turnover is occurring.

Exhibit 14.5 shows some representative data that might be used for assessing turnover across a variety of employees. The breakouts are based on various characteristics of employees for a hypothetical organization that produces gourmet roast coffee beans sold locally at coffee shops and online. The results show that among individuals with less than five years of experience, turnover is exceptionally high,

EXHIBIT 14.5 **Example Turnover Breakout Results**

		Annual Turnover Rate
Experience Level	Less than three years	35%
	Three to five years	21%
	More than five years	13%
Department	Customer service	45%
	Sales	36%
	Marketing	13%
	Product development	11%
	Administrative support	14%
Survey Data	Low organizational commitment	49%
	Moderate organizational commitment	15%
	High organizational commitment	8%

whereas turnover is less common among high-tenure employees. There are also substantial differences across departments, with customer service and sales employees being more prone to turnover relative to employees in marketing, product development, and administrative support. Finally, data from employee self-reported levels of organizational commitment show that those who feel low levels of commitment are much more likely to leave the organization.

Other, more analytically precise techniques are also available for assessing the predictors of turnover.[7] Multiple regression analysis, which we described in the planning chapter as a tool for predicting workforce demand, can also be used as a tool for predicting the likelihood that an employee will turn over. Employee turnover at either the individual or group level is the dependent variable, and factors like pay rates, supervisor leadership behavior, perceived alternative job opportunities, or job characteristics are used as predictors. Much of the research described throughout this chapter is based on exactly these types of statistical relationships.

Some basic breakouts of turnover rates and regression analyses are easily accomplished with the routine reports from HRIS. External vendors and consultants are able to provide more sophisticated statistical consulting when needed. Advanced analytical tools also can help visualize data relationships by showing scatterplots, trends of turnover across time, and heatmaps of where turnover is most problematic across regions.

Costs and Benefits

Costs and benefits may be estimated for each of the three types of turnover. Some of the costs and benefits may be estimated through accounting measures of expenditures on selection, training, wages, and benefits. Operational outcomes affected by turnover, like production and sales, should also be evaluated. To get the full picture, such analyses must be supplemented with a careful consideration of strategic and cultural costs and benefits. It may very well be that these less tangible costs and benefits are more important for organizational performance.

Voluntary Turnover

Voluntary turnover can be extremely expensive. Research consistently shows that organizations with high turnover have a low stock price, a low return on investment, low revenues, and other low financial returns.[8] Exhibit 14.6 shows the major types of costs and benefits that can occur when an employee leaves the organization. An assessment of these costs and benefits will help determine how far the organization should go to enhance retention. The costs and benefits assessment could be separately developed for the work or business unit, division, or total organization. The results could be used to communicate with top management about the nature and severity of employee turnover, and to help develop retention strategies and tactics.

Exhibit 14.6 shows that on the cost side there are separation, replacement, and training costs. The financial costs mainly involve the cost of people's time, the cost

EXHIBIT 14.6   Voluntary Turnover: Costs and Benefits

I. Separation Costs

  A. Financial Costs
  - HR staff time (e.g., exit interview, payroll, benefits)
  - Manager's time (e.g., retention attempts, exit interview)
  - Accrued paid time off (e.g., vacation, sick pay)
  - Temporary coverage (e.g., temporary employee, overtime pay for current employees)

  B. Other Costs
  - Production and customer service delays or quality decreases
  - Lost or unacquired clients
  - Employee goes to competitor or forms competitive business
  - Contagion—other employees decide to leave
  - Teamwork disruptions
  - Loss of workforce diversity

II. Replacement Costs
  - Staffing costs for new hire (e.g., cost-per-hire calculations)
  - Hiring inducements (e.g., bonus, relocation, perks)
  - Hiring manager and work-unit employee time
  - Orientation program time and materials
  - HR staff induction costs (e.g., payroll, benefits enrollment)

III. Training Costs
  - Formal training (trainee and instruction time, materials, equipment)
  - On-the-job training (supervisor and employee time)
  - Mentoring (mentor's time)
  - Socialization (time of other employees, travel)
  - Productivity loss (loss of production until full proficient employee)

IV. Benefits
  - Replacement employee better performer and organization citizen than last employee
  - New KSAO and motivation infusion to organization
  - Opportunity to restructure work unit
  - Savings from not replacing employee
  - Vacancy creates transfer or promotion opportunity for others
  - Replacement less expensive in salary and seniority-based benefits

of materials and equipment, cash outlays, and productivity losses. The other costs are harder to estimate, but may entail large negative impacts on organizational effectiveness. These other costs include loss of clients, lower customer satisfaction, and reduced efficiency. A number of benefits may result from turnover, however, including finding a higher-quality, less expensive replacement for the departing employee.

Materials and equipment costs are likely to be most prevalent in replacement and training costs. Recruitment brochures and testing materials, orientation program materials, and induction materials such as benefits enrollment forms all add to staffing costs. Formal training may involve the use of both materials and equipment that must be accounted for. Cash outlays include paying for (1) the departing employee's accrued but unused paid time off, (2) possible temporary coverage for the departing employee, and (3) hiring inducements for the replacement employee.

On the benefits side, the primary immediate benefit is the labor cost savings from not having the departing employee on the payroll. This will save the organization labor costs until a permanent replacement is hired (if ever). The organization will also save on labor costs if a temporary replacement at a lower pay rate can fill the position until a permanent replacement is acquired. The permanent replacement may be hired at a lower wage or salary than the departing employee, resulting in additional pay and benefit savings. The other benefits shown in Exhibit 14.6 are less tangible but potentially very important in a longer-run sense of improved work-unit and organizational effectiveness.

Exhibit 14.7 shows the cost estimates for a single incident of voluntary turnover in a hypothetical industrial supplies organization that employs 40 salespeople who receive $20/hour on average and bring in approximately eight million dollars in total annual sales. The three categories of the turnover and replacement process (separation, replacement, and training) are described in terms of their time costs, materials and equipment costs, and other costs.

While individual turnover cost estimates require considerable judgment and guesstimates, this example illustrates some expected costs that are "hidden" in (1) the time demands placed on the many employees who must handle the separation, replacement, and training activities, and (2) the sales or productivity losses experienced. Such costs might be offset, at least in part, through the acquisition of less expensive temporary and permanent replacement employees, at least for a while. Also note that when turnover costs for a single employee loss are aggregated to an annual level for multiple losses, the costs can be substantial. In this example, if the sales unit experienced just a 20% annual voluntary turnover rate, it would lose eight employees at a total cost of $519,000, or 6.5% of annual sales.

While this illustration shows significant financial costs from individual turnover for a specific job, some recent research suggests that there may be even more substantial system-wide effects. Interruptions in productivity due to vacancies can be quite substantial, and the productivity of the business unit as a whole can be impacted for a long time.[9] One study showed how the turnover of a single employee in a bank branch led to immediate and negative performance for the branch as a whole. These effects were especially dramatic when turnover occurred among managers. Branch-level performance did recover over time after a lower-level employee departed, but when higher-level employees left, the downturn in performance lasted for many months. Other studies demonstrate that turnover reduces innovation and performance by increasing conflict, disrupting projects,

EXHIBIT 14.7 Example of Financial Cost Estimates for One Voluntary Turnover

	Time			
	Hours	Cost ($)	Materials and Equipment ($)	Other Costs ($)
A. Separation Costs				
Staffing manager	1	25		
HR staff	1	15		
Employee's manager	3	120		
Accrued paid time off	160	2,400		
Processing			30	
B. Replacement Costs				
Temporary replacement				
Compensation difference	160	(800)		
Staffing manager	1	25		
Employee's manager	1	40		
Staffing firm fee (markup)				800
Permanent replacement				
Compensation difference	960	(4,800)		
Cost-per-hire				4,500
Hiring bonus				3,000
Laptop computer				2,000
Employee's manager	3	120		
Orientation	8	160		
C. Training Costs				
Training program				
Trainee	80	1,200		
Instructor	100	1,600	1,000	
Mentor	52	1,040		
Productivity/sales loss				
Permanent replacement				50,000
Temporary replacement				2,000
D. Total Costs		1,145	1,030	62,300

and creating holes in communication networks. The implication is clear: turnover of key employees can have long-term operational effects far beyond the immediately apparent costs associated with recruiting, selection, and training.

Discharge

At the aggregate level, there is not a relationship between involuntary turnover rates and firm performance.[10] This could be because of the complex balance of costs and benefits we outline below. Managing discharge is even harder than managing retention.

Some of the costs and benefits accompanying discharge are the same as those for voluntary turnover. Exhibit 14.8 shows that separation, replacement, and training costs are still incurred. There may be an additional separation cost for a contract buyout of guarantees (salary, benefits, and perks) common for high-level executives and public sector leaders such as school superintendents. As described in the chapter on final match, these guarantees can make the hiring package more

---

EXHIBIT 14.8   Discharge: Costs and Benefits

I. Separation Costs

A. Financial Costs

- Same as for voluntary turnover plus possible contract buyout (salary, benefits, perks)

B. Other Costs

- Manager and HR staff time handling problem employee
- Grievance, alternative dispute resolution
- Possibility of lawsuit, loss of lawsuit, settlement or remedy
- Damage to labor–management relations

II. Replacement Costs

- Same as for voluntary turnover

III. Training Costs

- Same as for voluntary turnover

IV. Benefits

- Departure of low-value employee
- High-value employee replacement possibility
- Reduced disruption for manager and work unit
- Improved performance management and disciplinary skills

attractive, but they drive up the costs of discharge substantially if the employee needs to be terminated.

Supervisors usually make a discharge decision based on the premise that the company is better off without the problem employee. This decision could have a positive effect if the supervisor is effectively able to identify and discharge low-value employees.[11] Most obviously, the organization can hire a better qualified and more motivated replacement. Removal of low performers may motivate those who remain to work harder to avoid a similar fate. The dismissal of hostile or uncooperative coworkers may also improve morale among those who remain, increasing their collective motivation and coordination efforts.

Even though discharge may be seen as a "valued exit," the costs should not be overlooked.[12] The disruption in group processes because of discharge can be just as substantial as that for voluntary turnover. The need to hire and train a replacement remains. A discharge is usually preceded by the supervisor and others spending considerable time, often unpleasant and acrimonious, with the employee, seeking to change the person's behavior. The possibility of a lawsuit means that all steps in the termination process need to be carefully documented, taking up more administrative time. Finally, discharge can erode relationships with remaining employees if they feel the procedure was unfair. In short, discharge turnover can be a costly and unpleasant process.

The preceding discussion highlights the role of accurate performance measurement in managing discharge. The expected positive effects of discharge are obtained only if problem employees are reliably identified and selectively terminated. If there is not a clear link between performance and discharge decisions, disruptions will be significant, morale will be damaged, and replacement hires may not be any better than the terminated employee. An employee who actively undermines the work process and morale through negative behavior, such as a serial harasser or bully, is one instance where discharge will be especially positive. In sum, the key to managing discharge is accurately identifying which employees are harming organizational effectiveness. Because of the importance of this issue, the performance management process is covered in depth later in this chapter.

Downsizing

Downsizing costs are concentrated in separation costs for a permanent RIF since there will presumably be no replacement hiring and training. These costs are shown in Exhibit 14.9, along with potential benefits. The major economic cost areas are time costs, cash outlays for various severance and buyout packages, and increased unemployment compensation insurance premiums. The time costs involve both HR staff and managers' time in planning, implementing, and handling the RIF. RIF turnover has an especially strong negative relationship with organizational performance relative to other forms of involuntary turnover.[13]

Severance costs may take numerous forms. First, employees can be paid for accrued time off. Second, early retirement packages may be offered to employees

---

EXHIBIT 14.9   Downsizing: Costs and Benefits

I. Separation Costs

A. Financial Costs
- HR staff time in planning and implementing layoff
- Managers' time in handling layoff
- Accrued paid time off (e.g., vacation, sick pay)
- Early retirement package
- Voluntary severance package (e.g., one week's pay/year of service, continued health insurance, outplacement assistance)
- Involuntary severance package
- Contract buyouts for fulfillment of guarantees
- Higher unemployment insurance premiums
- Change in control (CIC) guarantees for key executives during a merger or acquisition

B. Other Costs
- Shareholder value (stock price) may not improve
- Loss of critical employees and KSAOs
- Inability to respond quickly to surges in product and service demand; restaffing delays and costs
- Contagion—other employees leave
- Threat to harmonious labor–management relations
- Possibility of lawsuit, loss of lawsuit, costly settlement or remedy
- Decreased morale, increased feelings of job insecurity
- Difficulty in attracting new employees

II. Benefits
- Lower payroll and benefits costs
- Increased production and staffing flexibility
- Ability to relocate facilities
- Improved promotion and transfer opportunities for stayers
- Focus on core businesses, eliminate peripheral ones
- Spread risk by outsourcing activities to other organizations
- Flatten organization hierarchy—especially among managers
- Increase productivity

as an inducement to leave early. Third, employees who are ineligible for early retirement may be offered a voluntary severance package as an inducement to leave without being laid off. A typical severance package includes one week's pay for each year of service, continued health insurance coverage and premium payment, and outplacement assistance. A danger with both early retirement and voluntary severance packages is that their provisions may turn out to be so attractive that more employees take them and leave than had been planned for in the RIF.

Other costs of downsizing shown in Exhibit 14.9 may also be considerable. Shareholder value (stock price) may not improve, since downsizing can signal poor financial and operational health. There will be a critical talent loss and an inability to respond quickly to the need for workforce additions to cover new demand surges. A reputation for job instability will create added difficulties in attracting new employees. Terminated employees may pursue legal avenues, claiming, for example, that decisions about whom to lay off were tainted by age discrimination. Employees who survive the job cuts may have damaged morale and may fear even more cuts, which may harm performance and cause them to look for another job with a more secure organization.

Against this backdrop of heavy costs are many potential benefits. One such benefit will be lower payroll and benefits costs. The organization may gain production and staffing flexibility, an ability to outsource parts of the business that are not mission critical, and opportunities to redesign and relocate facilities. The restructuring may also entail a flattening of the organizational hierarchy by eliminating layers of management, leading to increased speed in decision making as well as boosts in productivity.

RETENTION INITIATIVES: VOLUNTARY TURNOVER

For most organizations, of the three types of turnover, voluntary turnover is the most prevalent and the one they choose to focus on in the continual "war for talent." Based on the causes of turnover model (Exhibit 14.2), ways to influence the three primary drivers of turnover—desirability of leaving, ease of leaving, and alternatives—are suggested for retention initiatives. After this broader discussion, we outline some typical examples of larger, organization-wide initiatives to retain employees.

Desirability of Leaving

Employees' desire to leave is influenced by their job satisfaction, shocks they experience, and personal (nonjob) reasons. Of these, only job satisfaction can usually be meaningfully influenced by the organization. Therefore, the first strategy for improving retention is to improve job satisfaction. The myriad examples of retention initiatives described above mostly represent attempts to improve job satisfaction through the delivery of various rewards to employees.

It is critical to understand that merely throwing more or new rewards at employees is not a sound retention initiative. Which rewards are chosen, and how they are delivered to employees, will determine how effective they are in improving job satisfaction. Accordingly, guidelines for reward choice and delivery are also described here. Exhibit 14.10 summarizes the guidelines for increasing job satisfaction and retention.

EXHIBIT 14.10   Guidelines for Increasing Job Satisfaction and Retention

A. Extrinsic Rewards
- Make rewards meaningful and unique
- Provide fair reward allocation systems
- Link rewards to retention behaviors
- Link rewards to performance

B. Intrinsic Rewards
- Create work characteristics that meet employee preferences
- Provide employees with organizational support
- Ensure supervisors and coworkers provide a positive social environment
- Enhance work/life balance

As discussed in the job analysis and rewards chapter, a variety of extrinsic and intrinsic rewards can be offered to potentially improve job satisfaction. One important point must be kept in mind for both intrinsic and extrinsic rewards. The person/job match model emphasizes that job satisfaction results from a fit between the rewards desired by the employee and the rewards provided by the job. Employee reward preferences may be assessed at all stages of the staffing process by (1) asking applicants what attracted them to the organization, (2) asking current employees about the most important sources of job satisfaction, and (3) assessing reasons for turnover during exit interviews.

Extrinsic Rewards

To have attraction and retention power, extrinsic rewards must be unique and unlikely to be offered by competitors. Surveys of employees consistently show that inadequate compensation and benefits are extremely powerful drivers of employee turnover decisions.[14] The organization must benchmark against its competitors to determine what others are offering. A survey of 1,223 employed adults also revealed that employee benefits are a key driver of employee retention. In particular, 40% of respondents indicated that 401(k) matching decreased their desire to leave; health care coverage and a competitive salary also topped the list.[15] Surveys also suggest that in a down economy, many employees see benefits like health insurance as a vital part of their personal safety net.[16]

Fair Allocation of Rewards.   If reward systems are to increase satisfaction, employees must know why the system was developed, the mechanics of the system, and the payouts to be expected. Such knowledge and understanding require continuous communication. Research shows that a very common form of employee dissatisfaction with reward systems is the failure to understand the underlying purpose or process.[17] Distributive justice requires that there be a rational and preferably measurable basis for reward decisions. Objective measures of job performance, such as sales figures, are likely to be accepted as legitimate. Rewards based on managerial performance reviews may be problematic if employees question the legitimacy of the performance measurement system, or if they believe these rewards create divisive comparisons among employees. The importance of system fairness has been demonstrated in many contexts. Although much of the research on justice has been conducted in the United States and Canada, studies from China, Korea, Japan, and Pakistan have also shown that perceived justice increases job satisfaction and decreases turnover intentions.[18]

Rewards for Retention.   Rewards can be even more powerfully attached to employee retention if they explicitly take seniority into account. For example, employees who have been with the organization longer may receive more vacation hours, career advancement opportunities, and increased job security. A subtler way of rewarding employee retention is to make the reward contingent on the person's base pay level. Base pay levels typically increase over time through a combination of promotions and merit pay increases. Specific retention bonuses are also used to encourage longer-term relationships.

Rewards for Performance.   Rewards can also be linked to employee job performance as a way to increase the retention of high performers. Organizations with a strong performance management culture thrive on high performance expectations, coupled with large base-pay raises, bonuses, commissions, and stock options for high performers. Because lesser performers receive lower wages in these organizations, they are more likely to leave, whereas superior performers are more likely to stay.[19] It should be noted, however, that many of these positive effects of differential pay have been investigated in individualistic countries. Individuals who have a more collectivistic orientation may be less positively disposed to differential rates of pay.

Intrinsic Rewards

The intrinsic rewards listed in Exhibit 14.10 should not be overlooked. There is consistent evidence that employees' dissatisfaction with the intrinsic quality of their jobs is strongly related to turnover.[20]

Work Characteristics.   A very large number of studies have shown that most people prefer work that contributes to an identifiable end product that is useful for someone else. When employees work on small, repetitive tasks that do not have a clear relationship with a finished product, they are not as intrinsically satisfied with their work. An automobile manufacturing employee will be more satisfied if they can see how their efforts lead to a finished car that is useful for a family, just as a customer service representative at a wireless Internet provider will be more satisfied if they can see how their efforts help a customer resolve a problem with a home connection.

Job redesign can improve the work environment. Managers might broaden the scope of tasks and responsibilities, allowing for personal growth on the job. Employees should be shown how their work contributes to the well-being of others. Job rotation programs help reduce perceived monotony and give employees a broader sense of the organization's purpose as a whole. Enhancing job autonomy might be facilitated by establishing formal performance goals for the job while giving employees minimal direction or oversight as to the methods required to achieve these goals.

Improving the work environment also involves assigning employees to jobs that better meet their intrinsic-reward preferences. For example, employees with high needs for skill variety could be assigned to more complex projects, or employees with high autonomy needs could be assigned to supervisors with a very hands-off style of leadership. One method for achieving a better fit is to perform "entry" surveys at the point of hire to learn about the new hires' experiences of engagement in previous work. Supervisors can then assign employees to tasks in the current job that provide a similar sense of fulfillment.[21]

Organizational Support. One of the closest correlates of employee commitment is the perception that the organization treats its employees fairly and provides them with support. Clear and honest communication is a vital component of support. Communication must begin early in the staffing process by providing employees with honest information about their job conditions. Continued communication, fair treatment, opportunities for mentoring, and investment in the relationship have all been shown to contribute to retention.[22] Other actions that can increase support from employers include provision of constructive feedback, benefits linked to health and well-being, and development.

On a broader level, communication regarding the organization's strategic direction can also reduce turnover. One large-scale study of high-tech companies in China found that when CEOs expressed a positive, inspirational vision for the organization and its goals, employee turnover was reduced.[23] This effect was related to a more collaborative human resources system, which encouraged more information sharing, collaboration, and group development. In this case, a sense of shared purpose linked with supportive HR systems led employees to stay with the organization.

Social Environment. It is said that employees do not quit their jobs, they quit their bosses. Thus, interpersonal compatibility or chemistry between the employee and the supervisor can be a critical part of the employee's decision to stay or leave. The same could be said for coworkers. Employees who believe they fit with the social environment in which they work are more likely to see their job as a source of significant social rewards.[24] The resultant sense of camaraderie with the supervisor and coworkers may make them reluctant to leave the organization. In fact, among high-turnover employees, like servers in chain restaurants, social relationships with coworkers have been shown to be among the strongest deterrents of turnover. Research confirms that individuals whose coworkers are searching for alternative jobs will also increase their own job search efforts.

The supervisor is also a source of perceptions of justice because of their role as a direct source of reward or punishment.[25] This is because the supervisor decides the process for assessing employees, as well as the amount of rewards to be provided based on these assessments. Supervisors have a key role to play in describing the purpose of an employee's job and giving the employee the resources to meet the job requirements. If supervisors communicate the purpose and mechanics of the performance evaluation system, employees will be able to understand the process of reward distribution and what they need to do to meet expectations. Supervisors who treat subordinates with respect and concern can also help reduce turnover. There are diversity implications for a positive social environment as well. Employees who are isolated from others in their racial, ethnic, or gender group are more likely to leave, whereas pro-diversity workplace climates tend to reduce turnover intentions.

Supervisors and coworkers in the social setting can engage in abusive or harassing behaviors that are threatening or discomforting to an employee. Research suggests that employees who believe their supervisors are abusive are more likely to leave.[26] Examples of abusive supervisor behavior that are frequently cited in surveys include "tells me my thoughts and feelings are stupid," "puts me down in front of others," and "tells me I'm incompetent." More extreme behaviors, such as sexual harassment, have an even stronger negative impact on an employee's desire to remain on the job. Turnover due to interpersonal conflict at work tends to come especially quickly; many employees who have such conflict will bypass the process of searching for and considering alternative jobs and will instead quit immediately. Subjects of abusive behavior may not just quit quietly. Employees who feel abused at work are more likely to resign in a public manner that calls out supervisors for their negative behavior, deliberately interrupt the workplace during their termination event, or initiate lawsuits soon after leaving.

Work/Life Balance. For many employees, trying to balance their work lives with their personal lives contributes to stress, dissatisfaction, and a desire to leave.[27] In an effort to reduce turnover, many organizations have developed programs to help employees integrate their work and nonwork lives. These work/life balance programs allow employees to take time off from work if needed, create flexible scheduling options, and facilitate opportunities to work from remote locations. Many organizations have made family-friendly benefits and flexible work arrangements centerpieces of their retention strategies, and surveys suggest that making efforts to help employees balance their work and family lives can pay off in terms of lower turnover. Data from 2,769 individuals who responded to the National Study of the Changing Workforce revealed that employees who had access to family-friendly work benefits experienced less stress and had lower turnover intentions relative to employees who did not have access to these benefits.[28] In a survey of over 200 HR professionals, 67% of respondents said that they believe flexible work arrangements have a positive impact on employee retention.[29] Despite evidence supporting their use, it should be remembered that work/life programs do not come without costs. Restructuring the workforce can disrupt productivity and may require investments in new technology to facilitate off-site work. Some employees who choose not to take advantage of telecommuting options resent their coworkers who are not in the office regularly, and this resentment can lead to increased intention to leave.[30]

Individual Dispositions

Although organizations often try to influence turnover rates by providing intrinsically and extrinsically satisfying working conditions, a growing body of evidence suggests that some employees are more likely to quit because of their personality dispositions. In other words, some people are just more prone to quit than others. We have already noted that a variety of tools like standardized tests and interviews can be used to identify the characteristics of job applicants. Organizations that are especially concerned about turnover might consider assessing applicants' propensity to quit voluntarily as part of their selection system.

One approach to identifying individuals who are likely to quit is to explicitly ask applicants how often they have changed jobs, whether they have any friends or relatives working at the organization, and whether they have been referred by a current employee. Although the effects are not large, these types of biodata questions are related to turnover rates.[31] Another approach to identifying employees with high turnover propensity is to assess conscientiousness, agreeableness, and emotional stability, as some research has shown that individuals with these traits are less likely to quit.[32]

Ease of Leaving

Ease of leaving may be reduced in two ways: providing organization-specific training and increasing the cost of leaving. A third factor, labor market conditions, cannot be influenced and represents a variable that will continuously influence the organization's voluntary turnover.

Organization-Specific Training and Development

Training and development activities provide KSAOs to employees that they did not possess when they entered the organization as new hires. Training and development seek to increase labor quality in ways that enhance employees' effectiveness. As shown previously, training represents a substantial investment (cost) that evaporates when an employee leaves the organization.

The organization may invest in training to provide KSAOs that vary along a continuum of general to organization-specific. The more general the KSAOs, the more transferable they are to other organizations, thus increasing the likelihood of improving the employee's marketability and raising the probability of leaving. Organization-specific KSAOs are not transferable, and possession of them does not improve employee marketability. Hence, it is possible to lower the employee's ease of leaving by providing, as much as possible, only organization-specific training content that has value only as long as the employee remains with the organization.

This strategy needs to be coupled with a selection strategy in which any general KSAOs required for the job are assessed and used in selection decisions so that they will not have to be invested in once the employee is on the job. For example, applicants for an entry-level sales job might be assessed and selected for general sales competencies such as written and verbal communication and interpersonal skills. Those hired may then receive more specialized training in such areas as product knowledge, specific software, and knowledge of territories. To the extent that such organization-specific KSAOs become an increasingly large proportion of the employee's total KSAO package over time, they help restrict the employee's mobility.

Once employees have gone through training and development programs, replacement and succession plans should be developed that take advantage of these enhanced KSAO levels. As we noted in the internal recruiting chapter, talent management systems that help employees learn about what KSAOs are needed to advance can be mutually beneficial. The organization naturally benefits from having employees who are efficient and effective in their jobs. Employees gain the ability to chart out their own progress within the organization and will have more incentive to remain when these growth opportunities are made explicit.

Increased Cost of Leaving

Driving up the cost of leaving is another way to make it harder to leave. Providing above-market pay and benefits is one way to do this, since employees will have a hard time finding better-paying jobs elsewhere. Any form of deferred compensation, such as deferred bonuses, will also raise the cost of leaving, since the compensation will be lost if the employee leaves before becoming eligible to receive it.

Retention bonuses might also be used. Normally, these are keyed to high-value employees whose loss would wreak organizational havoc. Such may be the case during mergers and acquisitions, when retention of key managers is essential to a smooth transition.

Another long-term way to make leaving costly is to locate the organization's facilities in an area where it is the dominant employer and other amenities (housing, schools, and health care) are accessible and affordable. This may entail location in the outer rings of suburban areas or relatively small and rural communities. Once employees move to and settle into these locations, the cost of leaving is high because of the lack of alternative jobs within the area and the need to make a costly geographic move in order to obtain a new job.

Alternatives

In confronting outside alternatives available to employees, the organization must fashion ways to make even better internal alternatives available and desirable. Two key ways to do this involve internal staffing and responding to outside job offers.

Internal Staffing

The nature and operation of internal staffing systems have already been explored. It is important to reiterate that open systems serve as a safety valve, retention-wise, in that employees are encouraged to look internally for new job opportunities, and managers benefit by seeking internal candidates rather than going outside the organization. The organization should also think of ways outside the realm of its traditional internal staffing systems to provide attractive internal alternatives to its employees.

Internal transfers are one way to address turnover concerns. A study of 205 individuals employed in diverse work settings found that those who were unhappy with their work environments did not translate this dissatisfaction into an intention to leave if they believed that there were opportunities for mobility within their organization. In a sense, one could say that these dissatisfied individuals saw internal transfers as a way to quit a disliked job, but without the costs to the employer that typically come with turnover.[33] To enhance the likelihood that employees will seek their next employment within the organization, professional connections among employees should be fostered. One study found that employees who engaged in more internal networking were indeed more likely to remain in their own organization over time, while those who turned to colleagues outside the organization for networking were more likely to leave.[34]

Response to Job Offers

When employees receive an outside job offer or are on the verge of receiving one, they clearly have a solid job alternative in hand. How should the organization respond, if at all, in order to make itself the preferred alternative?

The organization should confront this dilemma with a policy that has been carefully thought through in advance. This will help prevent impulsive, potentially regrettable actions being taken on the spot when an employee brings forth a job offer and wants to use it for leverage.

The organization should decide whether it will respond to job offers. Some organizations choose not to, thereby avoiding bidding wars and counteroffer games. Even if the organization successfully retains the employee, the employee may lack commitment to the organization, and other employees may resent the special retention deal that was cut. Other organizations choose to respond to job offers, not wanting to automatically close out an opportunity to at least respond to, and hopefully retain, the employee. The price for such openness to outside offers is that it may encourage employees to actively solicit them in order to try to squeeze a counteroffer out of the organization, thus improving the "deal."

Current Practices and Deciding to Act

Turnover analysis does not end with the collection and analysis of data. These activities are merely a precursor to the critical decision of whether to act to solve a perceived turnover problem. If the organization chooses to act, it must decide how to intervene to attack the problem and ultimately assess how effective the intervention was. Presented first are some examples of organization retention initiatives that illustrate the breadth and depth of attempts to address retention concerns. Then a systematic decision process for retention initiatives is provided as a framework to help with deciding whether to act. Such decision guidance is necessary given the complexity of the retention issue and the lack of demonstrated best practices for improving retention.

Decision Process

Exhibit 14.11 provides a suggested decision process that can help organizations navigate the complex trade-offs inherent in developing retention initiatives.

The first question—Do we think turnover is a problem?—requires the consideration and analysis of several types of data. The organization must judge whether turnover rates are increasing and/or high relative to internal and external benchmarks such as industry or direct competitor data. Managers complaining about retention problems, high-value employees leaving, and demographic disparities among those who leave are important signals that actions to reduce turnover are needed. The final analysis should involve the type of cost/benefit analysis described earlier. Even though turnover may be high, it is only a problem if its costs are judged to exceed its benefits in the final analysis.

The second question—How might we attack the problem?—requires consideration of the desirability of leaving, ease of leaving, and alternatives available to the employee. In addition, within each of these areas, which specific factors are possible to change? In Exhibit 14.11, factors such as increasing job satisfaction, improving organizational justice, and improving the social environment might reduce the desirability of leaving, but it is likely not possible to change personal shocks or personal reasons for leaving. Likewise, it is possible to avoid providing general KSAOs and to increase the cost of leaving for the employee in order to reduce the ease of leaving.

Question three asks, "What do we need to decide?" This requires choosing retention initiatives and making plans for implementation. First, develop specific

---

EXHIBIT 14.11   Decision Process for Retention Initiatives

Do We Think Turnover Is a Problem?	How Might We Attack the Problem?	What Do We Need to Decide?	How Should We Evaluate the Initiatives?
• Turnover high or increasing relative to internal and external benchmarks • Managers complain about retention problems • High-value employees are leaving • Demographic disparities among those who leave • Overall costs exceed benefits of turnover	• Lower desirability of leaving? Increase job satisfaction—yes Decrease shocks—no Personal reasons—no Improve organizational justice—yes Improve social environment at work—yes • Lower ease of leaving? Change market conditions—no Decrease provision of general KSAOs—yes Make leaving more costly—yes • Change alternatives? Promotion and transfers—yes Respond to outside job offers—yes	• Turnover goals • Targeted to units and groups • High-value employees • General and targeted retention initiatives • Lead, match, or lag the market • Supplement or supplant • HR and managers' roles	• Lower proportion of turnover if avoidable • Turnover low or decreasing compared with benchmarks • Fewer complaints about retention problems • Fewer high-value employees leaving • Reduced demographic disparities • Lower turnover costs relative to benefits

numerical turnover (retention) goals in the form of desired turnover rates. Then decide whether retention programs will be applied across the board, targeted to specific organizational units and employee groups, or applied to both. Examples of targeted groups include job categories in which turnover is particularly troublesome, underrepresented demographic groups, and recently hired individuals. Next, consider if and how high-value employees will be treated. Many organizations develop special retention initiatives for high-value employees on top of other retention programs. Such programs are most effective when there is a clear effort to select and develop high-potential candidates, align their development with strategy, and give them a clear path for developing their careers within the organization.[35]

Having established retention goals for organizational units, targeted groups, and high-value employees, retention program specifics must be designed. These may be general initiatives applicable to all employees, or they may be targeted. It must then be decided how to position the organization's initiatives relative to the marketplace. For example, will base pay on average be higher than the market average (lead), be the same as the market average (match), or be lower than the market average (lag)? Likewise, will new variable pay plans try to outdo competitors' plans (e.g., a more favorable stock option plan) or simply match them?

Adding to the complexity of the decision process is the delicate issue of whether new retention initiatives will supplement (add on to) or supplant (replace) existing rewards and programs. If the latter, the organization should be prepared for the possibility of employee backlash against what employees may perceive as "take backs" of rewards they currently have and must give up.

Finally, the respective roles of executives, HR, and individual managers will have to be worked out, and this may vary among the retention initiatives. Initiatives that involve wholesale work and compensation system redesign will involve action by top executives. If the initiative involves responding to outside job offers, for example, line managers may demand a heavy or even exclusive hand in this process. Alternatively, some initiatives may be HR driven; examples here include hours of work and variable pay plans.

The final question—How should we evaluate the initiatives?—should be considered *before* any plan is implemented. Answers will lend focus to the design of the intervention and agreed-upon criteria on which to later judge intervention effectiveness. Ideally, the same criteria that led to the conclusion that turnover is a problem (question one) will be used to determine whether the chosen solution actually works (question four).

What Do Organizations Do?

Several descriptive surveys provide glimpses into the actions that organizations take to address retention. These examples come mostly from relatively large organizations, so what happens in small organizations is less known. Nonetheless, the data provide interesting illustrations of organizational tenacity and ingenuity, along with the willingness of organizations to commit resources, in various approaches, to retention.

Review of Organizational Practices. Although there are many anecdotal stories about which retention practices are or are not effective, the most compelling evidence on this topic comes from a comprehensive examination of the effects of various organizational practices on organizational turnover rates across thousands of workplaces.[36] The results of this study showed that some practices were clearly more effective than others. The most and least effective retention initiatives are listed in Exhibit 14.12. We discuss the specific components of retention bundles in greater detail later in this chapter, but for now, it should be emphasized that these initiatives included not just single, isolated practices but a combined system of practices that worked together to encourage employees to remain. It is also interesting to note that increased investment in training as a stand-alone practice was actually associated with increases in turnover. This is consistent with our earlier discussion proposing that higher levels of general, transferable KSAOs can increase the ease of leaving.

WorldatWork Survey.   WorldatWork conducts regular surveys of HR managers regarding the implementation and success of retention initiatives. A survey conducted with a sample of 526 respondents in 2012 focused on the role of rewards in retaining key talent.[37] The great majority of respondents indicated that their organizations identified their key talent and focused their retention efforts on those individuals. Discussing future opportunities, creating succession plans, providing meaningful and enriching job designs, and paying key employees above the market rate were all identified as particularly effective retention methods. One of the least effective methods was providing tuition reimbursement and other educational opportunities. Such activities can actually increase the level of general human capital possessed by employees, thereby making it easier for them to find jobs elsewhere. Most managers also felt that simply tracking employee satisfaction was not particularly useful, perhaps because the tracking activities often were not accompanied by tangible efforts to improve problem situations.

EXHIBIT 14.12   Most and Least Effective Retention Initiatives

Most Effective Retention Initiatives

- Retention bundles (high-commitment HR systems)
- Benefits
- Dispute resolution
- Participation-enhancing work design

Least Effective Retention Initiatives

- Relative pay
- Sophisticated selection system
- Variable pay
- Training

The 100 Best Companies.   Each year *Fortune* publishes the report "The 100 Best Companies to Work For."[38] Organizations apply to be on the list, and their scores are based on randomly chosen employees' responses to the Great Place to Work Trust Index survey and an evaluation of a Culture Audit. Winners are ranked according to their final scores, and brief descriptions are provided about the number of US employees, job growth, annual number of job applicants and voluntary turnover rate, average number of employee training hours, entry-level salary for production and professional employees, revenues, and what makes the organization stand out.

Hilton, which placed at the top of the list for both 2020 and 2019, has focused on providing benefits that are desirable for all employees. In particular, an extended parental leave and other child care programs have created an inclusive and welcoming culture, while travel programs have tied employees to the organization's brand. Other top-ranked organizations, such as Accenture and Synchrony, have focused on skill development—a practice consistent with our earlier discussion of providing a robust internal labor market that provides employees a chance to work in new jobs without turning to external options. Workday, a major HR software provider, has built loyalty by giving targeted opportunities to qualified candidates who might otherwise be overlooked, such as those who have nontraditional educational or work histories or who have financial constraints. Finally, companies such as Salesforce and the Cheesecake Factory have directed their efforts toward developing leaders who are able to create inclusive and inspiring cultures.

Retention Bundles.   The retention initiatives up to this point have been described in terms of individual practices, such as providing rewards linked to tenure or matching offers from other organizations. This should not be taken to suggest that retention initiatives should be offered in isolation. To be effective, retention practices need to be integrated into a comprehensive system, or as a "bundle" of practices.

As an example, research has shown that the best performers are least likely to quit when an organization both rewards performance with higher compensation *and* widely communicates its compensation practices. Focusing on only compensation or communication in isolation does not have these effects—the procedures are much more effective as a bundle.[39] Other research found that the level of both voluntary and involuntary turnover is lower in organizations that make long-term investments in employees through a combination of employment security, internal mobility opportunities, and pensions for long-term employees.[40] Bundles appear to be effective in part because they demonstrate organizational support, which fits with our earlier discussion of employee commitment.[41] In summary, large-scale reviews of organizational practices and turnover rates clearly indicate that the most effective tool for improving retention is to provide integrated systems that involve careful selection, adequate training, satisfying work conditions, and rewards for retention.[42]

In practical terms, managers need to examine all the characteristics in the work environment that might lead to turnover and address them in a comprehensive manner. Organizations with strong investments in their staffing methods may find their investments are lost if they do not support this strategy with an equally strong commitment to providing newcomers with sufficient orientation material to adjust to their new jobs. Organizations that provide numerous benefits in a poorly integrated fashion may similarly find that the intended effects are lost if managers and employees believe that the programs fail to address their needs.

RETENTION INITIATIVES: DISCHARGE

Performance Management

Many organizations use performance management to link employee motivation and behavior to organizational strategy. Such systems also facilitate employee performance improvement and competency growth.[43] Having a performance management system in place also allows the organization to systematically detect and treat performance problems before those problems become so harmful and intractable that discharge is the only recourse. A well-documented record of efforts to communicate and address performance problems can also help an organization successfully defend itself against legal challenges to discharges.

Process Design

Exhibit 14.13 portrays the performance management process. Organization strategy drives work-unit plans, which in turn become operational for employees through a four-stage process:

- Stage one—performance planning—involves setting specific behavioral performance goals for each employee.
- Stage two—performance execution—focuses on actually performing the job. Resources to aid in job performance should be coupled with coaching and feedback from the employee's manager, peers, and others. Performance feedback should be provided frequently, accompanied by specific suggestions for improvement.
- Stage three—performance appraisal—establishes a regular performance review at the end of the performance period. The employee's success in reaching established goals is assessed, ratings of the employee's competencies are made, written comments are developed to explain ratings and provide suggestions for performance improvement, and feedback from the assessment is provided to the employee.
- Stage four—performance decisions—takes the information collected during the performance review and uses it to help make decisions related to the employee's performance. These decisions can pertain to pay raises, training, and career plans. They may also pertain to formal identification of performance problems, where the employee has shown, or is headed toward, unacceptable performance.

EXHIBIT 14.13 Performance Management Process

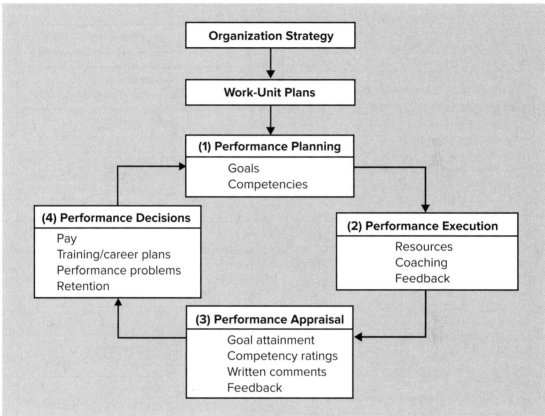

During stage four, it may be decided that an employee has severe performance problems, which can set in motion a focused performance-improvement process through the next performance management cycle. The process of performance counseling and discipline can be conceptualized in six stages, as shown in Exhibit 14.14. It is important for managers to consider different types of performance problems when developing a counseling and disciplinary plan, because each dimension requires different responses.[44]

The model in Exhibit 14.14 breaks down job performance into three categories that have been identified as useful targets for performance management interventions.[45] Task performance includes the completion of job tasks that are specifically included in the job description. Citizenship reflects the psychological and social environment of work created by employees, which might be only indirectly reflected in written job descriptions but is important for maintaining a smoothly functioning work group. Counterproductivity represents actions that directly violate

EXHIBIT 14.14   **Performance Counseling and Disciplinary Processes**

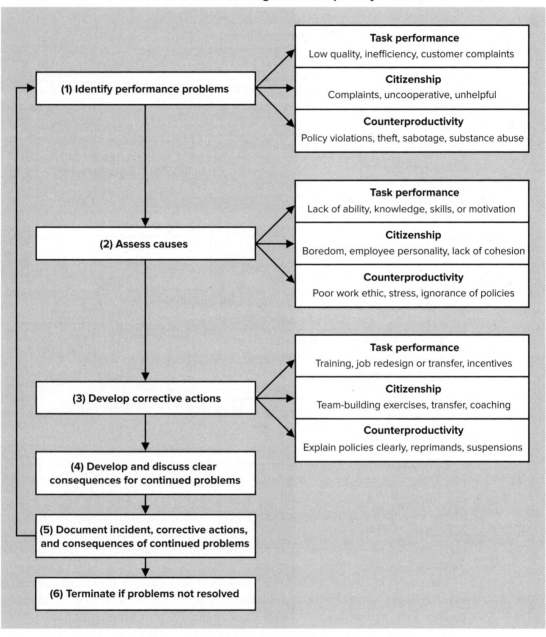

organizational rules or undermine performance. As the exhibit shows, each type of performance problem has distinct causes and distinct corrective actions.

The first imperative for managers is to continually monitor employee performance and identify problems. Next, managers should determine why employee performance has become unacceptable. This process should involve the employee's input as well. If problems are occurring because of a lack of knowledge or skills, it may be possible to use corrective action based on training or counseling. Problems involving a lack of motivation or a negative attitude require the use of rewards and punishments, while problems involving personality or lack of ability may require reassignment to a different job. Regardless of which corrective actions are taken, employees need to be clearly informed about the consequences of continued failure to perform adequately, and the entire counseling and disciplinary process needs to be documented. It is hoped that performance will improve, but if it does not, the organization will need to consider terminating employment.

Manager Training

A successful performance management system requires many components. Probably none is more critical than training the managers who will use the performance management system with employees in their work units.[46]

Performance management requires managers to possess a complex set of skills and knowledge. Examples of training content include purposes of performance management, policies and procedures of the performance management system, appraisal forms and how to complete them, keeping records of employee performance incidents, rating accuracy, coaching techniques, finding and providing resources, methods of providing feedback, goal setting, and legal compliance requirements. It is especially important to stress exactly why and how performance management is to be used as a retention initiative that seeks to prevent discharge through intensive performance improvement attempts.

Another important part of training should be concerned with employee termination. Here, managers must come to understand that a decision to discharge an employee for performance problems falls outside the normal performance management process (Exhibit 14.13) and is not a decision that can or should be made by the individual manager alone. Terminations require separate procedural and decision-making processes. These could also be covered as part of a regular performance management training program, or a separate program devoted to termination could be conducted.

Progressive Discipline

Although performance management strategies can be useful tools for improving employee performance and reducing the need for discharge, there are times when discharge is necessary. Many organizations have adopted progressive discipline procedures as a method to encourage fair treatment of employees and to ensure that when terminations do occur, there is clear documentation of a standardized, transparent process. An organization that adheres to standardized policies and criteria for employee discipline encourages supervisors to focus on job-relevant behavior. As discussed in the social and legal environment chapter, this focus on job requirements helps offset implicit biases based on protected characteristics, and therefore progressive discipline systems can be part of a diversity and inclusion strategy. The use of well-defined stages for specific performance failures also lays the groundwork for an effective legal defense.[47]

The classic progressive discipline model has its origins in the National Labor Relations Act. The act outlines stages of progressive discipline that increase in severity if performance issues are not resolved, starting with an informal warning and proceeding through written warnings, suspensions, and dismissal.[48] These stages remain the core of a progressive discipline approach. Job-relevant criteria for entering the progressive discipline cycle should be outlined and communicated to all employees and their supervisors. Such criteria can include consistently low levels of productivity, low levels of cooperation, failure to communicate, customer complaints, noncompliance with safety procedures, lateness, absenteeism, or violations of other policies. Employees receive notice and are given opportunities to rectify the problems; termination is a last resort. Best practices in progressive discipline encourage employers to inform employees about disciplinary talks in advance, give employees a clear sense of the objective of the talk, and provide employees with documentation of the reason for the meeting.[49] Many progressive discipline programs also have a formal mechanism for employees to provide their own evidence or to appeal decisions. Provisions should also be made for actions that will result in immediate dismissal, such as theft, dishonesty, sexual harassment, or violence.

Positive discipline is a procedure that blends the stage approach of progressive discipline with the more developmental perspective of performance management.[50] Methods of documentation and stages in positive discipline are similar to those of progressive discipline but also incorporate guarantees that employees have the opportunity to change their behavior by following a specific developmental program. In other words, rather than simply increasing in severity with each performance failure, an equally clear system is developed to allow employees to move toward a positive standing. Such systems tend to reframe the process as a problem-solving one rather than an adversarial one, while retaining the principles of clear consequences for performance success and failure. If an employee does not follow the steps to improve performance outlined in a positive discipline procedure, the termination decision becomes much easier to make.

Progressive discipline strategies are not without their detractors.[51] Some labor relations experts describe cases in which employees attempt to game the system. Employees may deliberately take actions to enter the discipline system with the expectation that the organization will violate written procedures. Supervisor failure to adhere to progressive discipline procedures can be grounds for a legal claim or part of a media campaign against the employer.

Is there a solution to this dilemma? Several strategies have developed over time to ensure disciplinary procedures achieve their goals without the risks described above.[52] As we saw with performance management, providing supervisors with ongoing training in following progressive discipline policies and procedures is also needed. Most cases of progressive discipline handled incorrectly occur when a supervisor acts in the heat of the moment, unaware of the policies that the organization has established. Supervisor compliance with policy should then be monitored. If supervisors are selectively enforcing the organization's policies to benefit favored subordinates or target those they do not like, the progressive discipline system provides a mechanism by which employees can appeal these decisions. Supervisors may well find themselves on the receiving end of progressive discipline for violating policy.

RETENTION INITIATIVES: DOWNSIZING

Downsizing involves reducing the organization's staffing levels through layoffs or elimination of job categories. Many factors contribute to layoff occurrences: decline in profits, restructuring of the organization, substitution of the core workforce with a flexible workforce, an obsolete job or work unit, mergers and acquisitions, loss of contracts and clients, technological advances, productivity improvements, shortened product life cycles, and financial markets that favor downsizing as a positive organizational action.[53] While downsizing obviously involves the elimination of jobs, it also encompasses several retention matters that involve balancing the advantages and disadvantages of downsizing, staffing levels and quality, alternatives to layoffs, and dealing with employees who remain after downsizing.

Weighing Advantages and Disadvantages

Downsizing has multiple benefits and costs (as can be seen in Exhibit 14.9). For one, research suggests that the presumed and hoped-for benefits of downsizing might not be as great as they seem.[54] There are many factors that jointly influence whether the costs or benefits of downsizing tend to dominate. Financial markets tend to have relatively neutral reactions to low-magnitude downsizing in firms that have a recent positive performance trend, but large downsizing events in firms that are doing poorly result in major decreases in share price.[55] Downsizing can have negative effects on performance because the loss of coworkers disrupts established work group routines. Effort directed toward adjustment means productivity suffers, sometimes for a long period of time.[56]

In short, downsizing is not a panacea for poor financial health. It has many negative impacts on employees and should be combined with a well-planned total restructuring if it is to be effective. Such conclusions suggest the organization should carefully ponder whether it should downsize, and if so, by how much, and which employees it should seek to retain.

Staffing Levels and Quality

Reductions in staffing levels should be mindful of retention in at least two ways. First, enthusiasm for a financial quick fix needs to be tempered by a realization that, once let go, many downsized employees may be unlikely to return later if economic circumstances improve. The organization will then have to engage in costly re-staffing as opposed to potentially less costly and quicker retention initiatives. At a minimum, the organization should consider alternatives to downsizing simultaneously with downsizing planning. Such an exercise may well lead to less downsizing and greater retention.

Second, staffing level reductions should be thought of in selective or targeted terms, rather than across the board. Such an approach is a logical outgrowth of HR planning, through which it is invariably discovered that the forecasted labor demand and supply figures lead to differing HR head-count requirements across organizational units and job categories. Indeed, it is possible that some units or job categories will be confronting layoffs while others are actually hiring.

If cuts are to be made, who should be retained? Staffing quality and employee acceptance concerns influence the decision. Retaining the most senior employees in each work unit signals job security commitments to long-term employees. An alternative plan would be to make performance-based retention decisions.[57] Employees' current and possibly past performance appraisals would be consulted in each work unit. The lowest-performing employees would be designated for layoff. This approach assumes that the current crop of best performers will continue to be so in the future, even though job requirements might change. It also assumes that the evaluation of who is or is not a high-quality employee is accurate. Legal challenges may also arise, as discussed later.

Alternatives to Downsizing

A no-layoff or guaranteed employment policy as an organization strategy is the most dramatic alternative to downsizing. A no-layoff strategy requires considerable organization and HR planning, along with a commitment to a set of programs necessary for successfully implementing the strategy. This strategy also requires a gamble and a bet that, if lost, could severely damage employee loyalty and trust. During the deep recession of 2007–2009, many employers that had previously pursued a no-layoff strategy abandoned this policy and significantly reduced their workforces.[58]

Some organizations are unwilling to make a no-layoff guarantee but pursue layoff minimization through many different programs. Exhibit 14.15 provides an exam-

EXHIBIT 14.15   **Alternative Methods for Cost Minimization**

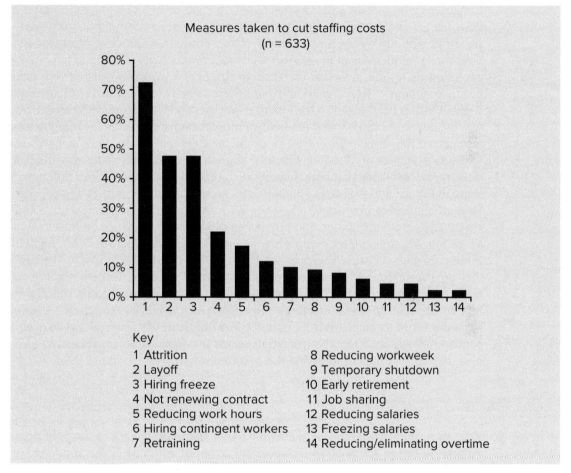

Measures taken to cut staffing costs
(n = 633)

Key
1 Attrition
2 Layoff
3 Hiring freeze
4 Not renewing contract
5 Reducing work hours
6 Hiring contingent workers
7 Retraining
8 Reducing workweek
9 Temporary shutdown
10 Early retirement
11 Job sharing
12 Reducing salaries
13 Freezing salaries
14 Reducing/eliminating overtime

SOURCE: Society for Human Resource Management, *The Impact of 2008 U.S. Economy on Businesses* (Alexandria, VA: author, 2008).

ple based on a survey of 633 organizations. It can be seen that multiple steps were taken as alternatives to layoffs, headed by attrition (not replacing employees who leave), hiring freezes, and nonrenewal of contract workers. A series of direct and indirect pay changes (e.g., salary reduction, early retirement) also played a role in their layoff minimization. Other actions are also possible, such as a temporary layoff with some proportion of pay and benefits continued, substitution of stock options for bonuses, conversion of regular employees to independent contractors, temporary assignments at a reduced time (and pay) commitment, and off-site employees who temporarily work at home on a reduced time (and pay) basis.[59]

Employees Who Remain

Employees who remain either in their pre-layoff job or in a redeployed job after a downsizing must not be ignored. Doing otherwise creates a new retention problem—survivors who are stressed and critical of the downsizing process. Many studies have shown reductions in the performance and productivity of remaining employees following layoffs, as well as increases in absence, work process disruptions, and health problems.[60] Researchers attribute these negative results to layoff survivor stress, which is heightened by the loss of coworkers and friends, a heavier workload, new locations and work hours, new and/or more responsibilities, and fear of job loss just around the corner.

These examples of "survivor sickness" suggest a need to anticipate and attack it directly in downsizing planning. Experts recommend that organizations take active steps to reduce survivor stress. Supervisors are an important part of the process. Laid-off employees experience less strain when supervisors communicate in a consistent and accurate manner, and provide employees with guidance on how to seek a new job. These seem like commonsense suggestions, but supervisors often fail in these core tasks because they are not prepared for negative reactions or because they are too anxious about delivering bad news to be effective. To help supervisors with the difficult task of a layoff meeting, they should be given formal training in how to conduct dismissal meetings and engage in role-playing exercises.[61] Unless steps are taken to help survivors plan for and adjust to the new realities they will confront, heightened job dissatisfaction seems inevitable. In turn, voluntary turnover may spike, further increasing the cost of downsizing.[62]

LEGAL ISSUES

Retention initiatives are closely entwined with the occurrence of employee separations, since the result of an unsuccessful retention initiative is the voluntary or involuntary separation of the employee from the organization. The organization's retention initiatives thus must be guided in part by the laws and regulations governing separations. A brief overview of these is provided. Then a detailed look at the role of performance appraisal in separation is presented, since performance-based retention is a thrust of this chapter.

Separation Laws and Regulations

As noted in the coverage of employment-at-will in the social and legal environment chapter, employment law in the United States protects the right of either employers or employees to end the employment relationship when desired without having to demonstrate why the separation is occurring. However, over time myriad laws and regulations have arisen to limit the employer's rights to terminate employees under certain specific conditions.[63] Employers cannot terminate individual employees (as in discharge) or groups of employees (as in layoffs or downsizings) based on protected characteristics, such as race, gender, national origin, religion, age over 40, or disability status. Separation procedures also need to follow stipulations in labor contracts or other formal agreements. Finally, large employers need to provide employees with 60 days of advance warning for large layoffs.

A basic tenet underlying restrictions on employee separation is the need for fair and consistent treatment of employees. Included here are concerns for ensuring procedural fairness and having a legitimate basis for separations, such as merit, seniority, or performance. The organization should be thoroughly familiar with these numerous laws and regulations, and their underlying principles, as it designs and administers its separation initiatives.[64]

Performance Appraisal

Organizations often favor retention and separation systems and decisions that are driven by employee performance. Laws and regulations generally uphold or even encourage such a role for performance. However, the law as interpreted also insists that performance appraisals, and the performance appraisal system generally, be fairly and equitably applied to employees undergoing separation. Interpretations come about from a combination of court decisions and governmental regulations that have evolved around the issue of performance appraisal in practice.

Based on these decisions and regulations, numerous specific suggestions have been put forth to guide the organization in the design and use of its performance management system:[65]

- Appraisal criteria should be job related, specific, and communicated in advance to the employee.
- The rater should receive training in the performance appraisal process and in how to avoid common rating errors.
- The manager should be familiar with the employee's job description and actual performance.
- Raters should agree in their evaluation of the employee's performance.
- Evaluations should include supporting documentation.
- The employee should be able to review the evaluation and comment on it before it becomes final.
- The employee should receive timely feedback about the evaluation and an explanation for any outcome decision.
- There should be an appeals system for employees who are dissatisfied with their evaluation.

Conforming to these recommendations will help provide a fair evaluation process that will hold up under legal scrutiny.

SUMMARY

Retention management seeks to control the numbers and types of employees who remain with or leave the organization. Voluntary turnover is caused by a combination of perceived desirability of leaving, ease of leaving, and alternatives to one's current job. Some of these reasons are avoidable, but others are not. Discharge occurs for performance- and discipline-related problems. Downsizing or RIF occurs because the organization is, or is projected to be, overstaffed in head-count terms.

It is important for the organization to conduct thorough analyses of its turnover. Turnover rates can be broken down by type of turnover, types of employees, job categories, and geographic location. It is also useful to benchmark the organization's turnover rates internally and externally. Reasons for turnover can be evaluated through exit interviews, post-exit surveys, and employee satisfaction surveys. The costs and benefits of each of the three types of turnover can be broken down into separation, replacement, and training categories. A thorough understanding of costs and benefits will help the organization determine where and among whom turnover is the most worrisome.

To reduce voluntary turnover, organizations engage in numerous retention initiatives centered on direct and variable pay programs, benefits, work schedules, and training and development. Little is known about attempts to increase intrinsic rewards. The process of deciding whether to act to reduce turnover is guided by four basic questions: Do we think turnover is a problem? How might we attack the problem? What do we need to decide? How should we evaluate the programs? To influence the desirability of leaving, the organization must raise job satisfaction by providing both extrinsic and intrinsic rewards. Ease of leaving can possibly be reduced by providing organization-specific training and increasing the cost of leaving. Finally, retention might be improved by providing more internal job alternatives to employees and by responding intentionally to other job offers they receive.

Involuntary turnover should also be managed thoughtfully. Discharges might be reduced through formal performance management and progressive discipline systems. A performance management system that involves performance planning, performance execution, performance appraisal, and performance decisions can help prevent and correct performance problems. A progressive discipline system addresses behavioral conduct problems that violate rules, procedures, laws, and professional and moral standards. While downsizing has obvious cost-saving benefits, research indicates that there are many costs as well. Staffing levels should be achieved in a targeted way rather than across the board. Alternatives to downsizing can be pursued as a way to reduce involuntary job loss. Attention must be paid to employees who survive a downsizing, or they might create a new retention problem for the organization by starting to leave.

Employee separation, especially on an involuntary basis, is subject to myriad laws and regulations. If the organization wishes to base retention decisions on employees' job performance, performance management systems should be demonstrably fair and equitable. Regulations and court decisions provide guidance for developing a performance management system that can withstand legal scrutiny.

DISCUSSION QUESTIONS

1. For the three primary causes of voluntary turnover (desirability of leaving, ease of leaving, alternatives), might their relative importance depend on the type of employee or type of job? Explain.

2. Which of the costs and benefits of voluntary turnover are most likely to vary according to type of job? Give examples.

3. If someone said to you, "It's easy to reduce turnover—just pay people more money," what would your response be?

4. Why should an organization seek to retain employees with performance or discipline problems? Why not just fire them?

5. Discuss some potential problems with downsizing as an organization's first response to a need to cut labor costs.

ETHICAL ISSUES

1. Imagine your organization is doing exit interviews and has promised confidentiality to all who respond. You are responsible for conducting the exit interviews. Your supervisor has asked you to give her the name of each respondent so she can assess the information in conjunction with the person's supervisor. What obligation do corporate HR employees have to keep information confidential in such circumstances?

2. Firing an employee has numerous potential negative organizational consequences, including the discomfort of the supervisor who delivers the termination information, conflict or sabotage from the departing employee, and the filing of a lawsuit. To avoid this, many supervisors give problem employees unpleasant work tasks, reduce their working hours, or otherwise negatively modify their jobs in hopes that they will simply quit. What are the ethical issues raised by this strategy?

APPLICATIONS

Managerial Turnover: A Problem?

HealthCareLaunderCare (HCLC) is a company that specializes in picking up, cleaning, and delivering laundry for health care providers, especially hospitals, nursing homes, and assisted care facilities. Basically, these health care providers have outsourced their total laundry operations to HCLC. In this very competitive business, a typical contract between HCLC and a health care provider is only two years, and HCLC experiences a contract nonrenewal rate of 10%. Most nonrenewals occur because of dissatisfaction with service costs and especially quality (e.g., surgical garb that is not completely sterilized).

HCLC has 20 laundry facilities throughout the country, mostly in large metropolitan areas. Each laundry facility is headed by a site manager, and there are unit supervisors for the intake, washing, drying, inspection and repair, and delivery areas. An average of 100 nonexempt employees are employed at each site.

The operation of the facilities is technologically sophisticated and very health- and safety-sensitive. In the intake area, for example, employees wear protective clothing, gloves, and eyewear because of all the blood, tissue, and germs on laundry that comes in. The washing area is composed of huge washers in 35-foot stainless steel tunnels with screws that move the laundry through various wash cycles. Workers in this area are exposed to high temperatures and must be proficient in the operation of the computer control systems. Laundry is lifted out of the tunnels by robots and moved to the drying room area, where it is dried, ironed, and folded by machines tended by employees. In the inspection and repair area, quality inspection and assurance occurs. Laundry is inspected for germs and pinholes (pinholes in surgical garb could allow blood and fluids to come into contact with the surgeon), and employees complete repairs on torn clothing and sheets. In the delivery area, the laundry is hermetically sealed in packages and placed in delivery vans for transport.

HCLC's vice president of operations, Tyrone Williams, manages the sites—and site and unit managers—with an iron fist. Williams monitors each site with weekly reports on a set of cost, quality, and safety indicators for each of the five areas. When he spots what he thinks are problems or undesirable trends, he has a conference call with both the site manager and the unit supervisor. In the decidedly one-way conversation, marching orders are delivered and are expected to be fulfilled. If a turnaround in the "numbers" does not show up in the next weekly report, Williams gives the manager and the supervisor one more week to improve. If sufficient improvement is not forthcoming, various punitive actions are taken, including base pay cuts, demotions, reassignments, and terminations. Williams feels such quick and harsh justice is necessary to keep HCLC competitive and to continually drive home to all employees the importance of working "by the numbers." Fed up with this management system, many managers have opted to say "Bye-bye, numbers!" and leave HCLC.

Recently, the issue of site and unit manager retention came up on the radar screen of HCLC's president, Roman Dublinski. Dublinski glanced at a payroll report showing that 30 of 120 site and unit managers had left HCLC in the past year, though no reasons for leaving were given. In addition, Dublinski received copies of a few angry resignation letters written to Williams. Having never confronted or thought about possible employee retention problems or how to deal with them, Dublinski calls to ask you (the corporate manager of staffing) to prepare a brief written analysis that will then be used as the basis for a meeting between the two of you and the vice president of HR, Debra Angle (Angle recommended this). Address the following questions in your report:

1. Is the loss of 30 managers out of 120 in one year cause for concern?
2. What additional data should be gathered to learn more about managerial turnover?
3. What are the costs of this turnover? Might there be any benefits?
4. Are there any lurking legal problems?
5. If retention is a serious problem for HCLC, what are the main ways we might address it?

Retention: Deciding to Act

Wally's Wonder Wash (WWW) is a full-service, high-tech, high-touch car wash company owned solely by Wally Wheelspoke. Located in a midwestern city of 200,000 people (with another 100,000 in suburbs and more rural towns throughout the county), WWW currently has four facilities within the city. Wally plans to add four more facilities within the city in the next two years, and later on he plans to begin placing facilities in suburban locations and rural towns. Major competitors in the city include two other full–service car washes (different owners), plus three touchless automatic facilities (same owner).

Wally's critical strategy is to provide the very best to customers who want and relish extremely clean and "spiffy" vehicles and to ensure they have a positive experience each time they come to WWW. To do this, WWW seeks to provide high-quality car washes and car detailing and to generate considerable repeat business through competitive prices combined with attention to customers. To make itself accessible to customers, WWW is open seven days a week, 8:00 a.m. to 8:00 p.m. Peak periods, volume-wise, are after 1:00 p.m. on weekdays and from 10:00 a.m. to 5:00 p.m. on weekends. In addition, Wally uses his workforce to drive his strategy. Though untrained in HR, Wally knows that he must recruit and retain a stable, high-quality workforce if his current facilities, let alone his ambitious expansion plans, are to succeed.

WWW has a strong preference for full-time employees, who work either 7:30 a.m. to 4:00 p.m. or 11:00 a.m. to 8:00 p.m. Part-timers are used occasionally during peak demand times and during the summer when full-timers are on vacation. There are two major jobs at WWW: attendant (washer) and custom service specialist (detailer). Practicing promotion from within, WWW promotes all specialists from the attendant ranks. There are currently 70 attendants and 20 custom service specialists at WWW. In addition, each facility has a manager. Wally has filled the manager jobs by promotion from within (from either the attendant or custom service specialist ranks), but he is unsure if he will be able to continue doing this as he expands.

The job of attendant is a demanding one. Attendants vacuum vehicles from front to rear (and trunk if requested by the customer), wash and dry windows and mirrors, dry vehicles with hand towels, apply special cleaning compounds to tires, wipe down the vehicle's interior, and wash or vacuum floor mats. In addition, attendants wash and fold towels, lift heavy barrels of cleaning compounds and waxes, and perform light maintenance and repair work on the machinery. Finally, and very important, attendants consistently provide customer service by asking customers if they have special requests and by making small talk with them. A unique feature of customer service at WWW is that the attendant must ask the customer to personally inspect the vehicle before leaving to ensure that the vehicle has been satisfactorily cleaned (attendants also correct any mistakes pointed out by the customer). The attendants work as a team, with each attendant expected to be able to perform all of the above tasks.

Attendants start at a base wage of $8.00/hour, with automatic $.50 raises at six months and one year. They receive brief training from the manager before starting work. Custom service specialists start at $9.00/hour, with $.50 raises after six months and one year. Neither attendants nor custom service specialists receive performance reviews. Managers receive a salary of $27,000, plus an annual "merit" raise based on a very casual performance review conducted by Wally (whenever he gets around to it). All attendants share equally in a customer tip pool; custom service specialists receive individual tips. The benefits package is composed of the following: (1) major medical health insurance with a 20% employee co-pay on the premium, (2) paid holidays for Christmas, Easter, July 4, and Martin Luther King Jr.'s birthday, and (3) a generous paid sick-pay plan of two days per month (in recognition of high illness rates due to extreme working conditions).

In terms of turnover, Wally has spotty and general data only. In the past year WWW experienced an overall turnover rate of 65% for attendants and 20% for custom service specialists; no managers left the company. Though lacking data further back, Wally thinks the turnover rate for attendants has been increasing. WWW's managers constantly complain to Wally about the high level of turnover among attendants and the problems it creates, especially in fulfilling the strong customer service orientation for WWW. Though the managers have not conducted exit interviews, the major complaints they hear from attendants are (1) the pay is not competitive relative to the other full-service car washes and many other entry-level jobs in the area, (2) the training is hit-or-miss at best, (3) promotion opportunities are limited, (4) managers provide no feedback or coaching, and (5) customer complaints and mistreatment of attendants by customers are on the rise.

Wally is frustrated by attendant turnover and its threat to his customer service and expansion strategies. He calls on you for assistance in figuring out what to do about the problem. Use the decision process shown in Exhibit 14.11 to help develop a retention initiative for WWW. Address each of the questions in the process:

1. Do we think turnover is a problem?
2. How might we attack the problem?
3. What do we need to decide?
4. How should we evaluate the initiatives?

ENDNOTES

1. US Department of Labor, "Employee Tenure in 2012," *TED: The Economics Daily*, Sept. 20, 2012; US Department of Labor, "Number of Jobs Held, Labor Market Activity, and Earnings Growth Among the Youngest Baby Boomers: Results From a Longitudinal Survey" (USDL-10-1243), *BLS News Release*, Sept. 10, 2010.

2. D. G. Allen and P. C. Bryant, *Managing Employee Turnover: Dispelling Myths and Fostering Evidence-Based Retention Strategies* (New York: Business Expert Press, 2012).

3. A. L. Rubenstein, M. B. Eberly, T. W. Lee, and T. R. Mitchell, "Surveying the Forest: A Meta-Analysis, Moderator Investigation, and Future-Oriented Discussion of the Antecedents of Voluntary Employee Turnover," *Personnel Psychology*, 2018, 71, pp. 23–65; R. P. Steel and J. W. Lounsbury, "Turnover Process Models: Review and Synthesis of a Conceptual Literature," *Human Resource Management Review*, 2009, 19, pp. 271–282; B. C. Holtom, T. R. Mitchell, T. W. Lee, and M. B. Eberly, "Turnover and Retention Research: A Glance at the Past, a Closer Review of the Present, and a Venture Into the Future," *Academy of Management Annals*, 2008, 2, pp. 231–274.

4. K. Jiang, D. Liu, P. F. McKay, T. W. Lee, and T. R. Mitchell, "When and How Is Job Embeddedness Predictive of Turnover? A Meta-Analytic Investigation," *Journal of Applied Psychology*, 2012, 97, pp. 1077–1096; K. Kiazad, B. C. Holtom, P. W. Hom, and A. Newman, "Job Embeddedness: A Mutlifoci Theoretical Extension," *Journal of Applied Psychology*, 2015, 100, pp. 641–659.

5. E. Spain and B. Groysberg, "Making Exit Interviews Count," *Harvard Business Review*, Apr. 2016, pp. 88–95; R. Maurer, "Using Exit Interviews to Prevent Disaster," *Society for Human Resource Management Risk Management*, Apr. 5, 2013 (*www.shrm.com*).

6. S. Givens-Skeaton and L. R. Ford, "Exit Interviews: The Impact of Perceived Sensitivity and Perceived Threat on Individuals' Willingness to Disclose," *Journal of Organizational Psychology*, 2018, 18, pp. 85–107; M. A. Campion, "Meaning and Measurement of Turnover: Comparison and Recommendations for Research," *Journal of Applied Psychology*, 1991, 76, pp. 199–212.

7. D. Zielinski, "New HR Analytics Tools Help Mine Big Data," *HR Magazine*, Nov. 1, 2014 (*www.shrm.org*); J. H. Dulebohn and R. D. Johnson, "Human Resource Metrics and Decision Support: A Classification Framework," *Human Resource Management Review*, 2013, 13, pp. 71–83; D. L. Stone, D. L. Deadrick, K. M. Lukaszewski, and R. Johnson, "The Influence of Technology on the Future of Human Resource Management," *Human Resource Management Review*, 2015, 25, pp. 216–231.

8. T.-Y. Park and J. D. Shaw, "Turnover Rates and Organizational Performance: A Meta-Analysis," *Journal of Applied Psychology*, 2013, 98, pp. 268–309.

9. D. Hale, R. E. Ployhart, and W. Shepherd, "A Two-Phase Longitudinal Model of a Turnover Event: Disruption, Recovery Rates, and Moderators of Collective Performance," *Academy of Management Journal*, 2016, 59, pp. 906–929; T. Wang, B. Zhao, and S. Thornhill, "Pay Dispersion and Organizational Innovation: The Mediation Effects of Employee Participation and Voluntary

Turnover," *Human Relations*, 2015, 68, pp. 1155-1181; T. Kuypers, H. Guenter, and H. van Emmerik, "Team Turnover and Task Conflict: A Longitudinal Study on the Moderating Effects of Collective Experience," *Journal of Management*, 2015, online first (*jom.sagepub.com*).

10. Park and Shaw, "Turnover Rates and Organizational Performance: A Meta-Analysis."

11. M. A. Maltarich, G. Reilly, and C. DeRose, "A Theoretical Assessment of Dismissal Rates and Unit Performance, With Empirical Evidence," *Journal of Applied Psychology*, 2020, 105(5), pp. 527-537.

12. C. O. Trevor and R. Piyanontalee, "Discharges, Poor-Performer Quits, and Layoffs as Valued Exits: Is It Really Addition by Subtraction?" *Annual Review of Organizational Psychology and Organizational Behavior*, 2020, 7, pp. 181-211.

13. Park and Shaw, "Turnover Rates and Organizational Performance."

14. S. Miller, "What Do Employees Want? Not Always What Employers Think," Mar. 2007 (*www.shrm.org*).

15. Harris Interactive, *Working in America: The Key to Employee Satisfaction* (Rochester, NY: author, 2007).

16. M. Schoeff, "Retention Edges Cost Reduction as Benefits Objective," *Workforce Management Online*, Mar. 24, 2009 (*www.workforce.com*).

17. N. E. Day, "Perceived Pay Communication, Justice, and Pay Satisfaction," *Employee Relations*, 2011, 33, pp. 476-497; D. Pohler and J. A. Schmidt, "Does Pay-for-Performance Strain the Employment Relationship? The Effect of Manager Bonus Eligibility on Nonmanager Employee Turnover," *Personnel Psychology*, 2016, 69(2), pp. 395-429.

18. J. Choi and C. C. Chen, "The Relationships of Distributive Justice and Compensation System Fairness to Employee Attitudes in International Joint Ventures," *Journal of Organizational Behavior*, 2007, 28, pp. 687-703; T. Kim and K. Leung, "Forming and Reacting to Overall Fairness: A Cross-Cultural Comparison," *Organizational Behavior and Human Decision Processes*, 2007, 104, pp. 83-95; D. G. Allen, R. W. Griffeth, J. M. Vardaman, K. Aquino, S. Gaertner, and M. Lee, "Structural Validity and Generalizability of a Referent Cognitions Model of Turnover Decisions," *Applied Psychology: An International Review*, 2009, 58, pp. 709-728.

19. J. D. Shaw, B. R. Dineen, R. Fang, and R. F. Vellella, "Employee-Organization Exchange Relationships, HRM Practices, and Quit Rates of Good and Poor Performers," *Academy of Management Journal*, 2009, 52, pp. 1016-1033; S. J. Peterson and F. Luthans, "The Impact of Financial and Nonfinancial Incentives on Business-Unit Outcomes Over Time," *Journal of Applied Psychology*, 2006, 91, pp. 156-165; W. He, L. Long, and B. Kuzaas, "Workgroup Salary Dispersion and Turnover Intention in China: A Contingent Examination of Individual Differences and the Dual Deprivation Path Explanation," *Human Resource Management*, 2016, 55, pp. 301-320.

20. Rubenstein, Eberly, Lee, and Mitchell, "Surveying the Forest: A Meta-Analysis, Moderator Investigation, and Future-Oriented Discussion of the Antecedents of Voluntary Employee Turnover"; P. W. Hom, T. W. Lee, J. D. Shaw, and J. P. Hausknecht, "One Hundred Years of Employee Turnover Theory and Research," *Journal of Applied Psychology*, 2017, 102, pp. 530-545.

21. L. Goler, J. Gale, B. Harrington, and A. Grant, "The Real Reason People Quit Their Jobs," *Society for Human Resource Management Employee Relations*, Jan. 23, 2018 (*www.shrm.com*).

22. D. Wang, P. W. Hom, and D. G. Allen, "Coping With Newcomer 'Hangover': How Socialization Tactics Affect Declining Job Satisfaction During Early Employment," *Journal of Vocational Behavior*, 2017, 100, pp. 196-210; D. R. Earnest, D. G. Allen, and R. S. Landis, "Mechanisms Linking Realistic Job Previews With Turnover: A Meta-Analytic Path Analysis," *Personnel Psychology*, 2011, 64, pp. 865-897; Rubenstein, Eberly, Lee, and Mitchell, "Surveying the Forest: A Meta-Analysis, Moderator Investigation, and Future-Oriented Discussion of the Antecedents of Voluntary Employee Turnover."

23. Z.-X. Su, Z. Wang, and S. Chen, "The Impact of CEO Transformational Leadership on Organizational Voluntary Turnover and Employee Innovative Behavior: The Mediating Role of Collaborative HRM," *Asia Pacific Journal of Human Resources*, 2020, 58, pp. 197–219.

24. J. E. Ellingson, M. J. Tews, and A. M. Dachner, "Constituent Attachment and Voluntary Turnover in Low-Wage/Low-Skill Service Work," *Journal of Applied Psychology*, 2016, 101, pp. 129–140; W. Felps, T. R. Mitchell, D. R. Hekman, T. W. Lee, B. C. Holtom, and W. S. Harman, "Turnover Contagion: How Coworkers, Job Embeddedness and Job Search Behaviors Influence Quitting," *Academy of Management Journal*, 2009, 52, pp. 545–561.

25. L. H. Nishii and D. M. Mayer, "Do Inclusive Leaders Help to Reduce Turnover in Diverse Groups?" *Journal of Applied Psychology*, 2009, 94, pp. 1412–1426; J. S. Leonard and D. I. Levine, "The Effect of Diversity on Turnover: A Large Case Study," *Industrial and Labor Relations Review*, 2006, 59, pp. 547–572; P. F. McKay, D. R. Avery, S. Tonidandel, M. A. Morris, M. Hernandez, and M. R. Hebl, "Racial Differences in Employee Retention: Are Diversity Climate Perceptions the Key?" *Personnel Psychology*, 2007, 60, pp. 35–62.

26. B. J. Tepper, "Consequences of Abusive Supervision," *Academy of Management Journal*, 2000, 43, pp. 178–190; A. C. Klotz and M. Bolino, "Saying Goodbye: The Nature, Causes, and Consequences of Employee Resignation Styles," *Journal of Applied Psychology*, 2016, 101, pp. 1386–1404.

27. C. A. Thompson and D. J. Prottas, "Relationships Among Organizational Family Support, Job Autonomy, Perceived Control, and Employee Well-Being," *Journal of Occupational Health Psychology*, 2006, 11, pp. 100–118; L. B. Hammer, E. E. Kossek, W. K. Anger, T. Bodner, and K. L. Zimmerman, "Clarifying Work-Family Intervention Processes: The Roles of Work-Family Conflict and Family-Supportive Supervisor Behaviors," *Journal of Applied Psychology*, 2011, 96, pp. 134–150; T. D. Golden, "Avoiding Depletion in Virtual Work: Telework and the Intervening Impact of Work Exhaustion on Commitment and Turnover Intentions," *Journal of Vocational Behavior*, 2006, 69, pp. 176–187.

28. K. Aumann and E. Galinsky, *The State of Health in the American Workforce* (New York: Families and Work Institute, 2009).

29. Society for Human Resource Management, *Workplace Flexibility in the 21st Century* (Alexandria, VA: author, 2008).

30. B. A. Lautsch, E. E. Kossek, and S. C. Eaton, "Supervisory Approaches and Paradoxes in Managing Telecommuting Implementation," *Human Relations*, 2009, 62, pp. 795–827.

31. A. L. Rubenstein, J. D. Kammeyer-Mueller, M. Wang, and T. G. Thundiyil, "'Embedded' at Hire? Predicting the Voluntary and Involuntary Turnover of New Employees," *Journal of Organizational Behavior*, 2019, 40, pp. 342–359; M. R. Barrick and R. D. Zimmerman, "Reducing Voluntary, Avoidable Turnover Through Selection," *Journal of Applied Psychology*, 2005, 90, pp. 159–166.

32. R. D. Zimmerman, "Understanding the Impact of Personality Traits on Individuals' Turnover Decisions: A Meta-Analytic Path Model," *Personnel Psychology*, 2008, 61, pp. 309–348; M. R. Barrick and R. D. Zimmerman, "Hiring for Retention and Performance," *Human Resource Management*, 2009, 48, pp. 183–206.

33. A. R. Wheeler, V. C. Gallagher, R. L. Brover, and C. J. Sablynski, "When Person-Organization (Mis)fit and (Dis)satisfaction Lead to Turnover: The Moderating Role of Perceived Job Mobility," *Journal of Managerial Psychology*, 2007, 22, pp. 203–219.

34. C. M. Porter, S. E. Woo, and M. A. Campion, "Internal and External Networking Differentially Predict Turnover Through Embeddedness and Job Offers," *Personnel Psychology*, 2016, 69, pp. 635–672.

35. C. Fernandez Araoz, B. Groysberg, and N. Nohria, "How to Hang On to Your High Potentials," *Harvard Business Review*, Oct. 2011, pp. 77–83.

36. A. L. Heavey, J. A. Holwerda, and J. P. Hausknecht, "Causes and Consequences of Collective Turnover: A Meta-Analytic Review," *Journal of Applied Psychology*, 2013, 98, pp. 412–453.

37. WorldatWork, *Retention of Key Talent and the Role of Rewards* (Scottsdale, AZ: author, 2012).

38. A. Sraders, R. Mashayekhi, S. Fitzgerald, A. Jenkins, L. Lambert, P. Marinova, N. G. Mcelroy, S. Mukherjee, A. Pressman, J. J. Roberts, L. Shen, and J. Vanian, "100 Best Companies to Work For 2020," *Fortune*, Mar. 2020, 181, pp. 115–120.

39. J. D. Shaw and N. Gupta, "Pay System Characteristics and Quit Patterns of Good, Average, and Poor Performers," *Personnel Psychology*, 2007, 60, pp. 903–928.

40. R. Batt and A. J. S. Colvin, "An Employment Systems Approach to Turnover: Human Resources Practices, Quits, Dismissals, and Performance," *Academy of Management Journal*, 2011, 54, pp. 695–717.

41. T. M. Gardner, P. M. Wright, and L. M. Moynihan, "The Impact of Motivation, Empowerment, and Skill-Enhancing Practices on Aggregate Voluntary Turnover: The Mediating Effect of Collective Affective Commitment," *Personnel Psychology*, 2011, 64, pp. 315–350.

42. Heavey, Holwerda, and Hausknecht, "Causes and Consequences of Collective Turnover: A Meta-Analytic Review."

43. D. J. Schleicher, H. M. Baumann, D. W. Sullivan, P. E. Levy, D. C. Hargrove, and B. A. Barros-Rivera, "Putting the System Into Performance Management Systems: A Review and Agenda for Performance Management Research," *Journal of Management*, 2018, 44, pp. 2209–2245; H. Aguinis, *Performance Management*, 3rd ed. (Upper Saddle River, NJ: Pearson Prentice Hall, 2019).

44. Aguinis, *Performance Management*.

45. J. Y. Choi, C. Miao, I.-S. Oh, C. M. Berry, and K. Kim, "Relative Importance of Major Job Performance Dimensions in Determining Supervisors' Overall Job Performance Ratings," *Canadian Journal of Administrative Sciences*, 2019, 36, pp. 377–389; C. A. Gorman, J. P. Meriac, S. G. Roch, J. L. Ray, and J. S. Gamble, "An Exploratory Study of Current Performance Management Practices: Human Resource Executives' Perspectives," *International Journal of Selection and Assessment*, 2017, 25, pp. 193–202; M. Rotundo and P. R. Sackett, "The Relative Importance of Task, Citizenship, and Counterproductive Performance to Global Ratings of Job Performance: A Policy Capturing Approach," *Journal of Applied Psychology*, 2002, 87, pp. 66–80.

46. K. Tyler, "Train Managers, Maximize Appraisals," *HR Magazine*, Dec. 2012, pp. 68–69.

47. Society for Human Resource Management, "Understanding Employee Discipline" (*www.shrm.org*), accessed Apr. 21, 2020; J. D. Allen Smith, "13 Ways to Improve Written Warnings and Manage Employees Better," *SHRM Employment Law*, Dec. 12, 2018 (*www.shrm.org*).

48. M. Bugdol, *A Different Approach to Work Discipline: Models, Manifestation, and Methods of Behaviour Modification* (London: Springer International, 2018); D. D. Bennett-Alexander and L. P. Hartman, *Employment Law for Business*, 9th ed. (New York: McGraw-Hill Education, 2019).

49. R. R. Hastings, "Designing a Progressive Discipline Policy," *Society for Human Resource Management*, Jan. 26, 2010 (*www.shrm.org*).

50. Bugdol, *A Different Approach to Work Discipline: Models, Manifestation, and Methods of Behaviour Modification*; J. Janove "Fire Progressive Discipline," *Society for Human Resource Management*, July 24, 2019 (*www.shrm.org*).

51. Bennett-Alexander and Hartman, *Employment Law for Business*; Allen Smith, "13 Ways to Improve Written Warnings and Manage Employees Better."

52. Society for Human Resource Management, "Understanding Employee Discipline" (*www.shrm.org*), accessed Apr. 21, 2020; Hastings, "Designing a Progressive Discipline Policy."

53. D. K. Datta, J. P. Guthrie, D. Basuil, and A. Pandey, "Causes and Effects of Employee Downsizing: A Review and Synthesis," *Journal of Management*, 2010, 36, pp. 281–348.

54. J. P. Guthrie and D. K. Datta, "Dumb and Dumber: The Impact of Downsizing on Firm Performance as Moderated by Industry Conditions," *Organization Science*, 2008, 19, pp. 108–123.

55. M. Brauer and M. Zimmermann, "Investor Response to Workforce Downsizing: The Influence of Industry Waves, Macroeconomic Outlook, and Firm Performance," *Journal of Management*, 2017, 45, pp. 1775–1801.

56. Datta, Guthrie, Basuil, and Pandey, "Causes and Effects of Employee Downsizing: A Review and Synthesis"; M. Brauer and T. Laamanen, "Workforce Downsizing and Firm Performance: An Organizational Routine Perspective," *Journal of Management Studies*, 2014, 51, pp. 1311–1333; D. van Dierendonck and G. Jacobs, "Survivors and Victims, a Meta-Analytical Review of Fairness and Organizational Commitment After Downsizing," *British Journal of Management*, 2012, 23, pp. 96–109.

57. A. Fox, "Prune Employees Carefully," *HR Magazine*, Apr. 2008 (*www.shrm.org*).

58. C. Tuna, "No-Layoff Policies Crumble," *Wall Street Journal*, Dec. 29, 2008, p. B1.

59. B. Mirza, "Look at Alternatives to Layoffs," *HR News*, Dec. 29, 2008 (*www.shrm.org*).

60. M. K. Shoss, L. Jiang, and T. M. Probst, "Bending Without Breaking: A Two-Study Examination of Employee Resilience in the Face of Job Insecurity," *Journal of Occupational Health Psychology*, 2018, 23, pp. 112–126; H. Wang, C. Lu, and O. Siu, "Job Insecurity and Job Performance: The Moderating Role of Organizational Justice and the Mediating Role of Work Engagement," *Journal of Applied Psychology*, 2015, 100, pp. 1249–1258; K. O. Strunk, D. Goldhaber, D. S. Knight, and N. Brown, "Are There Hidden Costs Associated With Conducting Layoffs? The Impact of Reduction-in-Force and Layoff Notices on Teacher Effectiveness," *Journal of Policy Analysis and Management*, 2018. 37, pp. 755–782.

61. M. Richter, C. J. König, C. Koppermann, and M. Schilling, "Displaying Fairness While Delivering Bad News: Testing the Effectiveness of Organizational Bad News Training in the Layoff Context," *Journal of Applied Psychology*, 2016, 101, pp. 779–792.

62. C. O. Trevor and A. J. Nyberg, "Keeping Your Headcount When All About You Are Losing Theirs: Downsizing, Voluntary Turnover Rates, and the Moderating Role of HR Practices," *Academy of Management Journal*, 2008, 51, pp. 259–276; A. K. Mishra, K. E. Mishra, and G. M. Spreitzer, "Downsizing the Company Without Downsizing Morale," *MIT Sloan Management Review*, 2009, 50(3), pp. 39–44; E. Andreeva, L. L. Magnusson Hanson, H. Westerlund, T. Theorell, and M. H. Brenner, "Depressive Symptoms as a Cause and Effect of Job Loss in Men and Women: Evidence in the Context of Organisational Downsizing From the Swedish Longitudinal Occupational Survey of Health," *BMC Public Health*, 2015, 15, p. 1045.

63. Bennett Alexander and Hartman, *Employment Law for Business*.

64. D. J. Walsh, *Employment Law for Human Resource Practice*, 6th ed. (Boston: Cengage Learning, 2019).

65. Aguinis, *Performance Management*; C. H. Fleischer, *The SHRM Essential Guide to Employment Law* (Alexandria, VA: Society for Human Resource Management, 2018).

NAME INDEX

Greenstone Miller, J., 148
Greenwald, J., 426
Greenwald, J. M., 259
Greenwald, N., 92
Greguras, G., 257, 505
Greguras, G. J., 256, 513
Grelle, D., 365
Grensing-Pophal, L., 559
Griepentrog, B., 606
Griffeth, R. W., 565, 752
Griffith, J. A., 557
Grijalva, E., 515
Grimaldi, E. M., 510
Grossman, R. J., 256
Groysberg, B., 29, 751, 753
Grubb, A., 363
Grubb, W. L., 499
Gruman, J. A., 656
Guadagno, A., 43–44
Guan, L., 509
Guan, Y., 44
Guay, R. P., 513
Gudanowski, D. M., 565
Guenole, N., 499
Guenter, H., 752
Guil, R., 505
Guion, R. M., 363, 498, 510
Gully, S. M., 43, 257
Gündemir, S., 515
Gunnigle, P., 558
Gupta, N., 754
Gurbuz, S., 558
Gurchiek, K., 45, 149, 421, 656
Guseh, J. S., 517
Guterman, H. A., 563
Guthrie, J. P., 754, 755

Haaland, S., 563
Habiboglu, O. S., 558
Hable, S. Z., 428
Hackney, K. J., 505, 559
Haden, J., 559
Hagen, M., 380, 383
Hajro, A., 92
Hale, D., 751
Half, R., 420
Hallam, G. L., 498
Hamel, G., 43
Hammer, L. B., 753
Hamori, M., 44, 260
Hampton, S. A., 43
Han, K., 257
Handler, L., 365
Hanges, P. J., 94, 149
Hanisch, K. A., 498
Hansell, S., 425
Hansen, F., 148, 255, 656, 657
Hansen, J.-I. C., 498
Hansen, S. D., 91, 92, 654
Hanson, J. R., 559
Harari, M. B., 607
Haraway, W. M., III, 516
Harding, M., 427
Hardtke, D., 420
Hargis, M. B., 606
Hargreaves, S., 147
Hargrove, D. C., 560, 754
Harman, W. S., 753

Harold, C. M., 513, 564
Harrell, E., 148, 149
Harrick, E. J., 339
Harrington, B., 752
Harris, J., 699
Harris, S. G., 421
Harris, T. B., 427
Harrison, T., 258
Harsch, K., 558
Harter, J. K., 196
Hartman, C. P., 428, 429
Hartman, L. P., 92, 94, 150, 517, 608, 657, 754, 755
Hartman, N. S., 499
Hartmann, K., 196, 514
Hartog, D. N. Den, 198
Hartwell, C. J., 149, 500
Harville, D. L., 498
Harwell, D., 427
Hastie, R., 606
Hastings, R. R., 93, 754
Hauenstein, N.M.A., 502
Hausdorf, P., 561
Hau[knecht, J. P., 428, 502, 504, 511, 752, 754
Hausmann, R., 298
Hayes, T. L., 196
Hazucha, J. F., 564
He, W., 752
Heathfield, S. M., 422, 559
Heavey, A. L., 754
Hebl, M. R., 149, 423, 425–426, 427, 753
Heckman, R. J., 558
Heetderks, T. D., 43, 297, 557
Heffner, T. S., 501
Heggestad, E. D., 510
Heilman, M. E., 560
Heise, S. R., 563
Hekman, D. R., 753
Heller, D., 508
Helliker, K., 517
Hellwig, S., 506
Henderson, N., 504
Heneman, H. G., III, 364
Heneman, R. L., 363
Henle, C. A., 420, 607
Henneman, T., 607
Hennessey, H W., Jr., 562
Henning, J. B., 499–500
Hentze, I., 518
Heo, C-G., 513
Hermelin, E., 562
Hernandez, M., 149, 655, 753
Hersby, M. D., 565
Hertel, G., 196, 499, 514
Hesketh, B., 198
Hewick, D., 516
Hiemstra, A.M.F., 421, 423
Higgins, C. A., 425
Highhouse, S., 257, 500, 510, 516, 606
Hill, A. D., 508
Hill, E. T., 364
Hill, P. C., 425
Hilmer, M. J., 423
Hinkin, T. R., 364
Hirsh, E., 149
Hitt, M. A., 196, 607
Ho, V. T., 655
Hoag, J. P., 429

Hoffman, B. J., 363, 503, 560, 561, 562, 563
Hofmans, J., 91, 297, 298, 558, 654
Hogan, A., 147
Hogan, J., 504, 511
Hogan, R., 43, 511
Hollenbeck, J. R., 509
Holmes, D. E., 258
Holtbrügge, D., 424
Holtom, B. C., 259, 751, 753
Holtrop, D., 510
Holtz, B. C., 365, 504, 606, 607
Holwerda, J. A., 754
Hom, P. W., 751, 752
Homan, A. C., 515
Hong, D-S., 514
Hong, Y., 699
Hong, Y-Y., 515
Hoobler, J. M., 560
Hooijberg, R., 298
Hornung, S., 655
Horovitz, B., 421
Horwitz, I. B., 93
Horwitz, S. K., 93
Hotchkiss, J. L., 149
Hough, L. M., 507, 509
Hout, M., 654
Howard, A., 423
Howes, S. S., 516
Howland, A. C., 563
Hsu, A.-J., 422
Hu, J., 514, 699
Huang, T-C., 422
Huber, K., 503
Huffcutt, A. I., 197–198, 363, 500, 501, 502
Hüffmeier, J., 499
Hugg, J., 362
Hughes, D., 499
Hughes, D. J., 506
Hughes, W., 342
Hui, C., 560
Hulin, C. L., 498, 557
Hull, R., 560
Hülsheger, U. R., 425, 428, 498, 502, 504, 510, 511, 512
Humphrey, R. H., 506
Humphrey, S. E., 513
Humphreys, L. G., 557
Hunt, S. T., 699
Hunter, J., 364
Hunter, J. E., 424, 503, 504, 505, 513, 559
Hunter, R. F., 424, 513
Hurtz, G. M., 607
Huselid, M. A., 700
Huxtable, J., 298
Hyland, M. M., 255
Hymes, R. W., 421

Iacono, W. G., 511
Idalski, A. A., 92
Ihsan, Z., 420, 421
Ilescu, D., 513
Ilie, A., 507, 513
Ilies, R., 503, 508
Illiescu, D., 507
Illingworth, A. J., 365
Imber, A., 256, 502
Inesi, M. E., 560
Ingold, P. V., 501, 561, 562, 563

SUBJECT INDEX